DARING TO HOPE

The Diaries and Letters of
Violet Bonham Carter
1946–1969

Kennedy assassinated

"Item" (I thought it was the [illegible] revival of the [illegible] Stage). Jamie dropped me back — very good Jelley on Education with Peterson, Crossman & Edward Boyle, Friday 22nd November

One of the most shattering evenings of my life. I am still stunned by its impact — I had been out by myself to see the T.V. film by the Boulting Brothers "I'm all right Jack" — which I had missed in its heyday & which Raymond told me was having a short revival at Studio One — I came back by bus — got lost in thought & passed the [illegible] stop by about a mile & about walked back arriving late for dinner & found Cressida in the dining room having hers — I was about to explain my muddle & expatiate on the brilliance of "I'm all right Jack" when she stopped me & said: "Kennedy has been shot — he was killed" — My heart stopped — (Only yesterday I posted him my [illegible])

Violet's diary entry for Friday 22 November 1963, recording the news of President John F. Kennedy's assassination.

DARING TO HOPE

The Diaries and Letters of Violet Bonham Carter 1946–1969

Edited by

Mark Pottle

John Connell:	And now, Lady Violet, looking back and looking forward, if you had to offer a philosophy to the three of us, what would you say?
Violet Bonham Carter:	Well, I've lived, you see, without any conscious philosophy of life. But I think I've followed a kind of current in my being. And I suppose I've felt, if I were true to that, I shouldn't lose the way.
John Connell:	Could you possibly analyse or describe that current in your life?
Violet Bonham Carter:	Always daring to hope, I think, and often realising it.

BBC Radio Home Service; *Frankly Speaking,*
with John Connell, Margaret Lane and Tony Benn,
recorded in London, 18 December 1957

Weidenfeld & Nicolson

LONDON

First published in Great Britain in 2000
by Weidenfeld & Nicolson

A CIP catalogue record for this book
is available from the British Library.

ISBN 0 297 81651 9

Typeset by Selwood Systems, Midsomer Norton
Set in ITC Stone Serif
Printed in Great Britain by
Butler & Tanner Ltd, Frome and London

Weidenfeld & Nicolson

The Orion Publishing Group Ltd
Orion House
5 Upper Saint Martin's Lane
London, WC2H 9EA

Dedicated to Michael Brock

CONTENTS

ILLUSTRATIONS

A section of photographs appears between pages 224 and 225. Unless otherwise stated, the originals are among the Bonham Carter papers. The editor is grateful to all those who have allowed, and assisted in, the reproduction of these images.

PREFACE

Daring to Hope is the final volume of the edited diaries and letters of Violet Bonham Carter. It covers the years in which she was most active in public life, from 1946 until her death in February 1969, aged nearly eighty-two. Though illness took its toll in her later years her vitality remained strong throughout: she kept her diary constantly and wrote her last entry just four days before she died.

The volume thus brings to an end the work started by Violet Bonham Carter's eldest son, Mark, in the years before his untimely death in 1994. He envisaged a trilogy that would allow his mother and her contemporaries to 'speak for themselves': the emphasis was to be very strongly on *their* words. In this book and its two predecessors the ratio of source material to editorial text has been kept as high as possible, roughly four-fifths to one fifth. The editorial comment tries to be unobtrusive and yet informative. Extracts from diaries and letters have been chosen for their broad biographical and historical interest. The aim has been to create a readable narrative that accurately depicts a 'life and times'. The contemporary nature of this last volume has meant that some material has been omitted on the ground that it might hurt the feelings of those still living. Such expurgation has been kept to a minimum and, as with the previous two volumes, all excisions have been marked.

The constant support since 1994 of Mark Bonham Carter's family has enabled his vision to be realised after his death. I am grateful to the many who have assisted, and especially to Mark's widow Leslie. She has shown steadfast faith in the value of the work and has lent her judgement, style and sensitivity to its creation. Her children Jane, Eliza and Virginia have all given vital support as the literary executors of their father's estate. Virginia has also shouldered an administrative burden, while managing to convey the impression that she enjoyed it, for which I am especially indebted. I cannot adequately thank Raymond and Elena Bonham Carter for all of their kindness; their great efforts on my behalf have lately been seconded by their children Edward and Helena, to whom I am also extremely grateful. Raymond's determination to see this work finished has been deeply moving and inspiring. It is a great tribute to his fidelity both as a brother and as a son.

Daring to Hope is the final product of eight years of research supported by numerous institutions and I am most grateful to: the Joseph Rowntree Reform Trust; the Leverhulme Trust; the Wolfson Foundation; the Rhodes Trust; the Warden and Fellows of Nuffield College, Oxford; the President and Fellows of Wolfson College, Oxford. To all of the staff and members of the latter college, I am particularly indebted. The volume includes extracts from twenty letters written to Violet, and I would like to acknowledge the kindness of the following copyright holders in allowing me to publish them: Eliza, Virginia and Jane Bonham Carter; Grizelda, John and Magnus Grimond; Sir John Leslie; Alexander Murray; Nigel Nicolson; Lord Oxford and Asquith; John Rous; Lord Thurso. The staff of a number of libraries have dealt expertly with my queries and I would particularly like to thank those at: Balliol College, Oxford; the Bodleian Library, Oxford; Churchill Archives Centre, Cambridge; Hertfordshire Record Office; *The Huddersfield Daily Examiner*; King's College, Cambridge; Nuffield College, Oxford; Trinity College, Cambridge; Wolfson College, Oxford. I am grateful also to Jackson & Dennett, Oxford bookbinders.

Many individuals have responded helpfully to my appeals, or otherwise given assistance, and I would especially like to thank: Tony Benn, Lady Boothby, Sue Boothby, Steve Carter, Mike Edge, Rachel Edge, Elizabeth English, Caroline Fryer, John Grigg, Donald Haley, Henry Hardy, Marigold Honey, Lord Jenkins of Hillhead, Bryan Magee, Riffat Mohammad, Nigel Nicolson, Lord Oxford and Asquith, Rt Hon. Sir Michael Palliser, John Penney, Sir Patrick Reilly, John Rous, Mrs Mary Rous, Fiona Ryan, Kate Shearman, John Saumarez Smith, Lady (Rose) Stephenson, Lady Williams of Elvel, Lord Wolfson of Marylebone. Comments made on the text by Mark Curthoys, Meike Hensmann and Isabelle Phan have been specially valuable. My family and friends have sustained me with their encouragement: like all gifts, it is unrepayable.

Each of the previous two volumes includes an impressive introduction written by an individual who had an insider's knowledge of the subject. Roy Jenkins and John Grigg knew Violet Bonham Carter and understood her times. The same is true of Mary Soames and I was especially pleased when she agreed to write the introduction to this volume. The presentation of the text has been much improved by Peter James, who has again undertaken an expert piece of copy-editing. I am grateful to Rachel Leyshon at Weidenfeld & Nicolson, who has given valuable assistance throughout the work. And also to Alice Hunt, Alison Provan and Bud Maclennan, who have helped with the final stages. For Ion Trewin, publisher, I reserve special thanks. He has helped improve the quality of the work, as well as providing the medium through which Violet and her contemporaries have been able 'to speak' to this and to later generations.

My own connection with Violet Bonham Carter began in the summer of 1991 when Dr Michael Brock, then warden of St George's House in Windsor Castle, suggested to Mark Bonham Carter that he contact me with a view to helping him with work on his mother's papers. Having recommended me Dr Brock naturally took an interest in my progress, but he could not have imagined that he would become as closely involved as he has done. Since Mark Bonham Carter's death he has taken on the role of mentor and consultant. He and Eleanor, his wife, have encouraged and advised, sharing with me their vast knowledge of history and their expertise in editing. They have brought out of me much better books than I would ever have been capable of producing on my own. It is with special pleasure therefore that I am able to make this acknowledgement to them both and especially to Dr Michael Brock – to whom this volume is dedicated. He has laboured at my affairs when his own were pressing.

Looking back on three volumes I can see some things that I would now do differently, but I hope that the work stands as a fitting memorial to a truly remarkable woman. The task of recording her 'life and times' began with her son, Mark Bonham Carter, and it is with a salute to his memory that I would like to end.

Mark Pottle, January 2000
Wolfson College, Oxford

EDITORIAL NOTE

Daring to Hope comprises about 175,000 words of which roughly 150,000 are edited diaries and letters and 25,000 preliminaries and appendices. Of the edited text about four-fifths is source material and one-fifth editorial. The source material is mostly diaries, with the remainder correspondence, most of it *from* VBC rather than *to* her. The diary entries have been selected from a series of journals that cover 1946–69 in an almost unbroken sequence – perhaps in excess of two million words. Of this it has only been possible to select a small amount, perhaps 5 per cent. Correspondence has been chosen from thousands of letters (there have not been the means to count them) which are spread fairly evenly over the period, with concentrations around events of obvious importance: VBC's peerage, December 1964; her eightieth birthday, April 1967; and so on.

The editing has tried to retain a sense of the continuity of a life while at the same time alighting on major themes: the division of the volume into three parts, and the inclusion of two years in each chapter, reflects this. Where relevant there are linking passages that help explain themes. The first volume of diaries and letters, *Lantern Slides*, dealt with the Edwardian era, and the second, *Champion Redoubtable*, with the three great epochs immediately following – the first world war, the inter-war years and the second world war. *Daring to Hope* covers the post-war world, the Suez era and the 1960s. It is an age of great interest, in which Britain's decline as an imperial and world power became starkly apparent. Violet was well placed to record this.

Diary entries and letters have been chosen for their historical interest as well as their biographical significance. The work is not a biography, nor could it be: editors seldom have as much freedom as biographers to contextualize, interpret and invent. The two endeavours, though, are complementary, each offering its own perspective of the past. Mark Bonham Carter and I both felt that the first presentation of his mother's life should be in the form of an edition of her papers; and that in due course her diaries and letters – which will be in the public domain – will be fruitful material for future biographers and historians.

Inevitably with a diary written late in life, and sometimes during passages of quite severe illness, there are errors of syntax and meaning, confusion of dates, repetition of words and occasionally even whole entries. More than with the previous two volumes, therefore, the editor has had to intervene to make the text intelligible. Difficulties in punctuation and errors in spelling and grammar have generally been silently corrected. Occasionally a change has been made to improve the style – for example, substituting 'he' or 'she' for a name, or vice versa; introducing a paragraph break; adding underlining to a word to emphasise the meaning of a sentence where it would not otherwise be obvious. Some idiosyncrasies have been kept – for example Violet's habitual use of the dash, as a kind of halfway house between a full stop and a comma; also the ampersand, which gives an impression of the speed and spontaneity with which Violet wrote. Where editorial information is supplied in the text it is enclosed in square brackets.

The dates given for the diary entries are generally those recorded by Violet herself. Some of the entries, however, were clearly written some time – days and, less often, weeks – after the event. The dates given here therefore apply to the timing of events, rather than to the writing about them. In a similar way the 'location' given in the diary entry headings refers to the place in which the action occurred, and not necessarily the place where the entry was written, though of course they were generally the same. All excisions have been marked, with either a three or a four point ellipsis. A four point ellipsis (. . . .) indicates the omission of the rest of a line (and/or) paragraph (and/or) ensuing paragraphs. At the end of a letter, it indicates the omission of a postscript. A three point ellipsis indicates omissions (of a line/paragraph/paragraphs) preceding the ellipsis – for example, the beginning of a paragraph. It is also used to indicate an omission occurring within a sentence.

Footnotes offer relevant biographical information and an appendix provides brief biographies of frequently mentioned individuals and prominent historical figures. The index can be used to locate both. In order to keep the editorial text to a minimum the biographical and historical information given has been made deliberately concise: as a rule only the most senior order of peerage or knighthood, conferred on one individual, is recorded. Where the title of a peerage differs from the surname, the former may be given in brackets. The date of the succession to a peerage is given where this occurs 1946–69. Editorial linking passages and other appendices have also had to be kept concise. General cultural references (for example, 'Pompeii & Herculaneum') and prominent figures mentioned only in passing (for example, Hitler, Napoleon) have generally not been elucidated where they can be found in *Encyclopaedia Britannica.*

A note on the appendices: the Glossary, Biographical notes and Notes on houses and places

After 1945 the diary is virtually uninterrupted and Violet made increasing use of abbreviations and foreign words and phrases in her daily entries. A note on all of these can be found in the Glossary below, Appendix A. Included in the Biographical notes, Appendix B, are concise biographies of the prominent figures mentioned in the text. There is also a note here on all of the correspondents whose letters are included in the work – for example, Barbara Freyberg and Gilbert Murray. A note on the houses and places mentioned in the text can be found in Appendix C.

A LIST OF CHRISTIAN NAMES, INITIALS AND NICKNAMES APPEARING IN THE TEXT

For biographical details of those mentioned see Appendix B: Biographical notes, and also the index – for page numbers (italicized) of biographical footnotes in the text.

Aunt Bett Betty Asquith
Adam Adam Ridley
Aga H. H. Asquith
A.J.B. Arthur James Balfour
Andrew Andrew Grimond
Aneurin Aneurin Bevan
Anthony Anthony Eden
Archie Archibald Sinclair
B. Maurice Bonham Carter (Bongie)
B.D. Bloody Duck (VBC)
Bett Betty Asquith
Bongie Maurice Bonham Carter
C. Cressida Ridley
Clem Clement Davies
Clemmie Clementine Churchill
Cressida Cressida Ridley
Cys Cyril Asquith
Dingle Dingle Foot
Duncan Duncan Sandys
Edward Edward Bonham Carter
Elena Elena Bonham Carter
Eliza Eliza Bonham Carter
Father H. H. Asquith
Ghima Violet Bonham Carter [that is, 'Grandma']
Gelda Grizelda Grimond
Gladwyn Gladwyn Jebb [Lord Gladwyn]
Hatchie Harold Nicolson
Harold Harold Macmillan
Helena Helena Bonham Carter
Ike Dwight D. Eisenhower
Isaiah Isaiah Berlin
Jag Andrew Grimond
Jane Jane Bonham Carter
Jeremy Jeremy Thorpe
Jo Jo Grimond
Johnny John Grimond
K. Katharine Asquith/K. Elliot
Katharine Katharine Asquith
Laura Laura Grimond; Laura St Just
Law Rose Law
L.G./Ll.G. David Lloyd George
M. Mark Bonham Carter
Magna/Magnus Magnus Grimond
Margot Margot Asquith
Marigold Marigold Sinclair
Mark Mark Bonham Carter
Mary Mary Rous (née Asquith)
Maynard John Maynard Keynes
Megan Megan Lloyd George
Michael Michael Padev/Michael Stratton
Moucher dowager Duchess of Devonshire
Nannie Ada Bentley
Priscilla Priscilla Hodgson (*née* Bibesco)
Puff/Puffin Anthony Asquith
R. Raymond Bonham Carter
Rab R. A. Butler
Randolph Randolph Churchill
Ray Raymond Bonham Carter
Roy Roy Jenkins
Sheila Sheila Wrathall
Sieg/Siegfried Siegfried Sassoon
Toad John Grimond
Tom Thomas Bonham Carter
Virginia Virginia Bonham Carter
Vites Vita Sackville-West
W./Winston Winston Churchill
Wilfrid Wilfrid Roberts

Asquith and Bonham Carter family tree, 1969

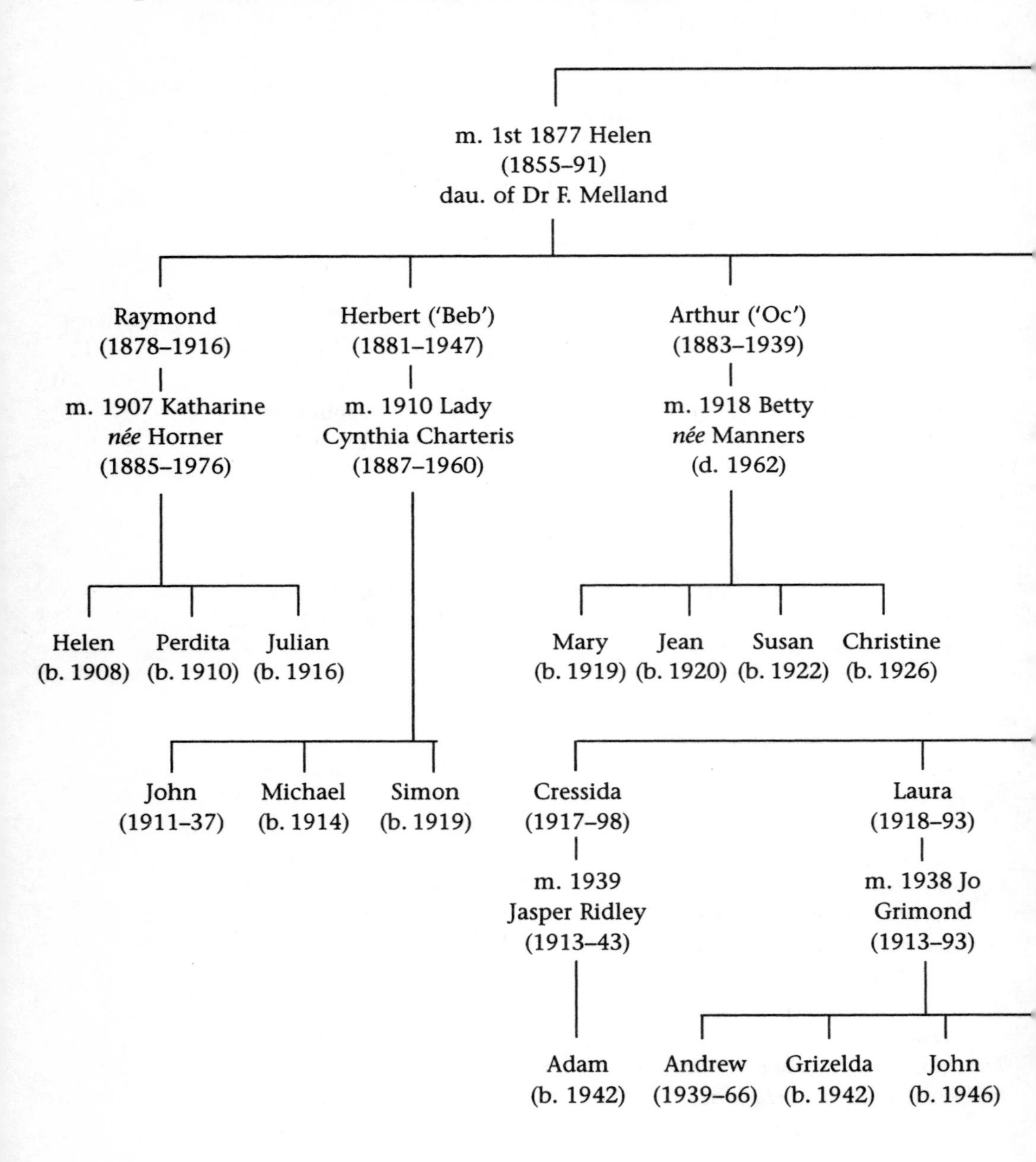

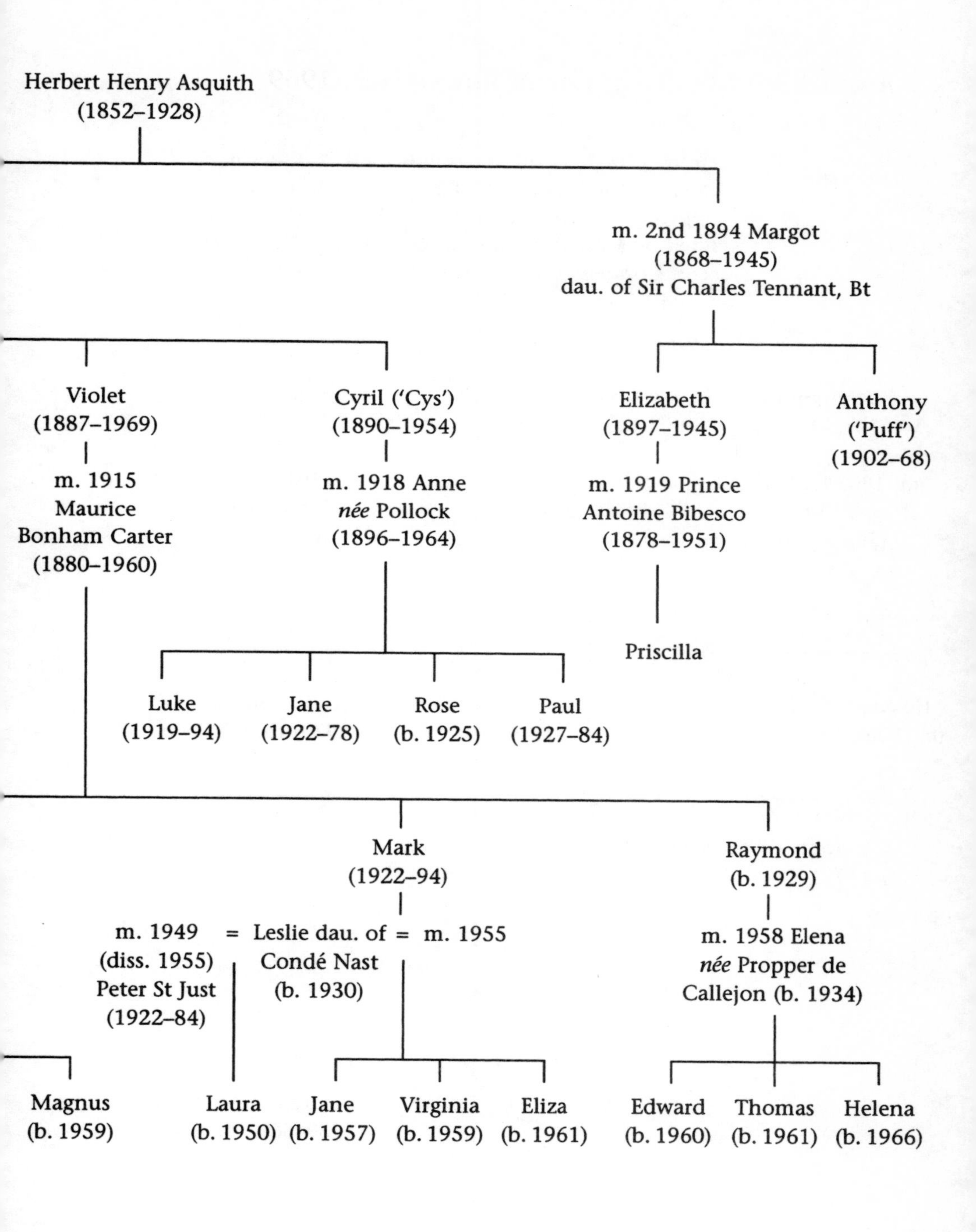

Herbert Henry Asquith
(1852–1928)
m. 2nd 1894 Margot
(1868–1945)
dau. of Sir Charles Tennant, Bt
Violet
(1887–1969)
m. 1915
Maurice
Bonham Carter
(1880–1960)
Cyril ('Cys')
(1890–1954)
m. 1918 Anne
née Pollock
(1896–1964)
Elizabeth
(1897–1945)
m. 1919 Prince
Antoine Bibesco
(1878–1951)
Anthony
('Puff')
(1902–68)
Luke
(1919–94)
Jane
(1922–78)
Rose
(b. 1925)
Paul
(1927–84)
Priscilla
Mark
(1922–94)
Raymond
(b. 1929)
m. 1949
(diss. 1955)
Peter St Just
(1922–84)
= Leslie dau. of = m. 1955
Condé Nast
(b. 1930)
m. 1958 Elena
née Propper de
Callejon (b. 1934)
Magnus
(b. 1959)
Laura
(b. 1950)
Jane
(b. 1957)
Virginia
(b. 1959)
Eliza
(b. 1961)
Edward
(b. 1960)
Thomas
(b. 1961)
Helena
(b. 1966)

Daring to Hope is the third and final volume of the diaries and letters of Violet Bonham Carter. The first, *Lantern Slides*, covered the period 1904 to 1914. It was edited by Mark Bonham Carter and Mark Pottle. The second, *Champion Redoubtable*, covering 1914 to 1945, was edited by Mark Pottle.

INTRODUCTION

Mary Soames

The third and last volume of the diaries and letters of Violet Asquith (as she began and ended her days) covers the last twenty-four years of her life and career – the two were virtually synonymous. From 1961 Lady Violet (as she then was, and as I always thought of her) was increasingly afflicted by heart trouble, but she struggled valiantly on: aged 80, in November 1968, and within four months of her death, she was one of a deputation to the Prime Minister (Harold Wilson) on the humanitarian crisis in Biafra; on 2 February 1969, despite her failing strength, she recorded a quite arduous broadcast for the BBC before a live audience; three days later she struggled to the House of Lords through arctic weather to listen to a debate on chemical and biological warfare. Her last diary entry was on 15 February – four days before her death. Sadly this brilliant, gallant woman had faced her last New Year's day on a note of deep discouragement, writing in her diary:

> Feel like a clock run-down .... Pray this will be a better year for the world than last. Nothing can buy back life to the countless thousands – millions? – in Biafra. Can freedom be regained for Czechoslovakia? I see no way. There are no great men anywhere to lead. How lucky I have been to be born so long ago.

But those who have read the first two volumes of this series, *Lantern Slides* (which covers the years 1904–14) and *Champion Redoubtable* (1914–45), may surely have received the same strong overall impression as myself – the ardour (for no lesser word will do) of Violet Asquith's political beliefs and ideals which, kindled even in childhood, burned with undiminished intensity to her dying day. I had mistakenly imagined that this last volume, which opens in 1946 when she was 58, would show an abatement in her zeal, or some fading of the passion and energy with which she would break lances for causes – and chiefly that of Liberalism. Instead, one follows her endeavouring after World War II to make the Liberal Party keep in view, as goal and guide, the great principles of Liberalism to which she had been unfailingly loyal since the radical reforming days of the Edwardian decade, in which her father had played such a leading role.

Another most remarkable feature of this great woman's life is that she achieved her political celebrity and her degree of influence in the political world without any parliamentary power-base. Colin Coote described her as 'the best politically equipped person who never sat in Parliament'. Her life peerage in 1964, barely five years before her death, only confirmed her long achieved public position and was, in a sense, too late: she never really acclimatised to their Lordships' ways, and (to her) the tepid tenor of their debates. She once impatiently described the Upper House as 'the Corridors of Impotence'. Lady Violet's political interests were bred in the bone and nurtured from childhood, and no one was more fitted by temperament and antecedent for a parliamentary role, although one may wonder whether the constraints of the party machine or governmental responsibilities might have chafed her beyond endurance. Even as a child, and later in her youth, she had accompanied her father in his political campaignings. She effectively entered the hustings (which she greatly relished) on behalf of her father when he fought Paisley in 1920, re-entering the House of Commons after the humiliation of his defeat at East Fife in the 'Coupon' election of 1918. Her political capacity and her outstanding power as a public speaker and debater made her a 'draw' on platforms in the years before radio, and above all television, destroyed public meetings as the forum and focus of electoral fights and political opinion. But as the effectiveness of radio and television developed, she took easily to these new and powerful vehicles of thought, speech and debate. Her regular participation in the Brains Trust and various television programmes made her known to a much wider audience, and created for her a following beyond the steadily diminishing ranks of the Liberal Party.

It was Violet Asquith's own choice that she did not seek to enter Parliament in the twenties and thirties – deliberately setting her family life and four children first. Perhaps also, having seen parliamentary life so close, she had no illusions as to the sheer drudgery of a member of parliament's life: why should she, who already bore the palm, seek the dust? Later in life however, she stood twice as a parliamentary candidate – both times unsuccessfully. In 1945 she came third and last at Wells in Somerset, and in 1951 she lost a close contest at Colne Valley in Yorkshire. On the latter occasion as a Liberal with Conservative support marshalled at Winston Churchill's instigation.

But Lady Violet seemed quite as happy – perhaps happier – campaigning on behalf of others as for herself. In freezing February 1950 she divided her time between Archie Sinclair, fighting forlornly to regain his seat in Caithness and Sutherland, and her son-in-law Jo Grimond, weaving back and forth across Orkney and Shetland to help him to victory. In March 1958, aged seventy, she was with Mark and Leslie Bonham Carter throughout the by-election campaign in Torrington, where he famously won the seat by 219 votes. She returned to be with them later in the General Election – this time sharing all the bruising of a close fight and defeat.

I have personal experience of electioneering as a daughter, sister and wife, and I enjoyed Lady Violet's accounts of her campaignings on behalf of her family and 'the Cause', following her sallying forth in wind and weather. No car drive too long, no meeting too rowdy, or too insignificant, for her to give of her brilliant best; no stints of canvassing too tedious. I lived again the tensions and agonies of the 'count'; the exhilaration of victory, and the bitter disappointment and exhaustion of defeat – all vividly described in her diaries. And it was painful to feel her desolation and disappointment when in 1964 Mark simply forbade her, out of solicitude for her fragile health, from joining his third campaign in Torrington. But she was there for polling day and the count, when once more she would support Mark and Leslie in defeat.

Dubbed by Winston Churchill as her father's 'champion redoubtable' in the 1920s, she continued down the years to fulfil the same role for the Liberal Party: but her diaries reveal intense frustration at times, and she did not conceal from herself that the party political scene of the 1940s and 1950s was largely peopled by pygmies compared with the giants of old. Violet Asquith needed – and found – great causes: never a little Englander, she believed fervently in the League of Nations and its successor the United Nations. She was among the first of the all-too-few people in this country who in the inter-war years saw clearly the threat of the dictators, and particularly the menace of a swiftly re-arming Germany. From 1936 she was a member of 'Mr Churchill's Focus in Defence of Freedom and Peace' – which united people from across the political spectrum in opposition to appeasement.

In this volume we see her wholehearted involvement in the cause of a united Europe. She was Vice Chairman of the United Europe Movement from 1947, and later campaigned vigorously for Britain to enter the Common Market. This brought her allies here at home from all parties; and abroad, through conferences and assemblies, she came to be known and respected by European leaders involved in this great crusade.

Nor did Lady Violet stand aloof from involvement in other ways in the issues and controversies of these later years. I am amazed to read of her in her seventies, and already suffering the onset of heart trouble, joining in anti-apartheid Black Sash demonstrations, and marching in 1961 from Speakers' Corner to Trafalgar Square. In the 1963 march she did take a taxi from Bond Street, but then valiantly struggled on to the plinth of Nelson's column to show solidarity, and to listen to the speeches.

Talleyrand's dry maxim 'Surtout, pas trop de zèle' would have struck no note with her: indeed those two minds and sets of values would have had little in common! Her heart seems usually to have commanded her brain – not for her the devices of tactical voting. In November 1956 in a letter to Nigel Nicolson, after he had lost the support of his local Conservative Association over his anti-government stance on Suez, she wrote: 'The only purpose of politics (or so it seems to me) is the expression of one's own deepest convictions – & their translation into facts.' This maxim had informed her utterances and actions during the whole time she had participated in the political life of this country – a span by then of more than 30 years. The Suez crisis in particular evoked her passionate opposition to the Government. She roundly reproached her Conservative friends (in and out of office) who, despite the deep misgivings felt by many of them, lent their support to the Government: she deemed this to be a totally false sense of loyalty. Nor could she forgive those who forbore to voice their criticisms because British troops were committed to action.

Throughout her life Violet Asquith formed 'enthusiasms' for people – usually men, although she had long and loyal friendships with women. As Roy Jenkins put it in his introduction to *Lantern Slides*: 'she had a natural gift for admiration'. But beyond enthusiasms – some of which chilled, usually when the object of her admiration fell from political grace in her eyes – she needed, and found, heroes. Foremost and lastingly among these was her father – Herbert Henry Asquith.

Violet was four when her mother Helen died; she was the fourth of five children – and the only girl. The older boys were soon hived off to school and from her earliest years she was the close companion of her father. It is a touching picture – that of the small girl greeting her father on his return from the House of Commons, gravely enquiring as to whether Mr Gladstone had spoken that day. In the ranks of filial love and loyalty Violet Asquith remains pre-eminent. She adored her father uncritically, and although when this volume opens Asquith had been dead for nearly 18 years, her veneration for him had not dimmed; her redoubtable champion's lance was ever ready to be drawn in his defence, at one word of criticism – or even lack of appreciation.

Undoubtedly therefore, it was for her an extreme emotional shock when in early 1964 she read the manuscript of Roy Jenkins's *Asquith*, sent to her in batches by her elder son Mark who was the publisher. Roy Jenkins was the first person to have unfettered access to, and use of, the letters written by her father when he was Prime Minister to his daughter's close friend and contemporary, Venetia Stanley. They were made available to Roy Jenkins by Venetia's only child, Judy Montagu (Mrs Milton Gendel), who had the possession of them, and by Mark Bonham Carter who owned the copyright. Lady Violet's letters and diaries for February and March of that year make painful reading since her shock and distress are so palpable.

Her sense of outrage was first aroused by (to her) the dismissive manner in which Roy Jenkins had described her mother, and her parents' marriage, writing in her diary: 'He describes her patronisingly as "rather good looking" .... suggests that when Father writes "our sun went down in an unclouded sky" the sun had not gone down one whit too soon for the good of his career.' But further trauma lay in store for Lady Violet when she reached the chapter dealing extensively with Mr Asquith's 'great epistolary friendship' with Venetia Stanley, which revealed a surprising degree of intimacy between them.

Subsequently Lady Violet read all the letters in this long correspondence and her shock and dismay are evident. As she would tell Roy Jenkins 'she had not hitherto had the slightest idea of any special relationship' existing between her father and Venetia Stanley – the fact of which emerges clearly from the 540 or so letters, written between 1910 and 1915: Asquith was then Prime Minister, turning 60 and more than twice the age of his daughter's friend. In his introduction to *Lantern Slides* Roy Jenkins describes vividly the embarrassment of his meeting with Lady Violet: 'the atmosphere was distinctly fraught'. He confesses he found implausible her statement that she had no idea of the relationship revealed in the letters, since he knew that at the relevant period Violet and Venetia had been intimate friends. However he became inclined to be convinced when, instead of advancing a routine protest and denial that such a situation could have existed, Lady Violet exclaimed: 'It cannot be true. Venetia was so plain' (forgetting, surely, that beauty lies in the beholder's eye.) John Grigg in his introduction to *Champion Redoubtable* also discusses this situation, and also remains unconvinced, writing: 'Readers of this volume will be forced to conclude that she [Violet Asquith] was a victim of selective memory or self deception . . . .'.

This relationship, upon which Mr Asquith had undoubtably come to rely, had been dramatically ruptured on 12 May 1915 when Venetia Stanley wrote to tell him of her intention of marrying Edwin Montagu, his close friend, protégé and government colleague. Venetia was at home ill when she wrote her letter, and so could not have known that her hammer blow would fall at a time of political crisis which would lead, in one chaotic week, to the end of Asquith's Liberal government and the forming of his Coalition administration. Asquith was stunned, and it has even been argued that his personal distress may have affected his judgement and actions during that fateful week.

It is clear the womenfolk at No. 10 were equally astounded by Venetia's news. Edwin Montagu had long been one of the Downing Street coterie, but clearly Venetia had not confided to Violet, any more than she had to Mr Asquith, that her long friendship with Edwin, during which he had been known to court her unsuccessfully, was about to become something quite different – marriage. Having read Lady Violet's early diaries and letters, and her reaction recorded half a century later when her father's letters to Venetia were about to be made public, I personally believe she must have known that her father nurtured tender feelings for Venetia. Since he was a great letter writer, particularly to his numerous women friends, she would have thought it quite natural that there would be letters between them. Perhaps also Lady Violet allowed her memory a measure of 'selectiveness'. But in my opinion she had no conception of the extent of the correspondence – and certainly not of the intensity of her father's feelings which are revealed in it. For the letters are not, as she had supposed they might be, solely 'an interesting account of political events, colleagues etc.': they are also *love letters*, as any perusal of them reveals.[1]

Lady Violet's reaction to Roy Jenkins's book and the use of the letters was one of outrage and I suspect, painful embarassment, and *my* daughterly heart bled for her as I read her diary entry for Friday 6 March 1964: 'I cannot believe that Mark cld have contemplated publishing it. It is a betrayal of the intimacies of private life second to none – i.e. a publication of his letters to Venetia at the time of their break – when she decided to marry Edwin. I am appalled that anyone shld have read them.' As she continued reading the letters her 'pain and astonishment' mounted:

> 'It is so strange to *know* that I was quite unaware of what was passing between 2 human beings – one of whom was closer to me in intimacy than any other (except perhaps Cys[2]) has ever been in my whole life – & the other my most intimate female friend.' (Tuesday 17 March)

Venetia had died in 1953: perhaps it was as well she would not know her great friend's dismay and sense of betrayal.

Violet's protectiveness towards her father bursts out in a letter to Mark on Thursday 6 March: 'I naturally long *not* to expose HHA's "infatuation" to the eyes of thousands – for it must inevitably cheapen him & reduce his stature to posterity .... I am sure you understand what this whole business means to me – for apart from the *closest* intimacy & love he was to me throughout my life a standard & a touchstone of all values'.

And in a later diary entry we get another inkling that her paragon had slipped ever so little in her esteem: 'I reminded Mark of my demand that letters written during Cabinet Sessions shd not be given as such. (This would shock others terribly as indeed it has shocked me).' (13 July 1964). Mark was able to write to reassure her 'as to *Asquith*, I do want you to know how aware I have been throughout of your feelings, and of how well I understand them – and respect them'. (Wed 12 August). The published version of the biography reflected some modifications made to meet Lady Violet's personal and deeply felt objections. It was published in early November 1964: Lady Violet reviewed it for *The Times*, and showed admirable detachment. She found much to praise, but took reasoned issue with the author on a number of historical points and on his interpretation of the motivation of some of Asquith's actions. She sedulously refrained

[1] H. H. Asquith, *Letters to Venetia Stanley*, Michael and Eleanor Brock (eds)., 1982.
[2] Her younger brother Cyril.

from any mention of 'the letters' or of the 'special relationship' between her father and Venetia Stanley.

The other 'star' in Violet Asquith's firmament, who became for her a hero, was Winston Churchill. They first met at a dinner party in 1906, when she was 19 and he 32 and a junior minister in Campbell-Bannerman's Liberal government. In her brilliant book *Winston Churchill as I Knew Him*, published in 1965 shortly after his death, Violet tells how at their very first meeting she instantly recognised in him the quality of genius:

> 'Until the end of dinner I listened to him spellbound. I can remember thinking: *This* is what people mean when they talk of "seeing stars" – that is what I am doing now .... I knew only I had "seen a great light". I recognised it as the light of genius.'

Years later in April 1963 she experienced a similar sensation when she met and had a long private talk with President Kennedy at the White House, of which she gave a full and riveting account in her diary. Almost exactly seven months later she recorded her feelings at his brutal assassination – 'I have never felt the death of any "public figure" with such stabbing poignancy & such obsessive grief.' And she remembered the deep impression that the President had made on her: 'And above all I had the sense of greatness – in a greater degree than I have felt it about anyone since I first met Winston at the age of 19.'

After their first meeting Violet and Winston gravitated towards each other's company at parties or weekend visits. Mr Asquith had for some time recognised Churchill's talents, and after he became Prime Minister in April 1908 Violet was delighted when her father told her that he intended to bring Winston at a bound into the Cabinet, from the under secretaryship at the Colonial Office to be the new President of the Board of Trade. Violet's sitting room in 10 Downing Street was on the ground floor, immediately to the right of the garden entrance door, and Winston would often drop in casually for a gossip on his fairly frequent visits to the Prime Minister.

There has been speculation as to the real nature of the relationship between Violet and Winston in those early days. I think neither was drawn to the other physically – but there was a *fervour* in their friendship: in her he found an 'insider' to the political world he inhabited, who because she herself had a passion for politics made the perfect listener and 'sounding board'. Yet her admiration for Winston, unlike her attitude to her father, would never be uncritical – which made her friendship all the more valuable to him. I think John Grigg has judged the situation between them rightly, when he wrote in his introduction to *Champion Redoubtable*:

'It is a fair surmise that she would have married him if he had proposed to her while he was a bachelor in her father's government.' But in the summer of 1908 Winston became engaged to the beautiful, poor and virtuous Clementine Hozier, and they married in September of that year.

My mother told me that in the early days of their marriage, when 'the young Churchills' were very much a part of the Asquith set, she felt (unaccountably at the time) distinctly wary of the Violet–Venetia duet. Clementine had already been 'out' for two years when Violet made her debut in 1905 – a significant bench mark in those days – and although they knew each other they moved in different time warps. But Venetia, although the same vintage as Violet, was Clementine's first cousin: from the days of their childhood they had spent many holiday times together, mostly at Penrhos, the Stanleys' home in Anglesey. But just how right Clementine was in her sense of 'wariness' is revealed in Violet's diary and in her letters to Venetia at that time, and also in several of Asquith's letters to Venetia. The comments and tone in discussing Clementine are dismissive – indeed they verge on the contemptuous: and Venetia would not seem to have taken her cousin's part to any degree. I only came to understand all these years later (and twenty years after my mother's death) just how acutely tuned her 'antennae' had been. On hearing from Winston of his engagement to Clementine, Violet wrote to Venetia on 14 August:

> I must say I am much gladder for her sake than I am sorry for his. His wife could never be more to him than an ornamental sideboard as I have often said & she is unexacting enough not to mind not being more. Whether he will ultimately mind her being stupid as an owl I don't know .... Father thinks it spells disaster for them both.[1] I don't know that it does that. He did not wish for — though he needs it badly – a critical, reformatory wife who would stop up the lacunas in his taste etc. and hold him back from blunders.

But Lady Violet was too intelligent and fair-minded not to see as time went on that Clementine was (miraculously and thankfully) just the woman for Winston. Four years later she would write: 'I love her so much now – more than W.'

The friendship between Winston and Violet would survive the passage of over half a century, during which there were deep political differences between them and a long 'stand-off' from 1916 to the early thirties, which started with Violet's passionate partisanship of her father in the wake of his ousting by the Lloyd George cabal in the winter of 1916. In the early

[1] Roy Jenkins comments in his introduction to *Lantern Slides*: 'Not one of Asquith's more prescient judgements'.

days of their acquaintance Violet acknowledged Lloyd George's charm, but from 1916 she would nurse an enduring hatred for him. And although Violet was acclimatised to politicians' ambitions, yet she deplored Winston's accepting office (as Minister of Munitions) in 1917 and serving in Lloyd George's government. For his part Winston did not disguise from Violet that he felt Asquith, in letting him go from the Cabinet without a fight in May 1915, had bowed too easily to Conservative demands that he must leave the Admiralty as part of their price for joining a Coalition government. Winston's journey from Liberalism back to Conservatism in the early 1920s, and his acceptance of office (Chancellor of the Exchequer) in Baldwin's government, further maintained the distance between him and Violet. Of these years she wrote:

> 'Though we never lost our way into each other's minds .... there were times when our passionate disagreements were vehemently expressed: others when our differences seemed to be too deep to be bridged by words, and silence fell between us.'[1]

But the thirties – which brought the perils of Hitler and Germany's rearmament (to which Britain remained so long purblind) and the fatal fallacies of appeasement – kindled their friendship to life again. Its flame would burn brightly thereafter.

It is of course particularly fascinating for me to be able now to follow the course of these relationships. Although Lady Violet came to acknowledge the uniquely important role Clementine would play in Winston's life, and developed a genuine affection for her, yet Winston was always the lodestar. But as Clementine became established in her role as Winston's wife, and increasingly sure of his unwavering love for her, and conscious of her own power to help him, she seems to have accepted without difficulty the 'special relationship' between Winston and Violet. And any element of 'threat' disappeared with Violet's own marriage to Maurice Bonham Carter ('Bongie') in 1915. Bongie provided the rock-like relationship that brought Violet not only the fulfilments of family life, but also the emotional security that carried her through the vicissitudes of her public political career. In this volume Bongie (or plain 'B') seems largely invisible – but his invisibility belies the role he played in her life for 45 years. Violet had no need to explain it to herself, and what her husband meant to her is spelt out for us – the outer world – most poignantly in the months after his illness and death in June 1960, when her feeling of utter alone-ness emerges, despite many activities, a loving family and many friends. On the anniversary of Bongie's death she wrote: 'It is a whole year

[1] *Winston Churchill as I knew him* p. 466.

since we parted – a year of great loneliness & desolation in which I have not learned to live alone.'

As time went on Violet and Clementine came to share another important bond, for Clementine remained a truer Liberal than her husband. In the biography of my mother I wrote:

> When Winston reunited himself with the Conservative party, she [Clementine] understood his political evolution, and followed his line of thought .... But if with her reason Clementine may have 'crossed the floor of the House' with Winston, in her heart she remained to the end of her days a rather old-fashioned radical.

During World War II Violet lunched quite often with Winston and Clementine, at first in Admiralty House and later in the fortified garden rooms at No 10 (where so many years before Violet had had her sitting room). She clearly admired Clementine's demeanour in those crisis days, although she describes one brisk squall at a party over the Vichy leader Admiral Darlan, who had been appointed High Commissioner of French North Africa (for purely strategic political reasons):

'I had a short interchange with Clemmie over Darlan in which she – to my amazement – completely lost her temper & nearly emptied a glass of champagne over herself & me saying "I used to think you were an intelligent woman!"[1]'

I suspect my mother's outburst was symptomatic of tension, and moreover that, in different circumstances, she would certainly have taken Violet's and the Liberal-left view! However harmony was soon restored, and when less than a month later Violet lunched at No. 10 she recorded in her diary: 'Clemmie very mellow & conciliatory.'

In fact, Violet and Clementine often had the same reactions to events or to issues in which Winston was involved. In one example in August 1944 Violet 'gave good marks' to Clementine for piping up 'with great courage' during a discussion of the impending General Election, when she (Clementine) said: 'W – I think you shld resign the leadership of the Tory Party before the Election. You shouldn't use your great prestige to get them in again. They don't deserve it.' *Realpolitik* was foreign to both women's natures. Although Violet and Clementine had a genuine affection and friendship for each other, yet it is impossible not to detect in Violet's diaries as the years go on an element of occasional, mild irritation on her part towards Clementine: the ghost of the patronising attitude of the earlier years and always a clear sense of her own intellectual superiority. Clementine seems to have been unaware of this – I do indeed hope so.

[1] Diary for Tuesday 15 December 1942; *Champion Redoubtable*, p. 248.

After the war Violet and Winston once more were closely and actively allied in the crusade for European unity. And as the hope and prospect of overturning the 1945 Labour landslide grew brighter, both did their utmost with their parties to bring about a realistic forging of a common front against Socialism. For the most part they met with unwillingness from their respective party caucuses, when the actual nuts and bolts for arrangements had to become reality. Lady Violet's Liberal candidature at Colne Valley in 1951 was based upon Conservative support, promoted and engineered by Winston, who came and spoke on her platform. It was a close contest and had she been victorious there is no doubt that Winston would have offered her a seat in his Cabinet. It is likely she would have accepted such an offer, even though it would have meant the disapproval of her party, a section of which had already bitterly criticized her for her willingness to ally herself with the Conservatives on a broad anti-socialist front.

From her diaries it emerges how Winston in these later years harked back to his Liberal days: both of them surveying the political scene in the light of long memory. In August 1953, when discussing with Violet the possibility of her standing again as a Liberal with Conservative backing (which she understandably declined to contemplate) Winston said 'After all there is very little difference betwen Conservatism today & what yr. Father & Grey stood for in the past.' Her reply is revealing: 'Yes – but that was 40 years ago. Time moves on. One can't afford to follow events with a time-lag of 40 years.'

When Winston resigned as Prime Minister in April 1955 Violet and Clementine were united in their true understanding of what this final leaving of the stage really meant for him, even though Clementine had long tried to persuade him to retire. As the twilight slowly deepened, Violet was a faithful and welcome visitor, stimulating his interest and eliciting his views on events and personalities present and past. Rather touchingly the diaries make quite plain how pleased she was when she had Winston to herself: Clementine would sometimes ask her to come and keep him company if she herself was away; and Violet also records occasions when Clementine with consummate tact left them alone at the end of a meal. As the shade deepened, I know she shared the sadness of his gradual distancing from us all, and from life.

Violet saw Winston during his last illness in January 1965, nine days before he died: he was beyond speech. And on that cold, cold Sunday morning, 24 January, at my mother's bidding I telephoned Lady Violet to tell her my father had died a short while before. That afternoon I received her, and led her to my father's room, and left her alone with that majestic peaceful presence, to take her last leave.

ONE

The Post-War World

1946–1953

CHRONOLOGY OF EVENTS 1946–1953

1946	March	5 Churchill's 'Iron Curtain' speech at Fulton, Missouri
	July	– nationalization of coal industry (effective January 1947)
		22 blowing up of the British military HQ in the King David Hotel in Jerusalem by Irgun terrorists, leaving 91 dead
	September	19 Churchill's speech at Zurich calling for a 'United States of Europe'
	November	– National Health Service Act passed (effective July 1948)
1947	February	18 Bevin announces in Commons that the Palestine question is to be referred to the United Nations
	April	30 Royal Commission on the Press convenes
	May	14 launch of the United Europe Movement at the Albert Hall
	June	5 General Marshall's speech at Harvard outlining 'Marshall Aid' plan
		27 Paris Conference begins, at which Bevin, Molotov and Bidault discuss Russian involvement in Marshall plan (ends 2 July)
	August	15 partition of the Indian sub-continent: India and Pakistan become independent states and full members of the Commonwealth
	September	20 cabinet accepts principle of surrender of Palestine mandate and withdrawal of troops
1948	January	– nationalization of railways
	March	17 Brussels Treaty – signed by Britain, France and Benelux countries
	April	– 'Marshall Aid' made available to Britain
		16 Organization for European Economic Co-operation established (OEEC)
	May	7–10 The Hague Congress meets
		14 proclamation of state of Israel
		15 British forces withdraw from Palestine after the surrender of the Mandate there
		27 victory for Malan's combined Nationalist and Afrikaner Party in the South African general election: inaugurates era of *apartheid*

	June	– end of bread rationing
		24 Russians stop road and rail traffic from entering and leaving Berlin
		26 beginning of the Berlin airlift
	December	21 Republic of Ireland Act (Dublin): Éire becomes the Republic of Ireland and leaves the Commonwealth (18 April 1949)
1949	January	29 Britain recognizes *de facto* the state of Israel
	March	– end of clothes rationing
	April	4 Treaty of Washington establishes NATO
		18 Éire leaves the Commonwealth
	May	12 lifting of the Berlin blockade
		23 Federal Republic of Germany comes into being
	June	2 Ireland Act declares the special relationship of Irish citizens to the United Kingdom and guarantees that Northern Ireland will remain in the Union unless its parliament decides otherwise
	July	– report of Royal Commission on the Press debated in Commons
	August	10 first meeting of Consultative Assembly of Council of Europe at Strasbourg
	September	18 devaluation of sterling: pound drops from $4.03 to $2.80
		23 Washington announces that the Soviet Union has the atomic bomb
	November	– nationalization of Iron and Steel industry (with effect January 1951)
1950	February	23 general election gives Labour 5 seat majority: 315 Labour, 299 Conservative, 9 Liberal, 2 other; Attlee remains premier
	May	– end of petrol rationing
		9 Schuman Plan for European Coal and Steel Community (ECSC)
	June	– British government decides against joining Schuman Plan
		25 North Korean troops invade South Korea: emergency meeting of UN security council authorizes military aid to South Korea; American forces committed to defence of South Korea
		28 British Far East Fleet sent to aid South Korea
	August	29 British troops engaged in Korean war

	October	24 Pleven Plan for European Defence Community (EDC)
1951	January	– large scale rearmament announced by government
	April	18 Treaty of Paris establishes ECSC
	October	25 general election gives Conservatives 17 seat majority: 321 Conservative, 295 Labour, 6 Liberal, 3 other; Churchill becomes premier
1952	February	6 death of George VI, accession of Elizabeth II
		15 funeral of George VI
	May	27 treaty to create EDC
	October	– Britain explodes its first atom bomb, off Western Australia
		– British Kenya government declares state of emergency and begins 4 years of military operations against Kikuyu 'Mau Mau' rebels
1953	March	5 death of Stalin, in Moscow
	June	2 coronation of Elizabeth II
	July	27 armistice in Korean war
	August	– Central African Federation established: Nyasaland united with Northern and Southern Rhodesia
	September	– end of sugar rationing

ONE

The Cold War

1946–1947

Diary – New Year's Day 1946 – Manor Farm, Stockton, Wiltshire

Cold hard white frost without & icy cold within! except for the drawing-room where Mark works & in which we keep our solitary electric heater! Cressida told me that sweet Adam had a temperature of 99.8 & that his cough was worse, so we decided to keep him in bed downstairs by the dining-room fire....

I stayed in all day till nearly tea-time when I went for a quick walk in the dusk. The ground was hard as iron & all the puddles glass. I started up Long Hedges but the wind was so cold that I turned back & walked into Stockton Park – along the terrace & about the silent lawns & College garden. Ray spent the day in Salisbury with the Sykeses.[1] It is strange that I feel so much more apprehension about the future on this first New Year of peace than I ever did during the 6 New Years of war. It seems more incalculable & uncontrollable than anything we have had to face.

Diary – Wednesday 16 January – 40 Gloucester Square, W.2

Keynes & Lydia lunched with Mark & me today to talk about the American loan.[2] He was very interesting & amusing. The gravamen of his defence was that no other course was open to us – the sterling area didn't want to go on lending us money – & wldn't hold. He surprised me by not attributing much importance to the shortening of the transition period, which I shld have thought important.[3] I asked him if he thought it possible that

[1] Frank Sykes (1903–80), Wiltshire farmer, and his wife Barbara (*née* Yeatman Biggs).

[2] In December 1945 John Maynard Keynes had negotiated a long-term American loan to Britain of $3,750 million, repayable at 2 per cent interest. The deal was unpopular in Britain, where it was felt that the loan should be interest-free. Keynes was in sympathy with this thinking, but he defended the deal as the best that he could get. For a biographical note of Keynes and his wife Lydia Lopokova ('Loppy') see the Biographical notes (Appendix B).

[3] One of the disputed terms of the December 1945 Washington Agreement, negotiated by Keynes, was the time allowed for sterling to become fully convertible into other currencies or gold. Britain sought, unsuccessfully, to lengthen this period beyond December 1946, the date stipulated in the agreement.

we cld increase our exports by 75 p.c. He said 60 p.c. wld do – unless we wanted to live like fighting cocks. He told amusing stories of Bevin. Talking to Lionel Robbins[1] of Anthony Eden, B. said 'He is all right – but after dinner it was cliche, cliche, cliche.' Bevin has developed historic gout & the traditional gout-stool at the F.O. has been produced for him. Maynard found him with his leg resting on this. He said 'They're lunching me to death. It's the wine.'....

Diary – Thursday 24 January – 40 Gloucester Square, W.2

Laura arrived by 11.15 – frozen after an arctic journey. I went off to B.B.C.... Every European country has now been 'handed back' to us except Austria, Germany, Italy & Greece. I raised the question as to whether, in view of the really poisonous anti-British Russian propaganda (contained in our Monitoring Reports), we ought not to link up our service to Europe a little more closely with the atmosphere created by these allegations; whether we do not perhaps err on the side of objectivity? Haley takes the high line & I daresay he is right. Dined at the French Embassy with the Massiglis[2] – where we had a tremendous feast for Attlee & Mrs A.... The food was exquisite – Consommé, Lobster & Rice, Chicken & (really green!) Peas, Ices. B. said the wines were equally delicious. After dinner I talked to Mrs Attlee – rather nice looking & very nice – quite un 'prétentieux'. She went on saying 'I know I'm no good to Clem as P.M.'s wife. I'm quite unpolitical. I didn't even join the Labour Party till 5 years after I had married.' When I asked her whether she wasn't very busy & hard-worked she replied disarmingly 'Oh no it's such a rest. I've put on a stone in weight. I've got so little to do. I have a secretary & a cook who does all the shopping.' Attlee is a tiny tot. I thanked him for re-instating me at B.B.C....[3]

[1] Lionel Charles Robbins (1898–1984), cr. life peer, 1959; a leading economist and academic, he helped negotiate the Washington Agreement of 1945.

[2] René Massigli (1888–1988), French ambassador to Britain, 1944–55; m. 1932 Odette *née* Boissier.

[3] In order to stand at the 1945 general election Violet had been obliged to resign from the board of governors of the BBC. She did so under the impression that if she failed to gain election, which she thought probable, she would be automatically reappointed. But this proved not to be the case and after her defeat her future as a governor rested with Clement Attlee, who chose to reappoint her.

Diary – Friday 25 January – 40 Gloucester Square, W.2

Lunched with Puff – Ansermet,[1] Miss Helen Henschel & one Chegrin (a musician) at Mirabelle. Ansermet very amusing about Russian music & Dialectical Materialism. He says the Russian System is destroying the human ethic 'Ils n'ont plus d'épine dorsale'.[2] Two years ago Russians were sent to prison for having Xmas Trees! This year they wld be sent to prison for not having them. Laura picked me up & we went for a long house-hunt together....

Diary – Saturday 26 January – 40 Gloucester Square, W.2

Edgar Mowrer[3] lunched with us, Jo & Laura. The burning blue of his eyes has faded – but not so the colours of his mind & conversation, which are as vivid as ever. We had a long discussion at luncheon about Germany, over which he takes a surprisingly unenlightened & Vansittart-ite line – thinking that we were sorrier for starving German children than for Dutch ones, etc. He is pessimistic about UNO & thinks that it will very likely have to fail before we get something better. He says the sessions have been so like dim echoes & ghosts of L. of N. He thinks the Russians are fanatical & out for everything....

Diary – Wednesday 30 January – 40 Gloucester Square, W.2

A thrilling day. In the afternoon I attended the meeting of the Security Council & heard the Persian Appeal, Vyshinsky's reply,[4] Bevin, Stettinius, Wellington Koo & Bidault.[5] They met in a biggish room in Church House &

[1] Ernest Ansermet (1883–1969), the world-renowned Swiss conductor, who had arrived in England to conduct the London Philharmonic Orchestra.

[2] 'They have no backbone any more.'

[3] Edgar Ansel Mowrer (1892–1977), distinguished American journalist, the European correspondent for the *Chicago Daily News* between the wars.

[4] On 19 January the Iranian government lodged a complaint with the UN Security Council over Soviet interference in the country's internal affairs. Bevin backed Iran and demanded an inquiry, which the Soviet Union resisted. Its permanent representative at the UN, 1945–9 and 1953–4, was Andrei Vyshinsky (1883–1954), jurist and politician, notorious as the public prosecutor during the state trials in the Soviet Union, 1936–8. He was Soviet foreign minister, 1949–53.

[5] Edward R. Stettinius (1900–49), industrialist and statesman, first US delegate to the UN, of which he was a founder. V. K. Wellington Koo (1888–1985), Chinese statesman, ambassador to UK 1941–6; to United States, 1946–56. Georges Bidault (1899–1983), French statesman; prime minister, 1946, 1949–50.

sat round a Horse Shoe Table – Makin (Australia) in the Chair then Stettinius, Bevin & Vyshinsky. Each delegate had their country's name on a bit of white cardboard erected in front of his place. The Persian delegate opened in rather pathetic English & in a slightly tenuous & quavering voice. It was extraordinarily like the La Fontaine fable *Le Loup et l'Agneau.*[1]

Vyshinsky, who doesn't look at all Russian or even Slav but might well be a black-coated professional man of any nation, replied in a long speech in Russian which was translated into English & French. It was a bad lawyer's speech – making small & false points & never facing the real issue. He cld have been answered sentence by sentence. He ended by saying that to submit this matter to the jurisdiction of the Security Council was against the dignity of the U.S.S.R. It shld be settled by bilateral negotiation between Persia & Russia.

Bevin made an admirable speech. It really moved me. He alone spoke with any force & courage or based his appeal on any sort of principle. He said that when a small Power is negotiating with a big one it enhances the dignity of the Great Power to make sure that the small power shall not do so under unfavourable conditions & shld have the help of the Council. Stettinius backed Bevin in a very colourless speech. Wellington Koo & Bidault were equally dim, weak and effaré. I had to go after Bidault had spoken. I thanked Heaven we had Bevin to speak for us. Anthony cld not have done so equally effectively, even if he had used the same words. Bevin has personality. I went straight on to *Uncle Vanya* with B. at Old Vic. brilliantly acted by Ralph Richardson & Laurence Olivier.

Diary – Friday 1 February – 40 Gloucester Square, W.2

Lunched at the Savoy (our old Peace & Freedom Focus Iolanthe Room) with Geoffrey Crowther[2] to meet Mr Spaak. . . . He was a nice solid sensible man without much sparkle. We talked about Communism in Europe & I asked him whether he thought the breath of public opinion from the outer world was getting through to the Russians at all. He thought it was & that Gromyko[3] had begun to be a little educated in the procedure of

[1]La Fontaine's fable *The Wolf and the Lamb* begins: 'Might is right: the verdict goes to the strong. To prove the point won't take me very long.' The wolf falsely accuses the lamb of muddying its drinking water and, ignoring its protestations of innocence, eats it: 'There was no right of appeal.'

[2]Geoffrey Crowther (1907–72), cr. life peer, 1968; journalist and economist; editor of *The Economist*, 1938–56.

[3]Andrei Gromyko (1909–89), permanent Soviet representative to the Security Council; minister of foreign affairs, 1957–85; president of the Soviet Union, 1985–8.

discussion by the time he left. Unfortunately as soon as they become educated they are withdrawn! G. Crowther said so truly that the real issue today is not between Capitalism & Socialism but between Totalitarianism & Freedom – or what we call Democracy. He was writing a book ... about our hopes for the world but is not too discouraged to go on with it.[1]

Spent another thrilling & moving afternoon at the Security Council. Vyshinsky launched his attack on us for threatening the peace of Europe by remaining in Greece.[2] It was translated paragraph by paragraph. Bevin made a long but absolutely shattering reply. The absence of 'diplomatic' language & clichés is such an intense relief. Also his candour & courage.

Diary – Sunday 3 February – 40 Gloucester Square, W.2

A wet day. Lunched with Puff & Padev[3] & had a long argument about Greece in which Padev was rather boring & revealed his 'C.P.' sympathies. The *Daily Worker* on Bevin is quite appalling – accusing him of being anti-democratic & anti-Soviet (to them synonymous terms) & saying that he was the worst Foreign Secretary since Lord Simon! G. M. Young[4] came to tea. I enjoy the old boy's society. He is writing Baldwin's life & said he came across an amusing letter from Father among his papers – welcoming him back from the 'land of the long-winded & short-sighted' (i.e. U.S.A.). He is very gloomy about the future....

Diary – Friday 8 February – 40 Gloucester Square, W.2

Uneventful day. Lunched at Savoy with Puff to meet Philip Bond, Vice-President of his Union of Film Workers, who Puff had told me is a Communist. Priscilla & Padev were there & I felt more than ever sure he is a crypto C.P. We had a violent hammer & tongs argument all thro' luncheon, in which I soon gave up the struggle of trying to make myself heard. Bond & Padev both said things I shld have thought unsayable – &

[1] It nevertheless appears not to have been published.

[2] In 1944 Britain had intervened in the civil war in Greece to prevent the Communists from seizing power. The Soviet Union did not then intervene, but in the changed post-war atmosphere it lodged a formal complaint against the presence of British troops in Greece.

[3] Michael Padev, the Bulgarian husband of Margot Asquith's granddaughter Priscilla *née* Bibesco (later Mrs Priscilla Hodgson).

[4] George Malcolm Young (1882–1959), eminent scholar, the author of *Victorian England* (1936) and *Stanley Baldwin* (1952). Young had served at the board of education 1908–11, when Violet's father was premier.

still more unthinkable. Instances: 'Right & Wrong is a bourgeois slogan' (Bond). 'Principles are useless' (Padev). 'It is right & justifiable to murder one's political opponents' etc. Both thought an E.L.A.S. régime established by force was right for Greece & are furious with us for having stopped it. I came away appalled at the thought of any country being at the mercy of such people....

Diary – Monday 11 February – 40 Gloucester Square, W.2

Lunched with Cys at an hôtel in Sloane Square called the Royal Court. Talked about Equal Pay, his domestic front, the black international prospect & the 'drab' outlook at home. Everything getting harder rather than easier – & no 'contrepoids de la gloire' to help one through. The food situation is very grave everywhere. There is a real world shortage....

Diary – Tuesday 12 February – 40 Gloucester Square, W.2

Lunched with Herbert Morrison in a mysterious little Cabinet Particulier which he keeps at a place called Howard's Hôtel, Norfolk St. I was ushered down long dark passages – up stairs – then a key turned in a lock & I found myself in a small sitting-room with a table laid for 2 – fire burning in the grate & a door leading into another room. He turned up a little late & we had quite an interesting lunch in which he discussed his Party's prospects, policy & personnel. Praise of Bevin didn't bring a glow to his cheek! I discussed the Russian attitude to us & he said it had coincided exactly with the advent of a Labour Govt & that there was a drive against Socialists all over Europe. I told him that the signing on the dotted line for their [Labour's] long term policy was what wld prevent me from ever joining up with them. He pretended to have forgotten the formula! He asked me if I shld mind Mark becoming a Socialist. I said not if he were a Socialist. He is a gay old hat & very friendly. Went with Puff to *Peter Grimes* at Sadler's Wells – a work of genius – astounding – shattering – deeply moving – one of the greatest works of art of this generation. Supped at Causerie.

Diary – Tuesday 26 February – 40 Gloucester Square, W.2

Pouring wet day of snow & rain & slush. I didn't put my nose out of the house – rare for me. Worked at my speech etc. lunched in alone. Terrible article in the *M.G.* about the enforcement of Communism in the Russian

Zone in Germany – with the Gestapo etc. & the whole Nazi machinery, including Concentration Camps. How have we deserved this? After giving our all at the very highest level – are we to go only out of the frying-pan into the fire?...

Diary – Friday 8 March – 40 Gloucester Square, W.2

Mark turned up early in the morning to my great joy. He has come up for the Buckingham Palace dance & is dining there & (he tells me) going on to Windsor (Royal Lodge) for the week-end.[1] Great fun for him. He looked rather tired but no worse than at Xmas-time & seemed in very good spirits & enjoying himself enormously at Oxford – obviously immersed in his work & loving it. He admits he never has a breath of air or exercise! I saw Allendale[2] in the morning & talked to him about Reconstruction Report & money. He is the most completely unspoilt rich man I know. I spent the afternoon working at tiresome odds & ends & went out with Cressida after tea to see *Brief Encounter*, the most perfectly restrained & flawless film I think I have ever seen. Celia Johnson's performance is exquisite throughout. There is not one wrong note. It could not have been produced in America. It is on a level with the very best French films. Came back to dine with B. Brigid[3] & C[ressida]. Mark had gone off....

Diary – Easter Sunday, 21 April – Stockton, Wiltshire

Lovely day tho' much colder. Went to early service with Laura & Ray. The church all primroses & moss – birdsong from without breaking into Mrs Hutching's yodelling. Back to breakfast & barely time to wash up before returning with Jag & Gelda to morning service....

B. rang me up after tea with the tragic news of Keynes's sudden death. Ray & I had seen him at *The Importance of Being Earnest* only last week. He killed himself by work. How strange that selflessness shld have been the cause of his death. I remember when everyone thought him a selfish

[1] Mark Bonham Carter had become friendly with the royal family while on garrison duty at Windsor Castle in 1944, and he was afterwards invited to spend some weekends and holidays with them. In 1946 he had resumed his studies in PPE at Balliol College, Oxford, which he had begun in 1940, before joining the army.

[2] Wentworth Henry Beaumont (1890–1956), 2nd Viscount Allendale; president of the Northern Liberal Federation, 1925–49.

[3] Brigid Balfour was a paying guest at 40 Gloucester Square, of whom Violet and Bongie were very fond. She qualified as a doctor during the war.

man – while conceding all his other obvious qualities. He had dictated our financial policy all thro' the war & will leave a great void there & elsewhere. I love to think that he had the joy of that 1st night at the Ballet, when he was so proud & happy.[1] John Anderson[2] did a tribute to him on the B.B.C. – just a 'straight' official one with no attempt at intimacy. My heart aches for Loppy. . . .

Diary – Tuesday 4 June – 40 Gloucester Square, W.2

Pouring wet day. Stayed in & worked all day. Went for short wet walk in Ken. Gardens & saw the poor damp soldiers of all colours in their tents, looking most un-victorious happy & glorious.[3] Dined in alone with Brigid. Bevin spoke on Foreign Affairs & relations with Russia (which are Foreign Affairs today!). . . .

Diary – Friday 7 June – 40 Gloucester Square, W.2

A lovely hot day. Walked in the Square for an hour before lunch. Went to have my hair washed at Selfridges afterwards. Streets crowded & a good deal of bunting. . . .

Archie [Sinclair] arrived at the Savoy this morning, rang me up & came to tea. He looked well & weather-beaten & was in good form. He told me of an extraordinary row which had taken place between Winston & Hugh Sherwood[4] in the smoking-room of the H. of C. The plebiscite on the Monarchy was taking place in Italy & W. expressed the hope that the King wld win.[5] Hugh S. said he hoped he wld be beaten – adding that he wld like to get rid of all Kings – & that he had always been a Republican. At this Winston blazed up & said – going off the deep end – 'Then I'm

[1] Keynes was chairman of the committee that oversaw the triumphant re-opening of the Royal Opera House after the war. He invited Violet to the first night, on 20 February, when there was a Royal Gala performance of *Sleeping Beauty* (Moggridge, *Maynard Keynes*, 705).

[2] Sir John Anderson (1882–1958), KCB, 1919; cr. 1st Viscount Waverley, 1952; statesman and administrator; MP (Nat.) Scottish Universities, 1938–50; chancellor of the exchequer, 1943–5.

[3] The soldiers were preparing for the extensive victory celebrations in London on Saturday 8 June, involving military parades, a fly-past and an evening of fireworks and dances.

[4] Hugh Michael Seely (1898–1970), cr. 1st Baron Sherwood, 1941; former Liberal MP for Berwick-on-Tweed and an additional parliamentary under-secretary at the air ministry, 1941–5.

[5] In early June 1946 there was a referendum in Italy on the future of the monarchy. A clear majority voted for a republic and Umberto II left the country for exile.

delighted that Archie was defeated in Caithness & that yr. Party has been placed in its present ignominious position.'[1] Hugh S. said that he ought not to say such things of Archie, who had always been his most loyal supporter. W. retorted 'The happiest moment I had in the whole Election was when I heard that Archie was beaten.' Hugh S. leapt to his feet & shouted at W. 'You ought to be dead.' Bob Boothby witnessed this interchange so it will no doubt be broadcast. When the 2 protagonists staggered blind with rage to the doorway they ran into each other!

Diary – Friday 21 June – 40 Gloucester Square, W.2

Worked most of the day at my speech.[2] It was warm & I was able to sit out in the Square. Puff came round to fetch me at ¼ to 9 to see him get the *Daily Mail* award for the best film of the year – *The Way to the Stars*. Nearly 600,000 people voted. We drove to the Dorchester where there was a vast mob waiting to see the 'stars' arrive. They rushed round the cars like hungry animals & gave a yowl of rage & disappointment on noting the contents of ours. We were hardly able to get out. But a most typical English policeman of the wisest sort said to them firmly but soothingly 'Now this is only an ordinary man & an ordinary woman so please let them get out' – which we then did with ease.

We were the first to be ushered into a blazing room with arc lights focused on one wherever one went & television in full swing (which adds a new hazard to life). We were received by Rothermere & Ann[3] looking very enamelled & curled & rich – & got into the shade (such as it was) as soon as we cld. We were then offered glasses of champagne! which was such an unfamiliar sight to me that I asked what it was. Puff introduced me to Stanley Holloway[4] a delightful man – as delightful off, as on, the screen. The arrival of Margaret Lockwood[5] (the female prize-winner) was

[1]Churchill was then deeply upset with the Liberal Party, which he believed had run an irresponsibly ambitious campaign in the 1945 general election, contributing to the Labour landslide. For a while he was even estranged from such close Liberal friends as Violet and Archie Sinclair. Sinclair had been his second in command with the 6th Royal Scots Fusiliers in 1916, and his secretary of state for air, 1940–5: see the Biographical notes below.

[2]Violet gave a speech to West Country Liberals at Stroud in Gloucestershire the following day.

[3]Esmond Cecil Harmsworth (1898–1978), 2nd Viscount Rothermere; newspaper proprietor and owner of the *Daily Mail*; m. (2nd) 1945, Ann *née* Charteris (divorced 1952), widow of 3rd Baron O'Neill (she later married the novelist Ian Fleming; see below, p 162).

[4]Stanley Augustus Holloway (1890–1982), actor and singer; appeared in *Brief Encounter* (1946), *The Way to the Stars* (1945), *My Fair Lady* (1964).

[5]Margaret Mary Lockwood (1916–90), actress; starred in *The Wicked Lady* (1945); winner of *Daily Mail* film award for best actress in a British film 1946, 1947 and 1948.

just what the crowd was waiting for. She looked quite absurd! but just what a film-star shld look like. A vast orchid – a white fur coat – a white dress covered with tinsel stars – & an erection on her head which was certainly not diamonds. Rosamund John[1] looked better.

The awards were then made by the Rothermeres on a stage – Ann presenting 3 absolutely monstrous silver 'statuettes' – which as Tolly de Grünwald said were like Maud Cunard naked.[2] Puff got a very good reception & was called on to speak (which he hadn't gone prepared for – but did quite well) & we then adjourned, roasted by arc-lights, into the large ball-room in which the *News Chronicle* supper was held – sat down at round tables & got a very good supper. Rivers of champagne flowed, people danced & a French Cabaret artist who had been flown over from Paris sang – probably quite well – but with agonizing effect thro' a microphone! I got home soon after 12 leaving Puff & the Party behind. He was quite all right – & de Grünwald, who I sat next to, spoke well of him & said he meant to hold on to him.[3] I liked him better than I have ever done before. I was introduced to Rank[4] – a very queer looking cove.

Diary – Friday 19 July – 40 Gloucester Square, W.2

Spent the whole day writing frenziedly to catch up on my last 2 days of unanswered letters. Telephoned to 8 Agencies to try & get a cook for Laura & failed. Olsson of the Swedish Service of the B.B.C. came to see me & discuss a broadcast to the Swedes, Finns & Norwegians about Foreign Policy. He was amazed by my 'simple' views 're' principle & expediency & I was amazed by his revelation of the scepticism & cynicism rampant in Europe today – & the complete mistrust by the 'small nations' of the Gt. Powers.

[1] Nora Rosamund Jones (1913–98), British actress who appeared under the screen name 'Rosamund John'; starred in *The First of the Few* (1942), *The Way to the Stars* (1945).

[2] Anatole ('Tolly') de Grünwald (1910–67), film writer and producer; he collaborated with Puff Asquith on *The Way to the Stars* (1945) and they worked together on many films over three decades, including *The Winslow Boy* (1948), *Libel* (1959) and *The V.I.P.'s* (1963). Maud Cunard (1872–1948), an 'exotic, cultivated American .... married to Sir Bache Cunard, heir to the shipping fortune' (M. and E. Brock (eds), *Venetia Stanley*, 632).

[3] Violet alludes here to Puff's battle with alcoholism. She was extremely supportive of his efforts to beat this addiction and helped him to find a cure in 1953; see below, p 336.

[4] (Joseph) Arthur Rank (1888–1972), cr. Baron, 1957; leading figure in the British film industry, the founder and owner of Pinewood Studios, and owner of the Odeon-Gaumont cinema chain.

Diary – Friday 2 August – Liberal Summer School, Cambridge

Left at 9 o'clock with Geoffrey Crowther to motor to Cambridge for Liberal Summer School. Very good talk driving down. He has immense point & a most strange T'ang Buddha face. I asked what he wld do if he were a Liberal (which he actually is – tho' may not declare it. He told me he always voted Liberal & sometimes subscribed to Party funds.) He said he often asked himself that question. He thought one ought to keep 'in being' at all costs – as a split might occur in either of the other two Parties of which we might be the heirs. I said what we lacked & needed most were men of distinction & personality & he asked: was it cause or effect? Was the Party in low water because it had no outstanding personalities? or did personalities fight shy of it because it was in low water? We had a lovely drive & went to Grantchester which I passionately wanted to see. A most romantic colour-washed house, with a bosky garden & the river at the edge, which we had hoped was the Old Vicarage[1] – proved not to be! We arrived at the Univ. Arms to find B. & Ray arrived & waiting for us & were ushered upstairs thro' crowds of old familiar faces....

Diary – Friday 20 September – 40 Gloucester Square, W.2

My first day free of Committees – a real luxury. Wrote all morning – lunched with Cressida – who went off to see [Isaiah] Berlin & thence to Mockbeggars. Spent the afternoon looking for a dressing-jacket for Laura & having my hair washed. Mark rang up. He returns Sunday night on the Royal train. Terrific gale blowing – I don't think I have ever heard one like it in London. Jo came in after dinner & said that huge branches from the plane trees in the Square were lying across the street & he & B. went out to drag them in. Brigid came in later. She had been seeing Oliver Lyttelton[2] who said that Bevin was a dying man – & that both Morrison and Bevan had taken to drink. I hope the first is not true.

Diary – Tuesday 29 October – 40 Gloucester Square, W.2

Stayed in bed till luncheon. Mark arrived soon after & we spent some time tidying up the house – arranging vases of beech-leaves – hips & haws &

[1] The subject of Rupert Brooke's 1912 poem 'The Old Vicarage, Grantchester'.

[2] Oliver Lyttelton (1893–1972), cr. 1st Viscount Chandos, 1954; MP (Con.) Aldershot, 1940–54; member of the war cabinet, 1941–5; secretary of state for colonies, 1951–4; president, Institute of Directors, 1954–63; first chairman of National Theatre, 1962–71.

sloes here & there, storing away litter.... At 10 they arrived & B went down to greet them in the hall. I waited on the landing & took them up to my bedroom where I left them. Pss E. is much prettier than any photograph because she has real bloom of youth – beauté de diable. She had a rather pretty white dress – silver-spangled. Pss Margaret tiny & really pretty in her blue bridesmaid's dress – very gay – natural & impulsive. They all went down to supper – & B & I had an hour over crossword & wireless – during part of which he slept! We heard loud bursts of laughter – followed by song – Pss Margaret singing 'The Bonnie Earl of Moray' at the top of her voice! Then they all came up & we played games.... They were wildly keen – amused & unblasé – so that it was real fun to play with them.... They stayed till 1.30 – & then rolled home – after a most successful & amusing evening.

Diary – Friday 20 December – 40 Gloucester Square, W.2

Arctic cold continues – snow on the ground. Old Vic Board in the afternoon. Soon over. Little done. Day shadowed by a heavy blow. Mark returned from Oxford & I noticed directly he arrived that he looked very unhappy – & I thought he felt he had done badly in his viva, so asked him no questions. Dined in alone with him & Ray & Edward Bell. Going to bed he came into my bedroom as usual. I finally said – 'Did you have a long viva?' – & he replied – 'The thing is that I have got a Second – after 1¾ hours' viva.'[1] It is a terrible blow to him – & of course to me thro' him. It is so hard – after all his work – & with his 1st class mind. Apparently the Examiners said he was a First-Class Man. The extraordinary thing is that he got alpha for his philosophy of which he knows very little.... I cannot write about it as I feel so sad for him. I wld have given the whole world for it not to happen.

'Listening is, at best, a chilly occupation!'
Lecturing in Germany, 25 January–8 February 1947

At the end of January 1947 Violet began a two-week lecture tour of the British zone of Germany, in which she addressed seven public meetings at the principal universities there. She offered an English Liberal perspective of the way ahead, with a talk appropriately entitled 'Ein neues Beginnen'. The lecture tour was one of a number organized by the British Control Commission, which

[1] Mark Bonham Carter had taken one of the 'shortened honours' degree courses at Oxford, intended for those returning from war service.

paid the speaker's expenses and offered a modest honorarium of 10 guineas a week. The tours were intended to help fill the ideological vacuum created by the collapse of Nazism. Violet was specially well qualified to participate in this programme, having been a vociferous opponent of 'Hitlerism' in the 1930s, but an ardent supporter of the Weimar democracy that had preceded it. In 1923 she had travelled to Germany to see firsthand the effects of the French occupation of the Ruhr. While there she witnessed terrible poverty among ordinary Germans: the experience convinced her that Europe needed a free, prosperous and stable Germany, which Britain must help to bring about. It was ironic that twenty-four years later her message should be the same. She informed readers of the *Star* newspaper in February 1947: 'During the last week in England we have been learning what it is to feel cold. But while I was in Germany people were dying of cold.... We face the cold with food inside us, clothes on our backs, shoes on our feet. To get a bare sufficiency of any of these things Germans are driven to the Black Market.' The ruin of Germany was of course a German tragedy: 'But it is also, alas! our own. The tragedy of a lost opportunity which may never come again, the opportunity of solving not the problem of Germany alone, but of the future peace of Europe.' Democracy in Germany could not be allowed to fail a second time, and none had a greater responsibility for ensuring its survival than the Germans themselves: 'You have rights, you have minds, you have youth, you will one day have power. Use them. Do not this time blindly or passively accept the future which is offered you by Fate or any Government or Leader. Make your own.' And Violet was heartened by the clear signs that Germans were doing just that. During her visit she sensed a spiritual and intellectual reawakening: 'I travelled by car in a spell of arctic weather, through a snow and ice-bound country, and my lectures were all given in quite unheated halls – ice-boxes – in a temperature which had to be felt to be believed. Listening is, at best, a chilly occupation. Yet, I always had crowded audiences....'[1]

[1] I. V. Copeland (Control Commission for Germany) to VBC, 26 September 1946; TSS of articles for the *Star* and *News Chronicle*, February 1947; see also text of BBC broadcast on the Third Programme, Tuesday 29 April 1947.

Diary – Friday 24 January 1947 – On board a train to the Rhineland

Snow lying in the Square. A very cold day. Said goodbye to C. Adam & Mark. Dictated 2 last letters. B. drove me to Victoria picking up Military Warrant on the way. We had over an hour & a quarter's wait on an icy platform among B.A.O.R. drafts going back. I gazed at the Officers in a wild surmise. They all seemed drawn by Osbert Lancaster. Never have I seen such faces. Even a Caucasian D.P. cld hardly have mistaken them for Herren Volk. B. was not allowed to cross the barrier with me & I finally got into an unheated train with a very nice Officer's wife going to take up a job in Germany.

We drove thro' snowy Kent – white hop-yards & oast houses – queued for a sandwich & a very Sacchariney cup of tea at a N.A.A.F.I. (I was refused a cup not being an officer!) – arrived at Dover under snow-laden sky & embarked on a small & terribly crowded boat. No possibility of shelter. Arctic crossing but I didn't feel ill tho' some were sick. Decks littered with soldiers in every kind of position. Wind like a knife. Reached Calais under orange sky. Too preoccupied with disembarkation to be able to inspect damage. Finally reached Rhineland Special – a rather shabby old German train in a blasted station with the old, old warnings in the carriages 'Nicht Herauslehnen' – 'È pericoloso sporgersi' etc. Carriages not very warm – but warmer than the ship! I clung to tepid pipes. Dinner at 7. Quite good but no undue luxury. Had some red wine – & tipped both waiter & porter with cigarettes. Now in bed & warm.

Diary – Saturday 25 January – Bünde, Germany

Called soon after 8 & breakfasted on tea & bacon. Snowy German country – all looking fairly normal. Two pathetic old Grausses[?] at one station picking up little bits of coke & coal on the line & putting them in a sack. Reached Bad Oynhausen about 10.30 & got a message to await a car in the Officers' Waiting Room – which I did to background music from Light Programme. The Osbert Lancasters of both sexes collapsed in various attitudes of unconsciousness around me. I was finally fetched by a very competent short dark stocky uniformed figure, Mrs Hochberger – my Interpreter. She looked Semitic & not quite English – but she spoke as tho' English & told me that her husband had died in a Concentration Camp. We drove to Bünde where I am staying at the Transit Hôtel. . . .

Diary – Sunday 26 January – Cologne

Left Bünde at 9.45 by car with Mrs. Hochberger for Cologne – a long day's drive thro' the snow – of great interest & some beauty. We went first thro' the Teutoburger Wald – very German forest country – broad open stretches – a marvellously good Autobahn. Then we entered the Ruhr – chimneys & slagheaps – Lancashire, but so much better country. Curiously enough, in spite of bombing, the chimneys & church spires were all intact. The first town we came to was Dortmund – appalling devastation – then Bochum – more ruins – vast heaps of rubble piled along the streets – then on to Recklinghausen where we saw directions stuck up – 'Sausage Factory' & 'War Crimes Trial' in equally big print. Long hunt for Officers' Club which we found closed. We were however most hospitably entertained at a mess by some very nice officers. . . .

On thro' Duisburg where we saw many Communist Election Posters – 'Gegen Chaos und Not. Für Arbeit und Brot'[1] etc. Then Düsseldorf – again a scene of ruin & rubble. Finally arrival at Cologne which is quite indescribable. Far the most dramatically complete thing I have seen yet. The whole town one vast ruin. The Hauptbahnhof a skeleton – the shattered Cathedral standing beside it. It stands, but is I think a hollow shell. A red sun was setting behind it & I heard sounds of singing from within & went up into a side door where people were attending a rather touching little service (Catholic) packed into a Chapel full of Xmas Trees (undecorated – just the plain trees). I cld not get through into the main building & we had to go on to find our billets in the falling dusk. . . .

Diary – Monday 27 January – Bonn

Started at 10 with Mr MacMillan & Mrs Hochberger for my 1st lecture to Bonn Univ. Arrived there & met the very nice Education Officer Mr Smith (in a quite unheated office) who took us on to Bad Godesberg(!) There I was introduced to the Professor, Friesenhahn – a very nice youngish man who introduced me. I spoke from a platform with a kind of lectern. The hall was packed out. I shld think there were 5 or 6 hundred there. Very courteous audience & responsive. Only a small proportion knew English & the translation naturally slowed things down – but it 'went' quite well, tho' it took (with the introduction) about 1 hour & 10 minutes. Then questions followed – very lively ones about the Iron Curtain – Liberalism in England – the Saar etc. I then went to see them eating in their Canteen – potatoes & soup etc. – well cooked. They said their difficulty was not

[1] 'Against chaos and need. For work and bread.'

having enough coupons for the food. Some students from the East have nothing – not even a pair of socks. . . .

Diary – Wednesday 29 January – Düsseldorf

I went out at 10.45 with a Major Campbell & Mrs Hochberger to visit the Bunker School – one of the most moving & terrible experiences I have had here. It is a great concrete-block building – completely cut off from both light & air – a stifling atmosphere in which 816 children are taught – & in which many live as well. Tho' it is considered dangerous to health to be in the Bunker for more than $3\frac{1}{4}$ hours some spend 24 hours there & owing to lack of shoes & stockings are unable even to go out. We saw one little girl standing barefoot & barelegged on the icy concrete floor & when we asked her she said she had neither shoes, socks nor stockings. I was much impressed by the head-mistress – full of sympathetic efficiency & quite uncomplaining. The children were queuing up in the snow outside with their mugs & tins for the Schulspeise – their pint of soup – when we arrived. One little boy – one of a family of 7 – looked very ill & they said he was too tired to be taught. I came away feeling terribly harrowed & helpless. . . .

Diary – Monday 3 February – Altenholz, near Kiel

Started at 9.30 for Kiel & saw the Canal again in full daylight & the Eckernförder bay. Arctic cold. . . . Luncheon at Yacht Club – given by Miss C. Cunningham. Sat between a Colonel Randall & Colonel Donnelly (Public Health – Irish name & Scotch accent) who took me afterwards to see a Camp of 'Flüchtlinge' – a really unforgettable experience. We motored to a camp just outside Kiel which (I was told) was by no means a 'bad' one. It looked very like what I imagine Siberia to be like – a collection of flat-roofed huts in an expanse of frozen snow. We knocked at the door of the 1st & went in. Thirty people were living in it – of both sexes & touching the extremes of age & childhood. The 'young people' – at least the young men – were missing. They had been held in forced labour or sent east as slaves. Every function of life was performed communally within these 4 walls – eating, sleeping, cooking, washing, children at play (without anything to play with), the old lying on their bunks or wandering aimlessly about on the damp boarded floor.

I asked a woman where they had come from? 'From Pomerania.' And why? 'We have been expelled – by the Poles. They gave us 10 minutes (or an hour as the case may be). We were not allowed to take anything – only what would fit in the rucksack. The children were all thrown onto the carriages. We went on foot.' It was the same tragic story time after time – like a gramophone record. They had been turned out of house & home – deprived & despoiled of everything they possessed – their life's treasures & belongings. Some asked pathetically 'Gehen wir bald nach Hause?'[1] They were amazingly brave – & orderly – in spite of cabbages under the bed & drying washing & clothes, & here & there a lovely crucifix – tenderly carried all that way. The fate of the old was most poignant. The children will forget. They had such patience – hope – & harmony – & the apple faces of country people – old apples & young.... I asked a woman 'Are these all your children?' 'Nein – 3 sind von meiner Schwester.' 'Wo ist sie?' 'Sie ist von den Russen gestorben.'[2] I went back feeling that in subscribing at Yalta & Potsdam to the Partition of Poland we had connived at one of the greatest crimes in history....[3]

Diary – Thursday 6 February – Berlin

I had a free morning till 12 o'clock.... I first dropped Maud Russell's[4] parcel on her half-sister – who I longed to see, but she was out.... I waited for a bit in front of the house in the car – & then had to go on.

I now drove round Berlin – an indescribable experience. It has the inconsequence of a dream – almost a nightmare, in which nothing is related to anything else. Solid heavy prosperity turned into ruin, before which Pompeii & Herculaneum pale. The streets are heaped high with gigantic mountains of rubble. Some houses stand precariously – but every one is a skeleton. The most extraordinary sight is the great triumphal way ... which leads thro' the Tiergarten up to the Sieges Säule & on to the Brandenburger Tor. On each side, where the Tiergarten shld be, there is a waste. The trees are all gone. Here & there one sees some strange survival, like the statue of a girl astride a (very tame) horse. The snow covered a desolation which wld have looked far worse without it. On the top of the Sieges Säule, waving, was the Tricolor. On the right is a huge monument erected by the Russians to the Soviet Army – rather impressive – dominated

[1] 'Are we going home soon?'

[2] 'No – 3 are my sister's.' 'Where is she?' 'She was killed by the Russians.'

[3] At Yalta in February 1945, and at Potsdam in July-August, the Western Allies reluctantly accepted the redrawing of Poland's boundaries by the Soviet Union. Having taken land from eastern Poland in 1939, which it refused to surrender, the Soviet Union proposed that Poland should be compensated with territory in the west, at Germany's expense. The new border encompassed much of what was then eastern Germany, causing a mass migration of ethnic Germans from east of the Oder and Neisse rivers.

[4] Maud Russell *née* Nelke, wife of Gilbert Russell, jobber; old friends of the Bonham Carters.

by one vast bronze Red Army soldier. Standing below, one on each side, are 2 absolutely immobile Russian guards – so still that I took them to be part of the monument until I was told that they were real. At the end is the Brandenburger Tor – with a crumpled chariot on the top. The Soviet flag is gone.

One of the strangest sights is the Sieges Allee of Hohenzollern statues. These have been chopped & chipped & blasted & defaced & present a most strange Surrealist aspect. Some are precariously balanced on their bases – as tho' a child had built his bricks up badly – one square of stone just overlaps the other. On the top you may see a headless Emperor with outstretched arms – or even a pair of feet in strangely mincing positions. One realises suddenly as one looks at them – & at the odd gamut of Travel Bureaux, Cigarren Laden, etc. – in complete confusion, disorder & incoherent fragments, that one is looking on at the suicide of a civilization. . . .

Diary – Friday 7 February – Berlin

. . . I picked up Mrs Hochberger on my way home at her German friend's. I had sent her my last 1lb of coffee to give her. . . . When she saw it she burst into tears & said 'Now I can go to the dentist again. You realise that I cannot drink it. It is worth 500 Marks to me.' Black Market of course – but what are these people to do in their dire need? It was the 1st time Mrs H. had seen her since the fall of Berlin. . . .

She told Mrs H. the most terrible stories of the entry of the Russians into Berlin. Everybody took to their cellars – but the Russians usually found them out & raped every woman – no matter what her age & condition – en masse. This woman's care-taker & wife had a girl of 16 who was the apple of their eye & to whom they had given secondary school education & of whom they were very proud. She was raped every day by 10 and 12 Russians – before the eyes of her parents – & finally one of them shot her & told her Mother to bury her in the garden. . . . Tom Creighton told me an English officer friend of his saw a German woman clinging to a lamp-post & a Russian trying to pull her off. He was near enough to see the hope & appeal in her eyes as she saw an Englishman approaching. But he was unarmed & so did nothing, as he said the Russian wld. certainly have shot him. . . .

The horror & hatred with which Berliners regard the Russians is understandable – & also indelible. It will never be forgotten or wiped out. Russia might have made a Communist Germany – but she threw away her chance thro' barbarity & bestiality which have sunk the S.E.D. – & Communist prospects everywhere. (Have we sacrificed our chance thro' unimaginative muddle & lack of policy?) Mrs H's friend said she had been in a railway carriage full of Germans where a Russian officer asked very courteously the name of the next station. Not a soul wld. answer him. She told him Potsdam & he thanked her. The rest of the carriage glared at her as tho' she were a blackleg. But the stories one hears make one understand it. It is almost impossible to believe that they belong to this century. The mot d'ordre now is for Russians to behave better.

Diary – Saturday 8 February – Berlin

I hurried off to keep an appt. at 11 at the Chancellery, made for me by Elizabeth Wyndham, with a Russian officer who was to show me over it. I arrived there 5 minutes late to find not a soul! So I wandered in alone with my nice military chauffeur & we roamed through the Babylonian ruins – attended by a poor old shivering, gibbering German beggar who reminded me of the Russian idiot left in the snow at the end of *Prince Igor*. He said to me 'Wir sind ja bettel arm – bettel arm' & when I asked for Hitler's bunker where he died – 'Aber der Hitler der ist nicht gestorben.'[1] I went out into the snowy garden beyond & found there a quite sensible German .... who seemed to know all about it & who took me down into the Bunker by the light of a guttering candle & my very dim torch. The rooms are all bare & stripped. They were once (according to my guide) marvellously furnished....

I shall never forget the intense & bitter cold in the Chancellery that morning. One literally felt as tho' one's features wld drop off one's face! I had one more look at the Sieges Allee & Sieges Säule etc. & then went back to the city before lunch with the Steels. My nice military chauffeur said to me on the way 'I have no time for the Russians. They ought to go away for 100 years & then come back before they are ready to talk to us.' Their lack of civilization has clearly been a great shock to our people....

We left about 9.30. I showered most of my remaining cigarettes on lift-men & housemaids. It is strange to have so much cheap bounty at one's disposal. I liked the Berliners – much better than the Hamburgers. We got into separate carriages on the Night-Train.... I slept alone but had an arctic night as my window was 'caput' & had to be lashed to the rack with a handkerchief & so remained ajar on a night which was certainly 20 degrees below zero. Light was dim & water non-existent.

[1] 'We are poor as beggars – poor as beggars.' 'But Hitler – he didn't die.'

Diary – Tuesday 11 February – 40 Gloucester Square, W.2

Mark's birthday. But no presents for him alas! I was terribly busy getting thro' letters etc. & cldn't 'make' the Liberal Party Committee.... I have returned to the Fuel Crisis at its height. The snow & ice have put the lid on Shinwell's incompetence & improvidence[1] – & after a policy of sporadic cuts we are now warned that the Power system of the country is at breaking-point & that we must not use any electricity from 9 to 12 & from 2 to 4 on pain of £100 fine or imprisonment! Shinwell has come very badly out of the whole thing & it is the worst knock the Govt have had....

Diary – Wednesday 12 March – 40 Gloucester Square, W.2

Went to see Mr Luker at B.B.C. & arranged to broadcast on 29th about my German University experience....[2] The U.S.A. is taking over our commitments in Greece. This has brought home our plight to me more than anything else. Without the U.S.A. Greece & Turkey wld be in the Communist maw. I was stunned by announcement in *News Chronicle* that Hatchie has joined the Labour Party! It is a bad 'rat' – not from any other Party – but from himself – for he is a much further cry from them than even I am.

'Let Europe arise again in glory':
the United Europe Movement

In a debate in the House of Commons on foreign affairs, on 5 June 1946, Winston Churchill expressed his grave fears for the future of post-war Europe, across which the 'iron curtain' had fallen. If the mistakes of the inter-war years were not to be repeated, he argued, Britain must take a lead: 'We cannot impose our will on our Allies, but we can, at least, proclaim our own convictions. Let us proclaim them fearlessly. Let Germany live.

[1] Emanuel Shinwell (1884–1986), cr. life peer, 1970; Labour politician first elected to parliament, 1922; later MP for Seaham Division, Durham, 1935–50; Easington, Durham, 1950–70; as Labour minister for fuel and power, 1945–7, Shinwell was severely criticized for failing to solve problems of coal production, which exacerbated public hardship during an exceptionally severe winter.

[2] Violet's talk 'Empty Vessels' was broadcast on the Third Programme on 29 April: 'I have come back from Germany convinced that the only sure way of turning War Potential into Peace Potential is by the education of a generation of German Youth which will refuse to accept the possibility of war. And that solution may lie within our power to achieve.' She found great interest there in the 'united Europe' idea that Churchill was then espousing.

Let Austria and Hungary be freed. Let Italy resume her place in the European system. Let Europe arise again in glory, and by her strength and unity ensure the peace of the world.' The idea of European unity gathered pace throughout 1946 and in an important speech at Zurich in September Churchill gave it further impetus, calling for the creation of a 'United States of Europe'. At home that winter he drew together a small number of like-minded pro-Europeans in a steering-committee, which Violet joined in March 1947. From this emerged the 'United Europe Movement', officially launched on 14 May 1947 at a packed meeting in the Albert Hall. It was presided over by the archbishop of Canterbury, who symbolized Churchill's desire that there should be a strong spiritual dimension to the movement, which he also hoped would attract popular support. And in her speech to the meeting Violet drew attention to the diverse backgrounds and beliefs of those gathered: 'Whatever our differences we feel the common need to declare a common faith, the need to defend that civilisation which is the common heritage of us all. Twice in our lifetimes the best and bravest of Europe's children have fought and died to save her freedom and assure her peace. Twice we have won a war and twice seen what we called victory crumbling to dust and ashes in our hands. And because we cannot, dare not, throw away this second chance – which may well be our last – we appeal to you to join with us in our resolve to seek and find a new way out – the way of unity.'[1]

Diary – Tuesday 18 March – 40 Gloucester Square, W.2

Liberal Party Committee in H. of L. . . . I dashed off to the Savoy where, in a Gilbert & Sullivan room, I had my 1st luncheon with the United Europe Committee – which I have now decided to join. As I hurried down the passage W. got out of the lift – looking, I thought, older & heavier – with a rather moist eye. He greeted me affectionately. In the private room I found an extraordinary assortment – Duncan Sandys, Gilbert Murray, Dr Berry (of the Free Churches) & Bob Boothby, Lady Rhys Williams, Victor Gollancz, the Dean of St Paul's – a figure who I suppose was Maxwell

[1] *Hansard*, vol. 423, cols. 2032–3; Gilbert, *Never Despair*, 265–7, 278–9, 290–1; CAC, CHUR 2/18; text of Third Programme broadcast, 29 April 1947.

Fyfe[1] – Bertrand Russell. . . . We had cocktails & nibbled potatoes & then settled down to lunch. I sat next Winston who was very sweet. Rather emotional. As usual discursive when it came to business – rambling off into long passages of purple prose. I feel that his mind has lost any tight executive quality – but I may be wrong. He is of course terribly gloomy about the country, which he feels is sliding to ruin.

Ly Rhys Williams drove me away to Gayfere St. & poured into my ears a flood of excited talk about the certainty of a coming General Election. The Lib. Party wld be wiped out. Winston wld give us 35 seats – 2 seats in the Cabinet – Under Secretaryships etc. I pointed out that we cldn't deliver the goods even if we wld. . . .

V.B.C. to W.S.C. ***Tuesday 18 March***
40 Gloucester Square, W.2

My dearest Winston.

It was such a deep joy to see you again to-day – & to feel that we were once more going forward together, side by side, on a great new adventure. So much, so bravely won, has turned to dust & ashes in our hands. So many faiths lie broken & buried in the rubble that once was Europe. Our first task should be to teach men to hope once more. They have almost forgotten how.

My constant love. Ever yr B.D. – Violet

Diary – Sunday 23 March – 40 Gloucester Square, W.2

Peaceful day. B. & [?] went to Bach Passion Music. Gerrard came to luncheon. Michael Padev to tea. . . . He talked to me for nearly 2 hours about Bulgaria – & indeed the Iron Curtain part of Europe. He is completely open-eyed now about the terror which reigns there & was so upset by his visit to Paris to see his friend the Foreign Minister that he had to see doctors when he returned. His friend never moves without a revolver & poison. Padev is now in Communist black books himself. What he told me is too long to write here. He ranks the Terror-stricken countries in this

[1] Rev. Sidney Malcolm Berry (1881–1961), DD Glasgow; former moderator of Free Church Federal Council (1934–7). Lady (Juliet Evangeline) Rhys Williams (1898–1964), DBE 1937; contested Ilford North (Lib.), 1945; hon. sec. UEM, 1947–58. Very Rev. Walter Robert Matthews (1881–1973), dean of St Paul's, 1934–67. David Patrick Maxwell Fyfe (1900–67), cr. Viscount Kilmuir, 1954; 1st Earl, 1962; MP (Con.) Liverpool, West Derby, 1935–54, afterwards lord chancellor.

order 1) Yugoslavia 2) Poland 3) Bulgaria 4) Hungary 5) Czechoslovakia 6) & best Rumania – because it is most corrupt. What he told me was a nightmare.

Diary – Thursday 27 March – 40 Gloucester Square, W.2

Very busy day. Long but interesting Old Vic Sub-Committee at which I failed to recognize Laurence Olivier![1] whose hair was dyed bright gamboge! literally orange – as he is being filmed in Hamlet. He revealed that they don't achieve more than one minute a day!... Rushed to Fortnum's to try & get a summer coat & failed.... Then on to Curtis Committee at Lib H.Q. after which Ly Rhys Williams made an impassioned appeal to me to make a pact with Winston, who she said wld give me anything I asked – including Electoral Reform & 35 seats if we wld agree to fight in alliance with the Conservatives at the election.

I pointed out that apart from all else we cldn't deliver the goods. Our Progressives wld go Labour. Unless there were some compulsive issue which welded us together it wld be an impossible strategic decision to take in cold blood. We cldn't carry the Party. Furthermore I thought the Election was not coming in the autumn – & the more we built up our strength & funds meanwhile the better our bargaining position wld be. She takes the view that the Tories are weak now & prepared to make terms – but that as Labour plunges deeper into the mire their position will get stronger & our terms will go down. I had to admit to her that if an Election came this autumn the whole Liberal Parliamentary Party might be wiped out. I wld do a good deal for Electoral Reform, as I think on Electoral Reform depends the ultimate survival of a Liberal Party in England. But can one buy survival with dishonour? I hurried home exhausted & feeling that a leech had sucked my blood....

Diary – Saturday 29 March – 40 Gloucester Square, W.2

...International Youth Council meeting at Beaver Hall. It was raining cats & dogs – literally floods (this on the top of existing floods will put the lid on). B & I went by tube to the Bank & paddled on to the Hall. There was a very small audience – I shld think about 150 – & nearly all

[1]Sir Laurence Olivier (1907–89), Kt, 1947; first actor to become a life peer, 1970; joint director of the Old Vic Theatre Company, 1944–8, and later first director of the National Theatre, 1962–73. He produced, directed and played the lead in the film version of *Hamlet* (1948).

Communists. The 2 Labour M.P.s had both failed to appear but the Chair was taken by a very nice Labour man called Hughes. I spoke 1st after him & tried to put a few home-truths between the lines, but cld not dot 'i's nor cross 't's with a Soviet delegate on the platform. A young Czech spoke next for about half an hour, then the Russian followed – a mask-like face without one glint of humanity.

He read like a Robot from a type-script, long lists of statistics describing Soviet losses, followed by even longer ones celebrating Soviet achievements – 'our system of Govt which renders Unemployment impossible' etc. Then a very green & innocent young American, Ed Hawley, got up & made a typically Anglo-Saxon self-deprecatory speech – describing how many calories young Americans eat, how much petrol they used, how tho' they had democratic forms of Govt. 'a lot went on behind the scenes' (what goes on behind the scenes in Russia I shld like to know?) & sent all the Communists home quite happy to bed – leaving me with the sense of having been the unwilling accomplice of a deception. We swam home thro' the rain. It is heavenly to feel I needn't make another speech for 3 whole weeks.

Diary – Tuesday 22 April – 40 Gloucester Square, W.2

. . . Attended a United Europe Committee Meeting in Winston's room at the H. of C. Present: W., self, Walter Layton, Gollancz, Ly Rhys Williams, Gibson. . . .[1] Winston discussed the [Albert Hall] meeting [on 14 May] – which he wants to open with 'When wilt thou save thy People' – a hymn he remembers being sung in old Limehouse days. He looks back nostalgically to his old Liberal past. He repeated some of the things he said last time . . . 'why shouldn't the people live, poor things – & enjoy a little happiness & food & family & simple things' etc. Order of speakers was arranged. I am to second the resolution, which Gibson is moving.

Then he asked me to stay behind & talk to him – & I knew what was coming. He stressed the need for Lib. Independence – no alliances etc. – but 'Lay off a little against us. We might help each other – make some arrangements which wld be mutually convenient etc.' I said that only an issue cld determine such an alignment – not a cold-blooded arrangement. I cldn't deliver the goods. Could he do so? Cld he for instance 'deliver' Electoral Reform? He couldn't say 'yes'. He wld speak to his party about it etc. – but I felt that he was not confident. He touches me very much & I feel a certain pathos about him. He harks back to his beginnings – & I think

[1] George Gibson (1885–1953), General Council of TUC, 1928–48; director, Bank of England, 1946–8.

he definitely – emotionally – desires a rapprochement with Liberals....

Diary – Tuesday 29 April – 40 Gloucester Square, W.2

Attended a meeting of our United Europe committee in Duncan Sandys' charming house in Vincent Square. Present D.S., Self, Victor Gollancz & Oliver Stanley. Victor Gollancz rather put the cat among the pigeons by suggesting that he was going to say that the only hope for a United Europe lay in a United Socialist Europe. I pointed out that if we all said something of the kind in our own political idiom it wld not 'go' very well. Also that one cld not demand political 'Gleichschaltung' from the various European Nations. He eventually said he might temper it down to something like 'social democracy'....

Diary – Sunday 15 June – 40 Gloucester Square, W.2

Grey, cold day. B & I & Mark here. Mark went off after luncheon to see Ettie.[1] B & I had a short 'duty' blow in Kensington Gardens. Michael Padev came to me. Tragically interesting about Eastern Europe. He is now on the Black List of his own country & much embarrassed by letters from his old father (aged 70) telling him that the Govt are gangsters & murderers etc. He knows that these letters are opened read & photographed. He writes in vain to his father that 'he is not interested in politics' but cannot stop him. He wants to save his mother – who is only 53 – & is trying to get her a visa to U.S.A. where he has a sister. If she goes she will never see his father again. They wld never both be allowed to go. One hostage is kept so that the one who goes cannot attack the régime abroad....

Michael says he cannot get his Bulgarian friends to come & speak to him in his flat – even here. They are afraid it is 'wired' & will only meet him in the Park. I had an inkling of the terror for others which operates in all their minds when I suggested he shld see Wilfrid Roberts....[2] He said 'Is he not a tall man? With a pale long face? I have seen him somewhere. I have seen him with Claud Cockburn.[3] No I cannot see him he might give me away.'.... I am terribly sorry for him as I think he is really worried about his future....

[1] Ethel 'Ettie' Grenfell, Lady Desborough (1867–1952), an old and dear friend of Violet; Ettie was one of the 'Souls' and a contemporary of Margot Asquith.

[2] Wilfrid Hubert Wace Roberts (1900–91), MP (Lib.) North Cumberland, 1935–50.

[3] (Francis) Claud Cockburn (1904–81), author and journalist, on staff of *Daily Worker*, 1935–46; joined the Communist Party in 1932.

Diary – Wednesday 25 June – 40 Gloucester Square, W.2

Most futile F.A. committee at H. of L. in the morning. Only Eric Perth,[1] Walford Selby[2] & Sheila Newsome present. We discussed the paper which had been written to me by a Czech Journalist complaining of the stamping out of liberty in Czechoslovakia. Sheila at once branded him as a German & a reactionary tho' she had to admit that she didn't even know his name. I had asked for Dick Stokes to be called as a witness but he wasn't. After ¾ of an hour it was generally admitted that the Secret Police was operating there actually under Czech not Russian control & Sheila remarked 'But there is a Secret Police in all countries. Look at it here – at the B.B.C.!' We all roared with laughter & I then left saying I was too busy for such fun. We ought to reform the Committee. . . .

Diary – Wednesday 30 July – 40 Gloucester Square, W.2

Edward Stinnes, who had sent us food parcels from U.S.A. all thro' the war, came to tea & stayed an unconscionable time! He thinks we all look tired, underfed & over-patient of our queues. I must say his appearance is that of a man from a different world – so fat & pink. Perhaps we don't realise what we look like to others. I certainly don't feel underfed & shldn't feel tired if I didn't have to make so many speeches. . . .

Diary – Thursday 14 August – Stockton, Wiltshire

Raymond came back in time for lunch. We had tea at the Rectory & went out after tea in the water meadows with Frank Barbara & Tristram [Sykes] to shoot duck. It was a most lovely evening – still hot but with a little breeze – the meadows very flowery tho' dry & hard. Tristram shot one astonishingly high duck. He dined with us. Ray & I sat up late talking about his interview etc.[3] He says that Mark winced at his recital of his candour with the Colonel! & told him that what got him in was his

[1] (James) Eric Drummond (1876–1951), 16th Earl of Perth, 1937; first secretary-general to League of Nations, 1919–33; British ambassador to Italy, 1933–9. Eric Perth was an old friend of Violet, having been private secretary to her father, 1912–15.

[2] Sir Walford Selby (1881–1965), diplomat and civil servant; formerly assistant private secretary to Sir Edward Grey, 1911–15.

[3] Raymond was due to embark on his military service and had recently been interviewed for officer entry to the Irish Guards. He joined the regiment on 7 September.

saying – about David Montgomery – 'He's a very nice chap & quite different from his father!'[1]

Diary – Saturday 16 August – Stockton, Wiltshire

The sun still burns & the whole earth glows. I can't remember such a summer since 1940 – Battle of Britain. . . . B. & I & Mark walked thro' the Park to the ford & took the bus to Heytesbury to have tea with Siegfried [Sassoon]. The Park looked extraordinarily beautiful – with large clumps of trees laden with all the greens that ever were. And the grey square house – cool as a vault as we walked into it out of the sun. At first I thought it was empty – tho' all the lovely rooms were open. Then just as we were going down to the cricket field – S. appeared in white shirt & flannels, looking I thought rather younger & less harassed. We sat outside gazing up at the 'hanger' of woods beyond – heavy with summer beauty & talked till nearly 6.30. . . .

We went all over the house which Mark admired enormously. It is I must say most lovely – every mantelpiece & door & moulding, & the proportions of the windows, which flood it with light. The 'best bedroom' is one of the loveliest I have seen anywhere, with a rounded end over the library. I can't think why the Royal Family don't buy houses like that instead of places like 'Sunninghill Park'. He finally drove us home, after fetching out of the cellar – & giving B. – a bottle of very good Burgundy – which B. & Mark drank at dinner. Ray had gone over to Shrewton for the night. Winston broadcast on the Economic Crisis – quietly & well but said nothing positive or constructive.

Diary – Monday 25 August – Stockton, Wiltshire

. . . Another radiant day. I went over to Heytesbury to spend the evening with Siegfried – arriving about 6. He leaned out of his bedroom window in the large great front & called to me to go round to the library as the front door was locked. Soon he came down in riding-clothes. We went to the stables & he cantered off on his mare along the green valley behind the house. I sat out in the evening sun & gazed up at the 'hanger' of woods – piled green upon green – & read *I Chose Freedom*[2] – a strange

[1] Raymond had been at Winchester with David Bernard (later 2nd Viscount) Montogmery (b. 1928), son of Field Marshal Sir Bernard Montogmery, 1st Viscount Montgomery of El Alamein.

[2] Viktor A. Kravchenko, *I Chose Freedom: the personal and political life of a Soviet Official* (1947).

contrast. I walked round the big walled garden but all the doors were locked. The walk round it is delicious however – shrubs & herbaceous border – & a little rose-garden with a hedge of box.

Siegfried came in & we had dinner together in the library. Delicious buttered eggs – a cold duck – cream & grapes & nectarines. We had a long talk about his poetry & way of writing. He hates being 'written off' as a war-poet – as tho' he had 'stopped there' – & says the public know him mainly as the author of the *Foxhunting Man*. He has a vol. of Collected Poems just coming out. Many of them are I think supremely good. . . . He doesn't care for the Moderns – Day-Lewis etc. & their complications. He says he is an old-fashioned poet – straightforward & simple & therefore out of tune with the Times. He talked with his usual uninhibited candour & simplicity about himself. 'There's nothing ever been written better than that – it's a great poem' etc. & 'There's De La Mare – there's Hodgson – there's myself – who else is there?'. . . .

. . . We also had an amusing patch about Ottoline[1] & both agreed she wasn't really 'wicked'. But he told me that when in the First War she asked him to tea on one occasion, before he went back to the Front, she suddenly got up & embraced him passionately, covering him with kisses, 'bouche & all' he muttered. A terrifying thought! He ordered the village car for me & I drove back thro' the dark – & saw the lights flash as so often in the past in Stockton's diamond windows. Read Ciano's diary in bed.[2]

Diary – Wednesday 10 September – 40 Gloucester Square, W.2

After early lunch here I started with Mark for Waterloo.[3] When we reached Marble Arch he said 'How empty the taxi seems' – it contained Ray's vast blue trunk, 2 suit-cases & a bag of golf-clubs. But we had forgotten his black tin box full of books! Luckily we had started early so we had time to go back for it. He is only allowed £5 in cash for the journey – hardly enough for tips & drinks – & no one is allowed to see him off for fear of smuggling currency, jewels etc. I had hoped to go to Southampton. We found the Commonwealth carriages & some rather dim little fellow-

[1] Lady Ottoline Morrell (1873–1938), *née* Cavendish-Bentinck, a Bohemian figure prominent in Edwardian literary and artistic circles. She married, 1903, Philip Edward Morrell, later a Liberal MP (1906–18). In her youth Violet had been friendly with Ottoline.

[2] Conte Galeazzo Ciano (1903–44), Italian fascist executed by pro-Mussolini partisans in 1944; his diary was published in England in 1947 as *Ciano's diary, 1939–43*.

[3] Mark was bound for the University of Chicago, having won a Commonwealth Fund Scholarship for a year of study there.

travellers – all scientists.[1] I met Kenneth Rae – seeing someone off. The usual 'boat-train' people – with terribly expensive luggage & 'stage' travelling clothes. Not long to wait till he was gone. What a hole in life! ...

V.B.C. to Mark Bonham Carter ***Wednesday 10 September***
40 Gloucester Square, W.2

My Darling

One line of goodbye – & every wish & prayer that you may have a wonderful year of adventure & new exciting experience. I have never felt more sure of anything than that this is the 'right thing to do' – & I feel that however much you enjoy – or dis-enjoy – some aspects of it you will never regret having done it.

How much I shall miss you is unsayable & (as yet) unimaginable. Sharing your life is such an intense vicarious joy to me & you are so infinitely generous in sharing so much of it with me. It is lovely, when one is almost at the end of everything that can 'happen' to oneself, to be at the very beginning of everything that can happen to someone who matters to one as much – or more – than oneself....

Try to overcome yr. letter-writing repugnance enough to give me a real sense of your surroundings & re-action to them. Don't fly (this is my only injunction – as I am not afraid of whisky for you!! the only other risk the U.S. holds!) We shall moulder on here in a way you can imagine very vividly – & will hear about all too often. This year without you will be a very bleak one – but I shall live it partly vicariously & buoyed up by the sense that at least you are warm & fed – & I hope amused & interested....

All my dearest love & constant thoughts go with you – with the seagulls & beyond. Ever yr Mama ....

Diary – Saturday 4 October – 40 Gloucester Square, W.2

Most lovely autumn day. Ray & Micky O'Brien polishing weapons & equipment in the basement. The polishing fever pursues them even in this brief respite. Lunch – B & I & Ray. Then he wrote letters & I worked in the Square. Ray & I went to *Peace in our Time* – an indifferent Noel Coward play....

[1]One of the 'dim scientists' was John Freeman Dyson (b. 1923), who went on to become professor of the School of Natural Sciences at Princeton. During the journey he fascinated Mark by likening the sudden illumination of an original insight to chasing a firefly – the light would fluctuate tantalizingly, and sometimes disappear altogether.

Diary – Sunday 5 October – 40 Gloucester Square, W.2

Ray very amusing about his army life & full of excellent 'Imitas' of Sergt Renton – who curses them up hill & down dale all day: accuses them of 'dumb insolence' – told Ray to stand 'closer to his razor' – & says 'I'd like to know your thoughts & if I knew your thoughts I'd place you under close arrest.' People are marched off to the cells for having a spot of Blanco on their collars. In spite of this Ray is a 'Recruit Leader' & obviously anxious to keep his job – for he spent the whole afternoon polishing his boots on the drawing-room sofa (a pathetic sight!) till they shone like ebony. He then said they were 'still quite dozy'. He & Micky had a vast tea at 5.30 – devoured a lobster & 2 boiled eggs – & girded each other into their belts (which have to be so tight that there isn't room for a finger to be poked in). It was like seeing a Victorian débutante 'tight-laced' – tho' very differently achieved. Then we saw them off to Victoria on the bus.

V.B.C. to Barbara Freyberg[1] ***Monday 6 October***
40 Gloucester Square, W.2

My darling Barbara ... How can I thank you for the wonderful shower of largesse which has again descended on us from your New Zealand Heaven? Wonderful soups & sauces (we have started on the celery which is delicious) & a tin labelled 'Biscuits' which I have not yet opened – as I am keeping it for a Xmas or some great 'grand-children' occasion. It is angelic of you both to think of us & be so generous. We are not starving! – but eating terribly dull food (like hake for fish for instance!) & have only a pint of milk a head a week to drink & cook with – which also presents a problem. Things are certainly going to get much worse – the Spring is supposed to be the time when the real pinch will come.

At present I am sure it is true that the ordinary 'man in the street' is far from recognizing the gravity of the position.... Disastrously as the Govt. have done I don't believe we shld gain by turning them out now – even if we could. The Conservatives wld have to face far greater hostility from organized Labour – which are the 'crux' of our difficulties to-day. Also I think it is far better that Labour shld have to face the music of their own difficulties & (in the process) gain some economic education from harsh reality.

In foreign affairs the other Parties are solid behind Bevin. But if Eden were trying to carry out the same policy the sniping from the Left wld be

[1]For Barbara Freyberg and her husband Sir Bernard Freyberg, governor-general of New Zealand, see the Biographical notes below.

much worse. The international outlook is dark indeed & the horrors going on in Eastern Europe haunt one as Hitler's did in pre-war days. But one feels even more helpless than one did then. How tragic that after a war fought & won for human freedom there is probably less freedom in Europe today than there was in 1939.

B & I are – like you & Bernard – childless. Mark in Chicago – having an absorbingly interesting time. Ray in the Irish Guards – just moving from Caterham to Pirbright. Laura now living in Scotland. . . .

Darling – I must stop. Once more my love & blessing to you both – deep gratitude & endless 'missing'. Ever yr Violet.

V.B.C. to Mark Bonham Carter ***Tuesday 7 October***
40 Gloucester Square, W.2

Darling – Yr. second letter from Chicago (dated 1st) arrived yesterday. It gave me a very good & vivid aperçu of the human atmosphere & temperature.

By an odd co-incidence I went (directly after getting it) to a Third Programme anniversary dinner at the B.B.C. I was introduced on arrival to a very nice don called Coghill[1] . . . who immediately spoke to me about America, where he had been in 1945, & said in your words 'The prevailing attitude to us is one of Schadenfreude.' It must be rather annoying – especially as they are probably quite unaware that we notice it (or indeed perhaps that they feel it!) Americans always strike me as having the least sensitive 'receivers' of almost any people. I don't know whether they become more 'receptive' when one lives amongst them? Possibly one acquires new powers of 'penetration'. . . .

I daren't write more for fear of weight. You are missing nothing here. Dada says don't bother to write to him as I show him my letters from you. Ray might perhaps enjoy one when you have time. I feel a growing sense of personal political futility as I am now convinced the Libs. can do no good at the next Election & that our one chance of survival as a Party in the immediate future wld be a deal over seats & P.R. . . .

Love – blessing – missing – Ever yr Mama

[1]Nevil Henry Coghill (1899–1980), fellow and tutor of Exeter College, Oxford, 1925–57; later Merton professor of English literature, 1957–66.

Diary – Monday 13 October – 40 Gloucester Square, W.2

Again lovely hot day. Spent the whole day at work except for a break at luncheon when I went down to the H of C to see Frank Byers.[1] We lunched together in a quite empty dining-room on potted shrimps & roast beef. I spoke to him very frankly about the Party position & the choice which seemed to face us. We must face the possibility of being completely wiped out at the next Election as a Parliamentary force. . . .

The alternative wld be a deal over seats with the Tories with P.R. as a condition & an agreed programme. I shldn't like it & it might split the Party in half & give the Left Wing to Labour. I see all the rocks & shoals very clearly but I fear complete Parliamentary extinction. Frank sees it all too. He was very sensible. We agreed that anyway we were in too low water at this moment to do anything but try & strengthen our position – whether for independence or a bargain.

He then sounded me on the question of making Clem the official leader of the Party – on the ground that he (Frank) cld control him better in this capacity. I said I cldn't possibly accept him as my political Pope to give the 'Party line' as I had no respect for his political judgement. I told Frank how he wanted us to go into Opposition a fortnight before El Alamein. . . .

Diary – Thursday 23 October – 40 Gloucester Square, W.2

. . . United Europe meeting in Winston's room at the H. of C. . . . W. in great form – very anxious to keep us out of all economics – 'If we get caught up into a squalid scramble for a place in the queue we shall be like a banana caught in a cog-wheel. We must stick to our sentimental line – the spiritual, cultural side. Let hatreds die.' etc. This was a blow to many – Sandys, Layton & Ly R.W. who spoke – with tears in her voice – about Currency Reform! When I spoke I got home to him, I think by sheer verbal ruse. I said I agreed with most of what he said – the Soul of Europe was our business – its body is the Govt's pigeon. 'Very well said' said W. I then rounded my corner by saying that it was impossible to reach the soul of those whose body was obsessed by hunger, cold etc. – & that in this state they were unable to entertain ideas – or attach importance to 'values'. We cld only talk reasonably round this table because we had something inside us. If we failed to save the human bodies of Europeans, the Communists shd get their souls. This was where economics overlapped with our 'spiritual' aims. He was placated & I think to some extent convinced. Sandys

[1] For Frank Byers, Liberal chief whip, see the Biographical notes below.

wants us to join up with the Van Zeeland group[1] & the Federalists. Others are doubtful. We finally took refuge in a 'co-ordinating Committee'....

Diary – Sunday 26 October – 40 Gloucester Square, W.2

Day spent working till 5 when I went to the B.B.C. & delivered my broadcast on 'the Souls'. I had a very nice Announcer & made him stay with me, as an experiment, in my Martian cubicle – & I felt it definitely helped to have a human being there to 'strike' on. His name is Pemberton. I think it went well.

Diary – Tuesday 28 October – 40 Gloucester Square, W.2

Liberal Party Committee – the new body, which is certainly not an improvement on the old.... I told them the figures Byers & I had had worked out, calculating Lib. chances at the next Election – in which if we added to every Lib. candidate 15 p.c. of the Labour votes & 10 p.c. of the Tory vote we shld gain exactly 6 seats. I also pointed out that this did not budget for any losses in 3 cornered fights for our 10 existing survivors – only 2 of which had not had straight fights. I came away feeling that we were not a Party – but just a collection of individuals – & not very bright ones at that....

Betty Asquith to V.B.C. ***Wednesday 29 October***
Clovelly Court, nr Bideford, N. Devon

My dear Violet, I had the usual awful steeplechase from the Twinnery to the kitchen with the Radio to try & 'select' your voice in your 'Souls' talk. In despair I got on to Mary at Penhaven & she put her Radio against the Telephone & I heard you that way – dimly but very well. I thought it quite excellent & beautifully done, just right – human & true & lively & interesting. It was terribly good because there was so little real substance to go on. How lucky, glad & envious I am of our own young lives. Isn't it awful to think our children are completely starved mentally & physically of those life-giving times....

[1] Paul van Zeeland, the former Belgian prime minister and later minister for foreign affairs and president of the OEEC, was closely involved in the early steps towards European union. His approach was 'functional' rather than 'federalist' and he founded the European League for Economic Co-operation in May 1946.

Don't answer as I expect you have a fan mail. I'm longing to hear how Mark is getting on.... Love Bett

W. R. McLaughlin to V.B.C. ***Monday 10 November***
Millwood House, Mill Lane, Grays, Essex

Dear Madam. Your broadcast on The Souls reported in last week's *Listener* reminds me that in 1904 I had to live in the East End of London – in Poplar to be exact. There was an industrial depression at that time. Unskilled labour was paid 25/- a week and skilled mechanics 37/6 for a 54 hour week. When sacked they were given one hour's notice and there was no dole. In the winter the children used to stand outside the pastry cooks' shops in their pinafores and bare feet in the rain, looking in through the steaming windows. But they were not queuing to go inside – they had no chance of that. And in the Industrial Districts of England it was worse than in London.

In the meanwhile the Souls, who included Prime Ministers as well as Leaders of the Opposition, played at Clumps. They did not go into Committees but talked of spiritual matters, having been well fed. They were in fact the brilliant froth that came to the top and was supported by an oppressed nation. And make no mistake, it was not the Liberal Administration of 1906 that began to improve the condition of the people, but the Great War of 1914 that did it. That war put stockings on the children's feet, when the Souls cared for none of those things. (Surely if they had it could have been done more cheaply than by means of a world war and 20 million lives.) The war in fact was a fitting & inevitable end to such a period and there is nothing for us to regret in it now except that it ever existed.

I am yours truly, W. R. McLaughlin

Diary – Monday 17 November – 40 Gloucester Square, W.2

Just back from Albert Hall [Liberal] meeting – which lasted from 7.30 to 10.15 – a Marathon feat of endurance. Something like 12–14 speeches. Megan was good on Electoral Reform – & (oddly enough) Elliott Dodds[1] on Ownership for all. Frank Byers wound up at the end. All the old cries about 'imperishable faith' etc. rang rather hollow on my ears when I

[1] George Elliott Dodds (1889–1977), former editor and director of the *Huddersfield Examiner*; five times unsuccessful Liberal candidate, 1922–35; president, Liberal Party Organization, 1948–9.

thought we were going to be wiped off the slate at the next General Election, which I fear we shall be. We raised £3,500 which was good – considering how the barrel bottom has been scraped. Fothergill[1] & Graham White[2] were both absent thro' illness which let us off 2 speeches – or we shld still be there.

Diary – Sunday 23 November – 40 Gloucester Square, W.2

Edgar Mowrer & Michael Padev came to luncheon – & we talked about everything – terror in the East – Atom-bomb consciousness (which as Edgar says only exists in the U.S.A.) – the Govt.'s position here – Stafford Cripps – American feelings towards us, etc. Edgar gave very amusing accounts of the Russians at U.N.O. He is in excellent form & only dangerous when he gets on to World Govt. Short walk before tea. Then I had the amusing experience of hearing the recorded 'repeat' of my Souls broadcast. It went well & my own recorded voice didn't give me the usual reaction of horror, tho' it does sound a very 'Oxford accent'! . . .

[1] (Charles) Philip Fothergill (1906–59), merchant; leading figure in the Liberal Party machine; president, Liberal Party Organization, 1950–2, vice-president, 1952–5.

[2] (Henry) Graham White (d. 1965), MP (Lib.) Birkenhead East, 1929–45.

Two

United Europe

1948–1949

Diary – Tuesday 27 January 1948 – 40 Gloucester Square, W.2

Went to hear Bertrand Russell at Chatham House speaking on Atomic Energy in the luncheon-hour. He was extraordinarily good – so courageous – never hedged or wobbled or skidded on anything. He clearly thinks war is inevitable sooner or later – & that the only way to avoid the extermination of the human race is a monopoly of all power & war-like weapons. This can be achieved either by agreement among nations – international control – or by force – one nation conquering all the others & imposing World Govt. He does not believe it will come by agreement because of Russia. He thinks U.N.O. no good because of the [Security Council] Veto & because Russia doesn't want it to succeed.

Questions. He was asked one on Pacifism & said he was a Pacifist in the last war but was now quite convinced that Pacifism wld only work if you were dealing with decent people not with toughs. He was asked by a hostile questioner if he wld advocate emigration to Australia & the building up of Germany as a buffer state & replied the answer to both is in the affirmative. He was asked if he favoured a preventive war & said he thought we shld be quite justified in telling Russia that she must accept international control of the Atom, or we shld make war on her – but that he knew public opinion in neither country (U.S.A. or here) wld accept such a course, so it was not practical politics.[1] Lionel Curtis[2] made a woolly foolish optimistic speech which was loudly cheered....

[1] Russell's readiness to contemplate a preventive atomic war against Russia contrasts markedly with his later championship of CND. His biographer Ronald Clark has written: 'Russell was one of the comparatively few who quickly realised the full implications of the atomic bomb.... The result was a realism that drove him into a succession of positions later swamped by the rising tide of nuclear protest' (*Bertrand Russell*, 517–30).

[2] Lionel George Curtis (1872–1955), CH, 1949; colonial administrator; member of British delegation at the Paris Peace Conference, 1919; founded, 1920–1, the (Royal) Institute for International Affairs; author of *Civitas Dei* (3 vols, 1934–7), advocating world unity under democratic institutions.

Diary – Friday 30 January – 40 Gloucester Square, W.2

I was lunching with Cruikshank[1] at the Carlton Grill. He came in a minute or two late & said 'The most terrible news has just broken. Gandhi has been assassinated.' It was done he thinks by a Hindu extremist (this was confirmed later) & not by a Moslem. This minimises the appalling vendetta of reprisals which wld otherwise follow. We had a very good talk about his 'sainthood' which I always felt was streaked with political slyness. Cruikshank said he agreed, but that Halifax[2] felt it strongly. I said Halifax's high-church conscience gave him a kind of kinship with, & understanding of, Gandhi....

We then got on to the Party business. He thinks the right thing is for Walter [Layton] & me to approach Winston personally & privately & try & get him to make an unconditional offer of Electoral Reform. He is a delightful man. I pointed out how difficult it wld be for us to offer him any quid pro quo....

Diary – Wednesday 4 February – 40 Gloucester Square, W.2

...United Europe meeting at H. of C. in Winston's room. Two thorny issues presented themselves immediately (1) That great friction was going on between Gordon Lang[3] & Duncan Sandys – & (2) that many members of the Committee were in revolt against D.S.... Winston began by being full of 'sweet reasonableness' & patience but after the attacks on Sandys – when Sandys said he was ready to 'fade out' – he blazed forth 'I am not going to "fade out" whatever happens. I shall go to the Hague[4] – if need be alone – & make a speech which will be read & heard all over the world. I can make Bevin a laughing stock. I can gain great credit for the Conservative Party. That is not my object however. My aim is to build a United Europe.'

We didn't have a very long sitting – & I didn't see Winston alone. I walked away with Victor Gollancz & we both mingled our tears over the fate of our Parties. Mine which is going steadily forward towards extinc-

[1] Robert James Cruikshank (1898–1956), journalist; editor of *News Chronicle*, 1948–54.

[2] Edward Frederick Lindley Wood (1881–1959), cr. 1st Earl Halifax, 1944; statesman; viceroy of India, 1926–31; foreign secretary, 1938–40; British ambassador in Washington, 1941–6.

[3] (Rev.) Gordon Lang (1893–1981), MP (Lab.) Stalybridge and Hyde, Cheshire, 1945–51; honorary secretary of UEM.

[4] Churchill refers to the great 'congress' of European organizations that was to be held at The Hague early in May, and at which his United Europe Movement would be strongly represented.

tion – his which has turned its back on all its old idealism.

Diary – Friday 6 February – 40 Gloucester Square, W.2

...Dined in the evening with Maud Russell. Party: Bertrand Russell, B & I & Raymond Russell. It cldn't have been more amusing. Bertrand Russell is brilliantly amusing – such a good sense of humour & perfect intellectual manners. As spry & limber as if he were a 2 year old, tho' actually 76 – married to his 3rd wife & 2nd Secretary.... He thought Maynard untrue to his own beliefs (in Pacifism) in the last war. He thinks the Russian Govt the worst & most terrible thing that has ever happened in the history of man – & described a terrible book by Kellin on forced labour. In a part of Siberia 4 times the size of France there is a gold mine & millions of forced labourers have been poured into it. They are worked during the summer months & allowed to die in the arctic cold of autumn & winter & then replenished with a fresh stock. He was very funny about the Americans, who bore him to extinction, & said that if he ever prayed (which he doesn't) he wld pray to be able to love the Americans. Maud goes to South Africa in a week.

Diary – Wednesday 18 February – 40 Gloucester Square, W.2

Press Commission all day.[1] A quite dull morning ... & after lunch the *Daily Worker*, who excelled themselves. We got them to admit that in their view 'a premise' equals 'a fact'. It was in fact 'calling a spade a spade'. Also that they wld allow freedom to one type of Govt but not another. Mr Hutt[2] was as good as a play. Went on to a most interesting evening in *Daily Express* office. We were received by Mr Robertson & Mr Christiansen[3] (Manager & Editor) & shown all over it while the paper went to Press.... I saw one machine which cost £50,000 & which cld turn out 50,000 copies an hour, but which is not allowed to turn out more than 35,000 by the man who sits beside it. It is not only men who may not work to their utmost capacity, but they are not even allowed to allow machines to do so. How can we ever recover while this goes on?

[1] Violet was a member of the 1947–9 Royal Commission on the freedom of the press.

[2] Allen Hutt, a renowned newspaper typographer, on the staff of the *Daily Worker*.

[3] Arthur Christiansen (1904–63), editor, *Daily Express*, 1933–57; director, Beaverbrook Newspapers, 1941-59.

Diary – Wednesday 25 February – 40 Gloucester Square, W.2

. . . The news from Czechoslovakia very bad – & to-night at 9 on the news we heard that Benes had capitulated to Gottwald, accepted the Cabinet he had dictated & that Masaryk was coming into it.[1] How can they? They will be just prisoners of the Communists. Free Press has already been forbidden & all the frontiers closed so that no one can get out. The trap has closed on another country. The Czech bastion has fallen for the 2nd time – but this time not by an assault from without – but 'betrayed by what is false within'.[2] Why shld those who love freedom fight for it less well than those who love tyranny? . . .

Diary – Wednesday 3 March – 40 Gloucester Square, W.2

Very full day – starting with Press Commission (*Yorkshire Post* – Rupert Beckett & Co) then dashing to Savoy to lunch with United Europe. Winston was there in spite of his cold – & looking fairly well tho' he coughed a little & blew his nose from time to time. When I arrived he was talking to Mr Kerstens – a very nice Dutch Senator who was a member of their Govt here in the war – & who is making all the arrangements for us at the Hague. I sat down beside them & tried to have a word about the Electoral Reform Bill & their possible support of it.[3] I felt very strongly that our bargaining power had sadly dropped. He talked of getting back to the Two Party system but then added that he wanted to see more Liberals in the House. I felt however that he was thinking in terms of a deal in seats without Electoral Reform – & this wld only mean uneasy survival for one more Parlt without any prospect of ultimate independence. I sat next to him at lunch, with Bertrand Russell on my other side. . . .

[1] On 25 February the Czechoslovakian Communists, led by Klement Gottwald (1896–1953), staged a coup, forcing the president Eduard Beneš (1884–1948) to endorse a new cabinet which gave them power. Jan Masaryk (1886–1948), son of the pre-war Czech leader Thomas Masaryk, retained the post of foreign minister. Violet had known him before the war and had greatly admired him. On 10 March he was found dead in the grounds of his residence, and there was speculation as to whether he had committed suicide or had been murdered by Communists.

[2] From *Modern Love* (1862) by George Meredith, xliii: 'In tragic life, God wot, / No villain need be! Passions spin the plot: / We are betrayed by what is false within.'

[3] On 29 January the Labour government introduced its Electoral Reform bill, which proposed the abolition of the business premises vote and of university seats, as well as a redistribution of seats. It received the royal assent at the end of July.

We talked about the Atom & prospects of peace & war.[1] W. said 'It is for America to decide. She has the bomb in her keeping.' Bertrand Russell advanced to me the theory that Stalin did not really know what was happening in the world outside – that he was helpless. I asked Winston whether he thought that he cld personally negotiate effectively with Stalin. He said chuckling 'If I went there they'd never let me out again! But this apart I cld certainly talk quite plainly to him & in words that he wld understand. He wldn't take offence if I told him plainly that we cldn't wait to get a settlement until they got the bomb.' Speeches followed. . . .

Diary – Good Friday, 26 March – 40 Gloucester Square, W.2

I think this is the 1st Easter I can ever remember spending in London – except possibly the one before Cressida was born. It is glorious, hot, sunny spring-like weather & must be heavenly in Wiltshire. We have been at Stockton practically every Easter since Laura first went there 5 years ago. Though I mind missing its beauty, it is a marvellous feeling to have 4 free days given one without packing, travelling, Committees, appts, engagements of any kind & thank Heaven neither a script nor a speech to prepare. . . .

Diary – Easter Sunday, 28 March – 40 Gloucester Square, W.2

B. & I went to St Paul's for the Communion Service & listened to the music – lovely as ever – & just the same as it was in the days of my childhood – the same 'Our Father' at the end that was sung when I used to go there with Father & Margot. Back to luncheon. . . . Then Michael [Padev] looked in with an American called Harris who had worked in political warfare before the war & who said to me exactly what I said to [William] Haley last night – i.e. that the B.B.C. must give light once more to those who sit in darkness – as it did in the war. It cannot go on giving a mere 'Reuters service' to the Iron Curtain countries. To Bulgaria he said we had given last night: a history of British football, an excursion to the docks & the bare fact that 24 Communists had been executed – without comment or explanation.

[1] There was then much debate over whether Britain and America should share atom-bomb technology with the Soviet Union, in the interests of world peace. Churchill believed that nothing should be given away without a clear gesture of reciprocity from the Soviet Union.

Diary – Monday 5 April – 40 Gloucester Square, W.2

Worked all day. Dined with the *Economist* at Brown's Hôtel.... Hatchie drove on with us to the party at the American Embassy for Mrs Roosevelt.[1] He said 'Do you mind arriving with a Hot Red?' I said 'I shouldn't – but you are a very cool pink.' The Party was quite an amusing one. Most of the Cabinet were there.... I had an amusing talk with Frank Pakenham. We were interrupted first by a man who rushed up & asked him how he cld 'take shares' in Germany & secondly by Massigli, who was in a state I have never seen him in before – of wild excitement & such volubility that we cld hardly get in a word edgeways. His contention was that the Russians cld make life impossible for us in Berlin & that we must retreat.[2] To make a stand there wld send the Russians swarming over into France – '[We have] only 2 divisions' he went on saying, 'only 2 divisions.' 'Then wld you retreat if they invaded our zones?' we asked. 'Ah no – that wld be different.' 'But there wld still be only 2 divisions.' This conversation went on hammer & tongs à tue-tête for some time – Frank meanwhile pressing champagne on him. Frank said afterwards that he thought he must have been drunk. But he showed no signs of it whatever! The only reassuring thing was that he said he was not speaking for his Govt! We saw Isaiah Berlin afterwards. Sir R. Mayer[3] dropped us home.

V.B.C. to Mark Bonham Carter — *Sunday 18 April, 40 Gloucester Square, W.2*

Darling – Yr letter arrived yesterday. I was so glad to get it.... David Astor & George Barnes came to luncheon.[4] David much pinker, heavier & thicker than when I saw him last. In very good form I thought. He 'showed up' & George was quiet. We talked about Russia & the possibilities of war almost the whole time. David agreed that it might well suit the Russians to strike

[1] (Anna) Eleanor Roosevelt *née* Roosevelt (1884–1962), widow of Franklin D. Roosevelt (her cousin); a renowned political campaigner in her own right.

[2] In early 1948 the Russians exerted increasing pressure on the Western Allies in Berlin in an attempt to force them to abandon the city. In June road and rail traffic was effectively stopped – the beginning of the 'Berlin blockade'. On 5 April there was considerable tension after a Soviet fighter collided with a British airliner at Gatow airport in the British zone, killing the Soviet pilot and all fourteen on board the airliner. There had been reports of Soviet planes 'buzzing' British aircraft trying to land at Gatow.

[3] Sir Robert Mayer (1879–1985), Kt, 1939; businessman, philanthropist and patron of music.

[4] Hon. (Francis) David Astor (b. 1912), foreign editor *Observer*, 1946–8; editor, 1948–75. Sir George (Reginald) Barnes (1904–60), head of BBC Third Programme, 1946–8; later director, BBC TV, 1950–6; from 1956 principal of University College of North Staffordshire (Keele).

soon, if they meant to strike at all, before Western Union got strong & American conscription came into play. They cld race across Europe – there was nothing to stop them – & if we atom-bombed their rear they cld destroy Paris & thousands of European hostages. There is something in it. Ray says Monty visited them for 1½ hours only & spoke breezily of the storm-clouds which might burst in 2 weeks, 2 months or 2 years – & Ray heard afterwards from senior officers that in his talk with them Monty had been rather ominous (they even said 'indiscreet')....

Only 5 months now till you are back. Did you say you arrived 14th Sept – & will you go then to Balmoral? I only ask because we shall be vaguely thinking about holiday plans. All my love, Yr Mama

V.B.C. to Mark Bonham Carter ***Wednesday 28 April***
40 Gloucester Square, W.2

Darling – 1000 thanks for yr. last letter (dated 18th) which I found on my return from b—-y old Blackpool where I stayed with great endurance from Tuesday evening till Sat. morning.[1] The Libs. excelled themselves in folly! Wednesday I spoke to the women on the Marshall offer (they were quite sensible about this) & I got a very good Press. But later on they (the women) passed a resolution entitling every woman to half her husband's income – earned or unearned – by law. I pointed out that this wld endow female butterflies, spivs & drones who happened to be the wives of millionaires with a cool £50,000 a year – while the working housewives, drudges etc. who married poor men wld get the skinny leg of a very skinny chicken. It was however passed....

Last night we went to the ball for the Silver Wedding at Buckingham Palace, to which you were asked. It was really great fun – even for Dada & me – & you wld have had a high old time. It was a big Party – about 1200 & held in the big, grand Throne-Room like the old Court Balls.... I have never seen Pss E. look better. She looked really pretty (as well as having, as she has always had, a very 'nice' face).... She spoke to me, asked after you & said you hadn't written to her for ages & she wanted news of you. She strikes me as being rather 'délié' by marriage – with fewer 'stops'. Pss Margaret on the other hand has none – as you have always said. Talking to her is not like talking to a 'royalty'. She also talked about you....

We went in to eat in that vast room where the gold plate used to be, but now no longer is, & there we saw & talked to Alexander – so nice – Osbert

[1]The Blackpool assembly was opened by Elliott Dodds, president of the Liberal Party Organization, who urged the Liberals 'to fight as a new party for recognition, not as an old one struggling for survival' (*The Times*, 23 April 1948).

Sitwell – Peter Fleming etc.[1] Aneurin Bevan was there in plain clothes – such an affectation – swilling enough champagne to pay for many evening suits. (What is the 'class' distinction between champagne & evening dress? making one permissible & the other not?) We went home at 1.30. I longed for you to have been there.

I went this afternoon to the H. of C. to get marching orders for the Hague. We shall be 140 strong – 70 M.P.s No policy was discussed at all. I was invited by a complete stranger, Mr Beddington-Behrens, to fly with him, Harold Macmillan & Sir Harold Butler[2] in his private plane – & accepted gladly as it will save me £15. I go next week returning on 11th....

All our love to you darling, Ever yr Mama

Adam pass thro' on Monday. I said 'Raymond is a soldier now & may go to Palestine.' He said with the sweetest 'social' smile 'Yes – he's sure to get killed isn't he Ghima?' Just as one says 'It's sure to rain.' Actually I think they will be out of Palestine before R. is ready. The situation there is a nightmare....[3]

Diary – Friday 30 April – 40 Gloucester Square, W.2

Went to Guildhall at 1 o'clock to hear Anthony Eden speak on United Europe. Packed hall – audience quite unresponsive until the end when they clapped loud & long. One lunatic made a strong interjection – & had a quite incomprehensible colloquy with Anthony – advancing towards the platform....

We had a rather good buffet sandwich lunch afterwards & I had some talk with Anthony about the prospects of war. He is one of the few people who had dealt with Stalin so his comments are interesting. He said he thought Stalin wld see further ahead than to believe that just to reach the Channel Ports wld do him much good in the long-run. I asked whether he still had power & this he cldn't say. He was critical of the F.O. as he said it seemed to have given up any attempts to keep in any sort of touch with the Russians. He agreed the Berlin situation was very ticklish & the worst danger-point. We cldn't move out – but the Russians might force us

[1] Harold Rupert Alexander (1891–1969), cr. 1st Viscount Alexander of Tunis, 1946; 1st Earl, 1952; field marshal; gov.-gen. of Canada, 1946–52. Sir Osbert Sitwell (1892–1969), 5th Bt, poet and novelist. (Robert) Peter Fleming (1907–71), writer and traveller; joined *The Times*, 1936; m. 1935 Celia Johnson, actress.

[2] Sir Harold Beresford Butler (1883–1951), KCMG, 1946; public servant; first warden of Nuffield College, Oxford, 1939–43; minister at HM Embassy, Washington, 1942–6.

[3] A state of war was then effective in Palestine as Arabs and Jews vied for control in advance of the British withdrawal on 18 May.

to seem to take the offensive. Home to tea – & worked at my article for The *Star* on the Hague Congress.

The Hague Congress, 7–10 May 1948

In December 1947 an international committee was convened to give shape to the amorphous movement for European unity which had evolved in the previous two years. The outcome was a more clearly defined 'European Movement' which quickly achieved a remarkable coup, organizing a great congress to be held at The Hague. On 7 May 1948 around 800 delegates duly gathered there – the representatives of governments, political parties and voluntary associations. Present were several former prime ministers, twenty-nine former foreign ministers and a sprinkling of famous figures such as Bertrand Russell and John Masefield. All strands of political opinion, except the Communists, were represented. And among the 140 British participants were 22 Labour MPs who had defied their Party leadership by attending. Attlee's government was not opposed to the idea of European unity itself, but feared that the concept 'might become corrupted in the hands of reaction' at The Hague. Given the size and diversity of the Congress, and the lack of precedent or of administrative support, the real danger was that it would disintegrate into farce. Its proceedings were indeed 'amateurish and often disorderly' and Harold Macmillan remembered that the bulk of delegates 'wandered about, like students at a university, from one classroom to another', looking for something that would capture their interest. There was also the potential for major discord, with a 'federalist' group demanding the creation of a single European state. The federalists were doubtless encouraged by Churchill's inspiring but vague rhetoric about a 'United States of Europe'. And the majority of delegates at The Hague aspired to something much less ambitious. Measured against their goals, at least, the Congress was a triumph of improvisation, which gave rise to a permanent 'European Assembly'. Churchill had called for this in his speech at the first plenary meeting of the Congress and he later pressed the idea on the Labour government. This pressure bore fruit and in January 1949 Britain reached agreement with France and the Benelux countries on the establishment of a 'Council of Europe'. Its membership was later considerably widened, while its remit was limited to non-binding agreements on human rights, the environment and cultural affairs. Put bluntly, it was a 'talking-shop'. But it did lead to the convening of a 'Consultative Assembly' of parliamentarians drawn from the participating states, and this opened in Strasbourg on 10 August 1949. If it was a far cry from the federalists' dream, it provided an important seed-bed for the idea of European union in the decade to come.[1]

Diary – Friday 7 to Monday 10 May – The Congress of Europe at The Hague

After a breathless 10 days to the Hague & back I must try & write up the bones of what happened there. I left at 20 to 8 on Friday (7th) morning – picked up Dorothy Layton at Marsham Court & embarked at Croydon Airport in a lovely silver Dove plane with our host Beddington-Behrens, Harold Macmillan, Peter Thorneycroft[2] & Harold Butler. We made a successful flight in brilliant weather. As we neared the Dutch coast I saw patches of what looked like golden fire all over the countryside. It was the sun shining on the greenhouses. We flew over carpets of tulips & came down at Valkenburg – drove from there thro' the Hague to Scheveningen – found we were at the Kurhaus & after a feverishly quick unpack & change started for the Hague to lunch before the Plenary Session.

We all lunched at an enormous table in a kind of Club called the Nieuw Witte in a Square. I sat near Bertrand Russell & Ld. Moran[3] so I was very happy. Every kind of known face surrounded one ... & of course innumerable MPs. We went on to the Ridderzaal – their Parliament – a large & beautiful hall of great dignity with a dais & a back-cloth of beautiful old red velvet. The Burgomeister – Prince Bernhard & Pss Juliana[4] arrived – & finally Winston who got a tremendous reception & made a very good speech. He looked benign & Pickwickian. We then dashed home again & went to a reception given by the Netherlands Govt. More familiar faces – Josephy[5] etc. We were presented to Princess Juliana & Prince Bernhard in the order – Laytons, Ly Rhys Williams, self, Mackay,[6] Josephy &

[1] Gilbert, *Never Despair*, 405–9; Harris, *Attlee*, 311; Macmillan, *Tides of Fortune*, 158–63.

[2] Peter Thorneycroft (1909–94), cr. life peer, 1967; MP (Con.) Stafford 1938–45; Monmouth, 1945–66; chancellor of the exchequer, 1957–8 (resigned); later defence secretary, 1964, and Conservative Party chairman.

[3] Charles McMoran Wilson (1882–1977), cr. Baron Moran, 1943; m. 1919 Dorothy *née* Dufton; personal physician to Churchill and president of the Royal College of Physicians, 1941–50.

[4] Princess Juliana (b. 1909), only child of Queen Wilhelmina of the Netherlands; m. 1937, Prince Bernhard of Lippe-Biesterfeld; she succeeded to the throne in 1948.

[5] Miss F. L. Josephy, chairman of the executive of the Federal Union, a British group committed to bringing about the political, social and economic integration of Europe.

[6] Ronald William Mackay (1902–60), Australian-educated solicitor, MP (Lab.) Hull North West, 1945–50; North Reading, 1950–1; an ardent European and author of *Federal Europe* (1940).

one or two others who I forget. Finally got away in a taxi with Harold Butler & one or two others – & dined at the Kurhaus where tables miles long stretched almost out of sight. As at the Folies [Bergère] one didn't know where real men ended & sham ones began. . . .

Saturday 8 May. We assembled very appropriately at the zoo for the meeting of the Political Commission. Mackay was making a 25 minutes speech to what looked like a mass meeting of some 500. [Paul] Ramadier in the Chair. The procedure chaotic & quite incomprehensible. Occasionally a bleat wld break from an Anglo Saxon delegate 'Sur un point d'ordre M le President'. His only reply was to strike a deafening blow upon the table with a hammer the size of a croquet mallet. One was asked to say at breakfast time exactly at what time one intended to speak. This was impossible as one had no inkling what business wld then be on the tapis. An attaché from the Embassy sought me out & found me to ask me to lunch there. It was a nice interlude. A lovely cool – spacious house – with vast tubs & bowls of tulips everywhere. I found Anthony alone downstairs when I arrived, with an attaché, & had a few words with him about how things are going. He is very definitely not a Federalist. At lunch I sat with Lionel Curtis (who is one). . . . Anthony reappeared after lunching with the Queen & we drove back together to the Political Commission. I discussed with him the possibility that Winston might be put in a very different position if the Congress pledged itself to whole-hogging Federation. He said that W. had said to him 'Nothing will induce me to be a Federalist'. . . .

Sunday 9 May. Another radiantly hot & brilliant day. I attended Plenary Session of Cultural Commission – Madariaga[1] presiding made a very good speech & so did Kenneth Lindsay.[2] I went out during the translation into the sunshine & met Harrod[3] who asked me to go to Haarlem with him en route for Amsterdam for Winston's open air meeting. . . . We got there [Amsterdam] before the special train of delegates. The streets were all lined as tho' for a King. We got thro' the crowds with our delegates tickets & into the Dam. A most beautifully decorated platform was erected in front of the Royal Palace festooned with orange white & blue flowers. The delegates chairs were in the centre of the Square – the rest packed with people & every window full. We took seats bang in front in the 5th row.

After a time Sir John Anderson arrived with Ava[4] & H. Macmillan. The

[1] Señor Don Salvador de Madariaga, closely involved in the early days of the movement for European unity.

[2] Kenneth Martin Lindsay (1897–1991), MP (Nat. Lab.) Kilmarnock Burghs, 1933–43; (Ind. Nat.) 1943–5; (Ind.) Combined English Universities, 1945–50; involved in the development of the Arts Council.

[3] (Sir) Roy Forbes Harrod (1900–78), Oxford economist and biographer of John Maynard Keynes.

[4] Ava, Lady Waverley *née* Bodley (d. 1966), wife of Sir John Anderson (later Viscount

Dutch police prevented him from sitting in the front row & shooed him away to the back saying front seats were reserved for only very important people. I dashed forward & saved them, explaining to the police in my synthetic Dutch – a shandigaff of German & English – that Sir J.A. was very 'important' indeed! a rôle I never dreamt I should live to fill. Ava thanked me with passionate gratitude! There was an hour's speaking before W. got up. Ramadier's endless French oratory palled, Brugmann's was interrupted by an accompaniment of bells, there was a good Belgian Liberal & a good Belgian Socialist, but they were all waiting for Winston & when he got up he had a marvellous reception. He spoke quietly & most impressively. The Archbishop or prelate at the end asked him to give the V sign which was understood by all & received with acclamation.[1] We got back to Scheveningen directly by the special train. . . .

Back after dinner to the Commission. Looked in on the Economic which was in a much smaller room & obviously far better conducted than the political – Van Zeeland an excellent Chairman. Then back to the Political again & home to pack & bed. The Economic sat all night till 6.30! I have never felt so short of sleep.

Monday 10 May. Went to the Moritz House in the morning & saw the Van Meers. . . . Then Plenary Session Political Commission. It was very dramatic though not on account of the speeches. Van Zeeland made a very good & moving speech but when an old French economist called Servys was at the rostrum a crashing thunderstorm broke out – Egyptian darkness fell – lightning flashed – deafening thunder rolled – but Servys stayed on at the microphone talking & gesticulating unheard. Winston arrived later & it abated. Ly Grant spoke well (the same speech as in the Economic Committee!) & soon afterwards Harold Butler & I had to leave so we missed the row made later by the French Syndicalists. . . .[2]

Waverley). After her husband's death, in 1958, she became a close friend and confidante of Harold Macmillan.

[1] 'He was asked to give the V Sign at the end & gave it to thunderous applause – sucking his cigar the while (as Peter Fleming said – "like a Giant Panda with a bamboo shoot")' (VBC to MRBC, 19 May 1948).

[2] Violet's return journey in Beddington-Behrens's private plane was eventful as its undercarriage failed, and it was forced to make a crash landing at Croydon airport after circling to use up its fuel. Harold Macmillan, badly burned in a plane accident in 1943, recalled: 'Lady Violet and Layton happily discussed the future of the Liberal Party for over an hour, scarcely noticing that anything was amiss. Butler & Thorneycroft argued about economics. My host and I watched the familiar rolling out of the fire-engines with what nonchalance we could assume' (Macmillan, *Tides of Fortune*, 162).

V.B.C. to Mark Bonham Carter ***Thursday 3 June***
40 Gloucester Square, W.2

Darling – 1000 thanks for your letter of 29th which arrived (with incredible speed) on 1st June. I have been plunged in bed for a week with a raging temp. but no other symptoms (except a few aches & pains). 'Flu I shld think. . . .

My last act before going to bed was to do a broadcast (repeat of my 'coming-out')[1] & my first act on Tuesday was to do another, quite short one, for the Pacific Service. I have also written this week an article for the *Sunday Times* on the incredibly dreary theme (handled a week or two ago with typical serio-dreariness & dreario-seriousness by one Mrs Stocks[2] – Principal of Westfield College): 'Why have women not produced bigger & better fruits from the Tree of their Emancipation?' I have handled it with candour & some levity & fully expect to get a shower of brickbats from the Feminists. One cannot dodge the fact that no woman of alpha quality has so far appeared on the political scene. Eleanor Rathbone[3] the only one who had a touch of 'greatness'. I have never seen a woman who cld be P.M., Foreign Secretary or Chancellor of the Exchequer. I will send you the article when it comes out. . . .

Ray is here having his embarkation leave (tho' he won't go away till July probably). He is I hope enjoying himself, but his name has naturally not got on to any of the dance lists yet & he wld so passionately love to go to them. Invitations pour in for you from Bowes-Lyons, Rex Bensons, etc. & it seems ironical that he can't go instead! . . .

All my love darling, yr. Mama

Diary – Saturday 26 June – 40 Gloucester Square, W.2

A boiling hot day – quite suddenly. B & C went off to the Test Match. I went to see the Courtauld pictures at the Tate. Worked in the Square all the afternoon. Went to Olivier Wormser's farewell cocktail party in a nice little house in St Leonard's Terrace. Talked to Toto[4] there about Berlin

[1] Violet had made a broadcast for the BBC about her experience of 'coming out' as an Edwardian debutante.

[2] Mary Danvers Stocks (1891–1975), cr. life peer, 1966; broadcaster and principal of Westfield College, University of London, 1939–51.

[3] Eleanor Rathbone (d. 1946), MP (Ind.) Combined English Universities, 1929–46; during the war Violet had served with Rathbone on the 'national committee for rescue from Nazi terror', of which Rathbone was vice chairman.

[4] Alphonse ('Toto') Morhange (1893–1976), French banker who left Paris to join the Free French in exile in 1940; later director of finance with European office of UNRRA; a good friend of the Bonham Carters and the Grimonds.

position – which he thinks quite untenable for us. He says that we have nothing to offer the Russians in negotiation – which is true. We cannot now retreat – or have 2 million civilians starving on our hands. I do not see the answer but I imagine that our Govt. & the Americans must have foreseen this possibility & must have some plan of campaign.[1] He says an English officer driving along the road to Berlin was held up 2 hours & when he went into the Russian Post covered by Tommy Guns....

Diary – Monday 28 June – 40 Gloucester Square, W.2

Lunched with Haley at Claridges.... We talked about Trusts, Press Commission, Reuters & finally the Berlin situation. I said I thought it was 50–50 war & peace. He didn't feel this quite. Ensor[2] on the other hand told me at the [Liberal] Policy Committee that he has always thought the Russians intend to make war this year – in August & Sept during the [American] Presidential Elections. I do not see how we can move – we certainly are committed. Nor do I see how they can. And they don't need to move. They have only got to sit tight. They can force us to take the offensive & we have nothing to offer them. Only by a threat which we are too civilized to implement can we get them out....

Diary – Wednesday 7 July – 40 Gloucester Square, W.2

...I got home & found that B had heard from Miss Willis that Ray really is sailing for Tripoli the day after to-morrow. It gave me quite a shock as I had counted on another postponement. He came up in time for dinner looking very well & quite unperturbed – packed & sorted – strummed the piano & caught the 10.57. I cannot believe that he will be going so far for so long – & I am haunted by the fear that war might break out while he is away & that he might be hurried to some awful front. Heaven forbid. Starting on my AJB script.[3]

[1] In response to the Russian blockade of Berlin the Western Allies began the 'Berlin airlift' on 26 June, keeping the city supplied with essential goods until the blockade was lifted, 12 May 1949.

[2] Sir Robert Charles Kirkwood Ensor (1877–1958), Kt, 1955; journalist and historian; a Winchester and Balliol contemporary of Violet's eldest brother Raymond; author of the acclaimed *England, 1870–1914* (1936).

[3] Violet's thirty-minute talk on Arthur James Balfour, prime minister 1902–5, was broadcast on the Third Programme on 25 July.

Diary – Monday 18 July – 40 Gloucester Square, W.2

Went to rehearse my AJB script at B.B.C. & got thro' in 19 minutes – but of course it will take longer. Rushed back & on to the American Embassy, who had a party to meet the unspeakable Mr McCormick of the *Chicago Sun*. I didn't however 'meet' him – only his wife. I had a long talk with Rothermere about Berlin on the usual lines. He feels as I do about it – that the Govt give the appearance of improvising – that the arrival of the American Bombers shld be played up, not down – that demobilization shld be stopped etc. This is the kind of gesture which wld impress the Russians. I then started a talk with Geoffrey Crowther on Western Union & the Govt's attitude & we were in full cry about this when Herbert Morrison came up. I tackled him about their cold-water attitude to United Europe & said the obvious things about Western Union & the need to mobilize public opinion. He said 'Well Winston is rather difficult.' I also asked him if he considered me verminous or sub-verminous. He is obviously aware of what Aneurin Bevan is losing for the party....

Later on I had a most disturbing talk with Geoffrey Crowther about Berlin. He began by saying there wldn't be war (this was not disturbing!) & went on to say that we shld keep Berlin fed till the autumn & then back out. When I expressed horror & reminded him of the betrayal of the $2\frac{1}{2}$ million Germans he said 'Better their betrayal than the death & ruin of several hundred million Europeans!' I was appalled by these Chamberlainesque ethics. He said people were too much obsessed by Munich. He seemed to remember it too little....

Diary – Thursday 12 August – Stockton, Wiltshire

At last a day of glorious hot still sunshine. I went up to London in the rain with B. by 10.5 – dropped luggage at G. Square & found a lovely letter from Ray with 2 boxes of chocolates & a tin of biscuits sent from Malta (very sweet of him with his straitened resources)....

Winston & Clemmie sent the car for me at 7 & I found them in their new lovely house in H. P. Gate which is being painted from top to bottom.... W. looked well – very calm. We had some champagne & sandwiches then left in a car for the film. There were large crowds in Leicester Square & he got a great reception outside the theatre. We were received by the Ranks & innumerable photographers flashlighting at every turn. Another great reception in the theatre. I sat between W. & Clemmie & Norman Collins the author of the film beyond. It was not a very good film *London belongs to me* – well acted by Fay Compton, Richard Attenborough etc. W. watched it like a child – arguing with the story 'But it wasn't murder – he didn't murder her.' Then we drove back to the Savoy where we had supper in a private room. . . .

I sat next W. & tried to get his views on 2 matters – (1) The internat. outlook. He thinks that Russia fears the Atom Bomb too much to face war – & that even if she overran Europe her communications cld be cut by air & her armies wld rapidly become helpless. On the other hand he is not sure of the firmness of the Govt & does not rule 'appeasement' out of court as a possibility they might contemplate. 'If I were there they wld know very well what to expect from me.' He never had any hope that their talks wld succeed. (2) I tried to find out what he really thinks of a Federal solution. He seemed to think a Parlt of Europe quite impracticable but it was clear that he did not want to think the thing out in detail & had not done so. 'I want Europeans to think of themselves as Europeans – to feel a loyalty to Europe' etc. Attlee had written him a 'dusty answer' to his letter about the European Assembly, saying that if convened it shld be by Govts not Parlts & that this critical time was not the moment to do it. . . .

We didn't break up till 12.30. W. is going to Aix en Provence till 15th Sept when Parlt is meeting. They motored back to Westerham. . . .

Diary – Saturday 14 August – Stockton, Wiltshire

Glorious day of hot, still sunshine. We went over to Heytesbury after luncheon to see Sieg. Missed our bus but caught the next. Found him on his lovely cricket-ground surrounded by 'flannelled fools'[1] all dressed in pre-war snow-white – Radstock v. Heytesbury. Watched a bit sitting on a fence, then had tea in his lovely white book-lined room – consisting of a very 'rich damp cake' or rather the remains of it, sent to him last Xmas by an Australian fan. He talked to us steadily for 2½ hours or so – then drove us home & sat on talking here till ¼ to 8 – his form improving all the time. He leads such a hermit-crab life that when one first meets him one finds him jerky & disconnected – then a détente comes & he begins to relax & enjoy talking & ends by begging one to come again. I am going again on Wed. . . .

[1] From Rudyard Kipling, 'The Islanders' (1902): 'Then ye returned to your trinkets; then ye contented your souls / With the flannelled fools at the wicket or the muddied oafs at the goals.'

Diary – Wednesday 18 August – Stockton, Wiltshire

Did my Polish script in the morning – boring. After lunch went by bus to Siegfried. Found the poor old bird in a terrible to do – as his woodcutter had just given notice because the wife of another employee – a Mrs Johnson – talked too much & got on his nerves! He calmed down & poured out his soul to me for some 2 hours – George[1] – Hester – his work, his worries etc. A great deal of Hester this time. He told me that never having liked drink, she drove him at one time to drinking hot whisky & orange juice before going to bed at night – in a vain attempt to numb himself & sleep. At times by releasing inhibitions it made him write some quite good poems. Then it began to lose its effect. He saw that he wld have to increase the dose & he cut it off – entirely. It interested me as a proof of what women can do to men. I think it does him good to disembowel himself. When I got up at 6 he said – 'We needn't go yet – let's stay another 20 minutes' & on he ripped. Then he drove me back – came in & had a drink. . . .

Diary – Tuesday 14 September – 40 Gloucester Square, W.2

Mark returned to-day. I was so excited that I slept very little last night. B & I went to Waterloo to meet the 12.20 which the Cunard C° told us was the train, but missed him as he had come by an earlier one, & found him at home when we got back. He looked very well – quite a different colour – whether from food or sun I don't know (but even thinner than before he went – he says he has lost weight). We all lunched together here & talked & unpacked all the afternoon. There is so much to tell & hear – one can't make a plan about it – it tumbles out all over the place. It is heavenly to have him back. . . . We dined alone & drank some champagne Bong had hoarded for the occasion. Talked till nearly 2 o'clock.

Diary – Saturday 11 December – 40 Gloucester Square, W.2

Grim Day. Liberal Council in the morning – back to lunch & on to Fulham to open a Fête there with Gervase Long. It was a pathetic bazaar – about 30 people mostly very old. The candidate – a retired bank-manager & a very tired one – began his speech 'Whom the Lord loveth he Chasteneth. When we had a garden party it rained. When we had a dance the fog was

[1]George Sassoon was the only child of Siegfried and his wife Hester: see the Biographical notes below.

too thick to reach it' – the moral being that the Lord loved Liberals. I was given a bouquet of heavily wired chrysanthemums & sparrow grass & got home with infinite relief to tea.

Diary – Wednesday 5 January 1949 – 40 Gloucester Square, W.2

Mrs Hochberger came to tea & had a very enjoyable jaw with me about Germany where she has been interpreting for Lindsay[1] whom she loves – & who she said had been the greatest possible success there. She went to Berlin with him for a few days. She says morale there is magnificent. They are showing a kind of 'Cockney' heroism, but their hardships are appalling – 2 hours' light only between 2 & 4 in the morning. She saw one family which had had no coal allocation at all. She told me an amusing story about Montgomery giving a shy-making harangue to a lot of Germans who had assembled, for a different purpose, at Robertson's[2] house – telling them that discipline was what they really wanted & needed, not this civilian mess-up. She had to translate this to her great embarrassment. Robertson, to his great credit, added a footnote – 'That is what we mean by democracy.' She assures me that the Germans saw & understood the irony. After Monty had bustled away they crowded round her & asked 'Wer war denn der kleine Offizier?' How I long for Monty to know! . . .

Diary – Tuesday 24 January – 40 Gloucester Square, W.2

. . . One lovely surprise – I got a letter from Ray saying that they have received orders to sail for home on 15th March! Will have disembarkation leave in April – & start on 1st May practising for the King's birthday parade! i.e. the Trooping! His childhood dream of being in scarlet in a busby will be realised! Mark turned up after tea having had a wonderful time at Sandringham & very good shooting – with 6 guns they got over 200 pheasants twice. The King was well enough to shoot. . . . One night he sat next to Queen Mary[3] who asked him family questions – very like a B.C.

[1] Alexander Dunlop Lindsay (1879–1952), cr. Baron, 1945; master of Balliol College, Oxford, 1924–49; principal, University College of North Staffordshire (Keele), 1949–52; Violet supported his candidature in the Oxford by-election in October 1938 when he ran as an anti-Munich candidate against Quintin Hogg (Lord Hailsham), who was elected.

[2] General Brian Hubert Robertson (1896–1974), cr. Baron, 1961; commander-in-chief and military governor, Control Commission, Germany, 1947–9.

[3] The widow of King George V (they married in 1893), formerly Princess Victoria Mary of Teck (1867–1953).

relation. She said how dull London was now with no entertaining. [Prince] Philip he said was obviously ill at ease with 'young men about town'.... On the other hand he is quite intelligent about politics & has pushed Pss E. into a position 'left' of the Queen! The Queen gave him (Mark) Winston's book on painting & wrote his name into it – very sweet of her.[1]

Britain and Israel, January 1949

The British withdrawal from Palestine in May 1948 had been preceded, by a matter of hours, by the proclamation of the state of Israel. The new state was at once plunged into a war for survival with its Arab neighbours. It gained immediate recognition from the United States, but not from the British government, even though the Labour Party was traditionally thought friendly to the Zionist cause. British policy in this volatile area was determined by Ernest Bevin at the foreign office. He sought to protect British interests and maintain the stability of Palestine by applying an 'even handed' approach to the interests of both Jews and Arabs. To this end he sought to limit Jewish immigration to the region. It was a policy deemed by many to be inhumane, given that the immigrants were mostly Holocaust survivors fleeing post-Holocaust Europe. For all his efforts at impartiality, Bevin found himself accused of anti-semitism. But in spite of this, and strong pressure from Zionists in Britain and America, he remained unwilling to recognize the Jewish state without some provision for the Palestinian Arabs. Israel's victory in the 1948–9 war, however, made this policy redundant and Bevin was forced, belatedly, to come to terms with the *fact* of Israel. Recognition came far too late for Bevin's critics and in a House of Commons debate, on 26 January, the extent of opposition to his Palestine policy was revealed when seventy Labour members rebelled by abstaining. He also faced a withering attack from Churchill, for, whatever the ethical basis of his policy, it had clearly failed. Without securing a settlement of the Palestine problem, Britain had alienated Israel, which was destined to be a key player in the politics of the Middle East.[2]

[1] W. S. Churchill, *Painting as a Pastime* (illustrated; 1948).

[2] Bullock, *Bevin*, 648–51; Gilbert, *Never Despair*, 453–8; VBC to RHBC, 13 February 1949.

Diary – Thursday 27 January – 40 Gloucester Square, W.2

Went to Lib. Press Conference at Caxton Hall & talked to *M.G., Glasgow Herald* & *Daily Herald* representatives. The *M.G.* man told me that Michael Foot[1] had been going about the lobbies last night telling them that the Govt. wld fall & that the King wld then send for Morrison who wld form a Govt with Dalton[2] & Bevan! I was amazed that he cld have talked such ignorant rot – as Morrison, Dalton & Bevan are all equally implicated in the Govt's Palestine policy. The majority was down to 80 last night & the abstentions on their own side must have been a nasty shock to them. Winston made a terrific onslaught & was so 'zionist' that I am surprised that his own Party took it lying down. No one made the vital point that the Jews have used force to acquire territory in defiance of the Security Council's edict – & that the Security Council appears to accept this fait accompli & to condone it. At least it has uttered no word of protest or condemnation....

Diary – Thursday 10 February – 40 Gloucester Square, W.2

...To-day attended Old Vic Executive & then went on to H. of C. for U.E.M. General Purposes Committee in Winston's room. He left us for the 1st hour during which we discussed the magazine: the suggestion of leasing a few pages in a Hulton Magazine *World Review* was turned down. Present: Lady R.W., Duncan Sandys, Bob Boothby, Mr Amery, Gollancz, Mr Gordon Lang, Harold Macmillan, Walter Layton. Winston returned & we then discussed the Govt.'s ridiculous attitude against all-party representation on the European Assembly.[3] W. had been bombarding Attlee with questions in the House about it & also about the 221 million supplementary estimates & there had been several 'breezes'. The question of Palestine then came up & Winston began to talk a lot of very foolish & wrong nonsense about the present situation – saying that he was glad that it had ended in a battle, he had always been on that side & the fact that it was the winning side made it none the worse etc. – like a bloodthirsty private

[1]Michael Foot (b. 1913), journalist and politician; columnist, *Daily Herald*, 1944–64; MP (Lab.) Devonport, Plymouth, 1945–55; Ebbw Vale, 1960–83; Blaenau, Gwent, 1983–92; leader of the Labour Party, 1980–3; brother of Dingle, Hugh (Lord Caradon) and John (see below).

[2]Hugh Dalton (1887–1962), cr. life peer, 1960; MP (Lab.) Camberwell, 1924–9; Bishop Auckland, 1929–31, 1935–59; chancellor of the exchequer, 1945–7.

[3]The government did in fact later nominate an all-party group to attend the inaugural meeting of the Consultative Assembly of the Council of Europe at Strasbourg, 10 August. It included eleven Labour MPs, six Conservatives and one Liberal (Walter Layton) (*The Times*, 24 February 1949; Macmillan, *Tides of Fortune*, 164–5).

schoolboy. He is a strange mixture between magnanimity & vindictiveness – greatness & smallness. The fact that it was a good stick to beat Bevin with had apparently blinded his eyes & queered the pitch of his conscience to all the tragic realities of the situation.

I intervened saying that I had always been on the side of the Jews – 'Yes I know you have' (enthusiastically from Winston) – 'But now I was not – because I hated terrorism murder & brute force as much in their hands as in anyone else's. What was going to happen to the 700,000 Arabs they had dispossessed? It was a disgrace that these had not even been mentioned in the H. of C. debate.' W. took my outburst quite calmly & good naturedly. But I was outraged by the lack of moral courage of all his colleagues who sat round him purring without raising their voices. Not a syllable of protest from any of them – & not even from Walter Layton.

I went out afterwards with Gollancz who of course agreed with me & is profoundly unhappy. But he had said nothing. I went back into W.'s room where he was alone with Duncan Sandys & tackled him again. He was very sweet – came up to me & kissed me saying 'I know one oughtn't to do this at Committees but I can't see you without kissing you.' I reminded him of how the Americans had bedevilled Bevin's policy by demanding the admission of 100,000 Jews when he was on the very verge of a settlement – how in U.S.A. a Jew is not allowed on a golf-course, etc. He admitted it all & cldn't have been sweeter – only saying 'Don't let's get worked up about these things – when there is so much else going on in the world.' I drove away with Walter Layton who dropped me at Charing X underground. B & I dined in alone.

Shane Leslie to V.B.C. ***Wednesday 16 February***
Glaslough, Éire

My dear Violet.

If you are alive I presume there is still a Liberal Party!

I have been speaking through Ulster on the Nationalist platform.[1] Personally I am where I was in the Elections of 1910 when we were allied to your father's party. It is of course a deadlock all round, but now that Attlee is in the Orange camp I pointed out that the proper room for manoeuvre

[1] In the Northern Ireland general election on 11 February the Unionists secured thirty-five of the forty-eight seats at the Stormont assembly. In their terms it was a resounding vote for 'King' over 'Republic'. But, as O. Sheehy Skeffington, a Dublin correspondent to *The Times*, pointed out, in three of the six counties (Armagh, Fermanagh and Tyrone) the Nationalists had secured a majority of votes: would they, he asked, be allowed to exercise self-determination and opt out of the Union? (*The Times*, 12 and 16 February 1949.)

is in the English Constituencies, where the Irish vote just turns the balance. A very moderate gesture towards an Irish Unity, as outlined by the old Liberals, would turn that vote and you might swing 40 seats away from Tory and Labour into the Liberal fold.

I enclose my Derry speech which emphasizes the point.... I shall be over in London by St Patrick's Day and would be glad to give your inner circle the idea as it stands in the aftermath of this Ulster Election. Now that Labour have been eliminated you might once more put up Liberal members in Ulster. In any case I believe it is your one chance of a fighting programme and possibly of survival!

Yrs as ever, Shane Leslie

V.B.C. to Shane Leslie[1]

Wednesday 23 February
40 Gloucester Square, W.2

My dear Shane,

It was delightful to hear from you again – though I wish your letter could have been about something else, as I could then have written you a more welcome reply. You write: 'Personally I am where I was in the Elections of 1910.' Are you really? If so you must be almost alone in performing such a remarkable feat – physical and intellectual. Everyone else I know – including myself – is living in 1949.

When my Father and I and other Liberals fought the battle for Irish Home Rule we believed that the Irish people cared – and cared passionately – for the freedom and independence of all small nations, not for their own alone. We believed that they hated tyranny – anywhere and everywhere. Alas! the years between 1939 and 1945 have made nonsense of our belief and of their history. You know what happened. While we fought, sometimes alone, sometimes with others, for the freedom of Czechs, Poles, Greeks, Norwegians, Belgians, Dutch, Danes, etc. – Ireland stood aside, nestled in snug neutrality under the lee of England – and wouldn't even give us bases to help us feed ourselves and her own people. While bombs rained on us the Swastika flew in Dublin. Ulster felt, and acted differently. She felt and acted as we did. Now Eire has severed her last link (a tenuous and symbolic one I grant you) with the Commonwealth.[2] Neither this last action nor her war record are calculated to make the prospect of Union more acceptable to Ulster. You would be the first to agree that the only way to bring Ulster in is to make her want to come in.

[1] This transcription is taken from a typescript copy of VBC's letter to Shane Leslie, kept among the Bonham Carter papers.

[2] Notice had been given in December of Éire's intention to quit the Commonwealth in April.

Coercion would be as abhorrent and as futile in your eyes if applied to Ulster as to Southern Ireland.

As to the glittering bait of votes and seats for the Liberal Party, which you dangle before me, I want neither – on these terms. I only want votes to be given and seats to be won for the things I believe in. I know that if I had a vote in Ulster to-day, whether I was Liberal, Tory, Socialist, Protestant or Catholic, I wouldn't cast if for union with Southern Ireland, which unlike Norway is not even willing to join the Atlantic Pact against Communist Russia; or indeed for union with any other State which is 'neutral' when freedom is at stake.

I should love to see you round about St Patrick's Day. But I don't expect you to want to see me now you know my views!

Ever yours, [Violet]

Diary – Wednesday 23 February – 40 Gloucester Square, W.2

Had a very interesting lunch with Gollancz at the Ivy. We talked about 2 things – the Palestine situation & Mark. On Palestine he sees absolutely clear – in fact the fact that he is a Jew makes him mind the thing more than if he weren't. He really minds about values not races & is fighting a hard battle with his own people – trying to raise funds to relieve the Arabs etc. (The accounts of their camps are heartbreaking.) . . .

'Every genuine Liberal':
the Liberal Party and the creation of the state of Israel

> The inauguration of Dr Chaim Weizmann as the first president of Israel, 17 February 1949, was greeted by the Liberal *News Chronicle* with a short leading article entitled 'Hopeful'. While noting that Israel had been 'compelled to use force to establish itself', the article observed that too many Israelis had 'acquired an exaggerated sense of the value of violence as a means to desirable ends'. Weizmann's election, however, suggested that 'wiser counsels' would now prevail, and the paper looked to the future with optimism. Violet disagreed strongly with this editorial and in a letter to the editor, published on 24 February, she drew attention to the legacy of Zionist terrorism and to the plight of the Palestinian refugees: 'This is the picture which is described as "hopeful". If ever milk had to be mixed with water it could not have been done more thoroughly.' Her letter drew an immediate response from the Liberal chief whip Frank Byers, whose reply had the appearance of an official rebuke: 'I deplore the substance and tone of Lady Violet

Bonham Carter's letter, and so must every genuine Liberal in the country.' Now was the time, Byers argued, to look to the future and encourage Israel, 'so that it can make the fullest contribution to the progress and welfare of all peoples in the Middle East'. Violet was indignant that Byers should use his office to cast aspersions on her Liberalism, and the matter was debated at a highly charged Party meeting in March. Senior party figures defended Violet, notably the ex-leader Archie Sinclair, who pointed out that her comments only echoed those previously published in a *Manchester Guardian* leader. And the affair was closed when Byers agreed to make it clear, in the pages of the *News Chronicle*, that he had not meant to question a colleague's Liberalism. It was a hollow gesture, for he clearly had, and the affair intensified Violet's disillusionment with the Party and its leadership.[1] The episode did not in fact represent her true feelings for the Jewish state, which she came greatly to admire and would visit three times in the years ahead – as a guest of the Israeli government.

Diary – Thursday 24 February – 40 Gloucester Square, W.2

Walter Layton rang me up last night & urged me to allow them to publish my letter in the *News Chronicle* – as Cruikshank very much wanted to & he (Walter) thought it a very good letter. I of course said they cld if they wanted to. My only hesitation had been about attacking the *N.C.* publicly when I had so constantly praised it in private. It duly appeared this morning – framed in a box! I went to Old Vic Committee – & drove on with Oliver Esher[2] to the Tate....

Diary – Saturday 26 February – 40 Gloucester Square, W.2

Received about 10 letters fan-mail for my letter to *N.C.* & 3 critical & cursing (all with foreign names!) One was from my old Becket Williams (who used to plague my life at the BBC) in which he alluded to a letter by Frank Byers with which he intensely disagreed. I had not observed it but sent for the *N.C.* of yesterday in which I found a letter from Byers saying that 'every genuine Liberal must deplore my letter'. I must say the suggestion coming from Byers that I am not a 'genuine Liberal' wld make me

[1] *News Chronicle*, 19, 24, 25 February; 14 March 1949.

[2] Oliver Sylvain Brett (1881–1963), 3rd Viscount Esher; m. 1912 Antoinette *née* Heckscher.

laugh if it were not so outrageous. I have drafted a letter to Clement Davies asking if this is to be taken as the official view of the Parliamentary Party. . . .

Diary – Tuesday 8 March – 40 Gloucester Square, W.2

Temp down thanks to Aspirin but not feeling very grand. Got up & drove to H. of C. arriving at 11 in one of the bigger Committee Rooms. Large attendance. Clem Davies (obviously having the 'wind up') opened with references to my health & my having come there with 'my usual courage'(!). Then read a lengthy 'factual' survey – including our correspondence & Layton's letter to Byers – which was a very valuable knock-out blow at the outset as it proved (1) that I had not asked for publication of my letter (2) that Layton & Cruikshank had asked me to allow it in the public interest. So that the *N.C.* ranged itself by my side & that 2 most distinguished Liberals did not 'deplore' my letter. I then opened the ball. I read a short & excellent extract from a letter to me by Eric Perth which cld not have put the case better & more succinctly & then proceeded myself to put Clem & Byers 'on the spot'. I took up the tale where Walter had left off – i.e. from the moment when my fan-mail on Sat. announced to me the existence of Byers's letter which, as I said, might well have been date-lined Moscow. . . .

I ended by asking for a 'public repudiation'. I cannot remember the exact order in which people spoke. Not one voice was raised in defence of the statement. Reading[1] made a most impressive contribution. Jimmy Rothschild[2] a poor one. Dingle[3] of course admirable & unanswerable – describing it as 'quite indefensible'. Hopkin Morris[4] equally intransigent but less effective saying 'No one has defended these words – not even their own authors. They shld be withdrawn.' [Lord] Samuel looking terribly sheepish & shamefaced said they were used rhetorically as one might say 'every genuine lover of peace'. It then somehow transpired that the charge of Anti-Semitism had been struck out by Samuel – & that of Racial Discrimination by Cruikshank. These 2 charges were seriously brought against me.

[1] Gerald Rufus Isaacs (1889–1960), 2nd Marquess of Reading; the following year Reading left the Liberal Party in frustration and took the Conservative whip in the Lords; he became minister of state for foreign affairs, 1953–7.

[2] James A. de Rothschild (d. 1957), MP (Lib.) Isle of Ely, 1929–45.

[3] (Sir) Dingle (Mackintosh) Foot (1905–78), Kt, 1964; QC, 1954; MP (Lib.) Dundee, 1931–45; joined Labour Party, 1956; MP (Lab.) Ipswich, 1957–70; solicitor-general, 1964–7; the brother of Hugh (Lord Caradon), John and Michael.

[4] Sir Rhys Hopkin Morris (1888–1956), Kt, 1954; QC, 1946; barrister; MP (Ind. Lib.) Cardiganshire, 1923–32; (Lib.) Carmarthen, 1945–56.

I blazed out my record of service to the Jewish cause & asked Clem & Byers how many Jewish Refugees they had each personally guaranteed?... A. MacFadyean[1] spoke well & said my letter cld not possibly be accused of Anti-Semitism. Dorothy Layton supported me strongly. Suddenly old Percy[2] burst into a spontaneous from-the-heart tribute to me saying how fantastic any aspersion on my Liberalism was – how nobody had a finer record all thro' the Appeasement days etc. – which met with a warm response & Samuel then said they certainly owed me an apology & withdrawal & an agreed statement shld be prepared. This was accepted & we broke up – Byers looking hot red & speechless & Clem inexpressibly foolish. Dingle dropped me home & I was glad to get into bed again.

Diary – Tuesday 15 March – 40 Gloucester Square, W.2

Got up in the evening & dined out at American Embassy in my new black dress.... I sat between Mr Bevin & Harold Wilson & started off with Harold Wilson, who didn't attract me at all. He is short, fat, podgy & rather pushing & seemed anxious to be 'in on' every conversation that was going – & to tell his own stories instead of listening to Bevin's when Bevin turned to me. I enjoyed my talk with him extremely. He was just as I had imagined him – only less (apparently) vain. Absolutely natural, solid, 3-dimensional, with real human enjoyment of his own jokes & the champagne ('Might do no harm' when he was offered it) – & extremely friendly....

He was frank about their colleagues & Party members – 'Someone saw Kingsley Martin[3] going off to Moss Bros. – "What is K. M. going to Moss Bros for?" "K. M. is going to Moss Bros to be measured for his Crown of Thorns."' Of Cripps – 'Cripps gets on his halo & binds himself up to the stake & waits – & nothing happens. Finally he shouts "Will no one ever put a match to these faggots?"' Someone had asked him to classify Crossman politically – 'I shld call him a Jay Walker' – rather a good description.

He was very interesting about Molotov[4] who he evidently doesn't dislike

[1]Sir Andrew MacFadyean (1887–1974), Kt 1925; treasury official, diplomat, businessman; contested City of London (Lib.), 1945; Finchley, 1950; senior officer in Liberal Party Organization from 1936, vice president, 1950–60.

[2]Sir Percy Harris (1876–1952), cr. Bt, 1932; MP (Lib.) Hanborough, Leics., 1916–18; South West Bethnal Green, 1922–45; chief Liberal whip, 1935–45; deputy leader, 1940–5.

[3](Basil) Kingsley Martin (1897–1969), editor *New Statesman*, 1930–60; 'the archetypal Englishman of the intellectual Left' (*DNB*).

[4]Vyacheslav Molotov (1890–1986), Soviet statesman; prime minister, 1930–41; deputy minister from 1941; foreign minister, 1939–49, 1953–6; regarded as one of the chief protagonists in the Cold War.

but regards as the victim of his superiors. He described the Conference in Paris when the Marshall offer was first made.[1] Molotov discussed it for 3 days quite seriously, rationally & soberly. Arrangements for exchange of coal with Poland etc. & the other satellites who were longing to come in. On the 3rd day a telegram arrived & was handed to him as he sat at the Conference table. 'He has a way sometimes of turning yellow & a kind of bump on his forehead shoots out. Well, when he got this telegram he turned bright yellow & the lump shot out. And from that moment onwards he had to turn everything down flat. He'd got his marching orders. He started threatening poor little Bidault – telling him all the dreadful things that wld happen to him if he went in to the Marshall Plan (I like little Bidault. I don't like de Gaulle – a man who wants to cash in when his country's in a mess). Well I had to take the brunt. I said "I belong to a country that's used to being threatened."' I asked him about the Communist infiltration into the T.U. movement – & he of course rated it very low. (This wld naturally be his brief.) I asked how the Communists got all the key positions. 'Because the others are lazy & don't attend.' Just as I was going out he said a word about Palestine – 'The situation is very serious there – more serious than people know.'...

Diary – Thursday 26 May – 40 Gloucester Square, W.2

Our Cocktail Party. Terrific furniture shiftings – tidyings up – arrangement of flowers – counting of glasses – distribution of functions, etc. At 6 we were all 5 in the drawing-room – 'all dressed up' for what seemed like ages. We felt such deep sympathy for the 1st arrival - - - who should it be but the Finletters! followed by Eddie Marsh[2] – & Kenneth Rae. Then they all poured in. I don't think there were more than 57 altogether but they all stayed all the time & we didn't get the last ones out of the house till 10 to 9!... Mark insisted on having Martinis – & made them mix them very strong ($\frac{3}{4}$ gin instead of half & half) with the result that Eddie Marsh literally reeled from the house & wld I am sure have fallen down the stairs had not B. escorted him & put him in a taxi. Even I (proverbially blind to the drunk) realised that he was half-seas over! Mark & Ray tell me that several others were drunkish! Micky O'Brien amongst them. However it

[1]At the Paris conference, June-July 1947, Bevin, Bidault and Molotov discussed Russia's possible involvement in the Marshall plan. But the meeting ended with a stern Russian warning that the plan threatened to divide, rather than unite, Europe, and the talks have been seen as marking an important step in the Cold War.

[2]Sir Edward Howard ('Eddie') Marsh (1872–1953), KCVO, 1937; formerly private secretary to Winston Churchill; an old friend of the Bonham Carters.

was generally agreed to have been 'a great success' – tho' many of my favourite people cld not come. . . .

Diary – Sunday 28 August – 40 Gloucester Square, W.2

Another hot & lovely day. B & I & Nannie drove to Buckingham Palace to see Ray mount the Guard for the last time. The crowds were enormous – the Queen Victoria monument covered as tho' for a Coronation or a Jubilee. More crowds 20 or 30 deep pressing up against the railings. We watched from the forecourt. Ray was carrying the Colours. Nannie enjoyed it all enormously I think. We went back to the Mess but as it was only 11.30 we felt we cldn't bother them (& ourselves?) till lunch so went off to the Marlborough Club to fetch B's umbrella & found (to our amazement) that I cld go upstairs with him & sit in a very nice library till lunch-time. I felt the point of a men's club. The absolute peace & silence & uninterruptibility. Also the pathos of the very old men poring passionately over their crosswords with heavy dictionaries. Yet a women's club wld not have the same point – or peace – even if they were silent. I shld like to belong to a men's club. . . .

'Going for Malan's policy hip & thigh'
The 1949 Commonwealth Relations Conference, Canada

In September 1949 Violet attended an unofficial 'Commonwealth Relations Conference' in Muskoka, Canada, as a member of a cross-party British delegation. The conference was held under the auspices of national branches of the Institute of International Affairs and aimed to promote better understanding within the Commonwealth. A range of controversial issues were discussed over ten days of talks: the dispute between Pakistan and India over Kashmir was debated, and an Irish delegation – there to 'observe' proceedings – made a protest against the partition of Ireland. But for Violet the most important debate was on 'the native question' in South Africa. In May of the previous year D. F. Malan's Nationalist party had won a landmark victory in the South African general election. His party had campaigned on the 'race issue' and *The Times* expressed deep concern at his success: 'Dr Malan's doctrine of apartheid requires the permanent repression of native aspirations of equality. It is a denial of the first principle of British imperialism; and there can be no burking the fact that the victory of its advocates is a setback for the ideas on which the Commonwealth is founded.' At the Commonwealth Conference Violet launched her own attack on apartheid, 'going for Malan's policy hip & thigh'. Her language anticipated Harold Macmillan's famous 'wind of change' speech in Cape Town more than a decade later: 'We cannot fight history. Politically and economically the Africans are advancing. We can't stay that advance – & we shldn't wish to do so.' It was the beginning of a long personal protest.[1]

Diary – Monday 29 August – 40 Gloucester Square, W.2

My very last day. I had a most agreeable luncheon with Haley in his room at the B.B.C. . . . I went on to Carter Braine then Selfridge to get a cheap case for my books. Home – finished finally with Wrathall.[2] Then – a real windfall – Isaiah Berlin came to see me – in marvellous form & terribly amusing about us & America. He says that 'isolation' is stone-dead – that so far from disliking us, they like us – but are maddened & distressed by our behaviour. They know they can never let us go under, which makes it worse. It is like a Catholic marriage. Divorce is unthinkable. We are the hysterical, unreasonable wife – always threatening to cut loose from them rather than endure support which is an affront to our pride, to marry the Russians, anything. They have to coax, placate, try & save us from our own folly. The ultimate end he foresees is that we shall be absorbed – at least the Commonwealth will be – in the American orbit. We can never recover as Crowther wld wish us to. People here will never work & boost & push & struggle. They have become too civilized to do so. They prefer leisure to money. We are becoming rather like the Austrians. Yet unlike the Austrians he thinks we might still be able to play a directing part in the whole concern. . . . I enjoyed seeing him enormously. Dinner with Mark – B – & Brigid. Now at last in bed. . . . (Breakfast at 7 to-morrow morning alas! alack!)

Diary – Tuesday 30 August – On board the Empress of Canada, *bound for Quebec*

Woke at ¼ to 7, with much less pain than I expected to feel, on a lovely radiant morning – the Square mistily green in the early sunlight. . . .

[1] Albert Luthuli, *Let My People Go* (1962), 96; *The Times*, 29 May 1948; typescript of speech, Bonham Carter Papers. Along with the host nation and the United Kingdom six other countries were represented: Australia, Ceylon, India, New Zealand, Pakistan and South Africa.

[2] Sheila Wrathall, Bongie and Violet's 'delightful and highly competent secretary' (Raymond Bonham Carter). Most of her time was taken up by Violet.

Mark came down in his dressing gown to say goodbye (Ray was on Guard at St James's Palace). I said goodbye to Nannie, Law, Alice, Mrs Lock[1] – & B & I drove off to Euston with 4 suit-cases – 2 attaché cases groaning with books & papers, & a hat box! It was a blow to find that the whole delegation was stabled together in a 'Plummer' – packed as tight as teeth in a râtelier. Stray members littered the platform & we were photographed by batteries of cameramen – the favourite trio being Rab Butler, Miss Sutherland[2] & myself! (not a beauty chorus) Lionel Curtis, to whom I gave a wide berth, looked very like an old Ophelia with dishevelled locks & a wild Federal light in his eye. . . .

V.B.C. to Bongie[3] ***Saturday 3 September***
***The* Empress of Canada**

[Darling] – I thought it no good writing till to-day & hope to post this by Air-Mail from Quebec or Montreal. Our journey up-to-date has not been all my fancy pictured! We started in bright hot sunshine, sitting out of doors on deck, watching a lovely misty, hilly Welsh coast recede. Next day started sunny too, but then grey skies & violent hurricanes of wind began & until last night it has been rougher than I can ever remember, at least the ship has been more violently convulsed. My journeys to U.S.A. & back in mid-winter [1912–13] didn't compare with it.

On Thursday night I hardly slept a wink. The whole ship cracked & creaked like a rheumatic giant, everything in my cabin glissaded about the floor as on a skating rink – objects on shelves clattered down & about, above, below, all round one. I in my bunk was tossed like a pancake, rolled from side to side, heaved up & down to & fro in every conceivable permutation of motion, but though aching with these physical jerks & unable to 'bat' anything but an eyelid, I neither was, nor felt, actually sick, by some strange miracle. I crawled out of bed & dressed (gymnastically) next morning & staggered upstairs to attend a 'group' meeting of our delegation, all looking very battered & the worse for wear. (Rab Butler actually always looks as though he'd had a night like that.) Poor Professor

[1]Rose Law was Violet's beloved maid; Alice one of the domestic helps at 40 Gloucester Square; and Mrs Lock the Bonham Carters' formidable cook.

[2]Lucy Stuart Sutherland (1903–80), DBE, 1969; historian and administrator; principal of Lady Margaret Hall, Oxford, 1945–71.

[3]The transcriptions of this letter, and that of 7–8 September (below), are taken from typescript copies of Violet's originals, probably made by Bongie for family circulation and kept among the Bonham Carter papers.

Mansergh[1] looked at the last gasp. Maurice Webb[2] didn't get up at all. To-day thank Heaven the sun has re-appeared & it is warmer again, & we have had a quiet night to restore us. Apart from this battery of bad weather, comfort is extreme....

My companions: those whose society I enjoy are Sir William FitzGerald,[3] a perfectly delightful Irishman, Colonial Administrator of great experience & most enlightened views. Palestine was his last assignment. (He is my ally over S. Africa.) Bob Brand,[4] who gave us a very good dissertation on the Dollar Gap this morning, which can't have been very palatable to some of our Socialist colleagues. H. V. Hodson,[5] sensible & nice, though unexciting. Sir Ian Jacob ditto.[6] He is obviously able, but reveals his 'military' limitations when he gets off his own terrain in conversation. Soldiers feel it part of their duty not to think about a great many things. Jakie Astor's most charming & pretty & delightful young (South American?) wife.[7] She is called Jacquita, & has great tact & exquisite manners to everyone. Denis Healey is able & nice, though 'party-bound' on a good many issues. Maurice Webb very friendly & terribly crippled with his one leg. I haven't had much truck with the two Ll. Georges. Gwilym[8] is very fat, & rather a 'floating kidney' in the delegation as he is not an 'expert' & does not represent any group or Party or particular point of view. My female colleague, Miss Sutherland, is quite nice but fairly bleak....

We are due at Montreal on Tuesday where we shall be met by the Canadian 'Chatham House' people & entertained in various ways, press

[1] Nicholas Mansergh (1910–91), research professor of British Commonwealth relations, Chatham House, 1947–53; master of St John's College, Cambridge, 1969–79.

[2] Maurice Webb (1904–56), political journalist and broadcaster; MP (Lab.) Central Bradford, 1945–55; chairman of Parliamentary Labour Party, 1946–50.

[3] Sir William James FitzGerald (1894–1989), Kt, 1944; born Co. Tipperary; served 1914–18 war (MC); afterwards judicial officer in Africa; chief justice of Palestine, 1944–8; president, Lands Tribunal, 1950–65.

[4] Robert Henry 'Bob' Brand (1878–1963), cr. Baron, 1946; banker and public servant: helped regulate Allied food supply during war.

[5] Henry Vincent Hodson (b. 1906), assistant editor, *Sunday Times*, 1946–50; editor, 1950–61; provost of Ditchley, 1961–71; author of *The British Commonwealth and the Future* (1939).

[6] Lt-Gen. Sir Ian Jacob (1899–1993), military assistant to war cabinet, 1939–46; director overseas services, BBC, 1947–52; director-general, BBC, 1952–60.

[7] Ana Inez Astor *née* Carcano (d. 1992); m. 1944 (diss. 1972) Major (Sir) John (Jacob) Astor (b. 1918), MP (Con.) Sutton, Plymouth, 1951–9. The Astors went along as secretaries to the British delegation at the conference.

[8] Gwilym Lloyd George (1894–1967), cr. Viscount Tenby, 1957; younger son of David Lloyd George; former National Liberal MP who gravitated to Conservatism, representing Pembrokeshire as a 'National Liberal and Conservative', 1945–50; afterwards Newcastle-upon-Tyne (North), 1951–7; home secretary, 1954–7.

Conference, Cocktail Party, etc. We leave for Toronto at night & travel all next day by rail, bus & ferry to Bigwin Island. I shall write next to you from there. It seems a hundred years since I left home instead of being four days. Doing something different is the way to prolong life, without a doubt. How are you? I miss you all, you, Mark, Ray. Ray will be at Oakley this weekend. Mark possibly but improbably at Balmoral. You possibly picking blackberries at Stockton, Adam & Cressida passing through London. There is nothing in the world I want you to do! . . .

V.B.C. to Bongie ***Wednesday 7 to Thursday 8 September***
Bigwin Inn, Lake of Bays, Ontario

[Darling] – I start this letter on the last lap of our journey, feeling rather battered from travel (night journey last night), a day in Montreal yesterday, & all the extraordinary complications of travel in this country. (It really has given me an 'up' with our railway system with all its faults.). . . The scale of the country is very impressive, but both in the towns & in the country the houses all seem to be 'villas', rather than cottages or mansions. There is a general pervasive sense of suburbia, but suburbia minus a metropolis. . . .

8th September, Bigwin Inn. Here at last! after two long last laps, one by a rattling bus, the other by a ferry, with a lot more luggage ritual en route. . . . We staggered into a Cocktail Party in a 'Ye Olde' hall fraught with beams & jutting stones & 'old-world' gadgets, where I had long talks with Pakistanis, Canadians, etc. feeling giddy & gaga with fatigue. Then dinner with my dear FitzGerald (whom I dote upon) & two very nice (strange) Canadians. Then up to bed & unpacking. No luggage lost, but I don't think I have ever felt more tired in my life. Others are similarly affected. Gwilym Lloyd George took to bed at 7 p.m. No letters for me to my surprise, but your two dated 1st & 3rd reached me this morning. A thousand thanks.

We had another long seance all this afternoon. Each delegation making 'general' points about its position. We only got as far as India (alphabetical order) who of course were very eloquent & long & full of verbal balloons which lent themselves well to pricking. They said they did not wish to raise the racial issue with S. Africa or their difficulties with Pakistan! I don't know whether Pakistan will say ditto to this. 'God Save the King' was played at dinner to-night & I was amused to see the Irish stand up!. . .

Diary – Friday 9 September – Bigwin Inn, Lake of Bays, Ontario

Discussion began thank Heaven this morning, after the formal speeches had ended.... After lunch I had to repack! to be moved again! from the East to the West Wing. This took up all the short time I might have spent out of doors – & the sun was out for once! Then on to a discussion on U.N.A. Denis Healey opened most unfortunately. He was patronising – talked of 'old' & 'young' nations – said that the old ones regarded UNO as a nuisance – gave an impression of weary cynicism & disillusionment & generally infuriated the Canadians. This is just exactly what we ought not to do – & tho' I hadn't meant to speak I had made a few notes, & did so I think with success in dispelling the illusion that faith & hope were dead in a tired, sceptical old country. Dear old Hall, the miner, who sat beside me, said to me with emotion 'You did well my dear – you did well. Yours is the greatest contribution our delegation has made. You pop in on that note whenever you can.' Ian Jacob spoke also very drily I thought – my opinion of him gets lower & lower – he is just a narrow, dry as dust official. Brand spoke too with gentle defeatism. He has the least fiery belly I know. There is no red blood in our delegation except in my veins & those of Sir W. FitzGerald. I had dinner with Lionel Curtis & his wife.... Now in bed in my new room – daren't look at the time!

Diary – Saturday 10 September – Bigwin Inn, Lake of Bays, Ontario

A sunny day at last! Morning spent on strategy & Communism – afternoon on economics.... Dined very drearily. It is dangerous to sit down at a table alone. You may be joined by anyone. I was joined by 3 women – Miss Sutherland, Mrs Schuller (whom I like) & the N.Z. delegate Miss Gwendolen Carter. When I asked after Freyberg she said 'Has he been in N.Z. lately?' I said 'He has been Governor General for 3 years' – which seemed news to her. There was a film afterwards. I watched only the S. African part – which only showed one black, near a blazing furnace, & said 'These cheerful negroes revel in the cosy heat' or words to that effect. Long talk with FitzGerald before going to bed. He is a most human, individual & attractive man. Now bed – have taken my 1st draught since leaving England. To-morrow thank Heaven is Sunday – but I shall be called by telephone at 8.30!

Diary – Wednesday 14 September – Bigwin Inn, Lake of Bays, Ontario

Very cold day indeed. (I needn't have brought any cotton clothes!) Discussion on Indian & Pacific Strategy – Japan etc. Lunched with one Neil Morrison who wanted to talk about the Press Commission's report. I think he must be an official of C.B.C. Stayed in all the afternoon. Then resumed Conference – FitzGerald & I sitting side by side & waiting to go over the top on S. Africa. The Far East dragged on till 5.15 – then FitzGerald was called & made a very good statement on the Colonies saying just the right things. Then Ceylon spoke & then I weighed in – paying tribute to the Liberal personal attitude of the S. African delegation & then going for Malan's policy hip & thigh. My speech was greeted with rounds of applause, which I think emanated from the delegations of India, Pakistan & Ceylon. Malherbe answered – very gently – not controverting any of my points. One Canadian businessman described the good condition of the Natives in the Reservations, whilst admitting that Johannesburg presented a very different picture. FitzGerald was delighted & Dr Reo rushed up to congratulate me warmly & said 'If only your speech cld be made at U.N.O.! what an effect it wld have on public relations' etc. I daresay that with the Indians it wld!! FitzGerald & I now feel 'Nunc Dimittis' & that we have done our duty.[1]

After dinner poor old Lionel Curtis made a speech to us all on his one & only theme of World Govt. He cldn't have talked more nonsense with greater solemnity. The irrepressible Reo of course leapt to his feet & asked him the pertinent question, which I have often put to our Federalists: what wld the franchise be? If 'one man, one vote' the smaller & more enlightened nations wld be swamped. This was clearly rather a teaser for L.C. but he finally said people shld vote according to their taxable capacity – in other words, we shld have a world Plutocracy dominated by the rich nations. Not a Chink or a Hindu wld ever get a glimpse of a voting paper. I missed alas! the only row that has taken place – between India & Pakistan – while I went to the telephone to answer a call from British Information Services in New York. . . .[2]

[1] Rab Butler later commented: 'The native question in South Africa was discussed against a Table Mountain of statistics and to the accompaniment of such notes of pure English liberalism from one of our number that the voices of the Indian delegates were temporarily stilled' (*The Times*, 29 September 1949).

[2] After the Commonwealth Conference ended Violet embarked on a short lecture tour in the United States. This was handled by British Information Services, a British government information agency operating from New York. She lectured on the theme of 'Britain Today – the Liberal approach to our problems'.

Diary – Saturday 15 October – on board the Queen Mary *bound for Southampton*

Sunny day – still – quite smooth.... Sat on promenade deck & wrote thanking letters to U.S.A. of which I have a packet. Instead of long tracts of peace & idleness I find there is constantly something to be done on board ship. Lifeboat drill or filling in a form or something for one's passport. I tried to cash a £2 Travellers Cheque at the Midland Bank & they began by refusing to do it – saying that they weren't allowed to give any change. I said 'But then what is the good of a Traveller's Cheque?' They said it must be paid as a unit. I objected that I cldn't afford to pay £2 for a stamp – which I happened to want at the moment! They cld not explain their reason, except that stewards might sell pound notes on the Black Market. I pointed out that it wld be a very unprofitable occupation at this moment.[1] Finally I said that on the *Empress of Canada* coming out we had all changed our cheques without the slightest difficulty. Their reply was wonderful – 'Ah, but you see Madam, there wasn't a Bank on that ship'!! Alice in Wonderland! A Bank exists now to prevent you from cashing cheques. Where there is no Bank you can cash them. No wonder the world finds it difficult to do business with us....

[1] Weeks earlier there had been a dramatic devaluation of the pound from $4.03 to $2.80.

THREE

Two General Elections

1950–1951

The Liberals and the 1950 general election

On 10 January 1950 Clement Attlee announced a general election for the following month. The campaign was expected to be a close contest, and a straight fight, between Labour and the Conservatives. But the issue was confused by an extensive Liberal challenge. After the Party's humiliation in 1945 the new leader, Clement Davies, planned an ambitious programme of recovery. He was determined not to compromise on Liberal independence and quashed rumours of a pact with the Conservatives. 'Let Liberals of little or no faith leave the party' he declared to the 1948 Liberal assembly, expressing contempt for 'the Quislings who had been among them'. This was alarming news for Churchill, who was concerned at the possible effect of Liberal candidacies on potential Conservative votes. He wrote to Davies shortly before the dissolution in 1950 urging an arrangement between their parties: 'There is a real measure of agreement between modern Tory democracy and the mass of Liberals who see in Socialism all that their most famous thinkers and leaders have fought against in the past.' Davies, though, dismissed the idea as 'unworthy subterfuge' and the Liberals proceeded to put up 475 candidates. To Churchill it was 'a policy of vote-splitting on a fantastic scale', and one that might easily tip the scales towards Labour. During the election he appealed to Liberals throughout the country to vote 'against the establishment of the Socialist state' – in effect to vote 'tactically' for a Conservative. And he was even prepared to offer one of the Conservative election broadcasts to Violet, a Liberal whom he knew to be strongly anti-Socialist. She had not been chosen to speak by her party and was forbidden from accepting Churchill's tantalizing offer, on the grounds that it might damage Liberal prospects. Disappointed with this decision she travelled north to campaign for her old friend (and Churchill's) Archie Sinclair, at Caithness, and also her son-in-law Jo Grimond, in neighbouring

Orkney and Shetland. Both Sinclair and Grimond were viable candidates, but Churchill's fears about their many colleagues proved to be well founded. Even the Liberal leadership must have had serious doubts, for insurance had been taken out against a maximum of 250 lost deposits. In the event 319 were lost and only 9 Liberals elected, against 315 Labour and 299 Conservative. Labour had thus won a narrow majority, for which the Conservatives inevitably blamed the Liberals, who were left to rue their worst ever electoral performance.[1]

Archie Sinclair to V.B.C. ***Sunday 8 January 1950***
Dalnawillan, Altnabreac, Caithness

Dearest Violet.

I hate to remind you of your noble and angelic promise to come & speak for me during the election. It seems almost like taking an advantage of your kindness! True it is that we are now enjoying an untimely summer. The sun has been shining all day and I have just come in from a walk with Marigold without a coat on! But if the election comes next month or in March – all Marigold & I can say is that we will take the greatest possible pains to shield you from the worst rigours of electioneering in the winter, and see that you have plenty of hot baths and a warm bed at night...

Clem wrote to me the other day a very nice letter asking me to join the Liberal Committee. I wrote back explaining that I simply could not spare three days out of every fortnight away from here in the immediate pre-election period, and with great reluctance and regret declined his invitation. The following day I saw my name in the newspapers as a member of the Committee! However I wasn't annoyed for I know these things happen to other people – & worse!... Of course, they are much understaffed and work under other big handicaps; and, whereas David only had to fight one Goliath, they have got to fight two....

With love from us both to you & Bongie, Archie

Diary – Wednesday 11 January – Clovelly Court, nr Bideford, Devon

B & I sat in the Twinnery answering our post & did not look up when the papers were brought in. It was only just before lunch that we opened our newspapers & saw that the General Election date had been announced for Feb. 23rd & that Parlt. wld not meet again.... I feel little zest about plunging into the fray – but it is as well to know the worst....

[1] Gilbert, *Never Despair*, 503–5, 507; Howard, *Butler*, 167–72; Cook, *Short History of the Liberal Party*, 132- 3; *The Times*, 26 April 1948.

Diary – Monday 16 January – 40 Gloucester Square, W.2

Just before I left Clovelly on Sat. morning Winston came thro' to me, just back from Madeira. He asked me how the Liberal Broadcasts had been allotted & I told him: Clem Davies 20 minutes, Megan[1] & [Herbert] Samuel 10 minutes each. He then said he felt it vital that my voice shld be heard in the National Debate & that he wished to offer me, quite unconditionally, one of the allocation of 5 which had been made to them. I cld say what I liked. He trusted me to be anti-Socialist. He was very sweet & asked me to come down on Monday to discuss it, which I accepted by telegram.

Today his car called for me at 12 & I drove down to Chartwell on a most lovely & sunny morning. I was ushered first into a luxurious downstairs bedroom (Clemmie's) where I tidied up then was taken upstairs by a Secretary. He came in & led me into the dining-room where we had luncheon tête-à-tête & a bottle of champagne. I told him that I had taken counsel with Walter Layton who was against it – saying that the prejudice in the Liberal mind wld be so great against my taking on the 'Tory air' that nothing I said there – however 'Liberal' & well-expressed – could undo it. I fully realised that by many I shld be regarded as a Quisling, a Tory puppet, a ventriloquist's doll.

Against this he said that I shld testify to the faith that was in me, that when great events were afoot one shld take a part in them. Here was a chance of throwing my influence into the scales with great effect, which might never come again. Feeling as I did, it was my duty not to stand aside. One must be crucified for something. The integrity of my character & record cld not be assailed. I was hard put to it, for I felt the moral force of his argument, & I also longed to do what he asked for my great love's sake & because this might be the last thing he wld ever ask me that I could do....

He showed me his pictures, his tanks of tiny gold fish & we walked out in the winter sunshine accompanied by his detective Sergeant MacDougall – with his hands full of large slices of bread for the black swans, which had been given him by Australia & which were floating on the lake – black with red backs – 8 of them divided by Iron Curtains into 3 different compounds. He fed them – only 2 wld take it from his hand tho' he coaxed them with every lure. There were gold fish in other pools & some rocks transported by lorry from Wales & fitted into the earth to make the setting for another pool. It was a child's nursery of his own delights. I drove away sorely torn. His last words – 'When great events are moving

[1] Lady Megan Lloyd George (1902–66), youngest child of Earl Lloyd-George of Dwyfor; MP (Lib.) Anglesey, 1929–31; (Ind. Lib.) 1931–45; (Lib.) 1945–51; deputy leader of Parliamentary Liberal Party, 1949–51; joined Labour Party; MP for Carmarthen, 1957–66.

one must play a part in them.' He told me a good Russian proverb Stalin had told him: 'One must walk with the Devil till one gets to the end of the bridge.' He longs for a bridge with the Liberals. He had told Anthony & Rab Butler of his plan but no one else. I said I felt sure my colleagues wld demur. He said 'They will screech – but you must not heed them. Only tell them when your own mind is made up.' Easier said than done.

... Talked to Mark & B about my problem after dinner. Mark said to me, when I said I might defeat my own object, by destroying my influence with those that trusted me: 'What is the good of your influence if you don't throw it into the scales at a vital moment? In politics every individual is a straw – & there are only a few moments when the straw can weight the balance. This is one of them.'

Diary – Wednesday 18 January – 40 Gloucester Square, W.2

Rang up Clem early this morning who of course was wholly negative & ended by offering me his own broadcast if I desisted – an empty gesture – for of course I cld not take it. He begged me to ask Samuel's advice & B. got thro' to him while I was dressing for departure. Samuel was even more negative – said it wld be quite disastrous etc. etc. On this B. felt I shld refuse, which I did with a leaden heart. W. was obviously terribly dashed & disappointed – begged me to reconsider it – said that so great an opportunity of playing a decisive part might never come again etc.

I had to go straight off to Barnsley – where I had a grim arrival at a dark, black, unlit, porter-less, taxi-less station. Thence to an arctic room in the Queens Hôtel which I remembered of yore. I drove to Wombwell – a mining village 4 miles off – with a very nice man called Makridge. Audience of about 100 in an icy school house. Very nice people – & so touching that in that grim & grimy spot – heavy with coal-dust – they shld wish to hear about the 'Spoken & the Written Word'.[1]

V.B.C. to Winston Churchill

Monday 23 January
40 Gloucester Square, W.2

Dearest dear Winston –

I know that B. has written to you to tell you of the infinite sorrow & disappointment I felt in refusing the opportunity you offered me so generously. I still don't know whether what I did – or rather what I didn't

[1] Violet made modest but regular income from paid speaking engagements, and this was one of a number of lectures that she offered.

do – was right or wrong. I think that it was probably politically right, but possibly morally wrong.

It was not my colleagues' judgement (nor their screams!) which influenced me (though Walter Layton's opinion had some weight). It was the fear that all the humble, loyal, rank-&-file Liberals in the country who trust me & believe in me, would feel that on the eve of battle I had stabbed them in the back....

Dearest Winston – apart from all moral & political considerations what I minded most was not to do anything in the world you asked of me. Please believe this.

Your drooping, moulting & bedraggled Bloody Duck – Violet

Diary – Wednesday 1 February – 40 Gloucester Square, W.2

Spent the day working on my speech & dictating letters – broken by a long visit from the *N.C.* photographer at 3.30 which robbed me of an hour. After tea another bad break. The *M.G.* rang up to say that Winston – who Byers had attacked in his last night's broadcast for 'trying to prevent' Libs. from getting a fair allocation of time – had issued a statement to the Press saying that he had offered me 20 minutes of their allocation & that I had been prevented by the Clement Davies group from accepting it. They asked me for my comment. I said 'Mr Churchill's statement is perfectly true & accurate. I have no comment to make.' I then gave him 'off the record' a little 'background' & asked him in justice to Winston to pass it on to Wadsworth[1] – i.e. how completely unfettered I shld have been – free to say anything I liked....

Diary – Tuesday 7 February – Inverness

Left London 9.45 for Manchester (narrowly escaped standing all the way as, tho' travelling 1st, I hadn't reserved a seat). Was met by Roger Fulford[2] & car & several journalists & photographers. Changed my clothes at Liberal Club Rochdale & then on to Town Hall which was packed out & many turned away. This amazed them as it was Monday afternoon – washing day for women & working day for men. I had a nice female Chairman Mrs

[1] Alfred Powell Wadsworth (1891–1956), journalist and economic historian; editor, *Manchester Guardian*, 1944–56.

[2] (Sir) Roger Thomas Fulford (1902–83), Kt, 1980; on editorial staff of *The Times* from 1933; unsuccessful Liberal parliamentary candidate, 1929, 1945 and 1950; president of Liberal Party, 1964–5.

Councillor Radcliffe & my speech 'went' very well.... I caught 8.30 to Crewe & had a longish wait there as Scotch express was late. Comfortable night tho' I didn't sleep much & out at Inverness where I had time for the usual wildly expensive breakfast....

Diary – Friday 10 February – Thurso Castle, Caithness

...I write in a large 4-poster bed in a vast & rather cold room by the light of 3 candles – a wood-fire flickering. We had a delightful meeting at Hallkirk, after dining at the well-known Vobster Arms. I really liked it the best of all my meetings. It was so intimate & friendly & there were some dear old traditional Radicals there. I had a sweet Chairman called Forbes – the local News-Agent. I dealt with David Robertson's[1] address (which is fantastic – he must be an ego-maniac) & this gave me & others a new wind & a little change & went down well. We then all repaired to the Vobster Arms & drank orangeade – & had a crack – & drove back across icy roads. It is freezing hard again – & really arctically cold. I have just heard Archie return from his tour. He has been touring distant parts – taking 4 meetings a day....

Diary – Wednesday 15 February – Lerwick, Shetland

Tuesday really was the coldest day ever at Thurso. I spent the morning doing very complicated packing – as I am sending 2 cases back to London. The afternoon finishing off things & working a little on my speech. Then we drove into Wick, dined (Marigold & I) at a very nice little hôtel called Mackeys. Then we had a marvellously good meeting – the best & biggest yet. Town Hall packed out – followed by tea & a party at the Hôtel – then a long wait, then Archie's arrival from another meeting. I was dog-tired – & tho' very comfy slept badly because my windows rattled like teeth. Up early this morning, packed & was taken to the Aerodrome....

Nothing was stirring. It was a wild morning with sheets of rain but they turned up at 9.15 & weighed me & I squeezed with difficulty into the front seat of a tiny plane (holding about 5) & flew over islands & seas coming down at Kirkwall about 10. Laura was on the telephone telling me that the connecting plane was delayed & that she & Jo wld come out & fetch me which they did.... Then an hour's flight over islands, seas, bays,

[1]Sir David Robertson (1890–1970), Kt, 1945; company director; MP (Con.) Streatham, Wandsworth, 1939–50; victorious at Caithness and Sutherland in 1950, he represented the constituency until 1964.

inlets & down at Lerwick where we drove thro' rather Caithness country – more grass than heather – to the house of Dr & Mrs Hamilton – a charming pair. Laura & I are sharing a room. I don't think I have ever felt more tired than when I arrived. Bad night – early rise. Aeroplane buzz in the head – alternations of bitter cold with the heat of the plane. I just put my ill-thought-out notes in order & lay down on my bed with a hot water bottle – drew the curtains & lay stunned with fatigue till tea-time when tea somewhat revived me – then off 15 miles in the dark & rain to our Lerwick meeting.

The hall was full – holding I shld think about 110. The audience seemed unresponsive to me compared to Caithness – but I was told that they were really friendly. We had heckling afterwards which might have been quite amusing except that 2 Socialists monopolized the whole proceedings – & in time grew rather boring. I think I answered quite well. . . . Then home. I realised to my horror that I had got a cold & had rather a bad & snuffly night.

Diary – Thursday 16 February – Lerwick, Shetland

Took aspirin & stayed in bed till after lunch today, then embarked for another tea with the Lamonts & on about 30 miles to a Women's Institute meeting at a distant spot called Barrowburgh. We disembarked in pouring rain & I spoke to about 40 people in a school-house gathered round a stove. About 30 women knitting Fair Isle jerseys & some men in the corner. All very friendly. Women wldn't ask questions but 2 very nice men – one old, one young – did – about timber decontrol & taking the purchase tax off Shetland tweeds. Drove home 30 miles in sheets of rain. Supper & now in bed. Dr Hamilton was out till 5 this morning having gone to Fair Isle in the Lifeboat to bring back a woman with a perforated appendix. They have no doctor or hospital there. Everything is done by wireless. At the Lamonts we heard the coast guard trying to get into touch with the lifeboat – but cldn't hear the replies.

Bongie to V.B.C.

Friday 17 February
40 Gloucester Square, W.2

I telegraphed to you today to say that we are posting letters to Laura's cottage at Merbister Orkney. I do not trust the post to reach you tomorrow in Shetland. There is nothing which you need bother about. . . .

W. R. Davies has rung up to ask Mark to address an eve of the poll meeting at Purley which is in W.R.D.'s own home town. I do not think

Mark will do it, he is 'browned off' with present Liberal politics & those who are responsible, as indeed you must be.... Again I say that the most extraordinary thing about this 'momentous election' is the total lack of public interest & certainly excitement in it. A Labour canvasser called here & was dealt with by Alice who asked him if he knew who were the owners? He said of course 'I know they are the BC's and I have "ticked them off my list" but I came to speak to the others.' Alice replied that he had best tick them off too.

I am going to *Peter Grimes* tonight with Maud Russell. My love always. I do hope you are not so cold & uncomfortable. B.

Diary – Wednesday 22 February – Merbister, Orkney

Eve of the Poll at last! The very last lap. Laura & I lunched with Dr & Mrs MacLure.... They are non-political – or Tory – very nice. He a very good surgeon. We then went on (Laura & I) to Jo's afternoon meeting. He had arrived from Shetland this morning. It was the first & only time I had ever heard him speak. It was not a very full meeting being at 3 o'clock in the afternoon. He looked extremely good-looking & spoke well. As often happens he seemed quite a different person when speaking – his voice much louder than one expected. Very good with hecklers. Obviously adored by his followers....[1]

We went back to tea at the hôtel & then Jo went off for his 2 Eve of the Poll meetings at Stromness & Birkie, & Laura & I to mine at Finstown & Dounby. Mine were quite excellent.... The name of Gladstone still stirs echoes. Neven-Spence[2] told Jo that a dear old woman living on his property – a traditional Liberal – was appealed to, by him, to give him her vote, on personal grounds, & promised to do so. After the Poll he said to her: 'Well – did you vote for me?' & she replied with tears that she hadn't. Just as she was leaving her house to vote her eyes were caught by a picture of Mr Gladstone on the wall & the appeal it made to her conscience was so strong that she couldn't resist it! Nunc Dimittis! My last speech made!

[1] Jo Grimond later recalled: 'The election meetings in 1950 were the most crowded I can remember. Not that any were large, but four times a night I would find several rows of black-suited and black-capped crofters waiting in the halls or schools. They sat patiently, often in desks designed for the infant class – like large birds on small nests' (Grimond, *Memoirs*, 143–4).

[2] Col. Sir Basil Hamilton Hebden Neven-Spence (1888–1974), Kt, 1945; landowner and soldier (RAMC); MP (Con.) Orkney and Shetland, 1935–50; Jo Grimond's Conservative opponent in 1950.

V.B.C. to Laura Grimond

Friday 24 February
Inverness Station Hôtel

My Darling – One line from the Station Hôtel while awaiting my train. I had a most lovely flight over the Islands to Wick in sunshine & crystal clear 'visibility' – & everything visible was almost unbelievably beautiful. I can't tell you what a coup de foudre the Islands have given me. I have fallen in love with them, & so dearly long to return to them & to feel a foothold there. . . .

I feel an odd mixture of emotions – the immediately prevailing one being an intense sympathy for you & Jo in having to face your supporters in the next few days. I can remember facing the same thing in a minor degree last time[1] – when I went straight from the declaration (where I was bottom – expecting to be 2nd – & my supporters of course hoping, as they always do, to win) to visit them assembled in their various centres. After weeks of drudgery & sacrifice – addressing envelopes all night etc. – giving up all their time & all their rooms & cars – it is so hard to face defeat for them – plus a bewilderment in the Triumph of Wrong (which of course one didn't wholly share oneself – because one saw the reasons for it).

Last time there were fewer reasons – we didn't deserve our fate – as in a sense I think we partly do to-day. I think the people at the top have been 'irresponsible' – & that their attempts to convince the public that we could form a govt. have been either fraudulent or so blankly out of touch with reality as to disqualify those who made them from any claim to political sense. . . .

I must stop. I can't tell you darling how I loved your people – it was an unforgettable experience to meet them – & what a tribute to Jo their touching faith & enthusiasm & devotion to him. I do think it is an extraordinary feat on his part to have inspired it. (His 'mug' helped!!! But it had strong backing from what it contained – & much else besides.) He is made for them & they for him. Oh how I pray he wins! . . .

Thank you darling for all yr luxurious care of me. I do hope I wasn't a fardel to you. Ever yr Mama

Diary – Friday 24 February – train from Inverness to London

It is all over – at least not quite all – for there are still about 150 seats to come in. On Thursday – Polling Day – we awoke in Laura's arctic cottage at Merbister – Dounby – romantically placed on the edge of a lake, but un-

[1] A reference to Violet's disappointing third place at Wells in the 1945 general election.

servanted, unheated & unlit by anything but Aladdin lamps & guttering candles. . . .

We awoke with horror to a very cold day – & the news that there was snow in Shetland – & that it was lying. This is sinister – because in Shetland the Polling Booths are sometimes 7 & even 12 miles away – & the poor Lib. crofters are very old (unlike the lefty young Socialists) & Jo is only allowed 10 cars for each island – a hopelessly inadequate number. This snow may make a real difference to Jo's vote & it was cruel indeed that it shld have chosen Polling Day to fall after some very good & relatively warm days before. We set out on our tour of the Polling Booths rather late. . . . We went to Kirkwall first & visited the Committee Rooms & the Polling Station. Things didn't look brisk there & the few figures we saw plodding up the hill with angry faces looked unmistakably Conservative. Then we set out on our tour round the island. . . . The roads were deserted. We hardly saw a car except once or twice one of our own. We went back to lunch at the Kirkwall Hôtel – then Laura went on a duty at the Polling Station (she had been sworn in) to help 'illiterate' voters. We were told a charming story about one man who cld neither read nor write but who turned up with a photograph of Jo & said 'That's the man I want to vote for'. . . .

[Evening] When Jo came back we turned on a wireless he had hired for the results, which started coming in at 11 o'clock. The 1st we heard (the 2nd which was announced) was the defeat of Horabin.[1] Then followed an almost unbroken series of Labour victories with large majorities – broken by a few Conservative ones – all ending with the knell 'The Lib. candidate forfeited his deposit.' It was quite appalling. When we went to bed at 2.30 there was only one Liberal in – Donald Wade[2] – as a result of his pact. . . .

We climbed up to bed with our guttering candles in our hands, & our hearts in our boots, & I lay like a sausage hugging my hot water bottles & not daring to move a limb because of the icy sheets. Woken this morning by Laura's tactful alarm clock. Got up & found snow lying quite deep all over the country. It had come silently down in the night & was still falling. We wondered if my aircraft wld fly & were finally told it wld. Motored to Kirkwall where the Airways Office is just opposite our Committee Rooms. Two of our dear supporters slunk in with a *N.C.* looking shattered. One hardly dared look at them. It was like meeting after a death. I said goodbye

[1] Thomas Lewis Horabin (1896–1956), MP (Ind. Lib.) North Cornwall, 1939–47; (Lib.) 1947–50; Liberal chief whip, 1945.

[2] Donald William Wade (1904–88), cr. life peer, 1964; MP (Lib.) Huddersfield West, 1950–64; deputy leader of parliamentary Party, 1962–4; Liberal deputy whip, House of Lords, 1965–7.

to Laura & Jo with a very tight heart, feeling vaguely for them the same responsibility as they felt for their followers. Not that I have ever urged them forward along a Liberal path – but I somehow feel that the heritage which meant such glory in my youth has been frustration & a lost cause to them.

Diary – Sunday 26 February – 40 Gloucester Square, W.2

B. met me at Euston with the news that Archie had been defeated by 200 odd votes by Sir David Robertson! I feel heart-broken for them & for the Party. He wld have made all the difference.... Winston rang me last night & also this morning again wanting to talk things over & also anxious that Archie shld come south & see him. 'He is the only one of the whole lot I want to talk to.'.... I told him it was much better for him [Winston] to be out by 12 than in by 12. He thinks the Lib. vote has robbed them of victory – & mentioned 60 seats they might have won.

Archie Sinclair to V.B.C.

Sunday 26 February
Thurso Castle, Thurso

Dearest Violet,

Our gratitude for your generous help is beyond all words to describe. I am grateful, Marigold is grateful and we are proud, too, that you thought our friendship worthy of so lavish a display of your brilliant gifts on our humble village platforms. The Caithness and Sutherland Liberals are deeply grateful too. Your speeches will be remembered and talked of months and years to come. Few of them have heard any great orator before, except on the wireless, or are likely to hear one again. So at least you have given many hundreds of people in Caithness and Sutherland an experience which they will remember all their lives....

My meetings seemed to get better and David Robertson's to get less good – the contrast being most marked on the eve of the poll at Thurso & Wick, when both my opponents had poor & noisy meetings, while ours were terrifically successful – ending up with a packed audience largely standing in the biggest hall in Wick singing 'Auld Lang Syne'! But that 'silent Tory vote' – a phrase from your letter which we have often repeated to ourselves – & frightened anti-Socialists, & mutts who fell for Sir David's promises, won the day.

Yours always and most gratefully, Archie....

Diary – Monday 27 February – 40 Gloucester Square, W.2

Woke up with an awful needle knowing that it was the day of the Orkney result.[1] It shld be declared at 2. In my heart of hearts I expected Neven-Spence to be in....

B. was waiting at Brooks's on the tape. At 3 he rang me up to say that it was not yet through & he must leave. A recount? or just delayed boxes? I rang Lib. H.Q. & asked them to let me know when it came through. Then B. came through again. Sheila took off the telephone & handed it to me. He said 'He's in by 2,950!' I cldn't believe my ears – just under 3,000 majority![2] I rang up Mark & told him – told Mr Cruikshank at the *N.C.* – telegraphed to Jo & Laura – telegraphed to Raymond. I don't think I have felt such ecstasy since Mark got his top Balliol scholarship. Where Jo has pulled out these thousands of votes from I don't know.... And we had the snow against us too! The old boys in Shetland must have tramped manfully. It is an amazing personal performance....

Diary – Tuesday 28 March – 40 Gloucester Square, W.2

...Back to tea with A. J. Cummings[3] & talk about the Party which he thinks is finished. He agrees with me that Pressure Groups are no good. He also agrees that Electoral Reform might give us one last chance. He is however very pessimistic about W. being able to get it thro' his Party. He says there was a meeting of the 22 Club – a quite important Tory Club – & that W. met & spoke to them & they were very hostile with some exceptions.... Quintin Hogg, Orr Ewing[4] & others spoke strongly against. Here they felt was a chance of wiping the Liberal Party off the block once & for all. This is what I terribly fear the next Election may do. Dined in with Brigid. Going to Wolverhampton to-morrow.

[1] The result at Orkney and Shetland was declared four days after polling day, 'so long did it take the boats to bring in the boxes from the outlying islands' (Grimond, *Memoirs*, 146).

[2] The figures were: J. Grimond (Lib.) 9,237; Sir B. Neven-Spence (Con.) 6,281; H. R. Leslie (Lab.) 4,198. The winning majority was 2,956.

[3] Arthur James Cummings (d. 1957), political editor and chief commentator, *News Chronicle*, 1932–55.

[4] Sir Ian Leslie Orr Ewing (1893–1958), Kt, 1953; MP (Con. Nat.) Weston-super-Mare, Somerset, 1934–50; (Con.), 1950–8.

'A constitutional injustice':
Churchill, the Liberals and electoral reform

Soon after the 1950 general election Churchill surprised Violet by confiding to her that he intended to call for a parliamentary inquiry into electoral reform. In the debate on the address, 7 March, he duly spoke of 'the constitutional injustice' done to the 2.6 million electors who had voted Liberal: 9 per cent of the electorate had secured only nine members of parliament. Churchill's support for electoral reform offered Liberals a lifeline, which Violet at once grabbed. In return she agreed to explore with R. A. Butler the common ground on which Liberals and Conservatives might fight at the next election. Butler subsequently produced an 'Overlap Prospectus' of areas of mutual interest, but to Violet's great disappointment it made no mention of electoral reform. Butler, though, knew that Churchill's initiative found no favour with the Conservative rank and file. The very fact that the Liberals *needed* electoral reform made them unwilling to give it: here was a chance to eliminate the struggling third party in politics and capture its votes. Churchill's motives in proposing the inquiry are complex. He may have been trying to woo Liberal votes, conscious that another election would soon be held which might be equally as close as the last. But the proposal was also consistent with his avowed belief that modern Conservatism and Liberalism were natural allies against socialism. It is ironic that Conservatives suspected their leader of wanting to support an independent Liberal Party at the very moment that most Liberals suspected him of wanting to destroy it. For her part Violet did not doubt the sincerity of Churchill's affinity with the Party of his youth, in which he had first entered the cabinet. But she felt keenly the dilemma that he did not: how could the Liberals form an alliance with the Conservatives, without being swallowed up by them?

Diary – Tuesday 18 April – 40 Gloucester Square, W.2

Jo & I lunched with Winston at 28 H.P. Gate. He came into the room in his siren suit with a new marmalade kitten perched on his shoulder with which he was obviously delighted. 'It only cost 7/6 – why the collar itself must have been worth more than that.' After some kitten talk we went down to lunch in the dining-room giving on the garden. Jo & I sat opposite W. side by side & he cldn't have been sweeter & more amusing. . . . He then told us in absolute confidence that he had set up a Committee over which Rab Butler was presiding to work out plans – Election & otherwise – for collaboration with the Liberals. They (the Party as a whole) were at present very averse to Electoral Reform. . . . He wanted the survival of an independent Party not absorption. He sees further than the Tories of course & realises that a 3rd Party with a progressive creed will be an invaluable buffer against Socialism. He said we shld know more about dissolution & Election prospects after the Budget. . . .

He said some very amusing things. About Seretse Khama:[1] 'I believe firmly in 2 principles (1) Christian marriage & (2) the bond of strong animal passion between husband & wife. Both exist in this case.' He told an amusing story about Cripps when they were colleagues & he came down to Chequers in the war. 'I thought I wld take a leaf out of

[1] In September 1948 Seretse Khama, chief-designate of the Bamangwato tribe in the Protectorate of Bechuanaland, South Africa, married an Englishwoman, Ruth Williams, whom he had met while studying in London. His uncle then contested his succession and in March 1950 the British government, having ultimate authority in the matter, condemned both to 'at least' five years' exile. *The Times* was not alone in questioning whether Seretse Khama's marriage to a white woman, and the need to appease South African opinion on this point, had influenced the government's decision. Churchill voiced his own concern about Khama's treatment in a Commons debate on 8 March (*Hansard*, vol. 472, col. 295). Only by renouncing his claim to be chief was Seretse Khama finally allowed to return to his homeland, which he did in September 1956, with his wife.

his book so I said to him: "I am the humble servant of the Lord Jesus Christ & of the House of Commons." "I hope" said Cripps "you treat Jesus Christ better than you treat the H. of C."' 'All my life now is an anti-climax' Winston said to me, 'I only stay on as you do – because I don't like seeing things done wrong – & neither do you. That's why we're there.'...

He cldn't have been sweeter – plied Jo with champagne & brandy – described a cigar he had had at the Dss of Kent's the day before – 'It was so dry I had to dip it in my coffee – & I cld blow the dust through it ' After luncheon he showed us the book factory where 2 female beavers sat at work & where there was rather a good picture of himself & Roosevelt on the Atlantic Charter ship.[1] Finally went off at ¼ to 3 to change out of his siren suit for the House – sending us in his car as far as a taxi....

Diary – Monday 12 June – 40 Gloucester Square, W.2

Went away Sat. to Mon. to stay with Brigid & her Father. We cldn't have had a more heavenly visit. Perfect weather – heat – sunshine – peace.... Back this morning – found Jo here – & we both set out on our 'Naval Expedition'[2] at 11.30. We went down by train from Victoria as W's car had to meet Clemmie that afternoon at an Air Port. Rab joined us & we had some talk with him on the way down.... We drove from Oxted in brilliant sunshine. I ran upstairs & found Winston looking very sweet in his siren suit. He kissed me – & I then went in & had some tomato juice till the others arrived & we went in to the usual voluptuous lunch with cham pagne etc. & bottles circulating all the time. The Party – W. self R.A.B. – Jo & Soames....

W. was very pleased with my speech & said I hadn't put a foot wrong so far as he was concerned.[3] He was not in a very 'executive' mood &

[1] The 'book factory' refers to the production of Churchill's war memoirs, *The Second World War*, which appeared in six volumes 1948–54. The picture of Churchill and Roosevelt that is referred to is probably the famous photograph of them joining in divine service on board HMS *The Prince of Wales*, Sunday 10 August 1941, during the Atlantic Charter negotiations.

[2] A cryptic reference to a visit to see Churchill, making a play on his days at the admiralty.

[3] On Tuesday 6 June Violet had given a speech at the Oxford University Liberal Club in which she alluded to Churchill's proposals for an inquiry into electoral reform: 'Mr Churchill has made a move which may transform the whole pattern of British politics. Whether it does so or not depends on the response of the Conservative Party to the lead he has given.' She was happy to declare her faith in Churchill, if not in his party: 'the word "Conservative" certainly does not and never will describe him. He has never been assimilated by any political party.'

Rab was not cheering as to the attitude of his party. I urged that their full dress Electoral Reform inquiry shld be publicized as soon as may be to show Liberals that they did mean business – or at least were sitting up & taking notice. He agreed at once & said to Rab 'See that it is done immediately.'.... [He] was more unsound on Black & White issues than last time. I reminded him about his classic dictum about Seretse – which placated him! He said 'You always make me feel – & seem – unregenerate!' Then we went on to Germany & her part in rebuilding Europe & he had a marvellous bit about 'I wld like to speak to the Germans standing among the ruins I have created & tell them that it is now their great mission to save the Europe they have destroyed! Build on the sublime! Do you hear Rab? Build on the Sublime – great slabs of it!' Poor Rab looked uninspired.

Driving back Rab told us how strong Eden's position was with the Party compared to W's – which often made him anxious.[1] He said that if only W. had not sprung Electoral Reform on the Party without any consultation all cld have gone much better. He said he had really been rather pathetic in his final appeal to the 22 Committee saying to them – 'After all, I did something for you all in the War. You might just do this little thing for me.' But it didn't go well – they were quite unmoved.[2] W. was rather touching talking to me & saying 'I can't bear to feel I am letting you down. I feel my honour is at stake. If they don't take care I shall go. After all I can be quite happy here' pointing to a large bank of flowering Ponticums. But I cldn't see him retiring into them. Jo & I were dropped at H. Park Gate & walked back across the Park.

Diary – Saturday 22 July – 40 Gloucester Square, W.2

A most exhausting, exasperating & futile day spent in Conference with the European Movement Executive at the H. P. Hôtel.[3] Rarely, if ever,

[1] Violet had met Nancy Astor the previous month: '[She] began her usual "Now Violet you must bring the Liberals & Conservatives together" etc. – & then said (quoting others) . . . "We shall never win another Election so long as Winston leads us."' Violet observed: 'It is really alarming hearing this from one Tory after another' (diary, 11 May).

[2] In February 1963 Violet met (Sir) Nigel Fisher, a Conservative MP first elected in 1950, who had witnessed Churchill – 'to him an all-powerful God' – appear before the 1922 Committee to plead the cause of Electoral Reform: 'Winston was given a terrible time – & Nigel Fisher marvelled at seeing this Colossus, who had swayed & saved the world, rebuffed & turned down' (diary, 1 February 1963).

[3] The previous evening there had been a large United Europe meeting at the Albert Hall, at which Violet made a short appeal for funds: 'It was a Marathon meeting – 7.30 to 10.15! 8 speeches! The hall was packed out & W. got a great reception.'

have I felt such despair about European Unity! The Latins behave quite impossibly. Duncan Sandys was in the Chair – as Spaak is kept in Belgium by [King] Leopold's return & its attendant complications & possible disorders.[1] He behaved with exemplary patience & fortitude – but in spite of this there was a deafening brouhaha & when we had voted by a majority that a resolution be put, & he proceeded to put it, one Frenchman threatened to leave the room if it was voted on & Madariaga threatened the British delegation with dire results if they carried it.

Harold Macmillan did his best to appease. The waste of time was quite frightful. We sat from 10 till 6 on procedure alone. The line of cleavage was of course the Federalists v. the Rest – the Federalists being the French & other Latins – the Rest Great Britain & the Scandinavians. We just won every time by the skin of our teeth. There were some abstentions. I sat with my U.E.M. colleagues – Walter Layton, Harold Macmillan, Ly Rhys Williams, Chambers. Walter spoke with more passion than I have ever heard him! Miss Josephy of course led the Federalists with one Frency – a Frenchman who seemed to disagree with everything that was proposed! The worst of it is that they are a sham façade & probably represent nothing & nobody in their countries. I went on, exhausted, to meet them again at a cocktail party at Duncan Sandys'. I had a good talk with Bucerius[2] – the very nice German who spoke at the Albert Hall & who said that he thought mine was far the best speech. I didn't mention that Winston angelically gave me £25 as a result of my appeal. To bed – very tired.

Diary – 2 August – 40 Gloucester Square, W.2

I got a message asking me to go to tea with W. at 5.15. Found an exquisite 'Tischleindeckdich' for two on which tea was spread & a message from him that he had been summoned to see Attlee (from Chartwell) & might be a few minutes late. Meanwhile dear Mrs Landemare[3] came in & had a chat with me. Then W. arrived hot from Attlee (if one can be such a thing), looking pink & well & without the bulging, lowering

[1] Leopold III (1901–83) ended a six year exile by returning to Belgium with his two sons on 22 July 1950. He had controversially capitulated to the invading German army in 1940, and there were riots in Brussels after his return. Paul-Henri Spaak supported calls for the king's abdication, and the following year he stood down in favour of his son, Baudouin, who ruled 1951–93.

[2] Dr Gert Bucerius, a member of the Federal German Parliament.

[3] Mrs G. Landemare, Churchill's cook housekeeper.

look of doom about his forehead which I thought the world situation warranted. . . .[1]

I asked him whether he thought Attlee was feeling the Atlas weight of his responsibility. 'Yes' he said, 'his hand shook as I was talking to him to-day. My hand doesn't shake – look at it – it's quite steady.' And it was. I said how difficult it was for us to strike in time – even with the bomb. If we allowed catastrophe to happen there was only retaliation. 'If a man in that street' he said, pointing out of the window 'was threatening us two with a Howitzer shldn't we be right to shoot him before he pulled the trigger?' 'Yes – but how could we ever prove that he was going to pull the trigger – to the satisfaction of our own consciences – & other people's?' There is the snag of the Preventive War. Bertie Russell is the only man who has ever had the moral courage to preach it – & that only in private.[2] 'When in the past cld we have justified ourselves in striking first?' He thought a little & then said 'Perhaps over Czechoslovakia.' Here I disagreed. There was nothing to prove that the internal coup had taken place under Russian orders, tho' we all knew it to be the case.[3]

We agreed that the General Election was off for the autumn & that we had a little more time to fix our Party plans. . . . He then went on to say that he had seen the 22 Committee & that he thought their attitude had improved. 'They were very hostile the first time I addressed them & I was very angry with them. But I've forgotten all that. This time they seemed to see the point of collaborating with the Liberals. I said to them – it's not a question of seats. It's a question of 2 Parties against one.' Then to me 'What I want is your witness.' I said that Rab had sent me the 'Overlap Prospectus' which contained a lot of unexceptionable generalities – but the first thing Liberals wld look for in it (& not find) was any reference to Electoral Reform. I must assume that that battle was now lost. If so I ought to tell my people. I stood in the same relation to them as he to me. We didn't want to let down or mislead those who trusted us.

He said 'I don't think the battle is yet lost. I'm still fighting it. Opposition only makes me keener. I'm not going to give up. I still believe we may get something.' He then said 'Look. I promise that I will let you know in a month how things stand. One month from now.' On this we compounded.

[1] Violet refers to the Korean war, which had begun on 25 June with the invasion of South Korea by Communist forces from the North. An American-led UN force was raised to defend the South and in late June the Royal Navy was sent to the region. By August the British army was engaged in the conflict.

[2] A reference to Russell's Chatham House speech, 27 January 1948 (above). On another occasion Russell's remarks *were* made 'public', attracting press criticism. *Reynolds News* observed drily: 'Lord Russell, the famous philosopher, advances the oldest and most blood-drenched fallacy in History: "the war to end wars"' (Clark, *Bertrand Russell*, 524–5).

[3] See above, p. 43 and n. 1.

I said 'I want to be in the line with you.' He said 'I want you in the line.' On this note we parted. He sent me back across the Park in his car. I arrived just in time to set out for another intoxicating evening at *Top Hat* – with Jo – Brigid & B – the second night running! I enjoyed it even more than last time – & want to go again to-morrow. I don't know which gives me the greatest kick – Winston or Fred Astaire.

Diary – Friday 24 November – Council of Europe, Strasbourg

Was met at the station at 11.45 p.m. by Clement Davies' nice but rather chetif son. To my infinite relief a room had been got for me in a rather one-horse, but quite clean hôtel called Union.... Still I was thankful to roll into bed at about 1 o'clock, dog-tired. Went to the Assembly next morning after arranging to transfer to the Maison Rouge where I am getting Bob Boothby's empty room. Very interesting. Heard Schuman[1] – very good – Dalton (short & perfunctory), a German, a Turk, Duncan Sandys, & several French. Spaak presiding & silent. Back to lunch at Maison Rouge with Harold Macmillan. Had the native dish – foie gras – & couldn't eat another thing....

Went back to my hôtel – packed, transferred clothes to Maison Rouge & back to the Assembly in Harold Macmillan's car which he very kindly sent for me. The debate was on Duncan Sandys' motion for a European Army. The official Germans wouldn't support it unless it was a Federal Army. I don't know whether this is through mistrust of themselves or because they think that they would dominate the Federal Army. One German took a different tune. Reynaud[2] spoke well – then Harold Macmillan. His stuff is always excellent – but he cannot appear spontaneous & thus any attempt at emotion always rings false. Passionate speech by Guy Mollet[3] against rearming Germany – frankly admitting that he still mistrusted her & could not forget the past – showing also some mistrust of America – as regarding war as inevitable. An 'unsound' speech & the only one with a note of real passion. It was now about 7 p.m....

[1] Robert Schuman (1886–1963), French statesman and premier, 1947–8; foreign minister, 1948–53; his 'Schuman Plan' led to the creation of the European Coal and Steel Community, 1951.

[2] Paul Reynaud (1878–1966), French statesman and premier in 1940; imprisoned by Germans during war he afterwards returned to politics and was a French delegate to the Council of Europe.

[3] Guy Alcide Mollet (1907–75), French socialist leader and president of the European Assembly, 1955; prime minister of France, 1956–7.

Diary – Saturday 25 November – Council of Europe, Strasbourg

Tremendous Committee day. Met at the Chambre des Commerce at 10 o'clock. Pouring rain – Walter Layton drove us there. Full International Committee – Spaak in the Chair. Interminably boring discussion on structure – the Federalists obstructing & resisting everything & even abstaining from voting on the motion to have a Treasurer! Miss Josephy sat amidst a little cluster of four of whom the male leader is a very pathological Resistance Frenchman called Frency who has already left the room more than once in the past.

We returned after luncheon having left in the middle of a struggle over a small Executive Committee of nine – whom it was suggested that Spaak should nominate & choose himself for ad hoc consultation. This was resisted by the Federalists who said that it must represent all the various 'Movements' concerned. Walter Layton pointed out that nine people could not reproduce seventeen countries & all their ideologies & beliefs & 'movements' ... but in vain. Going home to luncheon Duncan Sandys said he thought the Federalists were playing for a show-down that afternoon. He only wished (as we all did) that they would walk out – but feared they wouldn't.

After luncheon it came. The struggle began again. Spaak became exasperated. His patience – like Hitler's – was exhausted.[1] He said 'Listen, that does not interest me – everything you have been talking about for the last three hours is of no interest to me whatever. I don't even recognize the initials of these movements. We only meet in order to arrange a further meeting for us to have an even better argument. I no longer wish to be your President in these circumstances' – & he tried to resign. There were of course loud cries of protest from all but the Federalists. Duncan made a good appeal – everyone rose – gesticulated & talked at once & finally Spaak left the room pursued by some despairing followers.

Consternation among the disunited Europeans. I went out & suggested to Harold Macmillan that we should all pass, in Spaak's absence, a resolution of confidence – if necessary dissolve & reconstitute the Movement – without the Federalists. Meanwhile Spaak had been driven into a corner with his back to the window. He looked like a large Queen Bee with the swarm around him. Everyone pressed, coaxed, cajoled, entreated, implored him. Finally, & most unexpectedly to me, he came back. Loud applause except from the Federalists. He then read out the names of his Committee of ten – Frency being one of them. Everyone voted for them – the Federalists abstaining. Spaak then asked them if they accepted the names &

[1] At the Berlin Sportpalast, September 1938, Hitler declared: 'With regard to the problem of the Sudeten Germans, my patience is now at an end!'

if Frency accepted the position. He replied that he could not do so without consulting his Movement. Spaak said he must have his answer 'yes' or 'no' at once. He couldn't allow hours of time to elapse while everyone referred back decisions to their movements. Frency asked if he could be represented by a substitute. Spaak said 'No.' He was appointed as an individual not as representing a movement. He warned Frency that if he went away to consult his movement his place would be filled. A German Federalist made a great appeal to Frency to accept & remain. In spite of this he walked out followed by Josephy (obviously reluctant I thought) & another – on the absurd errand of consulting people who were not there about a post which was no longer open.

Everyone heaved a sigh of relief when they disappeared (alas! they will probably come back!) Spaak then filled the place with one Bicket – of the Nouvelles Equippes – who, though accepting, was very rude & made a condition of acceptance that it should be inscribed in the Minutes that the President had made a grave error in not inviting them from the start. (Bicket is a Catholic & therefore anti-Spaak.) Spaak with humour & bitterness asked that these words be inscribed adding that the President had tried to repair his grave error by inviting M. Bicket to join the Committee. We then went ahead with the business & reeled out exhausted about 7.30 p.m. I dined with Lady Rhys Williams, Duncan & Harold Butler. Said goodbye to Harold Macmillan, Julian Amery[1] & Butler in H. Macmillan's sitting-room. I have decided to fly straight home tomorrow afternoon with B. Behrens in his Chartered Plane. . . .

V.B.C. to William Haley ***Thursday 21 December***
40 Gloucester Square, W.2

My dear Sir William

Your book [gift] has just reached me – with its lovely inscription & with it your letter which I value more than I can say. . . . One grew up among such sure & steadfast standards – & never had a doubt that one was going forward – & now it is hard not to feel recession. And while events grow & tower above us – men seem to shrink.

Winston has many faults but he is the one great forest tree that still stands in this world of saplings & shrubs. When I am with him I feel the

[1]Julian Amery (1919–96), cr. life peer, 1992; MP (Con.) Preston North, 1950–66; Brighton Pavilion, 1969–92; delegate to the consultative assembly of the Council of Europe, 1950–3 and 1956; the son of Leo Amery – see below, p. 108.

perspective of history – which my Father gave me – & which I miss so much.

But as you so truly say we must live in the faith that the future is 'susceptible to individual effort'. And the knowledge that you feel it gives me heart & courage. It is like keeping step with a friend in the dark....

Ever yrs gratefully, Violet Bonham Carter

Might we not drop pre-fixes?

'A Liberal without prefix or suffix'
Contesting Colne Valley at the 1951 general election

At every general election from 1922 to 1959 Violet campaigned for Liberal candidates, but only on two occasions did she stand herself. The first was at Wells in July 1945, where she had no prospect of winning and came a distant third. The second was at Colne Valley in October 1951, and here an electoral pact with the Conservatives ensured a real chance of success. The general election was announced by Clement Attlee on 19 September, signalling the premature end of the Labour government elected in February of the previous year. That government had survived for nineteen months with the slimmest of majorities, but after the resignation, illness and death of cabinet colleagues Attlee sought an early election for 25 October. The campaign came at a difficult time for the Liberals. Morale and funds were low and only 109 candidates could be fielded, less than a quarter of the previous year's total. The 1950 defeat had demonstrated that Liberals had virtually no chance of winning in a three-way contest and Violet only agreed to stand at Colne Valley once she was assured of Conservative support in a straight fight against Labour. Churchill strongly endorsed this arrangement, which was consistent with his desire for an anti-socialist alliance. Personal loyalty to an old friend must also have influenced him. In December 1950, while on holiday in Marrakech, he sent a cryptic telegram to the Conservative Party chairman Lord Woolton: 'Hope the Violet is growing all right in that valley.' Woolton's reply indicated difficulties: 'Violet still under glass. Gardeners watching developments. Awaiting favourable conditions for planting out.'[1] A group of local Conservatives stubbornly refused to obey the Party leadership and support a Liberal candidate. Others demanded that, as a quid pro quo, the Liberal should stand down in favour of the Conservative in two neigh-

[1] CHUR 2/111/92 WSC to Lord Woolton, 27 December 1950, telegram; CHUR 2/111/91 Lord Woolton to WSC, 1 January 1951, telegram; Gilbert, *Never Despair*, 601.

bouring constituencies. Such a deal would have fatally compromised Violet within her own party, where there was strong feeling against any electoral pact with the Conservatives. It would be difficult enough to defend her own position, but it would be impossible if it entailed the sacrifice of another Liberal's chances. Churchill was adamant that she should not be subjected to any such pact and on 25 March he wrote to Clementine Churchill: 'I have fixed it up all right for Violet in Colne Valley.' She did indeed secure the crucial support of the local Conservative Association, but only by 33 votes to 26. It was an inauspicious start. Between March and October she campaigned as often as she could in 'the Valley', a vast constituency straddling the Pennines. She was disadvantaged by being a woman and an outsider in this industrial seat, held by the experienced Labour member William Glenvil Hall. Politically her greatest challenge was to woo the Conservatives without losing radical Liberal votes. It was a task to which she was not ideally suited. Early on in the campaign she declared herself unequivocally 'a Liberal "without prefix or suffix"'. Trimming was not in her nature, which probably lost her Conservative support; but then neither was disloyalty, and when Churchill offered to speak on her platform she would not refuse – although she knew it would cost Liberal votes.

V.B.C. to Gilbert Murray ***Whit Monday, 14 May 1951***
The Manor House, Mells, Frome, Somerset

Dear Gilbert – I got your letter just as I was leaving London. I am so enchanted that you have consented to unveil Father's tablet – & I am so grateful to you for doing it....

I went up to Colne Valley & fired my first shot at a very good meeting on 1st May. I spent the 2 subsequent days touring a bit of this widely scattered division & liked the people enormously. They are hard-headed & warm-hearted – the country is wild, bleak, bare & rather Brontë-ish & beautiful I thought – great desolate moors & small industrial towns here & there – weaving, a little coal-mining & some agriculture. The Conservatives I met were very friendly – & I shall probably want to be friendlier with them than my organization will want me to be!...

All my love & blessings & gratitude for doing the unveiling. Someday I shall ask you to send me a message to C.V. Ever yrs Violet

V.B.C. to Winston Churchill ***Friday 22 June***
40 Gloucester Square, W.2

Dearest Winston.... In Colne Valley everything is going like a wedding bell. I had a magnificent meeting in Huddersfield Town Hall, which was packed out, and where my reference to yourself got the biggest cheer of the evening. It brought down the house, and the Liberals almost out-cheered the Conservatives. (They also enjoyed – in quite a different way – my reference to Harold Wilson, who springs from those parts and being well-known is naturally unpopular.)

I have visited Dr. Stephens, the new Conservative President (who is a delightful man), and many other groups of Conservatives including Mrs. Smith (the late candidate),[1] and they could not be more friendly, welcoming and helpful. I also had a very amusing secret meeting with twenty-two of the dissentient Conservatives (the followers of Sir Gilbert Tanner),[2] grumpy old Tory Troglodytes, encased like armadillos in impenetrable shells. They inhabit a different world from you and me – and from Colonel Whitehead[3] and his civilized and enlightened followers. I don't think they have ever entertained an idea in their lives. They only recognise colours and labels. I tried – and failed – to prize open their heads – but we had a good hard-hitting three hours together and though they had no use for me as a candidate, I think they felt a reluctant respect for me as a pugilist. We parted on good terms and I shouldn't be a bit surprised if some of them vote for me in the end.

Your help and support have of course been invaluable to me. Some of the rank and file Conservatives who I thanked said to me rather touchingly: 'We must do what our Leader wants'.

All my love and infinite gratitude. Ever yr B.D. Violet

P.S. It is interesting that I have had nothing but favourable reactions from Liberal and – so-called – Radical quarters throughout the country. Not a breath of criticism up to date. 'Pourvou que ca dure!'

[1] Mrs E. E. Smith was Conservative candidate for Colne Valley at the 1950 general election, when she secured 15,826 votes against Glenvil Hall's 24,910, and the Liberal R. F. Leslie's 9,654.

[2] Col. Sir Gilbert Tanner (1877–1953), Kt, 1937; cotton manufacturer and soldier; he rebelled against his Party leadership over Violet's candidature, and was replaced as president of the Colne Valley Conservative Association by the Dr Stephens mentioned above.

[3] Col. James Buckley Whitehead (1898–1983), cotton spinner and soldier; served in Great War (10th Manchester Regiment; MC, 1918) and 1939–45 (Royal Tank Regiment); a senior Colne Valley Conservative.

Diary – Thursday 27 September to Sunday 28 October – Colne Valley, Yorkshire[1]

The General Election & its aftermath have rolled over us since I wrote last – & not a breathing-space to record things far more important than my daily chronicle of trivialities. I must try & piece together the fragments as best as I can. . . .

Thursday 27 September. I left Dalnawillan on Thursday morning to come south – leaving B. behind.[2] At Inverness I went to the Station Master's office to claim my sleeper & was 'winded' by being handed a telegram from Winston 'Am reserving next Wed. 3rd for Colne Valley – wire me, whether you want a joint meeting of Liberals & Conservatives or any other kind.' I wired back saying I did not know whether any halls were free & wld. discuss it at luncheon with him next day! . . .

Friday 28 September. W. was in wonderful form – obsessed by C.V. We spent 2½ hours with him. . . . Col. Whitehead was most good & firm & loyal. He had provisionally booked Huddersfield Town Hall for 15th. W. angelically said he wld sleep in the station that night in his special carriage & go on to Newcastle next morning. I said 'Won't you be tired?' 'Oh no I'll take my pill.' His energy is amazing. He is booked for every single night throughout the whole Election – with broadcasts & an El Alamein celebration thrown in. When he prepares – Heaven only knows. He was very excited by their Election Manifesto which he showed me in confidence & particularly pleased at having dished the Socialists by proposing that E.P.T. shld be re-imposed. 'How do you like that Colonel?' he asked Whitehead breezily. Whitehead looked rather blue! . . .

Tuesday 2 October. I left for Colne Valley for my Adoption Meeting at Slaithwaite. Meanwhile the Executive there had been gravely disturbed by the problem of W.'s meeting – & wanted to see me before my meeting. This I refused to do. I said I wld see them next day. My adoption meeting went off well. Attlee had spoken at Slaithwaite a few nights before & given me a good opening by comparing me to a 'dead fly in the Tory web' & calling me a Conservative by another name. I was able to make some play with both these accusations & ask him if he was a Bevanite by another name. . . .

Wednesday 3 October. I can't remember how I spent the 3rd – except for a long & very difficult Executive Meeting in the evening. It all ended

[1] These entries were written on, or soon after, 23 November, when Violet was staying at Mottisfont Abbey in Hampshire.

[2] Violet and Bongie had been staying with Archie and Marigold Sinclair, after spending a week in Orkney.

happily – with everyone voting for it [Winston's meeting] – except the rather ill-conditioned Jamieson who was 'nem. con.' & who afterwards tried to resign & make all the trouble he cld. I quite realised that it may on balance lose me votes. But even if it did I cld not humanly inflict such a wound on W. as to ask him not to come. Also how can I accept 16,000 Conservative votes & then refuse to have their leader on my platform? Decided that the meeting wld be Liberal – with a Liberal Chairman. . . .

Friday 5 October. Three meetings – Wellhouse, Linthwaite & Meltham – all excellent. Directly Winston's meeting was announced our H.Q. was literally stormed by Libs & Conservatives alike. 700 people invaded the place personally on the 1st morning. We were threatened 'No seat, no vote' by both Parties alike. Miss Furness, one of our old stalwarts, who had opposed the meeting, ordered 100 tickets! There were terrible heart-burnings because a husband & a wife cld not both go, etc. . . .[1]

Tuesday 9 October. I had 3 wonderful meetings at Kirkheaton, Lepton & Kirkburton. The Kirkburton one – which I only reached about ¼ to 10 – was one of the best I have ever had. The hall was packed out. I literally had to fight my way into it. There was no standing room – all the passages round the hall were blocked. There wasn't a spare inch. . . .

Monday 15 October. The day of Winston's meeting. . . . Mr Haigh[2] & I started for the meeting about ¼ to 7. Vast crowds thronged the streets & large areas of the town were roped off – throngs of police etc. We were given a great reception by the crowd. Went to the Mayor's Parlour where B. & Walter Layton had already arrived. Winston & Col Whitehead came shortly before 7.30. W. in wonderful looks & form – very calm & Pickwickian. He got a tremendous reception from the crowd. We went on to the platform & the whole hall rose – cheering wildly – 'Land of Hope & Glory' – then Haigh spoke, very well, then W. – whose speech cldn't have been better for the occasion & was rapturously received by Libs & Conservatives alike. He described me as having 'Come "out of the blue" – how lucky I didn't say "into the blue"!'

I followed for half an hour – then Walter Layton made a most admirable speech vindicating Winston's international record & showing that since 1946 he has been the great architect of Peace (Fulton – Zurich – reconciliation with Germany – European Army – talks with Stalin).[3] I have never heard him speak better – partly because he read

[1] Violet later added: 'We were offered Nylon stockings for a seat – as precious as rubies.'

[2] William Haigh, mill owner and a leading Liberal in Colne Valley; married to 'Nan' Haigh. Violet stayed at their home Lea House, in Huddersfield, while campaigning.

[3] During the election, which took place against the background of the Korean war, Labour attempted to portray Churchill as a warmonger. Walter Layton's speech was designed to counteract that impression.

his speech. He reads better than he speaks. I have never seen such an audience. They were like a loaded gun – going off at full-cock whenever the trigger was touched. When it was over we went up onto the balcony which was floodlit & W. spoke to the crowds for a few minutes – followed by a few sentences from me. There were 7000 I am told who had stood all thro' the meeting. His reception was tremendous & very moving. Walter & I & B. then went to his railway carriage, drawn up in a siding of Huddersfield station, & had a voluptuous meal. Only Col. Whitehead was there besides. Champagne & brandy flowed – innumerable attendants male & female appeared & put thro' telephone calls at W.'s behest. He was in marvellous form. He said to Walter 'If I am ever in the dock I shall have you to defend me.' He said he cldn't get Electoral Reform past his people.

He went on to talk about the past with Russia & its effect on the fate of Europe. I said that Roosevelt had let him down at Yalta & Teheran. He was too loyal to admit this & said the Russians had gone back on all their agreements. He said that after Roosevelt's death the wires had fused between us & U.S.A. for 2 or 3 months. He said 'I blame myself. I shld have gone over to see Truman.' He was terribly busy at the time & had sent Anthony instead. We didn't leave him till after midnight. He shunts off to Newcastle at 8 o'clock next morning.

V.B.C. to Winston Churchill ***Thursday 18 October***
Lea House, New Mill, Huddersfield

Beloved Winston. The Valley is still aglow with your presence and the echoes of your speech are still ringing through it. What I owe you cannot be expressed – but you know it. I am proud and happy to be 'in the line' with you. It is wonderful to think that a week to-morrow you may be leading the country again and that this crazy crew on their leaking craft may be sunk 'full fathom five'. No one will hail the result with greater joy than,

Your grateful & Bloody Duck, V. . . .

[Diary continues]

Friday 19 October. After a heavy day's broadcasting & a Mill Meeting (Mr Haigh's other Mill) I gave my 'Great Figures' lecture at Slaithwaite to a Baptist Men's Club. It went very well. My cough is very bad at nights, when I get paroxysms – & my voice is beginning to suffer. Mark, B. & Ray arrived late at night at the George having motored up. The boys are spending the last week here.

Saturday 20 October. It was lovely to see the boys. Mark came over in the morning & helped me by vetting an article for the *Daily Mail* which I must send off to-day. They went off broadcasting together, tho' Sat is a bad day, & I went with Miss Haigh. We all dined together at the George. My morale has risen with the boys' arrival. I felt all-in last night. Breather on Sunday.

Monday 22 October. Works meeting – broadcasting all day. Meetings at Upper Whitley & Flockton – a great Miners' place – very Labour. But we had a good meeting. Mark preceding me at meetings. He & Ray are broadcasting all day & have been 'Over the Top'.[1] Clifford [Haigh's driver] is full of admiration at Ray's complete absence of shyness. He had a good talk with a miner, who was also a cricketer, to whom he said 'What do you do when everything is going wrong?' The man said 'Change the bowling.' Ray said 'That is just what we ought to do now.' I spoke at Liversidge's works. He is not popular. One of his men said to me 'If my Boss voted Labour I wld vote Tory.'

Tuesday 23 October. Went to Dobroyd in the luncheon hour & spoke. Long tour with Miss Haigh with loudspeaker. War-Monger scare is doing deadly work. One woman said to me 'I'm fed up with this Govt & wld like to vote for you – but I've got 2 sons of military age.' One man in a Mill said 'America is starving us of raw materials to create Unemployment here. Only one man sees through them – Nye Bevan.' Facts cut no ice....

Thursday 25 October. Polling Day. We were to have started at 9.30 am (I had pleaded for 9.00) to visit some 80 odd Polling Stations & Committee Rooms. However when I got down at 9.30 Mr Haigh (who has no sense of time & lived without a watch for year) had gone to the mill. We didn't start till 10 & Mr Holland had not yet arrived! I insisted on starting without him & off we went. It was a lovely sparkling day – no excuse in the weather for anything. We stopped at every polling station (in the big places like Holmfirth there were often as many as 4) visited the workers in the Committee Rooms etc. The polling was heaviest in the small places in the morning. We met Mark & B. at Marsden where we had a sandwich lunch – then on. I was urging pace all the time – Mr Haigh & Mr Holland urging me to have a cup of tea or see a supporter of 90 & assuring me there was no hurry.

As evening came on I felt convinced we shldn't get thro' all the 'Over the Top' places before 9 o'clock when the booths closed – so we skipped

[1] Places like Delph and Saddleworth were practically on the other side of the Pennines and to reach them one went 'over the top'. Mark and Raymond's election message was: 'Vote for Victory for Violet in the Valley.'

Scapegoat Hill & one other place & got through just in time – visiting Greenfield (I think it was?) 3 minutes before the booths closed. Then we were lured into a Lib. Club – I think at Delph – against our better judgement. We were both very hungry & absolutely exhausted, having got in & out of the car some 100 or 200 times – & meant to go straight home. Once there Mr Haigh began to eat pork pies & was really too exhausted to move. At last we got off – & tumbled out at once at Lea House where we found B. & Mark – dead to the world.

Friday 26 October. The count began at Holmfirth at 9.30 – but B & I did not go there till about 11. Mark was scrutineering, also Sheila.... The tension was frightful – 'Neck to neck' I was told when I asked how it was going – & neck to neck it remained until the last half hour. At one moment there were 18,000 votes for each of us out on the long tables. We were not nearly thro' by 1 o'clock when the declaration shld have been made. In the last half hour Glenvil Hall[1] pulled out 1500 extra votes. I was warned of this by Dilmot & knew I was out by something like 2,000. (The figure was actually 2,189.)[2] So I was prepared.

We went out onto the top of the steps outside the Town Hall. It was 3 o'clock by then – so most of the crowd had dispersed & there was only a comparatively small one – most of the Labour supporters with bright red rosettes. Glenvil Hall made a short, colourless speech, thanking the police & everyone & I then advanced to speak & was howled down from the very first sentence – in which I said that I was glad it had been a straight fight. There were cries of 'Nothing straight about it' etc. I paid a tribute to Glenvil Hall's fairness (which he had not done to me!) & the only reference to the issues I made was to say that Labour had fought the Election on fear & I had tried to fight with facts, which was more difficult. I have never seen a more disgraceful scene. Even at Paisley the defeated candidate was always listened to.[3] Glenvil Hall never intervened – which for a Quaker & a righteous man of peace was not too creditable. We drove home & had some food & a bit of a rest. Clifford had tears in his eyes as he helped me out of the car. Nan Haigh & Mrs Oldham very sweetly sent me some flowers. We dined in Huddersfield at the George. Next day 27th

[1] William Glenvil Hall (1887–1962), PC, 1947; a barrister and a Quaker, he had a long experience of parliamentary contests, fighting unsuccessfully four times as a Labour candidate, 1922–35; he represented Portsmouth Central, 1929–31, and Colne Valley, 1939–62. Violet first saw him that July and probably underestimated him, writing: 'I felt considerably reassured. He is a gentle, tired, edgeless, punchless, nice old sheep' (diary, 22 July 1951).

[2] The official result was: W. G. Hall (Lab.) 26,455; Lady Violet Bonham Carter (Lib.) 24,266.

[3] Paisley, on the outskirts of Glasgow, was won by H. H. Asquith at a famous by-election in 1920. He held the seat at two subsequent elections (1922, 1923) before losing in 1924. It was while campaigning for her father there that Violet first emerged as a substantial political figure in her own right.

B. & I & Mark drove up to London lunching en route.... When I arrived I didn't feel quite so exhausted as I subsequently became. I was like a doped horse which goes on running & then falls....

'It was a gallant fight'

Of the 109 Liberal candidates who contested the 1951 general election only six were elected. Another eight came within sight of victory but more than half – sixty-six in all – lost their deposit. For the third successive election the Liberal Party had registered its worst-ever performance. The modest number of Liberal candidates undoubtedly helped the Conservatives to victory. But their seventeen-seat majority was won with substantially *fewer* votes than Labour: the predicted anti-socialist swing had failed to materialize and this dealt a fatal blow to Violet's prospects at Colne Valley. There the Labour vote increased by around 1,500 while her own vote fell below expectations, as significant numbers of Liberals defected to Labour and Conservatives simply abstained. As one of her campaign workers later put it: 'I'm afraid that the oil of the die hard Tory & the vinegar of the extreme Radical would not mix.' Churchill sent a message of commiseration: 'It was a gallant fight.' He had invited the Liberal leader Clement Davies to join his cabinet and told Violet that she, too, would have been offered a ministerial post had she won. In the event Davies refused where she would probably have accepted, in keeping with her pragmatic approach to an alliance with the Conservatives. This made her unpopular with some of her more radical colleagues, and they made their feelings known at a Party meeting after the election. Their virulent criticism added insult to injury.

Diary – Thursday 8 November – 40 Gloucester Square, W.2

Fetched by Colin Coote & had a most amusing dinner with him & his French wife, Bob Boothby & Walter Elliot, far away in Golders Green. Bob & Walter have been rather pointedly left out of the Govt. They were amusingly frank & quite unbitter about it. Colin C. told me that at a Shadow Cabinet W.'s eyes wandered rather dissatisfiedly round the faces of his assembled colleagues & he said – as though thinking aloud – 'Very few of you will find places in my next Administration' – which in fact turned out to be true.... Randolph behaved most sadistically on the day of the Govt.-making – ringing up all the houses of the expectant & possible & leaving a message to say – 'Mr Churchill rang you up'!...

V.B.C. to Gilbert Murray ***Tuesday 20 November***
40 Gloucester Square, W.2

Dearest Gilbert.

Thank you so much for your letter. I had been meaning daily to write to you on exactly the same problem. I am deeply concerned at the attitude of the Party, which appears to be frozen in the anti-Toryism of 1906–1914 & quite unaware of all the water which has flowed under the bridge of the world since then. . . .

When I attended a terrible Liberal Jamboree ten days ago (consisting of the Council, with Liberal candidates thrown in), I was assailed on every side with accusations of having caused defeat & damage to Liberal candidates by having Winston on my platform at Colne Valley. I bided my time for an hour or two & then went for them! At the beginning of my speech I was barracked, interrupted & almost shouted down by what, in fairness I must admit, was a minority. I quelled them & towards the end got a good reception for what I said. (I will try & send you a short report of this from memory when I have a moment's time.) There was of course a saner element. But all the sane were silent. Not one colleague or friend weighed in on my side, though some of them expressed agreement, sympathy & congratulation afterwards. . . .

The shabby part of the whole proceeding was that not one protest about Winston's meeting had reached me during the Election & many candidates had written to me (including Byers himself), to ask me for messages of support, which they could publish. Why, as I asked them, did they seek to attach such a public smear to their own candidature? At the moment I feel strongly tempted to 'walk out', not perhaps of the Party, but of the Organisation, but I shall do nothing before having seen & consulted with you. . . .

I think the Liberals made a mistake in not accepting Winston's generous offer to join the Government.[1] The crisis is far graver than it was in 1931. Had I been returned, I should have gone in without any hesitation.

Ever yours, Violet

Diary – Friday 7 December – 40 Gloucester Square, W.2

Lunched with Winston & Clemmie at N° 10 – the first time I had seen him there. It was moving to me to go back over that familiar threshold –

[1] Violet noted in her diary in late November that one seat in the cabinet and two under-secretaryships were on offer: 'I think poor Clem longed to accept. I shld have gone in unhesitatingly. (I'm told I shld have been offered Education.)'

up in the old lift – much higher than usual – as they are living in a luxurious & very convenient flat arranged for the Attlees. They come down to what are now called the State Rooms on big occasions (W. is always wanting to!).... He asked me about our Party meeting & when I told him about my rough passage, & how I had told them that our meeting was one of my greatest & proudest experiences, his eyes filled with tears. He is an extraordinarily human being....

FOUR

King George, Queen Elizabeth

1952–1953

V.B.C. to Gilbert Murray ***Tuesday 8 January 1952***
40 Gloucester Square, W.2

Personal

My dear Gilbert,

Thank you so much for your letter & invitation to speak again this year for the United Nations Association at the Lord Mayor's Dinner on May 14th. I should love to do so. My only difficulty is that the Liberal Assembly is meeting in Hastings & the delegates are supposed to assemble that night. . . .

I do not know whether you saw the attack which has been made upon me by the Bethnal Green Liberal Association? They call upon me to resign from the Party & accuse me of 'stabbing every liberal candidate in the back' by inviting Winston to appear on my platform. (I did not of course 'invite' him – but was proud to accept his offer to come.) The *Daily Telegraph* report adds that the proposer of the motion said: 'We must make a thorough example of this woman to show good faith to the electorate. We cannot afford to be sentimental!'

Byers has issued a statement saying that this Resolution is 'most unlikely to be regarded with any favour whatsoever by the Executive of the Party in the light of the decision of the Convention,' (i.e. that rigid discipline should not be imposed upon the Party). This is quite good as far as it goes, but of course it does not go far enough. The Executive is meeting on Friday & unless they spontaneously make a statement which is satisfactory to me, I shall resign. . . .

If this were to happen I should of course feel quite free to speak on the 14th May. May I postpone my reply until after the Executive, i.e. the beginning of next week?

All my love, Ever yours, Violet

Diary – Tuesday 5 February – 40 Gloucester Square, W.2

Anglo-German [Friendship Society] meeting at H. of C. with Bellenger,[1] Frank Pakenham etc. Frau Milchsack to tea. Dashed home & back to a very interesting United Europe dinner at the House to discuss policy. Sat between Julian Amery & Duncan Sandys. Others present: Leo Amery[2] (presiding), Juliet Rhys Williams, Beddington-Behrens, Gordon Lang, Stephen King-Hall,[3] etc. – about 16 of us altogether. Very good discussion about future policy. Leo Amery made the frank confession that he was an 'aggressive Imperialist' & suggested that the periphery of Europe – Norway, Sweden, Turkey, Greece etc. – might join the Commonwealth & thus compensate for what we were losing elsewhere! I said I was all for enlarging the Commonwealth – but if this was an object we must re-christen ourselves & change our avowed aims! Julian Amery made much the most practical & constructive suggestion – i.e. that if other European countries wished to federate without us we shld give them our blessing – but if they failed to we shld aim at a Commonwealth or confederal solution.

Drove home with B.-B. who dropped me. Told Duncan I was thinking of resigning from Lib. Exec. He begged me to resign from nothing – stay in the Party & swing it if I cld. . . .

Diary – Wednesday 6 February – 40 Gloucester Square, W.2

About $\frac{1}{4}$ to 11 this morning I was rung up by Fothergill to ask if he cld come & see me at 4 today, instead of in the morning as arranged, about my impending resignation from the Executive. In the middle of the conversation he suddenly drew in his breath & said 'Oh can this be true? – a message from a "British Press" agency has just been placed before me saying that the King died in his sleep during the night.' . . .[4] It is infinitely tragic. He struggled so bravely against such odds – recording his Xmas broadcast sentence by sentence. . . . It means the break-up of such a gay – warm – happy – devoted family unit – who shed their happiness on all

[1] Probably Capt. Frederick John Bellenger (1894–1968), MP (Lab.) Bassetlaw, Nottinghamshire, 1935–68; secretary of state for war, 1946–7.

[2] Leo Stennett Amery (1873–1955), statesman, journalist and author; MP (Con.) Sparkbrook, Birmingham, 1911–45; secretary of state for colonies, 1924–9; for dominions, 1925–9; for Burma and India, 1940–5.

[3] (Sir) Stephen King-Hall (1893–1966), Kt, 1954; cr. life peer, 1966; RN retired; broadcaster and writer on international affairs.

[4] George VI died at Sandringham early in the morning of 6 February. The previous September he had undergone an operation to remove his left lung, following the discovery of a malignant growth.

around. I shld think Balmoral, Sandringham & even Windsor had never been so full of fun & sunshine. Mark owes them infinitely much in happiness. They have given him all his loveliest holidays.... Poor Pss E. – learning this news abroad[1] – & having a lifetime of hard labour laid on her shoulders at 25. It is very hard on her....

Diary – Friday 8 February – 40 Gloucester Square, W.2

Proclamation of Queen Elizabeth II. The new Queen held her accession council & took the oath – & was then proclaimed by the Heralds in St James's Palace Courtyard, at the Royal Exchange, Trafalgar Square & elsewhere. I remembered how Walter Elliot had taken Ray to hear the Proclamation last time, when he was a little boy of 7....

Diary – Friday 15 February – 40 Gloucester Square, W.2

The King's Funeral. I left home at 7.20 with B. in a car which was able to get thro' to the Downing St. steps without any difficulty. I had a pass, but only had to use it once or twice. I got to D. St about ¼ to 8.... It was a mother of pearl day – glints of silver light in a grey sky – very cold. At 9.30 exactly a vast Grenadier Officer in a long grey coat raised his arm in the middle of Whitehall & let it fall like a conductor & the distinguished foreigner contingent began to march – with some difficulty as there was then no music. The things which stand out in my memory are the pipe bands – Scottish & Irish with their saffron kilts – the Gun Carriage itself – pulled by Bluejackets who slow-marched as they pulled – the coffin still surmounted by the crown, sceptre & orb & the white wreath. Then came the Queen's carriage with scarlet coachmen & scarlet standing-men behind – like something out of a Fairy Tale – then the 4 marching Dukes – the Duke of Windsor – still pathetic wizened Eton boy (how exiled he must have felt by seeing his inheritance pass from him a second time!), the Duke of Kent – looking exactly like an actual lanky Eton boy (which is what he is!) top-hat well on the back of his head, then the other Royal carriages. Then marching Kings & Presidents – Field Marshals....

We rushed up to the top of Downing St to see the scarlet coaches winding their way past the Horse Guards Parade to the Mall. Winston came & sat beside me after the procession had begun & we talked a little.

[1] Princess Elizabeth learned of her father's death while on an official visit to Kenya with Prince Philip. They had left England on 31 January for a tour that was intended to take in East Africa, Australia and New Zealand.

For the first time I noticed his deafness when he asked me in a voice of thunder 'Who is that woman?', of Lady Digby who was just behind us. I was fortunately able to say I didn't know. It wld have been difficult to reply 'Randolph's first mother-in-law.'....

Diary – Saturday 1 March – 40 Gloucester Square, W.2

...Mrs Hochberger came to see me at 6 & talked about Germany. It is sad that the Germans becomes so intolerable directly they begin to recover & raise their heads from the dust. She says the Americans are terribly crude, naive & gullible & don't know 'good' Germans from bad. The 'good' Germans are all anti-rearmament because they fear that all the 'bad' ones will be in on it. Jo returned late Sat. night. Mark dined.

Diary – Wednesday 17 – Monday 21 April – Königswinter Conference

Intensely interesting visit to Königswinter on the Rhine – under the auspices of the Anglo-German Friendship Society (Frau Milchsack). We all assembled in the Palace Yard at 11.30 on Wed. morning in midsummer heat – & entrained in 2 busloads for an airport in Hampshire. We were about 30 strong – a mixed bag of M.P.'s of all complexions – Walter Elliot our doyen & leader – & then people like E. H. Carr,[1] Robert Birley,[2] & journalists (Wilson Harris,[3] McDonald[4] of the *Times*, etc.) thrown in....

We had a boiling bus drive of over an hour, a boiling wait at the Airport of an hour, a 2 hour flight – & then another long drive, so I arrived feeling rather fuzzy in the head. We were received by Frau Milchsack & Mrs Hochberger at our hôtel on the banks of the Rhine in a nice small forest town called Königswinter. We went straight in to dinner & there were speeches of welcome etc. & Uncle Walter spoke for us. Afterwards – when I was longing to go to bed – I was summoned by him to a small steering Committee to decide what we shld do in the way of procedure. Others on

[1] Edward Hallett Carr (1892–1982), diplomat, journalist and historian, best known for his monumental *History of Soviet Russia*; assistant editor and chief leader writer for *The Times*, 1941–6; tutor in politics at Balliol College, Oxford, 1953–5; fellow of Trinity College, Cambridge, from 1955.

[2] The headmaster of Eton: see the Biographical notes below.

[3] (Henry) Wilson Harris (1883–1955), MP (Ind.) Cambridge University, 1945–50; editor, *Spectator*, 1932–53.

[4] Iverach McDonald (b. 1908), on staff of *The Times* 1935–73, becoming foreign editor, 1952.

it were Hynd[1] for Labour, Frau Milchsack, Mrs Hochberger, Wilson Harris & Birley. We decided to have a plenary session to-morrow morning & one to wind up with on Sunday – & meanwhile back into 3 groups of mixed English & German, about 30 strong each, arrange a Chairman & a few key people in each & let others sign on to them. Hynd then (amazingly) said to Walter – 'I wish to ask one favour of you. Whichever group [Richard] Crossman is in either I or Woodrow Wyatt[2] must be on also – to counteract him.' That he shld have said this to a political opponent gives an idea of the bitterness of the divisions in the Labour camp.

To my horror I, Xtopher Hollis[3] & Kenneth Younger[4] were deputed to make the opening speeches next morning at 9.30! I wld far rather have weighed in later & above all wanted to have a quiet night! . . .

Next morning a German opened with a good but very long speech, then Younger, then I followed, then Xtopher Hollis – each for about 10 minutes. Then the general debate opened & Crossman made the most wicked speech I had ever heard delivered – allowing for the fact that we were abroad – & that our object was to pump courage & good sense into the Germans, who the Russian offer had obviously upset.[5] He began by calling our 3 speeches 'optimistic nonsense'. Then he told the Germans that the French had only made gestures of good-will towards them (like Schuman plan – European Army etc.) with one object – that of keeping Germany permanently weak & divided. He said that Germany had never turned to Europe except when she was down & out. When she got back on to her feet she had always become once more 'a nation'. (He said this as Hitler wld have said it – not opprobriously as one says 'nationalism'.) What cld United Europe do? If you add up 8 or 9 bankruptcies they don't become any more solvent than 1. The only hope for Germany was to cash in on the Russian offer. Otherwise war was inevitable – with Germany [like] Korea – East fighting against West.

Denis Healey replied – too mildly but fairly effectively. The other Labour people obviously suffered as much as I did – perhaps more because they felt responsible for Crossman. I immediately signed on to the group in

[1]John Burns Hynd (1902–71), MP (Lab.) Attercliffe, Sheffield, 1944–70; chairman, Anglo-German parliamentary group; he had been minister for Germany and Austria, 1945–7.

[2]Woodrow Lyle Wyatt (1918–96), cr. life peer, 1987; MP (Lab.) Aston, Birmingham, 1945–55; Bosworth, Leics., 1959–70; weekly newspaper columnist; later chairman of the Tote.

[3](Maurice) Christopher Hollis (1902–77), author, schoolmaster and politician; MP (Con.) Devizes, Wiltshire, 1945–55.

[4](Sir) Kenneth (Gilmour) Younger (1908–76), KBE, 1972; barrister; MP (Lab.) Grimsby, 1945–59; minister of state at foreign office under Bevin, 1950–1; director of Chatham House, 1959–71.

[5]In the spring of 1952 the Soviet Union proposed an international conference on German reunification, hoping to exploit divisions between the Western Allies.

which he was. . . . I challenged him repeatedly but the knock-out blow was given to him by Woodrow Wyatt, who reminded him how, during the Berlin Air-Lift, he had suggested (in an article in the *N.S.*) trading off Berlin against Vienna![1] Even the S.P.D.'s shrank away from him in horror at this revelation.

Even the 'good' Germans have a very odd make-up. When the 'Korean' analogy was being pursued I said that they were blowing the whole argument for German 'unity' sky-high by suggesting that Germany wld fight Germans at Russia's behest. Why shld they? A quite friendly German asked me 'But what else cld we do?' I said: 'What else? You cld do as the Czechs did in the 1st World War. Desert, give yourselves up, shoot yr officers – form a Legion as Masaryk formed the Czech Legion – one of the greatest epics in history.' The question we discussed at my suggestion was 'What price are you prepared to pay for German Unity?' I am glad to say that most of them discarded neutrality – which was the Russian price asked. . . .

Diary – Thursday 8 May – 15 York House, Kensington Church St., W.8[2]

. . . U.E.M. Council of Management at H. of C. . . . The Schuman countries think of uniting in a small Federation. Ly R.W. & Bob Boothby think we ought to fight this to the death. As Walter Layton & I pointed out, we shld incur the odium of the whole world if, having refused to federate ourselves, we tried to prevent others from doing so. Such 'dog in the mangerism' wld never be forgiven by America or Europe. Whether we like it or not it must have our blessing & co-operation.

Diary – Friday 9 May – 15 York House, Kensington Church St., W.8

Lunched at N°10 to meet the Austrian Chancellor – a heroic & delightful little man called Dr Figl.[3] Sat next to him with Herbert Morrison on my

[1] There is no such article by Crossman in the *New Statesman* for the months in question. And in a House of Commons debate on Germany, at the start of the airlift, he had argued that the Allies should *stay* in Berlin: 'if we came out of Berlin it would have disastrous repercussions in Western Germany' (*Hansard*, vol. 452, cols. 2239, 2315, 30 June 1948).

[2] On 10 April Violet and Bongie had moved out of 40 Gloucester Square, their home since 1935, while it was being converted into flats. They subsequently took one of these, with the address 21 Hyde Park Square, early in January 1953. In the interim they lived in a house in Kensington Church Street, W.8.

[3] Leopold Figl (1902–65), first post-war chancellor of Austria, 1945–53.

other side. Talked to Figl in German – he has a slight Austrian patois. I asked him how he had survived his 6 years in Buchenwald. He replied 'Ich habe sehr starke Nerven'.[1] He needed them as he was flogged & ill-treated in every conceivable way.

. . . W. leant across to speak to Figl & I had to interpret, as he knows no English. The question he asked was astonishing! 'Did he know that there were now more packs of fox-hounds in England than ever before?' I hadn't the heart to transmit this to Figl! Speeches followed. It was a vast official luncheon – Anthony Eden – Attlees etc etc – about 30. I had an amusing talk with W. & Herbert Morrison afterwards – in which H.M. accused W. of having a far greater attraction for me than he had (too true!) & of defeating his attempts to enlist me on their side. He (H.M.) always opens conversation with me with the words 'Well – have you been a good gurl lately?' to which I reply 'If by that you mean more friendly to your party – no.' W. looked well – tho' rather tired. I told him about Crossman & Germany. I went on later to a reception at the Austrian Embassy for Figl.

Diary – Tuesday 24 June – 15 York House, Kensington Church St., W.8

Took the Chair for Julian Amery at a U.E.M. luncheon. Good audience. His speech slightly disappointing. Went to vast Commonwealth Banquet given by the B.B.C. who are having a Commonwealth Conference on Broadcasting. To my great delight sat next to Haley! On my other side Gordon Walker who is my bête noire.[2] We most unfortunately got on to the Closed Shop early in the meal (via broadcasting) & he was so rude & impossible that after begging him in vain to talk about something else I had to ask him to talk to someone else. Talked to Haley for the rest of dinner. It is tragic for the B.B.C. that he is going to the *Times* – tho' it may be the redemption of the *Times*. . . .

Diary – Thursday 23 October – 15 York House, Kensington Church St., W.8

U.E.M. Forum luncheon. Bob Boothby spoke very well. Beddington-

[1] 'I have very strong nerves.'

[2] Patrick Gordon Walker (1907–80), cr. life peer (Gordon-Walker), 1974; politician, author and broadcaster; MP (Lab.) Smethwick, 1945–64; Leyton, 1966–74; Wilson's choice for foreign secretary in 1964, he failed to gain election and was forced to resign.

Behrens in the Chair. I talked a little 'shop' to Bob & said that Anthony had never come out whole heartedly for United Europe & indeed kept clear of our movement just as he (cautiously) did before the war of the Peace & Freedom Focus. Bob replied that Duncan Sandys had kept Anthony out of it deliberately – that the relations between them are bad & that he (Duncan) confidently expected to be Foreign Secretary. Coming from Bob I take all this with a pinch of salt – but one cannot rule out the possibility that there may be a sediment of truth in it. Went with Puff in the evening to the TeleKinema on the South Bank & sat between him & Michael Balcon.[1] They gave a revival of Puff's *Pygmalion* with Leslie Howard & Wendy Hiller which was most enjoyable. It wears admirably & doesn't 'date' at all – except in the pure Shavianism of Dr. Doolittle. . . .[2]

Diary – Wednesday 19 November – 15 York House, Kensington Church St., W.8

Went to Sibyl Colefax about yellow curtains – also Cyclax.[3] Worked at my Oxford Union speech for to-morrow. Things very bad in Kenya. I forgot to say that yesterday at Lib. Party Committee (where Jo took the Chair in Clem's absence) the decision of the Exec. to fight all 'marginal seats' was discussed. The idea is to use this threat as pressure on the Tories to give us Electoral Reform. I said I was entirely against using such a weapon, regardless of its political consequences. Shld we be prepared to put in Bevanites? regardless of the national & international situation? I also thought it an extremely bad prelude to our approach to W. & it cut right across the lines we had agreed on – i.e. to present the need for Electoral Reform in its national setting & not ask for it as a favour to the Lib. Party. I was supported by Jo. . . . Mrs Gomsky[?] remarked naïvely 'But we needn't tell the P.M. we are doing it'. I pointed out that he read the newspapers & drew his own conclusions. Byers was of course for the big stick! . . .

[1] Sir Michael Elias Balcon (1896–1977), Kt, 1948; film maker, the director and producer of Ealing Films 1938–59; he produced *Whisky Galore* (1949), *The Lavender Hill Mob* (1951) and *The Cruel Sea* (1953).

[2] Puff's *Pygmalion*, which appeared in 1938, was acclaimed by the critics and is regarded as among his best work.

[3] Sibyl Colefax *née* Halsey, famous London hostess and interior designer, the wife of Sir Arthur Colefax (d. 1936). 'Cyclax' was a cosmetics house popular with fashionable society used by Violet.

Diary – Wednesday 17 December – 15 York House, Kensington Church St., W.8

... Pertinax[1] came to tea – older – quite on the spot – but an amazing incarnation of the reactionary Right Wing Frenchman who (like Duff Cooper,[2] with whom he sees eye to eye) sees nothing but Germany as a danger. Russia doesn't exist for him. Communism in France he pooh-poohs. Adenauer[3] is the villain of the piece. Schuman perhaps even worse. He hates E.D.C. – Schuman Plan & the whole bag of tricks – & when I said to him 'But this was a French initiative, a French plan,' replied 'the plan of a group of men'. 'But that group of men were your Govt.' To Frenchmen a 'Govt' means nothing but a group of men whom they either like or dislike. He was quite bankrupt of alternatives – & when I said to him 'What wld you do?' replied 'I wld bind them very strongly with Treaties' – as tho' anyone kept a Treaty nowadays, unless they wanted to....

Diary – Monday 26 January 1953 – 21 Hyde Park Square, W.2

... Got back here in time to dine with Mark who had been at Sandringham for Sunday & enjoyed himself enormously. Anthony Eden was also there (the 2nd Sunday Mark has spent in his company – he met him with Clarissa at the Bensons last week). He says truly that A.E. never says anything about foreign affairs one hasn't read in the newspapers that morning! But he thinks him very dispassionate & unprejudiced – & of course quite uncharged with any emotion. He told Mark he had never formally invited Tito but had said casually to him 'You must come to England sometime,' upon which Tito had replied he wld come in March.[4] Mark said the Queen was in marvellous form & obviously adored 'reigning'. What she had lacked before was confidence – & now she knew she was being a success – the Opening of Parlt., her broadcast, etc. had gone so well. She complained

[1](Charles Joseph) André Géraud, 'Pertinax' (1882–1974), journalist; contributor to *Daily Telegraph* from 1912; foreign editor, *L'Echo de Paris*, 1917–38; diplomatic correspondent, *France-Soir*, Paris, from 1944.

[2]Alfred Duff Cooper (1890–1954), cr. 1st Viscount Norwich, 1952; politician, diplomat and author; British ambassador in Paris, 1944–7; author of *Talleyrand* (1932); lived at Vineuil near Chantilly.

[3]Konrad Adenauer (1876–1967), former lord mayor of Cologne, a founder of the CDU and first chancellor of the Federal Republic of Germany, 1949–63; foreign minister, 1951–5; Violet first met him when she visited the Ruhr in 1923.

[4]Marshal Tito, president of Yugoslavia, arrived in London on 16 March 1953 for a five-day visit. It was the first time that the head of a Communist government had visited Great Britain and there was heavy security surrounding his arrival.

that Anthony cld not or wld not talk to her & said she felt like writing to him when he got married to say 'I know how much you dislike women – but do try & forget that I am one & try & talk naturally to me.' He said the children were sweet – particularly Pss Anne who has almost white flaxen hair – very blue eyes & very pink cheeks – & (like all little girls) is far more fearless than her brother. They all went to see some pigs after lunch on Sunday & she ran towards them with hands spread out like stars to stroke them – while Prince Charles kept at a cautious distance. . . .

Diary – Tuesday 3 February – 21 Hyde Park Square, W.2

This evening at 5.45 we met in Jo's room for our deputation to W. on Electoral Reform at 6. Clem had just received his invitation to take part in the Conference the Govt has now announced it is setting up on H. of L. Reform. I think Simon's Bill for Life Peerages has acted as a spur.[1] We went along to W.'s room – Clem, Samuel, Dingle, Ronald Walker,[2] Jo & myself. On the other side of the table sat W. (looking as R.W. afterwards wrote to me 'like an outsize baby'), Crookshank[3] & Rab on either side of him. Rab (who had just made an excellent speech)[4] had a faint pink flush on his usually 'pasty' cheeks. W. looked rather sombre – & evaded rather than sought my eye.

Clem opened – rather wordy – very friendly & uncontroversial – not too bad. Samuel was asked to follow but demurred & handed the ball on to me. I said that W. knew all the arguments we had & shld address to him – backwards & forwards, inside out & upside down – & had probably used them himself with greater force & artistry than we shld do. I put the national case shortly . . . the appeals to us to stand down 'in the National interest' in places like West Wycombe[5] – & of how often we had done so

[1] Earlier that day the second reading of Lord Simon's Life Peerage bill had taken place in the Lords. The bill proposed the creation a number of 'life peers' each year, with a maximum of ten suggested. It met with considerable opposition, though, and the House deferred a decision by agreeing instead to the government proposal of an all-party conference on the subject: it was another five years before legislation was enacted (*The Times*, 4 February 1953).

[2] (Sir) Ronald Walker (1880–1971), Kt, 1953; company chairman; president, Yorkshire Liberal Party, 1947–60; president, Liberal Party, 1952.

[3] Harry Frederick Crookshank (1893–1961), cr. Viscount, 1956; diplomat; MP (Con.) Gainsborough, 1924–56; leader of House of Commons, 1951–2; lord privy seal, 1952–5.

[4] That afternoon Rab Butler had delivered a speech in the Commons on the implications of the recent Commonwealth Economic Conference.

[5] Wycombe, in Buckinghamshire, was an example of a constituency where the Liberal presence was likely to benefit Labour, at the expense of the Conservatives. In a three-cornered contest in 1950 the seat was won by Labour, the Liberal coming last. But in the next three elections, 1951, 1952 and 1955, in the absence of a Liberal candidate, the Conservatives won.

in order not to put in a Soc. or a Bevanite. But if we did so indefinitely our Party Organization wld lose heart – dwindle & disappear. It might be expedient that 'one man shld die for the people' – but cld it be concluded that it was the duty of one Party to die for the people? Surely if such a sacrifice was demanded others must make their contribution. It was for their contribution we had come to ask....

W. asked Butler to speak first. He asked some rather naive questions about the French system – which Samuel answered. Said that with what he described as 'friends like us' they wld feel quite safe, but that P.R. in the towns wld involve a risk & a sacrifice for them. I demurred at this & said that surely it was Labour that wld make the sacrifice. I also pointed out the loss to Parlt of the crushing out of all independent middle-of-the-road opinion. Where wld Linky Cecil or Eleanor Rathbone be today?[1] Parlt was the poorer without such great figures.

W. was obviously unhappy. He read us long passages from his past speeches advocating P.R. in the big towns as 'an expression of their collective personality' – & did not recede from what he had said. But he said you wldn't find 25 people in this Parlt who wld vote for it. Labour was dead against it. Legislation was out of the question. They were obviously going to turn down the Inquiry out of hand. Clem nipped in & pressed it. W. turned to Butler who looked dubious. I said to him: 'Do you really mean your people are even afraid to examine the facts?' We got them at least to leave the door open – & consider the Inquiry & communicate with us again. W. was obviously depressed & said he had never – even in the darkest moments of the war – felt the state of the world to be graver. When I said goodbye to him he had tears in his eyes. Fothergill came hobbling in to hear the news – hot on his gouty foot – & was naturally dashed. I had never had bright hopes. What alarms me is that the Tory Party shld still run so true to form.

Diary – Sunday 8 February – 21 Hyde Park Square, W.2

Laura & Johnny came to lunch & we went back with them to Kew afterwards.[2] It was a dark day – snowing slightly. The house itself is a dream but needs <u>everything</u> doing to it in the way of heat etc. Every room

[1]Hugh Richard Gascoyne-Cecil, 'Linky' (1869–1956), cr. Baron Quickswood, 1941; a Conservative MP, he was made a privy councillor in 1918, 'an exceptional honour for a backbench parliamentarian whose independence of mind .... unfitted him for the discipline of office' (*DNB*). Eleanor Rathbone sat as an independent during her parliamentary career.

[2]The Grimonds had just moved into the house which was to be their London home for many years, 71 Kew Green, Richmond.

has perfect proportions & the outlook both ways is heavenly. At present it is all papered. I shld infinitely prefer paint & distemper – the cornices & mouldings are so lovely. There is a big grand room upstairs looking out on the garden & perfect bedrooms. The cold was intense & not a trace of a fire or boiler on. My daughters have heroic fortitude, but also a genius for provoking & creating situations which it alone cld enable them to face.

Diary – Wednesday 4 March – 21 Hyde Park Square, W.2

Sheila greeted me with the dramatic news heard on the wireless that Stalin was fatally stricken – a stroke – haemorrhage of the brain – paralysed all down one side. It throws war & peace into the melting-pot – & perhaps the régime itself. It illuminates the purges etc. of the last months – clearly the struggle for power was being fought out behind the scenes. Left by 2.10 for Stratford for 'Town Forum'. . . . Good audience – not very exciting questions – not a single topical one – not even a word about Stalin. . . .

Diary – Tuesday 31 March – 21 Hyde Park Square, W.2

Mark to luncheon. Did a Far Eastern *Brains Trust* with Hailsham & Aneurin Bevan. It was the first time I had met him. He is a most curious phenomenon – softly bloated – giving one a sense of slight abnormality – of being not wholly virile. Extremely 'agreeable' & out to please – cooing like any sucking-dove to me & Hailsham – his main topic of conversation, the sins of Hartley Shawcross,[1] whom he clearly loathes. He told stories to his discredit until the last moment when we went on the air – & then started up again the moment we were off it. The questions put to us were not such as to allow him to extend himself. . . .

Diary – Good Friday, 3 April – 21 Hyde Park Square, W.2

Bob Boothby called for me by arrangement about 10 to drive me down to Minehead. To my amazement I saw a stowaway in the back of the car

[1] Sir Hartley William Shawcross (b. 1902), Kt, 1945; cr. life peer, 1959; QC, 1939; MP (Lab.) St Helen's, 1945–58; attorney-general, 1945–51; president of board of trade, 1951.

whom I recognized as Tom Driberg,[1] whom I knew to be one of the *Any Questions* team. I have never spent an odder Good Friday. We had a long & beautiful drive in a vast silver Jaguar of Bob's – on a most radiant day – the roads packed with Easter traffic to begin with – but clearing after we got past Basingstoke. We went the old familiar Andover–Amesbury road – Driberg bleating the whole time to be put down in a church & Bob firmly refusing. D. is apparently an Anglo-Catholic – loving Church Councils, Liturgies, & Masses & knowing by heart all the churches in which these things are practised.

Combined with his Churchiness is strong Bevanite loyalty & a tendresse for Communism. He tried to pour out to me all the stories about Hartley Shawcross's villainy I had heard from Bevan – & when I told him that I knew them & he cld take them as read he produced yet another i.e. how H.S. acting for an American firm had recovered 5 American planes from the Chinese Communists. I said I thought this was surely a good deed? To this he demurred. I asked if he wld have preferred the Chinese Communists to keep them & he said 'Yes, certainly.' I was completely winded but Bob, who knew his views, took them like cold pork. We lunched at Amesbury where lots of old tabby cats crawled out of corners in the hôtel & hailed Bob like a God. They had seen him on Television. Our waiter said 'In the News – & now in the George' – with infinite pride. Television fame beats all others.

When we resumed our drive Driberg talked tenderly about an American crooner, Ray by name, who is deaf & sings a song called 'Cry', who he is studying with a view to writing a profile in the *N.S.* Instead of debunking, as he is meant to do, he is clearly tempted to write him up. He was at a party with him till 5.30 this morning in spite of Good Friday.[2] At this point Bob began to drowse at the wheel & finally ran (not dangerously) into the side of the road. He said in self-defence – 'I was not even asleep.' What worse thing he cld have been he did not reveal. At Taunton we finally yielded to Driberg & allowed him to go into a church. (I cld not have gone with him – an à trois with him & the Almighty wld have been immonde) & meanwhile Bob took primrose coloured 'dexedrine' tablets & gave me one. Driberg came out saying he had prayed for us both!

We reached Minehead – a lovely place about 5.... We found Frank

[1] Thomas Edward Driberg (1905–76), cr. life peer, 1975 (Bradwell); politician, journalist and broadcaster; MP (Ind.) Maldon, Essex, 1942–45; (Lab.) 1945–55; (Lab.) Barking, 1959–74. Violet wrote to Raymond of Driberg: 'A most unholy man I thought. He is reputed to be a member of what Mark calls the "Homintern" but is nevertheless a very "High" Anglo-Catholic' (19 April 1953).

[2] 'Driberg was drunk and in alcoholic tears; he had fallen violently in love with the American singer, Johnny Ray, but the latter had indignantly resisted his advances' (Rhodes James, *Bob Boothby*, 409).

Gillard, Freddy Grisewood & A. G. Street,[1] who has become such an intolerable bore & of such inordinate vanity that I don't know how they can do with him. Large & good audience & not bad questions. Long talk afterwards. Then bed & off [to Clovelly] next morning.

Diary – Wednesday 15 April – 21 Hyde Park Square, W.2

My birthday – remembered by B – almost for the 1st time in our married life! I was bunched by him – Cressida & Adam & dear Haley....

I left early so as to be in time for lunch at Downing St where Clemmie had asked us to meet the Robertsons – High Commissioner for Canada. The Iain Macleods[2] were there & Mary & Xtopher Soames. We lunched downstairs in the breakfast-room now painted white, which leads out of the Pillar Room & into the big dining-room. Winston escapes as much as possible from the flat whose narrow confines he dislikes....

They are polling today in S. Africa & we talked a little of that & other Africa problems. He [Winston] was I thought rather on the defensive about them & said how easy it was for people who did not live in multi-racial communities to lay down laws for those who did. I agreed but said that those Whites who did must come to some terms with the Blacks they had chosen to live amongst – & that Malan's terms were impossible & that he was sowing the seeds of doom for himself & all Europeans in S.A. I told him of the S. Africans' own admission of their complete economic dependence on Black labour & said I thought the Dutch Church ought to be abolished. He became very Puckish & school-boyish & said 'Do you know why Black people don't wish to pray with White ones? Because they don't like their smell.' He was slightly mollified at hearing I was pro-Federation.[3]

[1] Francis George ('Frank') Gillard (1908–98), distinguished BBC war correspondent; head of west regional programmes, BBC, 1945–55. Frederick Henry Grisewood (1888–1972), broadcaster, famous as chairman of *Any Questions*. Arthur George Street (1892–1966), Wiltshire farmer, author and broadcaster: a 'fearless commentator on current affairs.... Among his blackest beasts were bureaucrats, egalitarians, anti-fox hunters, and every kind of snob' (*DNB*).

[2] Iain Norman Macleod (1913–70), MP (Con.) Enfield West, 1950–70; minister of health, 1952–5; minister of labour and national service, 1955–9; secretary of state for colonies, 1959–61; chancellor of duchy of Lancaster and leader of the house of commons, 1961–3; chancellor of the exchequer, 1970; m. 1941 Evelyn *née* Blois (b. 1915) – she was created a life peer in 1971, after her husband's death.

[3] The 'Federation' of Nyasaland with Northern and Southern Rhodesia had been outlined by Attlee's government (though Attlee later turned against the idea) and was implemented by Churchill's. Violet hoped, somewhat naively, that this Federation would lead to the greater integration of Africans in the government of the region. Instead it extended the influence of

We talked of the Budget & the rising tide of the Govt's popularity & he said to me in confidence 'Of course I don't mean to have an Election in the autumn. I mean to carry on & do the job' – & added 'We are still beset with many grievous dangers – hands raised against us right & left.' I said 'Even by the Egyptians.' He said 'Yes – but they won't push us out while I'm there.'[1] He is now doing the F.O. in Eden's absence (Eden is in a nursing-home having an operation for gall-stones – to which Butler's bumper Budget will certainly add some bitterness!) On Electoral reform he said to me – 'It can't be done. I cldn't get one vote for it.' And this I fear is true. He added some reproaches about Sunderland where we are standing. I pointed out that it was a Labour not a Conservative seat – & anybody's money – & that anyway we cldn't be expected to stand down everywhere.... He went on more seriously – 'The Socialists have a theme. We have no theme – we just have a way of life. You have a theme – but it has been taken by both the other Parties.' He was going on to elaborate this when we were alas! interrupted. He also said to me in confidence – 'Did you know yr. name had been put forward for an honour by your party?' I said I had no idea of it & that there was no honour I wanted.[2] I wld have liked to be in this H. of C. – but alas! there was no chance of this.

He said 'Alas! Well you have been recommended by Clement Davies to be made a Dame.' I said it was the last thing I desired to be. He replied 'Well – you'll get a letter from me. You can do what you like about it.' He seemed extraordinarily well & buoyant – a different creature from what he was last year. Not the least overburdened & a very good colour. He was very amused by the account of my drive to Minehead with Tom Driberg which he had heard from Bob Boothby. He said about ¼ of the H. of C. were anti-American. I had no talk with Iain Macleod tho' I shld have liked to. W. suddenly said how increasingly he loved animals – particularly cats & goldfish – & went into a rhapsody about cats, tho' he admitted their impersonal nature. I went on to Fortnums & then home....

the white Southern Rhodesians, and when riots broke out in Nyasaland in 1959 she accepted the case for ending the Federation.

[1] Egypt was then mounting a growing challenge to Britain's military presence on the Suez Canal. Churchill wanted a stronger line to be taken in response than Eden was prepared to pursue. In late January 1953 Jock Colville, Churchill's private secretary, reported that his chief was 'in a rage against A.E., speaking of "appeasement" and saying he never knew before that Munich was situated on the Nile' (Carlton, *Eden*, 325).

[2] Violet had in fact been told by Clem Davies several months earlier that he had put her name forward: 'I was annoyed to hear that he had mentioned my name [to Churchill]. The very last thing I want is to be a Dame!' (diary, 18 December 1952).

Diary – Wednesday 6 May – 21 Hyde Park Square, W.2

Coronation Production of *Henry VIII* by Tyrone Guthrie[1] at the Old Vic – to which the Queen & Duke of Edinburgh came. Very successful. The theatre very garlanded & gay. Sat in front row of Dress Circle. The Queen looked very well – & watched without much apparent reaction.... It is a bad play but a good pageant. The few Shakespeare patches are superb – but there are tracts of Fletcher.[2]

We had one interval of $\frac{1}{4}$ of an hour during which we went behind & met the Royal Party. I had a long talk with Philip who was very 'easy'. He has a touch of German 'thoroughness' – talking of a survey of a town in which boys' & girls' games had been analysed – the boys always playing in teams & the girls specializing in individual performance, like skipping. But I thought him lively, natural & agreeable. There is no doubt that the longer 'royalties' have had out of the compound the better they are at their job.

Diary – Monday 1 June – 21 Hyde Park Square, W.2

Honours List out in which I am made a D.B.E. I feel no glow alas! but others do for me.[3] Telegrams pour in all day from the most unexpected quarters. Adam, up for the Coronation, arrived after lunch & solemnly & very sweetly congratulated me....

V.B.C. to Raymond Bonham Carter — *Tuesday 16 June, 21 Hyde Park Square, W.2*

Darling Ray – I too haven't written to you for ages – one reason being that I had too much to say – & too little time to say it in. Now I have got yr 2 exciting letters written en route to the West – the 1st posted on 10th from Scott, Mississippi....[4]

[1] (Sir) (William) Tyrone Guthrie (1900–71), Kt, 1961; influential theatre director and designer, with the Old Vic 1933–47; he later moved away from traditional theatre to the open stage, and was the creator of the Stratford Ontario Festival, 1952.

[2] *Henry VIII* is thought to be a collaboration between Shakespeare and John Fletcher.

[3] One congratulatory letter observed that the honour was overdue, 'but that is the price of being a Liberal; honours have to wait for Coronations'. And Berta Hochberger, Violet's translator in Germany in 1947, wrote: 'I do feel that you have done so much for England at home and abroad that no-one could have deserved this public recognition of service more' ('Meessee' to VBC, n.d.; BH to VBC, 1 June 1953).

[4] Raymond was then in America, where he studied for an MBA at Harvard Business School.

The Coronation naturally made an immense hole in one's life. I know that B. has told you about it. The day cld not have been viler as apart from wet it was very cold. We were in our seats in a stand in the Mall by 7 o'clock & the crowds were most touching – wrapped in soaked newspapers & plastic macintoshes but burning with loyalty & full of good humour, tho' many had been there all night. (A woman of 73 & 5 others took up their stand in Trafalgar Sq. 2 nights before!) An Irish Guards band played near us – & the Mall was lined with Guardsmen. I can't tell you how beautiful the 'files of scarlet' looked when they marched down it thro' the trees. Even that grey day glowed with their colours. In sunlight it wld have been dazzling. (We were lucky in having no trees in front of us.) We saw the procession at the very start – when it left B. Palace & at the very end when it returned. The Queen's Golden Coach, drawn by the 8 greys in golden harness with golden Postilions. . . .

The best receptions – after the Queen – were given to Winston & the Queen of Tonga! a marvellous 6ft 2 coffee Charmeuse – who remained buoyant tho' drenched in an open carriage till the very end. We went indoors for the Television of the Service – which was most moving – but unfortunately our reception was very blurred. . . . There has been a good deal of indignation here over the introduction (on U.S.A. Television) of an interview with a Chimpanzee called Fred Muggs into the middle of the Abbey Communion Service – & the plugging of a 'deodorant' at the moment when the Bible was handed to the Queen by the Moderator![1] It has however given a good send-off to an anti-commercial television campaign in which I am engaged. . . .[2]

Adam saw the Coronation from Coutts Bank at H. P. Corner. He said to me 'One of the best things about it was that Dr Malan was booed.' I said 'I wonder how the crowd knew which carriage he was in?' Adam said 'Well I counted them on my programme & knew it was the 5th – & I started the boo & then the crowd took it up.' I thought it showed admirable political consciousness & instinct for a child of 11. . . .

I must stop as it is well past midnight. All my love my Darling & do send me all yr news & let me know what we can send you for yr birthday

[1] Anthony Nutting explained in the Commons the next day that the chimpanzee ('J. Fred Muggs') was a regular feature of the American NBC network's *Today* programme, which covered the coronation, and that the chimp was not interposed during the 'live' screening of the Abbey ceremony. Nevertheless there was strong criticism on both sides of the Atlantic of the commercial stations' coverage. Jack Gould, the *New York Times* critic, attacked 'a callousness in the injection of commercials that defied description' (*The Times*, 8, 18 June 1953).

[2] The campaign opposed commercial television as being 'fraught with dangers to those spiritual and intellectual values which the BBC has nobly striven to maintain'. It was launched with a letter in *The Times*, 4 June, and a meeting followed at Violet's home on the 18th: she became chairman, and Lord Waverley president, of the 'National Television Council'.

on which you won't have to pay duty. Have you got any of the various Coronation Supplements we sent? Love & missings, Yr Mama

Diary – Tuesday 7 July – 21 Hyde Park Square, W.2

. . . . Went to Old Vic Trust – had to leave early to get to B.B.C. by 6.45 for a Far Eastern *Brains Trust* with Bob Boothby & Aneurin Bevan. Bevan was in a completely different mood from last time. He was obviously in a very bad temper (he had possibly just heard the news we read in the papers next day, that Morrison was going to be nominated as Treasurer of the Labour Party). He began by declaring against the B.B.C., for making payments to M.P.s for expressing their opinions on the air. I asked if he were accepting payment for our present séance & suggested that if so he shld throw it on the table & Bob & I wld split it. He refused to answer this or any other argument – simply declaimed – dismissing objections by saying 'That's silly – that's superficial' etc. etc. Bob left me all the batting to do at dinner. I reproached him with this afterwards & he said 'Bevan is impossible to argue with. I'm no F.E. I like sitting back & sipping my whisky & soda.' Having blown off steam at dinner Bevan was more reasonable during the discussion – though I had to go for him once when he said that 'the people of Russia had never been held down'! I cannot see his power. I compare him constantly with LlG. who was so much more agile, able, witty, charming – & (perhaps) treacherous![1]

Diary – Sunday 12 July – 21 Hyde Park Square, W.2

Lunched with Laura & Jo & went with Laura & the children to Hampton Court – & back to tea with her. Andrew up for long leave. A horrible campaign has been raging in the Press during the last fortnight – led by the *People* – hotly followed by the *Daily Mirror* & the *Sunday Express* about Pss M. & Peter Townsend, who has been posted to Brussels.[2] The 'decent' papers like the *N.C.* have alas! limped – or scurried – as the case may be –

[1] Violet later revised her opinion of Bevan's abilities after watching him in a debate on Suez: see below, p. 180.

[2] Group Captain Peter Townsend (1914–95), served with distinction in RAF, 1939–45; equerry to George VI, 1944–52; to Elizabeth II, 1952–3. Shortly before the coronation Townsend and Princess Margaret had made known to the Queen their love for one another. But his 1951 divorce (he had married in 1941) presented an obstacle to their marrying, even though he was the innocent party by the standards of the day. They were asked to wait and in the meantime Townsend agreed to take a post as air attaché in Brussels.

after the indecent ones. It is a gross outrage & very cruel. What she must be feeling on her Rhodesian tour I shudder to think. Mark says the Palace have behaved very clumsily. The thing started abroad – in U.S.A., Canada & Europe. He says that P.T. told them that posting him to Brussels wld produce the explosion of gossip, rumour, speculation etc. which has in fact followed.

Diary – Friday 17 July – 21 Hyde Park Square, W.2

. . . Went to rather dreary party given by Anglo German Society in H. of C. It shld have been on the Terrace but was too wet – like everything this year. Never has there been such un-intermittent wind in London – & so much rain. I was pursued by an *Evening Standard* reporter who stood at my elbow taking short-hand notes of my conversation. I asked what she was doing & she replied with a Cheshire cat smile 'I am eavesdropping on your conversation. I hope you don't mind?' I replied that I minded extremely & she said 'You see I want a story for the *Evening Standard*.' I reported it to Bellenger who didn't seem at all shocked!

Diary – Monday 27 July – 21 Hyde Park Square, W.2

Returned from Stockton after a delicious Sunday there with C., B., self & Puff. Puff most well, sweet & amusing. . . . Siegfried came over bringing a cricketer called Silk.[1] He was rather amusing about his own state of neglect by the public. 'I try to gain esteem by silence. But with me it is out of sight out of mind.' K. [Elliot] came for the night. I went to meet Adlai Stevenson[2] at the Spearses[3] & found him enchanting. Not the least impressive looking. One wld not be aware of him in a room. Much smaller than his photographs suggest – but an amusing sensitive face. Never holds forth – is 'short' – such a rare quality among Americans. It was difficult to have any real talk with him as he was of course surrounded by a milling crowd trying to catch every syllable that fell from his lips – Oliver Lyttelton,

[1] Dennis Raoul Silk (b. 1931), captain of cricket at Cambridge; assistant master, Marlborough College, 1955–68; warden of Radley College, 1968–91; chairman of the Test and County Cricket Board, 1994–6.

[2] Adlai Stevenson (1900–65), American Democratic politician and lawyer; elected governor of Illinois, 1948; unsuccessful presidential candidate, 1952 and 1956.

[3] Major-General Sir Edward (Louis) Spears (1886–1974), KBE, 1942; cr. Bt, 1953; MP (Con.) Carlisle, 1931–45; on diplomatic missions in North Africa during war; m. 1918 Mary Borden, novelist.

Archie, Bob Boothby, Winston etc – but I got the flavour of him. Went with B & K to the *Apple-Cart* – not really very good – but quite amusing. Shaw no longer 'startles'. It is a dangerous line if one wants to survive.

'Every instinct armed to fight it out until the end'
Churchill's stroke and incapacity, August 1953

For several months in 1953 Britain was effectively without its prime minister and its foreign secretary, when both Churchill and Eden were incapacitated by illness. Eden underwent two unsuccessful operations for gallstones in April before a third, in June, restored him to a degree of health; he resumed his duties in October. In his absence Churchill became acting foreign secretary, a role that he relished. He was then deeply concerned about the implications for the world of atomic weapons, and was fully aware that research was under way on even more powerful devices. After Stalin's death in March 1953 he was eager to try a direct approach with the new regime in Moscow. The idea found no favour either with the foreign office or in the United States, where there were fears about the high risks that such a strategy entailed. In the short term the breakdown of Churchill's own health derailed the plan. On Tuesday 23 June he suffered a serious stroke that left him paralysed down the left side of his body. His physician, Lord Moran, doubted that he would survive. In fact Churchill staged a remarkable recovery and when Violet went to see him at Chequers in the first week of August he was already weighing his future prospects. The after-effects of the stroke were still apparent, but Violet was struck by his tremendous determination to continue his life's work, 'every instinct armed to fight it out until the end'.

Diary – Thursday 6 August – 21 Hyde Park Square, W.2

I drove down to Chequers through the green countryside steeling myself inwardly. How shld I find Winston? how much – or how little impaired? I knew the truth, that he had a stroke – had for a time been partially paralysed – was walking again – was recovering. But for what? Cld he go back to public life, take up the threads which had been severed by the shears so brutally – just when they seemed to be leading him to the heart of the labyrinth?[1]

[1] The 'labyrinth' being a détente with the Soviet Union and an agreement over the future of nuclear weapons.

I was taken through the dark Chequers hall where electric light perpetually burns – & which has a kind of bogus Beerbohm Tree atmosphere. Last time I arrived there was in the War when W. sent for me to come from Winchester to meet Harry Hopkins.[1] I found Clemmie in the rose-garden....

Clemmie said that she felt sure he ought to retire in the autumn & begged me not to urge him to stay on if he asked my advice. She said, truly, that the Conference with the Russians, which he longed for, wld not be just one Conference. It wld be the start of a long struggle which might last for years. His mind was quite clear but tired more easily. He shld go now rather than wait & peter out (these were not her words, only their sense). She was wonderfully brave, sensible & unemotional.

He was just getting up & came in to the big hall when we went in – dressed in his siren suit, walking with a stick but not too badly, his face quite normal – pink & no distortion. He kissed me & I said how well he looked. He said 'I'm better – but you know I've been quite paralysed. I cldn't walk. I had no pain – it was like a heavy weight all down one side. Now I can move my fingers – & my toes even.' At luncheon he spoke thickly sometimes & I noticed a very slight crookedness in his mouth – also occasionally a slight lack of control when he got excited....

At moments he became suddenly & unreasonably angry – like a violent child. He blazed forth against the B.B.C. 'I hate the B.B.C. It kept me off the air for 11 years. It is run by reds – '. Abuse of Reith followed – who cld certainly not be described as a 'red'.[2] 'I put in Alec Cadogan[3] – a man I knew I cld trust to serve his country.' I said I thought it was a shockingly bad appt – 'Who wld you have sent there?' I said I cld think of several – but suggested Cyril Radcliffe.[4] 'Never heard of him. The B.B.C. behaved very badly over the Chimpanzee in the Coronation – publicizing it.' 'It was not the B.B.C. but your friend Ld Beaverbrook who splashed it. I saw it first in the *Sunday Express*. The B.B.C. has no organ of publicity. And it was a fact.' 'Well I don't care tuppence about this business of Sponsored Television but I am not going to have anyone forced to vote for it. There

[1] This was probably in January 1941 when Hopkins (1890–1946), Roosevelt's special emissary, made his first visit to Churchill.

[2] John Charles Reith (1889–1971), GCVO, 1939; cr. Baron, 1940; creator of the BBC, director-general, 1927–38; dismissed by Churchill as minister of works and planning, 1942, after just ten days in the job: 'Reith's hatred of Churchill stayed virulent' (*DNB*).

[3] Sir Alexander Cadogan (1884–1968), GCMG, 1939; OM, 1951; permanent under-secretary of state, foreign office, 1938–46; permanent UK representative, UN, 1946–50; chairman, BBC, 1952–7.

[4] Cyril John Radcliffe (1899–1977), KBE, 1944; cr. life peer, 1949 (as lord of appeal in ordinary); cr. Viscount, 1962; lawyer and public servant, the chairman of the boundary commissions set up by the 1947 India Independence Act.

must be a free vote.' I was glad to hear this – glad also when he said 'Do you know that ever since Anthony went sick he has not expressed an opinion of any kind on politics or foreign policy. No message has been received from him of any kind, except one sentence, 'No sponsored Television.'

I teased him about his hostility to the B.B.C. & said 'If it is such a scrap-heap, such a dirty pool of sewage, why did you throw me upon it? Why did you make me a Governor?' He replied 'Because you are such a Bloody Duck!' He asked me where I stood on Black & White issues. I said I hated Malanism but – unlike my Party – was pro-Federation & had fought with them for it. He said 'Is there anything you still agree about with yr. Party?' He asked if I wld stand again. I said never. I cldn't get in & it wasn't worth fighting as a mere ritualistic act. He said 'Why not as a Nat. Liberal?' I said 'Never. They had never stood or fought for anything & had earned the contempt of all Parties. I shld find it easier to stand as a Conservative if I did make a change.' 'Well, if you wld do that I can get you any seat in the country – now. I may not always be able to do it – but now I cld. After all there is very little difference between Conservatism today & what yr Father & Grey stood for in the past.' 'Yes – but that was 40 years ago. Time moves on. One can't afford to follow events with a time-lag of 40 years.'

After luncheon we went out into the garden, after numerous little houris had been summoned with papers etc. & a nurse brought shoes & zipped them on. It was sunny & after a little pacing on the grass we sat down on a seat & discussed his future. It was terribly poignant for he obviously longs to keep his hold on the levers of power – & where wld he be without them? 'Othello's occupation gone.'[1] He said how terribly he minded giving up the F.O. (This he recurred to more than once.) He had obviously enjoyed it intensely. He felt that he had quickened the current – made our Foreign policy positive after Anthony's somewhat negative reign. . . .

He said: 'Can I go on? Can I address the Conservative Conference. . . . A leader who can't address the Party Conference can't carry on.' I said I thought it didn't matter one jot whether he addressed the Party Conference or not. The Party was in good heart & on the crest of the wave. Butler or Eden cld easily take his place. The H. of Commons was what mattered. He said 'Yes – can I face the H. of C.? If I went now people wld say nice things about me. I shld be complimented – praised. I shld go out with general approval & goodwill. If I wait I may be criticized – blamed – barracked. And even then it might only be for another year?' I begged

[1] *Othello*, act 3, scene 3: 'O farewell, / Farewell the neighing steed, and the shrill trump, / The spirit-stirring drum, the ear-piercing fife; / The royal banner, and all quality, / Pride, pomp, and circumstance of glorious war! / . . . . / Farewell! Othello's occupation's gone!'

him not to make a hurried decision. He had made marvellous progress in 6 weeks. He might make more....

We spoke of the thin-ness of the 2nd line – compared Rab & Anthony. He said 'It is Anthony's turn – he's been at it longer. Rab is younger & can wait. The 1922 Committee are divided between them, but if you asked the rank & file in the country which cld win a General Election they wld say Anthony unhesitatingly. Rab has behaved very well about Anthony.' I said I had gained great respect for Rab when I went with him on the Commonwealth Relations Conference – his industry, integrity & lack of vanity. I cld never forgive Anthony for his caution in fighting Appeasement. He was against it but he wldn't burn his boats. He never threw in his lot with us or our Peace & Freedom Focus. He was trammelled by his old Party tie. W. said – 'It wasn't that so much as the F.O. He was always bound by the F.O.'....

We discussed Cripps – his odd make up & violent swings of thought & mind & he attributed these partly to his odd diet![1] Clemmie agreed that he was starved & we compared notes about Crippsian hospitality & parsimony – which deeply shocked W. We said how Attlee missed him & Bevin, & how he had suffered from their loss. W. 'Yes. He has had to fall back on the resources of his own exuberant personality!' This was very like him.

The masseuse was announced at 4 – but now he didn't want to go in. He was happy where he was & wanted to go on talking. We had to coax him in. He went up the steps as he had gone down them – putting one foot above the other – not one by one [sic]. Then he took me to see his fish – 4 large tanks of them – illuminated – which he takes with him wherever he goes – to & fro from Chartwell where he returns next week. He showed me their markings – & the 'Neon' fish – a tiny strip of scarlet with a bright green streak on its back. 'There it is – the shops have got it now – but the fish had thought of it first.' Again I realised his eternal childhood. His passion for his toys....

I drove back feeling an unutterable sense of tragedy – at watching this last – great – ultimately losing fight against mortality. The light still burning – flashing – in its battered framework – the indomitable desire to live & act still militant & intact. Mind & will at bay with matter. At best a delaying action – but every instinct armed to fight it out until the end.

Epilogue

Churchill *did* address the Conservative Party conference at Margate in October and gave an impressive performance, as Harold Mac-

[1] Stafford Cripps was a vegetarian and, in Violet's experience, happy dining on raw vegetables.

millan observed: 'He spoke for 50 minutes in the best Churchillian vein.' Having cleared this hurdle he was encouraged to continue further and spoke of staying in office until May 1954, when the Queen would return from a long visit to Australia. His renewed vigour and lengthening horizons came as a bitter blow to his designated successor, Anthony Eden, who had long been pressing his chief for the date when he would retire. Churchill, however, was extremely reluctant to give up power, believing that a settlement with the Russians lay within his grasp. On 3 November he consolidated his political come-back with a successful speech in the House of Commons, remarking afterwards to his physician: 'Now, Charles, we can think of Moscow.' Balked over the timing of the succession, as well as the direction of foreign policy, Eden's relations with Churchill deteriorated. Harold Macmillan, who would later be forced to act 'as a sort of mediator' between them, knew both characters well. In the autumn of 1953 he believed that Churchill would not risk defeat at a general election, and was therefore certain to retire before the next dissolution:

> 'But he will go on as long as he can, always having a date ahead, which (when reached) can be extended for a new reason. Last autumn, he had to stay for Eden's return. Now he must stay to get him through the Egyptian trouble. Then it is the Queen's return. By next summer, another reason will be found. But it is at once so rusé and so naïve, that it is very engaging! Of course, I am no fair judge, for he does not worry me. With his mind on Russia, and the whole world, he leaves me alone so long as the result is good – which it is. But it must be difficult for Eden.'[1]

[1] Gilbert, *Never Despair*, 909; Macmillan, *Tides of Fortune*, 526–9, 544–5.

TWO

Suez and After

1954–1963

CHRONOLOGY OF EVENTS 1954–1963

1954	May	7 fall of French garrison at Diên Biên Phu to Viet Minh
	July	– end of all food rationing; Anglo-Egyptian Agreement on withdrawal of British troops from Suez
	August	30 European Defence Community plan rejected by French National Assembly
	October	23 Treaty creating Western European Union
1955	February	– British government decides to proceed with manufacture of hydrogen bomb
	April	– West Germany joins NATO
		5 Churchill resigns – succeeded by Eden
	May	26 general election gives Conservatives 54 seat majority: 345 Conservative, 277 Labour, 6 Liberal, 2 other; Eden premier
	June	1–3 Messina Conference: Germany, France, Italy and Benelux agree further integration
	December	– Clement Attlee retires as Labour leader, succeeded by Hugh Gaitskell
1956	February	– Commons rejects motion to abolish death penalty
	June	– British troops leave Suez
	July	26 Nasser nationalizes Suez Canal
	October	21 beginnings of the Hungarian revolution
		29 Israel attacks Egypt
		31 Britain and France begin air bombardment of Egyptian targets
	November	4 Soviet troops attack Hungarian revolutionaries in Budapest
		5–6 Anglo-French invasion of Suez
		6 ceasefire in Suez; Jo Grimond succeeds Clement Davies as Liberal leader
		14 Soviet forces re-establish control in Hungary
	December	– Anglo-French evacuation of Suez; Britain draws on IMF
1957	January	9 Anthony Eden resigns
		10 Harold Macmillan becomes prime minister
	March	27 Treaties of Rome, establishing the EEC and Euratom, signed by the 'Six'
	May	– first British hydrogen bomb test in Pacific

Year	Month	Event
	October	4 first Sputnik satellite launched
1958	January	1 Rome Treaties (establishing EEC, Euratom) come into force
	February	12 Rochdale by-election: Ludovic Kennedy's second place raises Liberal hopes
		– Britain and USA agree on American missile bases in Britain; CND established
	March	27 Torrington by-election: Mark Bonham Carter wins the seat for the Liberals
	April	– first Aldermarston march organized by CND
		30 Life Peerages Act given royal assent
	July	24 creation of first life peers: 10 men and 4 women nominated by Harold Macmillan
1959	January	– London Agreement on independence for Cyprus
	October	8 general election gives Conservatives 100-seat majority: 365 Conservative, 258 Labour, 6 Liberal, 1 other; Macmillan premier
	November	20 EFTA convention agreed by the 'Seven' – Britain, Austria, Portugal, Switzerland, Norway, Denmark, Sweden
1960	February	3 Macmillan's 'wind of change' speech in Cape Town to South African parliament
	March	21 South African police kill 69 and injure up to 180 after firing on a demonstration at Sharpeville outside Johannesburg; on same day 19 shot dead at Langa near Cape Town
	May	– EFTA Treaty comes into effect
	August	– Cyprus becomes independent
	October	– Federation of Nigeria becomes independent
1961	July	– Macmillan announces Britain's decision to apply for membership of EEC
	August	10 Britain requests negotiations with EEC for membership
		13 start of the building of the Berlin Wall
		31 Soviet Union announces it will resume the testing of nuclear devices
	September	18 Dag Hammarskjöld killed in plane crash in Northern Rhodesia
	November	8 negotiations begin on British entry into EEC

1962	March	14 Orpington by-election: Eric Lubbock elected as a Conservative majority of 14,760 is turned into Liberal majority of 7,855
	July	13 Macmillan's 'night of the long knives' cabinet reconstruction
		10 Telstar launched
	August	– Jamaica, Trinidad and Tobago become independent
1963	January	14 de Gaulle's press conference expressing his opposition to Britain's entry to the EEC
		18 death of Hugh Gaitskell
		29 France formally vetoes Britain's application to join the EEC; negotiations between Britain and the EEC are broken off
	February	– Harold Wilson elected Labour leader
	June	– Profumo Affair
	July	– Peerage Act enables hereditary peers to renounce titles
	October	19 Macmillan retires; Sir Alec Douglas-Home becomes premier
	December	31 independence for Kenya and Zanzibar; Central African Federation dissolved

FIVE

Churchill and Eden

1954–1955

Diary – Saturday 30 January 1954 – 21 Hyde Park Square, W.2

Colder than ever – & a piercing wind blowing. Wrote letters & worked in the morning. Mark lunched & stayed here till after tea. Then I reluctantly dressed up & went to another delegate's reception at French Embassy. Drove on to Leo Amery's dinner at Piccadilly Hôtel with Harrod who seemed to me madder than ever. Found a vast crowd of delegates making the din of a lion-house in a vast room. Then in to dinner.

Sat at top-table between Torrance (deputy High Commissioner for S.A.) & Hore Belisha,[1] who exchanged his card with that of a Frenchman who shld have sat next to me, & who actually turned out to be quite amusing.... We had innumerable speeches. Walter Layton first – who is a terribly bad speaker & got not a ripple of response from a very friendly audience. Then Spaak who was brilliantly amusing. Then Abs[2] – wisely not trying to be amusing – but making a very good speech. Then Duncan Sandys – very good. By now it was 11 o'clock & I was longing to go when Destu[?] was called. He is an elderly & arid looking economist but he made the most brilliant speech – witty, moving & 'finished' to the last degree. There is no doubt that the Latins speak as birds fly or fishes swim – & that we speak like people trying to learn to bicycle. Beddington-Behrens tricycled unsteadily for 5 minutes – & I faced the blast of Piccadilly & mercifully found a taxi home.

[1] Leslie Hore-Belisha (1893–1957), cr. Baron 1954; MP (Lib. Nat., later Ind.) Devonport, 1923–45; secretary of state for war, 1937–40.

[2] Probably Herman Joseph Abs, a financial expert and rising star within the German CDU.

V.B.C. to Raymond Bonham Carter — ***Tuesday 16 February***
21 Hyde Park Square, W.2

Darling Ray – Your very interesting letter in 2 instalments was a great joy & I was thrilled to hear of the various business vistas opening before you. . . .

I have been hideously busy – 8 lectures between 11th Jan & 8th Feb. & 2 broadcasts – including a Commercial T.V. discussion on the air with Muggeridge – Editor of *Punch*[1] – an agreeable but definitely un-nice man – ex-Communist – now pathologically 'anti-'. He 'smears' everyone & has just published a horrible cartoon of Winston – collapsing into senility – with a signed article opposite on the same theme. The *M.G.* had a magnificent leader slating him & the *Daily Mirror*, which has been on the same tack. I wrote a letter thanking them. If it wld amuse you to see the leader I will send it. . . .

I have just been reviewing for the *Observer* a book I must send you called *Mr Balfour's Poodle* – 'an account of the struggle between the House of Lords & Mr Asquith's Govt.' It is by a young Labour M.P. called Roy Jenkins & is extremely good reading, very amusing & very pro-Father. . . .

I must stop. All my love & blessing darling. Tell me when you write next about when you think you will be coming home – September? October? as I will make plans accordingly. Yr Mama

Diary – Saturday 29 to Sunday 30 May – Chartwell, Kent

B & I went down to St Ronan's for the Sports & Prize-giving (it has always burned in B's heart that I have never been invited to officiate before – the only thing he has ever resented on my behalf!). . . .[2]

Then Winston's car arrived & off I went to Chartwell.[3] I got there about 6.30 – was received by Mary[4] (who is expecting another baby in July, but looked very glowing & pretty) & went straight up to see W. He was in his siren suit & greeted me with great affection – plunged almost immediately into the subject of payment of members, which is obviously uppermost

[1] Malcolm (Thomas) Muggeridge (1903–90), journalist and broadcaster; deputy editor *Daily Telegraph*, 1950–2; the editor of *Punch*, 1953–7, to which he brought 'lively and satirical journalism' (*DNB*).

[2] St Ronan's was the preparatory school attended by Mark and Raymond Bonham Carter before going to Winchester.

[3] Bongie appears not to have accompanied Violet on this occasion.

[4] Mary Soames, Churchill's youngest daughter: see the Biographical notes below.

in his mind.[1] He was bitterly disappointed when I said I thought that any increase which was given – either in salary or expenses – shld apply only to the next Parlt. It wld be indecent for M.P.'s to grab a raise of 50 p.c. for themselves when so many were suffering far more acutely from the conditions which were hitting them: i.e. fall in money values, rise in prices, etc. He said 'This is the first time you have disappointed me by taking a reactionary view'....

He went off to have a short sleep before dinner & re-appeared in a black velvet siren suit which he made me feel. We had a delicious dinner with Pol Roger champagne of a vintage year '28 – of which he has been sent all the existing supply by Madame Pol Roger. He recalled that he had had some relations with the 'Veuve Clicquot' in the 1st war, but that she wasn't a patch on Pol Roger. After dinner we went down to see a film (he has one every night) in a large room entirely devoted to the purpose.... We went upstairs afterwards & talked till nearly 1 o'clock. His valet sat in the passage asleep with his head resting on his crossed arms on a table. We talked about Indo-China on which he took rather an odd line – 'Why shldn't the French give it up? We gave up India.'[2] 'But if Indo-China goes what about its neighbours? Wldn't you fight if Malaya was attacked?' 'Yes of course we shld.' This piecemeal strategy seemed to me to be inconsequent & uncharacteristic of him. But the real key to his attitude came out later when he said 'The battle of the Far East can only be won in Moscow.' He still hankers after the 'parley at the summit'....

W. did not seem to be much afraid of China. He said their industrialization had gone such a short way – they were so insufficiently equipped with Radar etc. The Russians fed them a little but not enough. He was not so annoyed with the Lab. Party visit as I thought he wld be.[3] 'I hate people with slit eyes & pig-tails. I don't like the look of them or the smell of them – but I suppose it does no great harm to have a look at them.' He was in good form but I noticed once or twice a slight confusion of memory, unlike him....

When he had telephoned asking me to come I said 'How are you?' He said 'All right – in the last lap.' That evening he told me that Beaverbrook

[1] In the House of Commons on 14 April Churchill proposed a debate on the salary of MPs, following a report from an all-party select committee recommending an increase. His support for the idea of a salary rise was at variance with the majority of Conservative MPs and *The Times* of 3 June captioned an article on the subject 'P.M. Criticized'.

[2] On 7 May the French garrison at Diên Biên Phu had fallen to Vietnamese Communist forces, a defeat of great significance for the region. The French had unsuccessfully sought American and British aid in the garrison's defence.

[3] In May 1954 it was announced that a Labour Party delegation would visit China in August: the group, led by Attlee, spent three weeks there and sought clarification of China's intentions in south-east Asia (*The Times*, 27 May 1954; Harris, *Attlee*, 520, 522).

had been to lunch with him that day & added: 'He wants me to stay. He & you are the only 2 people who want me to stay.' I said of course I wanted him to do so. . . . 'But there is Anthony. I've kept him waiting a long time. And he's very impatient.' I said this was the last consideration which shld tip the scales. Anthony was assured of the succession. He was playing a great hand at Foreign Secretary. In fact it might well be that this wld be his finest hour. No one cld foretell what he wld be as P.M. He was only 57. W. had had to wait till he was 66 – & in the wilderness.

I can see that W. is going through profound unhappiness & searching of heart in this Valley of Decision. He longs to stay on & dreams of reaching a settlement with the Russians – 'Peace – the last prize I have to win.' This wld round off his life. He is in a hurry about peace. He is in a hurry about payment of members! The thought of making this generous gesture to his opponents appeals to him. When I say 'let it become operative in the next Parlt' he won't consider it, because he knows he will not be in there. It is in this sense that he may be dangerous at the moment. He hears 'Time's wingèd chariot' all the time – & it disturbs his judgement. . . .[1]

Diary – Tuesday 24 August – Mottisfont Abbey, Romsey, Hampshire

Alas! rain again. Stayed in all morning writing etc. but went with Maud & B. to hunt mushroom (chanterelles – those very poisonous looking orange umbrellas – which are not poisonous but very tough to eat) in rather stuffy woods. . . .

We were just finishing dinner when I was called to the telephone. A 'Sloane' call, Ackerman the butler said, but they wld give no name. I went into the morning room & Anne [Asquith] came through. She told me that Cys had just died – about an hour before. He had not been ill – & spent a normal day tho' he seemed a little tired. He had come back from the Club after 7.30 & said he didn't want anything for dinner. She asked if he wld like to dine in bed & he said yes. She brought him a hot water bottle & his tray – & left him with it for 10 minutes or ¼ of an hour – not longer. When she came back he was dead. . . . She was very calm & composed. I

[1] Andrew Marvell, 'To his Coy Mistress': 'Had we but world enough, and time, / This coyness, lady, were no crime. / . . . / But at my back I always hear / Time's wingèd chariot hurrying near.' Harold Macmillan has written of Churchill that summer: 'he knew that if he, an old man, was to play the role of the saviour of mankind from the horrors of nuclear war, he could scarcely avoid seeming, in his father's phrase, "an old man in a hurry".' (*Tides of Fortune*, 533).

said I wld come up to-morrow. I felt physically stunned – as tho' my body realised it – tho' my mind refused to take it in....

V.B.C. to Mark Bonham Carter ***Tuesday 31 August***
Mottisfont Abbey, Romsey, Hampshire

Darling Mark – One line to thank you for your letter. I still feel stunned & reeling as from an almost physical shock. When Anne said to me on the telephone 'Cys is dead' I felt as tho' half of me had been killed – not gradually but by a blow. We were part of each other – & part of me is gone with him – & yet is not with him – wherever he has gone.

Ever since I can remember anything, he shared with me every experience, emotion, thought, joy & pain. He often said – about things great & small – 'unless you see the point of it, it can't be perfect or complete for me'. He was not my brother only – but my child – & needing me so infinitely more than one's real children do. It is not 'confidences' that bind one – but the need to make them. If only he had been happy! – & fulfilled & realised himself. In youth & childhood I cld. be his shield & buckler. But later I was powerless to protect him. And now he has gone into the dark I know he wld have feared – alone – & nothing I can do can help or reach him.

My love to you. Ever yr Mama.

Diary – Friday 8 October – 21 Hyde Park Square, W.2

Went to Lydney (Gloucestershire) for an *Any Questions*. Met Collin Brooks[1] in the train & travelled with him.... We stayed at the Feathers Hôtel. Ralph Wightman & Mrs Wightman[2] rolled up later – & at dinner a new member of the Team – George Brown – Attlee-ite Labour who was Minister of Works for about 8 months in the last Labour Govt. & Under Sec. at Agriculture for a time. Everyone was agreeable to him – but he was obviously lacking in 'touch' – or any kind of 'amenity' of intercourse. We all rolled off to the Hall in due course & had an audience of some 450.

It was (I thought) rather a dull programme as the questions were all on the heavy side & the team did little to lighten them.... George Brown's

[1] Probably (William) Collin Brooks (1893–1959), author and journalist, chairman and editor of *Truth*, 1940–53.

[2] Ralph Wightman (1901–71), West Country lecturer in agriculture who became a freelance journalist and broadcaster, specially associated with *Any Questions*; m. 1924 Margaret *née* Wiggins.

'form' cld not I thought have been worse. He made 2 really 'bad form' howlers – one a quite gratuitous & irrelevant insult to the Liberal Party – the other an allusion to my age! When we returned to the hôtel (our BBC hosts having left us) & we sat up talking he hectored & harangued us & addressed me repeatedly as 'my dear Violet'. I was frozen – but did not I fear freeze him. I have never before – in the course of an unsheltered life, spent among all sorts & conditions of men – met anyone so completely un-house-trained.

Diary – Friday 5 November – 21 Hyde Park Square, W.2

Worked. Was manicured (very badly!) Had a most moving letter from W. who had just got the Cassell book.[1] He writes of the various chapters: 'There is one which means more to me than all the remainder & which indeed moves me deeply. It seems that after all these years you still believe me to be a glow-worm. That is a compliment which I find entirely acceptable.' It has made me very proud & happy. Working hard at my T.U. speech.

Diary – Sunday 7 November – 21 Hyde Park Square, W.2

Got a telegram handed in by W. at 12.30 thanking me for my letter. The book reached me yesterday. Anthony's epilogue is a masterpiece of platitude – even from the Prince of them. Gilbert Murray's preface is good.... Some of the contributions – like the Aga Khan's for instance – are indeed easy money! The one which inflamed me was a highly controversial chapter by little [Leo] Amery comparing W. & LlG. as war-leaders – in which he smears my father & his Administration & puts forward his own highly contentious views. Had I known that such a chapter was to appear in the same cover as my own I certainly wld not have allowed my own to be included....[2]

[1] Violet had contributed a chapter to Sir James Marchant's tribute book *Winston Spencer Churchill, Servant of Crown and Commonwealth*. Her chapter was entitled 'Winston Churchill as I Know Him'.

[2] At the end of that month Violet attended a special parliamentary tribute to Churchill, at which Attlee made a much praised speech. He later recalled: 'Characteristically Violet Bonham Carter liked my speech except my allusion to the social reform of the Lloyd George era. She clearly thought that it should have been Asquith. I fear the feud has become an obsession' (Harris, *Attlee*, 525).

Diary – Tuesday 7 December – 21 Hyde Park Square, W.2

Dined at Ritz Grill with Puff & Harewoods.[1] Very amusing – lots of music shop. I cast the only cloud by remarking innocently how glad I was to see that John Christie[2] had got the Mozart Medal in Vienna. The hostility of Covent Garden to Glyndebourne at once became apparent. Harewood expatiated on John Christie's musical ignorance, 'chip on the shoulder' in relation to C.G., etc. I asked innocently why he shld have a 'chip' towards anyone or anything in view of his achievement – & said that 'erudition' did not alas guarantee results. We must judge John by his results – the triumph of Glyndebourne.

Went on to have my hair washed. Then home & then on to reception given at the H. of C. by Inter-Parliamentary Union for the German delegates. Came in while Hynd was welcoming them. Anthony followed with a few words. My dear Frau Luhdens followed. I then had a talk with Stoddart-Scott,[3] Conservative M.P. & Chairman of the Union, who was acting as host. He was very friendly & talked of Colne Valley [in 1951] – as he was President of the Conservative Yorkshire Federation he knew all about it. He told me that when they were thinking of putting up a Conservative candidate in C.V. Winston said to them: 'I warn you that if you do I shall come up & speak against him.' Winston also sent for Sir Gilbert Tanner & asked him to come up to London to see him. Sir Gilbert replied that he hadn't been to London since 1910 & he didn't see why he shld come now! Stoddart-Scott ended by saying – 'The P.M. offered your party 50 straight fights. I could never understand why you didn't take them.' Why indeed? Those who the Gods wish to destroy....

'The Last Asquithian .... a very formidable lady'

The indignation with which Violet greeted Leo Amery's criticism of her father, in his contribution to the Churchill tribute book published in November, was entirely characteristic. A year later she pursued the historian Robert Blake over his treatment of Asquith

[1]George Henry Lascelles (b. 1923), 7th Earl of Harewood; KBE, 1986; m. 1949 Marion *née* Stein (diss. 1967; she later married Jeremy Thorpe); a director of the Royal Opera House, Covent Garden, 1951–3; on staff, 1953–60; artistic adviser to Edinburgh International Festival, 1961–5.

[2]John Christie (1882–1962), founder – with his wife Audrey *née* St John-Mildmay – of Glyndebourne Opera. Christie was an old friend of Bongie and the Bonham Carters often attended Glyndebourne; in 1955 Violet became a trustee of the Glyndebourne Arts Trust.

[3]Col. Sir Malcolm Stoddart-Scott (1901–73), Kt, 1957; RAMC; MP (Con.) Pudsey and Otley, 1945–50; Ripon, West Riding, 1950–73; chairman of British Group of Inter Parliamentary Union, 1951–9; chairman of Yorkshire Conservative Association, 1957–65.

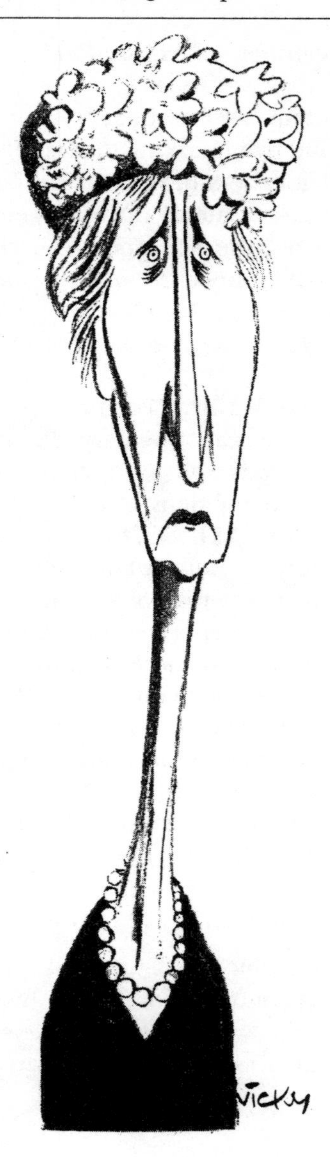

in his biography of Bonar Law, *The Unknown Prime Minister.* Their disagreement briefly blazed in the correspondence columns of *The Times* and Randolph Churchill wrote to Violet that the controversy had been the only thing worth reading in the paper for many months. Ten years on it was Roy Jenkins who came under fire, as he set about the writing of his biography *Asquith*. This filial loyalty, and the peremptory manner in which it could be displayed, was one aspect of Violet's character to be ridiculed in an unsigned article in the *New Statesman* early in December. Entitled 'Last Asquithian' it was accompanied by a full-page 'Vicky' cartoon depicting 'Lady Vi', as she was referred to throughout, looking forlorn. Having 'lived in the light of her father's sunset', it was suggested, she was now stranded in darkness, far from the 'promised land'. Gone was the narrow Edwardian world of her halcyon youth: 'the days when the world was worthy of the Liberal Party and there were parties every evening and good works every day'. She had become a 'fully conscious member of the ruling classes – without anyone to rule'. In the atmosphere of post-war Britain Violet was unmistakably the product of an earlier age and her manner must sometimes have given an impression of aristocratic condescension. But it was wrong to suggest that she lived in an idealized past. And she used such social standing as she had to fight for what she regarded as 'measures of ordinary human justice', whether at home or abroad. In December 1957 Tony Benn, alongside whom she would later march in anti-apartheid demonstrations, wrote candidly but affectionately of her: 'Although she is effusive, overpowering, goody-goody, and so much else that is awful, I still like her and admire her. She has a tremendous vitality and an unparalleled enthusiasm for life. She belongs to the "couldn't care more" brigade in contrast to so many of the bored people of today.' It was this 'couldn't care more' approach that perhaps made it 'easy to laugh at Lady Vi', as the readers of the *New Statesman* were invited to do. But even there it was grudgingly accepted that this 'Last Asquithian' was 'a very formidable lady'.[1]

Diary – Monday 13 December – 21 Hyde Park Square, W.2

... Went with B. to Raymond Mortimer's[2] party at his new & lovely house in Canonbury Place Islington. Directly the door opened on the wall-paper in the hall I knew it cld only be his.... It was very enjoyable except that much standing was involved. Eddie[3] & Raymond were seething with indignation – as was Jamie Hamilton[4] – over an odiously vulgar *New*

[1] *New Statesman*, 11 December 1954; Tony Benn, *Years of Hope*, 256.

[2] (Charles) Raymond (Bell) Mortimer (1895–1980), literary and art critic, and editor; with *New Statesman*, later *Sunday Times*.

[3] Edward Charles Sackville-West (1901–65), 5th Baron Sackville, 'man of letters' and first cousin of Vita Sackville-West.

[4] Hamish 'Jamie' Hamilton (1900–88), American-born, Scots-educated publisher, founder of Hamish Hamilton, publishers.

Statesman article about me (Jamie had already exploded to me about it in a letter). It is a 'smear' of a vulgarity one wld have thought the *N.S.* incapable. (I am alluded to throughout as 'Lady Vi' – as in what B. calls the 'Cads' Column' in the *Daily Express*.) It is instinct with an obsessional 'class-bruise' – patrician privilege being its theme. We were driven back by grace of Mary Hutchinson ... by a cousin of hers called 'Honey'. Just as we were starting M.H. called over the banisters 'I'm staying'. Then as we began getting out 'I'm coming'. I asked her what had lit the desire to stay & what had quenched it? She said she had seen Cyril Connolly[1] & longed to talk to him, then found he wanted to eat not talk, so (wisely) left him!

Diary – Tuesday 14 December – 21 Hyde Park Square, W.2

... Went to a farewell reception [for the Massiglis] at the French Embassy. Arrived very early to find the Massiglis & staff drawn up in a semi-circle ... Shane Leslie in a kilt. [Leo] Amery arrived while the ranks were still very thin! But they soon filled up & I had delightful talks with Isaiah ... & Hatchie – angrier than I have ever seen him over the *N.S.* He says that 'Vites' was beside herself & said to Ben & Nigs[2] that they must 'down pens' & never again write a line for such a paper. He said he had just come from a meeting at the London Library where Alan Pryce-Jones, Roger Fulford & Rose Macaulay[3] were boiling with indignation, particularly Rose Macaulay who expects to meet Kingsley Martin & 'tell him what she thinks'. I did not know that Hatchie cld react so violently & liked him for it.

Harold Nicolson to V.B.C. *Saturday 1 January 1955*
Sissinghurst Castle, Cranbrook, Kent

My dear Violet, Happy New Year to you, Bongey and the whole family.

Yes, Isaiah, Raymond, Rose and I signed a letter which may have been too late for insertion and which may be published next week. But if they

[1] Cyril Vernon Connolly (1903–74), literary critic and founder of *Horizon* magazine.

[2] Lionel Benedict ('Ben') Nicolson (1914–78), art historian and editor of the *Burlington Magazine*; elder son of Harold Nicolson and Vita Sackville-West ('Vites'). 'Nigs' is Nigel Nicolson, his younger brother (see Biographical notes below).

[3] Alan Pryce-Jones (1908–2000), author, journalist and critic; editor, *Times Literary Supplement*, 1948–59; director, Old Vic Trust, 1950–61. (Dame) (Emilie) Rose Macaulay (1881–1958), DBE, 1958; author and contributor to *New Statesman*.

do not publish it, then it is pretty stiff. But they must have had other letters on the same subject well in time for this issue and not to have published them is cowardly and dishonest. I know that John Sparrow wrote, because he showed me the letter. But he may not have sent it, since it concentrated on 'vulgarity' and 'Lady Vi' – which I thought not very good points, since you might as well reprove a rhinoceros for being impulsive as reprove the *New Statesman* for being a cad. But he was as angry as all of us....

You see it ought to be some solace when these things happen that so many friends are so very furious. But somehow it isn't. Bad behaviour is saddening all by itself and gives one an after-taste, as if one had scrunched a beetle when eating an apricot. But the shock passes off and one returns to the mood of judging life by its heroes, apricots by their customary savour, beauty by its eternal values, and friendship as something which has a real aesthetic as well as a moral quality. Goethe once wrote 'Life could not continue were it not so simple.' That surely is profound wisdom, since after we have been angered by a cat's cradle, we find it just another piece of string.

Bless you all, Yours ever, Harold

Diary – Friday 14 January – 21 Hyde Park Square, W.2

Papers full of trains stuck in snowdrifts – aircraft grounded – floods etc. Bright sunny sparkling day. Lunched with Puff & David Cecil[1] at H.P. Hôtel. Most amusing & delicious lunch – David in marvellous form describing the effect of bores upon him – the ex-husband of Jacquette Hawkes chief among them. Herbert Spencer used to quite frankly pull out a pair of earflaps & clap them on when bored.[2] We all wished we cld do something gentler – i.e. show an amber light. I asked him to tell the story about old Ld Salisbury,[3] David's mother saying to him in some crisis: 'But Ld Salisbury, doesn't it matter terribly?' And his replying 'Nothing matters very much.'

[1]Lord David (Gascoyne-) Cecil (1902–86), fellow of New College, Oxford, 1939–69, and Goldsmith's professor of English literature, 1948–69; younger son of the 4th Marquess of Salisbury.

[2]Herbert Spencer (1820–1903), philosopher. His use of 'earflaps' was, according to the *Dictionary of National Biography*, for precisely the opposite reason to the one given above: 'Among the peculiarities which nervous invalidism wrought in him was the use of ear-stoppers, with which he closed his ears when an exciting conversation, to which he was listening, threatened him with a sleepless night.'

[3]Robert Arthur Talbot Gascoyne-Cecil (1830–1903), 3rd Marquess of Salisbury; prime minister and foreign secretary, 1885–6; 1887–92; 1895–1900; prime minister and lord privy seal, 1900–2.

He also said on another occasion, when asked if he was not terribly worried about his decision 'No – I weigh the evidence in just the same way as I decide whether to take out an umbrella or not. If I don't take one & it rains it is not my fault.' We all went on to the Diaghilev exhibition then David left for Oxford. I went to Harrods Sale to see if I cld see anything nice ... came back thro' delicious cold still snowy air. In spite of the slush I love London under snow. Had a charming letter from John Sparrow 're' *N.S.* Dining in with B. & Ray.

V.B.C. to John Sparrow ***Saturday 15 January***
21 Hyde Park Square, W.2

Dear Mr. Sparrow....

Thank you so much for your letter & for all the trouble you have taken – which really touches me deeply. After a fortnight's delay the *N.S.* did finally 'cough up' the letter of the 4 signatories, which they had had since before Xmas. (The only sentence in it I demur to is the one in which they suggest that the paper itself has supported 'good' causes. It has always been instinct with rank defeatism on issues where a 'stand' was essential.)

I am sure your Secretary is mistaken in saying that the B.B.C. has ever referred to me as 'Lady Vi'. I am not famous enough to be mentioned by their low comedians – & in every other field of their activity they are meticulously careful to avoid lapses from austere 'respectability'. I have often heard producers of a 'discussion' implore speakers not to call each other by their Xtian names – with that dreadful hearty 'mateyness' affected by Barbara Castle & others. ('Now then Bob,' etc.) Admittedly it is not always observed – but I have never been a victim of it to my knowledge. My bitter enemies the *Expresses* have set the only precedent – in this, as in the suppression of criticism.

Thank you once more for all you have done. Ever yours Violet Bonham Carter....

Diary – Friday 1 April – 21 Hyde Park Square, W.2

Still no papers & no sign of the strike ending.[1] An abortive meeting took place in the Ministry of Labour at which the parties did not meet but each

[1] On Friday 25 March a month-long newspaper strike began, and Churchill's departure from 10 Downing Street on 5 April occurred amid a virtual newspaper blackout. Violet escaped the worst of the strike by being a subscriber to the *Manchester Guardian*, which continued to appear: copies were 'said to have changed hands on the black market in London for untold sums'.

stated their case. Dutifully went off to a small cocktail party at Barbara Bliss's in Chepstow Place – which was even grimmer than I feared it wld be.... Then home to dinner & on to Clemmie's 70th birthday party given by W. I felt a terrible pang at going & throughout – for this was Götterdämmerung – the last party they will give at N° 10 before he goes – except for Monday's dinner for the Queen. Clemmie wrote to me privately a fortnight ago that he hands in his seals of office the next day, Tuesday.

... I set off with a heavy heart – feeling as I entered that beloved house 'this is the last time I shall set foot in it with joy & pride – with the sense of home-coming it has always had for me since W. returned.' W. was alone at the door when I got to the top of the stairs – looking extraordinarily well – but I felt his emotion when he kissed me. I drifted thro' the people in the first room ... greeted Randolph – found Xtopher Soames & we sat down together & talked. He assured me in answer to my question that no one had behaved 'badly' – 'if they had he wld have fought like a tiger'.... He evidently felt no bitterness about W.'s going & said 'After all he is nearly 81. You see him at his best, but he cannot really face up to the tempo of all the routine work.'...

I saw Archie & Marigold & others – then Winston came & said 'I haven't had a word with you – we must talk' & we sat down side by side (constantly & maddeningly interrupted by people saying goodbye to him). I tried to tell him what I felt & of course he knew. He said he wld have been happy to stay till next Spring – 'But I've had my turn – a good turn. I can't keep others waiting about for ever. I wld have stayed on if there had been any chance of 4 Power meetings – but Ike won't have it. He's afraid – & there it is. I shall still exercise great influence....'.... Later he said – 'We must never get out of step with the Americans – never.' He spoke of death which I have never heard him do before. He said 'I don't really want to live very long. The spirit of man goes on eternally. But one can't live for ever.' I did not feel however that he was anywhere but in the midst of life!...

Diary – Tuesday 19 April – 21 Hyde Park Square, W.2

Very peaceful day. Got up late – worked, partly in the Square – saw a parlour-maid from Hunts (no good). Jo has a good 'press' in the *M.G.* for his speech to the Lib. Assembly. Signs of possible settlement in Press strike. Very nice letter from Harold Macmillan, to whom I wrote with a very good story about W's farewell to Anthony: 'Well – goodbye old boy. When the Election comes I mean to stand again for Woodford – probably as a Conservative.'

Diary – Sunday 24 April – 21 Hyde Park Square, W.2

Am trying to write all I can in advance of the Election – Colin Coote, *Daily Mail* & *N.C.* want articles. I don't think the very lean material will go round even if my time allowed. I groan at the idea of speaking in this Election. There is no issue – only the cold choice between 2 Govts. It is like being offered 2 plates of cold meat & asked 'ham or tongue, sir?'

The general election of 26 May 1955

The 1955 general election has been described as 'the least memorable of all the post-war contests'. That was Violet's reaction to it. Her speaking engagements were limited to an appearance at Westmorland and two in North Wales. Anthony Eden had sought a dissolution little more than a week after taking office and was confident of success. Polling day was on 26 May and the Conservatives duly increased their majority, more than trebling the margin of victory in 1951. The Labour vote fell significantly, in Attlee's last election as leader, while the Liberal vote increased, but by the smallest of margins – from 2.5 to 2.7 per cent. Although the Liberals had successfully defended the six seats that they held at the dissolution, no more had been won. And 60 of the Party's 110 candidates had lost their deposit. The Liberals seemed moribund under the leadership of Clement Davies and after the election thoughts inevitably turned to future strategy – as well as to past mistakes.[1]

Diary – Thursday 2 June – 21 Hyde Park Square, W.2

Attended a meeting of Officers at L.P.O. at 3 o'clock.... Election & future policy & tactics to be discussed. On this I asked 2 questions: (1) By how much had the Liberal vote increased? Both Fothergill (who was absent) & Ld Rea[2] claimed on the air that it had done so. It was then admitted that it had in fact fallen by 8000 – but our percentage of the national total had gone up. (2) I asked what had happened about the straight fights which C.D. had assured us were amiably fixed between him & the P.M. Fourteen had been mentioned as a possible figure. None had materialized....

Frank Byers then said that we ought to begin here & now laying the

[1] Cook, *Short History of the Liberal Party*, 134–5; Butler, *British General Elections since 1945*, 14–16.

[2] Philip Russell Rea (1900–81), 2nd Baron Rea (s. 1948); Liberal chief whip, House of Lords, 1950–5; Liberal leader, House of Lords, 1955–67; the son of the former Liberal chief whip Walter Rea.

foundations of what he called 'Operation Blackmail' for the next Election – i.e. putting in candidates whom we had the power to withdraw – who wld be prepared either to fight or not to fight, as it suited Party strategy. This wld be the only way to make terms for ourselves with the Conservatives for the next Election. Geoffrey Acland[1] declared himself opposed to any deal of any kind on any terms with anyone. I pointed out that this wld mean our having 3 instead of 6 M.P.s today – & that no one cld challenge the integrity of Arthur Holt,[2] Hopkin Morris or Donald Wade. I left before the end of the meeting. . . .

Diary – Friday 3 June – 21 Hyde Park Square, W.2

Was fetched at 2 o'clock by a B.B.C. car & driven down in pouring rain to the Haven Hôtel Poole . . . for an *Any Questions* programme – Michael Bowen, Freddy Grisewood & a very a-typical Conservative called Nabarro had arrived.[3] He was very proud of being of humble origin & told F.G. to announce him as having started life as a builder's labourer & been a private in the Army. We were later joined by A.G. Street . . . & the 4th member of the team James Callaghan. . . .

We all dined together & the conversation was painfully & tediously 'class-conscious' – one long harp on how many Etonians were in the Cabinet etc., in all of which Nabarro joined 'con amore'. According to him Miss Pat Hornsby-Smith[4] was the only sound proletarian in their set-up. He assured the Labour people (I thought quite unnecessarily) that there were rumblings of discontent & brewing storms in his own Party. We went off after dinner to a wonderful modern engineering factory – brand new (without a brick in it – or so we were assured) holding about 300 to 400 – all factory hands & their wives. We had a 'lively' programme – getting the strike as I had foreseen – as the 2nd question – i.e. 'Shld workers in nationalized Industries be allowed to strike? Ought they not to be like the police.'[5] Here we had a terrific slanging-match between Callaghan &

[1] Arthur Geoffrey Dyke Acland (1908–64), chairman of executive committee of the Liberal Party, 1954; a vice president of the Liberal Party, 1963.

[2] Arthur Frederick Holt (1914–95), MP (Lib.) Bolton West, 1951–64; Liberal chief whip, 1962–3.

[3] (Sir) Gerald (David) Nabarro (1913–73), Kt, 1963; politician, journalist, author and broadcaster; MP (Con.) Kidderminster, Worcs., 1950–64; South Worcs., 1966–73.

[4] Margaret Patricia Hornsby-Smith (1914–85), cr. life peer, 1974; MP (Con.) Chislehurst, Kent, 1950–66; 1970–4; parliamentary secretary, ministry of health, 1951–7.

[5] A rail strike was then in progress which had brought the railways to a virtual standstill. It ended on 14 June with a compromise agreement that brought increased wages for drivers. British Rail was then a nationalized industry and as well as extensive passenger inconvenience the strike had serious consequences for the economy.

Nabarro on the merits & demerits of nationalization – which was really out of order. Street then spoke in favour of differentials. I came next & pointed out the obvious difference between the old heroic strike of starving work people against Tyrannical & 'skin-flint' employers (to use a favourite adjective of Callaghan's!) & the present Inter-Union strikes of which the victims were not Bosses but the public & fellow-workers. . . .

The last question (2 minutes) was 'Why are people in the South of England surrounded by a high wall of shy reserve?' Arthur Street & I denied that they were. Callaghan – class-conscious as ever – said they were snobbish & bound by rigid class distinctions. Nabarro spoke next – I can't remember to what purpose – & as there was still time Freddy Grisewood asked Callaghan if he had anything more to say – & he returned again to the 'snob' theme saying there was far too much 'forelock touching' in the South etc. I then got in with one last punch – saying that I entirely disagreed – & that 'it takes a snob to see a snob'. This was received with thunderous applause. Callaghan attempted to reply but time was up & the programme closed. I think C. was distinctly annoyed – for he avoided saying goodbye to me! I drove back thro' the night. We missed the by-pass & drove thro' sleeping Winchester. Got back about 12.30.

Diary – Tuesday 7 June – 21 Hyde Park Square, W.2

. . . Attended a most extraordinary dinner given by Frank Owen[1] at the Hungaria. I had been asked to go by Lib. H.Q. . . . A good deal of drink was taken before dinner, then we sat down. I was between Jeremy Thorpe & Edwin Malindine (there cldn't be a nicer man & he did magnificently in North Cornwall . . .).[2] Jeremy did well at Barnstaple but he is a shade too confident & tells too many stories. He is however I must admit an amazingly good mimic. After dinner Frank Owen addressed the assembled company (seated) & said he wanted contributions from us all on the future of the Party – the methods to be adopted etc. The Election had shown a tremendous resurgence of Liberalism – Labour was demoralized etc. etc. – painting a very rosy picture with a flushed, rosy & rather gross face.

He then called on various members of the party to give their views –

[1] (Humphrey) Frank Owen (1905–79), journalist, broadcaster and author; MP (Lib.) Hereford, 1929–31; editor, *Daily Mail*, 1947–50; co-author (with Michael Foot and Peter Howard) of *Guilty Men* (1940), the bestselling indictment of the appeasers in British government in the 1930s.

[2] Edwin T. Malindine had come second at Cornwall North in 1955, just 1,604 votes behind the Conservative. In 1959 he narrowed the margin to 989 votes. He first stood as a Liberal candidate at Leyton East in 1935, and the 1955 contest was his sixth.

starting with John Arlott,[1] who did so at great length – meandering on about appealing to 'moral consciousness' etc. He had obviously had too much to drink & interrupted everybody else throughout the evening. Jeremy & Malindine were both to the point – especially Malindine – who stressed the importance of getting to grips with human issues. When I spoke I tried to stress the down-to-earth facts. Our job was to get people into Parlt. Malindine's & Bannerman's[2] near misses had been magnificent – but a miss was a bad as a mile 'qua' achieving results. Under our present electoral system we cld only hope for results in straight fights. Labour wld never give us these. The Tories wld only give them if it paid them, as well as us, to do so. We must capitalize & exploit real nuisance value. I asked Byers to expound his plan 'Operation Blackmail' which he did later in the evening.

Meanwhile Gilbert Harding[3] was asked to speak more than once & was I thought quite intolerable. . . . He has not an idea what politics are about – is determined to be anti-Conservative – does not specially want to be anti-Socialist. Described the Lib. Parl. Party (very pardonably) as 'risible' – but when he went on to describe Hopkin Morris in offensive terms I intervened & said that Hopkin Morris was a man of the highest intelligence & integrity. He then said 'another interruption!' & went away & stood in a corner of the room like a sulky child. I regretted it when he was coaxed to return. The Byerses left at one point to drive home – & a band of crooners' chorus struck up above us which competed successfully with the speakers. Lawrence Robson[4] (who was at least quiet) made an idiotic contribution – that Libs shld pledge themselves to reduce expenditure on armaments by 100 million & spend the saving on production. (This without any relation to the international situation.) John Arlott struck up again & Matthew Crosse[5] (who was quite drunk) bawled at him across the table – 'Oh John Arlott for God's sake stop talking. J. Arlott you are the bloodiest bore I ever listened to in my life. I heard the story you are telling now 25 years ago in Australia' etc. John Arlott got up & said he wld go if people wanted him to. They both went out – I hoped never to return.

[1] (Leslie Thomas) John Arlott (1914–91), broadcaster and writer, famous for his contributions on wine and sport, most notably cricket; contested Epping as a Liberal, 1955 and 1959.

[2] J. M. Bannerman came second at Inverness with 38.7 per cent of the poll, his best performance in four attempts to win the seat, 1950–9.

[3] Gilbert Charles Harding (1907–60), broadcaster, popular on radio's *Brains Trust* and later television, with *What's My Line?* He was of forthright anti-establishment views.

[4] (Sir) Lawrence William Robson (1904–82), Kt, 1982; accountant and public servant; president, Liberal Party Organization, 1953–4; chairman, Britain in Europe Committee, 1958–64.

[5] Matthew Crosse, Liberal candidate for Lowestoft, Suffolk East, in 1945, where he came third (to Labour) with 21.6 per cent of the vote.

'Vain hope & promise vain.'[1] I finally left about $\frac{1}{4}$ to 12. I have never attended such a party in my life & hope never to do so again.

Diary – Saturday 18 June – 21 Hyde Park Square, W.2

Went St. Louis.[2] Worked, read & sat out in the Square – dined in alone & did my Mother's letters. Mark's engagement in the *Times* & was rung up by *Evening Standard* asking to take a photograph – *Evening News* etc.[3] Ray lunched with me & went to Oxford for week-end.

Diary – Tuesday 21 June – 21 Hyde Park Square, W.2

Variegated & memorable day. B. & I drove to the Guildhall for the unveiling of Winston's statue. . . .[4] It depicts W. sitting back in a very 'rugged' arm-chair – his hands on the arms – a characteristic position – his head, face & expression remarkably good. He obviously likes it himself. He made an excellent & most characteristic speech. . . .

That evening I had the strange & rare experience of appearing at the Café de Paris to introduce Marlene Dietrich! They had asked me to do it some time ago – & invited me to bring a party of 4 or 6: B & I – Laura & Puff – Ray & a very nice young woman called Lady Arabella Stuart. We went about 10 – our table was alas! almost in the band – the music was non-stop & the heat & din terrific. . . . I cld not stand the din at the end of dinner & Puff & I took refuge in the relative cool of the 'lounge' which was at least quiet. I had coffee there & felt slightly revived. An official, Major Neville Willing, was in charge of me & of Marlene – & stood like a watch-dog outside the door of her dressing-room – ministering to me meanwhile. He finally at about midnight took me in to be introduced to her. She is still very beautiful – though 51. I didn't bother her by talking. We just greeted each other.

Then I went back to my table – the stage was built up – the band gave a premonitory rattle – & then ceased – the place was plunged into darkness, but for a spotlight, & I was led up onto the stage. My first reaction was

[1] An echo of Macaulay's *A Jacobite's Epitaph*: 'To my true King I offer'd free from stain / Courage and faith; vain faith, and courage vain.'

[2] Maison St Louis, a London dressmaker used by Violet.

[3] Mark had become engaged to Leslie St Just, the daughter of Condé Nast, whose marriage to Lord (Peter) St Just had been dissolved earlier that year. They were to be married in Chelsea registry office at the end of the month.

[4] The statue, then still in clay, was by the sculptor Oscar Nemon.

one of terror. I cld not see anyone or anything. I looked down into a black pit, which might have been empty, while a blinding spot-light played on me. I have rarely felt so unnerved. I then went 'over the top' & my short speech was a tremendous 'success'! – producing a loud response of laughter at all the right places etc. & ending with cheers – to my amazement.[1]

Then I left the stage & Marlene came on – & sang a series of songs – French – German – English – ending up with 'The Old Kent Road' – which was (deservedly) a furore – & brought down the house. It was terribly funny sung by her in pink chiffon dress – blue eyelids & a slight German accent! She then disappeared amid loud applause – & reappeared to my astonishment dressed as a man in evening clothes! a 'toff' with a topper & a white carnation in her button-hole. She sang 2 lovely German songs & one very good French one 'Tu me de'livrers'.

When she had finished she came to our table – kissed my hand & presented me with the white carnation from her button-hole & we – Puff & I – went up to her dressing-room & talked to her. She cld. not have been nicer – or more natural. Absolutely un-'star'-like – very matter of fact & sensible – saying 'Of course I've got no voice now'. She rather surprised me by saying she loved doing her present job. Puff extracted a signed photograph from her for 'Rita & Jim' at Catterick.[2] An extraordinary evening! I was abordéd by many strange fans....

Diary – Wednesday 29 June – 21 Hyde Park Square, W.2

...Davina Bowes Lyon dined with B. Ray & I & we went on to the Bensons' party[3] – which was a tremendous success. They had nobly turned out of their flat for the night & even had the beds moved to turn all the rooms into party space. B. & I went there on the tick at 9.30 – & soon a stream began to arrive.... I talked to George Barnes, had a very nice & long talk with Michael Astor[4] – largely about Anthony, of whom he is not a fan – &

[1] Violet's speech paid tribute to Marlene Dietrich's legendary beauty, but also to her 'integrity and courage'. She had opposed the rise of Nazism in her native Germany and, as Violet pointed out, this put her 'high up – very near the top – of Hitler's black-list of intended victims'. During the war she travelled extensively, entertaining Allied troops: 'For their delight and entertainment she even allowed herself on one occasion in North Africa to be sawn in half by Orson Welles. Well I'm sure that even one half of Marlene Dietrich would be very welcome to us all. And we should be hard put to it to know which half to choose. But tonight, thank Heaven for it, we haven't got to make that agonizing choice....'

[2] Close friends of Puff, who ran a transport café near Catterick.

[3] This was given in honour of Mark and Leslie's wedding, which was to take place next day, by Leslie's mother and step-father, Leslie and Rex Benson (see Biographical notes).

[4] Hon. Michael Langhorne Astor (1916–80), MP (Con.) East Surrey, 1945–51.

a long talk with Hugh Fraser[1] who thinks he is going to do very badly as P.M.! Cressida introduced Ray to Rose Macaulay – which was a great success. Leslie had a very pretty white lace dress & looked charming.

. . . At one stage Pss Margaret arrived looking really lovely – & Mark went to fetch me to have a word with her, as there was no one to receive her (Rex having waited downstairs for an hour & missed her & Mrs B. being in another room). I had a delicious bacon & eggs supper with Rex about ¼ to 1. Champagne was flowing freely. . . . At 1.15 B. & I made a move to go & Laura & C. dropped us home leaving a 'hard core' behind.

Diary – Thursday 30 June – 21 Hyde Park Square, W.2

Mark's wedding-day. B & I went to Chelsea Registry Office & arrived about 20 minutes before the appted hour of 3.30. There was an encampment of photographers waiting on the steps but they did not have time to erect their infernal machines – & were anyway waiting for bigger game in the shape of Mark & Leslie. The room was infinitely less bleak than Caxton Hall & much smaller. There were lots of better flowers – not too badly arranged & 2 officials rather like friendly undertakers. Nannie & Laura arrived next – Nannie most beautifully dressed in a very pretty black straw hat with a white rose, a glass handled sunshade & a fashionable film-star's bag with a stopper top – all borrowed she assured us. She wore her usual Nannie's grey & looked exactly like herself.

Next came the Bensons & then Leslie & Mark & Raymond. They staved off the photographers – promising to 'pose' when they came out. Leslie had a very pretty dress of stiff blue-green silk & a little pink feather hat. She & Mark sat down on 2 chairs opposite the Registrar with a table between. He first asked them to affirm that there was 'no just cause or impediment' etc – then they made one very simple pledge – repeating after the Registrar – & the whole thing was over in two-twos. I felt that I should not have felt 'married' after such a brief & business-like transaction. They then kissed each other very simply – Leslie taking the initiative – & went downstairs to face a battery of cameras. . . .[2]

[1] (Sir) Hugh (Charles) Fraser (1918–84), Kt, 1980; soldier and politician; with Lovat Scouts and Special Air Service, 1939–45; MP (Con.) Stone, Staffs., 1945–84; parl. under-secretary of state, war office, 1958–60; for colonies, 1960–2; secretary of state for air, 1962–4; married, 1956, Lady Antonia Pakenham (diss. 1977).

[2] After the wedding reception Mark and Leslie drove away to their honeymoon in Yugoslavia in Rex Benson's Armstrong Siddley Sapphire Jet.

Diary – Monday 4 July – 21, Hyde Park Square, W.2

Drove up with the Morans via Chartwell[1] – where he wanted to look in on W. & see how he was. We sat outside in the car & he came down to fetch us to see W. He was in bed – in a new small bedroom (with which he seemed pleased) propped up with pillows, pruning & correcting the proofs of his book *A history of the English-speaking peoples* (of which I had read the first 3 chapters when I stayed at Chartwell last summer) very neatly in red & blue ink.[2] He looked pink & well but I felt what he was feeling – in the sudden stillness of his new life. He said 'This is all I have to do now so I am staying down here. I shall motor up to vote this evening.' 'What about?' 'Oh I don't know. Something to do with Local Govt. I must help them to keep up their majority.' I said they had quite a comfortable one – nearly 60. He said 'Nearer 80.' 'Then why shld you bother to go?' 'Oh' rather wearily 'I suppose I ought to.' He said to Moran last week 'I'm paired for the whole week. What's the good of going there? one has no power.' But he was not plangent – or complaining. I felt an immense poignancy at seeing him there alone with his old MSS (it was written before the war), pruning & improving with tireless industry – but feeling the tide of events sweep by him....

Diary – Wednesday 20 July – 21 Hyde Park Square, W.2

...Ray has now decamped to Mark's flat. I miss him already more than I can say. It was heavenly to see him for a few minutes or more every night when he came in & sometimes before dinner as well – & sharing experiences. I suppose he will now come occasionally to dinner as Mark did – but it is an absolutely different relationship – like seeing a friend from time to time. One has forgotten all the things one wanted to share & tell. B. went to Dumbarton till Friday.

Diary – Thursday 11 August – 21 Hyde Park Square, W.2

Rain this morning! now a freakish event – but it soon stopped. Struggled with my post (how I miss Sheila!) sat in the Square & did some work.

[1] Violet and Bongie had spent Sunday at the Morans' house Marshalls Manor, near Maresfield in Kent. She knew Lord Moran, Churchill's physician, well and found him 'always amusingly critical of Winston!' But she later strongly disapproved of his much criticized book *Winston Churchill: The Struggle for Survival*, published the year after Churchill's death.

[2] This famous work was first published in four volumes, 1956–8.

Isaiah came in before dinner (of course over half an hour late). Ray came in later. We talked of W. – the Opera (he is now a Trustee of Covent Garden) – Russia – of which he is profoundly suspicious. He thinks they are going to make rings round us by smiles & back-slapping, conceding nothing. Anthony will fall for it – having always piqued himself on having 'a way with him' with Russia. At one point Isaiah said 'He will make no major stand – he cldn't do anything "major".' Isaiah thinks that the Middle East is the most dangerous area & the one in which a flare-up wld be most probable. They are not inhibited by nuclear considerations – for no war there wld be a nuclear war. He ended his visit with a masterly exposition of Einstein's theory for which I asked him. He said that E.'s greatest achievement was to revolutionize our concept of time & space. We used to conceive of space as a box (I still do!). . . . On his way out he said to Ray: 'When I see your Mother I want to talk to her about the gossip going on about me.' This made me regret I hadn't seen him alone. . . .

Diary – Thursday 18 August – The Glebe, Stockton

B & I walked to Codford to pick up sherry, coffee, etc., deposited by Wilson & Kennard. Called at P.O. Mr Parker is gone to my dismay! A lot of trees cut down by the bridge on the river. How I miss old familiar trees & men. We saw a delicious family of swans on the Domesday Bridge side. Gleaming white cob & pen – & 4 grey cygnets – all together on a soft green grassy verge. Then they took the water & sailed off in a procession like battleships. . . .

Diary – Friday 19 August – The Glebe, Stockton

Still, hot day – but no sun. Did a few chores & letters in the morning. . . . We were on our way up to Michael Stratton's to have sherry with him at the Manor Farm when he met us in his car & asked if we wld like to go up & see the combines at work on the top of Codford Down. I leapt at the idea. The evening sun had come up & the beauty of those fields of pure gold, like a Van Gogh picture, passes description. The red combine was driving its furrow through them in the distance – ploughing a golden road & scattering the straw in golden showers on each side of it. We passed the great amphi-theatre in the down – like a Greek theatre – & went to the very top – where I stood with Michael – a faint breeze blowing – looking down on the still, green, familiar valley – the water-meadows with our tall poplars standing sentinels – & beyond in the trees Stockton house, the square Victorian tower & the grey gables. I cld never love any bit of country more intimately & tenderly....

We watched the grain poured from a spout into another tractor – then went below & saw a vast erection (costing £20,000) where the corn was dried & stored & held – a kind of Corn Cathedral – filled with vast cylinders heated by oil. The tractor with the corn came down & tipped it out. I plunged my hand into the heap of gold. And gold it is – in the sordid sense! The 95 acre field we were in had a yield worth £3,000! ...

Diary – Sunday 24 September – 21 Hyde Park Square, W.2

Went round to see Randolph & talked to him about W. He agrees with me that he is unhappy & terribly bored. He misses power. He has no function, no raison d'être for the first time in his life. R. says that if he had a serious illness now he wld not try to live because the will to do so has left him....

Diary – Monday 17 October – 21 Hyde Park Square, W.2

...B & I were preparing for a quiet evening when I was rung up by the *Daily Herald* who asked whether I cld give them Mark's address & tel. no. as they had a 'personal matter' to discuss with him.[1] I told them that he wld never discuss 'personal matters' with the Press & asked what its nature was. He then asked me whether Mark was thinking of letting his house. I said he had only just got into it. I then discovered that they had got scent of the news that Pss M. & Townsend[2] were dining with Mark that night & wanted to get on the trail. I expressed my horror & said I wld have expected it of the Beaverbrook Press but not of them. I then tried to warn Mark. He was already at dinner....

Half-way through dinner the *Daily Sketch* came on – same technique & treatment by me. B. was amused when he heard me say 'I didn't think the *Daily Sketch* cld sink so low!' Next, to my amazement, came the *D.T.* – a 'gent' with a refined voice – called Adams. I greeted him in dulcet tones. 'The *D.T.* – is it Mr. Coote who wants to speak to me?' 'Well – no. His is another dept. I wondered if you cld tell me whether your son has moved?' 'Moved? moved where? do you mean moved to another job?' 'No, I meant his house.' 'No he hasn't moved his house – but why should it interest

[1] Mark and Leslie had just moved into their first home together.

[2] Group Captain Townsend had returned to Britain from Brussels the week before. He had not seen Princess Margaret in the preceding two years and there was intense speculation in the press about their future (Longford, *Elizabeth R*, 175–6).

you?' Then it came out. I expressed gasping amazement & horror that the *D.T.* – for which I had the honour of writing – whose Editor I admired & revered – shld behave just like the *Daily Sketch*. I mentioned the *M.G.* as a paper who wld never do such a thing – his last words to me were 'I hope you won't be rung up by the *M.G.*' I expressed complete confidence that I shld not be – nor by the *N.C.* – & both were justified. Then came the *Daily Mirror* – which I cursed up hill & down dale. A poor little under-dog said 'Thank you very much' at the end of it. Mark then rang me up. I told him all about it. He had taken off his telephone which is (luckily) under the name of Spicer. He said they were all round the house. What hell-hounds!

Diary – Monday 31 October – 21 Hyde Park Square, W.2

. . . Rushed home, changed & was called for by Puff at 7.15 to go to Royal Command Performance at the Odeon in Leicester Square: Puff had to remain in the Scrum of V.I.P.s stars etc. who were to be presented to the Queen. Many were in a foyer under blinding arclights. I meanwhile sat in peace & solitude in my seat for about half an hour. The presentations to the Queen were then televised & also some rather farcical & perhaps fortunately inaudible interviews. We then saw – first, a charming short film of Rowlandson's paintings of English life & then the film of the evening – a very bad & slow Hitchcock about a Cat Burglar.[1] We went back to the Savoy for supper with a nice young man in Ranks. . . .

We were very late & didn't come out of supper till well after one. Puff overheard someone saying something about Pss M. which sounded like 'off'. He went back & bought 2 early morning editions. They had banner headlines 'Pss Margaret decides not to marry Group Captain Townsend'. Underneath was a most poignant statement – perfectly expressed – basing their decision on the Church's teaching of the indissolubility of marriage & her duty to the Commonwealth. It is a heroic decision – & rends one's heart. She is so vital, human, warm & gay – made for happiness. And what she must be suffering doesn't bear thinking of.

Diary – Wednesday 21 December – 21 Hyde Park Square, W.2

Lunched at 1 Carlton Gardens with Harold Macmillan. The Govt reconstruction was in the papers that morning. A complete 'General Post' at the top. Butler leaves the exchequer for 'exalted brooding' – a thankless

[1] *To Catch a Thief*, starring Cary Grant and Grace Kelly.

task.[1] I think he is misguided to exchange a Dept. for what is in fact a high shelf. 'Planners' propose but departmental Ministers dispose & the Treasury is the greatest of all 'disposers'. As Cripps & others who tried it found there is no power in it. Harold Macmillan leaves the F.O. to take his place. I think this is a tragedy. He was doing brilliantly & clearly did not want to go. Julian Amery, with whom I had a word before luncheon, said that Anthony wanted to get back the F.O. under his own thumb. He (Julian) has got nothing out of the re-shuffle.

It was a vast lunch – so vast that I was able to talk to Harold privately. He was very loyal – but made no secret of the fact that he was sorry to go & that he felt no special aptitude for the Exchequer. (He said Anthony said he wanted someone to explain it to him!) He said he was beginning to build up a personal relationship with Dulles – & that in a way America was what he felt most worried about. . . .

Diary – Xmas Day, Sunday 25 December – The Glebe, Stockton

B & I & Ray went to early service. It was (miraculously) quite light – a green & orange sky – no lamps burning anywhere. Only one aisle of the church in use – the Pothecary one – & no organ music. Saw Muriel[2] Frank & Barbara. Back to 11 o'clock service (organ playing this time) with Cressida & Adam & went in afterwards to have sherry with Frank & Barbara. A tremendous Trollopian feud is raging over the Church Roof – aligned on class. The squirearchs wanting an alternative estimate to the £2,000 estimated by the Episcopal architect. 'The rest' saying nothing is too good for the House of God – & pointing to Frank's centrally heated hen-houses & Michael's Corn Cathedral, which cost £20,000. Their leader is Michael's farm manager Mr Hallett – a militant Churchman. We decided to have a mild lunch & eat our turkey in the evening. B & I went for a delicious walk towards Fisherton in the afternoon. We lit the Tree after tea & Frank came in & talked about his profit-sharing scheme for farm labourers. Then we all had our Xmas dinner by candlelight. . . . Mark rang us up from Drovers. Very happy Xmas. Ray in great form.

[1] Rab Butler left the exchequer to become lord privy seal and leader of the Commons and was replaced as chancellor by Harold Macmillan, whose post at the foreign office was taken by John Selwyn Lloyd.

[2] Muriel Yeatman Biggs *née* Swann, an old Stockton friend of Violet and Bongie, the mother of Barbara (Sykes); her husband William (d. 1952) had been a Winchester contemporary of Bongie.

SIX

The Suez Crisis

1956–1957

Diary – Wednesday 1 February 1956 – 21 Hyde Park Square, W.2

Arctic phenomenal cold here & throughout Europe. Stayed in & worked – went for short run in Park after luncheon. André Géraud (Pertinax) came to see me after tea. Still amusing & not much older.... Obviously very critical of Eden. I mentioned that he had been an excellent & expert Foreign Secretary & instanced his performance at the Geneva Conference.[1] He pooh-poohed this & suggested that Air Action by the Americans wld have saved Dien Bien Phu, but that we had refused to collaborate. I pointed out that it has since been made abundantly clear that Congress wld not have supported such action. He said 'But Congress wld not have been asked.' I tried to impress on him that neither in the U.S.A. nor here cld the Govt. take the risk of being involved in a war without the support of public opinion. The stupidity of the cleverest French people makes one despair. He was full of gossip about Clarissa & her rows with other women to which he (typically) attributes the anti-Eden movement here. B. got back from Dumbarton 2 hours late – just before midnight.

Diary – Saturday 18 February – 21 Hyde Park Square, W.2

Snowed at night. Spent the afternoon with Laura at Kew. Went into lovely spring flower house – cyclamens – camellias – blossoming trees. The

[1] At the Geneva Conference on Indochina, April-July 1954, Eden had been instrumental in securing an armistice between France and the Vietminh over their long-running conflict in Vietnam. But the arrangement left the region vulnerable to a Communist take-over and David Carlton, Eden's biographer, has questioned the achievement at Geneva: if not quite comparable to Chamberlain's at Munich, it was nevertheless 'unheroic' (Carlton, *Eden*, 352–6).

children & Didon[1] came in to tea, back from a film. Laura told me a touching story about Johnny whom she had taken out at Rowallan with Attie[2] & another young man with guns. They saw 2 snipe & shot them. Poor little Toad burst into tears of grief & horror. She took him home & tried to comfort him by assuring him that their death was instantaneous & that they had felt no pain. He said 'Yes – but they wld have had such lovely lives' & later 'It's not as if they killed them because they needed food. They killed them just for luxury.' She tried to distract him by saying 'Andrew is late. He said he was coming out to meet us.' Toad replied 'I'm glad he was too late to see the treachery of death' (such a good phrase). As Laura said, all his arguments were quite unanswerable. It gave her a realization of how we lose sight of truths & become hardened by custom to things we can't defend....

Diary – Tuesday 28 February – 21 Hyde Park Square, W.2

Went to lunch with W. Asked the butler on arrival how he was. 'Not too good this morning.' However when he came down he seemed serene & looked well – though very slow in movement & reaction & rather 'veiled' from life. He was sweet & loving & glad to see me. We lunched alone & I spent 2 hours with him. He had been in the H. of C. the day before for the F. Affairs debate & was – as ever – very loyal to Anthony – & said he made a good speech....

I spoke again with sympathy of Harold Macmillan's tough assignment. He said 'You needn't be sorry for him. He is in a position of tremendous power. If Anthony went, he wld succeed him.' I agreed that Rab had put himself in a position where he cld – & very likely wld – be by-passed. He then said 'Harold is a curious fellow. In some ways you can't depend on him.' I reacted defensively to this & said that on appeasement & United Europe he had been one of the most courageous & 'dependable' of W's adherents. He said 'Yes – but he did a very curious thing in '40 after I had taken office. He & Leo Amery went to see Ernest Bevin with proposals for some kind of Triumvirate Govt.'[3] – W. thinks headed by Ll.G. Bevin sent

[1] Hon. Diana Howard (later Hon. Mrs Faber), 'Didon' to her friends and family, the daughter of Lord and Lady Strathcona and Mount Royal; a friend of the Bonham Carters and Grimonds, she sometimes looked after Laura's children.

[2] 'Attie' (Thomas Anthony) Corbett, second son of Jo Grimond's brother-in-law Thomas Godfrey 'Billy' Corbett, 2nd Baron Rowallan. Attie had served alongside Mark Bonham Carter in northern Europe in 1945. 'Rowallan' was the Corbett family home in Kilmarnock.

[3] Seemingly a reference to the so-called 'under-secretaries' plot' of mid-June 1940, to which Leo Amery alludes in his wartime diary. Junior members of the government – including Macmillan and Bob Boothby – joined with Amery in pressing Churchill to devolve greater

them about their business saying 'Do you think I have just become a member of this Govt. in order to destroy it?' It seemed to me a most astonishing story – especially Harold's part in it. I can believe anything of Amery. W. begged me not to repeat the story....

Diary – Tuesday 13 March – 21 Hyde Park Square, W.2

...I felt disinclined to go to Quentin Crewe's party on his engagement but felt I must as I had promised & it is so gallant & unselfish of him to give it.[1] It was at Londonderry House....

I was very early & there was no one dancing when I arrived & only a few there, but a deafening band made all communication impossible. I tried to talk to Ben & others – but it was almost physical pain. Archie & Marigold arrived & I had some talk with Archie, then went down the stairs with them to go away – met Harold Macmillan & said 'Well what has happened to you all? What's up? I expect to hear that you are moving in to No 10 at any moment.'[2] He said 'I hope not – because I love N° 11 as a house.' I said 'But what's happened to you all?' He said 'The fact is we haven't got enough power to play our part in this world – we lack power everywhere.'

Diary – Wednesday 28 March – 21 Hyde Park Square, W.2

...We dined with Ann & Ian Fleming.[3] A most amusing & extraordinary evening. Party: 2 Gaitskells, Bob Boothby (rather muted & still I think

power to his ministers. They aimed at 'making wheels of the administration move faster' and not at displacing Churchill. The latter, though, gave them short shrift (Barnes and Nicholson (eds), *Empire at Bay*, 600–1, 625–6).

[1] Quentin Hugh Crewe (1926–99), writer and journalist; married, 1956, Mary *née* Sharp (diss. c. 1960); Crewe suffered from muscular dystrophy and he danced barefoot at his engagement party, because the condition made it difficult for him to balance.

[2] Anthony Eden's leadership was severely criticized in the press at the beginning of 1956 and on 7 March he gave an inept performance in the Commons in a debate on the Middle East, which was greeted with cries of 'resign' from the opposition.

[3] Ian Lancaster Fleming (1908–64), journalist on the *Sunday Times* and writer, the creator of 'James Bond'; m. 1952 Ann *née* Charteris (formerly Lady Rothermere).

a little shame faced vis-à-vis myself[1] – particularly when addressed as 'Dumpling' by Ann), Fred Warner who remained absolutely silent throughout the evening – & ourselves. I sat between Gaitskell & Ian Fleming – who was suffering from sciatica poor man & went to bed directly after dinner. Randolph then appeared & poured forth a flood of unprintable invective against Communists & homo-sexuals. Never have I heard so many words begin with 'B' repeated so often & so loud. The amusing thing about the evening was the demeanour of Gaitskell who was obviously basking & almost wallowing in it all – champagne – 'Annie' (as he called her)[2] – the foul language – the whole thing. His egalitarianism was obviously being eroded – almost exploded – before one's eyes. He must also have enjoyed the talk about Eden – the collapse of the Govt. front bench etc. Ann did not seriously try to keep its end up, but said to Randolph, more in sorrow than in anger, that it was sad to see the Conserv. Party destroying itself. Anthony was referred to as 'Jerk' by Randolph throughout....

Diary – Wednesday 11 April – 21 Hyde Park Square, W.2

Terrible last day rush.[3] Vast *Brains Trust* post – all letters on the 'personal survival after death' question. Hair waving. Trying on. When I came in late heard W. had rung me up & wanted me to ring him. I did so. He wanted me to lunch to-morrow – told him I was going away. Dine tonight? Told him Ray was coming – but he obviously wanted me to come so much that I said I wld – & wld go home early....

He came in in his grape-coloured velvet siren suit & kissed me. I admired it & said (truthfully) that I thought he was looking well.... We first talked about things at home – & in particular the steep & sudden dégringolade of the Govt. While observing complete lip-loyalty to Anthony he wld be less than human if he did not derive a little 'kick' from it. 'I feel like saying "Well you wanted me to go away. Well – I've gone away."'...

We then talked of the Middle East & the U.S.A.'s evasive references to

[1] Probably a legacy from the time when Boothby walked out of the Commons, 5 April 1954, in protest at Churchill's controversial speech on the hydrogen bomb. Violet described this at the time as 'a contemptible act' and nine months later it still rankled. She told Walter Elliot in January 1955 that Boothby's 'leaving the H. of C. when W. was being barracked had really finished him for me'.

[2] Gaitskell and Ann Fleming were in fact lovers: 'The couple used to meet for trysts at the house of Anthony Crosland .... and Ann used to joke that when she went to bed with Gaitskell, she liked to imagine she was with the more debonair Crosland' (Andrew Lycett, *Ian Fleming*, 296).

[3] Violet was leaving the following day for the Königswinter conference.

the Tripartite Agreement.[1] 'Supposing they refuse to take any action ... & supposing war flares up there (we can count the French out). Wld you be prepared for this country to "go it alone"?' He said 'I think I wld. – but it wld be very awkward if we had to fight the Israelis.'....

We talked of the decline of civilization – how differently people reacted in the past to horror, cruelty & tyranny – the Dreyfus case for instance – compared to their numb acceptance of the Slave Camps, torture & murder & deportation now. He agreed. I said 'If I cld be given 20 years of extra life I wld take it before I was born, not after I shall be dead.' He said 'No – no you wld have missed all your wonderful time with your father. For myself I don't want to go on living now.' And when I protested – 'You can see I can remember some things, not everything. I can understand & judge. But I have nothing original or creative left. No original idea.' I felt the tragedy of this.... I left sooner than he wanted – or I wanted. When I spoke of leaving him to prepare his speech he said 'I've got all to-morrow to do it in.' But I felt I must get home to Ray who was dining here – with my early start for Germany next morning. Yet I feel that every moment spent with him is as precious as jewels. And he tugs at my heart strings....

Diary – Monday 16 April – Hôtel Bristol, West Berlin

25 of us flew to Berlin [from Königswinter]. Many of the M.P.s ... had to get back for the Budget.... On arrival we were distributed in our various hôtels. I was in a very nice one called Hôtel Bristol, Grunefeld, with K. [Elliot], the Birleys, Mrs Emmet,[2] Berta [Hochberger], etc. We tidied up & went to a luncheon party given to us by Herr Willy Brandt....

We then made a tremendous tour of West Berlin in buses. It was pouring with rain & difficult to see much. The reconstruction is a miracle – compared to the days when I last saw it in '47 – a heap of rubble & ruins under snow. We were shown a lot of very boring things like gasometers etc. which are much the same everywhere. I was aching to get to the Refugee centre. This was intensely interesting – 5 to 6 hundred a day are

[1] The May 1950 'tripartite declaration' committed Britain, France and the United States to opposing the arming of Israel and the Arab states. It also held out the possibility of the three powers intervening militarily to prevent war in the region. In early 1956, though, Eden gained the impression that the Americans believed the declaration to be a dead letter, and that Britain was free to take unilateral action in the Middle East should the need arise (Bullock, *Bevin*, 776; Carlton, *Eden*, 394).

[2] Evelyn Violet Emmet (1899–1980), cr. life peer, 1964; MP (Con.) East Grinstead, East Sussex, 1955–64; chairman of the National Union of Conservatives, 1955–6.

still pouring through, bringing with them only what they stand up in. I saw & talked to men women & children. They are being dealt with [with] great imagination & humanity & no one – whatever he has done, is ever sent back.... I talked to some of the women who were joining their husbands who had already got a job in the West. The children said 'Wir gehen zum Westen' as one might say 'we are going to Heaven'....

Diary – Tuesday 17 April – Hôtel Bristol, West Berlin

We started at 9 & drove (again in pouring rain) thro' the Eastern Sector. This led us thro' the Tiergarten – much tidied up & replanted with young trees since I saw it last – & the Unter den Linden. The East is bleak & grim beyond words. The first thing one notices is the absence of advertisements. One hardly ever meets a car of any kind. The busses or trams are so small & archaic that they remind one of old English exhibitions of 'antique' out of date vehicles. The Stalin Allee is the pride of the East Zone, a long 'allee' of model workers' flats in which the pets & paragons of the régime are housed. Even here if you look down a side street you see squalor & ruins. Far less rebuilding has been done. We got out in pouring rain & looked at the vast memorial to the Soviet dead. It is impressive. We cldn't examine it in detail as we had to hurry to the Rathaus for our discussion with Herr Suhr, Willy Brandt, Parliamentarians & others....

Diary – Monday 30 April – 21 Hyde Park Square, W.2

B. went north. Tried on at Mendelssohn.[1] Went in the evening to a dinner given by Atlantic Union in Belgrave Square.... Glubb[2] (whom I had gone to hear) was quite first-rate. He speaks amazingly well. It was not 'a speech' but a quite simple talk with point & punch & truth in every word – & not one too little or too much. His major theme was that we are losing in the Middle East the war of words & of ideas. The friendship of Jordan – on which we have spent 90 millions (& the Americans 12) – has been stolen from us by the Russians & Egyptians, who have never given them a penny. Half the population are illiterate & listen to the blare of Cairo Radio....

The new War is the Govt of one country speaking to the people of

[1] Mendelssohn was a London dressmaker often used by Violet.

[2] Sir John Bagot Glubb (1897–1986), KCB, 1956; soldier, Arabist and author; a veteran of the Great War who became leader of the Arab Legion and adviser to the king of Jordan. His summary dismissal by King Hussein on 1 March 1956 greatly strained Anglo-Jordanian relations.

another. To this we are making no retort. We have been 'standing with our hands hanging at our sides'. We shld turn on a rival hose of propaganda & expose their lies.

Diary – Thursday 3 May – 21 Hyde Park Square, W.2

Lunched with H & Dorothy Macmillan at N° 11, which I had not been in for 20 or 30 years.... I sat between Harold & Leslie Rowan,[1] on Harold's right, & had a long & good talk with him. He was in very good form & said he was having a very smooth & easy passage with his Budget. We did not discuss it. He complained of being called 'Edwardian' because he belonged to an age where people thought it right to try & finish their sentences & attached some importance to form. Looking back on the past we both agreed that then Parlt was the real seat of power – now it had passed to the T.U.s. He was full of apprehension about the industrial future....

Harold told me one good W. story. During the '45 Parlt a Tory M.P. Colonel sat beside him in the Smoking Room & said 'Well, Attlee's coming on. He really made a good statesmanlike speech today.' W. (grunting) 'Do you think so?' The Colonel repeated & elaborated his opinion. W. 'Have you ever read Maeterlinck?"[2] The Col. 'No' (rather blankly). W. 'If you read Maeterlinck's *Life of a Bee* you will see that if you feed a grub on Royal Jelly – even a grub becomes a Queen'....

Diary – Saturday 19 May – Mottisfont Abbey, Romsey, Hampshire

Marvellous weather. Mottisfont looking a dream of beauty.... Lots of talk with Oliver [Lyttelton].... He had an amusing a/c of W. cross-examining Rab about a pamphlet which was being issued from Conserv. H.Q. – W. 'Is it simple?' Rab 'It sells at 3^{d} & is being circulated by etc. etc.' W. 'I ask – is it simple?' Rab 'I can assure you it is so simple that I can't understand it.' (Rare wit from Rab.) Oliver's summing up of Anthony & Rab's common deficiencies: 'They have neither of them ever been inside White's Club – or ever got drunk in their lives.' The only difference between them is – women. Sat out all day & went for usual river walk with Moira. B. arrived Sat. morning & the Brands soon after.

[1]Sir Leslie Rowan (1908–72), KCB, 1949; parliamentary private secretary to Churchill and to Attlee, 1941–7; second secretary, HM Treasury, 1951–8.

[2]Maurice Maeterlinck, *The Life of a Bee* (trans. Alfred Sutro; 1908).

Diary – Saturday 30 June – Birch Grove House, Sussex

The Queen coming to Glyndebourne. It was my night in the Box so John Christie asked me to combine with him.... *Figaro* was perfect as ever. The Queen had not read up her programme & was obviously considerably worried by the plot – which John tried to elucidate from time to time. The audience behaved perfectly – never turning round to look at her once. The row immediately in front keeping their nuques steadily turned. There was no crowding or apparent notice when we all went in to dinner. That at least had been arranged....

After the last Act we went into the Great Hall where Ebert,[1] the conductor & the company were presented to her & Pss Margaret. I discovered afterwards that Ebert had no idea that she was coming that night! John had never mentioned it to him! We had some difficulty in finding the car. I asked Moucher if she (H.M.) had enjoyed it. She said she thought she had, but that she was <u>very</u> practical & had probably been worried by being unable to unravel the plot! She is of course not half as musical as Pss M. We drove back to Birch Grove had more supper & went to bed.

Diary – Sunday 1 July – Birch Grove House, Sussex

.... We drove up after dinner [to London] in Harold's Ministerial car – he 'on the box' & we inside. I had a feeling that he was <u>terribly</u> overburdened & overcast. He had had to do [ministerial] boxes till 3.30 this morning & prepare an important speech for the H. of C. directly he woke up. I didn't like to talk to him about politics at all.... He looked tired to me & rather dispirited – not (I felt) 'enjoying' office at all. He feels the decline of power in politicians & indeed of Parlt (as who wldn't?) & commented again on being called 'Edwardian' because he tries to finish his sentences....

There has been a tragic rising in Poland at Poznan, where the World Fair is being held.[2] Hundreds of workers marched in a peaceful procession asking for 'Bread'. Their wages & living standards are desperate. They were fired on by the Security Police & desperate fighting ensued. Some of the

[1] (Anton) Charles Ebert (1887–1980), opera director; artistic director and producer, Glyndebourne Opera, 1934–59; producer, Edinburgh Festival, 1947–55.

[2] On 28 June 1956 some 50,000 workers marched in Poznán demanding 'bread and freedom'. Frustration at the slow pace of political reform in Poland lay behind the protest and in the ensuing riots the security police and Party offices were targeted. Order was restored by the military, leaving fifty-three demonstrators dead and more than 200 injured. The rioting stimulated the pro-democracy movement in Hungary.

soldiers handed over rifles & tanks to them. There has been heavy fighting & casualties – no one knows how many. The ice is breaking – but alas there is blood beneath it.

The Suez crisis

In 1954 Anthony Eden, then foreign secretary, reached a compromise with the Egyptian president, General Nasser, over the timing of Britain's military withdrawal from the Suez canal. The last troops would be due to leave in June 1956, while the waterway itself would be operated until 1968 by the Suez Canal Company, over which Britain had financial control, and in which France had a substantial interest. The deal was unpopular with the 'Suez Group' of Conservative backbenchers, who accused Eden of appeasing Egyptian nationalism at the expense of British influence in the Middle East. But Eden defended the withdrawal as a strategic necessity, which he hoped would be offset by improved relations with Egypt. The hope proved illusory and instead the two countries continued to regard one another with mutual suspicion. This culminated in Nasser's nationalization of the canal on 26 July 1956, in direct retaliation for the withdrawal by Britain and America of an offer to help finance the building of the Aswan Dam. Nasser's action was greeted with fury in Britain, where he was depicted as a megalomaniac dictator who threatened the peace of the Middle East. Feeling at Westminster ran strongly against 'appeasement'. Violet shared in the general indignation, but stopped short of believing that the use of force by Britain could be justified. Nasser had promised to compensate shareholders and keep the canal open to international trade, and in these circumstances she reluctantly accepted an audacious *fait accompli*. Eden's cabinet, though, did not. In August plans were made for a combined military operation with the French, who were eager to topple Nasser over his support for the rebellion against France in Algeria. Britain and France also colluded with Israel and at a highly secret meeting at Sèvres, 22–24 October, representatives of the three governments agreed the detail of a plan of attack on Egypt. Israel duly launched a preemptive strike against its hostile neighbour on 29 October, whereupon Britain and France issued – on the pretext of protecting the canal – an ultimatum to both powers to cease fire and accept a temporary Anglo-French occupation of the canal zone. When Egypt refused British planes began bombing Egyptian airfields, 31 October, in preparation for an Anglo-French invasion on 5 November. The Egyptian military offered less resistance than Eden had expected, but the international community quickly deployed its forces, and this determined the outcome. On 30 October Britain and France were forced to veto a Security Council resolution condemning the Israeli aggression. They could not, though, prevent the whole matter from being referred to the General Assembly, which voted overwhelmingly on 2 November for an immediate ceasefire. On 6 November, under extreme pressure from the United States government, Eden announced a unilateral ceasefire. France reluctantly followed the next day. The Anglo-French invasion thus ended, almost as soon as it had begun, in diplomatic humiliation: neither Britain nor France was permitted to participate in the United Nations peace-keeping force later sent to the region. The Suez crisis obsessed Violet as much as Munich had done nearly twenty years earlier: once again she felt intense shame over her government's actions, which she believed would have far-reaching and detrimental consequences for Britain. Her anger was intensified by the knowledge that Suez had provided the Soviet Union with cover for its brutal repression of Hungary. She laid the blame for the débâcle squarely, if not entirely fairly, at Anthony Eden's door, but she was not insensitive to the tragedy of his long-awaited premiership careering to a disastrous conclusion.[1]

Diary – Friday 27 July – 21 Hyde Park Square, W.2

... Bomb Shell in the morning papers. Nasser has seized the Suez Canal – breaking the agreement which does not lapse till '68. It is clearly a reprisal for the Anglo-American refusal to finance the dam. Great indignation in all parties in the H. of C. Paget compared him to Hitler.[2] Anthony pledged himself to act with 'firmness & care' – & said he was in touch with France, America & the Commonwealth & all other Govts affected. I don't know what effective steps we can take....

[1] Carlton, *Eden*, 356–9, 403–65; Gilbert, *Never Despair*, 914, 945, 1036.

[2] Reginald Thomas Paget (1908–90), cr. life peer, 1974; MP (Lab.) Northampton, 1945–74. 'Is the Prime Minister aware that this is a threat to strangle the whole industry of Europe? Is he further aware that this "weekend technique" is precisely the technique which we got used to in Hitler's day?' (*Hansard*, vol. 557, cols 779–80).

Diary – Monday 30 July – 21 Hyde Park Square, W.2

B. left Dumbarton en route for Stornoway at 11. I worked & had Mr Elath to see me at 6 about my visit to Israel. I shall go, but am not sure whether to do so in October or March – when the flowers are out. The political situation is the only argument for going in October. We discussed Suez. It is quite clear that the U.S.A. is 'dragging its feet'. The French are inflamed & wld I think like us to re-occupy the Canal Zone. The Suez Group wld be all for the same course. The irony of the situation is that the U.S.A. has put the fat in the fire by their abrupt refusal to finance the dam (we tagging along behind) & now they expect us to pull out the chestnuts. (Election year – American boys abroad – etc.) I feel unconvinced that the sanctions announced – freezing Egyptian credits, stopping export of arms etc. – will cause Egypt much discomfort. The French have 450 million invested there – so they must lose more than they gain by any punitive economic measure. What else remains to be done short of 'using force'? And what does that mean? Re-occupying the Canal Zone?

Diary – Tuesday 31 July – 21 Hyde Park Square, W.2

Terrible Lib. P. Committee. No one agreed on anything. Jo – describing himself as the Capt. Waterhouse[1] of the Lib. Party – is in favour of 'going it alone' & landing troops in the Canal Zone. He says Nasser's action is the parallel of Hitler's when he invaded the Rhineland & that unless we bring about his fall the whole Middle East will go his way – nationalize their oil, threaten to cut us off, etc. I think this is true.[2] Yet I hardly feel that we can 'go it alone' & align world opinion against us. . . .

Diary – Monday 6 August – Chartwell, Kent

After doing what work I cld without typing help I left for Chartwell by a 3.48 train. . . . Winston said he had lunched with Anthony & Clarissa, who were living in one room at Chequers (oil-heating is being installed). We talked about the Suez situation & I told him that I was gravely disturbed by all the sabre-rattling. What does 'using force' mean? 'It cannot surely mean that we are going to invade Egypt?' He replied: 'Yes – that's what

[1] Captain Charles Waterhouse (1893–1975), served in the Great War; influential Conservative backbencher, first elected in 1922; MP for East Leicester, 1950–7; Waterhouse symbolized Conservative opposition to the policy of 'scuttle' in Egypt.

[2] Much later Violet amended this to 'may be true'.

the Govt mean to do.' I said 'They are mad – they will align the whole public opinion of the world against us – risk Russian intervention & break our word – pledged by our signature to the U.N. Charter, by whom we run the risk of being branded as an aggressor. I cannot imagine a greater blunder.' W. seemed surprised at the mention of the U.N. – almost as tho' he had forgotten its existence. He said slowly 'Yes – there is the U.N.'[1] We discussed the debate.[2] I feel a slight delicacy in telling him what I think of Anthony because tho' I am sure he agrees in a large measure, he is so loyal that I feel I am putting him in a hole....

Diary – Thursday 16 August – Mottisfont Abbey, Romsey, Hampshire

...A nice old General Russell aged 82 with son & daughter-in-law came to dinner. I talked to him afterwards – very amusing & vital. Loves *Over the Bridge*[3] to my surprise – is a Die-Hard Tory (not however an admirer of Eden) & most surprising of all was at Sandhurst with W. – exactly his age. He says he was bumptious – 'held forth' – & was considered a bore by most people. In no sense considered a remarkable young soldier of promise. The General 'rather liked him', in spite of his jaw, because of his intense keenness. One day W. said to him 'Now I am known as the son of my father. It may be that one day it will be the other way round.' Amazing prescience! & what unshaken confidence in himself, for he had had nothing in life to encourage him. To a contemporary it must have seemed insane megalomania.

Diary – Wednesday 17 October – 21 Hyde Park Square, W.2

Worked all day. Dined with Mark & Leslie. He has had talks with Oliver Poole[4] about possibly joining the Conserv. Party. I was strongly in favour of this when W. was there but this is the last moment I shld choose to do it. I am sorry for Mark. Politics is his vocation & he has a real gift for it. It is cruel that he shld be compelled to enter politics if at all under a flag which is not really his own & under a leader about whom he has no illusions....

[1] Violet wrote to Bongie the following day about her Suez talk with Churchill: 'Alas! he is no longer the man he was – or I shld feel more hope in working through him.'

[2] There had been a debate on Suez in the House Commons on 2 August.

[3] Richard Church, *Over the Bridge: An Essay in Autobiography* (1955).

[4] Oliver Brian Poole (1911–93), cr. 1st Baron, 1958; MP (Con.) Oswestry, Salop, 1945–50; chairman, CPO, 1955–7; governor, Old Vic, 1948–63.

Diary – Sunday 21 October – 21 Hyde Park Square, W.2

Peaceful day (after a wonderful night). Walk in the Park. Went after dinner to see the Bolshoi on T.V. at the B.B.C. in the D.G.'s room. Not as good as the film. Extraordinary events in Poland & Hungary.[1] Poland seems to be winning all along the line. Russian troop movements have been halted. Russian ships denied entry to Danzig – Kruschev, Molotov . . . sent back to Moscow within 2 hours, after they arrived uninvited by plane, Rosokowsky deposed from the Cabinet, Gomulka acclaimed by the people. In Hungary there are riots in the streets & rumours of violence. It is difficult to know exactly what is happening – but it sounds more threatening. Alas! Nagy is no Gomulka.[2]

Diary – Monday 22 October – 21 Hyde Park Square, W.2

. . . Hungarian tumult grows. It looks as tho' the ice were breaking up all over Europe. The thaw will dissolve the satellite Empire. It is a thrilling moment.

Diary – Tuesday 30 October – 21 Hyde Park Square, W.2

Israel – which has been mobilizing for some days – & to whom Eisenhower addressed a stiff warning – has invaded Egypt. I went to Lib. Soc. Council to hear Samuel. His speech was mainly an account of the provocation Israel suffered & of her record of achievement. Nothing suggested of the action to be taken. The obvious step wld be to invoke the Tripartite Treaty. (But this wld not suit him as it wld mean defending Egypt against Israel.)

A few moments before he got up to speak Philip [Lord] Rea brought in a slip of paper from the H. of Lords with the news that at 4.30 in the H. of C. Anthony had informed the House that we were issuing an ultimatum to Egypt & Israel, to expire in 12 hours (by 4 p.m.), that unless they ceased fire & kept 10 miles from the Canal we & France shld intervene. In any

[1]The workers' rebellion in Poznán in Poland, in June 1956, stimulated resistance to Soviet rule and in October Wladyslaw Gomulka (1905–82), the former Polish Communist leader purged for being anti-Stalin, was reinstated as head of government. These events encouraged the nascent people's revolution in Hungary and on 24 October Imre Nagy (1896–1958), the reforming prime minister deposed in 1955, was also reinstated.

[2]In fact Nagy paid with his life for trying to free his country from Soviet control – he was executed after a secret trial in 1958 – while Gomulka, who ruled until 1968, lived to disappoint the reformers who had backed him in 1956.

case we meant to occupy Port Said, Suez & Ismailia to protect it. If Egypt refused we shld do so by force. It sounded to me like rank insanity. I do not see how we can defend it to the world – nor have I any idea whether we have taken counsel with U.S.A. As the Security Council is in session at this moment Gaitskell very sensibly suggested that we shld postpone any action for 48 hours until the matter had been submitted to them. This Anthony refused.

Diary – Wednesday 31 October – 21 Hyde Park Square, W.2

Our ultimatum has of course been rejected by Egypt. Meanwhile the agony of Hungary goes on – for the moment it looks as if they were winning. Nagy is acceding to their demands.[1] I must re-write my whole U.N.A. speech for Felixstowe – on Friday. I am convinced that we have made the biggest blunder in our history.

Diary – Thursday 1 November – 21 Hyde Park Square, W.2

Darling Bett [Asquith] came to luncheon. I cannot think of anything but the political situation. It obsesses me as nothing has done since Munich. I think the Govt. are mad. Anthony is author & begetter of this plan. He has always hankered after 'using force' since he was thwarted on 2nd Aug. – when I was at Chartwell. Things weren't ready militarily – or he wld have pushed the button then. They have been made ready since & the Israeli invasion gave him his chance....

Diary – Saturday 3 November – 21 Hyde Park Square, W.2

Went to Felixstowe yesterday for U.N.A. meeting. Stayed with a charming Mrs Clement Smith at a lovely old house outside the town called Walton Hall. Good meeting of about 700 – about half staunch Tories.... I denounced the whole Suez adventure in the most uncompromising terms. (I had warned my hosts that I shld do so & I was luckily covered by a U.N.A. Executive resolution passed on Wed. which took the soundest possible line.)... The Tories in the meeting were stunned & asked many bewildered & resentful questions – countered by Liberal & Labour questions. We finally passed a resolution supporting that of U.N.A. I returned this morning – very tired....

[1] On 30 October Nagy ended single-party rule in Hungary.

Diary – Sunday 4 November – 21 Hyde Park Square, W.2

...All through the day B & I & Ray listened to the most agonizing broadcasts from Hungary – now being crushed by Soviet forces – tanks are moving in everywhere & a massacre is going on.[1] All youth is rising & being mown down. Children are hurling grenades at tanks. It is an extraordinary example of sublime courage against hopeless odds. Heart-rending. One feels guilty at one's impotence – & our folly has distracted the attention of the world from this tragedy. I cannot forgive it.

Diary – Monday 5 November – 21 Hyde Park Square, W.2

We have landed troops – airborne & parachutists, & also sea-borne – & captured Port Said. We have been condemned as aggressors by a vote of 65 to 5 & ordered to cease fire by the [UN] Assembly. Only Australia & N.Z. supported us, the French & Israel. Russia also condemned.[2] We stand together in the dock.... Wrote a letter to the *Times* & sent it by hand in the morning – unable to contain my feelings....

V.B.C. to the Editor, *The Times*

Monday 5 November
21 Hyde Park Square, W.2

Sir, – I am one of millions who watching the martyrdom of Hungary and listening yesterday to the transmission of her agonized appeals for help (immediately followed by the description of our 'successful bombing' of Egyptian 'targets') have felt a humiliation, shame and anger which are beyond expression. At a moment when our moral authority and leadership are most direly needed to meet this brutal assault on freedom we find ourselves bereft of both by our own Government's action. For the first time in our history our country has been reduced to moral impotence.

We cannot order Soviet Russia to obey the edict of the United Nations which we ourselves have defied, nor to withdraw her tanks and guns from Hungary while we are bombing and invading Egypt. To-day we are

[1] On 4 November massive Soviet forces suppressed the Hungarian revolution. In response Nagy withdrew Hungary from the Warsaw Pact and proclaimed the country's neutrality, seeking assistance from the United Nations. None was forthcoming and by 14 November the Hungarian resistance had ended.

[2] On 4 November the UN General Assembly called upon the Soviet Union to withdraw all of its forces from Hungary at once. The resolution was passed amid reports of Russian planes bombing Budapest (*The Times*, 5 November 1956).

standing in the dock with Russia. Like us she claims to be conducting a 'police action'. We have coined a phrase which has already become part of the currency of aggression.

Never in my life-time has our name stood so low in the eyes of the world. Never have we stood so ingloriously alone. Our proud tradition has been tragically tarnished. We can restore it only by repudiating as a nation that which has been done in our name but without our consent – by changing our Government or its leadership.

Yours faithfully, Violet Bonham Carter

[Diary continues]

Went on to cocktail party at Gilbert Longden's[1] to meet Lilo Milchsack.... Poor Lilo disturbed at being pitch-forked into this volcano. Feeling in Germany is running high against us. Profound disillusionment. They had written the French off, but they believed in us.

Diary – Tuesday 6 November – 21 Hyde Park Square, W.2

My letter published in the *Times* just under one signed by Portal, Alanbrooke & Cunningham asking for no criticism while our troops were in action.[2] (I have written to Portal[3] about it.)

Lib. Party Committee – Lilo & Sir John Slessor[4] came to have sherry. He feels just as I do. I asked him to make some public demonstration but he is still on the active list & can't. The struggle now is to get us out of Egypt. The Govt. are stalling on the U.N. directive to cease fire. We turned on the 7 o'clock news & it said that a Cease Fire had been accepted by ourselves the French & the Israelis. Lilo & I were overwhelmed with relief. Poor Slessor put his head in his hands & said 'I can't bear it. As a Service Man I can't bear this humiliation.'...

[1] Sir Gilbert (James) Longden (b. 1902), Kt, 1972; MP (Con.) South West Herts., 1950–74; UK representative to the Council of Europe, 1953–4.

[2] The letter from the three service chiefs – Air Marshal Lord Portal, Field Marshal Lord Alanbrooke and Admiral Lord Cunningham – asked: 'Cannot the nation unite, at least temporarily, in wishing our forces complete and speedy success in their operations?'

[3] Charles Frederick Portal (1893–1971), cr. Viscount, 1946; OM, 1946; marshal of the RAF; chief of air staff during second world war. He and Violet afterwards engaged in a brief but lively correspondence about the expression of public dissent during time of war.

[4] Sir John Cotesworth Slessor (1897–1979), GCB, 1948; distinguished airman, marshal of the RAF, 1950; chief of air staff, 1950–3.

Diary – Wednesday 7 November – 21 Hyde Park Square, W.2

An enormous post of between 50 & 60 letters about my *Times* letter – mostly of ardent support – saying 'you have expressed our feelings exactly'. Many from Conservatives. About 8 calling me a traitor & saying I ought to be shot & shld be if I were in Hungary! (I hope I should.) Lunch at Lord Simon's[1] at Marsham Court to talk about Commercial T.V. . . . but we cld talk of nothing but the situation. I was told that Gaitskell had read my letter aloud in the H. of C., addressing himself to Winston. . . .[2]

Diary – Thursday 8 November – 21 Hyde Park Square, W.2

I lunched with W. & Clemmie. . . . Julian Sandys (nice son of Duncan – about 17) & Lady Norah (ex-Brassey & ex-Graham) were there so I did not see him alone & he greeted me rather coolly. . . .

I asked to see Toby the Budgerigar & he was brought down to hop about the table & perch on my finger & do his tricks. This made a slight détente & I was able to say to him, 'under cover' of the noise: 'I wrote my long letter to you in long-hand because I thought it was not suitable for dictation. I hope it was clear?'[3] He said 'Yes – it was beautifully written.' 'Are you applying the word "beautiful" to the calligraphy or to the "content"?' W. – with one of his old Puckish smiles – 'To the calligraphy.' I went on teasing him a little. 'I hear Mr Gaitskell read one of my letters aloud to you in the H. of C. That was very good for you. Shall I send him another to read to you?' He was now smiling & enjoying it: 'No. I don't want you to.' We parted quite sunnily when he went off to the H. of C.

When he had gone Clemmie said she thought my letter rather violent. She preferred the one above it signed by the 3 Chiefs of Staff saying there shld be no criticism while our troops were in action. I pointed out that they had in fact been out of action a few hours after my letter had been printed – but that I did not agree that there shld be no criticism of an unjust war. She said something about 'Well I think when one's country is

[1] Ernest Darwin Simon (1879–1960), cr. 1st Baron Simon of Wythenshawe, 1947; MP (Lib.) Withington, 1923–4, 1929–31.

[2] Addressing himself to Churchill, Gaitskell quoted about two-thirds of Violet's *Times* letter, and observed: 'He cannot really feel happy that one of his oldest friends should have been compelled to write in the terms which I have read' (*Hansard*, vol. 560, cols 37–38).

[3] On 3 November Churchill had issued a public statement of his support for the government over Suez and Violet was deeply upset, writing him a long letter of remonstrance the next day: 'I imagine that you have acted in response to appeals from ex-colleagues (now in a pit which they have dug, not only for themselves, but alas! for our country)' (VBC to WSC, 4 November 1956).

in a jam'. Had we been alone I shld have reminded her that it was 'a jam' – & the criticism of that 'jam' – which brought W. to power. When I said something about the Commonwealth being split she said 'Oh Violet, you do look on the dark side of things!' I replied that I read the news & cld if necessary quote the comments of the various Commonwealth P.M.s. . . .

Diary – Friday 9 November – 21 Hyde Park Square, W.2

U.N.A. Meeting at the Kingsway Hall. Speakers: myself, Arthur Henderson,[1] John Altrincham[2] & a Professor – an expert on Hungary. The Hall was not quite full & there were many dissentient Tories. Some had asked & been refused permission to speak – & they interrupted Arthur Henderson's speech several times though he made a very mild & unprovocative one. I was much stronger & more uncompromising in seizing & brandishing nettles – but I got along very well & aroused a strong 'Liberal' element who applauded loud & long. I led the Tories down the garden path by saying that of course we had been told that this was not a war. The P.M. had told us & told us truly that he had always been a 'man of peace'. (Tory applause.) He had not now become a man of War. (More Tory applause.) He had only become a man of 'Armed Conflict'. I had no more trouble with the meeting after that. John Altrincham was up & doing very well when alas I had to hurry off to Kingsway – T.V. House – to be televised. . . .

V.B.C. to Nigel Nicolson *Saturday 10 November 21 Hyde Park Square, W.2*

Personal

My dear Nigel – I must write you a line of heartfelt congratulation & relief at your action.[3] (I only wish you had been able to come to the

[1] Arthur Henderson (1893–1968), cr. life peer, 1966 (Rowley); Labour politician, first elected to parliament 1923 (South Cardiff); MP for Rowley Regis and Tipton, 1950–66.

[2] John (Edward Poynder) Grigg (b. 1924), son of 1st Baron Altrincham – Grigg renounced his peerage in 1963 after the passage of the Peerage Act of that year; writer and political commentator; contested Oldham West (Con.), 1951 and 1955; editor, *National and English Review*, 1954–60; columnist, the *Guardian*, 1960–70; biographer of Lloyd George.

[3] Nigel Nicolson was one of eight Conservatives who abstained in a vote of confidence in the government over Suez, 8 November. He had been under intense pressure to support the government and by refusing to do so effectively ended his political career: 'There can be few people who can identify the single most important moment in their lives. For me it was undoubtedly at 10 p.m. that evening when I sat in the House of Commons library as the division bells started to ring and Members trooped into the lobbies to vote' (Nicolson, *Long Life*, 165–6).

U.N.A. meeting at the Kingsway Hall last night. You wld have got a great reception.)

I am sure that you must be feeling much happier than you did when we met on Monday – in spite of the pain & embarrassment of the cleavage with your friends & – perhaps – the failure of some of them to understand your position & action. The only purpose of politics (or so it seems to me) is the expression of one's own deepest convictions – & their translation into facts. If one is to become a conscript of the Party Machine one might just as well join the Army. I am sure that this is an issue which – like Munich – has convulsed the conscience of the country. The present Govt. does not seem to recognize this fact. . . .

What is even stranger is that a man like Eden, who has spent his life immersed in foreign affairs, should be so impervious, or indifferent to our honour & good repute throughout the world. I do not believe that we shall ever recover them while he remains the titular leader & symbol of this country. His going wld be the 'outward visible sign' of our 'inward spiritual grace'.

But will he 'go quietly'? or at all? It is so sad that neither Harold nor Butler resigned. There is no 'Winston' in the bush. Once more my congratulations. Ever yrs Violet. . . .

Nigel Nicolson to V.B.C. ***Monday 12 November***
House of Commons

Dear Lady Violet,

How kind of you to write. My goodness, it is strange, isn't it? Here is a political party which has made a dogma out of the United Nations and respect for the spirit of its Charter. In fact, Anthony Eden wrote most of it himself. And without even a tremor, it suddenly chucks the whole thing aside, and a week later (feeling perhaps a little guilty under the lash of your letter to *The Times*) starts claiming that it had done the U.N. a good turn!

What has so appalled me is the facility with which good men have matched this bad deed with their principles – it must have needed Procrustean labour on Gilbert Murray's part.[1] Most of my constituents, besides swallowing the Govt. case whole, simplify the whole issue into 'loyalty to the boss'. In their eyes the Conservative Party is like a Regiment – you

[1]Murray was one of a number of senior Oxford dons who signed a letter to *The Times*, 6 November, expressing support for the government over Suez. Violet was amazed that Murray, who for so long had been her ally in fighting for liberal causes, should act in this way. She wrote him a characteristically strong letter of surprise and disappointment.

don't disobey the Colonel under fire, or you will get shot by your own side. By these standards, I have committed an unforgivable sin, and I don't think that I shall politically survive it – at least not in Bournemouth, and probably not in the Conservative Party. I was saying to Jo tonight, that I simply don't recognise it as the Party I joined. What on earth has happened to it? And to Harold and Butler?

I shall remember that phrase: 'The only purpose of politics is the expression of one's own deepest convictions – and their translation into facts.' That's just what I feel. And I shall always be grateful to you for steeling me on the night before the vote.

Your sincerely, Nigel Nicolson

Diary – Monday 26 November – 21 Hyde Park Square, W.2

. . . Horrible expulsions of English subjects – Maltese, Cypriots, Jews – are taking place in Egypt – the first bad tactical mistake Nasser has made. They are only allowed to take £20 out with them. As one old woman said pathetically to the *Times* correspondent in the plane '<u>This</u> is what they call protecting British lives & property.' Petrol rationing is forecast & shortage has begun. The London streets are like a desert. One buzzes through clear roads in a few minutes & gets everywhere too early! People with cars are beginning to think Suez <u>may</u> have been a mistake.

Diary – Monday 3 December – 21 Hyde Park Square, W.2

It now looks as tho' we were definitely going to clear out of Suez – waiving our conditions – an immense relief. There is an outcry from the Suez Group. They are all making mad-dog Anti-American speeches.[1] A spate of lunacy has been & is being poured out. . . .

Diary – Wednesday 5 December – 21 Hyde Park Square, W.2

Debate in H. of C. for which I luckily got a ticket in Strangers' Gallery.

[1] Violet wrote to Churchill urging him to use his influence to 'drown the yappings of the mad-dog pack': 'We are going to need American support and help – moral, material, economic – as never before. Your voice would reach and reassure them as no other could.' Churchill declined to intervene and wrote to her on 18 December: 'I think the moment has passed. I hope so.'

Uproarious House during questions. Walter Monckton made a statement on Suez casualties.... Then Selwyn Lloyd spoke – defending the Govt.'s action – amid a Babel of interruptions. He pretended to deal with collusion but evaded the issue – giving a long list of Israeli raids etc. & saying that of course the Govt feared & expected trouble. They had warned Israel against attacking Jordan. He did not explain why they had not been warned not to attack Egypt....

Then Bevan followed in a really masterly speech. I had never heard him 'good' before & was astonished at his performance. He was witty – almost 'urbane' – yet devastating, speaking very quietly & heard without interruption. Megan was sitting some rows behind me & caught my eye with sympathetic ecstasy! It was a really remarkable Parliamentary triumph & changed my estimate of his potential power (though it did nothing to reassure me about the way it might be used!)....

Diary – Thursday 6 December – 21 Hyde Park Square, W.2

Went to Hopkin Morris's Memorial Service at St Margaret's. Butler & Gaitskell there – Gaitskell sitting one off me. As we came out we had a short talk. I said 'There was not much left of them last night. I wish I were going to hear you to-night.' He said 'Well there isn't much left to say'.... I said that only Butler cld succeed Eden & that apart from being anathema to the Suez Group there seemed to be a general impression that he was 'slimy' & a hypocrite. G. said 'Yes he is, but not half such a hypocrite as Eden. At least he doesn't actually lie & Eden does. I wld rather have Butler a thousand times.' He evidently feels an intense dislike for Eden. He then said that the reaction in the country to the Suez issue had been most disappointing. I agreed & said how amazed I was that this shld be so....

Mark & Leslie dined. Leslie says that both Rex & her mother are 'unsound' – both adore Anthony (a very rare symptom). Lord Portal had said to her mother 'Poor little Leslie! – in that nest of vipers'! This infuriated her – suggesting as it did that she was wholly influenced by Mark, & Mark by me!... Mark had also had a crisp difference of opinion with the Queen Mother, who is of course thoroughly unsound. She didn't like it at all when he said that EOKA wld have done the landing better!...

[1]Sir Walter Turner Monckton (1891–1965), KCVO, 1937; cr. 1st Viscount, 1957; politician and lawyer – attorney-general to the Prince of Wales (King Edward VIII), 1932–6, and confidant to the king at the time of his abdication, December 1936; MP (Con.) Bristol West, 1951–7; paymaster-general, October 1956-January 1957.

Diary – Tuesday 11 December – 21 Hyde Park Square, W.2

...*Othello* at Covent Garden. B & I determined to see it after hearing the last Act broadcast. There was a most moving Desdemona called Bronwenstein who sang wonderfully. In one of the entractes I was approached by Kenneth Clark,[1] who hailed me as a blood-brother – or sister – about Suez. I was astounded. He was enthusiastic about my letter & generally 'on the boil'. He had just come from India & Siam where he said everyone was astounded & disillusioned. They just wrote off the French (as the Germans do). It was we who had fallen from our pedestal. I urged him to write a letter to the *Times* himself – as he said that letters & expressions of dissent did so much to reassure the world about ourselves....

Diary – Friday 28 December – 21 Hyde Park Square W.2

...Left for Chard in the afternoon for an *Any Questions* programme.... Nice little hôtel 'The George' – an old Inn run by good people – where I found Michael Bowen – Freddy Grisewood – John Connell[2] – Ralph Wightman & one Victor Mishcon[3] – a London County Council figure, whom I hadn't met before – Labour – very able – 'serious-minded' – fair-minded – nice. John Connell revealed himself to me in a most strange light. I knew that he was pro-Suez but did not expect to find him well to the right of Captain Waterhouse.

We had a very good audience but not (to my mind) very good questions. After one of those dreaded 'light' ones about Xmas we were suddenly plunged into the Moorhouse tragedy.[4] Had he been exposed to undue risks? Was the handling of the publicity at fault? etc. Ralph Wightman reminded the audience that 100 others had lost their lives in what he called this 'squalid adventure'. I confined myself strictly to the question

[1]Kenneth Mackenzie Clark (1903–83), KCB, 1938; cr. life peer, 1969; OM, 1976; director of the National Gallery, 1934–45; Slade professor of fine art, Oxford, 1946–50, 1961–2; chairman of the Arts Council of Great Britain, 1953–60.

[2]John Connell (1909–65), author and journalist; leader-writer, London *Evening News*, 1945–59.

[3]Victor Mishcon (b. 1915), cr. life peer, 1978; solicitor and later senior partner in Mishcon de Reya; member LCC (Brixton), 1946–65.

[4]Second-Lieutenant Anthony Gerard Moorhouse, a national serviceman in the West Yorkshire Regiment, was abducted at gunpoint in Port Said on 11 December. An extensive search failed to discover him and after weeks of uncertainty it was established that he had died on or around 15 December, probably from suffocation by being kept captive in a steel box. His fate was made public around the time of the Chard *Any Questions* (*The Times*, 12, 28, 29 and 31 December 1956).

saying that I knew nothing of the risks to which he had been exposed but that I was critical about the publication of the unverified reports which must have played such a cruel game of cat & mouse with the fears & hopes of his parents.

Then John Connell had a wild anti-Egyptian outburst – saying that we were fighting against cruel, cunning, treacherous people who wished to torture us etc. etc. – then suddenly switching to Israeli grievances – the whole thing incoherent & almost hysterical. He was very well & quietly answered by Victor Mishcon, whom I supported, & then he waved his arm wildly to come back again & shouted 'Between July & October our life was at stake' at which there was loud clapping from all the Blimps in the hall. When we were signing autographs afterwards he was called to the telephone. I said 'I hope his wife isn't ill.' Mishcon said 'No – I expect he is being rung up by a retired Colonel to say "It needed saying & by Gad, Sir, you've said it!"' When he returned we asked him & it was in fact a retired Major, who had used these very words!

After the rest had gone back to Bristol & Dorchester he & I & Mishcon sat up & talked – & Connell revealed a most extraordinary state of mind. He said the Govt had acted in a dishonourable, deceitful, shameful way – & that this country was now as a result facing ruin. We pointed out that if this was his real opinion he had grossly deceived his audience to-night & given them an utterly false impression of his position. He had given the impression that he supported the Govt's action without qualification or reservation. At this he seemed amazed. He described Eden as a poor deluded madman etc. etc. As I told him – the Tory Party today appear to me to be a set of crazy, mixed-up kids.

Diary – Thursday 3 January 1957 – 21 Hyde Park Square, W.2

Went to an interesting & amusing cocktail party at Douglas Jerrold's[1] in his new flat in Marsham Court. There were not many people there & few were known to me before but I enjoyed it enormously.... Talked to P. J. Grigg – ex-head of the War Office – & later Secretary of State for War.[2] He started in India & said he thought we cld. have held India for another generation. He agreed with me that our social arrogance – & particularly that of the 'memsahibs' as he called them – was responsible for our

[1]Douglas Jerrold (1893–1964), author and publisher; wrote a history of the Royal Naval Division, in which he served at Gallipoli.

[2]Sir (Percy) James Grigg (1890–1964), KCB, 1932; financial member of the Government of India, 1934–9; permanent under-secretary, war office, 1939-February 1942; secretary for war, 1942–5; MP (Nat.) East Cardiff, 1942–5.

difficulties there, far more than political ineptitude. He said he had always spoken frankly & bluntly to Indians including members of Congress. What they minded above all was being patronised.

Talking about present day politics he said there was no public man for whom he had more contempt than Anthony Eden.... I asked why Anthony was so disliked by those who worked with him. He replied 'Vanity, indecision, bullying people who could be bullied & collapsing before those who couldn't'....

Diary – Saturday 5 January – 21 Hyde Park Square, W.2

Stayed in all day & worked. Had a little dinner-party in the evening – George & Anne Barnes, Elizabeth Cavendish & Jimmy Smith. Moucher was to have come but she was suddenly attacked by flu after lunch & had to go to bed so Elizabeth came instead. George was in excellent form. I made him & Anne come early so that we cld have a private talk....

We talked a little Suez. He is 'sound' now & says he was never 'unsound'. He thought there must be some hidden explanation of the Govt.'s action & that we ought not to judge it out of hand – but every explanation that ensued made it worse. He was also rather amusing about the 'Blut und Boden' feeling of the Tories – shared by the 'lower classes' – but not by us the thinking slice between. In the journey of man between the monkey & the top-hat wearer they had not forgotten the monkey & understood his feelings. I said they still had some 'monkey' in them. Jimmy was very nice & easy & helpful – he is a good element in a party. Transport at night is now becoming very difficult thro' want of taxis. B & George had to go out & hunt for one.

Diary – Wednesday 9 January – 21 Hyde Park Square, W.2

Ordinary – uneventful day of work indoors.... Then just before dinner – a thunder-clap. Laura rang me up to say that she had just heard from Miss Preston that Anthony Eden had resigned. It had been on the 7 o'clock news.... I feel some relief – tho' no exhilaration at the prospect ahead. Relief because Anthony was the personal symbol of a policy – & his disappearance will help to restore our international position.

Diary – Thursday 10 January – 21 Hyde Park Square, W.2

. . . I went out about 3.30 & got on a bus in Edgware Rd. Rounding the corner of Oxford St I suddenly saw 'New Premier Official' on the news-boards. I longed to jump out but cldn't. . . . I possessed my soul with impatience till Oxford Circus & there got out & after hunting a little found a newspaper man. It was Macmillan! – with a prophetic article by Randolph predicting that by tea-time he wld be P.M. In spite of my mind being prepared for it I was astounded. Every newspaper of every complexion had pointed to Butler as a certainty. . . .[1]

I feel – who cldn't? – the tragic poignancy of Anthony's exit. Politics are his only interest. To be P.M. was his life's one aim. He waits – loyally but impatiently for W. to go ('those hungry eyes' as W. used to say to me). At last the cup is handed to him. He has a triumphant election. Then everything begins to go awry – but not catastrophically. Finally he himself accomplishes his own destruction by the suicidal blunder of Suez. (Was it health that drove him to this madness? And how far did that disaster contribute to the undermining of his health?) Now he faces a complete vacuum. Politics have always been his be-all & his end-all. He cares for nothing else. And he will have no chance of redeeming his reputation in the eyes of the present or of posterity. It is a Greek tragedy.

Diary – Tuesday 15 January – 21 Hyde Park Square, W.2

Lunched with W. Found Clemmie alone on arrival & we spoke of the tragedy of Anthony. I asked her how ill she thought he was. She didn't really know. . . . When Winston came in he kissed me & then said: 'Well you've won. You've won hands down & all along the line' – with the slightest tinge of resentment. (It reminded me of the time after the abdication when he had said to me 'Well you've got your way – you & Baldwin!' only that was far more resentful!)[2] I said that I hadn't had much to do

[1] When Eden resigned he did not recommend to the Queen who should be his successor. After taking 'hurriedly organized' polls of Conservatives the press guessed that it would be Rab Butler (Rhodes James, *Eden*, 599). But members of the cabinet, interviewed by Lord Salisbury and Lord Kilmuir, opted for Macmillan, and their preference was made known to the Queen.

[2] During the abdication crisis in 1936 Churchill supported Edward VIII, which Violet emphatically did not. She wrote to Churchill days before the abdication: 'I fully understand your emotional sympathies being aroused by this very moving human dilemma. But it is a dilemma which many other ordinary human beings have had to face & meet – with less at stake. Many – after all – have died for this country – not so long ago. The sacrifice now demanded falls far short of life – certainly in value & probably in duration' (VBC to WSC, 7 December 1936).

with 'winning'. World opinion had won – as I knew it must. We then turned to the new Govt. I said I was glad about Harold. He said with pleasure 'I thought you'd be glad about that' & we agreed that Butler had behaved well. . . .

I also said the so-called Suez Group were like the Tories he & I remembered from the 1st World War – stone-age men whom I thought had been bred out of the Tory Party. I said that I had ignorantly imagined that it had been 'liberalized' by him & others. He didn't rise to this but a little later said 'I've always been a Tory.' I said 'You've never been a Tory.' He said: 'I've been a Tory Democrat.' I said: 'You were once a Liberal – for quite a long time.' He said 'Liberal – it's the best name there ever was in politics.' Clemmie chirped in with 'Labour has been quite useful too.' He spoke with deep resentment of our leaving Suez & the Canal Zone in the first instance. . . . I think he is very sad about everything poor darling – & though he began by being critical & fully realizing the Govt's blunder, he now cannot endure or admit defeat for this country. . . .

Diary – Friday 18 January – 21 Hyde Park Square, W.2

. . . When I was trying to work between 11.30 & 12 I was rung up by Randolph – who was very amusing, defending himself from a criticism I had made on one of his articles in which he (1) slates the men of Munich – Butler in particular & (2) acclaims Hailsham as incomparably the finest addition to the Cabinet. I wrote reminding him that Hailsham had been a Municher & the Appeasement Candidate at the Oxford by-election. He said he wanted to support Harold & defeat Butler. I told him he was pushing an open – or shut – door for Butler was already defeated.

He told me one perfect story which I must record while I remember it. Betty Salisbury said to Lady Dorothea Head[1] 'Poor darling – don't worry – it's a very middle-class Cabinet anyway!' It's as good as her remark to old Lady Salisbury when her sister Sybil became engaged to a clergyman: 'Upon my soul, Lady Salisbury, I'd almost rather she married a doctor' – these two noble professions of healing body & soul representing to her the social nadir!

[1] Lady Dorothea Head (*née* Ashley-Cooper), daughter of 9th Earl of Shaftesbury. She married, 1935, Antony Henry Head (1906–83), cr. 1st Viscount Head, 1960; MP (Con.) Carshalton, Surrey, 1945–60; secretary of state for war, 1951–6; minister of defence, October 1956-January 1957. Head declined office under Macmillan but became the first UK high commissioner to the Federation of Nigeria, 1960–63.

Diary – Thursday 7 March – 21 Hyde Park Square, W.2

I lunched with Pertinax at L'Ecu de France. He is just like an incarnation of the old reactionary illusioned France, with the ex-Great Power complex, the belief in force, in the power of intriguing women to sway great events, etc. He was of course passionately pro-Suez & pro-conquering the whole of Egypt, wrong in all his facts, ignored the great facts of world opinion & the shift of World Power to the 2 Giants. I pointed out to him that we cld not even afford our 10 days' war & had to appeal to U.S.A. for a waiver on our loan to help to pay for it. . . . I like the old boy & we are wholly friendly, but he is a tragic reminder of one element in France which has been left far behind the march of events & stands grinding its teeth & shaking its fist at the future.

'The nation is in the making'
A visit to Israel, March 1957

In March 1957 Violet paid a week-long visit to Israel, the first of three such visits at the invitation of the Israeli government: she returned in May of the following year and again in October-November 1967. Her first and last visits came within months of an Israeli victory in a war with its Arab neighbours, and Violet regarded the young state's survival against heavy odds as a remarkable achievement. A decade earlier she had been a strong critic of Israel: now she was won over to the historic endeavour of a nation 'in the making'. It was not simply the effort taken to build new communities – in places such as Beersheba – that impressed her, it was the pooling of human resources that made this possible. Jewish peoples were coming together from across the world to create a homeland where they could be free from persecution. Violet was convinced not only that they were succeeding, but that in so doing they were transcending nationalism. She later wrote to Isaiah Berlin: 'Like you I find Israel intensely moving & exciting – & the only place where "internationalism", so eloquently talked about elsewhere, is truly practised.'[1] Her visit had been arranged at relatively short notice and entailed no speaking engagements, but there were meetings with civic leaders and government officials, including the premier David Ben-Gurion. There was also time for sight-seeing and on one of her last tours, before returning to London on 21 March, Violet glimpsed a camp of Palestinian refu-

[1] VBC to Isaiah Berlin, 9 May 1958.

gees. It was a poignant reminder of a human tragedy that, a decade earlier, she had urged her own countrymen not to forget, and which, a decade later, would revisit her even more forcefully.

Bongie to V.B.C. ***Night of Monday 11 March***
21 Hyde Park Square, W.2

Dearest dear girl. However untroubled one is by fears of any sort, a parting on a long journey, of one near & dear, always grips the heart a little – it is the symbol of a real parting. I am not necessarily thinking of death, but of the partings which we have suffered with our sons from time to time when they have moved away & will come back older & perhaps changed. You will come back only a fortnight older and I do not fear in any way changed, save by the addition of an intensely interesting experience and I trust one of great beauty. . . .

I am not yet bloody lonely but I do not want to be long without you.

My love & blessing. B.

Diary – Wednesday 13 March – Beersheba, Israel

Started at 9.30 on tour of Beersheba. Incredible conglomeration of people of every race & colour in this improvised straggling town in the making. . . . Patches of grass here & there now, but I am told that when the hot weather comes they shrivel & die & the sand reasserts itself. It is an amazing feat of reclamation from the desert. There is a station with a tiny brand-new Diesel train looking like a toy. Feathery Pepper trees line the sandy roads & streets – but all the building looks ugly & unplanned. The only beauty is in the Mosque in the Old City, with its quiet walled-in garden, palm trees, green lawn & a few fragments of old well-heads & stone vases. There is one building of great dignity & beauty belonging to Arab times, which used to be the house of the Mayor. Everything buzzes with work, hope, vitality, enthusiasm – but alas! no beauty. It is true that there was no time to make it beautiful, but wld the Jews ever have done so one wonders? They are a curious mixture of 'ur-alt' tradition & 'dernier cri' – living 2000 years ago & the day after to-morrow simultaneously. . . .

Diary – Thursday 14 March – Israel

. . . Arrived in Tel Aviv – brand-new modern town – only about 10 minutes before I was due to go & see Ben-Gurion. Mr Schmeerson fetched me &

took me to his house – a very homely & unpretentious one. . . .

He talked to me for an hour & a half of absorbing interest. He has tremendous personality, is completely natural & at ease with himself & others & has a curiously Biblical-cum-20th Century outlook. Prophet & politician in one – guided both by the Old Testament & by a shrewd appraisal of present-day forces & persons.

He welcomed me warmly & asked me a most surprising question at the very outset of our conversation. He wanted me to tell him about the Souls! Was I one of them? Who were they? Did Bernard Shaw & the Webbs belong to them? etc. I enlightened him. We got on to Arthur Balfour & I described his 'make-up' as a politician – how Zionism was the only cause that ever caught him & kindled his cool soul to a blaze. We then got on to the present situation – the difficulties he had had to face over withdrawal [from Gaza]. He feels he has been badly let down by the U.S.A. Ike had given him no concrete pledge – but an implied pledge of honour i.e. 'You will have no cause to regret it' (the withdrawal) but Dulles[1] had given a definite undertaking to Mrs Meir.[2] He had assured her that the Gaza Strip wld be 'de facto' internationalized. Since then the Egyptians had marched in & resumed control of the Civil Administration. Raids were beginning again already – a shepherd had been killed, a bit of railway blown up, a mine exploded under a car. The watch-towers I had seen on the edge of the Strip were now manned again. 'Did he feel great personal confidence in Ike?' 'I knew him as a General, not as a politician. He is a good, compassionate & human man. He behaved well over the D.P.'s in Germany.' But Dulles. . . .

Winston is his hero. He had heard him in London in 1940 make his great speech in the H. of C. 'We will fight upon the beaches' which he quoted with zest & fire. . . . We talked of the appeasement years & how even Ll.G. – the great Radical – had been hypnotized by Hitler. I told him how I marvelled at the welding of all the heterogeneous elements from every corner of the earth into one nation. . . . I left him feeling that I had seen a great man with the heart of a lion.

[1]John Foster Dulles (1888–1959), American secretary of state, 1953–9; fiercely anti-Communist, he was active in promoting the European defence community as a counter to Soviet influence.

[2]Golda Meir (1898–1978), one of the founders of the state of Israel, foreign minister, 1956–66, and prime minister, 1969–74.

Diary – Sunday 17 March – Haifa

...After luncheon we drove to Acre along the coast. It is a marvellous town – Crusader walls going down into a blue sea built round an Arab town. The Crusaders lived & ruled here for 200 years. There is a beautiful Mosque & Theological School with cloisters round a green garden. I went into the Mosque & saw one or two Arabs prostrating themselves with passionate devotion. They laid their foreheads again & again on the ground – one saw the tension even in the bare soles of their feet. I have never seen people pray so hard.... There are beautiful old Italianate houses & lots of small brightly dressed & dirty children playing in the sandy streets – all happy & well – clothes & faces of all colours – the darkest are the Abyssinian. Many fair blue-eyed Arabs are still to be seen, descended from the Crusaders. One longs to know how the Crusaders spent their time between their sallies on the Saracens....

A lovely drive back along the coast – a short rest & then dinner in the Zion Hôtel with Professor Ratner, Vice-Chancellor of the [Haifa Technion] University, & his wife. He is a delightful, sensitive & most distinguished man – a Russian who has been a General. He came here in 1926. His wife – much younger – is a German & left Germany in '33 feeling the coming terror. His political opinions were unorthodox so his parents thought it safer to have him educated at Heidelberg – for fear he shld be suspected in Russia of 'dangerous thoughts'. She begged her relations to leave Germany with her. They refused & were all killed. 'And one does not even know how' she said. He: 'And yet one wld like to know how.' He said that Jews are – & look – different here than in Europe because here they are afraid of nothing. In Russia – everywhere in Europe – there was a look in the eyes of a Jewish child which distinguished it from its fellows. It was not features or colouring but the look of fear which marked out the Jew. That look is not to be seen in Israel. The State is only 9 years old – & has today only 1,800,000 people. They are very poor still – experimenting in all directions & paying for their mistakes. The nation is in the making. There are 2 melting-pots welding it together. The education of the children of a myriad races together & the Army....

He spoke of the Jews' internal differences. There are too many parties. They will not compromise. They can only govern by coalition. What is coming he asked? What must they do to exist & survive? Yield again? Or fight again? And if they fight again, will they have on their consciences the starting of a new World War? He was a most moving & remarkable man. If only I had not been so tired I shld have longed to go on talking to him for hours.

Diary – Tuesday 19 March – Old Jerusalem

. . . Lunched with Mr Stewart our Consul-General – a rather nice looking young man – pro-Suez I gathered & not knowing anything about the place as he only came here from Korea a month ago. . . . I noticed the wishful-thinking 'blind eye' in both our Consuls. When I condoled with them on the collapse of their work in building good relations here (Stewart of course had done none) they both said 'Oh, but things aren't so bad. They're getting better. The Jordanians are awfully pleased with the way we've taken this thing.' 'This thing' being the abrogation of our treaty with, & the removal of our bases by, a state we have created & subsidized. . . .[1]

Stewart & I set off together . . . on the way out of Jerusalem to Bethlehem. We drove past Gethsemane & the Mount of Olives & on along a most perilous road, entirely composed of hairpin bends, which outdo any hairpin I have ever used. Frightful accidents occur there & 8 soldiers were killed last year when a lorry went over the side. The drive is infinitely beautiful. You look up at Jerusalem from below. There is a high mountain on which Herod's palace (or one of them) used to stand – & from a height one suddenly & (to me) astonishingly got a glimpse of the Dead Sea. I had no idea it was anywhere near! We saw the Jordanian end – past Sodom.

One tragic sight – the first camp of Arab Refugees – tents pitched by the roadside, which must have been saturated by the Monsoon-like rains of a few days ago. Wretched-looking Arabs, désoeuvré (& I am sure damp), huddled by the road-side with their poor little children poking about in the sand. They live on U.N. rations & do 'damn all' & the Jordan Govt. will not allow them to be resettled. Stewart said he thought they had very easily got used to doing nothing & on the whole preferred idleness to work. Whether they do or not it is tragic to see them rotting. . . .

Diary – Sunday 13 October – 21 Hyde Park Square, W.2

Brains Trust – John Furness's last. . . . I liked 'Freddie' Ayer,[2] whom I met

[1] The previous day Violet had watched a fancy dress parade in Jerusalem, part of the Purim festival, in which many political figures were depicted – Ben-Gurion, General Nasser, even Guy Mollet the French premier: 'Great Britain was quite unrepresented – neither vilified nor acclaimed. We have ceased to count here.'

[2] (Sir) Alfred Jules 'Freddie' Ayer (1910–89), Kt, 1970; philosopher and author; Grote professor of philosophy, University of London, 1946–59; afterwards Wykeham professor of logic at Oxford.

for the first time. The other 2 were Bronowski & Julian Huxley.[1] To my amazement the inevitable question about the satellite was handed to me.[2] I thought it was bound to go to one of the Scientists. I tried to deal with its earthly implications. . . .

I raised the question which obsesses me – whether the future destiny of mankind is to depend on a scientific fluke. Whether all the human resources of heroism & self-sacrifice will in future be at a discount – whether the survival of freedom of the world will lie not in the crucible of the human soul, but in the scientist's laboratory. Even Ayer (to my surprise) seemed prepared to trust all power to the scientist. I shld like to have come back & reminded him that scientists have been the docile tools & servants of dictators. They deal with means & do not determine ends. If Hitler had got the bomb before us he wld have won the war – in spite of W.'s lion heart & our 'finest hour' & the hopes & prayers of the bound & the free throughout the world. . . .

Diary – Tuesday 26 November – 21 Hyde Park Square, W.2

Lib. Party Committee at H. of C. at which Jo showed me an outrageous speech by Hailsham at the Garston by-election in which he said that if my father were alive today he wld be aligned with the Tory Party. . . . He combined this with an attack on the group of 'ill-assorted personalities' who make up the present Lib. Party & have no right whatever to its title etc. Accused the Parl. Party with sitting on the fence & voting two in one lobby & one in the other etc. Jo was off to Garston that afternoon. I spent the afternoon drafting a reply in the form of a letter to the candidate – one Dennis. I spoke to Harry Boardman & asked him to see that the *M.G.* gave space to it.

[1]Jacob Bronowski (1908–74), Polish-born mathematician and poet; deeply interested in the relationship between science and human values, he was the writer and presenter of the noted BBC series *The Ascent of Man*, filmed 1971–2. Sir Julian (Sorell) Huxley (1887–1975), Kt, 1958; biologist, academic and writer, brother of Aldous; director general of UNESCO, 1946–8; 'one of the most influential popularizers of science of his age' (*DNB*). Both men were *Brains Trust* regulars.

[2]The first of the Sputnik series of satellites had been launched from the Soviet Union on 4 October, inaugurating the 'Space Age'.

Diary – Thursday 28 November – 21 Hyde Park Square, W.2

...B & I went to a reception at the Goldsmiths' Hall.... I had a talk with Walter Monckton who congratulated me warmly on my reply to Hailsham, making boxing gestures at his jaw! He agreed with me (as he always does – perhaps with everyone?!) on the unwisdom of the appt. (H's).[1] I said so many things he had done surprised me.... Liberals were now more alienated by Conservatives than they had been since 1914. Winston had them feeding out of his hand. He said truly that W. had never been a Conservative & that when he asked him to join the Govt. Walter had said something about his [Winston's] party – & W. had replied 'Don't call them my party – they have never been that'....

Diary – Friday 6 December – 21 Hyde Park Square, W.2

Lunched at the Dorchester – a great Foyle's lunch in honour of Ld Samuel who has just at 87 published a book on philosophy called *In Search of Reality* which he began at the age of 83. He is a portent. I sat between Birkett (the Chairman) & Attlee, with whom I had a very good talk. I like his flavour – rather like a caraway seed. We talked of Suez & the Govt's extraordinary blunders – agreed that it stood with Munich as one of the great & lasting 'divides' in politics. He thinks that Hailsham will not last long – that he will overreach himself & commit some frightful blunder in the H. of L. He also spoke of Bevin with immense affection & admiration. Samuel spoke for a good 20 minutes perhaps more about his own life, ending up with a patch about philosophy & his difference with Einstein. I am told by those who know that philosophy is his weakest suit – but I am sure that he wld rather go down to posterity as a philosopher than anything else. We staggered out at 3.30.

Diary – New Year's Eve, Tuesday 31 December – 21 Hyde Park Square, W.2

In all day working at my article & writing letters. Mark came to lunch. Dined in alone with B.... What a dark & confused picture the curtain of the New Year goes up on. A definite Russian lead in Nuclear Power – with which we may not draw level for at least 3 years. Eisenhower an invalid,

[1] Lord Hailsham had been made chairman of the Conservative Party organisation in September. He in fact proved successful in reviving the popularity of the Conservative Party post-Suez.

Dulles a calamity, France still a hopeless casualty, unable to struggle out of the bog of error in Algeria, which is bringing her moral & financial ruin. A vacuum of leadership in Europe – meanwhile a kind of defeatism, neutralism, pacifism growing here – sometimes in the name of morality, sometimes of national independence & anti-Americanism.... Last year beginning with Suez & ending with the Sputnik was a bad one. I pray that this one may be better.

SEVEN

Torrington: Victory and Defeat

1958–1959

'I can see that Mark's mouth waters for the fray'
The Torrington by-election, March 1958

Under the inspirational leadership of Jo Grimond the Liberal Party began to show signs of recovery from the electoral disasters of the early 1950s. In by-elections in 1957 its share of the poll steadily increased and in February 1958, at Rochdale, the Liberal candidate Ludovic Kennedy finished a strong second behind Labour, with nearly twice as many votes as the Conservative. This encouraged ideas of a 'Liberal revival' but, as *The Times* observed, without an actual victory such talk 'rang a little hollow'. Great interest was therefore focused on the Torrington by-election in March, at which there was a real chance of Liberal success. The North Devon seat became vacant after the sitting member, George Lambert, succeeded to his father's peerage. It was a predominantly farming constituency which Lambert had represented as a 'National Liberal and Conservative'. Anthony Royle, the Conservative candidate who hoped to succeed him, was happy to accept this hybrid title in an attempt to retain 'National Liberal' votes. But it exposed him to the ridicule of the 'independent' Liberals, who showed no such confusion of identity. Because the by-election offered the prospect of a breakthrough, a high-profile Liberal candidate was sought. Mark Bonham Carter was an obvious choice. Since contesting Barnstaple in 1945 he had gained wide experience of Party organization. Like his brother-in-law, Jo Grimond, he epitomized modern, rejuvenated Liberalism. Upon hearing of the Torrington vacancy Violet wrote 'I can see that Mark's mouth waters for the fray.' He was duly adopted and his candidacy encouraged hopes of a historic victory: the Liberals had not won a seat at a by-election since 1929, the year after the death of his grandfather, H. H. Asquith.

Diary – Tuesday 18 March 1958 – 21 Hyde Park Square, W.2

The Queen & Duke of Edinburgh came to the Old Vic.[1] They were received in a small arctic room in the new Webber St. building – which is far from ready.... I had a nice & long talk with Prince Philip about T.V., Gallup Polls, etc. which I enjoyed. He is extraordinarily natural & easy. I also had some talk with Oliver Poole, who said to me about Torrington 'You're going to win.' He said it repeatedly in the course of our talk & added that he had never been wrong about a by-election result. He was extraordinarily frank & sensible about his party's position. He said the miracle was that the Govt had survived as they had done.... His last words to me were 'Well, don't do too well!'

Diary – Thursday 20 March – Royal Hôtel, Bideford, North Devon

I write up what I can remember of these dramatic days 'after the event'.[2] There was not one second to put pencil to paper while they were going on. B & I left by a 3.30 train to Exeter on Thursday 20th & were met there by a charming Mr Crow & his wife with their car. They were volunteers who had come from London to help. He was elderly & had always been a keen Liberal & left the Party because of Ll.G. She much younger – being 'inducted' into its mysteries. We had some tea in a charming Inn on the way to Okehampton, where I was to address a meeting of some 700 or 800 – met Mark in the dark street outside the hall & went straight onto the platform. It was a vast hall – packed to overflowing with a standing crowd at the back – a sort of overflow who heard, tho' they can't have seen much....

It was an extremely lively meeting with a high temperature & lots of women. We drove back through the dark to Bideford where we are all staying at the Royal Hôtel. Laura arrived in due course & finally Leslie & Mark & we all ate sandwiches ravenously in their bedroom, which is arctic. Mine is much warmer – tho' I haven't yet mastered the gas fire 6d-slot technique. Mark has a gruelling routine: home about midnight – press Conference 9.30 – off by 10 – loudspeaker work in villages all day followed by at least 4 evening meetings. Royle,[3] who has a perfect machine & has

[1] The Queen unveiled a plaque to mark the building of a new annexe to the Old Vic theatre.

[2] The entries 20–29 March, and perhaps 2 April also, were probably written at Easter when Violet and Bongie were staying at Clovelly in Devon. Although the record was not strictly contemporary Violet sometimes wrote as if it were, lapsing into the present tense.

[3] Anthony Henry Royle (b. 1927), cr. life peer, 1983; the Conservative candidate at Torrington, 1958; later MP (Con.) Richmond, 1959–83; vice-chairman, CPO, 1979–84; he married, 1957, Shirley Worthington.

been nursing it for $2\frac{1}{2}$ years, got off to a flying start & addressed 40 meetings before Mark had had time to open his mouth.

Diary – Saturday 22 March – Royal Hôtel, Bideford, North Devon

I had a wonderful meeting at Clovelly (in the primary school at Upper Clo.). I did not see the Cruses but they were all there. Jeremy [Thorpe] spoke till I came & all the press were there, including Gale.[1] I am taking meetings which Mark can't reach & taking questions for him. A howling gale of terrific force was blowing & one cld hardly struggle thro' it to the car. We went on thro' twisting turning lanes & over blasted heaths in search of Frithelstock. It was a real Macbeth night & I expected to see the Witches every moment. At last we reached it – a splendid meeting in a kind of barn lit by paraffin lamps – full of enthusiastic horny-handed supporters who had all turned out in strength.... Randolph has wired to Mark that he is coming, which fills us all with bale. Luckily there is no room for him in our Hôtel – where we live at very close quarters.

Diary – Sunday 23 March – Royal Hôtel, Bideford, North Devon

Marvellous respite for all except Mark, who had to prepare a questionnaire for broadcasting, with which I tried to help. Royle vetoed T.V. at Bristol fearing I suppose that he wld lose by it & announced ostentatiously that he was going to church. B. returned to London by 2.4....

A new Gallup Poll is coming out next Tuesday. A great deal will depend on it. I have the feeling that we shall win – but it is a kind of mystic's conviction – based on atmosphere. I feel 'it's in the air'. This is Liberal country – & we get a tremendous welcome everywhere. But – our organization has had to be improvised at lightning-speed & is I feel sure sketchy in the extreme....

Diary – Monday 24 March – Royal Hôtel, Bideford, North Devon

...Randolph suddenly turned up in the afternoon at our Hôtel! He is staying elsewhere but filled the 'lounge' with his views & presence. He has arrived determined that Royle will win. He was however in a 'douce' & reasonable mood for him. I had to scurry off to my meetings & did not

[1]George Stafford Gale (1927–90), journalist, author and broadcaster; special and foreign correspondent, *Daily Express*, 1955–67; later editor of *The Spectator*, 1970–3.

observe him at East-the-Water, my second one, a splendid packed meeting at which the Press was again fully represented, but he was there. Ambrose Fulford[1] in the Chair & Jeremy started it off until I came. It was one of the best meetings I have had. Questions are now freely 'planted' by the Tory Central Office & we get the same night after night. . . .

When I returned to the hôtel I found Randolph ensconced in the 'lounge' & he congratulated me fervently saying 'I was transported by your speaking. You looked beautiful – incandescent – you were speaking the truth – the truth as you had received it from God – from Mr Gladstone – from Mr Gladstone. And your words – your language – I wish I cld speak like that.' However as he drank more & more whiskies & sodas he became increasingly quarrelsome & difficult – furious if Laura & I did not give him our whole attention – shouting 'Listen to me – will no one listen?' & refusing to let us get in a word edgeways. When we finally asked for permission to ask a question each he reluctantly acceded & Laura asked him 'Do you honestly believe that even if Libs did not exist you wld beat the Socialists at the next Election?' (which he evaded) I asked 'Has not Rochdale convinced you that in some places we can beat the Socialist & you can't?' Here he replied 'Ah, now you are talking. We must make a deal.' From now on he became worse & worse & drank more & more – the 'bloodies' rippled from his tongue & I winced for Ambrose Fulford. The Press observed him from a corner of the room.

He was terribly rude both to the maid & to Mrs Middleton the manageress about a call to New York he wanted to put through, reversing the charge. We were hot with shame. Finally someone came in & said 'The *Daily Express* wishes to speak to Mr Randolph Churchill.' I said 'His Master's Voice'.[2] He blew up in fury – & while he was on the telephone I took evasive action & followed Laura upstairs to my bedroom leaving Col. Lort Phillips (who has arrived here) to warn Mark. I heard that he ranted about it the whole evening saying that he must have a written apology from me etc. etc. . . .

While he was still sober he had told me that he dined à quatre with Beaverbrook, Gilbert Harding & Michael Foot the night before & that B. had said to him 'Wld you like to have a poke at Lady Violet? Wld you like to beat her up?' R. had loyally replied no – that I was a great friend of his father's & his own. B. then said 'Well anyway, you will always allude to her as "Lady V." because she doesn't like that.' Randolph replied 'I wldn't even address your own daughter-in-law with such vulgarity.' So he had

[1] Ambrose Fulford was a local Liberal activist and had been the prospective candidate for Torrington before standing down in Mark Bonham Carter's favour.

[2] Implying that Randolph Churchill's 'master' was Lord Beaverbrook, proprietor of the *Daily Express* and the *Evening Standard*, for which Randolph wrote a political column.

done his bit! & therefore felt doubly outraged by my innocent tease.

Diary – Wednesday 26 March – Royal Hôtel, Bideford, North Devon

In the morning I met Randolph on the Bridge with 2 companions & 2 written prognostications in his hand – calculated on two different percentages of poll. In both Royle won by some 2 thousand. In the 2nd Lamb came second & Mark bottom of the Poll. I begged him to bet with me on this last – £100 – anything he liked. He said 'What odds will you give me?' I said 'Odds? – this is your own forecast. You are surely prepared to back it?' But he refused to do so. I wish now I had offered him almost any odds for I knew it was impossible that Lamb shld come second. Randolph arrived here with preconceived ideas & refused to be influenced by what he saw or heard. He told me that he wanted Royle to win. I asked why & he said because he loved Harold & didn't wish to send him to the Summit with 'Rochdale' on one shoulder & 'Torrington' on the other.[1] He also said he wld prefer Mark to be bottom of the Poll & Lamb 2nd. Again I asked why – as he was avowedly a strong anti-Socialist? He replied that if the Libs did well they wld be encouraged to put up candidates everywhere at the General Election.

He snatched the microphone from Royle in Crediton to-day to say that his father had been a 'Liberal & Conservative' (not mentioning that these states of mind were successive & not simultaneous!) but according to Gale he forgot to push the right button on the microphone so his words were inaudible. I drove with Laura & Roderic Bowen[2] to Crediton at 4.30 (their meeting started at 5.30 in the Town Hall). It was a marvellous meeting – one of the most enthusiastic we have had in the campaign – packed out & with masses of women. The chair was taken by a delightful Devonian agent George Foster. Laura was sitting in the audience & said the women were so delightful, nodding assent 'Yes, yes' or shaking their heads in dissent 'No, no'. Mark arrived towards the end of my speech.

It was then Mark's intention to pick up the crowds coming out of the Pannier Market meeting, which Royle was addressing, & Laura & I followed on but when we got back to Bideford we were told that they had had an awful rough house & that Socialists & Tories had almost come to blows. It wld be better to keep away & let them have it out with each other.... Royle has had a far rougher passage than we have ... & Andrew said he

[1] In the first months of 1958 Macmillan was trying to arrange a summit meeting with the United States and Soviet Union to discuss key issues, notably nuclear weapons. After protracted 'talks about talks', which lasted into the following year, the summit failed to materialize.

[2] (Evan) Roderic Bowen (b. 1913), QC, 1952; MP (Lib.) Cardiganshire, 1945–66.

looked really tired poor man. On the other hand his complacency & arrogance cld. not be greater. He asserted in print to-day that all the Gallup & Public Opinion Polls were rubbish (we had another good Gallup yesterday – leading by 9 points) & that he had a cast iron canvass which gave him 20,000 votes (this is the only thing that has shaken me at all throughout the Election – as I know how good his 'machine' is) & that Labour wld come second. He also said he was going to give the 'Independent Liberals' (sic) & Socialists 'the greatest thrashing they had ever had in their lives'.

Diary – Polling Day, Thursday 27 March – Royal Hôtel, Bideford, North Devon

Mark & Leslie started at 8 or soon after to go round the Polling Booths & Committee Rooms & Laura & I went to those they might not reach – Buckland Brewer, one of the nicest villages in the whole division where every child wears Liberal colours & the windows are papered with Mark's address. One nice thing was that every road-mender & steam-roller man we passed waved to us & wished us good luck.... Then Laura & I had a very late lunch in a Café with Andrew & then he & she drove off home to pack for Italy where she is going early next week. She has been invaluable & so angelically unselfish – doing all the hard & thankless & unshowy jobs like canvassing & arranging cars etc. & only speaking once at Okehampton. I longed to hear her speak which I have never done.

I got another car from the Lib. Committee Rooms & went round the remaining stations on my list....

Diary – Declaration of the Poll, Friday 28 March – Royal Hôtel, Bideford, North Devon

I dressed with a terrible needle. Mark & I & Leslie started about 11 to walk to the count. It took place in a large Municipal Building.... We were ushered into a large room in which about 8 long tables were aligned in 2 rows – littered with votes at which sat the counters closely watched by scrutineers. Everyone wore colours – the Nat. Lib. Cons. wore red white & blue – which I consider outrageous. (Royle entered meetings brandishing a Union Jack – & sometimes bearing a hand-bell – an accessory we did not grudge him.)...

I was introduced to Lord Lambert[1] who was rather like a swollen Arthur Penn[2] to look at. He sat down next to me & was very agréable – 'soapy' I felt in my present mood. After an interchange of smooth 'sweet nothings' I said to him: 'Lord Lambert – I must tell you how deeply we & our supporters resent the use of the national colours by your side as their party colours. How do you justify it?' He said 'Well you see when the fusion took place the [National] Liberal colours (violet & orange) didn't "go" very well with the Conservative ones. So we thought these looked better – prettier.' I said 'So it was on purely aesthetic grounds that you selected red, white & blue?' 'Yes.' 'It didn't occur to you that they had any symbolic significance?' 'No.' 'That they are usually associated, as is the Union Jack, with the nation?' 'No.' 'You have never in your youth heard a song called "Three Cheers for the Red, White & Blue"?' 'No.' 'Shall I sing it to you?' I had just begun to intone it when the 'counters' at the nearest table showed signs of distraction & we broke off our conversation! I felt cold with tension as the hours wore on. . . .

At last a blessed moment came when one of our people – I think George Foster – said to me 'We've got the edge on them – a slight edge.' I said 'How do you know?' He replied 'Ted winked.' Ted (Wheeler) was up on the high platform behind the long table. I felt infinitely cheered. Lamb had been 'out of it' for some time when this occurred. Royle looked visibly paler. Everyone began to expect a recount & at about 20 to 2 a recount was formally announced by the Sheriff. The Conservatives had (quite rightly) demanded it. . . . From the moment the recount started I knew we had won – & felt peace ineffable flooding every 'creek & inlet' of my being. . . . It was about 10 minutes to 3 when the High Sheriff rose on the platform & announced the figures . . . Liberal majority 219. It was a narrow shave – but we were in. Mark had wiped out a Govt. majority of 9000 odd & Labour was down by 2000. . . .[3]

We then went down into the tumult of the crowd. Mark was carried shoulder high (& managed to retain quite an effective position!) Leslie & I followed[4] with the help of friendly policemen (all the police & postmen were on our side throughout!) Our hands were grasped & wrung as we struggled towards the Rose of Torridge – a nice Labour man almost ground

[1] George Lambert (1909–89), 2nd Viscount (s. 1958); MP (Lib. Nat.), South Molton, 1945–50; (Nat. Lib.-Con.), Torrington, 1950–8. Lambert's succession to his father's viscountcy occasioned the Torrington by-election. His father had been Liberal National MP for South Molton, 1931–45, and so the family association with North Devon was very strong.

[2] Arthur Horace Penn (1886–1960), regimental adjutant of the Grenadier Guards when Mark Bonham Carter served in the regiment during the war.

[3] The official result was: M. R. Bonham Carter (Lib.) 13,408; A. H. F. Royle (Con.) 13,189; L. Lamb (Lab.) 8,697.

[4] Violet later added 'Attempts were made to hoist me up – which I gratefully resisted.'

my knuckles to powder saying 'I'm a Socialist but I'm glad you've won.' (Lamb said much the same to me inside. One of the nice things about this country is that Labour recognize & remember the old Lib.-Lab. alliance & feel that we are nearer to them than the Tories.)

. . . I was due to start for Bristol at 5.30 to take part in T.V. *Press Conference* but spent until ¼ to 5 going thro' points with Mark for his *The World Today* – a 12 minutes sound programme he was recording from the hôtel. I was sad to miss the Torch Light procession which had been (cagily & discreetly & hypothetically) planned by Dominic Le Foe.[1] I drove through the dark for 3 hours trying to collect what thoughts I had. They all seemed feelings. On arrival I found dear Frank Gillard who gave me coffee & sandwiches & a warm welcome in his room. Never have I been more glad of food & a friend! . . .[2]

Diary – Saturday 29 March – 21 Hyde Park Square, W.2

Mark & I & Leslie started about 10 & drove round the constituency getting marvellous receptions everywhere. . . . Dominic Le Foe drove ahead in a pilot car announcing Mark's arrival 'Here is Mark Bonham Carter – your new M.P. – the man who was going to be bottom of the Poll etc.' We met many old friends at Crediton, Hartland & Buckland Brewer. It was a fine day & the country looking lovely. The people are the nicest in the world. Mark is indeed blest in his constituency. I am so thankful that he has his heart's desire at last. Here he is, where he longed to be. 'Home is the Sailor – Home from the Sea & the Hunter Home from the Hill.'[3] Staggered up to bed & packed till about 1 o'clock. We started in the car for home about 9.30. . . .

[1]Dominic Le Foe was a tireless Liberal Party worker in North Devon, and central to Mark Bonham Carter's three Torrington campaigns, 1958, 1959 and 1964.

[2]Harold Nicolson wrote of Violet's performance that night: 'At 10.15 Violet appears on television, being interviewed by 3 journalists. Considering that she is not a young woman, has been electioneering for a fortnight, and has had an exciting and strained day, this is pretty sporting of her. She is excellent, and makes not one single foolish remark' (Nicolson, *Diaries and Letters, 1945–62*, 348).

[3]From Robert Louis Stevenson, 'Requiem': 'Under the wide and starry sky, / Dig the grave and let me lie. / Glad did I live and gladly die, And I laid me down with a will. // This be the verse you grave for me: / *Here he lies where he longed to be; / Home is the sailor, home from sea, / And the hunter home from the hill.*'

Diary – Monday 31 March – 21 Hyde Park Square, W.2

Tried to tackle & sort some of my mountains of telegrams & letters. Have to speak in Jo's absence at U.N.A. lunch to Hammarskjöld[1] – for 4 minutes. Harold & Gaitskell are taking only 5 & 4 each.... Mark takes his seat on Tuesday. Nat. Lib. Club luncheon before. The newspapers are a joy to read....

'Hold on – hold out – we are coming!'

The narrowness of the winning margin at Torrington did nothing to dampen Liberal enthusiasm about a revival. Violet was far from being immune to the infectious optimism that spread through the Party. At a celebratory luncheon at the National Liberal Club on 1 April she was asked to give a short speech, which she ended by repeating the message that she had delivered to a meeting of the same body nearly forty years earlier. In February 1920 she had helped her father to an equally famous by-election win at Paisley. It was a victory that signalled to the 'little gallant garrison' of Liberals then in Parliament that the country was mobilizing behind them. The 'message of Paisley' was 'Hold on – hold out – we are coming!' These same words now became the message of Torrington. Beleaguered Liberals across the land had a signal that help was on its way. It was an understandably emotional speech and Violet's words betrayed hope as much as conviction. Directly after the luncheon she went to the Commons to see Mark take his seat. There were just three Liberals in the Chamber to greet him, their 'scrannel cheers ... the only sounds that broke the sepulchral silence of the House'. It was a poignant moment and Violet inevitably cast her mind back: 'I remembered my father's introduction when he took his seat after Paisley & how faint the cheers of the survivors of the Liberal Party then sounded to me. But they at least were twenty-seven....'[2]

Diary – Wednesday 2 April – 21 Hyde Park Square, W.2

When I turned up at the Dorchester at 1.00 for 1.15 I was ushered into a private room reserved for the speakers & found myself in the presence of

[1] Dag Hjalmar Hammarskjöld (1905–61), UN secretary-general, 1953–61; Nobel Peace Prize winner, 1961.

[2] *Liberal Monthly*, April 1920, 8–10; *The Times*, 29 March 1958.

Harold & Gaitskell, with Hammarskjöld & Attlee lurking behind them – & Miss Courtney & General Lyne.[1] Harold gave me I thought a very 'old-fashioned look' & proffered no congratulations. Gaitskell & Attlee were much friendlier. . . .

Harold spoke first & had hardly got going when he was interrupted by a wild shout just behind him. There stood a member of the League of Empire Loyalists – 'bearded like the pard' – waving his arms & shouting at the top of his voice 'You are selling the Empire & the Commonwealth to a gang of Internationalists! Down with the United Nations' etc. He was led away & 'went quietly' – but Harold was naturally put rather out of his stride & asked us to drink the toast of Hammarskjöld without waiting for Gaitskell to second.

Gaitskell commented rather drily on this when he rose, adding that there was no reason he supposed why we shld not drink it again. Hammarskjöld followed & I then proposed the toast of U.N.A., stressing the fact that it was an independent body commanding the loyalty & support of all parties in this country, but dominated by none. Its first duty & its sole allegiance was to the principles of the U.N. Charter which it exists to serve. This in reply to Hailsham who has been lecturing it on its duties & scolding it for its resolutions on bomb testing etc.[2] The Laytons were just opposite me – very approving. General Lyne was delighted. Home to do 'last things' before Clovelly where we go to-morrow. Ray dined with us.

Diary – Thursday 24 April – 21 Hyde Park Square, W.2

Saw W. at last. I went to luncheon with him & Clemmie. Found him sitting in his usual chair – looking much paler & less roseate than usual. I had not seen him since all his illnesses. . . . He is being dieted – particularly with alcohol – & this has a depressing effect on him. We went into lunch – & as usual I found it terribly difficult to 'get through to him' in hearing etc. An à trois is really impossible to conduct with him. . . . Clemmie was most sweet & tactful to him but of course talked most of the time which made it more difficult for him to hear. About Torrington

[1]Kathleen Courtney (1878–1974), DBE, 1952; a veteran of the women's suffrage campaign; chairman and joint president, UNA, 1949–51. Maj.-Gen. Lewis Owen Lyne (1899–1970), distinguished soldier; on executive committee of UNA, 1951–7; joint president, UNA, 1957.

[2]In a letter to Conservative associations in England and Wales Hailsham had rebuked the UNA for a recent statement in favour of nuclear disarmament. This, he alleged, 'must hamper the government in its negotiations for peace'. The UNA replied to Hailsham by making clear that it did not support unilateral disarmament, but that it did back a suspension of British nuclear tests as a sign of good faith in advance of the international disarmament talks that were then pending (*The Times*, 31 March, 7 April 1958).

he said to me: 'They wanted me to send a message – in fact they sent me one to sign but I refused. I told them I was neutral.' He repeated this with emphasis. 'I said I was neutral.' I asked if Hailsham had ventured to approach him with this request. 'Hailsham! No not Hailsham – it came from higher up.' I wondered if this meant Harold. . . .

V.B.C. to Isaiah Berlin ***Friday 9 May***
21 Hyde Park Square, W.2

Dear Isaiah,

It was lovely to hear from you & I long to see you. Alas 15th & 16th I shall be out of the country. I am flying to Israel 13th-20th (my second visit – again as the guest of their Government) to speak at the dedication of a memorial in the Balfour Forest to Baffy Dugdale. . . .[1] Like you I find Israel intensely moving & exciting – & the only place where 'internationalism', so eloquently talked about elsewhere, is truly practised.

Mark in the H. of C! Raymond engaged![2] I am breathless with the pace of family events. Ray fell in love with Elena in U.S.A. after 2 brief meetings – one at a ball in London & one at Royaumont where he spent a night. He has never been in love before & is transfigured with happiness. His letters to me about her from U.S.A. made me sure that it was 'the real thing' (so-called) & that I shld. love her. And so I do. . . .

I heard Mark's maiden-speech in the House yesterday.[3] It went well – but I suffered from an acute vicarious 'needle' followed by relief.

My love. If the wedding is at Royaumont I hope that you & Aline will be there. Ever yrs Violet.

V.B.C. to W.S.C. ***Sunday 11 May***
21 Hyde Park Square, W.2

Dearest Winston,

I must write you a line of gratitude for your sweetness in sending for Mark in the House of Commons & talking to him. He was so touched. It

[1] Mrs Edgar Dugdale *née* Blanche 'Baffy' Balfour (d. 1948), niece and biographer of A. J. Balfour, and a passionate Zionist.

[2] Raymond and Elena Propper de Callejon had become engaged in New York in February. Elena's father, HE Señor Eduardo Propper de Callejon, had just ceased to be Spanish ambassador to Canada and was *en route* to take up a new post in Oslo.

[3] Mark Bonham Carter made his maiden speech on Thursday 8 May on the 'London Omnibus Dispute', which had been causing considerable inconvenience in the capital.

made up to him for the icy & surly reception he got when he took his seat. I was in the House to watch & I have never – in my long years of experience – seen any new member get such a reception. Deathly silence – not a murmur or a cheer (the 3 Liberals on the bench cld make barely audible noises) until he reached the table in front of the Speaker's Chair – then jeers from some of the Conservatives.[1] I could not 'catch' what they said – but the *Daily Telegraph*, which described the incident, said that some of them shouted 'Go back to Mummy'! What curious psychology! Is it so discreditable to wipe out a Govt. majority of 9½ thousand & take 2 thousand votes off Labour in the process? Is it disgraceful or ridiculous to possess a Mamma who is sufficiently articulate to lend a hand – or a tongue – in the process? (At a Private School – yes to both!)

All my dear love to you dearest Winston & to Clemmie. Ever your devoted Violet

Mark said you looked & seemed so well.

Diary – Thursday 24 July to Sunday 27 July – Royaumont, Seine-et-Oise

B. & I flew over on the 4 o'clock plane to Le Bourget, meeting Christopher Layton,[2] who was very kind & helped to carry the hat-boxes with which we were laden (B., who had pledged himself to Eduardo to dress 'en Ascot' at the wedding, was taking his white top hat). Alan Pryce-Jones met us at the Airport & we had a lovely drive thro' very French country, passing 2 beautiful châteaux on the way. Then Royaumont burst on us – a splendid square 'Palais Abbatial' – surrounded by avenues & lakes. Mrs Wooster[3] received us at the top of a flight of stone steps. . . .

Saturday 26th . . . B. & I drove to the church with Mrs W.[4] It was still fairly empty. Two splendid prie-dieux with red velvet cushions were in the centre of the little aisle. B & I sat in the 2 front seats behind them – on the right. Mark & Ray waited just in front of us. . . . Elena arrived at last. I shall never forget the moving radiance of her face. It outshone the 5 stars in her hair. Never have I seen such joy in any eyes – rarely such beauty. . . .

[1] Violet had written to William Haley: 'The glum & surly silence of both the Tory & the Labour benches was a strange welcome to my father's grandson. How differently Winston wld. have behaved' (11 April 1958).

[2] Christopher Walter Layton (b. 1929), editorial writer, *The Economist*, 1954–62; economic adviser to the Liberal Party, 1962–9; the son of Violet's Liberal Party colleague and friend, Walter Layton (1st Baron Layton).

[3] Mary Wooster *née* Springer, Elena's grandmother.

[4] The church service, at Viarmes, had been preceded by a civil service at the mairie at Asnières-sur-Oise the previous day.

The service was short – the responses only 'Oui – je le veux' firmly spoken by Raymond – less audibly by Elena.... A great deal of signing of books followed the ceremony – done at their prie-dieux before the altar. Then they went out into brilliant sunshine....

The afternoon passed in a kind of dream from which one felt one must wake up.... The sun shone – the Trompe de Chasse played in the avenue in front of the house – dressed in their traditional uniforms – standing with their backs to us so that we might not get the blast of their trumpets.... Elena went down & drank champagne with them. She wandered in her lovely dress across lawns – by the lake – over the bridge into the wood (pursued by photographers). We caught glimpses of her whiteness among the dark trees – then she disappeared & Bongie said 'I wonder if she has turned into a swan?' There were swans everywhere – floating & gliding on the lakes – & also sunning themselves on the grass.

The cake was cut – the health of the bride & bridegroom was proposed in one sentence by Mark & replied to in another by Raymond – & Elena disappeared to change. Many of the guests melted away. Those who stayed saw the loveliest, most lyrical & unexpected moment of all – Ray & Elena's departure. They came down the steps – saying their goodbyes & being embraced by all – a few perfunctory handfuls of rice were flung. At the foot of the staircase there awaited them a little open chaise drawn by a white horse garlanded with white flowers (even the spokes of the wheels were bound with white gladioli). Behind sat an old coachman of 84 who had served all his life at Royaumont. They got in side by side (nothing between them but the reins) – Elena put her arm round Ray – thus with a few goodbye waves they drove away into the future....

Diary – Tuesday 19 August – 21 Hyde Park Square, W.2

Did a broadcast programme for Associated Rediffusion at T.V. House Kingsway with Bob Boothby, John Connell, & Paul Johnson (*New Statesman*).[1] Subject: The Establishment. It was rather fun but wld have been much better had it been a debate. The procedure was that Gerald Fay of the *M.G.*, who was Chairman, made a preliminary statement. Then Bob Boothby took the stand & expressed his belief that there was an 'Establishment' – that it was sinister, that its members were high-minded but wrong-headed – that it had all kinds of underground ramifications & was a kind of spider's web which spread its tentacles throughout society. He stressed of course the Appeasement years & named All Souls & the Astors

[1] Paul (Bede) Johnson (b. 1928), author; on editorial staff, *New Statesman*, 1955; editor, 1965–70.

as among the strongholds from which its influence radiated.

I then followed him & said that tho' I was supposed to be a member of the Establishment I was not aware of its existence. It was not because of the Cliveden Set or All Souls that we had then pursued a disastrous policy, but because the P.M. of the day believed in it, & so did his Cabinet, & they were supported by the H. of C. The idea that I was in constant telepathic contact with the Archbishop of Canterbury & the Gov. of the Bank of England & the Editor of the *Times Literary Supplement* cld only be believed by people living in Cloud Cuckoo Land.

I also pointed out that Bob himself, who alleged that all thro' his career he had 'bumped up against the Establishment with disastrous results to himself', was himself a contradiction in terms of his own theory. Why there he is plastered with decorations – titles, Knighthoods & Life Peerages rain down on him.[1] He emerges drenched & dripping from the Fount of Honour & then shakes himself like a dog getting out of dirty water. . . .

After it was over we saw a run through. The photography I thought was appalling – particularly of myself. Technically they are far below the B.B.C. Bob was most mellow & pressing & said (I am sure untruly!) that the 2 programmes that lived in his memory were one he had done with me at the Isle of Wight (an *Any Questions*) & this one. He also said the one thing he had looked forward to was being in the H. of Lords with me. Of course I ought to have been there & shld be. I said I had no particular desire to be – but I thought it disgraceful of Harold not to have consulted the Liberals & allowed them to put up a list of nominations. Bob said 'No, he was frightfully bitter against the Liberals.' I didn't have time to ask him why.

He is quite childishly delighted with his peerage, chattering about his 'quarterings' etc. (just as K. Elliot does in her letter).[2] It is odd how much innocent pleasure it appears to give. I told him I was amazed that having a safe seat in the Commons he shld have forsaken it for the Lords. He replied that there were much better debates in the Lords & they were much better reported. He is an odd creature. He cld not have been more friendly. Having no loyalties he also has no rancour. . . .

[1]Boothby has been included in the first creation of life peers under the 1958 Life Peerages Act, 24 July.

[2]Kay Elliot, the half-sister of Violet's step-mother, Margot Asquith, was also among the first creation of life peers.

Diary – Thursday 18 September – 21 Hyde Park Square, W.2

Long meeting of the Old Vic Trust.... I had a short talk with Oliver Poole & teased him about Percy Browne's candidature at Torrington, which he has come to save from Socialism![1] He told me that we shld lose the seat next time – reminding me that he had prophesied that we shld win it this time. I persuaded him to bet me £5....

Diary – Thursday 7 May 1959 – 21 Hyde Park Square, W.2

...Borough Council Elections. Drove round in a Liberal car – with loud-speaker – with Sheldon Williams through the 'dark backward & abysm of Paddington' & visited 3 very sleepy Polling Stations with a few children leaning against the railings round them & hardly anyone going in or out. And this was supposed to be the 'rush-hour' for voting – between 8 & 9. I felt a certain pathos about poor Sheldon W. who has an almost fanatical light of faith in his eye & is I fear going to reap such a meagre harvest....

Diary – Monday 8 June – 21 Hyde Park Square, W.2

...N.A.T.O. party given by Beddington-Behrens & his new wife. Saw Walter Layton there & talked to him about the wreckage of our U. Europe hopes. Then Duncan Sandys came up & I continued the conversation with him. He shared my despair & anger. I said to him 'Tell me Duncan – why didn't Winston act when he came in in 1951 & had the power to do so? What hampered him? Why did he allow E.D.C., the Coal & Steel Community etc. to be turned down? His Govt. did no better than the Labour Party to support his own idea. What happened?' Duncan replied 'He never really understood it. When I was sitting next to him in a debate about the European Army he turned to me & asked "What does it mean?" He didn't understand it & Anthony was strongly against it. He & the F.O. never wanted anything of the kind.' I believe this to be dead true. W. was too old to grasp the practical implication of his own idea, & the F.O. – which hates all new ideas, led by Anthony – who never liked this one, sabotaged it. A real tragedy. We are now trying to build a still smaller one-horse group with the Scandinavian countries & Denmark.[2] I suppose as a bargaining-

[1] Percy Basil Browne (b. 1923), company director; the victorious Conservative candidate at Torrington in 1959, he went on to represent the seat until 1964.

[2] An allusion to the European Free Trade Association (EFTA), which was established in November 1959.

counter? But its immediate effect will be to divide Europe.

Diary – Wednesday 1 July – 21 Hyde Park Square, W.2

...Dined at Turkish Embassy.... After dinner talked first to my hostess – the Ambassador's mother – in French. She is a dear old girl & admired my dress (a long one in cyclamen satin) saying how she preferred them to short ones & adding 'You look like a Princess' (!! – the last thing I have ever been compared to!) I then had a long talk with Callaghan whom I liked very much – which I had not done when we met at an *Any Questions* & the programme had closed with my saying to him 'Takes a snob to see a snob' & he had been annoyed at not getting a chance to come back.[1] This time we gnashed our teeth in unison about Africa.[2] I told him how well I thought he spoke in winding up the Hola debate for the Opposition. We went in to all the horrors ... & he said how serious he thought it might be if the Tories get in again next time in view of the African situation. I agreed. Oliver Messel[3] who dropped me home was also boiling over Africa. He said he was a Conservative & didn't bother about Suez, but he just cldn't stand this. I was surprised to find he had any political reactions!

Diary – Tuesday 14 July – 21 Hyde Park Square, W.2

Saw a very moving documentary film about S. Africa shown privately in Wardour St. by the Africa Bureau – Michael Scott,[4] Sir Jock Campbell & other friends there. Sat between Jeremy Thorpe & the Africa correspondent of the *Times* – a very nice man.[5] I told him I had urged Haley to hurl a

[1] See above, p. 149.

[2] In early 1959 there were increasing signs of unrest in Britain's African colonies and on 3 March a riot at the Hola detention camp in Kenya resulted in eleven 'Mau Mau' prisoners being beaten to death by guards. The incident led to widespread criticism of the government's handling of colonial affairs. But Macmillan refused to accept the resignation of his colonial secretary, Alan Lennox-Boyd, and an opposition motion of censure was comfortably defeated in the Commons on 16 June. Macmillan later reflected that 'Hola' was 'an anxious, if minor, incident exaggerated by the hysterical attitude of some critics and the not unnatural desire of others to gain political advantage' (Macmillan, *Riding the Storm*, 735).

[3] Oliver Hilary Messel (1904–78), artist and stage designer; worked with Covent Garden and Glyndebourne.

[4] The Rev. Michael Scott, director of the 'Africa Bureau' and for many years one of the more militant supports of the anti-nuclear movement.

[5] Oliver Frederick Woods (1911–72), joined editorial staff of *The Times*, 1935; colonial editor and assistant foreign editor, 1956; assistant editor, 1961.

few more thunderbolts & thought the *Times* terribly moderate & mugwumpish about it....

Diary – Sunday 2 August – Liberal Summer School, Oxford

...Lord Elton arrived for dinner.[1] Why on earth he was chosen to give the Ramsay Muir lecture I cannot conceive. An ex-National Labour man who has written a book called *St George or the Dragon*. I believe that he now calls himself 'independent'. He gave us exactly what I had expected – a sugary dissertation on 'The British achievement'. Kipling without the punch. A hymn to the Empire of unadulterated praise, sprinkled freely with allusions to cricket, not a shadow on the picture – not the most indirect allusion to present-day events in Africa – with which all our minds & hearts & consciences were full. Poor Miss MacKinnon who presided was hard put to it to thank him....

Diary – Thursday 27 August – Belstone

My last day – a most beautiful one.... In the afternoon went down about 4 & said goodbye to the Westlakes & the Bins.[2] With the Bins I got – involuntarily & unfortunately – engaged in a fierce debate over Conservative-Liberal affinity. He likes to think that we are akin. I had to point out that there are things – like Suez, Cyprus, Hola – hanging, flogging & manifestations like Blackpool[3] – which divide us emotionally so deeply that any sort of get-together is impossible. Labour is muddle-headed – Socialism is antediluvian – but these issues do not stir us so deeply as the violence & blindness which leads to brutality & bullying on one side, & great loss of life on the other. He even resorted to the plea that the Hola

[1] Godfrey Elton (1892–1973), cr. Baron, 1934; fellow of Queen's College and lecturer in modern history, Oxford, 1919–39; unsuccessful Labour candidate 1924, 1929; expelled from Party as a follower of Ramsay MacDonald, 1931; author of *Saint George or the Dragon* (1942).

[2] Cyril Edward Robinson (b. 1884–?), classical scholar and house master at Winchester College, 1917–39; he married, 1923, Mary *née* Sealy; Mark Bonham Carter's house master for all but his (Mark's) last year at Winchester.

[3] On the closing day of the Conservative Party conference at Blackpool, October 1958, the prime minister faced organized heckling from members of the League of Empire Loyalists. The hecklers were ejected by stewards and later claimed to have been beaten up by them in a back room of the conference hall. Lord Hailsham rebutted these allegations in a letter to *The Times*, but argued that the heckling was 'calculated and intended to cause a breach of the peace': 'if I had behaved similarly .... I should have expected to receive physical violence, however unjustified' (*The Times*, 18 October 1958).

victims were murderers etc. – as tho' the character of the victim was relevant. It is the degradation of those who were able to beat them to death which matters. But I shld not have chosen this for a farewell talk! They have both been so sweet to us. . . .

'The Tories expect to win, or say they do'
– *Torrington and the 1959 general election.*

Mark Bonham Carter had been in the Commons for barely eighteen months when a general election was announced for 8 October 1959. His victory at Torrington had helped revive Liberal morale and the Party approached the coming campaign with renewed confidence. In all 216 candidates took the field, nearly double the number in 1955, while performances in recent by-elections suggested that fewer deposits would be lost. On the other hand, the Liberals had won only six seats and 2.7 per cent of the vote in 1955. This precarious electoral foothold was likely to come under sustained attack from a reinvigorated Labour Party. The Conservatives meanwhile were set to exploit the prosperity enjoyed by most voters in an era when, as Harold Macmillan famously put it, 'most of our people have never had it so good'. In these circumstances only the most optimistic Liberal could envisage a dramatic electoral breakthrough. At Torrington it would be a challenge simply to hold on to what had been won. Disgruntled Conservatives, who had abstained at the by-election, were now expected to return to the fold. Days before the poll, Violet detected renewed confidence in the opposition camp, writing to Bongie: 'The Tories expect to win, or say they do.' She put their son's chances at no better than even. It was a realistic assessment, which must have been especially hard for Bongie to bear. He was then chronically ill with prostate trouble and practically house-bound in London, awaiting an operation after the election.

Diary – Wednesday 16 September – 21 Hyde Park Square, W.2

Toad & Andrew to luncheon – dear little Toad in a brand-new suit & rather badly cut hair. It was a poignant thought to imagine what needle he might be feeling about going off to Eton – his first parting from home. He seemed very brave & composed & ate a good luncheon. Jo came in to fetch them afterwards to drive down in Elena's car, which she angelically brought round for them. To my amazement Jo urged me to come up to Orkney to help him! He has not done this since the '50 Election & I am hard put to it to refuse, but I know he is as safe as a church whereas Mark is fighting for his life at Torrington & Malindine & Jeremy might win seats. I don't know what to do.

Went with B. to see Sir Eric Riches[1] where we met [Dr] Rettie. B. saw him alone of course but I went up afterwards. He said that it was imperative for B. to have the operation – irrespective really of the state of his heart. There was no other way out.... He is very full up in the immediate future. This wld have the advantage of allowing me to help Mark in the Election. For B. it is of course a bore to wait on in discomfort. He wld rather get it over as soon as possible....

V.B.C. to Bongie ***Tuesday 22 September***
Royal Hôtel, Bideford, North Devon

Darling, Thank you for your letter. I had a good journey but there was not a crumb of food on the train (the tea carriage was switched off by the time I went along). However I had a little cold supper when I arrived, felt very tired & went to bed & was actually fast asleep by the time Mark came in from his 4 meetings & came to my bedroom. He went off early to London to-day for his T.V. programme & will be back on Wed. evening when he & I do 2 meetings together. To-day I shall be going round here, there & everywhere meeting people in High St., Market & various villages, seeing canvassers off, etc.

I think it will be a touch-&-go election as there is no obvious clear-cut issue & the people here according to George Foster (Agent) care more about what happens to themselves than about what happens to people in Africa & abroad. Percy Browne (Mark's opponent) is 'playing' the thing very soft & low which is the obvious tactic for a Tory. Mark's personal hold & record & status as a member is his first asset – & must be stressed. For the rest the issues are so far rather blurred. I hope you are not feeling too uncomfortable. I am glad Cressida will be with you soon....

Love always. In haste. V.

Diary – Tuesday 29 September – Royal Hôtel, Bideford, North Devon

Laurie Buck fetched me 2.15 & we had a stiff afternoon's canvassing at Crediton on a new Council House Estate (Winswood by name). The state of Crediton (always our weak spot) is well demonstrated by the fact that

[1] Sir Eric (William) Riches (1897–1987), Kt, 1958; surgeon and urologist to the Middlesex Hospital, where Bongie underwent a prostate operation in October.

we asked for 6 canvassers to meet us at the Liberal Club & come with us – & only 2 poor, gallant old women – one very deaf – turned up. Crediton simply won't canvass. It was nevertheless quite useful. I then rested at the house of a nice woman called Mrs Searle – who had an old father asleep in a chair (he had had a stroke). She gave me a room to myself & I was able to prepare my notes & tidy in peace. I spoke to her about canvassing & she said she thought it wld be interesting & exciting. But when I suggested she shld help in Crediton she said 'Anywhere but in Crediton – people wld know me & it wld hurt my husband's business. It has already suffered because we came out as Liberals at the by-election.' It is appalling that intimidation by the Tories shld exist on every level. Drove on to Shobrooke where I had an excellent meeting ... & then to Black Dog where I had another – both well attended.

Diary – Saturday 3 October – Royal Hôtel, Bideford, North Devon

Dominic Le Foe has arrived & we had a Circus of Cars – with him & a loud-speaker in front with music alternating with his priceless comments. Unfortunately the music went wrong (sabotage was suspected by a Tory mechanic in the Liberal works which had supplied it!) Ray drove Mark & Leslie – I followed with Laurie Buck. We visited Torrington, Hatherleigh, Okehampton & North Tawton – Mark & I speaking in each market-place or street, introduced by Dominic....

V.B.C. to Bongie ***Sunday 4 October***
Royal Hôtel, Bideford, North Devon

Darling, I have not had a second to write as the pace has been fast & furious as you can imagine....

Of the situation here I can say nothing. It is in the lap of the Gods. Browne (the Tory) is a good-looking pleasant cypher who never mentions Liberalism or Mark or gives us a ball of any sort to return. This makes the Election difficult to fight. He never speaks for more than 9 minutes. The first burst of strong feeling was produced by Lord Lambert appearing here to speak for Browne under the Tory flag. He was almost shouted down at Winkleigh & I shld think had a rough time at Okehampton last night....

The Tories expect to win or say they do. Our people tell us of increasing Labour voters coming over to us – but we have no means of knowing their numbers. I shld have said it was 50–50.... I shall be thankful when Thursday is over. This is the prize the Tories long for above all others. I cannot bear to think what it wld mean to Mark to lose. He has invested so much in it – his whole future....

All my love to you & missing. We had a much-needed day of rest to-day & went over to Clovelly in the afternoon. I am very tired but shall complete the course.

Diary – Monday 5 October – Royal Hôtel, Bideford, North Devon

...Canvassed in the afternoon with Miss Hutchinson at a place called Dolton & afterwards at Copplestone where everyone was Liberal (including a railway-man we called on) except one woman who thought voting wrong for religious issues. (Sheila thought she was a 'Plymouth brother'.) I asked her if she thought it wld be wrong to interfere (as I had once done) if she saw a man kicking his wife in the stomach. It acted like a kind of shock treatment. She shuddered – gasped – & held out her hand for the paper I had offered her to read. Went home & was driven – by dear Mr Heywood – very much against the grain & under protest to 2 widely separated villages – Throwleigh & Broadwood Kelly – a tiny remote village 25 miles off. It seemed such a waste of time.

Throwleigh was I think the most disagreeable meeting I have ever addressed. It was packed with solid, suet-faced Conservatives who made no sound or comment of any kind so that speaking was like a recitation without a prompter. There may, in fact must have been, a few timid Liberals interspersed with them but they were so terrified & terrorized that they did not dare to make any demonstration or sign of life.... An ex-Colonel (or so he looked) got up & asked some very foolish questions ... which I answered. But when he tried to ask a 4th I said I thought it was someone else's turn. (My Chairman had never been a 'Chairman' before & did not know what to do.) I rather enjoyed it when the Colonel made an attack on our lack of preparation for the 1st World War. I said how much worse we had been prepared by Conservative Govts for the Second – & recommended him to read the *World Crisis* by W.S.C. The gravamen of his charge was that the Lib. Govt had refused to listen to Ld Roberts' demand for Conscription. I told him that Lord Kitchener – a far greater soldier – & then Secretary of State for War had been against it.

This reduced him for a time to silence. But when I had to leave for my next meeting he complained that he had more to ask & that Mark at Chagford had refused to answer more questions on the grounds that he was tired (of course a lie). I said 'I expect he was tired of you' – upon which there was a sudden burst of laughter from the (till then) inanimate audience. When I got into my car in the dark a few terrified Libs clustered round me & gave me some flowers. I'm afraid I told them what I thought of Throwleigh! & asked them why they didn't show their colours. We then drove on thro' the dark for the best part of an hour to Broadwood Kelly getting there at 8.30 – the appted hour – only to find that all the people – except about 20 from Warkleigh who had arranged the meeting – were at a Harvest Festival Service! I had to sit in the car for 20 minutes till they came out of it. It was then quite a reasonably good meeting but there is apparently not one 'key' man or woman who can run anything there. They had complained that they had never had a meeting. One cannot wonder at it!

Diary – Eve of Poll, Wednesday 7 October – Royal Hôtel, Bideford, North Devon

They had another Circus on which I longed to go but was told that I must stay behind & canvas Bideford – to my disappointment. However it gave me a free morning to think over Eve of the Poll speeches. A Miss Pickard picked me up & we had a fairly futile afternoon. . . .

I did however have rather an alarming experience in 2 adjacent streets within the space of an hour. 3 people of very different kinds – an artist (Lloyd by name), a housewife & a 'half-way between' woman – all floaters with no political allegiances, each in their own idiom said to me 'We voted for your son last time – we think him incomparably the best candidate – he has done more for us & Bideford in 18 months than any other Member in our experience. But – we mean to vote Tory this time – as we feel we must keep Labour out at all costs – & only a Tory member can help to do so.' In vain I argued (though one of them I swayed). I told them that I felt sure the Tories were going to be returned (& this I believe). Their attitude was perfectly logical. But it showed me how the wind was blowing. . . .

Diary – Declaration of the Poll, Friday 9 October – Royal Hôtel, Bideford, North Devon

We had not meant to turn up till 12 o'clock but had a message that it might be declared between 11.30 & 12 so arrived earlier. Large crowd assembled in the Market Place. The Torrington Town Hall bristling with Tories with bright blue rosettes.

We were invited to go up into a Gallery which looked down on the Counting Room – but I did not do so as I cld not bear the thought of being mewed up with Mrs Browne etc. so I sat on one of 2 chairs (Leslie on the other) in a little ante-room where there was a buffet with urns of tea & buns. The Tories who came constantly through it cld not have behaved worse – showing themselves at the window & displaying their rosettes to the crowd. Mark went through into the count to see how things were going & came out saying to us: 'Laurie Buck says I'm out by 3,000. Labour has got a high vote.' I cld not bear it.... Poor Leslie. I think she was less braced for defeat than I was but she behaved with admirable calm. One single decent Conservative came through & when I automatically asked 'How is it going?' said 'Liberal & Conservative are neck to neck. Labour's nowhere.' It was some comfort.

Mr Dobson[1] the young Labour candidate came in looking very bouncy & confident. He sat down beside me & I had a very frank though friendly talk with him – pointing out some of the most dishonest features of his campaign.... I also asked him why – as he had told the *M.G.* – it was his main object to unseat the Liberal at this Election – when his predecessor Lamb had recognized that we were much closer ideologically than to the Conservatives. He did not deny it, but said Lab. must fight & establish itself everywhere as the alternative to Toryism & this involved wiping out the Liberal.

I have been told since that he expected to get 10,000 votes.... When the last pile had been counted he got 5,500 (or a little under). His poor little wife was in tears. We got 15,268 & the Tories just over 17,000....[2] The victory speech was made by Browne to a howling Tory mob. Mark followed very well & bravely. Then we staggered out into the crowd – poor Sheila Hutchinson in tears – some of our supporters borne towards us in the crowd – men with tape-recorders sticking them under Mark's face & mine.

At last we gained the car & drove back. It was nearly 3 o'clock. We sat down in the (mercifully empty) 'lounge' feeling bruised from head to foot. But at least it was over. I said: 'I feel as if I'd had a tooth out.' Mark said 'I feel as if I'd had an abscess lanced.' As he truly said the emotional strain of an election is so great. At one moment one is plunged into the depths, at the next tossed up to Heaven. Every contact, rumour, bit of news, plays cat & mouse with one's emotions....

[1] Raymond Francis Dobson (1925–80), trade union official with the Postal Workers' Union, 1950–66; MP (Lab.) Bristol North East, 1966–70; parliamentary secretary, ministry of technology, 1967–9.

[2] On a higher turnout than the previous year (86.2 per cent against 80.6) the official result was: P. B. Browne (Con.) 17,283; M. R. Bonham Carter (Lib.) 15,018; R. F. H. Dobson (Lab.) 5,633. The Conservative majority was thus 2,265.

Bongie to V.B.C.

Friday 9 October
21 Hyde Park Square, W.2

Darling – I have just heard that our Mark has lost his seat. In spite of the many hopeful Liberal results, as the Conservative gains grew & grew, it became almost impossible that he should retain it, yet one goes on hoping for a miracle. I sat up until 4 o'clock waiting for it and now I have just heard the result from the BBC report and I have no more interest in the bloody election. He has all my heartfelt sympathy and Leslie too, who has entered so fully into his political life.

I have little doubt that he will be offered many contests, and probably more advantageous ones, though it is difficult for a Liberal to win unless the Tories have a major disaster (as is quite possible in Africa); and of course I am thinking of you knowing what you are feeling and how much of every atom of your head and heart you have devoted to the fight, and how we both longed for him to represent Torrington, with its charming supporters & lovely lovely prospects.

It is of course the weakness of the Labour position, dominated by the Trades Unions, and resulting in the fear of inflation that has produced the result – it is horrible and so bitter that one cannot restrain one's hatreds. Forgive this disjointed & imperfect letter.

My love is with you both. B.

I do not expect you back until Sunday afternoon. I have to be in the Middlesex Hospital by 3 o'clock on Monday. Elena will take us if you wish to go.

Diary – Saturday 10 – Sunday 11 October – Royal Hôtel, Bideford, North Devon

We drove around without a time-table & I can't now remember all the places we went to – only so many people broken-hearted & in tears. . . . I had a long exhausting pack before going to bed. So far I hadn't cried – but when I said goodbye to the dear Middlelines on Sunday morning I felt unconquerable tears. Bert took my luggage & Gillian's[1] to the station – & I felt lacrimae rerum welling again when I said goodbye to him. He's been an angel to me. Then Gillian & I embarked for London & tears poured down my cheeks for many hours. Reached home after 5 & found B. waiting for me – very sad. He goes into Hospital to-morrow for his operation on Saturday. It is his 79th birthday – would that it could be a happier one.

[1] Gillian Jacomb-Hood, Mark's political secretary.

The aftermath of the 1959 general election

The Conservative triumph in the 1959 election was, in the words of Harold Macmillan, 'a staggering result'. No party in modern times had won three consecutive general elections with an increased majority at each. It was a personal victory for 'Supermac', who was rewarded with a 100 seat overall majority, nearly double the figure at the dissolution. Measured against this, the Liberal performance was highly creditable. Although only six seats were won, just fifty-six deposits were lost, a great improvement on previous polls. And the Party had attracted over 1.6 million votes, more than twice the total in 1955. But there were disappointments and notably at Torrington. Defeat there came as 'a heavy and ... unexpected blow' to Jo Grimond, depriving him of a particularly valuable member of his small parliamentary team. Violet's own sadness at Mark's defeat was quickly overshadowed by her concern about Bongie's health. He never fully recovered from his prostate operation that October and in the months ahead Violet was increasingly occupied in caring for him. This took its toll of her own health. When Mark contested Torrington in 1964 she was herself too ill to canvass. The 1959 general election thus proved to be her last. She had campaigned at twelve in a career spanning four decades, and few then alive could claim such political longevity.[1]

Diary – Tuesday 27 October – 21 Hyde Park Square, W.2

...A shattering day which I shall never forget. I had told [Dr] Rettie yesterday on the telephone how worried I was by B.'s lack of reaction, memory & any sort of real recovery – & I asked him to telephone me today before I went to the Hospital. To my horror he told me that he might have sustained thro' the shock of the operation some kind of injury or damage to the brain.... He said he cld not promise complete recovery. My heart seemed to stop beating.... I cld hardly stand when I put down the telephone. I felt stunned with despair & horror. There was no one to consult or ask advice from. Here was a nightmare staring us in the face – which to him wld be the worst imaginable. He has always feared his family's longevity & made me promise to give him a 'Bongie bean' if he showed any sign of surviving his faculties. I staggered to the Hospital, when I recovered myself enough. He said 'My whole life is a blur' – &

[1] Horne, *Macmillan, 1957–1986*, 152.

again 'Life is very difficult. People ask me questions & I don't know the answer.'

Mark Bonham Carter to V.B.C. ***Wednesday 28 October***
Villa Suveret, Valescure, St Raphaël

Dear Mama,

We arrived here safely last night, having picked up our car in Nice & driven along the twisty, beautiful coast road. The villa is vast & hideous, though standing in a magnificent position over-looking St Raphael & the sea....

Do let us have news of Bong. It is strange & disquieting to find someone whose pleasure in the ordinary things of life has always been so strong, & whose 'philosophy' seemed founded on some inner rock, overcome by so deep a lassitude. Your own feelings at this time must be so black & I only wish that you, & not we, had been given the opportunity for a break. You must long for it, & I cannot describe the love & admiration which I have felt during & since the election, watching your undying vitality and courage....

I also wish I could think of some way to bring home to him the fact that all of us want him to live – and need him. It is this that I think he disbelieves. He has convinced himself that he is no longer needed, & no longer necessary.... I don't think from a sense of over-weaning modesty he knows how many people love him, from Norman at Brooks's to Mr Luke at Okehampton, & to all of us. And these people want him to get better – but he is doing his best to deprive us of what we want. This is the first act of selfishness I have ever known him commit.

...Love from us both in these hard days, we long to see you, Love Mark

V.B.C. to Barbara Freyberg ***Christmas Day, Friday 25 December***
21 Hyde Park Square, W.2

Darling Barbara.

A thousand grateful thanks for lovely book-marker & card. I have been terribly handicapped in getting Xmas presents this year, & had to do most of them by telephone as I cld. so rarely get out, so forgive no card. The little Wedgwood ash-trays wld. I felt at least be useful, as one never has enough of them.

I am spending the 'stillest' Xmas of my life alone with B. here. I had not spent Xmas in London for 30 years! (I can only remember about 3 London Xmases in my life) & the hush of this silent Square in a silent town is very strange. B. is a little better. He still has a night-nurse & I look after him by day. The Drs say I must think of his recovery in terms of months rather than weeks. I do hope darling that you & Bernard are well & have had a lovely family Xmas? I have missed spending it at Stockton with Cressida & Adam as we usually do. . . .

My dear love to Bernard & you darling. Ever yrs Violet

Diary – New Year's Eve, Thursday 31 December – 21 Hyde Park Square, W.2

B. still very breathless. Every effort tires him. . . . Pouring wet dark day. Leslie & Mark came to pick me up to dine with them. We had been going to have a quiet evening but Ann Fleming asked us all to her party & knowing Mark wld like to go & wld not like to leave me, I went, tho' feeling ill-attuned & a ghost at the feast. Huge party – Bob Boothby – Diana Cooper – who I had a short talk with & liked better than I have almost ever done.[1] She talked of Duff & how she now felt that perhaps it had been best for him to die suddenly after only 30 hours of illness. Said how lonely she was. I had children & they were all near me & round me. She had only one son far-away whom she never saw. She was absolutely natural & rather touching. She said she felt old inside – no longer feeling things so strongly – ardour gone (these were not her words). She said – 'But you don't feel like that?' And it is true that I don't. . . . Home to find B. sleeping under his blue light. He stirred & spoke to me.

[1] Lady Diana Cooper *née* Manners (1892–1986), Viscountess Norwich; daughter of 8th Duke of Rutland; a society beauty and actress who married, 1919, Alfred Duff Cooper, 1st Viscount Norwich.

EIGHT
Widowhood
1960–1961

Diary – New Year's Day, Friday 1 January 1960 – 21 Hyde Park Square, W.2

The darkest I can remember – since 1910.[1] Rettie called & said B's pulse was down. Prescribed a white capsule (diuretic) to bring down the swelling in his legs & a day in bed to-morrow.... Read in the paper that W. goes to Riviera to-morrow. Telephoned him my love.

Diary – Saturday 23 January – 21 Hyde Park Square, W.2

Dr Rettie came in the morning & admitted that there had been a steep & sudden decline in his condition. He did not attempt to account for it but used Nurse Hayward's phrase 'He is failing.' I asked 'physically or mentally?' He said both. His heart was not bad but power of movement etc. had gone downhill. He gave no reason....

Diary – Tuesday 26 January – 21 Hyde Park Square, W.2

...Nurse Hayward came in to look after B. while I was out. She said to me with some insight 'He does not want to live.' It is tragically true – but can that affect him physically as it does? She thinks it can. He often says (as he did yesterday) 'Oh my body' – as though he longed to shed it....

[1] In the New Year of 1910 Violet was coming to terms with the death of her close friend and suitor, Archie Gordon, who had been involved in a serious motor-car accident. Bongie had been instrumental in helping her to overcome that loss: see *Lantern Slides*, chapter six.

Diary – Thursday 28 January – 21 Hyde Park Square, W.2

Terribly busy morning with tel. calls ... preparations for my broadcast, correspondence etc. Went to B.B.C. at 7 to broadcast on the Boycott & Apartheid in *Matters of Moment.*[1] It was the same kind of programme I had once taken part in when Trevelyan, the Film Censor, was in the box & had to give answers & reply to criticism from 3 questioners, of whom I was one. This time I was in the box to defend the Boycott of S. African goods. Percy Cudlipp[2] in the Chair & the questioners Paul Bareau[3] (economist – *News Chron.*), a journalist called Utley[4] – blind & very Right Wing, & a young S. African called Hertzog – grand-nephew of the General & P.M. He was a whole-hogging supporter of Apartheid & of course anti-boycott. The other 2 were anti-Apartheid & anti-boycott.

We had (what is called) a very 'lively' discussion with a good deal of interruption – almost barracking at times from my questioners.... Young Hertzog was not very skilful & had an impossible case. Paul Bareau rather inhibited because on the main issue he was on my side & I conceded in the first few sentences that a month's boycott cld not possibly be an effective economic weapon. We adjourned afterwards & talked quite friendlily about J. M. Barrie etc. Utley is an extraordinary character. He is clever & I liked him but his one hope is that we may now have Civil War in Kenya! I got home to find a sheaf of telephone messages & telegrams from complete strangers sprinkled about the country. 'Bravo. Four Cheers for democracy – in deep admiration.' 'God Bless you Lady Violet I am listening this moment' etc. etc. One very nice one from Margaret Lane.[5] Cressida came up from Stockton.

[1] Violet was then involved in the campaign for a month-long boycott of South African goods, in protest against apartheid.

[2] Percy Cudlipp (1905–62), journalist and broadcaster; columnist for *News Chronicle*, 1954–6; editor, *New Scientist*, from 1956.

[3] Paul Bareau, city editor of the *News Chronicle*.

[4] Thomas Edwin ('Peter') Utley (1921–88), journalist and commentator; leader writer with the *Sunday Times* and *The Times*; later assistant editor, *Daily Telegraph*; blind in one eye at birth, he lost sight in the other at the age of nine.

[5] Margaret Lane (1907–94), Countess of Huntingdon (m. 2nd 1944 15th Earl of Huntingdon); novelist, biographer and journalist; author of *The Tale of Beatrix Potter* (1946). Most of the listeners who wrote to Violet after this broadcast judged her the winner in the debate, and many drew attention to the fact that she was a single woman against three, at times rude, male interrogators. One correspondent wrote: 'At one point you seemed to be surrounded by a pack of angry dogs! Your triumph was all the greater for that' (Louise Morgan Theis to VBC, 29 January).

Diary – Saturday 30 January – 21 Hyde Park Square, W.2

...C. lunched & she & I & Law went on at ¼ to 4 to little Virginia's christening in St Faith's Chapel Westminster Abbey.... Virginia behaved admirably & only cried when very liberally sluiced with holy water.[1] We all went back to Victoria Road where we drank her health in champagne, then Ray & Elena dropped me, & Cressida drove off to Stockton with Maize.[2] I felt a great sadness at B's absence & worse still that he was not even well enough to regret not being there – or realise that he was missing it. The miss of sharing life with him is unutterable. When I said goodnight to him, last thing, he was (as he usually is) very clear & calm. He said to me rather pathetically: 'I asked Rettie whether I was getting better. He said I was – they all say so – so I suppose I am, though I sometimes wonder.'

Diary – Saturday 6 February – 21 Hyde Park Square, W.2

In the afternoon I went with Ray to the Italian Exhibition while Elena rested here. Worked at my Simon Marks article. Harold has made a speech in Cape Town (2 days ago) talking about Apartheid & dissociating us from it – with allusions to the 'Wind of Change'.[3] It has taken a long time to reach him – for most of us it has been blowing with hurricane force for some time now. Macleod said to me yesterday that it was a very brave speech. I said I wished it had been made earlier....

Diary – Wednesday 17 February – 21 Hyde Park Square, W.2

...lunch with W. & Clemmie, back from Onassisdom at Monte Carlo[4] – where Clemmie tells me that in 5 weeks they only had 5 fine days. They are off again on 4th March under the same flag – this time across the

[1] Christened Virginia Leslie, she had been born on 27 August 1959. She was Mark and Leslie Bonham Carter's second child – Jane Mary preceded her and Elizabeth Cressida ('Eliza') (b. 1961) followed.

[2] Maize was Cressida's labrador.

[3] Macmillan's keynote speech to the South African parliament in Cape Town on 3 February marked the fiftieth anniversary of the Union of South Africa: 'The wind of change is blowing through this continent, and, whether we like it or not, this growth of national consciousness is a political fact. We must all accept it as a fact, and our national policies must take account of it' (Horne, *Macmillan, 1957–1986*, 194–8).

[4] In the last years of his life Churchill spent a number of holidays in the company of the Greek shipping magnate Aristotle Onassis (1906–75), on this occasion at the Hôtel de Paris in Monte Carlo (Gilbert, *Never Despair*, 1277).

Atlantic to Florida, to anchor off Palm Beach. Nothing wld tempt me less. . . .[1] He looked well in face I thought – but very old & stiff & very deaf. I sat next him & opposite Clemmie & Sarah. Of course when they chattered together he didn't hear & consequently hardly spoke. Clemmie left me alone with him for ½ an hour after luncheon & we had a little talk – but he is very far away. Points which emerged – he is alas very anti-black & didn't like Harold's Cape Town speech. He remembers very little (did not for instance ask after B.). . .

He asked me to drive with him to the H. of C. & this was a delight – sitting beside him with our knees covered with his voluptuous Union Jack-lined rug, holding in his hands inside a long beaver muff (like a very old-fashioned women's one) a small heated water-tin to keep them warm. Here – I don't know how – we got on to Ireland (probably via Africa) & I asked him if he remembered his negotiations with Michael Collins. His face lit up 'I remember this well. I was Colonial Secretary. I conducted those negotiations – – I thought well of him & trusted him.' Those days were obviously more alive to him than yesterday or to-day. I kissed him goodbye & his car, after furling its flag, dropped me home. . . .

V.B.C. to Raymond Bonham Carter ***Tuesday 23 February***
21 Hyde Park Square, W.2

My darling Ray, One line of love & blessing & deepest gratitude for all you have done for me & been to me throughout this agonizing time. I shall miss you terribly during your 5 weeks' absence. I think that if a maleficent fiend or fate had been told to devise for me the innermost circle of the Inferno it wld be just this. To watch a mind & 'personality' (to use an odious word) with whom one has intimately shared everything for the best part of a lifetime crumbling to dust before one's eyes – so that there is really nothing left but a physical shell . . . is a nightmare – which fills every hour.

I cannot really share any thoughts with him – sometimes a memory is awakened – sometimes it fades away. I have really said goodbye to him (though I didn't know it) the night before the operation – a parting far crueller for both of us than death. You have both meant everything to me all these weary months. Your perfect happiness is one of the few streaks of light – & your coming child, to which I look forward so eagerly & with such joy & impatience.

[1] Churchill joined the Onassis yacht *Christina* early in March for a tour to the West Indies (but not, apparently, Florida): 'Comfort was the main aspect of life on board *Christina*, every aspect of which was adapted to pleasure and relaxation' (Gilbert, *Never Despair*, 1277, 1308).

Bassano portrait of Violet Bonham Carter, taken around 1945 and frequently used as a publicity photograph in the decade afterwards.

The Hague Congress, 7–10 May 1948. 'The procedure was chaotic & quite incomprehensible. Occasionally a bleat wld break from an Anglo Saxon delegate "Sur un point d'ordre M le President". His only reply was to strike a deafening blow upon the table with a hammer the size of a croquet mallet.'

With the Churchills at the London premier of *London Belongs To Me,* 12 August 1948. 'It was not a very good film ... Winston watched it like a child – arguing with the story "But it wasn't murder – he didn't murder her".'

At Euston Station, 30 August 1949, about to leave with the British delegation for the Commonwealth Relations Conference in Canada. 'Stray members littered the platform & we were photographed by batteries of cameramen – the favourite trio being Rab Butler, Miss Sutherland & myself! (not a beauty chorus).'

The 200th edition of London Forum, 28 April 1951, marked with a broadcast on human rights. Seated are (l. to r.) Bertrand Russell, Sir David Maxwell Fyffe, Violet, Eleanor Roosevelt, Lord Boyd Orr.

Violet with her younger son Raymond Bonham Carter, then in the Irish Guards, around 1947.

With her grandson Adam Ridley, elder son Mark Bonham Carter and elder daughter Cressida Ridley, at Cressida's home, The Glebe, in Stockton, Wiltshire, New Year 1954; the photograph was probably taken by Bongie.

Jo and Laura Grimond, Violet's son-in-law and daughter, being ferried in waters off the North Isles of Orkney, 1964.

Winston Churchill speaking at Huddersfield Town Hall, 15 October 1951, in support of Violet's candidature at Colne Valley: Violet is pictured sitting behind Churchill, and behind her is Sir Maurice Bonham Carter, 'Bongie'.

Participants at the April 1954 Königswinter Conference enjoy a break from the proceedings. Among the 'passengers' are (l. to r.) Robert Birley, Lilo Milchsack, Nigel Nicolson, Violet, Gilbert Longden, and Jo Grimond. The would-be stowaway is Sir John Slessor, marshal of the RAF.

With Bob Boothby and A.G. Street, at BBC radio's 'Any Questions', broadcast from Sandown, the Isle of Wight, 26 March 1954.

The Torrington by-election, March 1958: (top left) Mark Bonham Carter, the Liberal candidate; (bottom left) Mark with his wife, Leslie; (main picture) the victorious candidate being chaired by jubilant supporters after the declaration of the poll, Friday 28 March.

Violet with members of the Crediton Liberal Association, April 1959, six months before the general election. 'The state of Crediton (always our weak spot) is well demonstrated by the fact that we asked for 6 canvassers to meet us at the Liberal Club & come with us – & only 2 poor, gallant old women – one very deaf – turned up.' (September 1959)

Violet and her husband, Sir Maurice Bonham Carter ('Bongie'), pictured in the living room of their home at 21 Hyde Park Square, around 1957–8.

The inauguration of the memorial to Blanche Dugdale in the Balfour Forest, Israel, 15 May 1958. To the right of Violet is Mrs Vera Weizmann, widow of the first president of Israel, Chaim Weizmann.

Jo Grimond, Liberal leader, taking the applause after his speech at the Liberal Party assembly at Llandudno, September 1962. In the front row are (l. to r.) Lord Ogmore, Violet, Arthur Holt, Emlyn Hooson, Jo Grimond, Timothy Joyce, Felix Brunner and Lord Banks. Eric Lubbock, the victor at Orpington in the famous by-election of March that year, can be seen directly behind Brunner, while his campaign manager, Pratap Chitnis, can be seen between Holt and Hooson.

The procession of honorands at the University of Sussex, 11 June 1963: Harold Macmillan, Paul-Henri Spaak and Violet, all about to receive honorary doctorates, walk in line. 'We were robed in gold & then (I with regret) put on our black velvet chimney-pot hats. A small crowd, mostly of women, clapped sporadically & a thousand cameras were discharged & T.V.'s whirred.'

Addressing an Anti-Apartheid Movement rally from the plinth at Trafalgar Square, 3 November 1963; seated immediately behind Violet are (l. to r.) Vanessa Redgrave, Barbara Castle and Humphry Berkeley.

Violet leaving the Churchills' home at 28 Hyde Park, at the time of Sir Winston Churchill's final illness. 'I left him with a wrench & reeled out into the mob of press & flashlights.' (15 January 1965)

Violet becomes the first woman to address the Royal Academy dinner, 26 April 1967; to her left is Lord Goodman. 'At the end of a delicious dinner (uneaten by me), on which even the cheese was dated on the menu – the business of the evening began.'

Interviewed by Kenneth Harris, February 1967, for the BBC's eightieth birthday tribute, *As I Remember*, which was broadcast that April.

Baroness Asquith of Yarnbury, pictured outside parliament on the day of her introduction to the House of Lords, 23 December 1964. 'It is funny to open a new chapter of life at the age of 77!'

Bless you both, Ever yr Mama
Work is a help because it forces one to think of something else.

Diary – Friday 11 March – 21 Hyde Park Square, W.2

Mark lunched here with me as B. is spending these days in bed. He does not feel well enough to get up. Good talk with Mark who is working hard at L.P.O. as Chairman of the Standing Committee & speaking into the bargain – with Collins [publishers] as well. I cannot bear his exile from the House. I have had a very depressed letter from Jo who misses him terribly. Clem is no good, Roderic Bowen never turns up, Jeremy speaks often & is as active as a flea – but does too many outside things & doesn't sit there. Nor does he carry Mark's guns. . . .

Diary – Wednesday 16 March – 21 Hyde Park Square, W.2

I took part in a Boycott 'Brains Trust' in Kensington Town Hall. We had great alarms & excursions over the meeting, as Chelsea suddenly withdrew their Town Hall which we had booked, for fear the Mosleyites shld break up the furniture. Elizabeth Pakenham, who was the Chairman, & I signed a letter to the *Times*.[1] Kensington, which is the heart of the Mosley Territory, nobly offered theirs instead & there we went. I arrived early & found the pavement [lined] with Mosleyites selling *Action* & our people selling the *Boycott News*. In the Green Room rumours were flying about – that the hall wld have more Mosleyites than our supporters – that we shld have a Rough House etc. Then a scuffle on the Pavement outside was reported. However all went off smoothly without a ripple. Our Stewards knew the Mosleyites & picked them off one by one & ejected them from the Hall before it started. . . .

[1]The Chelsea Borough decision was doubtless influenced by a spate of violent attacks on the boycott movement, which faced opposition from Sir Oswald Mosley's Union Movement, rallying to the cry of 'Stand by the whites in South Africa.' Violet and Elizabeth Pakenham were nevertheless determined to challenge the Borough's action: 'What does this amount to? It means that the power of veto over the right of public assembly has in fact been granted to an undemocratic minority. . . . The boycott movement was founded to protest against the denial of civil liberties in South Africa. Let us also guard our own' (*The Times*, 14 March 1960).

Diary – Tuesday 22 March – 21 Hyde Park Square, W.2

Terrible news of a massacre in S.A. 65 Africans killed & 156 wounded are the latest figures. There were also minor riots in Cape Town.[1] Africans demonstrated against the Pass Laws at Vereeniging & elsewhere – asking to be arrested, having left their passes at home. They threw stones (& fruit!). They were of course unarmed. They were shot down by the police with Sten guns. There are terrible descriptions in all the papers. The U.S. has expressed regret – & implied censure. Our Govt refused to do so in H. of C. It was tragic & sickening reading. . . .[2]

Diary – Saturday 2 April – 21 Hyde Park Square, W.2

Rettie came in the morning – examined B. & then came in to see me. . . . He said I must think of his life in terms of weeks not months. For the first time with him I broke down. I told the boys – or rather Raymond who told Mark. Laura & Magnus & Gelda came in to see me which was a comfort & joy. . . .

Diary – Wednesday 6 April – 21 Hyde Park Square, W.2

. . . After dinner I went to a party at the French Embassy at the invitation of De Gaulle. The Queen etc. were dining there but they were to leave after dinner & we were to be received by the General. . . . Chauvel[3] came along & greeted me. . . . I explained that I wasn't going in the défilé – the General must be so tired. He said 'I will see that he speaks to you when he comes back' & though I begged him not to bother, went off. Within a few moments however the General appeared, made a literal 'faux pas' on the stairs & almost fell at my feet! He looked older – but above all much

[1]At Sharpeville outside Johannesburg, on 21 March, police opened fire on a crowd demonstrating against the hated 'pass laws', killing sixty-nine and injuring as many as 180. The same day another nineteen were killed at Langa township, near Cape Town, after police fired on demonstrators.

[2]In the House of Commons on 22 March the Labour Party and Liberal Party tabled separate motions strongly condemning the South African government over the Sharpeville massacre. Macmillan's government, though, would not be drawn into making a forthright statement either of censure or of regret, its Commons spokesman offering the observation that: 'Civil commotion at any time and in all parts of the world is always to be regretted' (*The Times*, 23 March 1960).

[3]Jean Michel Chauvel (1897–1979), hon. GCVO, 1957; French ambassador in London, 1955–62.

gentler & more benign & mellow than when I had last seen him – in the early days of the war – a prickly porcupine of an Ally – shy & costive as a talker – though I never felt his spikes, which dug so deeply into Winston. With a sense of duty done went home.... An oddly unreal interlude.

Diary – Tuesday 10 May – 21 Hyde Park Square, W.2

Lunched with W. & Clemmie. He looked very well I thought & walked slowly but firmly & without his stick. We had the usual delicious but unsatisfactory luncheon – Clemmie & I one side of the table & he the other – hearing nothing – while Clemmie chattered 19 to the dozen.... I talked to him a little about S. Africa & asked whether they had not made some firm provision for Native Rights in the original bill. I knew that there were reserved clauses which had been swept aside by a 'packed' Senate.[1] He said: 'It's all so long ago. I can't remember.' The issue which was clearly in & on his mind was Cyprus. 'Terrible that we shld have to surrender to these people after all we have already given way on' etc.[2] I said we were paying for the usual Tory failure to see ahead & act pre-emptively – as in Ireland long ago, we have sold the pass to violence. He didn't argue or agree but just repeated 'I mind it terribly.' Towards the end of our talk he said: 'Things are not well with us. We are going down. It is over.' And I knew what he meant by it – 'The power & the glory' of this country in the world – for to him, the glory is inseparable from the power. He cannot bow to a new dispensation – & it is merciful that it shld have come at the very end of his life....

Diary – Tuesday 24 May – 21 Hyde Park Square, W.2

Ray & Elena have a son![3] He rang me up this morning about 20 to 11 to

[1] The 'original' 1909 South Africa Act, creating the Union of South Africa, included a 'colour-bar' in the constitution. Only in Cape Province could Africans vote and there the franchise was left open to future constitutional amendment. In April 1936 the necessary two-thirds majorities were secured in both houses of the South African Assembly to pass the 'Natives' Representation Act', which took Africans off the Cape electoral roll.

[2] Britain was then in the final stages of difficult negotiations leading to independence for Cyprus. During the first half of 1960 Macmillan's government faced Cypriot pressure to reduce the size of the base areas that were to be retained by British forces on the island. This pressure was resisted, and Cyprus was formally given independence on 16 August (Horne, *Macmillan, 1957–1986*, 199–200).

[3] Christened Edward Henry. Edward was followed by a brother, Thomas David, and a sister, Helena (b. 1966).

say that Elena was now in the 2nd stage & that the baby might be born at 11! I held my breath & protected the telephone line with my life. Soon after 11 he rang to say that she had a son. (It was in fact born at 10.29 – but everyone was so busy with her that he didn't know when he first telephoned to me.) I felt flooded with overwhelming happiness for them both....

Mark came here to meet Rettie at 12.30 & to help me face the situation. He had examined B. before talking to us. He came in looking very grave & I can see that ... he is inwardly convinced that B. has cancer.... I felt this morning had held the whole of life in its span. The 'joy that came in the morning' – of a new life starting for us all – & then the shadow of death – far worse than death itself – when the way is paved with unimagined possibilities of pain & fear. Above all the gradual dimming of a light.

I told him of the baby's birth before I went to see it – & he understood – but was not able to grasp what wld have been his greatest joy. When I came back & tried to describe the baby to him his eyes closed. He hardly speaks at all these days. I think he feels an overwhelming lassitude. It was only a week ago that when I went in to see him late at night he said: 'Don't go away' & I stayed & talked to him. Alas! he may never say that to me again – he is drifting away – out of my reach. It was a terrible effort to dress & go to Glyndebourne – as I had to on the Opening Night. I was glad to be alone & in the train with strangers....

Diary – Tuesday 7 June – 21 Hyde Park Square, W.2

...Some time between 10 & 10.30 I went to fetch something from my bedroom & passing his door I heard an extraordinary sound of fast & noisy breathing. I went in. He was breathing very fast. I asked Nurse Hinde when it had started. She said at 9.30.... I longed to ask her 'Is he dying?' but somehow her youth inhibited me. I said 'Should I ring up the doctor do you think?' & she said 'Yes – I think you shld.' It was ¼ to 1 when I telephoned Rettie. I said I wasn't asking him to come, but I thought I ought to report the symptoms. He registered no surprise & simply said he wld come in the morning to-morrow instead of after tea. I thought 'Then perhaps he isn't dying? It may be a passing access like he used to have' & went back to him. Still no change.

He was like a runner putting all he had into the last lap of a race. Yet all the time I – strangely – felt no distress for him, as I had felt only a few hours earlier, when he had winced when he was moved. Then I had felt that he was feeling pain – now I felt that his body alone was struggling & fighting & that he himself was no longer part of it. I lay down on my bed for a little & asked Nurse Hinde to call me if there was any change. His temp. had come down to 100 – his pulse & respiration were the same. Towards 5 o'clock she came to me & said 'There is a change.' His breathing had quite suddenly become still. I put my hand upon his heart – it was still beating. Then under my hand it stopped. The race was over. He was dead. (I heard the nurse whisper '5.7')

I remember vaguely the Nurse asking me if she cld get me 'a hot drink or anything' & then – some time later – her saying there were things that she must do. I saw she wanted me to go away. I opened the shutters of my bedroom & the sun streamed in. I dressed. Everything was still & silent – everyone asleep – unknowing. Nurse Bates arrived some time later in response to a call from Nurse Hinde – about 7 I think. Then I went in to him again. They had drawn the curtains & covered up his face. I pulled them back & let the sun in & folded back the sheet. He looked transformed.

Suffering & years had vanished. His face was as it had been in youth – only more finely drawn & chiselled – with an ineffable serenity & on his lips a smile in which there almost lurked amusement. I felt an infinite sense of reassurance – & longed to hold fast this precious moment forever – & for there to be no other. When I touched his neck it was as warm as my own. I felt that he had been given back to me & to himself – intact in essence & in every feature. Time passed – & then – about half-past 8 I think – I telephoned the children. . . .

Bongie's death, Tuesday 7 June 1960

Violet received scores of letters of condolence on Bongie's death and characteristically answered every one. Among them was Maud Russell's: 'What can I say except that I loved Bongie, his sweetness of character, his gentleness & wisdom, the occasional – only very occasional – fire of indignation or revolt & all the expressions of his expressive face.' To some of Violet's friends and acquaintances Bongie had seemed a background figure in her life, but he was in reality an essential part of it. His good-humoured patience proved the perfect foil to her rapier sharpness and she deferred to his judgement more than was perhaps realised. She never learned to live without what she once described as his 'dumb, solid, minding, strong presence'. Bongie's funeral took place at St Andrew's church in Mells, Somerset, on Saturday 11 June. Violet left London early in the morning under grey skies and rain, but as she travelled west these cleared and the day filled with 'April lights & shadows & bright skies dappled with cloud'. St Andrew's lies within sight of the Manor House at Mells – the home of Katharine Asquith and scene of many happy memories for Violet and Bongie. It comforted her to think that he lay in the churchyard there: 'The place cld not have been more beautiful – under wide, open skies with the great tower standing four square above it – the tower which we have all heard ring in & out so many years.' On the Sunday evening Violet returned to London and a lonely house: 'It is strange that from habit I still tip-toe past his door – & think every moment that I ought to go to him. It is also strange to have the house empty of nurses for the first time for months. I feel drained & void of all content.' In the weeks ahead she was occupied with plans for a memorial service, which was held at Westminster Abbey on 5 July. Violet was uplifted by the numbers who attended and the love that Bongie had inspired: 'We have now done the last thing for him it is possible to do on earth.'

Diary – Saturday 9 July – 21 Hyde Park Square, W.2

Winston is going off to-morrow with Clemmie on a cruise on the Onassises' yacht which he joins at Venice. I wrote to Clemmie asking if I cld. come & say goodbye to him & she asked me to luncheon today. We were alone as usual. He was very sweet, tender & sympathetic. . . .

He asked if I felt very lonely & I said I did. It was so strange to sit in the evening in the room in which we had always sat together & see the chair in which he sat – still there unchanged – intact. Why shld chairs last for centuries & men vanish & perish? He then said (with more grasp than he had shown till now) 'But how terrible if we did – if we went on for ever. It's a dreadful thought.' I said 'Some people think it. Do you hope they're wrong? Wld you rather that death meant extinction?' He said he wld. – eternal life seemed to him to be a nightmare possibility – although he did not phrase it in these terms. I said 'But no one has had a more ardent, a more voracious appetite for life than you have.' He replied rather tragically 'Not for the last 5 years. During these I have had no appetite for life. No – when it comes to dying I shall not complain. I shall not miaow.' (This last most characteristic.). . .

Diary – Sunday 31 July – The Manor House, Mells, Somerset

Rainy day. Went to church & sat alone in a family pew. . . . We lead a very peaceful life. K. is a perfect companion. She sits indoors most of the day as she is terribly crippled poor darling. I have 'air-hunger' & try & spend every moment in the garden taking refuge in the loggia when the (frequent) showers come on. It was pouring when I went to church this morning. The garden is the most fragrant I know. Going to bed one night

I went into the hall in the dark & said to K. 'Even the hall smells of Rosemary & Tobacco Plant.' She said 'Is the garden door open?' And it was. How well I remembered the thrill of sleeping out in the loggia as a girl & waking early to see the thrushes hop across the dewy lawn. Sleeping out was the greatest thrill of my youth....

Diary – Monday 1 to Tuesday 2 August – The Manor House, Mells, Somerset

Monday showery – Tuesday a lovely day of hot sunshine. We had tea under the medlar in the garden.... I had a most memorable & pathetic talk with K. on my last night, when I took her to her room & we both agreed we had no fear of death. It arose from her saying that Ronald[1] – with all his faith – longed to go on living. We got on to the ethics of suicide. What one fears is not dying but the manner of one's death. The indignity of the decay of faculties & the heavy burden imposed on others. (The last Horner aunt died at the age of 99!) To K. of course taking the law into one's own hand was the worst sin imaginable. God alone had right to decide life & death. I said I recognized that for her it wld be sin. But wld it be for me if my conscience approved it? I knew that certain things wld be wrong for me which wld not be wrong for others. She conceded this. Then, I said, she must accept the converse. One's own conscience alone cld decide what was right or wrong for oneself. This strikes at the root of the difference between her faith & mine – the acceptance of authority.

But I was pleased & relieved by the calm with which she heard my case & put her own. Her faith has become infinitely gentler & I think a little broader. She then said a very poignant thing – which I have always suspected – & cannot doubt the truth of. She said 'I have wanted to die every day of my life since Raymond was killed.' I believe it to be absolutely true. Sept. 1916 – 44 years ago. She cannot have been more than 31. With what fidelity & integrity she has lived – refusing to compromise at any turn. She is a very rare human being.

V.B.C. to Katharine Asquith

Saturday 6 August
The Glebe, Stockton, Wiltshire

My Darling -

I don't know how to thank you for my lovely days at Mells. It was such

[1] Ronald Arbuthnott Knox (1888–1957), Roman Catholic priest, author and translator of the bible; Knox lived for many years at Mells, where he is buried.

a heavenly reprieve to be in the country – for the first time since last October – & such a luxury to be alone with you. I do hope I wasn't a burden. When I think of the courage & selflessness with which you have lived your life since Raymond's death put out its light so many years ago, it makes me feel ashamed of my own, & of any grief or faltering I feel today. I can only feel thankful for you that you have certainties – where I have only hopes – of what lies beyond death. I do not, cannot, think of it as an end. That, for me, would take all meaning out of life. But my imagination is so blind & finite that I cannot see beyond it. I could not, as dear Haldane could & did, be satisfied with being just an impersonal 'pulse in the eternal mind – no less'.[1] I cling to the thread of my own faulty identity & that of those I love – & clay & spirit are here so intimately interfused that I find it hard to unravel them in my heart.

I daresay that, if we only knew, there is less difference between what we call 'life' & 'death' than we imagine. Yet when I watch Cressida's stoical & lonely life I realise how profoundly she has been affected by being deprived, so young, of all that for her made life worth living.[2] A neighbour, Barbara Sykes, told me today that the shepherd here said he wld rather have Cressida than anyone to help him when he 'cut sheep's feet'! This is (according to Barbara) a most disagreeable, hard & dirty job. She asked Cressida why she did it & C. replied 'I like it – it unwinds me' – a strange symptom of the tension which she lives with....

My gratitude & constant love – & if ever you are in need of another 'body' in the house when you are alone do remember how I shld love to be with you for my own sake. Ever yr Violet

Diary – Tuesday 6 December – 21 Hyde Park Square, W.2

Lib. Party Committee at 11 with Wade in the chair instead of Jo – a poor orchestra with no conductor.... Dressed like lightning & went on to Atlantic European dinner for Edward Heath – a private one to talk about the Common Market. It was very interesting. He spoke conversationally, sitting. He obviously wants to make a 'go' of it – & that as soon as possible –

[1] From 'The Soldier' by Rupert Brooke: 'And think, this heart, all evil shed away / A pulse in the eternal mind, no less / Gives somewhere back the thoughts by England given.' In her youth Violet had discussed religion with Lord Haldane (1856–1928), her father's friend and lord chancellor: 'He is the only man I have ever met who seems really at home in the Infinite' (*Lantern Slides*, 336).

[2] Cressida's husband, Jasper 'Bubbles' Ridley, was killed in December 1943, after straying into a minefield while escaping from German captivity in Italy. Like her aunt Katharine, Cressida never remarried.

but thinks it important to choose the psychological moment. He thinks that Italy wants us in unreservedly, that Germany is friendly & welcoming (& says that the Germans & we ourselves are working out solutions to outstanding practical difficulties). France is the obstacle & it is difficult to know just what to offer her that wld be any good to her. We have no cards in our economic pack to play as inducements. Everyone there is at present absorbed in Algerian problems & there is no urge to get on with it.... I liked Heath – he is unpretentious, friendly, pink, 'bon coucheur', but as for being in the running for P.M.-ship – the idea is absurd! I see what a good Chief Whip he must have been. I can imagine him laughing people into voting for Suez.

Diary – New Year's Day, Sunday 1 January 1961 – 21 Hyde Park Square, W.2

Slept late – lunched alone. Ray walked on Hampstead Heath with Mark – & I went to him & Elena before 6 & had a heavenly hour with sweet Edward.... He is unimaginably perfect & I can't bear the thought of parting with him. He changes from week to week. I shall miss 2 whole years of him.[1] They dropped me back on their way out to dinner at the Connaught. I have a leaden sense about the New Year & the years that follow. They can hold nothing for me but dwindling powers. I want to finish my book so as not to let down my publishers & also for the money it may bring in for the children.[2] But all zest in it has gone. I feel that the 'virtue' has gone out of me. I do not feel old yet – on the contrary – achingly active – but old age must come. I have nothing to look forward to. Only things to dread – like becoming a duty or a burden to the children. Pray God I die before then. I should feel no pang if I were told that I shld. not wake up to-morrow.

Diary – Friday 24 February – Roxburghe Hôtel, Edinburgh

We left the Roxburghe at 9.15 & drove to the University – a most lovely Adams building. Were ushered into a beautiful 'Robing Room' full of Raeburns & thronged with Dons in most beautiful robes of all colours –

[1] Raymond had been posted to Washington for two years as the Bank of England's alternate executive director at the IMF. Violet was torn between joy at this considerable promotion and sadness at his (and Elena's) imminent departure.

[2] Violet was then working on her biography *Winston Churchill as I Knew Him*, published after his death in 1965.

plus other platform ticket-holders like K. Elliot ... & a charming young man called David Steel who is the President of the Students' Representative Council & has conducted & organized the campaign for Jo throughout.[1] Then the procession was marshalled – our names were called. We went in pairs on to the platform – Laura & I walking, tho' not sitting, together. The McEwan Hall is a splendid sight packed from floor to ceiling with students – the organ thundering – loud cheers & a sense of tremendous excitement....

Then David Steel advanced to the Lectern & 'presented' Jo to the assembled student Body. Jo, who had entered dressed in a plain black gown, like a crow among birds of Paradise, had meanwhile been re-gowned in his magnificent Rectorial garb with red velvet & gold shoulders & sleeves. He advanced to the Lectern looking splendid & amused – & delivered his Address triumphantly. The subject was 'Politics' – & it lasted about 35–40 minutes. There was of course some liveliness & interruption – paper streamers were flung across the hall from the boxes in serpentine coils – & little paper arrows darted about. But there was no rowdiness – not a tomato was flung – no flour, fish or live-stock & the audience was with him all the time....[2]

[After dinner] We then went on to the Ball given by the S.C.R. in the Union.... We spent most of the time in the Library talking to many of the delightful young men & women. They are far more uninhibited than the English & have absolutely no 'class' sense. I had a long talk with a highly interesting & intelligent young man, Mackintosh by name, who was going out to Nigeria to teach 'Politics & Government'.[3] He had rummaged among my father's papers at the Bodleian & had been coached at Oxford by Thomas Balogh[4] in Economics. (He did P.P.E.) I asked if Balogh still sucked a thermometer during Tutorials as in Mark's day. He said no – he lay on his back with a plastic tube in his mouth blowing

[1] Jo had been elected rector of the University of Edinburgh and Violet was present for his inauguration. For (Sir) David Steel, the future Liberal Party leader, see the Biographical notes below.

[2] Rectorial addresses could be riotous affairs. When Rab Butler prepared to deliver his, at Glasgow University in February 1958, he beheld students sitting under umbrellas: 'A tomato hit him square in the back. A flour bomb hit him full in the face. The barrage of missiles & noise continued throughout the ceremony and during Mr Butler's speech. Often he stood silent, waiting a rare chance to make himself heard' (Howard, *Butler*, 261).

[3] John Pitcairn Mackintosh (1929–78), politician, writer and professor of politics; lecturer in history, Edinburgh University, 1954–61; senior lecturer in government, Ibadan University, Nigeria, 1961–3; senior lecturer in politics, Glasgow University, 1963–5; MP (Lab.) Berwick and East Lothian, 1966–February 1974; October 1974–8.

[4] Thomas Balogh (1905–85), cr. life peer, 1968; Hungarian-born political economist; fellow of Balliol College, Oxford, 1945–73; economic adviser to the Labour government, 1964–7; consultant to the prime minister, 1968; minister of state, department of energy, 1974–5.

disgusting bubbles, making notes for a *New Statesman* article with one hand & occasionally telephoning – while his unfortunate pupil, who was trying to read him a paper he had written, protested vainly – 'I can do all this as well as listening to your rubbish, boy'....

Diary – Saturday 25 February – 21 Hyde Park Square, W.2

Had breakfast 7.30 – packed – said goodbye to Jo & Laura & flew home arriving here about 1.30. I wld not have missed my Edinburgh experience for anything & was more than ever impressed by Jo's public performance. His personality puts that of all other political leaders in the shade. To begin with – his very rare good looks – which hit one in the eye – his combination of almost schoolboy casualness & informality about clothes etc. with real dignity. He looks the part of a young 'great man'. Then the impact of his voice, delivery & gesture – his originality of thought & gesture, never falling into the almost inevitable trap of cliché. He has the goods & can deliver them matchlessly. As Mark says his sense of humour is almost too good for his job! Would that he cld be given by Fate a better armoury of material weapons, in the way of money & organization – & above all a group of abler followers & henchmen approaching his own stature. It is here that Mark's absence from Parlt. has left such a tragic void – though he is doing invaluable work in organization....

Diary – Sunday 5 March – 21 Hyde Park Square, W.2

Spent alone working at my broadcast for *Women's Hour* etc. Lovely day – sat in the Square for the first time. I don't know whether I recorded that Verwoerd – on being questioned by the Press on his arrival – described Apartheid as 'good neighbourliness'. One instinctively exclaimed 'I wldn't like to be his neighbour' & now to my delight Nehru has said it – when he arrived at the airport.[1] Saw a very moving T.V. film about Lincoln – the man I shld most have liked to know.

[1]The South African and Indian leaders were both in London for the Commonwealth Conference that month. South Africa effectively left the Commonwealth at this meeting, over member states' opposition to apartheid.

Diary – Sunday 19 March – 21 Hyde Park Square, W.2

Went to Speaker's Corner towards 2 & found a motley crowd – the nucleus of the Procession – & groups round individual rostrums listening to everything under the sun. Met Jo – & together we found Fenner Brockway, Barbara Castle, & the 2 Wedgwood Benns with a small folding pram & 4 children. We were formed up – Jo & a blackamoor[1] leading with a banner. We were given black sashes to tie over our shoulders & across our chests with 'Sharpeville' on one side & 'Langa' on the other. Then we marched about 2,000 strong down Oxford Street, Regent St., Haymarket & Pall Mall to Trafalgar Square.[2] The Square was already pretty full of people – nearly all white. I saw very few Charmeaux. Some of us scaled the plinth by a ladder – Mrs Castle was the Chairman & introduced the leader of the African United Front, followed by Wedgwood Benn, followed by Jo – each speaking for about 5 minutes. I was asked to speak but felt they had more than enough. Michael Scott came next & as I was told that there were 5 more speeches & it was arctically cold on the plinth (a north wind blowing) I climbed down at the back & drove home....

Diary – Wednesday 12 April – 21 Hyde Park Square, W.2

Spent yesterday & to-day in bed – yesterday in considerable discomfort & intermittent pain. Dr Hamilton had telephoned to me yesterday that the cardiogram revealed that my arteries were not '100 p.c. sound' & he said this morning that the chart was slightly ambiguous & open to 2 meanings. It was possible that I had a very slight coronary thrombosis....

V.B.C. to Raymond Bonham Carter — *Thursday 20 April, 21 Hyde Park Square, W.2*

Darling Ray – All my thanks & blessings for your birthday letter which reached me, as you said it wld., the evening before.... [Dr Rettie] does not think I have had a thrombosis but he says quite definitely that what I have got is angina. This is, of course, an incalculable disease. One might well live for years or one might die at any moment. If I have to have an

[1]Nana Mahomo, of the South African United Front, based in London.

[2]The march was heckled on its route by a loudspeaker van belonging to the League of Empire Loyalists. At Trafalgar Square there was a confrontation between marchers and members of Sir Oswald Mosley's Union Movement, resulting in twenty-nine arrests (*The Times*, 20 March 1961).

ailment I wld certainly choose it – for I have always thought 'sudden death' (which we foolishly pray to be 'delivered from' in the Litany) the most desirable of all ends – & B.'s long ordeal has made me even more convinced of it.

I hate writing this to you darling because I know it will worry you, but do believe me when I assure you that I am not disturbed by it. No one has loved life more than I have – but I have never been afraid of death. My one prayer has always been to die intact – & this gives me a good chance of doing so. The thing I mind is being so far away from you & Elena & beloved Edward when life may be short. . . .

I don't know quite what terms I am to make with my 'way of life'. My work has been my greatest solace & distraction since B. died & I could not bear to live at half-cock on a low gear. I have been in bed this last week but I got up on Tuesday evening & went to speak at an Albert Hall meeting for the Abolition of Capital Punishment to which I had been committed since January. . . . It is difficult to be selective because people will say 'if she can do "X" why can't she do "Z"?'

Wedgwood Benn is asking me to go to Bristol next week for his election & I long to go.[1] We have stopped the local Libs. standing & want them to support him on this big constitutional issue – in which justice & common-sense & the rights of the subject are all on his side. My personal life is so lonely & so empty – but my 'public' life is full of clamant demands & possibilities of helping people & things I believe in. It is 1 A.M. – I must stop & try to sleep. . . .

Ever Yr Mama . . . .

Diary – Wednesday 17 May – 21 Hyde Park Square, W.2

. . . John Osborne[2] came to see me (at the request of *Women's Day*!) to talk to me about 'Angry young men'. He never sees 'journalists' but said he wld like to come & see me which was nice of him. He cldn't have been more different from anything I expected. He was perfectly delightful – calm, robust, sensitive, natural & carrying his 'success' as tho' he was

[1] In November 1960 Tony Benn was debarred from the Commons after succeeding to his father's viscountcy, which he had previously tried unsuccessfully to renounce. A by-election was subsequently held in his Bristol seat, which he contested and won in May 1961. Finding himself debarred a second time he instigated the Peerage Act of 1963, to make possible the renunciation of a hereditary peerage: see below, p. 271.

[2] John (James) Osborne (1929–94), dramatist, actor and author (*Damn You, England: Collected Prose* (1994)). The staging of his play *Look Back in Anger*, first performed in May 1956, is seen as a key event in the post-war revival of British theatre. Violet read it and thought it 'squalid but moving'.

unaware of it. I had expected a far more highly-strung, fickle, excitable, nervously taut human being. I had such an absorbing talk with him that I feared to break the thread by taking notes or behaving in a 'business-like' way. I forgot business in the excitement of finding out what he really thought & felt.

He said the 'angry young men' were not a coherent group – in fact they had no common philosophy, aim or 'message' – only the bond of a common age. They had all been schoolboys during the war – & thus felt 'out of it' because they cld take no part. They were all left-minded – bitterly disappointed in the Lab Govt's record, on which they had set high hopes – & in the post-war world which was offered to them. I contrasted the lot of youth in my own generation – the appalling gap between wealth & poverty – the squalor, want, hunger, lack of security & opportunity – & yet the strange absence of 'anger' in those days – the high spirits & the far higher moral standards among the very poorest – no flick-knives, gangs, etc. Why has savagery taken the place of high spirits?

We both agreed that <u>real</u> civilization had gone down since material prosperity had risen. Was it sheer coincidence? or cause & effect? He said that in the <u>narrow</u> social sense the breaking down of barriers had created a greater malaise. In the past the classes were rigidly segregated – now they mixed & through this process class-consciousness was not diminished but increased. People felt 'different' from others whom they met on (supposedly) equal terms. 'I'm always conscious' he said 'whether I'm talking to someone middle-class, lower middle-class etc.'

I reflected how wrong one is to 'personalize' authors by incarnating them in those they write about. Because J.O. has created Jimmy Porter the public somehow identifies J.P.'s grudge against life with that of his creator. As I said, one might as well identify Shakespeare with Iago. I have never yet met anyone gentler, less 'angry' than John Osborne – except in the sense that he deeply cares. I told him that politics had always been the safety-valve for my 'anger' in youth. I cld see <u>effective</u> things being done to change the things that made me angry – by my own father. Later one felt more impotent – but the habit of public action & protest remained. I cld understand his saying & feeling 'What can one do? A letter to the *Times* – a Committee – a meeting – & what does it all lead to? A question in the H. of Commons.' That is true of all I can do now – but I remember better days. Anyway I feel that one must raise one's voice even if one can do no more. He feels passionately about the abolition of the Death Penalty & told me he had heard that I made a wonderful speech at the Albert Hall. . . . I felt when J.O. left that I had made a new friend. He is exactly Raymond's age – 31.

Diary – Sunday 21 May – 21 Hyde Park Square, W.2

A solitary day. Sat out a little on the balcony in the afternoon when the sun was out & read the papers. I have been opening 2 of my tin-boxes with a view to destroying my letters in case I die. When I did so I became lost in reading them & found it impossible to destroy the ones that mattered most. Destroying love-letters feels like destroying love.

Diary – Whit Monday, 22 May – 21 Hyde Park Square, W.2

A fine day. Sat out in the Square all afternoon & worked & read. More tin-boxes after dinner. It is strange how much of the detail of one's life one ostensibly forgets – & then finds safely tucked away when it is recalled – as vivid & intact as if it had happened yesterday. Everything – or nearly everything – shld be written down – because the subconscious memory keeps its secrets until they are demanded of it – & then yields them up as fresh as daisies.

Diary – Saturday 27 May – 21 Hyde Park Square, W.2

Spent the day dog-alone & went by myself at 6 to the brilliant revue of the 'Angry Young Men' called *Beyond the Fringe* at the small Fortune Theatre near Drury Lane. I had a good corner-seat in the Stalls which gave me an even greater sense of isolation. Laughing alone has always seemed to me to be an unnatural act – making one feel uncomfortable. One wants to get rid of one's amusement on others. But I sat & shook & writhed & shrieked & shouted with amusement for 2 hours by the clock. It was really brilliant.... The targets were Macmillan, the Church, philosophers, & there were very good musical parodies ... a terribly funny one of some pansies with plucking gestures, dressing in Sou' Westers to do a terrifically virile hearty T.V. advertisement for something like Lifebuoy Soap – & almost the funniest of all, 4 Clubmen meeting at their Club, making hearty gestures & quite inarticulate hearty noises, & finally sitting down together – to no food or drink. I got back by tube from Holborn which I was rather proud of finding my way to. I long to see the Show again with Adam – Mark – Laura.

Diary – Monday 29 May – 21 Hyde Park Square, W.2

Went to Church House where the W.E.U. is meeting in Assembly. Got there about 11 – a dim & dreary collection they looked from the Gallery –

awaiting Super-Mac. My morning was made by the fact that Desmond Donnelly[1] – whose society I delight in – came & sat next to me. We heard Mac's speech together. He said to me 'It might be Ramsay MacDonald' & I added – 'In his last phase.' It was the old, old story. Unity for Europe must grow. Nothing he cld say or do wld make it grow any faster. Then came the old stuff about the Commonwealth, our E.F.T.A. partners, British agriculture. There was one dreadful passage 'Let us count our blessings'. Can one imagine a more smug & sterile occupation? No wonder the Europeans distrust us! There was no impetus – no faith – not a breath of hope or urgency. To those who – like myself – remember the great days of the Congress of Europe, the early days of Strasbourg – the tide & the wind & the inspiration. All lost. A few cold ashes left on the floor of Church House & Harold with his watering-can putting out any smouldering embers. . . .

Diary – Wednesday 7 June – 21 Hyde Park Square, W.2

This is the anniversary of B.'s death. It is a whole year since we parted – a year of great loneliness & desolation in which I have not learned to live alone. It is for this reason that my illness seems a solution – though I cannot yet guess whether it means early death or life further handicapped. I am thankful that B. is not here as he wld. be so worried. . . .

V.B.C. to Raymond Bonham Carter

Friday 15 June
21 Hyde Park Square, W.2

My darling Ray – All my love & every blessing on your birthday. How well I remember the joy of it (your birth day) & what inexpressible happiness you have given me – every day & year of your life since. . . .

The sudden awakening 'en sursaut' of the Govt. & of the Press here to the importance of the Common Market (which has been for donkeys' years the most important issue for this country's future) is a terrible reflection on both.[2] One wld think it had only happened yesterday. Both

[1] Desmond Donnelly (1920–74), pro-European political commentator and columnist; MP (Lab.) Pembroke, 1950–68 (resigned over British withdrawal from 'east of Suez'); (Ind.) 1968–70; joined Conservative Party, 1971; 'an enjoyable companion, thoroughly sybaritic with an engaging touch of vulgarity' (*DNB*).

[2] The government was about to initiate negotiations on a British application to join the EEC. Macmillan had decided upon this momentous step the previous year, but he now faced a difficult task in trying to get his Party, and public opinion, behind him.

the major parties are, as you see, split down the middle about it & one understands exactly why. Many Tories still don't realise that we have already lost 'national sovereignty' – through N.A.T.O., U.N., Gatt, I.M.F. etc. etc. (Suez was a good practical demonstration of that fact.) The Labour Party are Jingo Little Englanders, economic Nationalists & xenophobes who dread the 'foreigner' – with his unpleasant habit of working hard & his 'mobility'. Liberals alone have been united in backing the Common Market – but they will get no credit for it, I fear!...

Goodbye my darling. I long to share your birthday. Ever yr Mama....

Diary – Friday 7 July – 21 Hyde Park Square, W.2

...C. & I dined together & started about 10 o'clock for Laura's ball. The ball rooms looked lovely.... The band was playing loudly, but nobody was there – all the young were crowded below in the library talking. Laura told me that this was nowadays 'the thing' – to have a band & a ball-room, but to treat a ball like a cocktail party! However they danced all right later on....

I sat on a sofa & talked to darling June & later on to K. [Elliot] who launched into a fierce personal attack on Gaitskell whom she dislikes strongly. I told her I liked him very much as a human being – modest, sensitive, etc. & showing dignity & grit in most painful circumstances & asked her what she minded about him. She said he wanted to abolish Oxford(!) & the Public Schools, having been there himself & sent his children there. I told her he had no sons & wanted (as far as I understood it) not to abolish them but share them more widely. (It was the old 'Traitor to your Class' cry which I remember hearing in the Lib. Govt.'s day before the 1st World War – particularly about Winston.) I was rather glad to be interrupted by Mrs Roy Jenkins when she (K.) got on to Gaitskell's 'love-affair' with Ann Fleming – but not before I had reminded her of all the divorces on the [government] Front Bench & her chaperonage of Bob Boothby & Dorothy Macmillan on their visits to Paris in the days of their youth!...

Diary – Tuesday 11 July – 21 Hyde Park Square, W.2

Listened to *Any Questions* pot-pourri repeat – & got up at 3 to see Gagarin's arrival on T.V.[1] He has I must say got a most charming personality – natural, friendly, modest & always smiling & happy. He came down the steps from the aeroplane clapping the crowd which applauded him – a

[1] The pioneering Soviet cosmonaut, Major Yuri Gagarin (1934–68), arrived in London on 11 July to a welcome that 'sometimes bordered on hysteria' (*The Times*).

very nice habit. I listened to his Press Conference. His replies to questions from the floor were masterly – diplomatic when necessary, usually quite 'straight' & not making the askers of foolish ones look foolish.[1] If only his native country were like he is, we shld be living in a far easier world....

Diary – Saturday 29 July – 21 Hyde Park Square, W.2

...Jo rang me up, which I had asked him to do, as I propose writing to Carleton Greene[2] (whom I don't know) about the exclusion of Libs. from all broadcasts about the Common Market – an issue on which Libs. alone have been united & backed from the word go. He came to lunch with me & we had a nice talk – but what a heavy burden he has to carry. Wade is ill, Jeremy is ill, Clem is a chronic absentee & useless when present. He wrote imploring Bowen to be with him for the Berlin debate on Monday & to speak – & Bowen replied that he had 'a function'. He does damn all in the House. As Jo says – why go into it? Jo is literally maid-of-all-work to the party. As he says, now that the *N.C.* is gone the word 'Liberal' is never mentioned in the Press.[3] The *Expresses, Pictorial, Daily Mail* never mention it in print. Millions of newspaper readers are given no evidence that the Party exists.

Diary – Sunday 13 August – The Glebe, Stockton, Wiltshire

Stayed late in bed & read the Sunday papers. Adam looked in later & told me he had heard very bad news on the wireless. The East German Govt. has suddenly erected a barbed wire fence guarded by soldiers & tanks across the frontier of their sector in Berlin to seal off the escape route of the Refugees. A record number of thousands had got over the day before.... One rather sinister feature is that Ulbricht[4] had just returned from a visit to Khrushchev (now on holiday near the Black Sea) so he must have got his marching orders straight from the horse's mouth....

[1] Asked how it felt to be a celebrity – he had been driven to the Russian embassy from London airport in a Rolls-Royce 'YG1', bearing the hammer and sickle flag – Gagarin observed that his 'Hero of the Soviet Union' gold star had number 11,175 on it: 'That means that 11,174 people accomplished something very notable before me. Mr Kruschchev has three gold stars and is a hero of socialist labour' (*The Times*, 12 July 1961).

[2] (Sir) Hugh Carleton Greene (1910–87), KCMG, 1964; journalist, broadcaster and publisher; joined BBC, 1940; director-general, 1960–9; brother of the writer Graham Greene.

[3] For the demise of the *News Chronicle* see the Glossary below.

[4] Walter Ulbricht (1893–1973), German Communist politician exiled mostly in the Soviet Union after the rise of Hitler; returned to Germany in 1945 and was largely responsible for the 'sovietization' of the East and the building of the Berlin Wall.

V.B.C. to Elena Bonham Carter ***Friday 1 September***
21 Hyde Park Square, W.2

My Darling – How can I thank you enough for your letter. . . . I am hungry for all your news. Leslie & Mark are going to U.S.A. about 6th Oct., he tells me, & will be a week in New York with her sister, a week in Chicago & hopes to be a week in Washington. World news very black with Berlin, & the Russians resuming tests.[1] Our generations, mine & yours, seem to be doomed to be rocked by earthquakes from the cradle to the grave. I count myself blessed to be old enough to remember a civilized world – whose peoples did not dream of war – & where such horrors as slavery & torture, concentration camps & atom bombs cld. not have been imagined.

I cannot help feeling sorry for poor Kennedy – faced with such odds – & from whom miracles of leadership are expected & demanded. And what a team he has to work with! De Gaulle – who refuses to enter negotiations – Adenauer 87 – whose vile attack on Willy Brandt for his illegitimacy makes me feel that he is no longer fit for responsibility[2] – & Macmillan – who has committed every imaginable gaffe at home – including the statement that the Berlin situation is 'got up by the Press'!

Ray writes me a lyrical description of your new house & says that you have 'filled it with atmosphere'. I must stop & send this quickly to catch a post. Goodbye my darling three, all my love & blessings & gratitude for the heavenly photographs of Edward. Ever your devoted Violet.

Diary – Monday 23 October – 21 Hyde Park Square, W.2

I went to a most moving Memorial Service for Hammarskjöld in Westminster Abbey. I sat with the U.N.A. representatives. . . .[3] I went on to hear Ted Heath at Chatham House talking about the Common Market. It was ironical to hear all the arguments we have used for the last 3 or 4 years trotted out – 'numbers of agricultural populations of European countries' etc. – 'wld they vote for their own damnation?' I felt as if I were listening to a well-known hymn-tune suddenly intoned by a pagan. I felt like

[1] The Soviet Union announced on 31 August that it intended to resume testing nuclear devices, blaming the necessity on NATO's 'threatening' posture in Europe.

[2] In a speech in Regensburg, 14 August, Adenauer had spoken disparagingly of 'Herr Brandt *alias* Frahm'. This was an allusion to the fact that Willy Brandt's father was unknown to him. Brandt took his mother's name 'Frahm' until he emigrated to Norway in 1933. Adenauer's attack reflected his bitter opposition to Brandt's proposal that the Western Allies and Soviet Union convene a conference to discuss the question of Berlin and of German reunification.

[3] Hammarskjöld had been killed in a plane crash in Northern Rhodesia on 18 September.

shouting out 'You're telling me! But why didn't you tell your party all this a few years ago?' I abstained with difficulty from putting awkward questions. Home & on to a Liberal meeting in Paddington. . . .

Diary – Thursday 2 November – 21 Hyde Park Square, W.2

Lunched with Jeremy at the H. of C. & a Mr Franklin – Chairman of the Northern Rhodesian Liberal Party. Talked N. Rhod. 'shop' all through. . . . On to Drury Lane (of all places!) where Martin & Anne Russell had very kindly asked me to go to a Gala Matinée (for the R.A.D.A.) with them to see the male Russian dancer Nureyev. . . .[1] I accepted less from any passionate desire to see him than from a feeling that it was so nice of them to ask me. Little did I dream that I was going to have one of the great, unforgettable experiences of my life.

The Matinée was for a Charity – & it was a hotch-potch of different pieces. The Danish Ballet who are over here did one or two very well. . . . Then came Nureyev. The dance was called *Poème Tragique* – music by Scriabin – choreography by Frederick Ashton.[2] The curtain went up. He was alone. He looked very young – about 19. He is actually 23. It is impossible to attempt to describe what followed. I can only say that it was the most inspired, exciting, convulsive experience I have had since Nijinsky. Like Nijinsky he seemed outside nature, belonging to a genus of his own – half faun. But the emotion he gave one (in the words of Cecil Beaton[3] whom I saw afterwards) 'cut like a whip-lash'. It was 'hors concours' – alpha plus plus – touching the summit of human performance in its chosen medium. The whole theatre was intoxicated & cheered like people possessed. The reaction was explosive – like firing a mine.

I could not look at what followed & my hopes of *Spectre de la Rose* (with Margot Fonteyn & John Gilpin) were dashed. It was charming & lovely but the leap from the window – which used to bring one's heart into one's mouth when Nijinsky did it – was a mere hop – & there was no bed – Margot Fonteyn dozed uneasily on a chair. I was sorry to see Nureyev again doing a pas de deux from *Swan Lake* with Roselle Hightower. He

[1] Rudolf Nureyev (1938–93), ballet dancer and choreographer; sought political asylum in Paris, June 1961, when touring with the Kirov ballet. The gala matinée in which he made his London debut was organized by (Dame) Margot Fonteyn (1919–91), his future partner at the Royal Ballet.

[2] (Sir) Frederick William Ashton (1904–88), Kt, 1962; founder-choreographer to Royal Ballet; director, 1963–70.

[3] (Sir) Cecil Walter Beaton (1904–80), Kt, 1972; photographer, artist, writer, scene and costume designer.

wore a rather bad blonde wig & tho' no doubt both danced exquisitely it was such a bathos after *Poème Tragique*. Raymond Mortimer came with us. Martin & Anne dropped me home. A Red Letter day in my life.

Diary – Saturday 4 November – 21 Hyde Park Square, W.2

Suddenly very cold. Abortive expedition to General Trading C° where there was no one to 'serve'. Worked in the afternoon. In the evening went to India House to meet Nehru (who travelled overnight from India & goes to-morrow morning to meet Kennedy in U.S.A.) at a pre-view of the Tagore Exhibition (Centenary Celebration).... I had a word with Nehru before he went away & asked him if he was going to plunge into the U.N. – the storm centre of the world. He said 'It certainly reflects the storms of the world. But the object of my visit is to see the President'. I asked him how much hope he had for the world? I said that I felt hope that we cld. bridge the immediate ditches by expedients but it was the long-term prospect which alarmed me. He said he felt rather the other way – that if we cld manage to get through the immediately impending crises there might be hope for the future. He looked very tired.

I shld like to have got his view on the extraordinary events in Russia. To-day she has exploded her 31st bomb. The optimists try & persuade themselves that these 31 bombs have been exploded in order to enable Khrushchev to pursue a moderate foreign policy & defeat the Stalinists on his home Front. Meanwhile the digging up of Stalin's body & its banishment from the Kremlin (for crimes in which most of the diggers played a part) has aroused fury in Albania – & (one imagines) in China. The Communist camp is therefore no longer monolithic. This is the comfort we can take to ourselves for the monstrous inhumanity of the Berlin Wall & the breach of the Geneva Agreement. The frightening thing to me is that the future of the world at the moment seems to depend on our dealing with people we understand as little as we do the Russians.

Diary – Thursday 23 November – 21 Hyde Park Square, W.2

Went to Foyle's lunch at the Dorchester in honour of Bertrand Russell who has published a new book – *Has Man a Future?*[1] It was of course thronged with unilateralists & sitters- & squatters- & liers-down. Mervyn Stockwood,

[1] Its subject was nuclear disarmament. Russell was by then a leading figure in public demonstrations against nuclear weapons, many of them utilizing the 'sit-down' protest.

Bishop of Southwark, in the Chair.[1] I had a word with B. Russell before luncheon. He is in a marvellous state of preservation – more limber & spare than Herbert Samuel & not apparently the least deaf. His sharp spare snipe-like face quite unchanged. . . .

At lunch I sat between Ld Attlee & Vicky[2] with whom I talked for most of lunch. . . . I liked Vicky & he was much more moderate & less *New-Statesman*-like than I had thought he wld be. He told me incidentally that he had coined the phrase 'Super-Mac' in one of his cartoons, & that it had then been used not to pillory but to boost its intended victim. Attlee asked me whether I had liked Harold Nicolson's tribute to my father. I said to him what I had written to Harold – & told him that I had asked him to name one achievement of the present Govt. which cld justify nominating H. Macmillan as the 'greatest peacetime P.M.' – adding that both his own '45 Govt. & my Father's pre-War Govt. had achieved far more than any other in this century – with which, needless to say, he heartily agreed!

B. Russell made a thoroughly bad speech – crisply & competently delivered – in which he said we only assessed & valued scientists according to their capacity to kill us & railed at the impotence & futility of politicians (rather ungrateful after Michael Foot's speech of unqualified adulation in proposing his health). He attacked America & wasted a lot of time reading out some obscure American idiot's remarks about deep shelters in U.S.A. – which were quite irrelevant to the issue. His logical sense has evidently decayed – but he never understood political issues, which often deal not so much with goals as means of reaching them. No one wants to be 'incinerated'. The question is how best to prevent it. Sitting down in Trafalgar Square does not seem to many of us the most effective means (& even on 'means' he has fallen down – since he dialled the police to remove 2 squatters from his own house who wished to persuade him by his own methods to heal the breach in C.N.D. by resuming contacts with Canon Collins!). . . .[3]

[1] (Arthur) Mervyn Stockwood (b. 1913), bishop of Southwark, 1959–80.

[2] Victor Weisz, 'Vicky' (1913–66), Berlin-born Hungarian-Jewish cartoonist; his early work attacked the Nazis and he left Germany for England; briefly with the *Daily Herald*, 1938; *News Chronicle*, 1939–53; afterwards *Daily Mail* and, from 1958, *Daily Express*; from 1954 he drew a weekly cartoon for the *New Statesman*: 'It was a labour of love for which his original fees barely covered the taxi fares' (*DNB*) – see his caricature of Violet, p. 141.

[3] Rev. Canon Lewis John Collins (1905–82), chairman of CND, 1958–64; later president of the International Defence and Aid Fund.

NINE

Liberal Dawn

1962–1963

Diary Tuesday 30 January 1962 – 21 Hyde Park Square, W.2

Lib. Party Committee at the House. Jo in the Chair.... We have a by-election impending at Orpington at which we may do well & about which the *Daily Mail* has again produced a National Poll which must warm the cockles of every Lib. heart – suggesting that we might win the seat. We are apparently neck to neck with the Conservatives. Home all afternoon – very cold. Cressida dined in. She has an awful catarrh poor darling.

Diary – Tuesday 13 February – 21 Hyde Park Square, W.2

L.P. Committee in the morning. I got there late thro' preparing some notes for our [Africa Bureau] delegation to Lord Home this afternoon.... At ¼ to 4 I met my colleagues at the Foreign Office – Ld. Hemingford, Peter Calvocoressi, Dr Roland Oliver, my new friend Colonel Draper[1] – the crippled lawyer who came to our preliminary meeting.... Dr Rita Hinden was also there.[2] After a short wait in a very grand room we were ushered into a still grander one where we found Ld Home, who received us very affably. We sat round a table. Ld Hemingford introduced us. Peter Calvocoressi spoke first, rapidly, fluently, but not very crisply or impressively. Then Roland Oliver weighed in, then Dr Rita Hinden – a Colonial expert – had a word.

[1] Dennis George Herbert (1904–82), 2nd Baron Hemingford; spent career as an educationalist in Africa; chairman, Africa Bureau, 1952–63; vice president 1963. Peter (John) Calvocoressi (b. 1912), author and publisher; contested Nuneaton (Lib.) 1945; chairman, Africa Bureau, 1963–71. Colonel Gerald Irving Draper (1914–89), barrister and soldier (retired); later professor of law, University of Sussex.

[2] Dr Rita Hinden, 'a gifted and idealistic South African Jewish emigrée', active in the Fabian Research Bureau (Morgan, *Labour in Power*, 189).

Then I spoke on our voting at the U.N. – refusing to condemn Apartheid, which we all abhor & openly condemn at home. . . . He [Hume] said that the Apartheid vote contained a proposal to impose sanctions. I said 'Why shldn't we impose economic sanctions?' 'Because India & Ceylon refused.' 'But they voted for the resolution.' 'Ah yes, that is the trouble. The Dominions are apt to vote for things they are against.'[1] I felt inclined to say that was no reason to prevent us from voting for things we were in favour of.

I got in a last shot about Portugal in the end, quoting a sentence from a speech . . . . in which he had said that while we, Britain & Portugal, had different methods of approach to our respective Colonies, 'We both had the same belief, in Africa, in respect for the human personality'. There was precious little respect for the human personality or for any human right in Portugal – not a vestige in Angola.[2] This discomfited him – for the 2nd time only. The first had been when Colonel Draper pointed out what aid & comfort we were giving to the Communists – & quoting at first hand from a Communist who said so. . . .

Home was throughout very smooth courteous & facile but I don't think his heart is in the right place. He sees the African leaders as ambitious self-seeking Nationalists. I reminded him of Kaunda, Nyere & Luthuli. Walking away with Col. Draper we congratulated each other on the shots which we felt had gone home. I said reflectively, thinking aloud, 'The object of a deputation is with tact & courtesy to inflict extreme pain.' He said 'That remark has made my afternoon!' I don't know if we did any good but it was at least a gesture.

Diary – Wednesday 21 February – 21 Hyde Park Square, W.2

Lunched with W. & Clemmie. He looked well & pink as usual but was very remote in mind. Said he had not painted for 18 months when I asked him. I think boredom is his most deadly enemy. It is so difficult to find anything that will reach or engage his mind. The past is blurred as well as the present. It must be a great strain for Clemmie to keep him 'in play' at all. He has not got the concentration to read. I had my usual half-hour alone with him before going [with him] to the House – this visit gives him his only 'break' & sense of being part of things. He had no idea what was

[1] In fact India had ceased being a dominion in 1950 (it had been an independent dominion from 1947 to 1950).

[2] The general movement for independence in the African colonies had spread, by 1962, to Portuguese-ruled Mozambique and Angola, where it was strongly resisted. In the latter half of 1961 Portuguese authorities had crushed a serious uprising in northern Angola.

going on there. He was as ever loving & sweet, kissed me goodbye with real emotion & turned as he always does, when the detective had helped him out & up the few steps at the door of the House, full round & took off his top-hat with the formal observance & ceremony of 40 years ago. . . .

Orpington and the Liberal revival, 1961–1962

The Liberal resurgence under Jo Grimond's leadership gained momentum in 1961 when the Party fought ten by-elections, gaining on average a quarter of the votes cast at each. A series of by-elections in March 1962 provided a further opportunity for advance. At Lincoln on 8 March the Liberals came only third behind Labour, but the Party had nevertheless performed creditably in a constituency that it had not fought since losing a deposit there in 1950. And prospects were brighter at Blackpool North on 13 March. Here the Liberal came within 973 votes of victory, a remarkable result that raised genuine hopes of an upset in the Conservative bastion of Orpington in Kent the following day. The Orpington Liberals had mounted an impressive campaign and were set to exploit their victory in the local government elections the previous year. They had a strong candidate in Eric Lubbock, a former local councillor whose family had a long association with the town. Lubbock's link with the past undoubtedly told in his favour, but he also epitomized the modern world. Jo Grimond later wrote that he was 'widely and rightly regarded as a representative of a new generation – Orpington-man – the generation which was classless, understood technology . . . and intended to apply to the management of the country the principles of modern science – political engineering'. Lubbock faced an able Conservative candidate, Peter Goldman, who was also backed by an energetic campaign. But for all his efforts, Goldman came across poorly to the Orpington electorate, his task made more difficult by an unquantifiable degree of anti-semitic prejudice (though an Anglican, he took pride in his Jewish descent). Goldman also had to contend with the deep unpopularity of the government, especially over its 'pay pause' policy. This was intended to help revive a faltering economy by reducing costs, but was widely resented, and perceived as being unfair to groups such as nurses. A potent blend of national and local factors thus converged at Orpington to threaten a normally impregnable Conservative majority of 15,000.[1]

[1]Grimond, *Memoirs*, 203; Young, 'Orpington', 167.

Diary – Wednesday 14 March – 21 Hyde Park Square, W.2

Polling Day at Orpington. Papers full of nothing else. Too many Tory cars – some had to be sent away there wasn't room for them. Terrific tension. . . .

Dined in with Cressida & at 11 o'clock we settled down to watch the Orpington programme on the T.V. screen. I was torn between wanting to see Mark on B.B.C. & Jo on I.T.V. I did a certain amount of switching but spent most of the time on B.B.C. as it is as a rule so much the best programme. They had (of course!) Robert McKenzie & David Butler[1] as psephologists, to fill in time, & a team consisting of Enoch Powell (rather dull & heavy), Mark, Woodrow Wyatt, William Deedes & Richard Taverne[2] (very good-looking & attractive). Jo had a dustier lot.

Between whiles we saw thrilling scenes of the count. I was amazed that they allowed the T.V. cameras in – knowing all the formalities I have had to go thro' at Torrington (signing a paper pledging myself to absolute secrecy etc.). . . Goldman[3] was a curiously repellent personality, dark, smug, with thick spectacles, very Semitic (this in itself not a criticism – but there are types & types), very slick, experienced & professional in every sense of the word. Eric Lubbock[4] was the perfect foil to him (or he to Lubbock?) diffident, decent, a little shy, un-glib – what Aunt Bett wld call 'a gent' to the finger-tips. He has a very pretty wife – obviously nervous – whereas Mrs Goldman – not unattractive – was assured & ready. Poor Jinkinson[5] didn't come into the picture much but George Brown was there to support him.

The hours crept. Woodrow Wyatt refused to bet on the result at which Mark ragged him as a 'gambling-man' (he keeps race-horses). William Deedes & Powell plumped for the Tory without hesitation, Mark backed the Liberal – saying 'I think that we shall just make it'. . . . Finally the

[1] Robert Trelford McKenzie (1917–81), Canadian-born political scientist and broadcaster; with LSE from 1949 (professor, 1964). David Edgeworth Butler (b. 1924), fellow of Nuffield College, Oxford, since 1954; expert on British parliamentary elections.

[2] William Francis Deedes (b. 1913), cr. life peer, 1986; MP (Con.) Ashford, Kent, 1950–74; minister without portfolio, 1962–4; later editor of *Daily Telegraph*. Richard ('Dick') Taverne (b. 1928), QC, 1965; victor at the Lincoln by-election on 8 March; MP (Lab.) Lincoln, 1962–72, resigned; (Dem. Lab.) March 1973–September 1974; SDP candidate, 1982, 1983.

[3] Peter Goldman (b. 1925), director, Conservative Political Centre, 1955–64; contested (Con.) West Ham South, 1959; Orpington, 1962; married, 1961, Cicely *née* Magnay (diss. 1969); later director of the Consumers' Association, 1964–87.

[4] Eric Reginald Lubbock (b. 1928), 4th Baron Avebury (s. 1971); management consultant; MP (Lib.) Orpington, 1962–70; Liberal whip, 1963–70; married, 1953, Kina Maria *née* de Gallagh (diss. 1983).

[5] Alan Raymond Jinkinson (b. 1935), the Labour candidate at Orpington; at education department of the National and Local Government Officers' Association; later general secretary of the public service union Unison, 1993.

Sheriff summoned the candidates & as they clustered round him showed them a bit of paper. He then read out the names & figures – my heart nearly dropped on the floor when the first word he uttered was 'Goldman 14,9–'! I thought he had won. (Mark had the same experience but he had time to realise that on an 80 p.c. plus poll the winning figure must be higher.) My moment of relief came when the second name 'Jinkinson 5,000 odd' was read. He then turned a little towards Eric Lubbock who was standing alone on his left & said 'Lubbock 22,—' I cldn't believe it. It was incredible – fantastic. Not only had he wiped out a majority of just under 15,000 but he was in with a majority of just under 8,000.[1] There was wild cheering & excitement.

I just had time to switch to Jo & hear him say a few words of congratulation to Lubbock – adding 'I congratulate them all – it's been a good fight' (or 'words to that effect') & then back to the B.B.C. – where they were all winded. Enoch Powell & Deedes had to wait a little to get their breath to tell us how it wld all come back at the General Election. Robin Day[2] appealed to Mark to compare it with Torrington & Mark said it was of course a far greater achievement than Torrington. There they had an old Liberal tradition, but in Orpington none. An unforgettable evening. I was too happy & excited to go to sleep & finally, thinking of to-morrow, took a seconal.

Diary – Thursday 15 March – 21 Hyde Park Square, W.2

Woke early & asked for all the papers & telephoned Mrs Honey[3] to bring *Express, D.T., Daily Mirror – Herald*. The *Herald* had the most grudging headlines. No mention of Libs. in large print there! *Telegraph, Mirror* & of course *Daily Mail* did us proud. Their Nat. Poll was over-vindicated. Mark rang me up late last night – over the moon. I rang Jo at 9 & heard real emotion in his voice. I must say they both deserve it. I love to think that they are reaping some reward for all their integrity & selfless grind. I was treading on air all day – returning again & again to the papers – sucking their headlines like delicious sweets. . . .

[1]The official result was: E. R. Lubbock (Lib.) 22,846; Peter Goldman (Con.) 14,991; A. R. Jinkinson (Lab.) 5,350 (lost deposit). The majority was 7,855. Violet wrote to Elena Bonham Carter on 14 April: 'We shld have been triumphant if the Liberal had got in by 10 votes.'

[2](Sir) Robin Day (b. 1923), Kt, 1981; television and radio journalist, famous for his robust style when interviewing the leading politicians of the day.

[3]Marigold Honey, Violet's personal secretary.

Diary – Tuesday 20 March – 21 Hyde Park Square, W.2

Tremendous Liberal day. Laura lunched with me & we drove together to the H. of C. to see Eric Lubbock take his seat. As we got out of the car in Palace Yard there was only one human being in it – Dingle! He looked extremely embarrassed & gave us a cracked smile.[1] Not a topical word passed between us but Laura & he were able to exchange views on safe African ground. . . . We went up to the Gallery after I had been introduced by Eric Lubbock to Mr Chitnis[2] his brilliant agent (of Indian birth) & 3 young sub-agents. Lubbock had arranged for all of them to see him take his seat – which I thought so nice of him. . . . I had warned him about Mark's reception after Torrington. To my amazement the Labour benches cheered him too. Deathly silence from the Tories. Macmillan had scuttled out before the ceremony, but I was amused at seeing him peeping from behind the Speaker's Chair. . . .

Diary – Tuesday 27 March – 21 Hyde Park Square, W.2

Went to Chatham House at 1.30 & heard a rather dull read speech by a German – Alfermann by name – about the German T.U.'s. He told one nothing one really wanted to know about them until Question Time when I was able to ask him about Closed Shop, Secret Ballot before Strikes, Political Levy, etc. I talked to him afterwards & he was quite nice & informative. His presentation was German at its worst – pages of figures which conveyed nothing & all the political pith omitted. It was a very small meeting. . . . Then on to Farewell Party of my nice friend the Turkish Ambassador who I took last year to Glyndebourne. Chauvel drove me home. I asked him on the way whether de Gaulle really wished to keep us out of the Common Market – as I & many others here believed. He said 'No – he only thought we shld find it very difficult to go in, in view of our Commonwealth obligations.' I said 'Then he thinks it desirable but impossible?' He replied (I don't know how 'diplomatically') 'No – not impossible – only very difficult.' I forgot to say that at Chauvel's own party yesterday I met Bob Boothby who said to me with enthusiasm 'I feel like joining the Liberal Party. I agreed with every word of Jo's article in the

[1] Violet regarded Dingle Foot as a renegade for having deserted the Liberal cause for Labour in 1956. Before the 1955 general election he had written an article in the *News Chronicle* urging Liberals to follow his example and vote Labour.

[2] Pratap Chidamber Chitnis (b. 1936), cr. life peer, 1977; central figure in Liberal Party Organization from 1960; chief executive and director, 1975–88; election agent in the Orpington campaign, 1962.

Times'.[1] I encouraged him – though I don't know whether the old rascal wld be an asset or a liability to us. He is of course a first-rate speaker & sound to the nth degree on the C.M. . . .

Diary – Monday 9 April – Hôtel Berlin, West Berlin

[Königswinter] Called at 7 – finished packing – luggage stacked in the hall – Berlin on one side – London on the other. Jo, Roy & many Parliamentarians & journalists going back for the Budget. Separated from the London party at the Air-port. . . . Arrived late at Berlin airport. Received as usual with lovely bouquets of red & white carnations – Dr Reif – Frau Krug. Driven to Hôtel Berlin. No time to do more than sketchy tidying before huge luncheon – mercifully in the hotel. . . .

Lunch didn't end till 3.30 so our tour of West Berlin was rather mercifully confined to what we really wished to see – i.e. the Wall. At first sight it is very much lower than one had imagined – tho' covered with barbed wire, broken glass etc. It runs for 30 miles – cutting across streets, churchyards – so that one sees pathetic withering wreaths hung on walls by people cut off from the graves of their dead. One refinement of human cruelty is that in places where a rise in the ground on either side enabled separated families & friends to see over the Wall & wave to each other, high match-board screens have been erected to cut them off even from the comfort & contact of this distant sight & greeting. In one street on the border-line – Bernauer Strasse – where the houses front on the East & back on the West we saw a green wreath tied with red ribbons lying on the pavement. I was told that this was where a woman had leapt from a 3rd storey window to her death. They were very high houses. She had put [thrown] a mattress down to jump on – heard the East German police battering on her door & jumped – missing the mattress. . . .

40 escapees have been shot dead by their own fellow-countrymen – the E. German police. This is what shocks one most deeply. It is so easy to miss. Many of course have missed & helped – actively or passively – & some have deserted. It is impossible to telephone to the East now, even via Frankfurt, & letters & parcels are opened. The inhumanity of Communism must surely defeat it in the end? . . .

[1] Jo Grimond's article 'New Breakdown of Parties Needed', in *The Times* of 17 March, criticized both the Conservatives and Labour: 'The divisions in politics fall in the wrong places. The natural breakdown should be into a Conservative Party – a small group of convinced Socialists in the full sense – and a broadly based progressive Party. It is the foundations of the last named that the Liberal Party seeks to provide.'

Diary – Tuesday 10 April – Hôtel Berlin, West Berlin

Hectic day. We started at 9.30 for the East Sector into which, after an endless examination of passports in a long hut on the East side of the barrier, we were allowed to proceed on foot. I went with Desmond Donnelly & a nice Adviser to the Bank of England who knows Ray, called Cunnell. The streets were grimmer, blacker, sadder & emptier than ever before. We gaped at a few shop windows where there was nothing one cld have desired to buy – went into one bookshop full of ideological literature, but completely devoid of fiction or light relief.

Tried to reach the Adlon Hôtel[1] which we saw in the distance but realised it was too far for the time available. The men, who had changed some money, wanted to spend it so we went into a café where they ordered beer & I asked for coffee. I took one tea-spoonful & nearly spat it out, it was quite undrinkable – not like the worst coffee there ever was – it wasn't coffee at all. I don't know what it can have been made of. It was actually lucky I didn't drink more. We heard afterwards there were 27,000 cases of dysentery (this figure probably an understatement) in the East Sector & it is also rife in the Eastern Zone. Prolonged re-examination of passports in the hut opposite the one they were vetted in when we entered the Sector. Seeing a bewildered official page-ing thro' my passport for the 100th time I said 'Wissen Sie was Sie suchen & wofür?' He replied frankly & pathetically 'Nein ich weiss es nicht.'. . . .[2]

Diary – Tuesday 17 April – 21 Hyde Park Square, W.2

Tried on Miss Joseph. Waited for North Derby result which was announced about 10.45. It is astounding – & most encouraging – the Liberal – Lyndon Irving – came second. . . .[3] It is, in its way, almost as bad a knock for the Govt. as Orpington. Our candidate was said to be a poor one (he played the trombone for hours on polling-day according to the press) but he must have been a 'character' with some attraction. He started absolutely from scratch. We had never fought the seat except once (in 1950) since it was created & he had no help to speak of from outside. Jo cldn't go there & Jeremy (inexcusably) chucked, pleading a cold. Yet he beat the Tory who had an entrenched position & a marvellous machine. If this can happen in an industrial stronghold like Derby North it can happen anywhere.

[1] A famous Berlin hotel, in which Violet had dined during her visit to Germany in 1923.

[2] 'Do you know what you are looking for and why?' 'No, I don't know.'

[3] The official result at Derby North, which polled on 17 April, was: N. MacDermot (Lab.) 16,497; L. Irving (Lib.) 8,479; T. M. Wray (Con.) 7,502.

Mark rang me up at 12.15 – ecstatically happy. He thinks (rightly) that something dynamic is taking place....

A Liberal dawn?

The euphoria surrounding Orpington encouraged Liberals to think in terms of the long-awaited electoral breakthrough. This time their hopes seemed justified by results. Harold Macmillan wrote in his diary ten days after the by-election, 'we have been swept off our feet by a *Liberal* revival'. And on 28 March a National Opinion Poll in the *Dail Mail* seemed to confirm this, putting the Liberals ahead of Labour and the Conservatives, albeit by the narrowest of margins. The political atmosphere had undoubtedly altered, as the Liberals exploited the deep unpopularity of the government to threaten Conservative seats. This proved to be a factor behind Macmillan's inept 'night of the long knives' cabinet reshuffle in mid-July, widely seen as an act of desperation from a failing government. But, for all the Conservative fears and the Liberal hopes, the Liberals had won only one seat in the run of recent by-elections, and had made virtually no gains at Labour's expense. Torrington showed the vulnerability of a Liberal victory based primarily on Conservative abstentions or defections, which might easily be reversed at the next general election. Ominously the Liberal share of the vote at by-elections fell from 28 per cent in 1962 to 17 per cent the following year. The downward trend was confirmed with a disappointing result at the general election in 1964, which showed the limits of the Liberal revival. Under Jo Grimond the Party had pulled itself back from the brink of electoral extinction, but it was far from the threshold of power.[1]

Diary – Thursday 5 July – 21 Hyde Park Square, W.2

U.N.A. Luncheon to U Thant[2] at which I was to speak, Jo being absent. Arrived at the Dorchester at 12.45 & was ushered, not into a small speaker's Green Room ... but into a large-ish room with a buffet & about 30–40 people in it – Nigel Nicolson & wife & Judd & dear Dame Kathleen

[1] The NOP poll gave the Liberals a 30 per cent rating; Labour 29.9 per cent; the Conservatives 29.2 per cent; Cook, *Short History of the Liberal Party*, 141; Young, 'Orpington', 157–79; Horne, *Macmillan, 1957–1986*, 335–45.

[2] U Thant (1909–74), permanent representative of Burma to the UN, 1957–61; became secretary general of the UN on death of Dag Hammarskjöld, 1961, and held that office until retiring in 1971; was influential in bringing peace to the Congo, 1963.

Courtney with whom I sat down after a time. We were joined by the Gaitskells.... We were given marching orders – the speakers to proceed last to the High Table etc. H. Macmillan finally arrived, but was met at the door & escorted ahead so there was no confrontation. I had been introduced to U Thant, who is full of charm & seemed (surprisingly) to know 'all about me' such things as there are to know – & I was delighted to find myself sitting next to him, with Gaitskell on my other side....

I had an excellent talk with U Thant about the U.N. & particularly about the Congo.[1] He is a Buddhist & one feels that he has a kind of core of peacefulness inside him – unlike we Westerners who are militant about it, if we care. Gaitskell was as ever delightful. I reminded him of last time – when Harold had forgotten to let him second the toast to Hammarskjöld who was with us – the guest of Honour – & when 3 bearded Empire Loyalists had appeared behind H.M.'s chair & interrupted him. Curiously enough his speech was again interrupted by them – less dramatically but far more effectively. They had somehow got tickets & were sprinkled all over the room in seats at the various tables. Harold looked exhausted & read a very dull speech from notes – without one ounce of 'go' or enthusiasm or brio. In fact I think the Loyalists were a help by leavening things up a bit. He got his best response – one laugh – by saying 'I don't believe you've paid your subscription' in answer to one interrupter. It was an immense relief to us all when he decided to leave after his own speech.... When he left U Thant spoke – reading from a type-script – very interestingly for 12–14 minutes – then Gaitskell – then I wound up by moving a vote of thanks to them all. It went well & I was congratulated by Gaitskell, U Thant, Gladwyn[2] etc. & many Liberal faithfuls who had come up from all parts of the country. Much autographing on Menus went on for ages. Finally got home at 20 to 4....

Dressed for Admiralty dinner[3] & was taken there by Mr Burnside. Arrived not too early – knowing that only the might of the U.N. cld have prized these portals open to me, I did not want to risk being the first.... I was given a fairly 'frapped flipper' by my host [Macmillan] & by Hailsham. Butler was 'urbane', regretted my not having seen him for so long etc....

After dinner I drifted very happily onto a sofa with Philippa Nicolson....

[1] The United Nations was then trying to execute a peace-keeping role in the Congo, where a bloody civil war had broken out after the region had gained independence from Belgium in 1960.

[2] Hubert Miles Gladwyn Jebb (1900–96), cr. 1st Baron Gladwyn, 1960; GCVO, 1957; diplomat; permanent representative of Britain at the UN, 1950–54; British ambassador in Paris, 1954–60; deputy Liberal leader and spokesman on foreign affairs and defence, House of Lords, 1965–88.

[3] From the summer of 1960 to the summer of 1963, while 10 Downing Street was being rebuilt, the prime minister's official residence was Admiralty House.

When the men came in Gaitskell & I settled on a sofa & he warned me that 2 of our fellow-guests were very drunk – Roy Harrod & John Wyndham[1] (Harold's Private Secretary & therefore one of our hosts).... We got on to the next General Election – the possibility of 2 give-away Budgets to restore the Govt's fallen fortunes. Gaitskell said 'I believe in the swing of the pendulum.' I said that it hadn't happened last time. At this moment Harrod approached us – literally swaying on his feet – his speech blurred – a glass of amber-coloured liquid in his hand which I was terrified he wld pour over us (as indeed he wld have done had I not warned him not to). He began by taxing Gaitskell very incoherently with his attempt to expel Bertie Russell.[2] Gaitskell reacted strongly & said that Russell had always been wrong & absurdly so on every political issue. Harrod talked on – tried to talk about his distinction in logic etc. But I have never in my life seen anyone so drunk in a private house. We finally got up to escape him but he followed us about.

Then Ly Drogheda came to consult me about suggesting to Mrs Gaitksell that she shld give the signal to depart. It was 5 to 11 & the P.M. was so tired that he yawned all thro' dinner. I agreed & after a time there was a slight movement towards departure. I said goodbye to my host, who tried to exchange a few words with me about grandchildren, saying he had 15 & one was playing in the Eton Eleven. I then tried to find Dorothy – a few people had already dribbled away – when my eye was suddenly arrested by an extraordinary sight. In the middle of the room John Wyndham was standing, having removed his dinner jacket, in a white shirt & a tie making strange lunging movements at a circle of puzzled guests. He was I think pretending to be a Toreador. It was an extraordinary curtain to this (wld-be) formal & dignified evening in honour of the Secretary General of the U.N. & I cldn't help wondering what the Buddhists thought of it. For a few moments I watched in frozen astonishment, then I followed some of them downstairs – Harrod still lurching & talking. I was terrified that he wld fall downstairs. I was driven home by Mr Jan Lindstrom & his wife. (I think he is a U.N.A. representative – he told me he lived here at Wim-

[1]John Edward Wyndham (1920–72), cr. 1st Baron Egremont, 1963; civil servant and author; with Conservative Research Department, 1947–52; private secretary to Harold Macmillan, 1957–63.

[2]In June 1962 the Labour Party sought to expel Bertrand Russell over his support for a Soviet-sponsored international conference on nuclear disarmament, to be held in Moscow. There was an outcry at his expulsion and it was subsequently claimed that Russell had left the Party voluntarily, not having paid his annual subscription. This explanation met with general derision and on 28 June there was a climb-down, when Russell was confirmed as a Labour Party member. Three years later, though, he publicly tore up his membership card in protest against the Vietnam war.

bledon. I met him at Chatham House with Dr Linner.) The end of a very full & strange day!

Diary – Saturday 14 July – 21 Hyde Park Square, W.2

Morning drenched in pouring rain – a cruel day for Laura's fête at Kew.... Newspapers announce the most dramatic & sweeping Govt. purge – for that is what it is. Gaitskell describes it truly as a 'massacre'. The chief sacrificial victim is Selwyn Lloyd! He leaves the Exchequer (with a C.H.) & is succeeded by Maudling....[1] The 'image' seems to me to remain the same because tho' 7 'old familiar faces' are gone the rest remain & meanwhile Supermac's 'image' of unflappability & implacable loyalty to colleagues is tarnished by this 'Night of the Long Knives'. It is also a curious repudiation of Cabinet responsibility. They all approved the Pay Pause policy, defended it root & branch – Mac first & foremost – & are now using poor old Celluloid as a scapegoat. I think they will find they have miscalculated & that their transformation scene will have little effect....

Diary – Monday 16 July – 21 Hyde Park Square, W.2

Newspapers full of the purge. The small fry are now being dealt with. Macmillan is seeing them at intervals of 8 to 10 minutes all through the day & a horde of press vultures flutter round the door of the Admiralty & guess from the faces of those who go in & out whether they have been axed or promoted – sometimes asking them direct or tendentious questions – to which the victims try to give cryptic replies....

Diary – Tuesday 17 July – 21 Hyde Park Square, W.2

Lunched with Moucher.... Very agreeable. Dropped Ava [Waverley] in Ld North St. & went to H. of C. to inquire about *Hansards*. As I was going along to the Whips' Room I came upon Gilbert Longden sitting talking to someone. Question time was just over & he told me he had asked Mac a question (it was Mac's first appearance in the House since the purge). He prefaced it with the words 'May I take this opportunity of personally congratulating the P.M. on having "kept his head while all about him

[1] Reginald Maudling (1917–79), MP (Con.) Barnet, Herts., 1950–74; Chipping Barnet, Barnet, 1974–9; secretary of state for the colonies, 1961–2; chancellor of the exchequer, 1962–4; later home secretary, 1970–2.

were losing theirs".' At this point (I heard afterwards) there was a roar from the whole House of laughter & applause which lasted over half a minute until the Speaker had to call it to order. Then Gilbert finished the quotation 'And blaming it on him.'[1] A new roar & the question finished with an inquiry about the political set-up in Europe. Selwyn had entered before questions & taken a back-bench seat. Mac was received in dead silence by his own side....

Diary – Sunday 22 July – 21 Hyde Park Square, W.2

The papers are most interesting reading – Rees-Mogg for once bad – completely ignoring the human factor in politics, & concentrating on the economic advantage of the changes, talking of sentimentality, tittle-tattle, gossip columns & not realizing that trust in, & respect for, one's leader is the essence of party solidarity....

I found Jo less exhilarated by the rumpus over the massacre than I had imagined he wld be.... He said he wasn't sure whether we ought to take part in the vote of Censure (which is of course idiotically inept).[2] We shld have to support it of course, but he was doubtful whether he wld speak. I was aghast – & said of course he must – & he cld. make the speech of his life. I poured out points – the Govt had moved a vote of censure on itself by the sackings – Cabinet responsibility had been thrown overboard (who was responsible for the Pay Pause policy if not the P.M.?) etc. etc. He said Gaitskell & H.M. wld speak first & take 3 hours. He wld not be called till late. I reminded him he was P.C.[3] 'Yes but the youngest – every older one will have the right to speak first.' I am sure he will in fact speak, but the thing that astounded me was that he shld not be burning to do so. The only ingredient he lacks as a political leader is passion. Andrew drove me home. Dined alone – read more papers. Listened to wireless music. Too sleepy to work – & too distracted by present events....

[1] From Rudyard Kipling's 'If': 'If you can keep your head when all about you / Are losing theirs and blaming it on you.'

[2] In response to Macmillan's purge the opposition tabled a motion of no confidence in the government, calling for a dissolution of parliament and an early general election. The motion was debated on 26 July.

[3] It was then customary for privy councillors to be given precedence over other members wishing to speak in a Commons debate, though it was never a matter of right.

Diary – Thursday 26 July – 21 Hyde Park Square, W.2

Vote of Censure day. Pelting, pouring, relentless rain. Tried several car hire companies in vain. Finally walked macintoshed to close on Paddington & got a taxi. Reached H. of C. in good time. Seat in Mrs Speaker's Gallery, 2nd row. Antonia Fraser[1] next me. Mrs Gaitskell & Catherine Amery[2] & Mrs Butler in front. Packed house. My disappointment was inability to see the Tory benches & the faces on them. (I knew just what Labour wld be looking like!) Three great bursts of cheering – the 2 loudest for Selwyn & Gaitskell – the least loud for Harold. Gaitskell made a good fighting speech to roars of back-bench cheering. Not really first-rate. He lacks the edge of wit which reaches the bone – Aneurin, LlG. & others had it – but he hasn't. Harold's speech interminable & unutterably dull. Not one spark in it. Praise of departed comrades he had pole-axed succeeded by shouts of 'Why sack him?'.... Jeremy counted 6 Tories fast asleep. Sat down to moderate cheers.

Shinwell up – having been called instead of Jo (who rose) & House emptied. Jeremy & Eric Lubbock fetched me for tea.... Up again to hear a maiden speech by one Biffen.[3] Then Jo got up – was called – & made the best speech I have ever heard him make in the House. He was loudly cheered by the Labour M.P.s as well as our own. It was delivered with great punch & energy. It was an all out attack on the Govt. – Harold's speech was that of an exhausted man – they had never told the truth from Suez onwards & this was the end of the road. It was magnificent....[4]

Diary – Saturday 28 July – 21 Hyde Park Square, W.2

...I had been rung up earlier by Jo asking if he cld come & see me. I asked him to dine at 7.30 knowing him to be alone & servantless at Kew. (Laura & the children had gone north by car on Thursday.) I had a long & good

[1] Lady Antonia Fraser (b. 1932), *née* Pakenham, daughter of 7th Earl of Longford; m. 1st, 1956, (Sir) Hugh Charles Fraser (diss. 1977); 2nd, 1980, Harold Pinter; writer, the author of *Mary Queen of Scots* (1969) and *The Weaker Vessel* (1984).

[2] Catherine Amery (1926–91), third of the four children of Harold and Dorothy Macmillan; she married, 1950, Julian Amery. Amery was promoted to minister of aviation in the reshuffle, but was not given a seat in cabinet.

[3] (William) John Biffen (b. 1930), MP (Con.) Oswestry, Salop, November 1961–83; Shropshire North, 1983–97; future cabinet minister and leader of the Commons.

[4] Jo Grimond argued that the most regrettable casualty of the whole affair was 'public confidence' – in politics and politicians – and he attacked Macmillan's government: 'No vote of confidence could be more effective than the one of sacking one-third of the Cabinet' (*The Times*, 27 July 1962).

talk with him about the whole party position. What he suffers from most he says is that so few Liberals even in the Parliamentary Party are really interested in politics!... Jo has immense charm & cldn't have a better sense of humour. I can't help feeling that he wld enjoy a little more cosseting & comfort & a few more 'signs'. I sent him a glowing note (through Eric Lubbock) directly after his speech & he clearly liked it.

Diary – Thursday 11 October – 21 Hyde Park Square, W.2

...Cressida came in before dinner & we dined together.... We listened to the account on sound & T.V. of the Tory Conference C.M. debate – & interviews with Heath, & Derek Walker-Smith[1] who led the Opposition, also Mark's commentary which was excellent. The Conservatives are sheep. Only about 50 hands were raised against the C.M. – they were all abusing us like pickpockets for supporting it about a year or 18 months ago. Butler – who said it 'wld not be suitable for Britain' – actually had the face to harangue the Conference in its favour! And not one of the opposition speakers had the guts to fling their sayings in their teeth.

Robert McKenzie put Heath thro' some very effective hoops in his interview. In a Freudian lapse Heath had had the imprudence to say how he wished he cld have been a Foundation member of the Six & R.M. pointed out that he cld have been & asked why his party had havered & wavered for so long & told him it was quite disingenuous to put the blame, as he did, on Labour's refusal to go into the Coal & Steel Community in 1950. Kenneth Harris[2] on T.V. embarked on the same course but handled him far less effectively & never closed his hand on him when the crunch came.

Diary – Saturday 17 November – 21 Hyde Park Square, W.2

Lunched with W. & C. He looking well & able with a great effort to get out of his chair alone. But alas! very very far-away in mind. It is now almost impossible to say anything to him which rings a bell. He knows nothing of what is going on in the world ... & even the distant past seems to be gradually fading.... What was very touching was that he went on

[1]Sir Derek Walker-Smith (1910–92), cr. life peer, 1983 (Broxbourne); Bt, 1960; MP (Con.) Hertford, 1945–55; Herts. East, 1955–83; minister of state, board of trade, 1957; minister of health, 1957–60.

[2](David) Kenneth Harris (b. 1919), journalist, author and broadcaster; on editorial staff, *Observer*, 1953–76; biographer of Clement Attlee.

stretching out his hand to mine & holding it fast – as though, like a child, he felt the need of love & its protection. I stayed with him till nearly 4....

Diary – Wednesday 5 December – 21 Hyde Park Square, W.2

Lunched with Bob Boothby in his delightful flat in Eaton Square. We had a most interesting talk.... Bob thinks – & indeed it must be apparent to all – that the Govt. is sinking – beset by troubles on all sides – soaring Unemployment, now over $\frac{1}{2}$ a million, which he thinks will reach the million mark, failing to get into the C.M., bungling everything it touches – riding for a tremendous fall at the next Election. He says that Dorothy tells him Harold is so cross & depressed one can hardly speak to him. Who is to succeed him? We discussed the barren possibilities....

Diary – Tuesday 11 December – 21 Hyde Park Square, W.2

Abortive shopping. Awful day of wind & rain. Had my hair washed. Ridiculous explosion of Jingo rage over a passage in a speech by Dean Acheson[1] saying that our rôle as an independent power is played out & that we are seeking a new rôle (wisely) in the C.M. Most thinking men & women wld admit the truth of every word he said & may have already said the same things themselves. H. Macmillan has replied to a (transparently) elicited letter of protest from Oliver Chandos – written as 'Chairman of the Institute of Directors' (which wld have come more appropriately from him in his capacity as 'Chairman of the National Theatre'!) To this H. Macmillan replies – comparing Dean Acheson to Philip II of Spain, Louis XIV, Napoleon & Hitler!...

Diary – Tuesday 1 January 1963 – 21 Hyde Park Square, W.2

The New Year came in under dark, heavy, snow-laden skies. I did not go out all day. Wrestled with work in the morning, wrote letters etc. in the afternoon.... Snow ice & piercing cold persist & the papers are full of stories of isolated villages, of helicopters dropping food & coal to stranded people & hay to starving animals, & lifting the ill to hospitals. An Orphan-

[1] Dean Gooderham Acheson (1893–1971), American lawyer and politician; US secretary of state, 1949–53; took a leading role in the establishment of the UNRRA and later the Marshall plan.

age at East Knoyle [West Wiltshire] has been completely cut off for days – 30 children under 7.

Diary – Wednesday 9 January – 21 Hyde Park Square, W.2

Arctic frost continues & there are electricity cuts from a 'Go Slow' among electrical workers – a really brutal act in this weather. We have not suffered but the Hospitals have, in some cases with dire results. This is what makes the T.U.'s so widely unpopular. . . .

Diary – Monday 14 January – 21 Hyde Park Square, W.2

. . . Spoke to Colin [Coote] on the telephone. He told me that de Gaulle had given his Press Conference this afternoon about which Toto had already warned me this morning. . . .[1] Toto predicted that de Gaulle's Press Conference wld be entirely hostile to our entry & explicitly so – an invitation to us to break off negotiations. This is in fact exactly what it has proved to be. I listened to excerpts on *Panorama* & afterwards to a very good interview with Xtopher Layton on sound. He said, I am sure rightly, that we shld not play de Gaulle's game, & go on negotiating with patience & determination. It is however rather a tough opening to poor Heath's new round of negotiations. I only hope that de Gaulle has overplayed his hand & that his move will rally the others to our side. . . . Colin said, when talking to me about de Gaulle today, that he only wished this Govt. wld go – they bungled everything they touched. It is nice to hear this from the Editor of the *D.T.*!

Diary – Thursday 17 January – 21 Hyde Park Square, W.2

Cld not sleep for thinking of Hugh Gaitskell. Switched on my little transistor at 8. He had had some periods of sleep in the night but the secondary infection had spread to his abdomen & kidneys. . . . I am haunted by this tragedy. Though I did not meet him often he 'revealed' himself to me in some of the talks we had – & this revelation always enhanced my respect &

[1] President de Gaulle gave a press conference at the Elysée Palace that day, adopting what Macmillan later described as his 'most majestic and "Louis Quatorze" style'. De Gaulle declared: 'Sentiments, as favourable as they might be and as they are, cannot be put forward in opposition to the real facts of the problem. . . . England is insular' (Horne, *Macmillan, 1957–1986*, 445–6).

admiration & affection for him. It is true to say that I loved him. He had pure integrity, which is the quality I value above all others....

Diary – Friday 18 January – 21 Hyde Park Square, W.2

Stayed in all day. It is colder than ever – freezing hard & a glacial East wind blowing.... C & I dined together. I switched on at 10 & heard the dreaded news – Hugh Gaitskell had died – just after 9.

Diary – Tuesday 22 January – 21 Hyde Park Square, W.2

Arctic conditions continue. Didn't budge out as I have very slight sinus remains of my chill last week. Papers full of 2 subjects: (1) de Gaulle, who is the target at present deflecting a few (deserved) brick-bats from the Govt. (2) Leadership of the Labour Party.... Brown v. Wilson presents a harsh choice between an often (though not always) drunken boor – rude, clumsy, devoid of finesse or subtlety, but an honest & loyal man – & a very able, clever, experienced but universally distrusted one, of proven disloyalty. One might I suppose have some affection for Brown, one cld. have nothing but distaste, dislike & mistrust for Wilson. The Tories are said to hope for Brown, as Wilson wld be so much more formidable. He is I think the most brilliant debater in the House. If Elections were decided by 'images' & personality either or both wld. throw Jo into glittering relief as a contrast....

Diary – Tuesday 29 January – 21 Hyde Park Square, W.2

On evening news came the dreaded but expected tidings – collapse of Common Market negotiations. France immovable has vetoed our entry. Devoured the papers with their funereal banner head-lines. All furious – except the unseen *Express* which Laura tells me has a head-line 'Hip Hip Hooray' which is an exact description of what it feels. And now where do we go from here? It is hard to see the way. Everyone will say: closer links with Commonwealth, E.F.T.A., U.S.A. But we have long weighed these alternatives & know them to be pis allers. Our economies are not complementary. My only hope is that in time the C.M. will break under the strain & that we shall enter one nearer to the heart's desire. If a Dictator's writ is to run it is not the place for us. The contempt de Gaulle has shown to his 5 partners is to me more shocking & revealing than our exclusion.

The concept of Monnet,[1] Spaak & R. Schuman is killed stone-dead....

Diary – Saturday 9 February – 21 Hyde Park Square, W.2

Lunched with W. & C. & béziqued all the afternoon. We had our usual half to ¾ of an hour tête-à-tête after lunch. At lunch itself he was very blank. I saw he had been dining at the Other Club & Clemmie told me he sat next to Hinch.[2] I said 'Did you have fun with Hinchingbrooke at dinner?' He said: 'Who is Hinchingbrooke?' Clemmie said 'Darling – you know who he is – he is coming to dine to-morrow.' But he remained blankly denying that he had ever heard of him. One flash of his old self surprised & brought me comfort. When I mentioned de Gaulle shutting us out of the Market he suddenly said – just like his old self – with real anger 'Dirty beast!' It was like a sudden spurt of flame from a sinking fire. When I got home I felt utterly exhausted – drained – the effort to 'reach' him is so great....

Diary – Monday 18 February – 21 Hyde Park Square, W.2

...lunch at the H. of C. in honour of Norman Angell's[3] birthday. When I arrived I found dear Norman – quite unchanged to look at – though 90! & a lot of dear 'old familiar faces' of the L.N.U., as well as newer U.N.A. ones, gathered round.... I had a word with Niggs who said 'I am sitting beside you.' I told him how glad I was – & he added 'On your other side is the Prime Minister.' I was startled & jumped visibly. 'Do you mind – do you want me to change you?' 'I don't mind for myself but it won't be a treat for him.'....

I went straight into de Gaulle & the failure of the Market – & asked him whether de G. had given him any inkling of his opposition at Ram-

[1]Jean Monnet (1888–1979), French economist and public official, a leading proponent of European union post-1945; president of the European Coal and Steel Community, 1952–5.

[2]Victor Montagu (1906–95), Viscount Hinchingbrooke, son of 9th Earl of Sandwich; succeeded to the earldom in 1962 but renounced the title in 1964; MP (Con./Ind. Con.) South Dorset, 1941–62.

[3]Sir Norman Angell (1872–1967), Kt, 1931; author of *The Great Illusion* (1910), which made his name, a pioneering work examining the practical reasons for preventing war; an originator of the League of Nations and winner of the Nobel Peace Prize, 1933.

bouillet?[1] Also whether he had had a witness there – a secretary or translator. He said he had. (I asked him because it is rumoured – Roy Jenkins said so on Saturday – that Harold thinks he speaks French better than he does, & that he did not realise how rude de Gaulle was being to him, & continued to make affable sounds of assent.) I am relieved to hear that even one witness was present. He said that de Gaulle spoke with the greatest contempt of his Allies – the 'provincials' of Bonn – 'Une petite ville de Province.' I do not know how it was led up to, but he made an allusion to the French condition after his demise or departure 'Alors – ils retournèrent aux délices de l'anarchie' – which is quite funny. He said that of course de Gaulle's idea of the E.E.C. was a means of allowing him to dominate Europe....

He went on – the tongue touching where the tooth ached – to talk of Pss Margaret's visit – saying he had been criticised for cancelling it.[2] I remained mute.... The criticism on this score seemed to 'needle' him more than other more important potential charges – since he went out of his way to introduce the subject & defend himself. I said I was all for reprisals but I thought they shld be on a big scale. He gave me the impression of being an exhausted man – particularly when the speeches began & he twice dozed off to sleep. When speaking himself for 3 minutes he hardly seemed to have the energy to propel the words past his lips. I shld think they were almost inaudible to those not at the High Table....

Diary – Good Friday, 12 April – Königswinter

Back Wed. evening from Königswinter & Berlin – where the pace was so fast & furious that I had no time or strength to scratch a line....

The final day [Sunday] – Marathon Plenary Session starting at 9.30 & going on till nearly 7! Reports of groups in the morning. Niagara of speeches in the afternoon. I told Birley I did not want to speak unless 'provoked'. I was provoked! Crossman turned one of his worst cartwheels! a speech delivered, as ever, with matchless fluency – saying what a debt we all owed to de Gaulle for having excluded us from the Market. Hardly

[1]On 15–16 December 1962 de Gaulle and Macmillan joined in talks at the château de Rambouillet, south-west of Paris, about Britain's application to enter the EEC. When de Gaulle made clear his opposition to Britain's entry Macmillan was roused to indignation: 'De Gaulle seemed rather shaken.... On this depressing note our conference ended' (Horne, *Macmillan, 1957–1986*, 431–2).

[2]Influenced by the Foreign Office and by public opinion Macmillan retaliated against de Gaulle's Common Market veto by cancelling Princess Margaret's impending official visit to Paris: 'It was an impulse of the moment .... and looking back on it he regretted the decision' (Horne, *Macmillan, 1957–1986*, 449).

anyone in England wanted to enter it. Parliament wld certainly have refused to accept its conditions. We shld do much better on our own etc. This after we had been trying to instil a sense of responsibility into the Germans!

I sent in my name & spoke last – saying Crossman's speech had been a delight to all. We got from him exactly what we had expected – a brilliant knock-about turn. He is the most brilliant knock-about artist in British politics to-day – & if there were a World Congress of such comedians I shld unhesitatingly nominate him to play for England. He wld probably return as Mr Europe – or as Mr World.... I urged that we shld find & establish some framework for joint consultation & discussion with the 5. Ended by saying that tho' de Gaulle lived in a dream world of Grand Delusion he was au fond a realist. He recognized the inevitable when he saw it....

Diary – Wednesday 17 April – 21 Hyde Park Square, W.2

Haley came to see me at 4 & we had a very good 1½ hours' talk covering a lot of ground. He says that Macmillan's decision to stay on had plunged a great many Tories in deep gloom. The reasons to stay are (1) his own desire (2) the absence of any obvious successor. We both agreed that Butler & Macleod are 'out'; the choice lies between Heath & Maudling. We (H. & I) were both Heath-ites – he surprised me by saying that Mac's man was Maudling. I always thought he adored Heath. (Dorothy says at every Bazaar 'What my husband owes to Mr Heath!')...

He was very amusing about 2 consecutive talks he had had with Adenauer & de Gaulle. Theme – the Franco-German Treaty.[1] Haley suggested to Adenauer that an exclusive bi-lateral Treaty might not be the best thing for Europe. Adenauer replied: 'Look at France – ravaged by 2 World Wars. Threatened with Civil War. Torn to bits by the Algerian struggle. This is the moment when we – who have been responsible for much that she has suffered – must hold out a hand to her' (or 'words to that effect'). When Haley saw de Gaulle he said almost exactly the same thing about Germany. 'Defeated in 2 wars – ground into powder – a pariah among nations etc. etc. This is the moment when France shld hold out her hand to Germany in a great gesture of forgiveness & reconciliation.' Both saw themselves as rescue workers! He told me a wonderful story of a short-hand writer at a Bonn Conference transferring extraordinary squiggles to paper. He asked

[1]In the week following the French veto on Britain's entry to the EEC Konrad Adenauer, chancellor of the Federal Republic of Germany, travelled to Paris to sign the Franco-German Treaty of Friendship.

what on earth she was doing? She replied: 'Our spokesmen always speak in clichés & always the same ones.' They therefore found it quicker & more labour-saving to illustrate with squiggles. He was in excellent form....

Diary – Friday 19 April – Washington, D.C.

Up early & drove to Airport – angelic Marigold [Honey] coming with me – a great moral support. To my horror had to pay £16 for excess luggage! I knew I had excess but cld not in my wildest dreams have guessed how much. Plane very empty to my relief.... Met Ray & Elena as I emerged from luggage room! Edward with them – angelic & quite unchanged. Heaven to see them again.... Little Tom was at home. He is lovely – with his vast sapphire lakes of eyes & flaxen hair like gosling's feathers. Very big & strong like a baby Hercules. I was reeling with tiredness.... Finally dropped into bed at what must have been 5 in the morning for me.

Diary – Friday 26 April – Washington, D.C.

Very social day. Elena angelically dropped me at the Embassy for large luncheon-party.... They sent me back in the car. Rested – then dressed for Acheson dinner.... Sat between Dean Acheson & Molloy & had an excellent talk with D.A. He pooh-poohed the idea that H. Wilson had had a 'rip-roaring success' here, saying that most people knew he was not to be trusted. He is obviously a qualified admirer of the President. He said himself that it was difficult to be dispassionate about the performance of people belonging to one's children's generation. About the group of highbrows & 'egg-heads' of the President's inner circle he said 'I only hope what happens to us will come in the form of a crisis – because these people are good improvisers – but if they are given time to think, Heaven help us!'...

Diary – Tuesday 14 May – Washington, D.C.

Arthur Schlesinger[1] telephoned Raymond yesterday that the President wld like to see me at 12.15 this morning. I was to be at the White House at ¼

[1] Arthur Schlesinger (b. 1917), American historian and author; special assistant and speech writer to the president, 1961–4. He had mooted the possibility of Violet meeting President Kennedy when she had visited Washington the previous year, telling her: 'He is keenly interested in British politics. I can easily arrange it for you' (25 May 1962).

to 12 – & Arthur Schlesinger wld see me first. Elena drove me to the East Gate in torrential rain. A large procession of tourists or aboriginals were forming up to be shown over the White House. We gave our names, which were checked by telephone, & I was taken to Arthur Schlesinger's room. I asked him the drill – i.e. ought I to make an attempt to leave or wld the President dismiss me? He said 'Leave it to chance – the President likes talking.' He had put forward the meeting to 12 o'clock so we started on a long walk through endless broad white corridors – red-carpeted – the walls hung with pictures & prints of past Presidents. . . .

He left me with the Secretary & at about 12.5 the President strode in to fetch me from the neighbouring room on the right. I must add that all the doors were open – in fact I wondered if they existed – that of the Secretary's room was wide open on the corridor & also the 2 others opening on the Cabinet room & the President's room. I asked her 'Do you live with open doors?' She said 'Yes, I like it – anyone can come in to talk to me.' The President took me into his own room – sat me on a sofa next to himself in his rocking chair & fired away. He has great simplicity, spontaneity, naturalness & charm – no 'high hat' or 'high horse', one feels immediately at ease & as though one had known him all one's life.

He started off by asking if I'd enjoyed my visit here. I told him every moment of it both last year & this – & what an enormous difference I had felt last year in the atmosphere since his régime started. I always thought it one of the most beautiful towns in the world, but for a seat of Govt I had before thought it strangely lulling – rather like Bath at home. This year & last I found it electric, as tho' the pulse of the world were beating here – as indeed it is. He went on to ask what relation I was to Raymond Asquith. I said he was my elder brother. He said he had read about him in John Buchan's *Memory Hold the Door* & also in Winston's *Great Contemporaries* & quoted the sentence about his striding 'into the crash & thunder of the Somme'.[1] I was amazed at his verbatim memory & the impression it had made on him. He asked if I had written or was writing my Memoirs. I said 'Not yet.' I had been asked to do so & might, but I found it difficult to tread the tight-rope between indecency & dullness. . . .

He asked me if I was speaking much. I said less than I used to, as Jo & Mark were there. He said he had seen Jo & added something nice about him. I said I was interested to know what impression Jo had made on

[1]John Buchan's *Memory hold-the-door* (1940) appeared in an American edition as *Pilgrim's Way*. Of Raymond Asquith, Churchill wrote: 'The War which found the measure of so many never got to the bottom of him, and when the Grenadiers strode into the crash and thunder of the Somme, he went to his fate cool, poised, resolute, matter-of-fact, debonair' (*Great Contemporaries* (1937), 98–9).

him & repeated to him some of the things McGeorge Bundy[1] had said to Raymond about him – 'Was he ambitious? was he serious? what was he after?' I said he was both serious & ambitious & it was a proof of his integrity that he shld have hitched his wagon to the least bright star in the political skies. Bundy had thought he was 'uninvolved'. The President was amused & said 'That is what we are always accused of – I & my team of helpers – uninvolvement!' I was amazed that such an accusation cld have been levelled against the President! . . .

He asked me if I liked H. Macmillan. I said I had both liked & admired him in the Thirties. We were politically intimate – tho' not personally intimate (I didn't know anyone with whom he cld be said to be personally intimate). He was against Appeasement, which was a close link in those days. He was also pro-European Unity when W. launched his U. Europe movement in the late '40s which was another bond. I said it was ironical looking back to remember that in those days I thought of him as a brave & independent man who never got his 'due'. He had long walrus moustachios, & high stiff collar, a limp, damp handshake & pince-nez – no political sex appeal & certainly no other kind either. How little I dreamed that he wld ever blossom into 'Super-Mac' – tho' that image was now fading. My breach with him was over Suez. . . .

I also cld not forgive him his cunctations, fumblings, hesitations over the C.M. Had we gone in at the start – what a difference it wld have made! 'Yes' he said 'even if you had applied one year earlier – before Algeria was settled, de Gaulle cldn't have stopped you.' He went on to describe how he (de G.) was now blocking all progress in Europe – in defence, economics etc. etc. I asked him how he thought this road-block cld be broken. He said 'The root of the matter is that not only you in Britain, but we in the U.S.A. have now become debtors & not, as we always used to be, creditors. The gold reserve has ebbed at the following rate (he then gave me the figures for the last few years). Europe is economically for the moment in a stronger position than we are. Naturally every nation has these fights for their own interests. This is a far graver position for us than any military threat presents at the moment. There is no danger of military aggression in Europe at present. This is the crux of the matter & our greatest present handicap. And it is a very complicated matter to deal with.'. . . .

He then asked me about my relationship with W. in the Thirties – hadn't we worked closely together? I said indeed we had – W. was then 'despised & rejected of men'. I told him about the Freedom Focus & our meetings at

[1] McGeorge Bundy (1919–96), educationalist and public official, special assistant (1961–6) to President Kennedy and President Johnson; an important voice in American foreign policy, Bundy played a prominent role in pursuing the Vietnam war; professor of history at New York University, 1966–79.

the Albert Hall, Manchester, etc. throughout the country – & in the H. of C. 'Did he make no impression?' I said: 'None. The country wanted poppy & mandragora. The Govts gave it. Awakening came with the fulfilment of the doom he prophesied.' I told him that I had this year read his book *Why England Slept* – now published in paperback – & what a just & fair appraisal it seemed to me to be of those years. I told him that I was staying with Raymond & Elena. He was under the impression that I was at the Embassy with David.[1] My impression was of a man well over life-size with power in reserve – who carried the world on his shoulders with buoyancy & gaiety & without a trace of self-importance or swollen head. Power had not gone to his head. His penultimate remark was 'I shall tell Bundy that you find him "uninvolved"!' He left me saying he must now deal with Alabama....

Diary – Wednesday 15 May – Washington, D.C.

Elena & I lunched with Mr Moorhead[2] (Democratic Congressman) & his very nice & able Research Assistant in Congress dining-room. This was not luxurious – in food or otherwise, but the luxury & comfort in which Congressmen live was brought home to me by his private working room with 2 secretaries (plus the Research Assistant) writing tables & telephones galore. After luncheon we went up & listened to the beginning of a debate.... What was interesting was that the prayer, read by a clergyman before the Session, opened with an allusion to the racial issue. The riots in Birmingham [Alabama] photographed in *Life* make one absolutely sick. Snarling Police Dogs ripping off the clothing of the Negroes & 3 policemen ill-treating a black woman lying on the pavement – one grinding his knee into her neck while 'Bull Connor' Head of the Police called the white crowd to gather round & 'watch our dogs working & the Niggers run'. What a problem for the President....

Diary – Monday 29 July – 21 Hyde Park Square, W.2

...Went to Tony Benn's party at the House, in celebration of the Peerage

[1] William David Ormsby-Gore (1918–85), 5th Baron Harlech (s. 1964); MP (Con.) Oswestry, Salop, 1950–61; minister of state for foreign affairs, 1957–61; British ambassador in Washington, 1961–5.

[2] William Singer Moorhead (1923–87), Democrat representative for Pennsylvania, 1959–81.

Bill, in the Members' Dining Room.[1] It is a real personal triumph. One man has changed the law of England by his courage, skill & pertinacity & that man is Tony. I felt a real emotion on seeing him & he paid tribute to me very generously as one of those who had helped him, in his excellent & most amusing speech.[2] (In the course of it he drew out of his pocket a small bottle of his blood which he had asked a Ghanaian Dr to extract when he was ill in Bristol last week. This was to illustrate the curious properties of the 'Life Commoner', who can transmit blue blood – tho' not one drop flows in his veins.)...

As I write Tony has just rung me up to give me the good news that St Clair[3] – his Tory opponent – is going to apply for the Chiltern Hundreds & he thinks this means the Tories will give him an unopposed walk-over. He asked about the Liberals & I said that of course it wld be unthinkable that they shld oppose him. I will try & get in touch with Jo directly he comes back from Stratford....

Diary – Friday 18 October – 21 Hyde Park Square, W.2

A really exciting day. I heard on the 1 o'clock news that Macmillan had sent in his resignation to the Queen at 9.45 this morning. The morning papers, with the one important exception of the *Times*, had all tipped Home.... Evening papers full of photographs of him being mobbed & 'shot' round N° 10.... I feel terribly sorry for poor Butler who has now – for the second time – been prevented from becoming P.M. by the same man. Macmillan must dislike him very much. I wonder why? He has slaved for the party & carried the can for them in many hot-spots. Andrew (who is leaving for U.S.A. to-morrow) came in for drinks & dinner & we watched a special *Panorama* programme on the Premiership with symposiums of Press & politicians in which Butlerites seemed rather unrepresented & Liberals not at all....

[1] The Peerage bill of 1963 gave those succeeding to a hereditary peerage the option of disclaiming the title for life, without this affecting the due succession of that title. It received the royal assent in July 1963.

[2] Tony Benn later recalled: 'I jumped on a chair and made a speech that lasted about ten minutes. I summarized the history of the case and how long it had taken, and thanked the Party.... Also the Young Liberals like Lady Violet and the Young Tories like Churchill' (Benn, *Out of the Wilderness*, 44).

[3] Malcolm Archibald St Clair (b. 1927), MP (Con.) Bristol South East, July 1961–August 1963. Benn was unopposed at the by-election following St Clair's resignation.

Diary – Monday 21 October – 21 Hyde Park Square, W.2

Received a message from the B.B.C. asking me to broadcast after the 10 o'clock news & comment on a broadcast by Home which is to follow it. Went to the B.B.C. about 9 & heard the broadcast twice & made some notes. He made one astonishing statement which I noted. When asked if he felt 'Any uneasiness at depriving Mr Butler of the leadership for the 2nd time' he replied 'No thought of competing for power ever entered Mr Butler's mind' & 'We (the Tory party) don't have these conflicts for power – if I may put it that way. We're friends, we're colleagues & partners in the Cabinet & the party.' I rubbed my eyes! He may be going to speak plainly to the nation – but is he going to speak the truth? My broadcast interview (only 6 minutes) was over before I cld say half of what I wanted to!

Diary – Sunday 3 November – 21 Hyde Park Square, W.2

Went to Speaker's Corner at 3 o'clock where I found the procession assembling – found Mrs [Barbara] Castle. The Stewards were late & I cld. not believe that it cld fall into the perfect order that it did when we started off preceded by a pipe-band – which had antecedents reaching back to the days of the Tolpuddle martyrs. In the front row marched the speakers – a Xhosa[1] bearing a wreath flanked on one side by Mrs Castle & on the other by myself – Woodrow Wyatt, Humphry Berkeley[2] & one or two others. At the end of the row Vanessa Redgrave.[3] I stayed the course as far as Bond St which they went down, then took a taxi to Trafalgar Square where I sat on a heap of ladders till I was hauled up the plinth by the Bishop of Southwark in his beautiful purple robes. We were soon hauled down again to go & lay the wreath on the doorstep of S. Africa House (appropriately facing the Square). Then we all scaled the plinth by ladder & Mrs Castle (very shortly) opened the proceedings with a very short speech as the Bishop had to go to a christening – leaving at 3.15. He spoke very well. The Square was packed & the whole audience stayed the course – standing for over 2 hours. It was fortunately a most lovely day of sunshine. I put on a thin coat to march in – & got very cold towards the end upon the plinth. . . .

[1]Violet's writing is unclear here and 'Xhosa' is a guess as to what she meant. Around 5,000 demonstrators marched in the anti-apartheid rally that is described here (*The Times*, 4 November 1963).

[2]Humphry John Berkeley (1926–94), author; MP (Con.) Lancaster, 1959–66; later joined Labour Party, 1970.

[3]Vanessa Redgrave (b. 1937), CBE, 1967; actress and political campaigner; with Royal Shakespeare Theatre Company; won an Academy Award (1977) for *Julia* (1976).

Diary – Tuesday 5 November – 21 Hyde Park Square, W.2

Spent the day at a U.K.C. Conference at the H. of C. – broken by a luncheon at the Waldorf Hôtel, to which B. Behrens gave me a lift & at which Duncan Sandys spoke. I sat between 2 'business men' (whom I imagine to be large subscribers to the U.K.C.) – on my right one Sir Leslie Gamage[1] – on my left a man called Staddiford – both unknown. Most unluckily in almost the first sentence that he uttered Gamage made some allusion to the Trafalgar Square meeting. I said 'Yes. I was there. I was on the plinth – speaking.' He looked at me with unutterable horror & said 'You were there – mixed up in this business?' I said I certainly was mixed up in it – up to the neck. There was nothing I felt more strongly about. He asked the usual question: 'Have you ever been to S. Africa?' I made the usual reply – that I never had been but that I knew many people who had lived there – & I also read the papers. Had he by chance read this week's *Observer*? It had a report of the torture now going on in South African prisons – very like the Algerian tortures practised by the French – with electricity etc. '*The Observer*?' he exclaimed 'I wldn't touch it.' He evidently regarded it as a subversive & unclean publication. I felt that we shld soon come to blows so I turned to my other neighbour. . . . I talked to him till the end of luncheon. Then Duncan spoke – very well & competently. B-B was in the Chair. I was furious with him when in his introductory remarks he quoted first Harold Wilson (a verbatim passage), then Harold Macmillan (also verbatim) to show that they both had the door open to European Unity – & then added 'And Mr Grimond also assented' knowing full well that Jo – so far from having said 'Et moi aussi' – had come out for applying for Membership directly the E.E.C. was signed. I rounded on him in the car coming back! & he professed penitence. . . .

Diary – Wednesday 6 November – 21 Hyde Park Square, W.2

Went to Chatham House luncheon hour meeting to hear Patrick Duncan[2] (whom I had never seen before) on South Africa. Very interesting – & I was interested that he made exactly the same points, of course at far greater length, as those I tried to make in Trafalgar Square – particularly

[1] Sir Leslie Gamage (1887–1972), Kt, 1959; a veteran of the first world war; with the General Electric Company from 1919; managing director, 1957–60.

[2] Patrick Duncan (1918–67), anti-apartheid activist; the son of a governor-general of South Africa, Duncan became a radical opponent of apartheid; he was deprived of his South African citizenship, 1964, after joining the militant Pan African Congress; author of *South Africa's Rule of Violence* (1964).

the 'internal' issue one – the comparison with the Nazi régime, as a threat to international peace, & the danger of violence & bloodshed spreading throughout Africa. I asked him when questions came whether he thought ... we shld invoke the help of the U.N. & ask them to send an observer force to watch the frontiers & tell the world what was happening. P.D. was strongly in favour of this course of action. He made one amusing slip. Describing Bechuanaland he said 'They are a very conservative people' – then, seeing some Conservatives – 'I am sorry. I shld have said they are a very backward people!' (I enjoyed the synonym!) I had a word with him afterwards....

The Rees-Moggs & Ray & Elena came to dinner & we had a very good talk. William said, I think truly, that Harold Wilson & Harold Macmillan were politicians of exactly the same type – adroit, skilful, ruthless, without personal loyalties, 'fixers' & manoeuvrers & manipulators. He did not think either of them wld make a real sacrifice of the nation's interests to further their own political ends, but they wld sacrifice most other things....

Diary – Friday 22 November – 21 Hyde Park Square, W.2

One of the most shattering evenings of my life. I am still stunned by its impact. I had been out by myself to see the T.U. film by the Boulting Brothers *I'm All Right Jack* – which I had missed in its heyday & which Raymond told me was having a short revival at Studio One.[1] I came back by bus – sat lost in thought & passed the Park West stop by about a mile & a half. Walked back arriving late for dinner & found Cressida in the dining room having hers. I was about to explain my muddle & expatiate on the brilliance of *I'm All Right Jack* – when she stopped me & said: 'Kennedy has been shot – he was killed.' My heart stopped. (Only yesterday I posted him my Romanes Lecture.)[2] I felt the personal stab of shock & horror more strongly than I cld. have thought possible ... & with it a sense of terror for the world, of which he was the Atlas – the only leader above life-size. His stature, power, courage & judgement gone – the extraordinary hold he had established over Khrushchev by his blend of strength & conciliation ... his fight for all the right things – above all Human Rights for Negroes. What was to happen to all these vital causes without him? The West is

[1] *I'm All Right Jack* (1959), one of the Boulting brothers' most successful films, a satire on 1950s British industrial relations and class, with Peter Sellers as a confrontational shop steward.

[2] In June 1963 Violet had become the first woman to give the Romanes Lecture at Oxford, speaking on 'The impact of personality in politics'. The lecture was subsequently published by the Clarendon Press.

orphaned – the world is orphaned. What had happened? Doris & Mrs Lock had heard a few words only on the news at 7.30 – & that he was in a car with Mrs Kennedy & others. The *Daily Express* had rung me up. That was all. We kept the wireless on – but nothing came through.... Lyndon Johnson as V.P. took the oath in the plane flying back. Poor little Jackie was flown back with his body. The horror passes belief. One could only imagine it was a segregationalist.

New bulletins went on on sound & sight till midnight.... Tributes were paid by Home & Harold Wilson & Jo. Jo coming last had the most difficult task – for so much had been said already. All were good. Home obviously 'senti'. H. Wilson much better than I thought he wld be – dwelling (characteristically) on his administrative efficiency & power. This is the anniversary of Gettysburg (it happened a few days ago). Abraham Lincoln's fate & aims were Kennedy's too – but he was not given time to realise them.

I have never felt the death of any 'public figure' with such stabbing poignancy & such obsessive grief. Though I only saw him once, for one hour this year in May at Washington, I feel a strong sense of personal loss. I felt as we talked that I had known him all my life – his charm, his vitality, responsiveness, impetus, momentum, complete absence of high-horse or high-hat or any form of vanity, was amazing in one wielding greater power than any human being had ever had, since the beginning of time. And above all I had the sense of greatness – in a greater degree than I have felt it about anyone since I first met Winston at the age of 19.

Diary – Saturday 23 November – 21 Hyde Park Square, W.2

I went with Raymond & Elena to the Requiem Mass in Westminster Cathedral at 12.30. It was most moving – the vast Cathedral packed with people – mostly poor & humble bringing their children with them. As Elena said to me 'C'est la base du peuple.' They had a Communion Service with unaccompanied singing – no organ music until the end when the organ suddenly peeled out the 'Star-Spangled Banner'.... 'God Save the Queen' followed – rather flatly – then Beethoven's *Funeral March.* Ray & Elena came back at 7.30 & we watched a Kennedy T.V. programme – not as good as yesterday's – & a late 'News-Extra' with rather touching man-in-the-street remarks. Then, as I was about to switch off, a half-hour of *T.W.T.W.* which I did not feel in the mood for, but which was surprisingly good & had no single lapse of taste (the only flaw a sentimental poem about Jackie recited by Sybil Thorndike).[1] One good point made was that Death does not make all men equal. On the news we had heard of the death of 60 poor old people burnt in an Old People's Home, which they were too crippled to get out of. I was aware how stonily I took this tragedy compared with Kennedy's death.

[1] Dame (Agnes) Sybil Thorndike (1882–1976), DBE 1931; actress, specially remembered for her interpretation of the lead role in Shaw's *St Joan* – a part that was written for her; she married, 1908, (Sir) Lewis Casson.

THREE

The House of Lords

1964–1969

CHRONOLOGY OF EVENTS 1964–1969

1964	June	6 Malawi (Nyasaland) becomes independent
	September	15 announcement of general election on 15 October
		25 dissolution of parliament
	October	15 general election gives Labour a narrow majority: 317 Labour, 304 Conservative, 9 Liberal; Wilson becomes premier
		24 Zambia (Northern Rhodesia) becomes independent
1965	January	24 death of Sir Winston Churchill
		30 funeral of Sir Winston Churchill
	February	– Gambia becomes independent; establishment of National Board for Prices and Incomes
	July	– Edward Heath succeeds Alec Douglas-Home as Conservative leader
	November	11 unilateral declaration of independence by Rhodesia (UDI); Britain begins economic sanctions against Rhodesia
1966	January	– government bans all trade with Rhodesia
	March	31 general election gives Labour 96-seat majority: 363 Labour, 253 Conservative, 12 Liberal, 2 other; Wilson remains premier
	November	10 Wilson announces intention to seek membership of the EEC
	December	– UN Security Council approve British resolution for mandatory sanctions against Rhodesia
1967	January	18 Jeremy Thorpe succeeds Jo Grimond as Liberal leader
	May	2 Harold Wilson announces the government decision to make a second application to join the EEC
		30 declaration of the Republic of Biafra
	June	– Arab-Israeli war; Arab oil embargo on Britain
	November	27 de Gaulle announces continued opposition to Britain joining EEC
1968	January	26 cuts in public expenditure announced
	March	1 Commonwealth Immigration Bill given royal assent

	April	4 Martin Luther King assassinated in Memphis, Tennessee
		20 Enoch Powell's 'rivers of blood' speech in Birmingham
		21 Heath sacks Powell from shadow cabinet
	May	16 French veto Britain's application to join EEC
	August	20 Soviet and Warsaw Pact forces invade Czechoslovakia
	October	– Race Relations Bill given royal assent
		27 large scale anti-Vietnam war protest in London
1969	February	15 the last diary entry
		19 Violet dies at her home in London
		22 Violet's funeral and burial at St Andrew's Church in Mells, Somerset
	March	19 memorial service at St Paul's

TEN

Life Peer

1964–1965

Diary – Tuesday 21 January 1964 – 21 Hyde Park Square, W.2

... Big banquet at Dorchester given by Foyle's to celebrate their Jubilee.... I sat between von Etzdorf[1] the German Ambassador & the Indian High Commissioner.... On the other side of Frau von Etzdorf was the Chairman – none other than Bob Boothby! – with the Attlees on his other side. I had a word with the old rogue before we sat down & he (most typically) launched into a lyrical paean of praise of Harold Wilson! describing him as a 'sweet fellow' – & a 'sweet man'. I told him I thought the adjective strangely ill-chosen. 'Oh no! I sat down to dinner with him at 9 o'clock & we didn't part till 2 in the morning.' 'But Bob – since when have you discovered this passionate affinity?' 'Well – since I knew he was going to become Prime Minister of course.' Disarmingly true.

Diary – Wednesday 22 January – 21 Hyde Park Square, W.2

... Lancaster House banquet for Signor Saragat[2] the Italian Foreign Minister who is over here. Vast party.... Dinner was in the big dining-room – at an immense horse-shoe table. I sat between Sir Harold Caccia[3] & a nice Italian diplomat called Otrano – to whom I talked very little because Caccia was at the end of a row in a cul-de-sac & had no one except me to talk to. We had a very agreeable talk about Anglo-German relations – the curiously (superficially) friendly amenities we establish with the Germans – so much more easily than we do with the French for instance – & yet the strange

[1] Hasso von Etzdorf (1900–89), (hon.) GCVO, 1964; married Katharina *née* Otto-Margonin; diplomat; German ambassador in London, 1961–5.

[2] Signor Giuseppe Saragat, foreign minister and later president, 1964–71, of the Italian Republic.

[3] Sir Harold Anthony Caccia (1905–90), GCVO, 1961; cr. life peer, 1965; career diplomat and later provost of Eton.

hang-over of national prejudice which has remained so much more deeply rooted here than in Europe – even in the countries who remember being occupied.

After dinner Moucher & I drifted together to my delight, but our fun – or at least mine – was soon spoiled by the Italian Ambassadress, a crisp & confident chatterer. When the men came in Peter Thorneycroft made a bee line for me & sat down beside me. I had not seen him to talk to since I came & visited him in the Middlesex Hospital when B. was there after his operation. I said what odd circumstances we always met in – aeroplane crashes & hospital wards. We had a good & unrestrained talk. I started off on Europe & the inexplicable course the Govt. had steered after '51. Why, with so many Europeans in it, had they behaved just like the Labour Party? He said that of course Anthony & the F.O. were the main obstruction. Duncan was not in the Cabinet, Harold entirely occupied by building 300,000 houses, W. appeared uninterested. He at the Bd of Trade had written a Memorandum on Europe which had not been taken up. When he went to the Treasury he was anxious to conduct the European discussions – all his officials were well-briefed. To his disappointment Harold gave the job to Maudling – with the results we know. . . .

Diary – Sunday 9 February – 21 Hyde Park Square, W.2

Slept late & read papers the whole afternoon. Mark rang me at dinner-time & said he & Laura were coming round to see me. (He leaves for a week in Torrington to-morrow.)[1] He brought with him the 10 first chapters of Roy Jenkins's book about my father & explained to me a most disturbing factor. . . . Both Beaverbrook & (possibly) Randolph are in possession (by what means we do not know) of my Father's correspondence with Venetia Montagu – i.e. his letters to her. A myrmidon of Beaverbrook approached Roy & intimated that they intended to publish these. Mark & Roy immediately disillusioned him on this score: as my Father's Literary Executor Mark was in a position to forbid publication. He obtained from Judy Montagu a copy of the letters – which are an interesting account of political events, colleagues, etc. – & he has arranged for Roy to publish these, or extracts from them, in order to pre-empt a more sensationally treated publication by Beaverbrook. . . .

I read the whole 10 Chapters in bed – the opening 2 rather dull & flat & quite without colour – then came the chapter about my Mother & her death – & this upset me so much that I was still wide awake & quivering

[1] After his defeat in 1959 Mark Bonham Carter remained Liberal candidate for Torrington and stood at the 1964 general election.

with indignation at 5.30 a.m. I took some seconal & slept a few hours but woke up exhausted & shattered.... He describes her patronisingly as 'rather good looking' ... suggests that when Father writes 'our sun went down in an unclouded sky' the sun had not gone down one whit too soon for the good of his career – & that she might well have been the 'never-to-be-seen Mrs Morley' – John Morley's wife ... who was reported to be dull, plain & wholly unpresentable & lived in Purdah in Wimbledon. I cannot conceive why Mark did not warn me. I have written to him – but he is away for a week.

Diary – Friday 6 March – 21 Hyde Park Square, W.2

...Ray dined in the dining-room next door & came in & talked to me afterwards. After he had gone I was reading some more R.J. Chapters, which had been sent to me, & got a terrible shock when I reached Chapter 22. I cannot believe that Mark cld have contemplated publishing it. It is a betrayal of the intimacies of private life second to none – i.e. a publication of Father's letters to Venetia at the time of their break – when she decided to marry Edwin. I am appalled that anyone shld have read them. I know that Mark's argument for publishing anything is that Beaverbrook wld otherwise paraphrase part of the correspondence. (He cannot by law do more than paraphrase even a very limited number of words.) But this seems to me like burning down your own house for fear an enemy might burn it down to-morrow! The remedy is worse than the disease. And it is certain – whereas the possibility of B.'s paraphrasing is uncertain. I am once more deeply distressed – but for a draught cld not have slept.

Diary – Monday 16 March – 21 Hyde Park Square, W.2

...Telephoned Mark about last batch of chapters. He has not yet seen Roy. He (Mark) is – very understanding. He is going to send me (or rather tell Roy to send me) all the letters to read. I shall feel a terrible sense of eavesdropping dishonour in doing so – but if they have already been exposed to so many prying eyes I must do so if only to protect him. Have now finished the whole book. The account of the fall of my father's Govt. is well done – more fully & fairly than any other account I have read so far.

Diary – Tuesday 17 March – 21 Hyde Park Square, W.2

. . . The letters have arrived & I have read a large proportion of the first batch. They give me pain – & astonishment. It is so strange to know that I was quite unaware of what was passing between 2 human beings – one of whom was closer to me in intimacy than any other (except perhaps Cys) has ever been in my whole life – & the other my closest & most intimate female friend. The 2nd batch for which I am steeling myself will be worse. . . .

V.B.C. to Mark Bonham Carter

Thursday 26 March
21 Hyde Park Square, W.2

Private

Darling Mark – I was worrying in bed last night over Roy's desire to publish that last letter. . . .

I naturally long not to expose H.H.A.'s 'infatuation' to the eyes of thousands – for it must inevitably cheapen him & reduce his stature to posterity. . . . I am sure you understand what this whole business means to me – for apart from the closest intimacy & love he was to me throughout my life a standard & a touchstone of all values – the only human being I accepted without any reservation whatsoever. His errors (with colleagues etc.) were due to a nobility which refused to make terms with baseness or even to admit that it existed.

I cannot bear to think that by this book he may be defaced with our acquiescence. If some things revealed by the letters have come as a shock to me – how much greater will be the impact on οἱ πολλοί?[1] This is of course my main & supreme anxiety. But I also feel (a long way after) that, it is a little hard on Margot? who never guessed (what of course I knew) how little she met his needs, & what exasperation she often caused him – in spite of her unwavering, tho' blind, devotion. One does owe something to the dead. I realise to the full what you are up against – i.e. blackmail. I also realise that Roy cannot be expected to feel as we do – nor can even you feel quite as I do – though you have shown an understanding & delicacy & imagination which I shall always bless you for.

From the age of 4 – a lonely, questioning & bewildered child – he made the climate of my life. It was because of him that I found it so impossibly difficult to marry anyone (although, unlike Venetia, I had an embarras de choix). He dwarfed them all. He also implored me not to, whenever I showed the slightest inclination to do so! I cldn't help laughing when I

[1] That is, *hoi polloi*, 'the many'.

read the letter in which he put Hugh[1] as second only to Raymond in desirability as a suitor (remembering that for 10 years he had pressed his suit & that my Father had told me with tears that it wld. break his heart if I acquiesced!) But this is by the way.

I think it is important that we shld. not be hurried. There is so much ground to cover – & then we must see the picture as a whole & calmly. One or two snatched afternoons will not suffice.

My love & gratitude. Yr Mama.

Diary – Friday 22 May – 21 Hyde Park Square, W.2

I insert this most important day which I forgot to enter.[2] I have been persecuted – (the word is not too strong) to take part in the B.B.C. programmes for Beaverbrook's 85th birthday on Monday. First 'sound' approached me. I explained that I regarded B. as the quintessence of evil & I did not think therefore that I was an appropriate person to speak to him across a birthday cake. Next T.V. got on to me for *Panorama* which is celebrating the same event. I gave the same explanation. They rang me the next day & the next. I told them I didn't want to take part. Finally they asked if they might bring their instruments here on Friday afternoon 2–4. I said they cld do it at their own risk. I reserved to myself the right to call the programme off if I didn't succeed in getting the right 'balance'...

Diary – Monday 25 May – 21 Hyde Park Square, W.2

Laura had asked me to dine to meet Max Freedman & Robert McKenzie. I said I wldn't dine as I wanted to watch *Panorama* but cld come afterwards. After several shots of Beaverbrook looking (as K. Martin wrote) 'as old as sin' & 600 others guzzling at the Grosvenor Hôtel ... & some retrospective shots of his boyhood I came on early in the programme. To my rage & amazement I found my interview (which lasted only 3½ minutes) had been 'edited' & cut in every way. Sometimes the end of a sentence had been lopped off. Many of the parts to which I attached the greatest importance had been omitted & many stings drawn. I was absolutely furious. When I exploded to Robert McKenzie at Laura's he said the B.B.C. constantly did this doctoring of programmes – the interviewer 'nodded' when there was

[1] Hugh John Godley (1877–1950), 2nd Baron Kilbracken, for many years Violet's suitor and a close friend and contemporary of both Raymond Asquith and Bongie. He was counsel to the chairman of committees, House of Lords, 1923–44.

[2] The entry was probably written on Monday 25 May.

a cut. I said it was as bad as forgery. One can distort the truth as much by omission as by insertion. I shall make a hell of a row about it to-morrow.

Diary – Tuesday 26 May – 21 Hyde Park Square, W.2

Windows cleaned at last! Spent the morning ringing up B.B.C. Rowlands in Paris. John Grest on a course. A Mr Paul Fox[1] – a high-up dealing with 'Public Affairs' – rang me in the afternoon & was very civil – apologetic & understanding. He said that 'someone had blundered' as I ought to have been warned in advance of the possibility of cuts. I said that if I had been so warned I shld. have called off the programme & they knew it. It rested on a delicate balance. Why shld I have made a row about the order of the questions if mutilation was contemplated? I thought the ethics of the business shocking. 'Sound' wld never dream of perpetuating such a deception....

Diary – Monday 13 July – 21 Hyde Park Square, W.2

...In the evening I watched on *Panorama* the start of the Republican Convention at San Francisco – returning to it at midnight for the Telstar transmission. It was an appalling revelation of an America I did not know & of which I had not suspected the existence. My 'image' of present-day America was incarnate in Kennedy & in those who surrounded & supported him – the civilized intellectuals & journalists I had seen & known during my 2 visits to Washington. I was thankful that the fate of the world was in their hands & none other. That Atlantic Alliance seemed to me to be the sheet-anchor of sanity & safety.

What I watched on the screen was a farcical harlequinade, a bad pantomime played by clowns to a rabble – waving balloons & placards under a shower of 'golden' confetti which descended from the roof, & shouting down the one Republican – Rockefeller[2] – for whom one still retains respect, when he tried to move an amendment ... asking for restraint on the violence & lawlessness of the John Birch Society. Goldwater[3] was

[1] (Sir) Paul Leonard Fox (b. 1925), Kt, 1991; joined BBC, 1950; head of public affairs, 1963; later controller of BBC1, 1967–73; director of programmes, 1973–84.

[2] Nelson Aldrich Rockefeller (1908–79), Republican governor of New York, 1959–73; vice-president of the United States (under 25th amendment), 1974–7; unsuccessfully sought the Republican nomination, 1960, 1964 and 1968.

[3] Barry Morris Goldwater (1909–98), Republican senator for Arizona, 1953–65, 1969–87; won the Republican nomination in 1964 but lost the presidential election.

hysterically acclaimed & it is clear now that he must win the nomination, possibly scoring 800 odd against Scranton's[1] 200. His programme is intensification of Cold War throughout the world; the threat of hot war on China, Viet-Nam & several other countries; the delegation to Military Commanders of the power to use Nuclear Weapons on their own responsibility; the cutting down (or off) of Aid programmes; the loosening of Federal responsibility (which means that the South can do what they like about Segregation); the turning of heat onto Neutrals, & every insanity imaginable. The enthusiasm he evoked & the manner in which it was displayed made me feel that America is au fond not an adult nation. Yet she remains the most powerful in the world. It is terrifying.

Diary – Wednesday 29 July – 21 Hyde Park Square, W.2

Took my diamond Star & pearls to Carrington to be re-threaded. Star passed as sound. Law feared the pin was bent. William Haley came to tea with me. He is leaving for a holiday end of week. We talked of the political situation. He wld like to want Labour to get in – but his desire is paralysed by the mediocrity of their Front Bench (apart from Wilson). It is always said that 'in 2 years he will get rid of his dead wood' – but what will happen to us in those crucial 2 years? On the other hand he thinks that the Tories do not deserve – after their 13 years' record – to get in again. I feel very much as he does. From our Party pt of view the Tories wld of course be best. A fourth defeat for Labour might lead to some realignment.

Dined alone with Mark & Leslie & saw little Virginia in bed.... Mark talked about his electoral prospects & facing the alternatives of defeat & victory.... His morale in this disappointing political prospect fills me with admiration. He has invested so much in Liberal fortunes & worked so hard for them. It is hard on Jo as well. He hasn't put a foot wrong....

Quite late, when Leslie went to bed, we got on to the still debated pages of the R.J. book. I want them further cut & he, I gather, is resisting. I feel sure that it wld have been better after Beaverbrook's death[2] (when the

[1] William Warren Scranton (b. 1917), Republican representative for Pennsylvania, 1961–3; governor of Pennsylvania, 1963–7; a candidate for the Republican presidential nomination, 1964.

[2] Violet believed, somewhat naively, that Lord Beaverbrook's death (9 June) meant that it was no longer necessary for extracts of her father's letters to Venetia Stanley to be 'pre-emptively' published in Roy Jenkins's *Asquith*. As a publisher Mark Bonham Carter knew that the letters could not be forever suppressed, and that they were in any case of such historical interest that no biography of Asquith could be complete without them. After his mother's death he took the decision to have a comprehensive edition published, with historical commentary, and this appeared in 1982 as *H. H. Asquith: Letters to Venetia Stanley* (OUP), edited by Michael and Eleanor Brock.

major threat of blackmail was removed) to apply the axe instead of the pruning-fork. The situation shld then have been drastically revised. But Mark was the negotiator with Roy & his instinct was the other way. I want the pages dealing with V.S.'s engagement written down – not dramatised. . . .

Diary – Friday 31 July – 21 Hyde Park Square, W.2

. . . Mark rang up – he had obviously had an unsatisfactory talk with Roy. He is naturally in a hurry to get out the book, but as he is away for 3 weeks there is not much more we can do about it. I reminded Mark of my demand that letters written during Cabinet Sessions shld not be given as such. (This wld shock others terribly, as indeed it has shocked me.) . . .[1]

Mark Bonham Carter to V.B.C.

Wednesday 12 August
Collins Publishers,
14 St James's Place,
London, S.W.1

Dear Mama,

Many thanks for your letter. . . . As to *Asquith*, I do want you to know how aware I have been throughout of your feelings, and of how well I understand them – & respect them. . . . From the start my preoccupation has been to minimize the pain which the book might inflict upon you & on this I have pondered endlessly ever since the problem of the Venetia letters emerged – & long before I told you about it. Of course I may be wrong & may have taken the wrong decision, but I still believe the book as a whole will support & increase Aga's[2] reputation. . . .

What I have attempted to do, doubtless without success, is to do the utmost within my powers to minimize the pain I always knew you would feel, while at the same time producing a book which was as near as could be invulnerable to the kind of criticism which I feared.

Love Mark.

[1] Violet had been alerted to this possibility by Bob Boothby two years earlier, in a letter in which Boothby poured out his own complicated feelings about Churchill: 'Don't delude yourself that Winston was loyal to your father. He told me, often, that he spent most of his time in the Dardanelles (later the War) Committee writing letters to Venetia Stanley; and that, if he had remained in charge of our affairs, we should have lost the war' (BB to VBC, 30 October 1962).

[2] Aga was a Bonham Carter family nickname for H. H. Asquith.

Diary – Tuesday 22 September – 21 Hyde Park Square, W.2

Worked all morning with Miss B. T. at my accumulations.[1] I have to give a 10 minutes [Liberal] national broadcast on Home Service on 2nd Oct. & went round to see Pratap Chitnis & ask him for some gen. He is a delightful & most able man. He summoned Mr Arnold who does research & they have promised to send me some facts & figures about Housing, Pensions, Site Values. Went on to Simpsons & bought a coat & skirt. Trying desperately to get au fait by reading up back Nos of papers.

Watched Jo on first of 3 T.V. programmes in which the 3 party leaders are being cross-examined on 3 following evenings. He was quite admirable I thought. Kenneth Harris – who I have always thought a very nice man – behaved in a very rude & bullying way & interrupted him 3 times! I was furious. William Rees-Mogg rang up later to congratulate me & we had an excellent talk. He too was indignant at Harris's behaviour, but said, quite truly, that it always puts the audience on the side of the interviewee. His opinion of Home is still abysmal & he has a 'foible' for Wilson which I deplore. I thanked him for his very nice & generous allusion to Mark in his *Sunday Times* leader. His guess is that Labour will just make it in the General Election. It is my fear too....

Diary – Thursday 24 September – 21 Hyde Park Square, W.2

Went to see Goldsmith in the afternoon as it occurs to me that my giddiness (on one side of my head) might be caused by eyes – or rather, my worse eye, which is that side. But he gave me a clean bill. My sight is exactly what it was last July year. Forgot to say that Wilson was on last night – very 'douce' & agreeable – obviously all out to show sincerity. K. Harris kept a civil tongue in his cheek which made me angrier than ever! To-night we had Home who was deplorable. (Probably over-tired poor man.) He didn't answer any of the questions even when he was not trying to evade & side-step them. He appeared to have no grasp either of words or thoughts – mixed up 'exports' and 'experts'. I have seldom seen a worse performance....

[1] Violet had returned from a fortnight's stay at Royaumont the previous evening. While she was in France it was announced that the long-awaited general election would be on 15 October.

Diary – Sunday 11 October – 21 Hyde Park Square, W.2

Jo very sweetly came in to see me about tea-time & we had a talk. I told him how splendidly & flawlessly he had conducted the campaign & stated our case. He was charmingly modest as ever & didn't look exhausted though he has had to carry the whole country & with it the whole burden of the campaign on his shoulders. . . .

Diary – Eve of Poll, Wednesday 14 October – Royal Hôtel, Bideford, North Devon

Left for Torrington[1] – or rather Exeter St David – by 2.30 from Paddington in a very comfy corner seat. At the very end of the journey I found Frank Byers & wife 2 carriages off. I had a little talk with them. Frank is speaking at Torrington for Mark & at Barnstaple for Jeremy. He very kindly took down my cases & gave them to a porter. I found my car & had a lovely drive to Bideford past Warkleigh Heath & Crediton under sunset skies. Found Elena at the Royal – & also Cressida – who was just leaving after 2 days there. Rested for a bit. Wanted to go to 2 meetings (eve of poll) one at Appledore and the last one on the Quay but Elena persuaded me to go straight to the Quay in a car so as to get a good place there. . . .

Mark arrived on time – his 4th meeting – & made a good short speech & then we all went home – everyone confident.

Diary – Declaration of the Poll, Friday 16 October – Royal Hôtel, Bideford, North Devon

I slept little – having a natural 'needle' but when we started for the count at Torrington I had no doubt that Mark was in. Ambrose Fulford had driven me round the Polling Stations yesterday evening (between 5.30 & 8). We visited about 7 in & near Bideford, including Appledore & Buckland Brewer, & all our supporters (including dear old Ambrose who knows the pitch better than anyone) were completely confident. . . . When we got into the counting-rooms & watched the silent tables I beckoned to Mary Hoskins – Mark's agent – who told me 'They are a bit ahead.' I said 'Are we half-through?' She said 'A little more.' This gave me my first misgiving. . . . Mark's stack of votes looked – & was – far the highest –

[1] Because of poor health Violet had been forbidden by Mark from travelling to Torrington to help with the election. She was bitterly disappointed and was only present for the very end of the campaign.

which cheered me – but I was told that Mills's[1] were laid out in breadth. My fears grew. I saw the radiant faces of the Tory principals & the awful truth was whispered to us. Mills was in by 2,000 odd votes. . . .[2]

Mark behaved magnificently. He was perfectly composed & calm & betrayed no surprise or other emotion. He said 'Poor Mary.' Then they went out onto the balcony & we heard the roar of the triumphant Tories. After giving them a decent interval to shout in we went out thro' the crowd – Mark's supporters gathering round him – almost too heart-broken to cheer. On the way out I saw poor Sheila Hutchinson with tears in her eyes & in the crowd dear Mary Rous[3] who came up & spoke to us. Then we drove away – Mark – Leslie, little Laura[4] & I to Bideford. Half way there a car stopped in front of us & drew across the road to stop us – & a man got out to speak to Mark. It was Baker – his old agent in his first fight for Barnstaple in 1945. After a hasty word of condolence he enlarged on their triumph in N. Devon in glowing terms![5] I thought I had never seen a more tactless gesture – tho' doubtless well-meant. We all lunched together – Mark indomitable & almost light-hearted in his way of showing it – poor Leslie very brave tho' quite exhausted. . . .

She has worked so wholeheartedly & hard – my heart aches for her & above all for Mark. He is doing a short tour of thanks to-morrow morning & then driving home staying one night at the Jellicoes' en route. Elena angelically motored to Exeter with them so that Mark shld not drive back alone. The end of a day of shattered hopes. Mark cld not of course fight Torrington ever again. But where else might a chance occur?

V.B.C. to Mark Bonham Carter ***Monday 19 October***
21 Hyde Park Square, W.2

My darling Mark – You will know without my telling you how bitterly I resent this cruel & senseless blow. That Fate shld. have chosen such a

[1] (Sir) Peter McLay Mills (1921–93), Kt, 1982; MP (Con.) Torrington, 1964–74; West Devon, 1974–83; Torridge and West Devon, 1983–7; parliamentary under-secretary of state, Northern Ireland Office, 1972–4.

[2] The majority was 2,068, the official result being: P. M. Mills (Con.) 16,899; M. R. Bonham Carter (Lib.) 14,831; Dr D. A. L. Owen (Lab.) 5,867. The Labour candidate, Dr David Owen (b. 1938), cr. life peer, 1992, went on to become Labour foreign secretary, and co-founder and leader of the SDP. He was first elected to parliament as member for Sutton, Plymouth, in 1966.

[3] Violet's niece, the daughter of her elder brother 'Oc' Asquith and his wife Betty.

[4] Hon. Laura Grenfell, Leslie's daughter from her first marriage to Peter Grenfell, Baron St Just.

[5] Jeremy Thorpe had significantly increased his majority at North Devon, from 362 in 1959 to 5,136 in 1964.

ridiculous ninepin as Mills as the instrument of its purpose (or lack of purpose) points clearly to the fact that (as I said) Torrington is Tory Country – & not (as the dear old farmer said in our first Election there) 'Liberal country'. I was always taken in by the tremendous loyalty & love which you inspired & by the ardour of our supporters there & saw it the other way round – i.e. as fundamentally & traditionally Liberal – with a feudal Tory upper-crust which the majority wanted to overthrow & where Labour wld never have much nuisance value.

This astonishing result has convinced me that I was wrong – & though I am sure you were right to stay there & fight again after the '59 Election – & you won much admiration & respect by doing so, you were in fact wasted there – & shld rightly have been in a more politically minded constituency where your great gifts of thought & speech wld have been understood, & taken tricks....

I feel that this Election has given a 'shake-up' to the mould & made the whole political scene more fluid. Unexpected fissures may occur & opportunities will present themselves.... I don't feel this Parlt. can last very long – unless Labour throws some of its cargo overboard – thus losing face with its Left & provoking disunity.[1]

All my dearest love Yr Mama.

I wld willingly have given the last years of my life to see you in.

Diary – Tuesday 20 October – 21 Hyde Park Square, W.2

Was sorry not to be able to go to W. H. Smith Award which went to Ernst Gombrich.[2] Lord Home has handed in his seals of Office & Wilson is already in N° 10 issuing lists of his Govt. which promises to be enormous. He is splitting several offices.... Ministers are multiplying like rabbits.... Wilson has made it clear that he neither needs nor desires co-operation with Liberals.

[1] The general election result was: Labour 317, Conservative 304, Liberal 9. The Liberal share of the vote was 11.2 per cent, more than double the 1959 total. But despite the narrowness of the Labour majority, Harold Wilson made no overtures for Liberal support.

[2] (Sir) Ernst Gombrich (b. 1909), Kt, 1972; OM, 1988; director of the Warburg Institute and professor of the history of the Classical Tradition, University of London, 1959–76; his *Meditations on a Hobby Horse* had been published the previous year.

Diary – Sunday 1 November – 21 Hyde Park Square, W.2

Terrible day. Roy's book (which comes out on 2nd Nov.) is reviewed by Sunday papers (*S. Telegraph*, which is serializing it, does not of course review it). *Sunday Times* had a very nice review by Raymond Mortimer – but when I read A. J. P. Taylor in the *Observer* it nearly killed me – a tissue of falsehood plastered together with smears & mud.... Nothing can undo the harm now done. I dare not look at the *Sunday Express* – & there are still the weeklies to face. I wish I had not lived to see this week – tho' long enough thank God to avert even worse things.[1]

Diary – Wednesday 25 November – 21 Hyde Park Square, W.2

... Colin Coote came to see me at 4.... He told me one story about Wilson (under a seal of absolute secrecy) which made my flesh creep. He (Colin) dined à trois with him (Wilson) & Bob Boothby (who has been an acharné Wilsonite from the moment he looked like becoming P.M.!) In Colin's presence Wilson pressed upon Bob first the Embassy in Washington & then the Embassy in Paris. To Bob's credit he had the common sense to refuse both. I cldn't have believed this story had Colin not told it to me. I had always thought of Wilson as a cool astute man. This proves him surely to be a naive greenhorn....

'The Corridors of Impotence'
Baroness Asquith of Yarnbury, December 1964

On Monday 9 November Violet learned from Jo Grimond that she had been offered a life peerage by Harold Wilson. She reacted with 'astonishment'. Although to many she had been a natural candidate for this honour ever since life peerages were first introduced in 1958, she had, like all Liberals, been overlooked during the years of Conservative rule. Not unnaturally she thought that her time had passed. Now, when the offer finally came, she was in failing health and doubted whether she could fulfil the duties that would be expected of her. When Jo Grimond explained this to Harold Wilson the prime minister generously offered to create three Liberal peerages, as Violet later put it: 'two "working" ones & my own – as "honorary" as I cared to make it'. Once her trusted

[1] Violet was later comforted by 'a really good article' on her father in the *Times Literary Supplement*, 'Master of Liberal Britain'; it showed 'real understanding in depth & must have been written .... by someone who knew & cared for him' (diary, 15 November 1964).

doctor, Dr Goldman, had given his approval, Violet accepted and her peerage was made public in the honours list of 4 December. Violet professed, unconvincingly, not to be excited at the thought of sitting in the Lords: 'frankly it is not an exhilarating prospect'. She took great pride in her title 'Asquith of Yarnbury' – with its dual evocation of her father's memory and the Wiltshire countryside that she so loved. And as 'Baroness Asquith' she proceeded to make her own mark on the parliamentary record. Four years on, in December 1968, the *Times* diarist 'PHS' reviewed the performance of Wilson's life peers, of which there were by then more than a hundred. The prime minister, it was noted, had 'effectively reformed the House of Lords avant le mot'. The 'working House' now had 'a majority of nominees' comprising 'people of ability from a wide variety of walks of life'. Violet was in sympathy with the spirit of this 'reformed' chamber and she proved a hard-working peer, in spite of bouts of serious ill-health. But she also experienced frustration at the lack of power exercised in what she would describe as 'the Corridors of Impotence', and in 1968 'PHS' wondered if she might perhaps have been 'more at home in the less genteel atmosphere' of the Commons. This was a fair surmise, but whatever its limitations the House of Lords provided Violet with a new platform at the very end of her life, and it was one that she used to the full.

Diary – Wednesday 23 December – 21 Hyde Park Square, W.2

'Der Tag' – Had breakfast rather earlier than usual & scrambled thro' necessary business with Mrs B.T. – put on black clothes (as I noticed yesterday when I went to have a squint at Mrs Morgan Phillips's[1] introduction that her pale blue sleeves did not look well poking through her red robe) & left by Minnecar at $\frac{1}{4}$ to 12. . . .

Lunch followed & then rehearsal in an empty house with Black Rod & Blue Mantle. Dear Frank [Longford] seemed as uninitiated as I was. We went through it twice with an interval for Byers & his sponsors. The oath I have to swear is on the clerks' table in enormous print. Then we went up & 'robed' ourselves. The black tricorne fitted me perfectly & was not one whit too big (I had brought tissue-paper to stuff into it as a

[1] Norah Mary Phillips *née* Lusher (1910–92), cr. life peer, 1964, after the death of her husband Morgan Phillips (1902–63), who was general secretary of the Labour Party, 1944–62.

precaution).[1] That angel Elena came to help me robe. Then we went downstairs & after prayers our solemn procession set out through the Peers' lobby. . . .

We entered the House in silence, bowed in turn when we reached a given spot, slightly on the right facing the Ld Chancellor[2] on his Woolsack with the House behind him. We then progressed with measured steps till we came abreast of the clerk's table. . . . [I] made my oath & declaration. . . . I stumbled slightly before 'Yarnbury' (I cldn't for a moment remember what the devil I was called!) but otherwise got through all right. Then I signed my name – 'Asquith of Yarnbury'. . . .

As we went out a friendly cheer – decorous but friendly – was raised. Unrobing – joined by Leslie & Elena – meeting downstairs with sweet little Edward, Jane, Virginia, Hélène, Eduardo (who were all in the Gallery). . . . I went in later to listen to the debate – asked where the Liberal Bench was & was shown to an empty strip of red leather near the door. I sat down on it & listened to Lord Strang[3] & Ld Colyton[4] & then a very good speech by Hugh Foot[5] (now Ld Caradon) on the U.N. I felt, as I have done before, that the atmosphere has no resonance. Your audience gives you nothing back. . . .

Home via Palace Yard & into bed very tired. It is funny to open a new chapter of life at the age of 77! The impression I got from the H. of Lords is that though it leaves much to be desired as a forum it is probably a very nice Club. Dear old Attlee, who strays about there all the time, is obviously very happy – like an old horse turned out to grass in a lush & peaceful meadow.

[1] Feeling obliged to 'spend something on becoming a peer of the realm' Violet had planned to have a tricorne made, at a cost of seven guineas. But on bumping into Kay Elliot in the peeresses' sitting-room the plan was scotched: "Nonsense" she said briskly "have Lady Wootton's' & she snatched a tricorne out of a cupboard & plonked it on my head. Tho' a little on the big side it fitted me. I was told it was the smallest peeress's hat in existence" (diary, Tuesday 15 December).

[2] Gerald Austin Gardiner (1900–90), cr. life peer, 1963; barrister; contested West Croydon (Lab.) 1951; chairman of Bar Council 1958, 1959; defended Penguin Books over the publication of *Lady Chatterley's Lover*, against a charge brought under the Obscene Publications Act (1959); lord chancellor, 1964–70.

[3] William Strang (1893–1978), cr. Baron Strang, 1954; diplomat; deputy speaker, House of Lords, 1962–78.

[4] Henry Lennox Hopkinson (1902–96), cr. Baron Colyton, 1956; MP (Con.) Taunton, Somerset, 1950–6; diplomat; minister of state for colonial affairs, 1952–5.

[5] Hugh Mackintosh Foot (1907–90), cr. life peer, 1964 (Caradon); colonial administrator and diplomat; British ambassador to UN, 1964–70; brother of Dingle, John and Michael.

Diary – Friday 14 January 1965 – 21 Hyde Park Square, W.2

Was just starting out when Sylvia[1] rang me up from H. P. Gate to tell me that beloved W. was very ill. They were trying to keep it secret till 7 o'clock news.... I felt stunned & drove to H.P. Gate – which I found packed with press-men & flashlight photographers & T.V. men, & one or two policemen who cleared a way for me. Winston's detective (Murray) let me in to the front door. I went into the drawing-room to write a letter to Clemmie. Asked to see dear Miss Hamblin.[2] She said he was suffering no pain or discomfort. Clemmie came down – very brave but looked worn out. She asked if I wld like to come & see him & I went into his bedroom. He was propped up on pillows – breathing quite easily & quietly & his beloved face looked at peace....

I sat beside him – longing to exchange one last thought or word. I know that he has left us gradually over the years – becoming more remote with the passing months this last year – but the thought of parting with him is just as hard, though one has faced it so often. His going seems to shrink the scale of things. While he still lived on this country shared his greatness – in some measure. When he is gone I shall feel 'that there is nothing left extraordinary under the visiting moon'.[3] I left him with a wrench & reeled out into the mob of press & flashlights – the reporters surrounded me 'How did you find him Lady Asquith?' I said 'very peaceful' & evaded a shower of questions by taking refuge in my taxi....

Diary – Sunday 24 January – 21 Hyde Park Square, W.2

Mary Soames telephoned to me early this morning to tell me that beloved Winston had died. They were called to his bedside about 6 – & he died quite peacefully – at 8.... It is so difficult to say & accept that this is the end. (And I know that he believed it wld be the end of all things – for I asked him once whether he thought we shld survive death – & he replied with great decision: 'No. I believe that death is the end.') I could not face parting from his earthly presence – knowing that after to-day I shld never see his face again.... I went to H.P. Gate at 2.30 – found Mary who was

[1] Sylvia Henley *née* Stanley (1882–1980), daughter of Lord Sheffield and sister of Venetia; the cousin and close friend of Clementine Churchill.

[2] Grace Hamblin, Clementine Churchill's personal secretary, who often helped Sir Winston Churchill with secretarial work. She had been with the Churchills since 1932.

[3] From *Antony and Cleopatra*, act iv, scene xvi: 'The odds is gone, / And there is nothing left remarkable / Beneath the visiting moon.'

most sweet – quite calm & most understanding. Mary told me I cld go in & see him & left me alone....[1]

Diary – Friday 29 January – 21 Hyde Park Square, W.2

Day of darkness cold & rain. I pray it won't be like this to-morrow.[2] Had my hair washed. In the evening went to Westminster Hall for the last time.... I telephoned Laura, who has come south from Scotland, to meet me in the Whips' Room at 10.20 & we cld go together at 10.30 when Wilson, Jo, Alec Home & the Speaker will be on guard for 5 minutes....[3]

Mark & I & Leslie drove there ... & then went to meet Laura. She had just come from a Colonial Office dinner to dark potentates given by Tony Greenwood.[4] I asked where Jo was. She replied: 'Borrowing a black waistcoat from the Serjeant-at-Arms. He borrows all his clothes from him – & even medals. The other night he had none for a dinner-party with decorations, so he borrowed a lot & found during the evening that he was wearing the Burma Star! (never having been in Burma in his life)'! (So like Jo.) Presently he appeared in a rather ill-fitting waistcoat (very short & slightly 'pouting' in the middle) & a tail-coat which I recognized as the one in which he was married – & which was then his Etonian tail-coat! No one cld accuse him of foppery! or of being in any way conscious of his good looks!

He also told me that the B.B.C. had sent him an urgent message asking him to record an obituary tribute to Harold Wilson! which seems rather

[1] The following day, Monday 25 January, Violet delivered a eulogy on her departed friend in her maiden speech in the House of Lords: 'I think it is hard to realise that that indomitable heart, to which we all owe our freedom and our very existence, has fought its long, last battle and is still. I count myself infinitely blessed in having known Winston Churchill as a close and dear and life-long friend. But, from the day of our first meeting in my early youth, I saw him always in a dual perspective. Through and beyond my friend, well known and dearly loved, I saw one of the greatest figures of all time upon the stage of history' (*Hansard*, vol. 262, cols 1069–70).

[2] The funeral service for Sir Winston Churchill took place on 30 January at St Paul's Cathedral, followed by a burial at Bladon in Oxfordshire. Prior to this there was a lying in state in Westminster Hall in the Palace of Westminster.

[3] Harold Wilson had arranged that the three Party leaders and the speaker of the Commons should together stand guard as a parliamentary tribute to Churchill. The speaker was Sir Harry Hylton-Foster (1905–65), Kt, 1954; MP (Con.) for York, 1950–9; London and Westminster, 1959–65; former solicitor-general, he was speaker, 1959–65.

[4] (Arthur William) Anthony Greenwood (1911–82), cr. life peer, 1970; MP (Lab.) Heywood and Radcliffe, 1946–50; Rossendale, 1950–70; secretary of state for colonial affairs, October 1964-December 1965; minister of overseas development, December 1965–August 1966; minister of housing and local government, 1966–70.

pre-emptive & an unnecessary addition to this week's broadcasting. Jo wondered whether Alec Home & Wilson had each got similar notes, so that each one of them wld have letters in their pockets asking for obituaries of the others. He said the original proposal had been that they shld stand for the normal period of guard – i.e. 20 minutes – upon which Alec Home said 'But that wld kill me!' & implored to have the time reduced to 5. We sat in the Round Lobby to watch them go through so as to follow them & be in the Hall before they went off guard. Soon they came through & Wilson gave me an extremely affable bow & smile. We followed at a respectful distance & then went through for the last time. We saw them leave their guard. (Jo of course looked by far the best in spite of his borrowed plumes!)

The unbroken human stream flowed on. It was so strange to think that W. was lying there – high up in that vast coffin – under its Union Jack – – – – He wld. have been moved by the people & the love he had inspired. I said to Mark afterwards that nothing has ever given me a more uncomfortable sense of undue 'privilege' than being able to slip in & out (& take anyone I like with me – up to 6 people) while these others had queued for miles & hours in icy rain & bitter wind. We went home, Mark & Leslie dropping me.

Diary – Tuesday 2 February – 21 Hyde Park Square, W.2

Worked all morning. Went to H. of Lords. Such a wasted afternoon! The old boys were discussing a 'Dogs Bill'! – to impose punitive measures on dogs who misbehaved on pavements instead of using gutters! I cldn't believe serious men cld waste an afternoon in such a frivolous yet boring occupation! Gladwyn joined me for a few minutes in solitude. Discussed with him measures for meetings & some concerted action....

Diary – Wednesday 10 March – 21 Hyde Park Square, W.2

Immigration debate in the H. of L. Dilhorne[1] made an attack on Philip Rea – accusing him of having made a 'party point' in his interjection yesterday (a question quite legitimate – asking whether the flow of illegal immigrants then being discussed had not taken place during the previous Govt's régime – which of course it had). His motion & his speech were

[1] (Sir) Reginald Edward Manningham-Buller (1905–80), cr. Viscount Dilhorne, 1964; Kt, 1951; MP (Con.) Daventry, Northants., 1943–50; South Northants., 1950–62; lord chancellor, 1962–4.

entirely negative & restrictive. I followed him & replied at once to his attack on Rea. He interrupted to say that I was making another 'party' point. I replied that Rea had merely stated an obvious fact & when Dilhorne wanted to interrupt again I refused to give way – & proceeded with my speech – which I think 'went' quite well – but of course so far as response is concerned one might just as well be talking in a mortuary. There is not a murmur either of assent or dissent.

I was followed by Ld Stonham[1] (for the Govt.) who said civil things about my speech. I sat through part of the debate tho' not all of it. I was amazed to hear a Labour Peer – Ld Brown[2] by name – accuse me of 'sentimentality' for saying that we owed a debt of gratitude to those emigrants who were now rendering essential services to our economy & our prosperity by rendering us essential services in hospitals, transport etc. I had to leave before the Ld Chancellor wound up – but was interested to read in *Hansard* that he had made many of the same points as I had – & that he was afterwards rebuked by Dilhorne for 'following the bad example of the absent Baroness'! (Dilhorne is an appalling man!). . . .

Diary – Tuesday 6 April – 21 Hyde Park Square, W.2

I must now 'write up' my diary from 1st April when we left for Königswinter till now. It was unfortunate that the date of the Conference coincided with the date of publication of my book[3] – & Mark felt in 2 minds whether we ought not both to have chucked. But apart from my 14 years' fidelity [to Königswinter] I felt we must keep faith with Lilo – & if we had both opted out the Conference wld have had no Lib. representation but Gladwyn. . . .

On Sunday 4 April – the awful ordeal of the Plenary Marathon. Did not attempt to speak – nor did Mark. But – the Sunday papers were nectar to me. Marvellous reviews of my book. Raymond Mortimer in the *Sunday Times* & Ld. Attlee's (headed 'Quite possibly a Classic') in the *Observer*. Both super-favourable. I was most deeply touched by Attlee's – 1) He had clearly enjoyed reading the book enormously. 2) He had obviously felt a real affection & appreciation for W. (which W. alas did not reciprocate!) 3) He said it had given him a new aperçu of my father. He had always

[1] Victor John Collins (1903–71), cr. life peer (Stonham), 1958; MP (Lab.) Taunton, Somerset, 1945–50; Shoreditch and Finsbury, 1954–8; minister of state at home office, 1967–9.

[2] Wilfrid Banks Brown (1908–85), cr. life peer, 1964; company director and chairman; minister of state, board of trade, 1965–70.

[3] *Winston Churchill as I Knew Him*, which Violet had been working on since 1959, was published in Britain in the first week of April and in the United States in mid-May.

thought him a great man of noble character – but this book convinced him that he had also been 'a man of decision'....

[Tuesday 6] Goldman[1] came to see me in the afternoon – said that my heart & blood-pressure were down to rock-bottom – & that I must not move – even to have a bath for at least a week. Terribly depressing but I am thankful I did not go on to Berlin. To my infinite disappointment I shall miss the War Damage Bill Committee Stage next week when we shall vote on the Liberal Amendments – the one debate I had really looked forward to with excitement.

Katharine Asquith to V.B.C. ***Tuesday 20 April***
Tynts Hill, Mells, Frome, Somerset

Dearest Violet.

I do long to know that you haven't been too badly ill & are better. I've just finished reading the book. I think it's a great achievement. How you could have marshalled all that material – diaries, letters, newspaper articles, & Winston's own books & your father's – seems to me wonderful & it confirms so many memories of that time which are engraved on my mind. I have been absorbed in it.

The end is very sad reading.[2] I don't wonder at your enduring bitterness about the Conservative Party – but, when I think that, I remember that L.G. was the worst of any, & your father's cabinet must have been very difficult.... It's so difficult to imagine how it must have seemed at the time & not read the after-events into one's feelings of indignation. I wish I could talk to you about it. I'm so in the dark.

Have you gone away for Easter – or are you in bed? I suppose I ought to have known that you could write a beautiful book just as well as you could make a beautiful speech – but they seldom go together.

Much love K.

[1] Violet placed great trust and faith in Dr Goldman, whom she first consulted in September 1964: 'I am really devoted to him as a human being quite apart from all that I owe him as a doctor' (diary, Tuesday 15 March 1966).

[2] Violet's biography of Churchill ends in June 1916 when he returned to the backbenches of the Commons from the trenches of the Western Front, determined to vindicate himself after his sacking the previous year, and prepared to oppose Asquith's government in the process.

V.B.C. to Katharine Asquith ***Wednesday 21 April***
21 Hyde Park Square, W.2

Darling K – Our letters crossed. I have to-day got yours of yesterday & am so enchanted to hear that you like my book. I started it some time in '59 – then came B.'s long & agonizing illness – & his death – & for more than a year after I cld. think of nothing else. I found it very difficult to 'get going' again – it seemed an impossible effort. . . .

About the political part – it is impossible to exaggerate the blind folly & obscurantism of the Tory party. You must remember as well as I do the terrible poverty of the days we grew up in – & the 'affluence' we all lived in. Even those of us who were not considered 'rich' by the standards of those days. I was haunted by it from early childhood onwards. The Liberals were a 'great party' in 1906 & onwards – judged by any standards – of quantity & quality. The reforms my father & his Govt. fought for – Old Age Pensions, Sickness and Unemployment Insurance, Trade Boards, Labour Exchanges, the abolition of Sweated Labour, Home Rule for Ireland, the end of the Veto of the H. of Lords (which had the power to block all progressive legislation) – all these measures of ordinary human justice were opposed with ferocity by the Tories. They were obliged to swallow them – & every one of them has since been generally accepted & built upon by successive Govts. We believed in these measures & we loved them. They accepted them under duress – because they cld. not well do otherwise.

The Appeasement years, when they had power, were another chapter of errors – in the field of foreign policy this time. You write 'Ll.G. was the worst of any'. With him it was his character which was at fault. He did not know what loyalty meant – either to a principle or to a friend. My father alas! was so immune from such defects that he cld not believe in them – & thus allowed himself (& his party) to be destroyed. His was the 'infirmity' of 'a noble mind' – a tragedy the Greeks, or Shakespeare, wld have understood.

Winston – thank Heaven – came into his own at last – but only through the catastrophe he had done his utmost to avert. He had to wait for power till he was 66. He was never even then loved by the Tory party – & he knew it. His great mistake was to accept its leadership (which he had once, wisely, refused).[1] His overwhelming defeat in 1945 (which he naturally

[1]Churchill became Conservative leader in October 1940 after Chamberlain, seriously ill with cancer, resigned. Chamberlain had offered Churchill the leadership the previous May but the latter declined, arguing that as head of a national government it would be better 'not to undertake the leadership of any one political Party'. Clementine Churchill advised him against his later change of heart (Gilbert, *Finest Hour*, 347–8).

minded bitterly) was not a vote against him but against the party which he led. What a terribly long letter! Poor darling you will never get through it.

My dear love to you & Helen & to all at Mells. Ever yr V. . . .

V.B.C. to Elena Bonham Carter ***Friday 27 August***
21 Hyde Park Square, W.2

My Darling

One line of love & gratitude for your telephone call. . . .[1] Words cannot tell you how much I miss you. You have done & meant more to me than anyone during these long 4 months. I shall always bless you for it.

A long illness is a very lonely experience in spite of friends & visitors & letters (though I value all) because one somehow feels 'different' & isolated from other people by one's physical state. (In reverse this may be the reason why animals ostracize & sometimes kill their fellows when sick?) One tries to behave normally – but one knows one is not 'normal'. . . . What I have found hard to endure are the 'false dawns' – followed by setbacks. Being an incorrigible optimist I always believe in the sunrise – & then feel déçue when it proves to have been a mirage. I want so much to live again – not just remain alive. . . .

My dearest love to you all. I miss you every hour.

Ever yr Devoted V . . . .

Diary – Sunday 28 November – 21 Hyde Park Square, W.2

. . . Laura blew in which was delicious & we had tea & a long political 'jaw' together – of course about Rhodesia[2] – which we both enjoyed to the nth degree. She & I have the same political views & temperature! Ray came in at the end & stayed on with me till dinner-time. After dinner I was rung up by Jeremy who talked to me for about ½ an hour. He is deeply anxious about Jo's desire to retire from the leadership of the party. It blew up before the [Liberal] Assembly in Sept – but he had such an ovation at the Assembly & seemed so cheered by it that Jeremy & others thought he had

[1] Raymond and Elena were then enjoying a family holiday at Royaumont, Asnières-et-Oise, in northern France.

[2] Weeks earlier the Rhodesian government had unilaterally declared the country's independence from Britain, refusing to accept British constitutional proposals for majority rule. Economic sanctions were imposed by Wilson's government, but failed to have any real effect. The crisis of 1965 became a long-term problem, which would not be settled in Violet's lifetime.

dismissed the thought. However at the end of the Lib. Party Committee which I attended [in October] ... he apparently made some remark (after I had gone) to the effect of 'Well by January I may no longer be your leader' – or 'words to that effect'.[1] Jeremy – who is devoted to him – thinks he is very tired both physically & mentally – has a feeling of 'staleness' – is worried about his deafness (which I never notice – tho' I know it exists) & also about his eyes – which I never knew had anything wrong with them.... He begged me to write to him – imagining (quite wrongly) that I have influence over him. I promised however to do so.

Diary – Monday 29 November – 21 Hyde Park Square, W.2

Dr Goldman came at 6 & gave me my shot in the arm. He is delighted with my condition & very 'sound' on Rhodesia.... Mark followed him. I had asked him to come & talk to me about Jo.... Mark said one can't force him to stay but one can & shld ask him to remain till after the next Election – which might well be only a year hence. Mark thought Jeremy was the only one who cld. possibly succeed him. (But dear Jeremy with all his gifts is not a politician in depth). No one cld replace Jo. He is the one great asset the Party possesses. It is cruel for him – as it is for Mark – that their integrity has robbed them of their chance of using their great political gifts.

Jo Grimond to V.B.C. ***Thursday 9 December House of Commons***

Dear Violet – I am immensely grateful for your letter. It is far too kind. I struck a reasonably high patch in the Liberal fortunes – but failed to get it over the hump. I have been most loyally and ably helped by such people as Mark, Frank, Jeremy, Eric [Lubbock] and Arthur Holt. Considering its tiny size and resources the staff at Headquarters has been wonderful.

I have no complaints against the Party and no disagreements. But I have done $9\frac{1}{4}$ years in one job – and that a job of projection, propaganda, encouragement, etc., and as you know in politics that is a long time.... Further, I have to manufacture all my own stuff. I want before I reach old age to do a different political job. Since the day after I was first elected to Parliament I have been whip or leader, tied to an endless succession of decisions, week-end tours, turning up day after day at questions and making speeches in and out of the Commons on all sorts of subjects,

[1] In fact Jo Grimond remained Liberal leader until January 1967; see below, p. 312.

about many of which I know little or nothing. I now want to concentrate on a few subjects....

I mentioned my desire to change a year ago. I was and am anxious to do it as conveniently as possible for the Party – but no one took much notice and I must press the matter.... Nor does there seem to be any half-way house. The Liberal Party is like a clock which has got to be constantly wound up. I explored the possibility of a deputy leader – but it fell through. So long as the party has a leader, it expects him to be constantly available. There are so few people available that he must continuously tour, follow up ideas, prowl committees etc. If he lets down for a few months, the whole machine slows up. If only Mark or Frank or both were in the House of Commons things would be different. But they are not.

Thank you very much for all your personal help, advice and encouragement. I am most grateful. Now I must prepare to go to Bristol! Love Jo

Diary – Thursday 16 December – 21 Hyde Park Square, W.2

Temp. down & cough going lower. Laura (that angel) came in to see me & we had a long talk. I mentioned Jo's decision to retire for the first time to her. We felt the same about it – complete understanding & regret. Her serenity & balance are amazing. I think she has one of the most flawless characters I know. How cld. I have played a part in her making?

ELEVEN

The Common Market

1966–1967

Diary – New Year's Day, Saturday 1 January 1966 – 21 Hyde Park Square, W.2

Spent the whole day in bed & listened to the news etc. on my new transistor – including an excellent play (dramatized short story) by Somerset Maugham called *The Letter.* Too tired to move. Viet Nam peace moves in all directions – Harriman[1] & other U.S.A. envoys circling the globe. So far Chinese & Vietcong seem adamant. (There was a short Xmas truce – broken by Vietcong.) Americans have stopped bombing the North while peace feelers are put out.

Diary – Friday 4 February – 21 Hyde Park Square, W.2

Dear Robert Birley came to see me at 4.30 & we had a marvellous talk about S.A. & Rhodesia. He never drew breath – pouring out his experience. He is teaching in an African school which he is <u>legally</u> forbidden to enter & had 2 narrow squeaks of being found out – but once it was a friendly African sub-Inspector & the other time a white superior – who had once been bribed with two £5 notes by an African woman.... So the white fanatics are corruptible on top of all else. He quoted to me a remark of an African Rhodesian who said to him of the Smith Govt. – 'At present we are being governed by the Committee of a Country Club' – a very true (& sophisticated) remark. Adam drove him back to the Travellers. How I long to be with him at Königswinter before he returns – but how I fear I shan't.

[1] W. Averell Harriman (1891–1986), American financier and diplomat; he led the US delegation that conducted preliminary peace talks with North Vietnam, 1968–9.

Diary – Friday 18 February – 21 Hyde Park Square, W.2

Sally came 3.15 – followed by Dr Goldman before 5. I wasn't expecting him till after 6. He gave me my piqûre of glucose. I told him how breathless I had been all that week – & asked him a long term question: was I ever going to get better? I wasn't worrying about sudden death. I had taken that in my stride for years. But what did worry me was that I didn't seem to get any stronger. I was just as exhausted after a small effort now as I was in mid-October when I got back from Orkney. And we were now in mid-February. The smallest grasshopper was still a burden & to walk a few hundred yards was as much as I cld. do. He said I shld get better as the warmer weather came. By the summer I shld be having easy mornings still – then up in the afternoon – & a little rest before dinner – & shld be able to go out to dinner. I only hope & pray that he is right. At present I feel quite stationary. Mark's appt. head-lined in *Times* – *M.G.* & *Daily Mail.*[1]

Diary – Friday 25 February – 21 Hyde Park Square, W.2

Adam came back from work at luncheon time with an awful cold – no temp. but wisely went to bed. Dr Goldman came at 4 & gave me a shot in the arm but told me to stay in bed. Laura came in later. Wilson has returned from Russia & the Election is certainly on – tho' not yet announced. Date suggested 31st March. I fear we shall do badly & I am sure the Tories will be steam-rollered – & tho' they continue to make 'brave' noises one feels their hearts are in their boots. It is Gelda's birthday to-morrow which I had forgotten.

Diary – Friday 4 March – 21 Hyde Park Square, W.2

Had a visit from Haley (whom I haven't seen once since my illness – tho' he has written to me frequently). We had a most interesting talk – mainly about the present political situation. He says the Gen. Election date was fixed 6 weeks ago. He was very good & percipient about Wilson (perhaps I say this because he sees him just as I do?) a virtuoso professional – living from day to day & hand to mouth without long term aims or ideology. George Brown against this is an ideologist – a man who wants to achieve certain definite aims & a man of great courage – who will stand up to opposition & not try & find his way round it. He agrees also of course

[1] Mark Bonham Carter had accepted the post of first chairman of the new Race Relations Board, established by the 1965 Race Relations Act.

about the dismal disarray in the Tory Party & intense disappointment with Heath's performance. . . .

Diary – Sunday 20 March – 21 Hyde Park Square, W.2

. . . Mark looked in after tea. He has been covering the whole country uncovered by Jo poor darling but seems to have weathered it well. He thinks we are not doing too badly. He had been to Barnstaple to speak for Jeremy – who must be as safe as a church. . . .

He showed me a terrible bit in the *Sunday Times* (a report – not article) saying 6 Tory Members had come out for restoring the Death Penalty, others for flogging. There was a nauseating hob-nob reported between Julian Amery & Iain Macleod – who had come to the conclusion that their views didn't differ much on Rhodesia. In his speech Iain Macleod said he wondered how Wilson had the impertinence to speak as he did to Ian Smith 'who was a fighter pilot in the last war'. As Mark says – the same might have been said of Goering. Have since heard that Selwyn Lloyd has come out for flogging! What a crowd!

Diary – Thursday 31 March – 21 Hyde Park Square, W.2

A very quiet day – I don't know why? Everyone cannot have been voting. Stayed in bed all day till ¼ to 9. Then Adam & I & a charming young woman friend of his (Chilean) called Lucia Santa Cruz went off to Ray & Elena's to hear the results. Poor darling Elena went early to bed – not feeling well. The rest of us stayed up till nearly 2. 'Labour gain' succeeded Labour gain. There was not one Conservative gain. Eric Lubbock is in thank Heaven – tho' his majority is down to a thousand odd. An astonishing fall in majority was Jeremy's. He has gone steadily up & was over 5000 last time. It is now about 1500. . . .[1]

Diary – Wednesday 6 April – 21 Hyde Park Square, W.2

Mr Vincent came at 1.15. Mark at 6 – interrupted by Goldman – who is going to Cannes for a week's holiday to-morrow. I had a 'long-term' talk

[1] Jeremy Thorpe's majority at Devon North was cut from 5,136 in 1964 to 1,166 in 1966; it fell further in 1970 to 369. Labour secured a comfortable majority at the polls with 363 seats against 253 Conservative and 12 Liberal.

with him of rather a depressing nature.... If one drew a graph between last April & this it wld contain many zig-zags but a steadily downward trend. I quoted to him the interchange in Rosmersholm I always remember (I saw it first in German – an excellent translation) where Rosmer meets a man one dark & gusty evening on a road & asks him 'Wo gehen sie so spät?' & he replies 'Berg ab.'[1] (So like Ibsen!) I felt that I was going steadily 'Berg ab'. He was as ever very sweet & tried to be comforting – not denying my facts – but saying 'I must think of something. I will think of something'....

Diary – Thursday 21 April – 21 Hyde Park Square, W.2

Opening of Parliament. Had very early breakfast (for me). Started 9.30 with Burnside[2] for the House of Lords – collected my robe in the Library & went in to the Chamber to find a seat soon after 10. It was full of wives in their tiaras.... It was beautifully done as ever – but when (the faithful Commons having been summoned) the Queen began her speech not one word was audible either to me or to Gladwyn.[3] I glanced at the ceiling & I saw that all the microphones hanging from the ceiling had been removed – presumably lest they shld clash with the T.V. transmission. Bobbety Salisbury came up to me when it was over & said 'Have I suddenly gone stone deaf? I didn't hear a word of the Queen's Speech.' I told him that we none of us heard it. It is an ironical result of transmission by T.V. that everyone with a 'set' heard the Queen's Speech except for the faithful Lords & Commons to whom it was addressed....

Diary – Wednesday 22 June – 21 Hyde Park Square, W.2

Felt rather tired & gave a miss to Agriculture in the H. of L. Richard Ollard[4] came to tea & was as usual delightful. We drove on together to the Collins Cocktail Party where I found Hatchie & was led straight to his chair & sat beside him.... Later Kenneth Harris (*Observer*) came up & told me that dear old Attlee constantly said to him – 'Do tell her to hurry up with her

[1] From act IV of *Rosmersholm* (1886) – Rosmer: 'Where are you going so late?' Brendel: 'Downhill.'

[2] One of Violet's regular taxi drivers.

[3] Gladwyn Jebb, the former diplomat who in 1960 became 1st Baron Gladwyn, taking the Liberal whip.

[4] Richard Laurence Ollard (b. 1923), author and editor; senior editor, Collins publishers, 1960–83.

2nd Volume. I can't live forever.' He also told me that he was going to ask me to take part in a 40-minute discussion programme (T.V.) about 'the past'. I asked 'What past? Political – social – personal?' He said 'All 3.' I said I shld welcome it – until I discovered that it was to take place between 4 women. Why women? Men shared the past with women in equal measure. I hated 'women's' programmes. He was slightly dashed but said he wld communicate with me later about it. . . .[1]

Diary – Thursday 22 September – 21 Hyde Park Square, W.2

Went to Miss Joseph with patterns of velvet & straight on from her to the Hospital to see Law. . . .[2] A charming young female Dr got up from a table where she was writing & took me into her room. She told me that Law's temp was 101. She had had anti-biotics, but cld she fight this infection, which had congested part of one lung, with her meagre reserves of strength? . . . She was still breathing quickly & her eyes were closed. I took her hand & tried vainly to get through to her. . . . I left her with an aching heart – only thankful that she was not suffering. That night when I was sitting in the drawing-room the telephone rang & the Sister told me she had 'passed peacefully away' at 11 o'clock. It was the end – of a life of selfless & devoted help & service to me & mine. For the last 44 years she has given herself to us – to me. Was I worthy of it? What did we give her in return? Like all gifts it is unrepayable. Like all great losses I cannot realise it to the full as yet.

Diary – Friday 23 September – 21 Hyde Park Square, W.2

Strange stunned night & all day to-day I have been expecting to see dear Law run into the room & ask 'Can I do anything for you?' She was a constant presence in every hour of my life. Fred came in to see me – very composed & brave. The funeral date cannot be fixed yet. . . .[3]

[1] From this discussion emanated the fifty-minute television interview *As I Remember*, recorded and broadcast on BBC1 the following year as an eightieth-birthday tribute; see below, 315.

[2] Rose Law, Violet's long-serving maid, had been admitted to the Middlesex Hospital on the previous Sunday, seriously ill with a chest complaint.

[3] 'Fred' cannot be identified. Rose Law's funeral took place at Willesden cemetery the following Wednesday. Violet had committed herself to complicated travel plans for a stay in Orkney and did not attend.

Diary – Tuesday 20 December – 21 Hyde Park Square, W.2

. . . Frank Byers dropped me at Lib. H.Q. Xmas Party, where I was alas only able to spend a very short time before going home to rest a little & dress for Laura's dance at Kew – given for Toad & Laura Grenfell jointly – a 'not yet out' party. Ray & Elena angelically picked me up & we got there by 11. In the doorway was dear Johnny, with a beatle hair-cut all over his forehead & neck. . . . Cressida warned me not to go upstairs where they were dancing – as one cldn't hear one another speak – so I sat in the drawing-room on a sofa & had nice talks with Florrie St Just[1] & some very sweet (& normal looking) 'young'. . . .

All wld have been well had not darling Laura (who was as aghast as I was by the fancy hair-dress of many of her guests) said to me – 'I think you ought to have just one peep upstairs & see them in action. It is such an extraordinary sight.' So up I went with June & never have I seen such a sight or experienced such acute physical agony. The noise of the percussion band, helped out by an amplifier, was so deafening that it nearly burst one's eardrums – even though I rammed a finger in each. The 'music' never stopped & never changed. The dancers shook their bodies & swung their arms a little – yards apart. . . . When I reeled downstairs again I had lost my balance & cld hardly stand!

Diary – Tuesday 17 January 1967 – 21 Hyde Park Square, W.2

H. of L. met again. Dull debate on Land Commission – mercifully interrupted by T.V. Committee where I saw Hugh Reay.[2] When I was sitting afterwards at one of the writing tables in the library a new batch of *Evening Standards* was dumped on the table beside me with large splashed headline 'Jo Grimond to resign?' I knew of course that Jo had hinted at this possibility in a Committee of 22 just before the last Election. . . . But I had heard no word to prepare me for this. I am quite ready to believe it though – as I can well understand his feeling stale & frustrated after 10 years gruelling work punctuated by so many false dawns. . . .

It is the end of a chapter & a bad blow for the Party. There is no one even approaching his stature to succeed him. If only the second election (in '66) had not given Labour its present large majority he might have realised his dream of realignment of the Left. 'Being right' about major issues has availed Libs. so little. . . .

[1]Florence St Just (1888–1971), the widow of Edward Grenfell, 1st Baron St Just.

[2]Hugh William Mackay (b. 1937), 14th Baron Reay.

Diary – Wednesday 18 January – 21 Hyde Park Square, W.2

... Went to H. of L. where the election of a new leader was already en train in the Whips' Room. Liberals in the country naturally resent the matter being settled with such haste over their heads & without any consultation with any of their 'bodies' & organizations. I understand their feeling this – but who to consult, & how, wld have presented insuperable difficulties & I think Jo is right in wanting to get it over in a hurry. It was over sooner than one cld have guessed. Between 3 & 3.30 Donald Wade – who had been counting the votes – appeared on the Bench & told me that Jeremy had got it. He wld have been my choice. He has got vitality & colour & passionate zest – & has the right slant in approaching issues. His judgement might well go wrong & he is not a thinker in depth – but he is so devoted to Jo that he will I'm sure always seek & take his advice. The other candidates were Emlyn Hooson[1] & Eric Lubbock. They got 3 votes each & Jeremy 6 on the first count....

Diary – Thursday 26 January – 21 Hyde Park Square, W.2

Spent a quiet day before my Israeli dinner, at which I am the Guest of Honour & give (i.e. 'present'!) certificates to those Founder Members who have contributed to W.S.C.'s memorial – a Chair of International Relations at the new University of Bar-Ilan....[2] I sat between the Chairman & the Ambassador. Long 'intoned' Jewish grace for which many put on their hats (we take ours off as a sign of respect). Then a long dinner followed by a mort of speeches – starting off with that of an M.P., Weitzman,[3] before he returned to the H. of C. I was amazed by the emphasis on Jewish Nationalism – a note struck again & again in the speeches. Had they been non-Jewish English speakers I shld have described them as extreme Jingoes. My turn finally came & I spoke for about 10 minutes stressing Internationalism (that after all was the object of the dinner...). To my amazement I received what is called 'a standing ovation' from the whole company.... I was finally sent home in a swift & sumptuous car – the drive along the Embankment was lovely – all the lights of London lying in the Thames. Dog-tired.

[1]Hugh Emlyn Hooson (b. 1925), cr. life peer, 1979; QC, 1960; MP (Lib.) Montgomery, 1962–79.

[2]Violet was a member of the committee supporting the establishment of the chair; other members included Clement Attlee, Anthony Eden, Jo Grimond, Edward Heath and Harold Wilson. The university was at Ramat Gan in Israel.

[3]David Weitzman (1898–1987), QC, 1951; MP (Lab.) Stoke Newington, 1945–50; Hackney North and Stoke Newington, 1950–79.

Diary – Tuesday 14 February – 21 Hyde Park Square, W.2

The first of 4 days during which I shall broadcast from 2–3 hours every afternoon. . . . I had luncheon in bed – dressed – make-up woman Miss Exelby at 2.15 – who dis-improved my appearance with yellowish powder – whitened me under the eyes (the usual T.V. make-up – they won't let one's face be white). . . . I then went into the drawing-room & found the infernal machines rigged up & in full blaze – manned by their attendant crews. K. Harris opposite me. . . . He cldn't have been easier & more sympathetic. I think we covered about 6 or 7 questions in between 2 to 3 hours. Drinks followed. They were to return at 2.30 to-morrow (make-up 2.15). . . .

Diary – Wednesday 15 February – 21 Hyde Park Square, W.2

Day exactly ditto. Cleared the 2nd lap. K. Harris kept up my morale by constant praise & encouragement. Some deviations made by him from prescribed route. He had asked me in advance whether I minded his asking me whether I had been in love with Winston. I said 'Not at all.' I shld reply – quite truthfully – that I had not been 'in love' – though I cld. not have loved him more – & that our relationship was an intimacy of minds – & words – & an emotional one. When I mentioned this to Mark he advised me to cut it out from the broadcast version – as all journalists & commentators wld head-line it. I told Harris this. He disagreed but said that I was of course free to cut anything out when I read the script.[1] Fell into bed & concentrated on the next day's route – with ebbing powers!

Diary – Thursday 16 February – 21 Hyde Park Square, W.2

3rd day. Very exhausted & when Goldman came to see me was sick from sheer fatigue! Disgusted with myself – for this lapse – but he took it quite naturally – & diagnosed it as sheer fatigue – which is what it was.

Diary – Friday 17 February – 21 Hyde Park Square, W.2

Last day! . . . The last question was a demand to compare past with present – politically – an immense question. There was so much to say – too much. I had to be rigidly selective. At the end I compared technological advance –

[1] This was later a point of dispute between Kenneth Harris and Mark Bonham Carter, who on his mother's behalf insisted that the question should be cut.

'the march of science' – with the failure of 'civilization' (in its human sense) to keep pace with it – & suddenly thought of the 'Bengal Rain' story – about the Indian bearers who laid down their burdens & said they must wait until their souls caught up with their bodies. 'I sometimes wonder whether we ought not to do the same.' At this K.H. cut off. It was a 'curtain-line' – whether the best I cld have chosen I cannot say. Was sick again! But it was over. Now I must await the script in fear & trembling for 3 weeks! We all had champagne in the dining-room to celebrate the end of the Marathon.

Diary – Monday 13 March – 21 Hyde Park Square, W.2

. . . I rang Humphrey Brooke[1] this morning. I had received an invitation to the Academy dinner – to which in its long history no women have ever been invited. I naturally wrote accepting. Now I get a letter from the President asking me to speak! Horror! I can't plead health as I had accepted the dinner. I explained to Humphrey my dilemma. He said: 'Well they asked you because they knew you were the best woman speaker. You will only have to speak for 4 or 5 minutes – & you will propose the health of the Royal Academy.' He promised to send me some gen. I shall receive it to-morrow – & then probably, reluctantly but inevitably, accept.

Diary – Thursday 13 April – 21 Hyde Park Square, W.2

Times photographer arrived ¼ of an hour late having lost his way – as he had not bothered to look at my address! I asked how he even got here? 'By looking at the telephone book.' 'Don't you usually do that before starting?' Apparently he didn't. Meeting of Lib. Peers. Heard Willy Brandt in Grand Committee. Tiny audience. W.B. terribly long-winded in answering questions – rambling – diffuse. All his crispness gone.

Adam & I dined in & at 9.15 Elena, Ray & Puff turned up – & we all watched my broadcast. They were all angelic about it – & of course I felt uncomfortably 'responsible' – & regretted the cuts – but I was on the whole relieved.[2]

[1] (Thomas) Humphrey Brooke (1914–88), secretary of the Royal Academy of Arts, 1952–68.

[2] *As I Remember* elicited what Violet later described as her 'favourite fan letter', from one Commander Henry Burrows, who wrote simply: 'It was the perfect T.V. broadcast – lovely appearance, entrancing voice and fascinating subject. Nothing but sport has held me before' (HB to VBC, 14 April 1967).

Diary – Friday 14 April – 21 Hyde Park Square, W.2

The deluge! Tel. calls began last night. To-day a spate of letters – telegrams – greetings cards – flowers pouring in. . . .

Diary – Eightieth birthday, Saturday 15 April 1967 – 21 Hyde Park Square, W.2

Went to Elena & Ray's & sat in their garden in the sun. He is going to Australia for 3 weeks to-morrow. The 2nd time in 3 months! Elena is afraid he is going to be 'Our man in Australia' for Warburgs – a grisly fate. The flood of flowers – letters & telegrams continues. I shld be absolutely helpless to cope with the flowers were it not for Adam. They are quite lovely but enormous. Maud Russell sent me a huge & lovely white sheaf – all lilies & white lilac. We are running out of vases.

Diary – Wednesday 26 April – 21 Hyde Park Square, W.2

Vincent came & washed my hair. Ursula[1] came at 6 & helped me to dress. . . . We had a terrible struggle with my Orders. The D.B.E. star is almost impossible to fix on a bust. I had to sacrifice my Star (H. of C.) & my Defence Medal. Mrs Berryman fetched me. I went up in a lift & there I was in the vast rooms papered with pictures – & kind Humphrey took me to a seat in one of them & I talked to John Sparrow & Kenneth Clark & other 'compatibles' while a band played – not too loud – & then we went in to dinner. I sat at a long high table – with minor tables radiating from it. Every Ambassador was there & several Dukes & other swells – & espied dear Martin Charteris[2] at one of the 'radiating' tables quite near to me & caught his reassuring eye. I sat between the President & Lord Goodman![3] – a gorilla of ugliness! (How Ann [Fleming] cld think of him – even as a 4th – husband!) The President modest & charming. Harold Wilson beyond him. . . .

I 'chatted' quite happily with Goodman whom I liked, but he did not set my heather on fire. At the end of a delicious dinner (uneaten by me),

[1] Ursula Businger, Violet's Swiss maid.

[2] Martin Michael Charteris (b. 1913), cr. life peer, 1978; assistant private secretary to the queen, 1952–72; private secretary, 1972–7.

[3] Arnold Abraham Goodman (1913–95), cr. life peer, 1965; personal solicitor to, and close confidant of, Harold Wilson; chairman of the Arts Council of Great Britain, 1965–72; later master of University College, Oxford, 1976–86.

on which even the cheese was dated on the menu – the business of the evening began. The President proposed 'Her M.'s Ministers' & Wilson replied in a long prepared brief – which I expect was handed to him that morning on his return from Bonn, where he had gone to Adenauer's funeral & (I expect) had put in a little business with de Gaulle. Next Ld Goodman replied for 'The Guests' – quite good – ample notes but not entirely read. High praise for Jennie Lee[1] who has been his Pygmalion. According to Kenneth Clark, Goodman's magnum opus at the Arts Council has been the creation of Jennie Lee. (She was there dressed in gold lamé from head to foot – shades of Aneurin Bevan!)[2]

Then my turn came to propose the R.A. of Arts.... My speech 'went' amazingly well. I did not have to glance at a note – it was audible because spoken to the audience – whom I found surprisingly responsive. (They had seemed rather dead before.) It was a speech I enjoyed delivering & everyone was most generous about it – the President in his following speech describing it as a 'work of art'. (It was not that!) Wilson was very congratulatory. I asked him about Common Market prospects & he was most sanguine – saying he had got the Cabinet solid '& you know what that means'....[3]

Diary – Tuesday 16 May – 21 Hyde Park Square, W.2

Extraordinarily nice letter from one Sir Charles Ponsonby who was at Balliol with Raymond & B. & knew them both well, also Oc & Cys. It was elicited by my broadcast, but mostly about my book. It ended with a marvellous story about W. arriving as a fugitive at Lourenco Marques [in 1899], where the British Consul gave him a bath & dinner & lent him a suit.[4] When they were going to bed W. asked for his clothes & was told by the Consul that he had burnt them as they were absolutely filthy. 'What

[1]Janet ('Jennie') Lee (1904–88), cr. life peer, 1970; MP (Lab.) North Lanark, 1929–31; Cannock, 1945–70; minister of state, 1967–70, 'in effect, Britain's first "minister for the arts"' (*DNB*).

[2]Jennie Lee and Aneurin Bevan were married in 1934 (he died 1960) and Violet appears to be comparing the inappropriateness of their dress for formal occasions; see above, p. 47.

[3]On 2 May Harold Wilson announced the government's intention of renewing its application to join the EEC. The proposal was supported by the leaders of all three main parties in the Commons debate a week later, where the vote was 488 to 62 in favour of the application.

[4]While reporting on the South African war in November 1899 Churchill was captured and held prisoner by Boer fighters. He later made a daring escape and on 21 December arrived at the British consulate in Portuguese Lourenço Marques, 'black as a sweep' from the coal dust at the bottom of the goods train in which he had hidden to cross the border (Gilbert, *Churchill*, 120).

a pity' said W. 'I wanted them for Madame Tussaud's!' It bears the stamp of absolute authenticity....

Diary – Monday 17 July – 21 Hyde Park Square, W.2

Went to H. of L. Abortion alas! comes on on Wed. when I am seeing Sir Philip Magnus[1] – at 6. Met Frank (Longford) who is passionately against it & engaged me in argument about it in the presence of Silkin.[2] Appalled at David Steel producing a foetus (half an inch long) in the H. of C.![3] 'What wld your Father have felt?' I said he wld have been deeply interested. I have never seen Frank so near real anger!... Burning heat – must go to bed & open my window – burglars or otherwise.

Diary – Wednesday 19 July – 21 Hyde Park Square, W.2

Abortion Bill debate. Opened by Ld Silkin.... Then (a body blow) my dear Archbishop.[4] He began by saying that the present laws of Abortion were shockingly bad – & urgently needed reform. But there were certain features of the present Bill he cld not support & he therefore felt obliged to abstain on the Second Reading. I felt despair because his leadership in this issue is so vital – & it might be followed by the whole Episcopal bench. Also his attitude was so illogical. What were the Committee & Report Stage for except to amend?

Frank Byers shared my feelings & sent me out to reason with him. By luck I found Beloe – his secretary – just outside the Prince's Chamber &

[1]Sir Philip Magnus(-Allcroft) (1906–88), 2nd Bt; writer; a revised edition of his biography *Kitchener – Portrait of an Imperialist*, was published the following year.

[2]Lewis Silkin (1889–1972), cr. Baron, 1950; MP (Lab.) Peckham, Camberwell, 1936–50; deputy leader of opposition, House of Lords, 1955–64. The 1967 abortion bill, sponsored by David Steel, sought to clarify the law regarding the medical termination of pregnancy; uncertainty about the legality of abortion bill drove many women to 'backstreet' abortion clinics, exposing them to health risks and financial exploitation.

[3]Steel produced the seven week-old embryo when moving the third reading of the Medical Termination of Pregnancy (Abortion) bill, after an all-night sitting of the Commons 13–14 July. He used it to emphasize the point that the bill allowed for abortion only at an early stage in pregnancy, before the embryo could be said to have a human form: 'This is what we are weighing against the life and welfare of the mother and family' (*Hansard* vol. 750, col. 1347).

[4]Arthur Michael Ramsey (1904–88), cr. life peer, 1974; archbishop of York, 1956–61; archbishop of Canterbury, 1961–74; as a young man, before deciding on holy orders, Ramsey had been an adherent to the Liberal Party and was adopted prospective candidate for Cambridgeshire.

he admitted me to his 'closet' – where I pled with him – pointing out that he wanted reform of the present laws – but wasn't satisfied with every clause for the reforming Bill as it stood. If however the Bill was killed on 2nd Reading there wld. be nothing left to reform or to amend. He replied soothingly (and confidently) 'But it will go through.' I said – 'Not if you lead people to abstain by your example.' What I longed to say to him was: 'Is it right to expect – & indeed to desire – other people to do for you what you will not sully your own hands (if that is how you see it) by doing for yourself.'[1]

However to my amazement & relief when the division was called it did go through – overwhelmingly! It had been a thinnish House throughout & the majority of the speakers had either been fierce indictments from the R.C. lobby (who turned out & spoke up in force) or critical & half-hearted support. The most moving speech in favour was from Lord Soper. . . .[2]

Of the R.C.'s Frank Longford made the most violent & the worst speech I thought. He usually lacks indignation to a fault – but this Bill really inflamed him & he dragged in Euthanasia & all sorts of irrelevancies – picturing moribund peers being carried in to the H. of L. & condemned to death – a far cry from the foetus! . . .

Diary – Tuesday 17 October – 21 Hyde Park Square, W.2

. . . On the news: 'There is anxiety about General de Gaulle's health. After he returned from Poland he developed arterio-sclerosis.' Adam & I cldn't repress a whoop of joy – of which I suppose I ought to feel ashamed – but hope is stronger. (What must the Govt be feeling!) Strikes are appalling – N.U.R. coming out on Thursday. . . . 100 ships are standing idle at Liverpool with rotting cargoes & Heaven knows what losses to our exports.

'The right to live dangerously'
A visit to Israel, 29 October-5 November 1967

In September 1967 Violet was invited by the Israeli government to attend a celebration of the fiftieth anniversary of the Balfour Declaration – regarded as the foundation stone of the Jewish state. Her health was then poor and before accepting she sought the approval of Dr Goldman. He, though, was 'crushingly negative',

[1] According to Violet's obituarist in the *Daily Express* (20 February 1969) she assailed Ramsey with the words: 'Michael, I never thought of you as a moral coward.'

[2] Rev. Donald Oliver Soper (1903–98), cr. life peer, 1965; methodist minister; superintendent of the West London Mission, Kingsway Hall, 1936–78; a regular speaker at 'Speaker's Corner' and a champion of liberal causes.

despite her obvious desire to go: 'For the first time I felt angry & estranged from him. He did not understand what it meant to me. I feel that at my age I have the right to "live dangerously".' Months earlier Israel had won a dramatic victory over the combined forces of Egypt, Syria and Jordan in the 'Six Day War'. It was a time, Violet felt, in which there was a special obligation to accept the invitation that had been extended. As she explained to Dr Goldman: 'I feel that this is a moment when all Israel's friends shld 'stand up & be counted" ' – & I am one of them.' Faced with such determination he eventually relented and she was allowed to travel, leaving London on 29 October.

Diary – Saturday 28 October – 21 Hyde Park Square, W.2

'Last day' – crowded with 'last things' & haunted by fears of forgetting something essential. . . . Miss Lock & I packed all the afternoon – or rather she packed & I crossed things off a list. I worked on a hypothetical speech with which I felt I ought to provide myself – wrote one or two last letters. Adam also stayed in & worked all day. . . . Mr Siven calls for me at 12 o'clock – & I hope (oh how I hope!) that I shall sleep in Jerusalem to-morrow night![1]

Diary – Monday 30 October – Jerusalem

Was called with breakfast by a most interesting waiter. He had fought for us in the desert war but was disabled by a wound which prevented him from being called up here. He was full of praise of Israel. 'So calm in the war – & so patriotic. No demonstrations – just everyone to his job. The children delivered part of the post. It was amazing how smoothly everything worked tho' everyone was called up. Very low casualties for such a decisive war – about 1000 in all. They're a splendid people.' I talked to my chamber-maid – a Pole. Her family had suffered untold miseries at the hands of Russians & Germans. She had somehow found her way here & intended to stay. 'Everyone is so free. I am so happy here. It is a new life.'

Packed & left with Mrs Goitien who has been attached to me as my escort – a hyper-efficient woman & very nice & kind. The drive to Jerusalem was so beautiful that I forgave last night's disappointment. We drove

[1] In fact Violet was disappointed in this wish, her travel plans going awry. She stayed instead in a hotel in Tel-Aviv on her first night, travelling to Jerusalem the next day.

through wonderful mountains along roads edged with eucalyptus trees – thro' orange groves – Cypresses & vines in terraces – very like Italy. I felt a deep emotion when Jerusalem came in to sight....

Diary – Wednesday 1 November – Jerusalem

A very strenuous day starting by a meeting of the 'Parliamentarians' with Mr Eshkol[1] the P.M. at his office. We all assembled there – Sir Barnett Janner[2] (Chairman) sat on his left & Mr Short[3] (the Govt's representative – Postmaster General) on his [Janner's] left. Pardoe[4] next to Janner & I next to Pardoe. Eshkol opened with a statement – then some questions were asked. Nothing very new or illuminating transpired until the very end. I was anxious to get on to Refugees but they were not touched upon until John Pardoe asked a question about them – received an unenlightening answer & I followed up with another. The 'illuminating' & (to me) 'give-away' sentence then came from Eshkol 'All wars result in an exchange of populations.' This made it clear to me (& Pardoe agreed with my interpretation when I checked with him later) that in fact the Israeli Govt did not desire a return of the Refugees who had fled to the East Bank in this war back to the West Bank. Admittedly they wld constitute an economic & political problem to the Israeli Govt. Hence I conclude that there may be some 'bureaucratic' & mechanical 'trip-wires' put in their way. We went straight on to the Knesset – a 'functional' but not ugly building in a beautiful position on the top of a hill....

I was [later] fetched by Ore[5] who dismayed me with the news that my programme for the afternoon (which was to have been a quiet one – a rest & possibly a quiet drive in the early afternoon) had been changed. Mrs Coney (my old acquaintance) was to take me to Ramalla to see a re-training Institute for 600 Refugee girls. This I did not want to see – interesting as it may be. I want to see a camp & talk to random Refugees – not to inspect an interesting but rare experiment. I reasoned – with some

[1] Levi Eshkol (1895–1969), Ukranian-born prime minister of Israel, 1963–9; minister of defence during the 'Six-Day War' of 1967.

[2] Sir Barnett Janner (1892–1982), Kt, 1961; cr. life peer, 1970; MP (Lib.) Whitechapel and St George's, Stepney, 1931–5; joined Labour Party, 1936; MP (Lab.) West Leics., 1945–50; North West Leics., 1950–70; president of the Board of Deputies of British Jews, 1955–64.

[3] Edward Watson Short (b. 1912), cr. life peer, 1977; MP (Lab.) Newcastle-upon-Tyne Central, 1951–76; postmaster general, 1966–8; later deputy Labour leader, 1972–6.

[4] John Wentworth Pardoe (b. 1934), MP (Lib.) Cornwall North, 1966–79; later company director and chairman.

[5] An unidentified female companion, perhaps working for the Israeli government or else attached to the British embassy, and delegated to accompany Violet during her visit.

heat – with Mrs Coney about this. However – the die was cast – & there was nothing I cld do about it. In fact the afternoon proved a most useful one – tho' quite different from anything I had expected. I talked for some 2½ hours with the Arabic Head Mistress of the Institute, with 3 of her younger assistants sitting by & occasionally intervening – & thus got a far better understanding of an Arab point of view from a highly intelligent, educated & civilized individual.

She is on terms of close friendship with Mrs Coney – whose husband is head of the Dept. dealing with Refugees. It was on his authority that the Institute (financed by U.N.R.R.A.) has been kept going – & that many (tho' not all) the girls have been allowed to return to it. The Head Mistress is a 1948 Refugee herself so she has seen the tragedy of displacement happen twice in her life. (She herself was dispossessed of her home.) We asked her first how far in her view the Jews had tried to stop the migration to the East Bank. She said (without accusing them of terrorism) that she felt the Jews had clearly welcomed the migration & had certainly done nothing to stop it. To this Mrs Coney replied that processions of trucks laden with Refugees were going East & that the Jews did try to stop them. She gave one concrete instance.... The school-mistress said 'There had been intimidation. Houses were searched after midnight – all the men being first turned out of them. Their inmates were naturally terrified.... She gave instances of intimidation. Stones thrown at windows. Busses on the way to Jericho stopped by Israeli soldiers & their passengers stripped & searched in sheds – then turned naked into the street to dress again. (This at check points run by the Army. Mrs C. afterwards suggested to me that it might have been done after there had been sniping.)... We had a final talk about the inculcation of hatred in very young Arab children (6 year olds). The Head Mistress said 'Ah. I know the example you are going to give.' (I had already heard it & wondered if it was a chestnut.) It was mental arithmetic taught as follows: 'Take 6 Jews. Kill 4 of them – how many are left to kill?' Mrs Coney said however that she herself has seen this & kindred lessons with her own eyes.

We all bid a friendly goodbye to each other. The Israeli chauffeur told Mrs Goitien afterwards however that while he had been waiting outside for us (some 2 hours) the girls of the school had showered insults upon him such as he had never before received in his life. He gave me one instance – 'What you & your kind need is another Hitler.' It is appalling that hatred shld be fanned in the young to such a pitch. We got home just in time for me to dress for the Minister of Posts dinner – a vast affair in a public hall....

Diary – Thursday 2 November – Israel

'Der Tag' – 50th Anniversary of Balfour Declaration. I started with Ore on the long drive to Rehovot – in burning heat & (fortunately) put on my black & white silk dress which 'does' for day or evening occasions. A fleet of cars was pressing along the dusty road between the rocks – & when we arrived the sun disappeared behind the clouds & it looked as tho' rain might fall. It mercifully didn't – for the ceremony was out of doors. . . .

I was in the second row. There was a défilé on to the platform – the Weizmann Institute Professors in their robes – the Chief Rabbi, The President, the politicians. . . . Many speeches were then made – mostly in English. I thought Ld Rothschild's (Victor)[1] one of the best. The Orchestra played the *Hallelujah Chorus* & later the *Fire Music* – & a very good professional singer (male) sang. The whole thing was beautifully staged & obviously deeply felt. We didn't get away (after an inevitable longish wait for cars) till about 6.30. The dinner at the Knesset was at 8 so I didn't attempt to change my dress – but just a quick wash & brush-up. . . .

The names of Balfour & Weizmann must have been mentioned several hundred times to-day. It is so strange that A.J.B. – who has left no mark on the memory of his own fellow countrymen (other than those who are old enough to have known him & are still alive, like myself – & on these not as a great statesman, but rather as a charming, distinguished & many-sided man) shld here be revered as a Saviour & the Founder of the State of Israel. It is true that it was the one great constructive achievement of his life – brought about by the fateful impact of Weizmann's personality.

Diary – Saturday 4 November – Israel

My last day – alas! Ore & I made our last (& successful) attempt on the Dome of the Rock. . . . We got back to the Hôtel. I 'tidied' in time to be fetched by Lord Samuel[2] to have luncheon with him. This I enjoyed enormously. He & his wife live in a smallish house in a quiet street – simple & very civilized. They are both quite delightful. . . .

There were only 5 of us at luncheon – & we had 'general conversation' all the time. There was not one dull moment. My fellow-guests were their

[1] (Nathaniel Mayer) Victor Rothschild (1910–90), 3rd Baron; Cambridge zoologist and public servant; honorary fellow, Weizmann Institute of Science, Rehovot, 1962.

[2] Edwin Herbert Samuel (1898–1978), 2nd Viscount (s. 1963); married, 1920, Hadassah Goor; colonial service, retired; senior lecturer in British Institutions, Hebrew University, Jerusalem, 1954–69.

very clever daughter-in-law Mrs David Samuel[1] – who is a teacher (or Professor?) at the Weizmann Institute at Rehovot & a fascinating Professor of Archaeology called Benjamin Masser[?] at the Hebrew University Jerusalem. We talked about the English attitude to Israel in her present crisis. The daughter-in-law, who has been in England visiting her husband, thinks there is a strong Anti-Semitic element in England. I tried to convince her that this is not the case.[2]

... I said that R.C.s had a strange culte for the Arabs – which might give an impression of Anti-Semitism. I did not know its origin. Samuel said that most Arab converts to Xtianity were R.C.s. I told them about my Father's hostility to R.C.-ism & his sorrow at Katharine & (above all) her children's conversion & Samuel said – truly I think – that converts are usually activated by stress of some kind. (They were amused by my accusation to my father that he had only 2 prejudices in life – R.C.-ism & eating rabbit! Masser thought I had said eating Rabbis!) They all hate the *M.G.* – & Mrs David made the right criticism of their perversity – 'If we had lost the war they wld have been on our side.' They also regard the *Observer* as an enemy paper. I loved the daughter-in-law's ardour – & said to her 'You are like me – a natural Protestant.' She said this was just what she was & asked me where I had made my 'protests'. I said 'Everywhere from "social" & personal life to the plinth of Nelson's column in Trafalgar Square'....

Samuel drove me back to the Hôtel & we started off on our last Refugee expedition to a place called Kalandia[3] recommended by Mr Coney. It was in a way the most repaying of all. I did see families of real 'refugees' – who had been driven by the war from their homes 35 kilometres off & had walked the whole way with their small children. One very young looking mother had a baby in arms & several 'toddlers' with sweet faces & large brown eyes – very beautiful & expressive....

I was wrung by their plight & asked the Head of the Camp – a nice Arab – to tell the young mother with the baby how deeply I sympathised with her – & how beautiful I thought her children were. She very touchingly took my hand & kissed it – then placed it on her forehead. I felt helpless in the face of human tragedy. Ore was quite steely (& rather bored I thought!) She told me constantly – 'They always live like that.' 'Yes – but in their own homes & by their own land which they love – & where their husbands have an occupation – & can earn their living.' No two peoples cld have less mutual understanding or compatibility than the Arabs & the Jews. I longed sometimes to quote to the Israelis what Gilbert Murray said

[1]Rinna *née* Grossman, second wife of Professor (later Lord) David Samuel, scientist; they married in 1960.

[2]Violet later added, 'The Belloc-Chesterton days are over.'

[3]A refugee camp on the West Bank, near the town of Ramallah.

to me about the Greeks: 'They wanted to understand their enemies as well as to defeat them.' But I 'understand' how difficult it is to do so in this particular case....

Diary – Sunday 5 November – 21 Hyde Park Square, W.2

Was called at 6 on the ticket – packed last things – met Ore in the hall & we embarked in our car for the long drive to Tel-Aviv. I refused to sit in my usual place in front by the chauffeur feeling that I shld spend these last hours with Ore on the back seat (she had always made me sit in front before – comfier, better view – easier to get in & out etc.). I little thought how much I shld owe to this change of position.

We were chattering away when I suddenly felt an almighty shock which flung me – in a tangle of twisted limbs – on to the floor of the car. I was conscious of acute pain in my left ankle & foot which was twisted somehow under me & which I cld not move. Ore tho' shaken & bruised remained on the seat. The chauffeur got out & between them they extricated my ankle & raised me to the seat again. What had happened was that a car in front of us had suddenly pulled up – so suddenly that our driver had to brake violently to avoid a crash. Had I been in front I must have been shot thro' the glass. (There were of course no passengers' seat belts.) We drove on & apart from acute pain in my ankle I felt no 'shock' – only some worry as to how I shld manage the journey as my foot felt quite powerless....

At London Air-Port I was carried like a baby off the plane by one of the crew – & there was dear Mrs Siven to meet me with a charming male colleague Mr Barton who carried me from the wheel-chair into the car – thence into my own house along the passage & laid me on my bed! The Israelis' kindness to their friends knows no bounds....

Dr Goldman came in to see me about 9.30 – examined my ankle, said he wld. arrange for X Rays & bring an orthopaedic surgeon in the evening. He was, I think, a little surprised to find me so well in myself & said 'There I was worrying about your heart & you return with a broken ankle!'....

Diary – Monday 6 November – 21 Hyde Park Square, W.2

X-Rays taken. Heard that Puff, who returned from Rome on Friday, was very unwell with pains inside – sick on Sat. morning....[1] Dr Russell stressed

[1] Puff had been in Rome preparing for the filming of *The Shoes of the Fisherman*, from the bestseller by Morris West, with Laurence Olivier and Anthony Quinn. He was unable to continue with the project after being diagnosed with cancer on his return to London, and direction of the film was taken over by Michael Anderson.

to me that he was very seriously ill. I asked 'dangerously'? 'No – but very seriously' – poor darling. He seemed so well & happy about his film before he went to Rome. Found a flood of work & Committee engagements I shall be unable alas! to fulfil. . . .

Diary – Tuesday 7 November – 21 Hyde Park Square, W.2

Rang up for news of Puff & to my amazement they offered to put me through to him! I refused, appalled, but the Sister said he had already had several calls – so I spoke to him. He was 'on top of the world' – said he was feeling perfectly well – the relief was enormous. He had no pain or discomfort except being a little thirsty & not allowed to drink. Later he wld like grapes but wld not yet be allowed to eat them. I was amazed & infinitely relieved. . . .

Diary – Friday 16 November – 21 Hyde Park Square, W.2

Did not attempt the H. of L. today to attend Peers Meeting as transport is so complicated & the 'Business of the House' was not compulsive. . . . Terrific economic crisis coming suddenly to a head. We are catastrophically in the red – everywhere – export-import imbalance – balance of payments worse – foreign debts to meet. Adam of course sees a patch of it behind the scenes at D.E.A. Stark alternatives between devaluation – 30 p.c. or 15 p.c.? – plus new borrowing from I.M.F., U.S.A. & European countries. And what conditions wld they impose? Alas! for the Common Market!

Diary – Monday 27 November – 21 Hyde Park Square, W.2

De Gaulle's Press Conference. Cld not wait to hear about it on the evening news. Dropped 2 coats & a dress to be shortened by dear Miss Joseph. *Panorama* entirely devoted to it. It amounts to a 2nd Veto. We had comments from Dr Lewis & a Round Table of Douglas Jay[1] (bad – & of course anti-Market), Gladwyn & Xtopher Soames – the last 2 good & very militant. I enjoyed it top-hole. . . .

[1]Douglas Patrick Jay (1907–96), cr. life peer, 1987; fellow of All Souls, Oxford, 1930–7, 1968–96; on staff of *The Times*, 1929–33; *Economist*, 1933–57; MP (Lab.) Battersea North, 1946–74; Wandsworth, Battersea North, 1974–83; president of board of trade, 1964–7.

'To insult de Gaulle in his own capital' – *December 1967*

President de Gaulle's second veto of Britain's second application to join the EEC, in November 1967, inevitably focused attention on Anglo-French relations. This gave rise, in mid-December, to a live television discussion in Paris, under the auspices of the state broadcasting service ORTF. The subject of discussion was to be the 'Entente Cordiale' and a panel of experts, principally French academics, was assembled. Violet had previously worked with ORTF on historical documentaries and was an obvious choice to participate. She had learned to speak French in Paris in 1904, the year of the 'Entente', and, through her father's position in politics, had personal recollections not just of the era but also of the characters involved. For the long historical perspective that the programme makers sought there was no-one better qualified to speak. Violet, though, was determined to discuss not the distant past of the Entente, but the immediate present of the veto. She went to Paris to defend the ideal of European unity that she and many others had embraced in the immediate post-war years. She was intent upon 'exposing de Gaulle to his own fellow countrymen'. It was not what ORTF had had in mind, but Violet's performance proved to be compelling television for thousands of French viewers, and made an impact on both sides of the Channel.

V.B.C. to Laura Grimond ***Friday 1 December***
21 Hyde Park Square, W.2

My Darling –

A thousand thanks for your letter.... My ankle slowly mending – not hurting only powerless & slightly vulnerable (I limped to the H. of L. all last week). Will you like an angel buy me a Xmas present for Magna & let me know what I owe you for it – as I cannot totter in the football match of shops & you will know his heart's desires....

I have been asked by T.V. Française in Paris (not their branch here) to go there on the 13th Dec. for a T.V. Round Table talk lasting 1½ hours on the theme of 'L'Entente Cordiale'! Nothing cld. be more enjoyable or a better safety-valve for one's feelings! To be able to insult de Gaulle in his own capital! If only my French were better! I know that I shall grope in vain for the 'mot juste'....

Damp, dark & grim here – so glad you are in lovely Orkney – for your own sake – & I hope having a rest. All my love – Ever yr Mama ....

Diary – Tuesday 5 December – 21 Hyde Park Square, W.2

. . . Went on to H. of L. Again a series of very dull Committee stages. Voted once on legitimizing 'bastards' in Scotland. Then home. K. Elliot rang me up. She saw Puff for the first time this morning & was shocked by his looks. She told me when I spoke about the 2nd operation 'I don't think he will ever have it.' I said 'Do you mean that he is dying?' That she thinks that, came as an overwhelming shock to me. . . .

Diary – Wednesday 13 December – Paris

Off to Paris by a 2 o'clock plane to which I was driven & 'escorted' by M. Chattard's nice young female employee & car. Wheelchair & all in order. Arrived at Le Bourget in a flash & was met there by another nice & competent young lady. Driven to Hôtel near the Champs Elysees – whence whom shld I find but Ray! The angel had waited for me passing on his way home from Switzerland. The joy & comfort of finding him was immense. . . . I had had a note from Miss Linda Blandford, who was 'covering' the event for the *Sunday Times*. Said goodbye to Ray & she & I drove off to the Studio where 6.45 was the appointed hour.

Anything more squalid than French T.V. it wld be difficult to imagine. We were taken straight into a burningly hot studio where the lights glared at one (it was being done in colour) & there I was introduced for the first time to the 4 Professors (historians) & Massigli, whom I remember of old – a nice but very dull man who used to be in London en poste. The Professors were: Chastenet, Durosil, Beauchon, & a German whose name I have forgotten. They were all old & as heavy as lead – the German the nicest. We were then informed that we shld have to watch a film on L'Entente Cordiale for the next hour & a half upstairs. I indicated my broken ankle & asked for a lift. The only lift available was one of those vast lifts for heavy luggage, meat & fish one sees in stations! In this we all embarked. But it wldn't move until at least 3 professors had got out. We sat in a long bare room upstairs on hard-backed wooden chairs – behind a long table 'où vous trouverez de la nourriture'. The only nourriture available were some pea-nuts. I asked for orangeade – I don't know whether the men had stronger drinks. The film was an old mid-thirties one – ineffably boring – 'starring' Edward VII, Ld Salisbury, Kitchener & a few other contemporary figures who were quite unrecognizable. . . .

The Professors nodded off quite soon. By 10 o'clock we were all abruti with boredom & fatigue. We then re-embarked in the lift – which, when the nice René-Clair-ish workman who managed it pressed the 'down' button, buzzed up. 'Voilà' said our conductor despairing but resigned –

'voilà la television Française' & he spread out both hands, palms upwards. Now we were in the studio's heat & glare. I sat on the Chairman's right.... A few perfunctory remarks about the film – & then the historians began – from the very beginning: Fashoda (who in France or England ever remembers the name?) For a long time we remained bogged down in these sands – the professors droned on – never speaking for less than 7 or 10 minutes each. It was assommant.

Finally I got a chance of opening my mouth & began with a rosy – nostalgic retrospect of the Entente – always a presence in my life – reassuring & precious. I remembered all that we had shared together 'conseils – ennuis – épreuves – triomphes' – always our mutual solidarité. Flying from London this afternoon I had asked myself one question unceasingly – 'Does the Entente Cordiale still exist?' & with the best will in the world my reply was 'forcément' – No. No one cld pretend that between our Govts there was either cordiality or understanding. And if I had not come dressed in mourning ... if I had dared to wear a dress 'd'une couleur quasi optimiste' – it was because this discussion might give me a spark of hope that, though dead to-day, the Entente might one day – who knows – be resurrected.

The programme was obviously derailed by this intervention & efforts were made to get back to Fashoda & more neutral & remote ground by the introduction of some questions – supposed to come from listeners – but clearly fabricated upstairs – which gave the professors another chance of mumbling 'historically'. My most effective break-through came towards the end when (neither of the Two World Wars nor the Thirties having been mentioned) I said that we had been talking of Entente & of Alliance but that no one had mentioned the moment when we might have become one nation. I then described de Gaulle's arrival in England in 1940 – England, which fortunately for us & for him was 'une isle'. Here he found friends & allies – not only an 'isle mais une base où il pouvait lever son étendard. Et grâce à la B.B.C. il pouvait faire appel à ceux de ses compatriotes qui voulait continuer la lutte pour la liberation de leur pays'.[1]

I then described Churchill's offer of an indissoluble union between our 2 countries – common citizenship & rights etc. – & General de Gaulle's welcome of this offer which he personally transmitted to Reynaud who wld have accepted it – but alas! had lost power to do so.[2] 'Churchill did

[1]Here he found not only an 'island but a base where he could raise his banner. And thanks to the BBC he could call on those of his countrymen who wanted to continue the fight for the liberation of their country.'

[2]The 1940 proposal of 'indissoluble union' emanated not from Churchill but from René Pleven and Jean Monnet, two of the architects of post-war European integration. During intergovernmental talks, 14–16 June, aimed at keeping France in the war, they interested members of Churchill's war cabinet in the idea of a union. Churchill consented to the plan for its

not ask "And how is your franc? Is he in good shape? And your reserves? It seems to me that your military and economic situation leaves much to be desired. But apart from those things – it would take you several years to adapt to British habits, attitudes, way of life." Churchill said: "Let us unite. Let us share everything. What is ours is yours. Our destiny is inseparable."' They all looked down their noses. I got in once more on de Gaulle's nationalism – a dead & dying creed. It was ironical that now we had abandoned isolation & wished to integrate ourselves in Europe he stood for the old order of L'Etat Seul. We saw a crude imitation of Gaullism in the German N.P.D. – de Gaulle had made nationalism respectable in Germany & Communism popular in France. At last it was over! & we staggered out into the darkness at midnight....

Diary – Thursday 14 December – 21 Hyde Park Square, W.2

Linda Blandford came in to see me & told me of the ferocious goings-on [last night] on the production floor above. The Director – a faceless voice – ordering the poor producer M. Gormot to stop or cut me off. The producer protesting 'But how can I control her?' He personally wanted a 'lively' programme & welcomed my incursions for this reason. Now I understand why the Chairman had constantly been called on a little black telephone under the table – & from that moment onwards had done his damnedest to prevent me from intervening! I gave my tips but forgot to pay my bill – drove alone to the Airport.... End of a well worth-while T.V. adventure.

Diary – Saturday 16 December – 21 Hyde Park Square, W.2

Miss Blandford came round to see some of my French fan-mail which is pouring in by every post.[1] (English ditto.) Delightful letters from Ld Birkenhead, Kenneth Younger & many others & actually a telegram from Randolph! 'Thousand congratulations on your magnificent broadcast in

obvious strategic value, but was 'less interested in the grandiose idea of a Franco-British union' (Gilbert, *Finest Hour*, 546–50, 558–61).

[1] Violet received many letters of praise and support following her broadcast, the bulk from correspondents in France. She also received a letter from the British ambassador Sir Patrick Reilly. He and his wife missed the programme, but he wrote: 'We heard on all sides that you were absolutely splendid. We have met quite a number of French people who saw you and there is no doubt at all that you made a tremendous impression. One or two of the people who have spoken to us about you were critical, but most of them were enthusiastic. It is of course quite exceptional for the French public to hear frank speaking of this kind and I dare say there have been some wigs on the green in the O.R.T.F.!' (15 December 1967)

Paris – happy Xmas etc. Randolph!' The ranks of Tuscany indeed.[1] The English letters are an explosion of passionate resentment & anger at the way we are being 'pushed around' & gratitude to me for 'expressing the feelings of millions'. The first voice to 'speak for England since Churchill' is the key-note (to me a blasphemous comparison!) No party inflections – sheer patriotic indignation & relief.

Diary – Monday 18 December – 21 Hyde Park Square, W.2

Attended the H. of L. Was almost embraced in the Library by many stout Peers I did not know by sight. They were in an (unusual) state of wild enthusiasm, over my attack on de Gaulle. One of them was almost hysterical with joy. 'Oh the joy of seeing his trousers taken down – & by you! How splendidly you did it' etc. . . . Not one member of my own party sent a single word to me about it.

Diary – Wednesday 20 December – 21 Hyde Park Square, W.2

Gelda & Cressida to luncheon. Was rung up by the 'Frost Programme' asking if I wld perform on it that night. I had never even seen it I am ashamed to say[2] – but I accepted as they wished to ask me questions about my de Gaulle broadcast & I felt this was a chance to further the good work . . . There was a live audience & it all went very easily & naturally. David Frost is not a politician & the 'niceties' of politics don't exist for him – but he is 'easy' 'natural' & unrattled & my theme was a very simple one to get across. I was to have had ¼ of an hour but D.F. let it run to 25 minutes – deviating at the end (rather to my regret) into personal questions. I forgot to say that when we were walking towards the platform he whispered to me 'Call me David – if you want to.' I didn't & afterwards was bunched by the Manager (I forget his name) who wrote me a very friendly letter saying 'You deserve these flowers – if only because you were

[1] Violet was then on bad terms with Randolph Churchill, for reasons that are not altogether clear. She quotes from Macaulay's *Lays of Ancient Rome* (1842), Horatius, lx: 'No sound of joy or sorrow / Was heard from either bank; / But friends and foes in dumb surprise, / With parted lips and straining eyes, / Stood gazing where he sank; / And when above the surges / They saw his crest appear, / All Rome sent forth a rapturous cry, / And even the ranks of Tuscany / Could scarce forbear to cheer.'

[2] *The Frost Report* was a popular topical television programme, named after its presenter (Sir) David (Paradine) Frost (b. 1939), Kt, 1993 – author, producer and columnist, and joint founder of London Weekend Television.

the first person this season to address D.F. as "Mr Frost" – which is of course what he is.' D.F. also bunched me with lovely flowers & I have got the inevitable 'fan mail' to answer.

TWELVE

The Good Fight

1968–1969

Diary – Monday 8 January 1968 – 21 Hyde Park Square, W.2

Was permed at 12 (badly needed but it took a chunk out of my day). Isabel angelically stayed all day & I was able to dictate letters to all my English 'fans'. (I only wrote 3 French ones after dinner alas! They are such good letters that one wants to answer rather than acknowledge them.) . . . Have agreed to write an article for *Envoy* for £100 – on Entente etc. – a grind – but I think worth doing.

Diary – Tuesday 16 January – 21 Hyde Park Square, W.2

Wilson made his statement about 'cuts' in the H. of C. I did not go (as the debate will take place to-morrow) but listened as they dribbled out on T.V. 1. East of Suez – Out by '71. 2. F-111 [bomber] plane ordered from U.S.A. cancelled. 3. Prescription charges re-introduced – with exceptions for the old, chronically sick, expectant mothers etc. 4. Dental charges raised on N.H.S. 5. Family Allowances – now paid to all will be refunded thro' taxation on well-to-do. 6. Raising of school [leaving] age postponed for 2 years from the appted. date. On this Frank Longford has resigned.[1] Jennie Lee – after making a lot of public fuss over prescription charges & striking attitudes – is staying on. Went to see Puff at 4.30 – & thought him rather tired. Cressida succeeded me.

Diary – Wednesday 17 January – 21 Hyde Park Square, W.2

Forgot to say that I was rung up by *l'Express* reporter who wanted me to comment on the cuts – particularly those abroad. We had an amusing talk about my broadcast. He said 'Vous avez fait une grande impression sur la

[1] Lord Longford resigned from the government on 16 February over the decision to defer for two years the raising of the school-leaving age to sixteen. He was leader of the House of Lords and the only cabinet minister to quit over the spending cuts.

France.' I read him aloud my last 'fan' letters comparing de Gaulle to 'notre deuxieme Hitler' & saying what a good bottle of champagne he was keeping in his 'fridge' 'pour boire à sa mort'.... Worked at my article for *Envoy*. All the house-parlourmaids have evaporated into thin air! without a word. Ethics & manners have vanished in this particular pursuit.

Diary – Saturday 20 January – 21 Hyde Park Square, W.2

Went to see Puff at 5. He was fast asleep & the Nurse told me he had been sleeping all day. I did not of course disturb him but waited outside on a chair in the passage for 10 minutes – then peeped in again & saw him still asleep. Found the Nurse to tell her I was going & to give him my love....

Diary – Monday 22 January – 21 Hyde Park Square, W.2

...Dark gloomy day & the political prospect ineffably dark. If only there was one man on the political scene who cld be a Deus ex Machina. I can't see one. Roy is full of good sense & sound judgement – but somehow he doesn't quite fill the bill. Wilson is punctured. Heath can't be inflated. He's like a balloon that won't blow up. H. of L. met. Consumer Protection Bill. Didn't spend long in the House....

Diary – Monday 5 February – 21 Hyde Park Square, W.2

...Terrible slaughter in Vietnam where the North Vietnamese & Viet Cong broke the truce on a holy day & penetrated Saigon.[1] It is held – but there is an all-out attack on the big cities. This after the Americans had ceased the bombing of the North. The photographs are heart-rending. The Refugees numbering 175,000. The people have not risen to back the North or greeted them as liberators. The slaughter is appalling.

[1] In the 'Tet offensive', launched on 31 January, North Vietnamese forces attacked more than 100 cities and military bases in the South. American and South Vietnamese forces eventually contained the offensive, but only at great cost. 'Tet' marked a turning point in the war, intensifying American popular opposition to the conflict.

Diary – Saturday 10 February – 21 Hyde Park Square, W.2

Spent the day in complete solitude. Puff's operation took place this morning.... I feel terribly anxious at the new assault on his strength. By a strange chance his film of years ago *The Young Lovers* was on at 7.30.[1] I shld not have known it but for Cressida – as it was on I.T.A. (& therefore not in the *Radio Times*). I watched it with real emotion. I had forgotten how moving it was – beautifully conceived & acted. My darling Puff – he is a real artist. I can't bear to think that he will never do another film....

Diary – Wednesday 14 February – 21 Hyde Park Square, W.2

Went to see Puff early after lunch. His colour a shade better but terribly weak. Felt he shld doze & left him after a few minutes. Was able to tell him about the *Young Lovers*. His mind quite clear – he remembered the names of Odile Versois & the young American. My violets had arrived. Left him to go to the H. of L.... Isaiah came at 6 & stayed 2 hours.... He was most amusing discussing other things & people. He is the best company in the world. I almost forgot my sorrows for an hour (almost – not quite – they ached below the skin.) Dined in alone.

Diary – Tuesday 20 February – 21 Hyde Park Square, W.2

Mrs Berryman drove me to luncheon with Moucher. If it had been anyone else I shld. have chucked, but she has been so angelic to Puff – sending him flowers a few days ago.... Went to H. of Lords for a short time & then back to him. C. fetched me & we sat with him alternately. He was quite lucid when he spoke to me – evidently thirsty – for he asked constantly for a drink called Lucozade in a glass by his bed....

C. & I finally left him & went home to dinner here – telling the night nurse (a very pretty Australian I had not seen before) to ring us without fail if there was any change for the worse. C. left me about 10 meaning to go home to Thurloe Square but looked in on him on the way & decided to stay. Towards 11 Ray fetched me in his car as he was rapidly growing weaker. When we reached him he was dead. He had begun breathing deeply – then he drew one or two short peaceful breaths & it was over. When I kissed his forehead it was as warm as it had been in his life. He

[1] *The Young Lovers* (1954), a 'Cold War' love story starring Odile Versois as Anna Sobek, the daughter of a Russian official who falls in love with an American code breaker, Ted Hutchins, played by David Knight.

looked as if he had found peace. But what he had longed for was life – more life – to fill to the brim. He had immense powers of enjoyment. K. told me that once, when in a 'general conversation' people were saying in the well-worn cliché 'I don't want to live till I am very old', Puff had said 'I do – I want to live till I am a hundred. I enjoy every moment of every day of my life'....

He had a quality of saintliness – never blaming or passing judgement. Its only flaw was that he felt more compassion for the wrong-doer than for the victim.... Ethically he was probably right. It is worse to be a malefactor than a victim. Yet I can't help feeling indignation against the malefactor & sympathy with the victim – coupled with the desire to confound the one & compensate the other. He did not re-act in this way. He was never a fighter.... Yet he cld show heroic courage – as during this terrible series of surgical ordeals – & in facing his cure with Dent. (It made me happy when he told Cressida that no one cld have persuaded him to do it except me.)[1] He never looked back since then – & told me once that he had never even felt tempted to do so. God bless & keep him – wherever he is. 'Would that I knew where I might find him.' – – – –

The 1968 Commonwealth Immigration Act

In early 1968, as a result of President Kenyatta's discriminatory 'Africanization' policy, the number of Kenyan Asians emigrating to Britain dramatically increased. On 22 February the British government announced that emergency legislation would be introduced to control the flow: there had been 7,000 new arrivals in the previous three months, more than the figure for the whole of 1966. The ensuing Commonwealth Immigration bill placed a barrier before every United Kingdom passport-holder who had 'no substantial connection' with the country – either by birth or by parentage. This covered virtually all of the Kenyan Asians, who would instead have to apply for a 'voucher' for entry: 1,500 would be made available each year (a single voucher covering the holder *and* their dependants). The legislation was passed by a large majority in the House of Commons on Tuesday 27 February, its passage expedited by a rare alliance between the government and opposition. There was however determined resistance from sixty-odd

[1]During the second world war Puff began drinking increasingly heavily and became an alcoholic. Violet was deeply concerned about him and in 1953 persuaded him to undertake a cure from a Dr Dent, involving a severe course of aversion therapy. Puff completed the course and never drank alcohol again.

MPs, drawn from all three main parties, who argued that the government must honour pledges of British citizenship given to the Kenyan Asians at the time of Kenya's independence in 1963. The same arguments were repeated in the House of Lords on Thursday 29 February, when the bill was due to pass all of its stages in a single marathon sitting and come into immediate effect. Though the final outcome of the Lords debate was never in doubt, the strength of the opposition represented a moral victory for opponents of the bill. If it was a battle lost, it was one that many peers – Violet among them – passionately believed was worth fighting.[1]

Diary – Thursday 22 February – 21 Hyde Park Square, W.2

Went to the House as I had to attend the Select Committee on the Televising of the House of Lords. Was impelled to ask the only 2 questions I have ever asked, arising out of a 'Statement' made by Eddie Shackleton[2] on the Kenyan Pakistanis. When Kenya was given Independence in '63 these Asians, along with some English, were given the choice between opting for Kenyan citizenship or for U.K. citizenship & some opted for U.K. citizenship & were given U.K. passports. The Kenyans are now trying to drive them out by refusing them work-permits & other rights.[3] This & some most unwise speeches by Duncan Sandys – who himself conferred these rights on them – & Enoch Powell – saying what a menace such a vast influx wld be to us & to Race Relations – has started a panic rush of Pakistanis to get into this country & they are arriving by plane-loads – realizing that they will otherwise be both Stateless & job-less.

It is reasonable to suggest that this influx shld. be 'phased'. But Shackleton accompanied this with the suggestion that 'belongers in' – i.e. people with a male English parent – shld be treated on a different basis – i.e. given priority on entry. I asked whether they wld not have to take their places

[1] *The Times*, 19 February 1968; *Hansard*, debate on the Commonwealth Immigration Act, 27 February 1968, vol. 759.

[2] Edward Arthur Shackleton (1911–94), cr. life peer, 1958; MP (Lab.) Preston, 1946–50; Preston South, 1950–5; lord privy seal, 1968; deputy leader of the House of Lords, 1967–8; leader, 1968–70.

[3] The Kenyan Asians had been given two years in which to take up Kenyan citizenship: the many who did not do so – and *The Times* estimated that there were 100,000 in February 1968 – remained eligible for British passports.

in what he had described as 'the queue' & got a very ambiguous reply.[1] I then pressed him to define more clearly the genus 'belongers in' – which was to me a new & incomprehensible word. If it was to be incorporated in an Act of Parlt we shld surely have a more precise definition of it. We got none. Fervent thanks [to Shackleton] & relief followed from the Tory benches. I feel that this is a most shocking breach of faith – & that belongers 'in' or 'to' is just a Colour Bar in disguise....

Diary – Saturday 24 February – 21 Hyde Park Square, W.2

Puff's funeral.[2] Letters & telegrams poured in all yesterday. Also flowers. I am sending mine with the coffin by Kenyon & so are the others. Birkett kindly ordered a car for me in which I asked Ray & Elena to come with me.... We stopped at the Red Lion at Henley ... & ate our sandwiches & drank some coffee from a Thermos. It was a day of bitter cold.... The service was perfect – simple & just as we had planned it – opening with 'Ye Holy Angels Bright'.... Out in the Church Yard the wreaths had been laid on each side of the grassy path leading to the grave – just beyond Father's & Margot's. The coffin was lowered – & I dropped my small bunch of violets into it. Then, after the committal prayer, we went away from the flower-lined path. I trembled for the poor clergy in their thin surplices in the bitter cold....

It was a moving day – one felt the love which went out to him & which he had inspired in all sorts & conditions of men throughout his life.... Cressida & Adam stayed in Oxford. How strange I thought, when I was left at home, that of us 7 I shld be the only one left.

Diary – Thursday 29 February – 21 Hyde Park Square, W.2

Immigration Bill. All night sitting. How will it go? Can we possibly defeat this Immigration Bill? I met Frank Longford in one of the Corridors of Impotence & sounded him about his personal position, saying how much

[1] Outlining the scope of the proposed legislation Shackleton had explained that those wishing to come from Kenya would now 'have to wait their turn'. Violet was moved to ask if 'white Kenya citizens holding British passports' would also be bound to take a place 'in the queue'. Shackleton's answer – 'it entirely depends on whether they fall within the definition of United Kingdom belongers' – was in effect a negative, since most white Kenyans would be able to claim a link to Britain by birth or parentage (*Hansard*, vol. 289, cols 589–91).

[2] Puff was buried in the churchyard at Sutton Courtenay in Berkshire, in which his parents are also buried. The Asquiths had for many years owned a river-side house in the village, called 'The Wharf'.

more important the principle appeared to me than the extra year of Education on which he had resigned.[1] He said he was all against it – but felt a personal hesitation about voting against the Govt. when he had just resigned from it. I said he must put principle before any such scruples (and felt sure he wldn't! I did him an injustice for in fact he did).

I also had a talk much later on with Dora Gaitskell in our little 'harem' room. She felt passionately against the Bill. She is a Jewess & as she said not a 'Belonger'. Neither her father nor her grandfather came from this country & only her father lived in it. But she felt one must support one's Party even if one did not agree with it. I said that for me this wld take all the purpose & meaning out of politics. (In fact she did in the end vote against them.) At $\frac{1}{4}$ to 3 Eddie Shackleton rose to move the procedural resolution that Standing Order 41 – which forbids taking any 2 stages of a Bill in one day – be dispensed with for the purpose of taking all the stages of the Bill thro' in one day. The House wld adjourn for half an hour at 8 o'clock. House dinners wld be served & if necessary breakfast from 6 p.m. (here he was corrected with interjections of 6 A.M.)...

The Ld Chancellor then opened the main debate in a very disingenuous speech – pretending that some 2 million people in other parts of the world had as good a right to descend upon this Island as the Asians in Kenya & completely ignoring the fact that most of them had dual nationality & wld not be rendered stateless. His noble face makes his disingenuousness more distasteful.... We then had soft soap from Ld Brooke of Cumnor[2] – for which the Ld C. expressed himself as being vastly obliged. The atmosphere of cosy collusion between the 2 Front Benches was very 'widerlich' to me throughout the debate. The Archbishop then weighed in on the side of the light.... Ld Brockway[3] then moved rejection of the bill which we proceeded to discuss until the small hours of the morning....

I went out to prepare my own speech & came back to hear the last half of a magnificent one by Ld Willis[4] – (Lab.) delivered with real fire & emotion. John Foot[5] also spoke well. He has the technique of a persuasive

[1] See above, p. 333.

[2] Henry Brooke (1903–84), cr. life peer, 1966; MP (Con.) West Lewisham, 1938–45; Hampstead, 1950–66; home secretary, 1962–4.

[3] (Archibald) Fenner Brockway (1888–1988), cr. life peer, 1964; MP (Lab.) East Layton, 1929–31; Eton and Slough, 1950–64; socialist campaigner, conscientious objector and parliamentarian: 'still at the age of 80, as one fellow-peer described him, "a continuous one-man Grosvenor Square demonstration"' (*The Times*, 30 December 1968).

[4] Edward Henry Willis (Ted Willis) (1918–92), cr. life peer, 1963; playwright, novelist, television and film script writer; author of the long-running television series *Dixon of Dock Green*.

[5] John Mackintosh Foot (b. 1909), cr. life peer, 1967; solicitor and four times unsuccessful Liberal candidate, 1934–50; later chairman, then president, of the UK Immigrants Advisory Service; brother of Dingle, Hugh (Lord Caradon) and Michael.

barrister. I slipped out to get a little food – & there was precious little to choose from – Gladwyn & Cynthia Jebb invited me to forage with them & I got a little cheese & some biscuits. Then back into the fray. I got up at 9.18 & spoke 10 minutes or so (some interchange with Eddie Shackleton about 'belongers'). Lord Hunt[1] spoke well about dispersal. Dora Gaitskell – who had missed her place in the debate – was chivalrously let in by Ld St Davids[2] – stressed her own non-'belonging' alien origin. The night wore on....

I will not meander through the Marathon debate – one of the most interesting I have ever taken part in because the cross-voting was so revealing. (Who wld have guessed for instance that Ld. Boyd[3] wld have been on the side of the light?) Lord Brockway wound up – very well – adumbrating the possibility of a Govt defeat. (How I prayed for one!) We divided at 2.30 A.M. Result. The Govt scraped home by 24 votes – [in opposition] every Liberal (15), the Archbishop of C. & Bishops of London & Chichester, several Cross Benchers, Ld James, Ld Hunt. I have not analyzed how many Tory v. Lab. dissentients. Supporting Govt. – both Front Benches, Blimps – & I regret to say a few – like Peter Thorneycroft – who shld have known better. Committee Stage then began in which we played an active part. I went home about 3.30. Palace Yard locked up so had to go to the Peers' Entrance. Nothing on wheels in sight. A policeman finally got me a taxi. Got home at 4 – very chilly. Wished I cld have stayed the course till breakfast. What shame many Labour 'loyalists' must have felt. I have never seen a more clear-cut line between the forces of Light & Darkness.

Diary – Friday 1 March – 21 Hyde Park Square, W.2

Very tired – spent most of the day in bed – thus missing Eliza's birthday party.

[1]John Hunt (1910–98), Kt, 1953; cr. life peer, 1966; distinguished soldier; leader of the British Everest Expedition, 1952–3; personal adviser to the prime minister during the civil war in Nigeria, 1968–70.

[2]Jestyn Reginald Philipps (1917–91), 2nd Viscount St Davids (s. 1938).

[3]Alan Tindal Lennox-Boyd (1904–83), cr. Viscount Boyd, 1960; MP (Con.) Mid-Beds., 1931–60; secretary of state for colonies, 1954–9.

Diary – Wednesday 3 April – Windsor Castle

Ursula appeared after luncheon & finished my (very sparse) packing & at 3.30 Mrs Berryman came for us & we started off – in a snow-storm – to Windsor (large flakes falling). As we approached our goal the sun suddenly came out & the Castle walls, turrets & towers stood out against a blue sky. What an inspired site the original 12th Century architect selected! It could not be more 'commanding' on its height ... Ray had, with his unfailing practical helpfulness, urged me to find out by which of the many gateways I approached it .... but we must have taken an unorthodox route as we were challenged by several policemen in different courtyards about our destination. 'Who are you going to see?' Alice-in-Wonderland answer: 'The Queen.'

At the right doorway 3 figures were there to receive us.... I was taken to my suite of rooms – bedroom – bathroom – sitting room – containing every comfort including the evening papers & assured that I shld be fetched & guided to the Green drawing-room, in which I was to meet my hosts & fellow-guests at 6. (Ursula was also fetched & shown her room 2 floors above – where my bell if rung wld give an instant bright signal.) At 6 I was duly fetched – & thank Heaven for it! We walked down miles of red or green carpeted corridors & galleries – hung with pictures one longed to linger by & gaze at – & finally reached a large room with green brocade curtains containing our fellow-guests.... The Queen & Duke of Edinburgh then came in, followed by the Prince of Wales & Pss Anne, & greeted us all & we broke into groups & talked.... Then we broke up to dress for dinner & I was once more conducted to my door in the Lancaster Tower – a long & beautiful walk....

Ursula helped me to dress in the black tulle dress lent to me by Elena which fitted me exactly – in fact better than my own clothes do. I wore my H. of C. star. I was fetched & delivered in another vast & lovely room opening into the dining-room & instructed to sit one off the Queen, beyond her, next to the Italian Ambassador. The Queen looked lovely in a pale blue brocade dress with a corsage of pearls. She is so much better-looking in life than in her photographs – which do not show her radiant complexion & the intense blue of her eyes. Princess Anne has become much better looking. She is tall & upright – a good figure – an obviously 'outdoor' girl. Prince Charles quite different – tall – shy – quite unlike either parent – but for me full of charm. We moved into dinner. I started with Lord Goodman, whom I liked much better than at the Academy dinner (the last time I had him as a neighbour) when he had a speech on his chest (& so had I!) He voted against the Immigration Bill which warmed my heart to him....

When we moved out I had a little talk with the Queen & she asked me whether I shld like to do a little tour after dinner or whether it wld be too tiring. I accepted with delight as I longed to see the treasures I had only had a glimpse of en route to & from my bedroom.

So off we all went in a drove & very soon I found Prince Charles beside me – pointing out a few things that he specially liked or that I might not have noticed. I was deeply touched by the courtesy which broke through his natural shyness – & by the sensibility & 'finger-tips' of his approach. He was 19. I was 80 & a complete stranger to him – yet we talked the same language. I felt he was as at ease with me as I was with him. (How had he guessed? or had he not guessed but just tried to be civil to a stranger his parents were entertaining?) I have rarely felt more drawn to or attracted by anyone so young & unknown. He is so different from his parents that one wonders where he has come from. Elena tells me, this after the event, that she hears . . . that they wld like him to be quite different – keen on Polo & Sailing like Princess Anne – tougher & rougher – & that they are not understanding & often critical. To send such a boy to Gordonstoun[1] rather bears this out – a school of toughness, hardening, where people are expected to practise 'adventurousness'. To have to be 'adventurous' as a duty & not from an impulse wld be a nightmare. He wld I imagine have been far happier at one of the traditional schools like Eton or Winchester – which (for all their defects) have beauty & 'patina'.

We wandered through the centuries in the galleries, where the variety of beauty & wonder amazed & constantly distracted. Everything was there – pictures – amazingly beautiful mirrors – Charles II – William & Mary – china – furniture – one cld not absorb, only blink & marvel. After a time my stamina began to fail & at the suggestion of Ld Plunket[2] I fell out & returned to the nice little relatively intimate drawing-room we started from. . . .

Then the Queen appeared saying that she was too tired to go on! This made me feel shriven. We had a delightful & very easy talk. I think she has become much more relaxed. I was able at one point to tell her the story of Betty Salisbury's letter to my father about his 'impudence' in daring to take the title of Oxford. 'However, it is only like a suburban villa calling itself Versailles.'[3] And his amused remark to me – 'I think there is more of the orange girl than the De Vere in that letter' (an allusion to her

[1] Prince Charles was educated at Cheam, Gordonstoun and Trinity College, Cambridge, with a term at Geelong Grammar, Australia; his father had been at Gordonstoun.

[2] Patrick Terence Plunket (1923–75), 7th Baron; equerry to the queen, 1952–75.

[3] On being made an earl in 1925 Asquith chose the title 'Earl of Oxford', which had been given by Queen Anne to her prime minister Robert Harley. He was compelled, though, to add 'and Asquith' to his title to distinguish his earldom from the earlier creation. The episode occasioned Lady Salisbury's cutting remark in a letter to Asquith, which is said to have amused him (Jenkins, *Asquith*, 507–8).

descent from Nell Gwynne via the St Albans). I shld not have hazarded this in old days! She cld not have been sweeter or easier. We all said goodnight – thanked & I was once more conducted back to my bedroom. . . .

Diary – Saturday 6 to Sunday 7 April – 21 Hyde Park Square, W.2

. . . The most appalling tragedy in the U.S.A. has shadowed all these days & blotted out all else. Martin Luther King has been murdered[1] – a saint – the one voice raised & listened to by many for non-violence. When I was in Washington with Ray & Elena in '63 he led a great Peace procession there & one was full of hope that he might achieve a great miracle of reconciliation. Alas! too little was done (tho' Johnson was sound on race). Black Power was born of impatience & hopelessness. In the Southern States the whites remained as savage & obscurantist as ever. He had 2 fronts to contend with. . . .

Since then appalling riots arson & looting have raged in most of the big cities – Washington worst of all. Troops were immediately called out & ringed the White House. Johnson postponed his visit to Honolulu for exploratory talks about Vietnam. Something like a civil war is raging in U.S.A. How ineffably tragic that the two men America had most dire need of – Kennedy & Luther King – shld be murdered by her own citizens.

The Funeral Service was attended by 100,000 people of both races – [Bobby] Kennedy, McCarthy, Nixon & Jacqueline Kennedy walked in the Procession. There was a most moving transmission on T.V. Our Race Relations Bill is just printed & about to be introduced.[2] I said to Mark 'Surely this tragedy will help it on its way. Even the blindest will understand what we want to prevent.' He replied (& alas! he may be right) 'By some it will be used as an argument against letting any more coloured immigrants into this country.' One can think of little else.

Diary – Thursday 11 April – 21 Hyde Park Square, W.2

Went by an afternoon train to Liphook where a very special *Any Questions* is to be recorded (& transmitted on Friday, its usual day) to celebrate dear

[1] Martin Luther King Jr (1929–68) was shot in Memphis, Tennessee, 4 April, when visiting the city to show support for striking sanitation workers.

[2] The bill extended the provisions of the 1965 Act, which had outlawed the 'colour bar' in public places. The 1968 Act made it illegal to discriminate racially in the allocation of housing and in employment practice. It was outlined in the queen's speech in October 1967 and received the royal assent a year later.

Freddy's 80th birthday – & retirement. . . . We had a question on Race – 'Wld it not be better to use Evangelism rather than legislation' or words to that effect. I am glad to say that except for C. A. Joyce, who thought that Evangelism wld do the trick better & used the inevitable cliché 'You can't compel people to love each other by law', we were all 'sound'. John Arlott – who spoke last – was violently so – saying that he had known a lot of very nasty white men, but never met a nasty black man – & then launched into a violent attack on the T.U.s – saying they pretended to be left wing & to fight for justice for the oppressed etc. & they were now trying to keep black men out of jobs & block their promotion as Inspectors on busses etc. All this was well received by the audience I was relieved to see – but I shudder to think of the post we shall get – particularly John Arlott. The last question was worded in such a way that we cld all pay our tributes to Freddy. . . .

Diary – Sunday 21 April – 21 Hyde Park Square, W.2

Another glorious day, the hottest April day since '49 according to the Wireless. Enoch Powell has made an appalling, blood-curdling speech about the Immigration Bill which will cook Heath's goose as Leader even more brown than it is cooked already. The 'Shadow Cabinet' is moving an amendment to the Bill, instead of supporting it in principle & strengthening it in Committee. Humphry Berkeley has resigned from the Tory Party. Now Enoch Powell comes out with a speech asking for the Immigrants already here to be shipped home – saying we are building our own Funeral Pyre & seeing rivers running red with blood.[1] Pray God that I am well enough to go to the debate on Tuesday.

Diary – Tuesday 23 April – 21 Hyde Park Square, W.2

Heath has repudiated Powell's insane speech & sacked him from Shadow Cabinet (the first sign of what Margot wld call 'temperament' the poor Grocer has given since he became leader).[2] In consequence he has a very

[1] Powell's speech at Birmingham on Saturday 20 April called not just for a halt in the flow of immigration, but for it to be reversed, with the voluntary repatriation of those immigrants already arrived. Alluding to the racial tension then evident in the United States he declared: 'Like the Roman, I seem to see the River Tiber foaming with much blood.' *The Times* leader called it 'an evil speech', commenting: 'The more closely one reads the text of Mr Powell's speech, the more shameful it seems' (*The Times*, 22 April 1968).

[2] Powell had been shadow defence secretary and was sacked on the Sunday evening. Heath had made soundings within his shadow cabinet before announcing the decision.

good press. Powell a very bad one naturally, but is deluged with thousands of fan letters & 1000 dockers 'downed' tools for 24 hours as a sign of approval. Other sporadic strikes broke out – a strange new symptom – striking because one approves of something. What with 'approval' & disapproval strikes our industry will soon be paralysed. Still much better but I think it wld be madness to go to the House, much as I shld love to. Mark went of course & telephoned to me about it. Everyone agrees that Hogg made the speech of the afternoon. Mark said it was masterly – particularly when he dealt with Enoch Powell.[1] There was not one Tory yelp of protest....

Diary – Monday 29 April – 21 Hyde Park Square, W.2

...To my great joy Lilo came to see me at H. of Lords – & we had tea together & a heavenly talk – mingling our tears over the state of mind of our 2 countries. In Germany the NDP has had a phenomenal success in the south gaining votes & seats. The SPD has lost seats & strength – the CDU has also lost some but nothing like so many. There is a sharp turn towards the right – in Germany the movement most to be feared. With us – the disgrace of Enoch Powell's speech & its terrible reaction. He has conjured up evil spirits & drawn out the worst that was in human nature in an unholy explosion. (Callaghan was on *Panorama* to-night with Robin Day – not fighting on the right ground in defending the Race Relations Bill – but congratulating himself on his part in the Immigration Act.)[2] I had a nice talk with Lord Soper before leaving the H. of L. He said he had had the roughest time ever at Speaker's Corner in Hyde Park yesterday. I do respect him.

[1]Speaking in the debate on the second reading of the Race Relations bill, 23 April, Hogg criticized Powell's judgement in making his controversial speech: 'If one is going to say, and goodness knows many of us have thought, that the streets of our country might one day run with blood .... then surely one ought to consider whether, in the more immediate future, one's words are more likely to make that happen, or less likely to make that happen' (*Hansard*, vol. 463, col. 74). Hogg also questioned Powell's loyalty to his Party in making such a controversial statement without warning his colleagues. Both men, however, voted against the second reading of the bill.

[2]In an effort to win over opponents to the 1968 Commonwealth Immigration bill, Callaghan had promised that the government would be flexible on the numbers of entry 'vouchers' that would be issued to the Kenyan Asians. He had declined, though, to write this undertaking into the bill itself (*The Times*, 28 February 1968).

Diary – Tuesday 21 May – 21 Hyde Park Square, W.2

Attended H. of L. I have not yet written a word about the astounding events in Paris. The students in the Quartier Latin have 'risen' – occupied their own Universities – the Sorbonne – also the Odeon Theatre – & the Opera. They are building barricades & lighting fires. The police are attacking them savagely – one student's head was blown off by a grenade & the 'tear gas' used is in some cases (according to the Press) something much worse. There are big casualties on both sides.... Meanwhile de Gaulle has gone off to Rumania on a State visit quite detachedly.

It must be a terrible blow to his pride that this near-revolution shld occur just as Paris has been chosen as a 'show-place' for the U.S.A.-Vietnam Summit. He preened himself on this & no doubt attributed it to his own masterly diplomacy.

Diary – Thursday 23 May – 21 Hyde Park Square, W.2

Attended Select Committee in the H. of Lords. Left after an hour to dash home to dress for my Reform Club dinner & speech.... Found Mr Haylon (the Secretary) awaiting me in the Hall & was ceremoniously escorted up in a lift into an enormous room filled by an enormous table – surrounded by about 45 to 50 men in dinner jackets. Was introduced to a percentage. None of them except dear Lord Amulree[1] – the Chairman of the Political Committee – appeared to be politicians. There were scientists & every other sort of specialist. It was – as was stressed – a revolutionary departure to ask a woman to attend this dinner & to speak. As I reminded them when I got up, 3 years ago the Reform Club had said it wld be quite unthinkable for me to join my colleagues there for their Eve of Session dinner. I don't know what caused them to scrap their cherished traditions. But they were all most kind & welcoming – & I think my speech went quite well. They cld not have been a more tolerant & responsive audience....

I was dazzled by the splendour & dignity of the Reform Club – with its vast mirrored vistas. I reflected on going home how many times I – an anti-feminist – had been the first to break virgin soil....

[1] Basil William Mackenzie (1900–83), 2nd Baron Amulree; physician; Liberal whip in House of Lords, 1955–77.

Diary – Saturday 25 May – 21 Hyde Park Square, W.2

... Dined in alone & watched scenes of fires blazing in the streets of Paris & mobs of students & police at logger-heads. Gaullism is certainly on its funeral pyre.[1] But how still it kept & for how long! The meaning of my astonishing fan-mail becomes daily clearer.

Biafra and Czechoslovakia

In June 1968 the scale of the humanitarian crisis unfolding in war-torn Biafra, eastern Nigeria, became known to the British public. Images of starving children appeared in the newspapers and on television, and were used to launch famine relief appeals by Oxfam and Christian Aid. The starvation was a direct result of the civil war that had followed Biafra's declaration of independence from the Nigerian federation on 30 May 1967. From the outset the British government supported fully the efforts of the federal forces, under General Yakubu Gowon, to crush the rebellion. But the brutality of the conflict, and in particular the use of famine by the federal army as a weapon of war, made many in Britain question their government's position. More than one million Biafrans died of starvation during the conflict, the majority of them children. Violet was deeply affected by this human suffering and demanded an end to the sale of arms to the Nigerian government, as a first step towards re-establishing peace in the region. Her concern over Biafra was paralleled that summer by her fears for the growing movement for democratic reform in Czechoslovakia. The so-called 'Prague Spring', led by Alexander Dubček, had caused alarm in Moscow and the Czech leader came under intense pressure to reverse the process of liberalization. In July he entered into talks with the Russians, but reached no agreement, and after weeks of tension and uncertainty five Warsaw Pact powers invaded Czechoslovakia on the night of 20–21 August. They quickly took control of the country, crushing democratic protest and re-establishing a regime acceptable to Moscow. It was bitter for Violet to see – at the very end of her life – the suppression of Czech freedom for a third time. She faced these troubled times with failing physical powers, but with her fighting spirit 'still militant and intact'.

[1] In the short term the 'students' revolution' of May 1968 did not bring down de Gaulle, whose party scored an overwhelming victory at the ensuing general election.

Diary – Saturday 8 June – 21 Hyde Park Square, W.2

Dined at Garrick Club with dear Neville Cardus[1] & enjoyed it immensely. He is such excellent company. At one moment we talked of all the unspeakable horrors that surrounded us in the world (Biafra is the ghost – no alas reality – which haunts me at present). What cld one believe in? We were reeling back to barbarism – but armed to the teeth with the lethal weapons provided by 'science & technology'. What cld one have faith in? He suddenly said 'When I look at that lovely face[2] & think of music – it is a sheet-anchor to my faith.' The Garrick had great atmosphere & 'time deposit' & the dining-room was papered with Zoffanys.

Diary – Wednesday 12 June – 21 Hyde Park Square, W.2

H. of Lords. Lib. Peers Meeting. Frank Byers was there but is soon leaving for abroad. I asked him to have a word with me alone afterwards. A much publicised 'revolt' against Jeremy's leadership is taking place in his absence on his honeymoon. The Young Liberals are at loggerheads with him for having alluded to them as 'Marxists' (where & when I don't know) & for saying that 'all capitalists are not callous'. ('Capitalist' is of course a dirty word in leftist circles.) I don't think 'Y.L.s' matter much, as they talk great nonsense & are perhaps best ignored, tho' they are an undoubted nuisance at Party Conferences. But what is serious is that one Richard Holme,[3] who is V. Chairman of the Executive, has now followed up their attack on Jeremy & this has been publicised thro' our own H.Q. machinery thro' an official hand-out!

Anything more lunatic one cannot imagine. I asked Frank (who of course has nothing to do with the Exec.) to give me the low-down on the situation.... He told me that there was criticism of Jeremy – partly owing to his 'social' activities. He has always been on the best of terms with Wilson (I have often told him he is the only man I know who really likes Wilson – & he admits it.) Wilson invites him to N°10 on Royal occasions & shows him off as a mimic. He does a dialogue between me & the Archbishop of C. to the Queen Mother, etc. Also he gate-crashed his fiancée into a party to which he had been asked, but at which there were no

[1] Sir Neville Cardus (1889–1975), Kt, 1967; music critic and cricket writer; on staff of *Manchester Guardian* from 1916.

[2] Perhaps an allusion to his wife, Edith Watton, who died that year.

[3] Richard Gordon Holme (b. 1936), cr. life peer, 1990; contested East Grinstead, 1964, 1965; Braintree, October 1974; Cheltenham, 1983; 1987 (Liberal/Alliance); vice chairman, Liberal Party Executive, 1966–7; president, Liberal Party, 1980–1.

women but the Queen (this was very foolish). Frank also thinks it is a mistake to give a party for 800 people at the Royal Academy – all in white ties – to celebrate his marriage. This is not a 'white tie' age – & many Libs. don't possess them. He is in danger of being considered a 'light weight'.... I am however furious at the wanton damage to the party caused by the attacks & I told Frank that I shld go down to the joint Lib. meeting at 6 that evening....

I duly did so. It was a very small & unrepresentative meeting. Emlyn Hooson first took the Chair – very well & was succeeded by Eric Lubbock. We heard to our horror (or at least to mine) that the Chairman of the Exec. – one Gruffyd [Evans] – is now taking up the cudgels in defence of his V. Chairman, Richard Holme, & has issued – again thro' our own Press machinery – a violent attack on Eric Lubbock! I went thro' the ceiling at this – told them what Eric had done for the Party – said that they deserved to be carpeted & must be animated by the death wish! Eric was obviously grateful for my onslaught & it commended the support of the President of the candidates' association....

Finally Donald Wade whose heart is in the right place but who hasn't got a tooth in his head was delegated to deal with the situation. I was sitting next to him but cld not forbear from pointing out that he had not got the requisite ferocity for the job – which he took in excellent part. I was thankful I went – as no one else cld have spoken with so little inhibition! & such genuine amazement at their madness – nor such rage! I cld see that it had helped Eric & that he was really grateful to me.

Diary – Tuesday 25 June – 21 Hyde Park Square, W.2

Lunched at H. of L. with Ld & Ly Samuel.... Am haunted by the appalling tragedy of Biafra, where the survivors of the massacre are now dying in thousands for lack of food & drugs. It is criminal that our Govt. shld still be feeding the Nigerians with arms. John Wells (who brought Sir Louis Mbanefo[1] to see me) has been in close & constant touch with me about it – & I am wondering what I can do to help to avert this ineffable tragedy. Children are dying at the rate of 400 a day. It is a race with death.

[1]Sir Louis Mbanefo (1911–77), Kt, 1961; Nigerian judge; chief justice of eastern region of Nigeria, 1959–67.

Diary – Thursday 27 June – 21 Hyde Park Square, W.2

Vincent came & shampooed me. Attended last meeting of the Select Committee & went through final stages of our Report. In the evening went to Jeremy's vast wedding party at the Academy. It reminded me of a *Tit-bits* question in my childhood which has always haunted me as a 'fact' – i.e. that the whole population of the world wld find room in the Isle of Wight – provided that they all stood up! This was not necessary in Jeremy's party – there was plenty of standing & sitting-room – but the numbers were astronomical – very close to a thousand. He was 'shaking hands' side by side with his very nice & nice-looking wife. Wandering thro' the rooms one met many old Lib. faithful – Mrs Clement Davies – the Leonard Behrens etc. – & many old retainers & widows – but suddenly Quintin Hogg with whom I had a long interesting & friendly talk (sitting down). All the cobwebs are now blown away between us by our rapprochement on Race – on which he has taken an enlightened line. . . .

I stayed the course till after 11.30 & got a taxi in the courtyard quite easily. Tho' criticized (by me) for 'white ties' & inviting Alec Home (of which he had boasted to me!) I rescinded my criticism – as Jeremy had not only invited the 'mighty from their seats' but also droves of the humble & meek.[1]

Diary – Monday 1 July – 21 Hyde Park Square, W.2

Still racked about Biafra. Telephoned Gillian Rees-Mogg, as the *Times* has not played up about it. John Wells tells me that their correspondent Roy Lewis is a committed pro-Nigerian. Poured out this to her & asked her to beg William, with my love, to make the *Times* show its paces & change its tune on this issue. Stressed the children side to her. . . .

Diary – Tuesday 2 July – 21 Hyde Park Square, W.2

So absorbed & harrowed by Biafra that I have never mentioned that the Railways are 'going slow' & that it is almost impossible to travel. Commuters are the worst victims. There is of course congestion of traffic & taxis are scarce & Minis in great demand. Fortunately the Govt. are not involved directly – as it is a struggle between the Railway Board – already 150 million in the red. Made the terrible mistake of writing Randolph's

[1] From the Magnificat, *Book of Common Prayer* version: 'He hath put down the mighty from their seats, and hath exalted the humble and meek'.

Memorial Service in on the wrong day – i.e. to-morrow – ordering Mrs Berryman etc. It happened to-day! & I missed it. I am sorry to have done this for Clemmie's sake – & for my own too. Grudges do not survive the grave.[1]

Diary – Friday 5 July – 21 Hyde Park Square, W.2

Did not attend the morning sitting of the H. of L. on Caravan sites.... Talked to John Wells on the tel. He had wanted me to chair a meeting in Trafalgar Square about Biafra – but I told him on Thursday that it was far too late to organize a good one & he agreed. The Nigerians now threaten to shoot down Biafran Relief planes – & contend that arms are being smuggled through. The horror grows.

Diary – Wednesday 10 July – 21 Hyde Park Square, W.2

...Went to H. of L. Transport Bill labouring through Committee & Report. Left in storms of rain after 20 minutes wait in the tel. box in Palace Yard. Wrote a note to Jeremy about Biafra – telling him truly – that he is one of the few people in this world who really likes Wilson & who Wilson really likes. He must go personally straight to Wilson & tell him this massacre by starvation – the worst human tragedy since Hitler – must stop. The sale of arms stop is the first essential step.

Diary – Friday 12 July – 21 Hyde Park Square, W.2

A day full of trivial necessities – i.e. hair-washing by Mr Vincent, visit by one David Montgomery from *Vogue* to photograph me (I submitted for the sake of Mrs O'Connell – once 'Miss *Times*' – who is an editress) & finally a long visit & talk with Mr Arengo Jones – again laden with lovely roses from his garden. We had a good 'jaw' but did very little business.[2] Haunted by Biafra nightmare. What can one do? I have asked several

[1] Randolph Churchill had died on 5 June. In his last years he had been on bad terms with Violet, which she attributed, at least in part, to resentment on his behalf at her biography of his father.

[2] Arengo Jones was to interview Violet (in German) for a German television programme about women and equal pay, to be recorded that August.

'questions' in the Lords – written to Shepherd,[1] written twice to Ld Goodman – John Wells is in constant touch with me. He too is crucified. I have asked Jeremy to see Wilson personally. He has done it & Wilson referred him to Thomson[2] & told him to 'come back' to him afterwards. One cannot move the adjournment of our House. One cld move a vote of censure on the Govt. But with this tight time-table it wld be strenuously resisted by the Govt.

Diary – Tuesday 23 July – 21 Hyde Park Square, W.2

H. of L. – Transport Bill in Committee. Voted in one Amendment Division which was victorious. Mind & heart torn with fear for Czechoslovakia where the Russians are mobilizing vast 'manoeuvres' on the frontier & making threatening pronouncements. Czechs calm & wise in every word. It is terrible to be able to do nothing at all – but I feel that the best thing to do is to let the Russians off the hook on which they have impaled themselves – to the horror of the Communist world as well as ours – with as little loss of face as possible. Therefore one must resist the temptation to say 'J'accuse'. It is tragic to know that we haven't now got the power to help them – whatever our will may be. Biafra is another bleeding wound – & here we are in the dock.

Went on from the House in a Minne (which did turn up at the Peers' Entrance) to Frank & Elizabeth Longford's party – in a tiny flat off the King's Road called Chesil Court. I put my coat brief-case umbrella & other impedimenta on Elizabeth's bed – already fairly thickly strewn & then went into a very small living-room next door thickly jammed with people – making a noise like a lion house. Found a small settee against the wall to sit on. Talked to a nice man (name unknown) about Cys whom he adored. He had in his Classics [studies] at Oxford studied from exquisite translations of his (Cys's) of the *Shropshire Lad* in Latin Elegiacs. He said many of them were much better than Housman.[3] Then Ld Goodman's vast form appeared & I hailed him to talk about Biafra & he slumped with relief onto the settee beside me – & we began a good talk till a female

[1]Malcolm Newton Shepherd (b. 1918), 2nd Baron Shepherd (s. 1954); government chief whip in House of Lords, 1964–7; minister of state, FCO, 1967–70; deputy leader (later leader), House of Lords, 1968–70.

[2](Sir) George Morgan Thomson (b. 1921), cr. life peer, 1977; Kt, 1981; MP (Lab.) Dundee East, 1952–72; chancellor of the duchy of Lancaster, 1966–7, 1969–70; secretary of state for commonwealth affairs, August 1967–October 1968; minister without portfolio, 1968–9.

[3]The poetry of A. E. Housman's *A Shropshire Lad* was popular in Violet's youth. Housman (1859–1936) was a classical scholar and professor of Latin at Cambridge.

'intervener' came & sat between us – ruined our talk & provided no substitute. (I've no idea who she was.) Was just wondering how I cld get away when Norman[1] appeared. Had a few words with him then said I must go when Hugh Fraser appeared. I covered him with praise for his speech on Biafra (he is as sound as a bell where any 'race' question is at stake – except on Rhodesia). I asked him to help me to go – excavated my clothes etc. now deeply buried on Elizabeth's bed full fathom five. Hugh told Frank I must have a taxi – Frank miraculously got me one – & I got home – alive – to my infinite relief – after a lethally dangerous experience.

Diary – Monday 29 July – 21 Hyde Park Square, W.2

Mr Vincent – then H. of Lords – our last week of toil – the Commons has risen. Transport & Town & Country Planning in Committee. How little they seem to have to do with the issues which absorb, & haunt & agonize one like Biafra & Czechoslovakia. One feels daily & hourly the humiliation of utter helplessness. We are selling arms for the destruction of a people which is starving to death. Czechoslovakia is putting up an inspired fight for mental freedom – the freedom of the human spirit. Dubcek[2] has issued a classic statement of their aims. Meanwhile vast armies are surrounding her – 10,000 Russians are on her soil. . . .

Diary – Wednesday 31 July – 21 Hyde Park Square, W.2

To the H. of L. – the last day but one – for we 'break up' on Thursday. . . . Shepherd was asked one question about Biafra. I got up to put in a supplementary, but Edith Summerskill[3] got in first with a good one. She is absolutely 'sound' – but how Labour can endure this barbarity I don't know. Shepherd looks so disgustingly fat – I shld like him to be starved for a few weeks.

[1]Norman Antony Francis St John-Stevas (b. 1929), cr. life peer, 1987 (St John of Fawsley); joined *Economist*, 1959; MP (Con.) Chelmsford, 1964–87; minister of state for the arts, 1973–4; leader of the House of Commons and minister of state for the arts, 1979–81; master of Emmanuel College, Cambridge, 1991–6; a close friend of Violet in her later years.

[2]Alexander Dubček (1921–92), Slovak Communist leader, elected first secretary of Czechoslovakian Communist Party, 5 January 1968. Dubček inaugurated the reforming era of the 'Prague Spring' but was later forced to capitulate to Soviet pressure and reverse the reforms, and was ultimately expelled from the Communist Party.

[3]Edith Clara Summerskill (1901–80), cr. life peer, 1961; MP (Lab.) West Fulham, 1938–55; Warrington, 1955–61; parliamentary secretary, ministry of food, 1945–50; minister of national insurance, 1950–1.

I sent a note to Ld Hunt & asked if I cld see him for 5 minutes. He found me & told me he had got to see a Biafran for half an hour, but we made a tryst in the Library & went out & sat in a lobby together. He is a perfectly delightful man & so attractive. I trust him utterly. He tried to get into Biafra – & the Head Red X man nearly succeeded – but when it was discovered that he was one of Hunt's – i.e the British Govt.'s mission – the Biafrans wldn't have him. As I said to Hunt – wld we have taken 'aid' from Hitler when the Battle of Britain was going on? There is no sanctity in 'legal' Govt.'s. Hitler's was a 'legal Govt' accomplished – as Gowon's[1] was – by a military coup. Secession is no crime. I reminded him of Ireland. These incompatible Federations – hastily clapped together by us – are fallen asunder right & left because they are composed of incompatible elements. . . .

By the time the Addis Ababa talks start thousands will be dead. I told him what I felt when Cressida as a baby was losing weight – & weighed as much at 5 months as she did at 5 weeks. The agony Biafran Mothers must be enduring in seeing their children die. He was so human I really loved him. But what can he do? He is too 'nice' I felt to treat the Govt. rough which is what they deserve. Came home late in showers of rain – lucky to get a taxi. They hadn't been able to get one for one hour in Palace Yard. . . .

Diary – Wednesday 21 August – 21 Hyde Park Square, W.2

A day of doom – when I was called I was told that Norman (St. J. Stevas) had rung me earlier to let me know that he had heard on the 8 o'clock news that Russia had invaded Czechoslovakia. I felt as if I had been knocked out. I just cldn't accept it, believe it. I was so sure the Czechs had won. I got through to Norman after a time & he told me the Russians had moved in at dawn in the dark – & not the Russians alone but the East Germans, the Hungarians, the Bulgarians & the Poles. What can we do to help them? Nothing. (We are not even strong enough to betray them again!) . . . .

Rang Lib. H.Q. The Young Libs plan to march in protest to the Soviet Embassy & hope to rally 5,000! – a good plan but I am sceptical about the numbers. Eric Lubbock may go with them. I told Pratap [Chitnis] to say that I wld come – but he said the entrance to Millionaires' Row is heavily guarded by police – & it may be impossible to get in there. Listened on my transistor to the heart-breaking accounts of the Russian Tanks rolling thro' Prague – students sitting in front of them. 'No fighting' is the order

[1]General Yakubu Gowon (b. 1934), leader of the Nigerian military regime that opposed the secession of Biafra, 1967–70; he was deposed in 1975.

of the day. How cld the Czech Army of 200,000 stop the cohorts numbering millions which are arrayed against them? Passive resistance is all they can hope for – poor – poor people. . . .

One of the darkest days I can remember. I wld willingly give my life – even if it were a longer one – to undo the crime that has been committed. I feel the hearts of the Czechs aching in mine. They looked & were so happy in their new-found freedom. Now they are handed over again to tyranny – for the 3rd time. And no people more deserved to be free.

Diary – Thursday 22 August – 21 Hyde Park Square, W.2

Went to a Lib. Foreign Affairs meeting in Whips Room H. of C. I had telephoned yesterday to Frank Byers to say that we shld ask for Parlt to be recalled. To my amazement he didn't agree. Jeremy however did & so did all the F.A. Meeting. (Since then Wilson has announced that it will be recalled on Monday & sit for 2 days.) We discussed – hopelessly – what we cld do – except condemn. Things are getting worse rather than better. People in the streets of Prague are shouting to Dubcek 'Tell us the truth.' The Czech people are amazing in their courage, humour, & pride – also in their ingenuity – taking down all signposts & names of streets to baffle Russians – teasing them – sometimes alas! with fatal results. There has been shooting – some estimated the deaths at 60 – others at 200. Dubcek tries to explain that some concessions will be necessary for a time. He is in a frightful dilemma. Either he must counsel resistance & remain intransigent in his promises of a free Press, Free Speech etc. – or, he must face replacement by a military tyranny who will arrest & execute & silence every voice which speaks for freedom. . . .

We have since heard that Dubcek was suddenly & brutally arrested in his office at gun- point – his telephone torn out by the roots. He & 4 others were thrown by Russian soldiers into a plane & flown to Moscow to negotiate. I am invited to speak at a U.N.A. protest meeting at Friends' House by Humphry Berkeley Sat. night. . . . I must do it & try & prepare my speech.

Diary – Monday 26 August – 21 Hyde Park Square, W.2

Houses both met. I got there at 2 o'clock for Lib. Peers meeting. Frank asked me to speak to-morrow when Biafra will be debated – & though it gives me little time to prepare, as I naturally want to hear the Czechoslovakia debate, I accepted feeling that I must do it. Debate opened by Shackleton followed (very well) by Jellicoe, then Byers – Anthony Eden (unremarkable – as he always is – but 'sound' of course – he looks very old because his looks are essentially 'jeune premier' & made for youth)....

Went out for a breather when Silkin rose. Came back for Watkinson,[1] Gladwyn who read his speech but very rapidly, then Bob Boothby as ever good & as usual right. It is odd that a man who always does the wrong thing in private life shld be so invariably right on political issues.... It was a reputable debate but not a great one. Partly because we are utterly helpless. Went back very tired & worked on my Biafra speech till 2 o'clock. We meet at 11 o'clock to-morrow. Not my finest hour!

Diary – Tuesday 27 August – 21 Hyde Park Square, W.2

Breakfast at 8.15 & scurried off to the House. I was down to speak third. Bessborough[2] opened.... He was followed by Shepherd who gave us what Ld Goodman later described as 'a child's guide history of Nigeria'. Dice loaded all the way through. I came next – & did not speak long (about 10 minutes) but did not pull my horse – & told them what I felt – or I tried to do so. Spoke for the first time from our Front Bench. Ld Hunt gave a factual report about the difficulties he had encountered. He had of course no chance as Biafra wld not receive him as he was the emissary of our Govt. Lord Head – who had been for 3 years Governor of Nigeria – made an excellent speech & came out quite unequivocally for suspending sale of arms. Lord Goodman made a brilliant speech which tore Shepherd's case to bits. I had suggested that the 'legality' of a Govt. (their excuse, or one of them, for the sale of arms) was not sacrosanct – & that the last 2 Govts of Nigeria had been established by 2 military coups – preceded by 2 murders which hardly gave them a claim to Divine Right. Goodman – an experienced lawyer – tore their claim to any 'legality' to bits. His speech was devastatingly good. I had to leave before the end alas to keep an appt. with Goldsmith for new spectacle lenses....

[1] Harold Arthur Watkinson (1910–95), cr. 1st Viscount, 1964; MP (Con.) Woking, Surrey, 1950–64; min. of transport and civil aviation, 1955–9; minister of defence, 1959–62; company director and later president of the CBI, 1976–7.

[2] Frederick Edward Ponsonby (1913–93), 10th Earl Bessborough (s. 1956); politician and author; Conservative front-bench spokesman on science, technology, power, foreign and commonwealth affairs, 1964–70.

Diary – Monday 7 October – The Old Manse of Firth, Orkney

. . . There have been riots in Ulster – by the Catholics in Londonderry – & there is a demand for a Commission of Inquiry into the conduct of the police.[1] Terence O'Neill[2] appeared in an interview refusing it & staunchly defending the Police. I fear there is a kind of Apartheid – on a religious basis – practised against the Catholics. Tried to pack before dinner. Feel sure I shall fail to get my things 'in'! Sad to be going home to-morrow. I shall never get used to living alone – tho' I try to come to terms with it.

Diary – Saturday 26 October – 21 Hyde Park Square, W.2

Vast Protest Demonstration (Vietnam) – Tariq Ali & C° – is impending here on Sunday so I asked Elena if I might go there to-day.[3] All 5 picked me up after a walk in Regent's Park & we drove there by the heath & round the donkey rank, just round the corner by the pond, & Edward & Tom went for a ride on 2 very sweet velvety-nosed ones. Helena was offered a ride but didn't fancy it. We had tea in the drawing-room – the boys – especially Thomas – acting as waiters. I said 'How well you wait. I must give you a tip.' His eyes shone with excitement & he said 'Oh yes do. I will put it in my bottle of money.' I asked why he kept a bottle of money & he said 'For Biafra' – which touched me deeply. I wonder if he has seen the starving children on T.V.[4] – or how he knows about it. Lovely evening with them all & then Ray drove me home.

[1] The riots followed the violent breaking-up by the police of a banned civil rights march in the city on Saturday 5 October. Three Labour MPs, who had been invited to witness the march, condemned the police action and called on the government for a public inquiry.

[2] Terence Marne O'Neill (1914–90), cr. life peer, 1970; prime minister of Northern Ireland, 1963–9.

[3] Around 50,000 were expected to join the demonstration, though only around half that number materialized. The bulk of the marchers followed the radical activist Tariq Ali, of the Vietnam Solidarity Campaign, to a peaceful rally in Hyde Park, though around 6,000 broke off to stage a noisy protest at the American embassy in Grosvenor Square.

[4] Television brought the Biafran crisis directly into British homes, a fact to which Violet referred in her speech in the House of Lords on 27 August. She called for an end to the sale of arms by Britain to the Nigerian government, as a first step towards ending the humanitarian catastrophe in Biafra: 'Thanks to the miracle of television we see history happening before our eyes. . . . We have no alibi. We see these things happening' (*Hansard*, vol. 296, cols 700–2).

Diary – Wednesday 6 November – 21 Hyde Park Square, W.2

...on to H. of L. where Economic Debate was taking place. Jellicoe[1] & Byers both spoke well. I shld have liked to stay on & hear Bob Boothby & Balogh but had to leave – first for a talk with Lord Brockway & then for our deputation to the Prime Minister on Biafra. After many refusals he has at last consented. It was not a high-powered delegation – Ld Brockway – Self – K. Elliot – & a Tory M.P. called Tilney[2] – not a very bright specimen who, while subscribing to our other aims, did not wish to protest against the sale of arms, which I thought was the fons & origo of our deputation – & David Steel.

We duly went to the P.M.'s room. He was flanked by that 'chubby lad' Ld Shepherd & an official. Fenner Brockway led off – asked for a Commonwealth Peace Keeping Force, a Cease Fire, Aid (instead of arms), all the essentials. But his native gentleness & incapacity to hit anyone between the eyes with any point made him ineffective. Tilney knew Nigeria well but is unfortunately pro the Sale of Arms! K. Elliot burbled – saying this was the moment to strike a bargain with de Gaulle (who is now arming Biafra). I spoke next & stressed the well-worn points. Our function & our duty in a Civil War was mediation. By arming one side we had abdicated from this rôle & indeed from all moral authority.

Govt.'s defence: (1) Legal Govt. must be supported.... (2) We shld lose all influence over Nigeria unless we sent her arms. But what has our influence accomplished? What have we to show for it? How many lives has our influence saved? And how many have our bullets killed? I then quoted from the European Women's League, Netherlands Sector ... begging their Govt to bring stronger pressure on ours to stop the sale of arms; & having pressed our case for entry into the E.E.C., they now ask themselves whether we are in fact fit & proper to enter Europe. David Steel said a few words. Then Wilson replied. His technique is exactly like that of a conjuror – 'patter' all the time – fluent patter like that of a conjuror who talks to divert you from his tricks. Nothing accomplished. Drove home in pouring rain. Streets so blocked it took me nearly an hour.

[1] George Patrick Jellicoe (b. 1918), 2nd Earl; son of Admiral Jellicoe, 1st Earl, and minister of defence, RN, 1964; deputy leader of opposition, House of Lords, 1967–70; leader of House of Lords, 1970–3.

[2] (Sir) John Tilney (1907–94), Kt, 1973; MP (Con.) Wavertree, Liverpool, 1950–74; parliamentary under-secretary of state, commonwealth relations, 1962–4.

Diary – Thursday 12 December – 21 Hyde Park Square, W.2

After dreary Fisheries, etc. Ld Ritchie-Calder[1] raised Biafra on an unstarred question & made a most impressive speech – backed not only by very comprehensive knowledge of the facts – including dietary & scientific facts – but of the whole terrible picture. He said comparable horrors might have taken place before in the world's history – but the world had not sat still & watched them happening. His idiom was sober but impregnated with deep feeling. Shepherd has gone to Lagos – ostensibly to get a 'Cease Fire' – the Govt put all their hope in a 'quick kill' – & it hasn't happened thanks to the arms Biafra has received from France & others. All the speeches were in a solemn key – but Ritchie Calder's was in a class apart. I went on at 6.30 to a party for the Aged in the Cholmondely Room.

Diary – Monday 30 December – 21 Hyde Park Square, W.2

Stayed in all day as still feel tight chest & rather giddy.... Goldman came at 6 & knew the moment he put his head round the door that I was not so well. He took my blood pressure which was down to 120 (the cause he thinks of my giddiness) sounded my chest & said I still had bronchitis & must not go out at all to-morrow. I longed in vain to be allowed to go to Mark's party. He rang up – & we are both very disappointed.

Diary – New Year's Day, Wednesday 1 January 1969 – 21 Hyde Park Square, W.2

Telegram of love & good wishes from Neville Cardus! one of the few people I shld rather like to see. Feel like a clock run down. C. an angel cooking for me etc. Pray this will be a better year for the world than last. Nothing can buy back life to the countless thousands – millions? – in Biafra. Can freedom be regained for Czechoslovakia? I see no way. There are no great men anywhere to lead. How lucky I have been to be born so long ago.

[1]Peter Ritchie-Calder (1906–82), cr. life peer, 1966 (Ritchie-Calder); science editor, *News Chronicle*, 1945–56; on editorial staff of *New Statesman*, 1945–58; Montague Burton professor of international relations, Edinburgh University, 1961–7; later a leader of CND.

Diary – Wednesday 15 January – 21 Hyde Park Square, W.2

In bed – as I have been now for a week. Yet I feel just as breathless & giddy as a week ago. Telephoned Goldman's Sec. to ask if he cld come in & see me this evening instead of Friday. He came – took my blood-pressure – down now to 115 – its lowest yet, in spite of a whole week's rest.... He says I must stay in bed another week – which is terribly depressing & also fills me with anxiety about the programme[1] – such a responsibility if I wasted their time & upset their plans. He will come again on Friday. I feel a sort of constant vibration at the back of my head.

Diary – Tuesday 21 January – 21 Hyde Park Square, W.2

H. of L. met but I was a defaulter. Terrible things happening in Czechoslovakia. A young student has poured petrol over himself & burnt to death as a protest.[2] As may be imagined it has had a profound effect on an already explosive situation. Crowds assemble in the Wenceslas Square & elsewhere in tears of grief & despair. Czechoslovakia is a nightmare – a Russian crime....

Diary – Wednesday 5 February – 21 Hyde Park Square, W.2

Struggled to the H. of L. as I wanted to hear what proved to be a very interesting debate on Chemical & biological warfare. It was interesting because only experts spoke.... Was terribly lucky in getting a taxi from H. of L. Entrance – because someone happened to drive up into it. I was afraid of getting chilled in Palace Yard – in this arctic weather.

Diary – Friday 7 February – 21 Hyde Park Square, W.2

...Dr Goldman came at 6 – his last visit till he goes away on holiday to Kenya (to-day week) for a fortnight's holiday. I am sure he needs it for he

[1]On 2 February Violet was due to appear before a live theatre audience to record *An Evening with Lady Asquith* for the BBC – a programme of prose and poetry recitals, elicited in conversation with George Rylands. Violet was sufficiently well to make the broadcast, which proved a great success with the live audience. It was broadcast soon after her death as a special tribute by the BBC: see below, p. 362.

[2]Jan Palach set himself on fire on 16 January, in protest at the erosion of freedom in Czechoslovakia.

has had gruelling work this winter. I complained to him about a pain I have just below my ribs – every day now. . . . He said it was an inflammation of the inner duodenum – caused by 'stress' – which is just what I've had for the last 4 weeks – & accentuated by eating too little. He ordered me some pills. I think sedative rather than curative.

Diary – Saturday 8 February – 21 Hyde Park Square, W.2

Arctically cold – the whole country snowed up. Stayed in bed all day – now up (after dinner) sitting in the drawing-room. Hoped to see Ice Skating Championship at Garmisch which has been on for 2 nights – but they found one Football Match in which snow hadn't stopped play & it has been going on ever since. . . .

Diary – Thursday 13 February – 21 Hyde Park Square, W.2

Ray & Elena have gone off to Austria for a fortnight ski-ing with a Swedish couple – he is a colleague at Warburgs. . . . I am thankful Ray will have a breather. . . . Still feeling inside discomfort & great fatigue – also very slight occasional heart pains. Goldman off to Kenya to-morrow – so I haven't worried him with complaints.

Diary – Saturday 15 February – 21 Hyde Park Square, W.2

Arctic cold continues. The whole country under snow & ice. Impassable roads etc. Lunched with Mary Wooster again at the Connaught. Again she was 'in the pink' – mellow & eating enormously. I cldn't resist drawing her attention to de Gaulle's rebuke in to-day's papers to W.E.U. who have had the temerity to meet without him here in London. . . . France was of course asked – but did not deign to attend – & now threatens to leave W.E.U. Toto came to see me at 4 followed (unexpectedly) by Mark – followed by Mary Hutchinson. So I did no work either on diaries or book. More comfortable day – less pain inside.

Epilogue

The diary entry for Saturday 15 February was the last that Violet wrote. Four days later, on Wednesday 19 February, she died of heart failure at her London home. Her death was widely reported in the press both in Britain and abroad. In the House of Lords on 20

February, during questions on peace proposals to end the Biafran war, one speaker after another took time to pay their respects. It was particularly apt, as Lord Brockway observed, that she should be thus remembered, during a debate on a subject 'about which she felt so deeply'.[1] The next day, Friday 21 February, the BBC delivered its own special tribute by screening ahead of schedule the programme of prose and poetry recitals that Violet had recorded earlier in the month with George Rylands. Her performance in *An Evening with Lady Asquith* ended with a recital of Keats's sonnet 'To Sleep' and on Saturday 22 February she was laid to rest in the churchyard of Mells, alongside Bongie in a double grave. The final act of remembrance was a memorial service at St Paul's, her favourite church, on Wednesday 19 March. The first hymn to be sung was 'Fight the Good Fight'.

[1] *Hansard*, vol. 299, cols 944–93.

APPENDIX A: *Glossary*

An explanatory list of words, phrases, names and abbreviations appearing in the text.

abruti – stupefied

Africa Bureau – a London-based humanitarian organization, active in the late 1950s and 1960s, with a watching brief on the government of Britain's African colonies; it included in its membership the Rev. Michael Scott (director), Lord Hemingford (chairman of its executive committee) and Lady (Elizabeth) Pakenham

Aladdin lamps – simple paraffin heaters for domestic use

All Souls – Oxford college, membership of which is regarded as a high academic distinction and confined to fellows (there are no undergraduates); there is a strong legal tradition at the College, which has produced many leading public figures; during the 1930s it was associated with appeasement through the actions of several prominent fellows (Lord Halifax, Lord Simon, Geoffrey Dawson)

Anglo-German Friendship Society (Deutsch-Englische Gesellschaft) – organization founded immediately after the second world war by Lilo Milchsack, with the support of Robert Birley, to promote Anglo-German relations; the annual Königswinter Conference was held under its auspices (*see also* Königswinter)

'Angry Young Men' – a phrase describing disillusioned youth in 1950s and 1960s Britain, typified by 'Jimmy Porter' in John Osborne's play *Look Back in Anger*

Any Questions – popular BBC radio programme, of which the *Brains Trust* was a begetter; it was first broadcast from Winchester in September 1949 and was the preserve of BBC west region until the death of its famous presenter Freddy Grisewood: 'under Grisewood's deeply appreciated chairmanship there was a strong rapport between chairman and local west country audiences' (*DNB*)

aperçu – summary, glance or rapid view

assommant – boring, tiresome

Atlantic Charter – an agreement between Churchill and Roosevelt, in August 1941, reached after five days of talks aboard naval vessels moored in the waters of the north Atlantic; it outlined a joint manifesto of common aims in world affairs, touching on (*inter alia*) the regulation of trade, freedom of the seas, promotion of peace and freedom

à tue-tête – at the top of one's voice

Bad Godesberg – scene of a meeting between Hitler and Chamberlain, 22–23 September 1938, over the 'Sudetenland' issue; to Violet it was synonymous with 'appeasement'

Balfour Declaration – November 1917 declaration by A. J. Balfour, then foreign secretary, committing Britain to 'the establishment in Palestine of a national home for the Jewish people'; although it also stated that nothing should be done to 'prejudice the civil and religious rights of existing non-Jewish communities in Palestine', the Declaration was widely interpreted as a pro- Zionist statement; it became an instrument of international policy after the first world war and was included in the British mandate over Palestine approved by the League of Nations

B.A.O.R. – British Army of the Rhine; second world war occupation army that went on to administer Britain's responsibilities in post-war Germany and Berlin

B.D. – *see* Bloody Duck

Beerbohm Tree atmosphere – an allusion to the stage effects of the famous Edwardian theatre manager Sir Herbert Beerbohm Tree

Benelux – refers collectively to Belgium, the Netherlands and Luxembourg; these countries formed a customs union, 29 October 1947

bézique – a card game for two or four players, using a double pack of sixty-four cards

Biafra – the name adopted by the secessionists in eastern Nigeria, whose Republic of Biafra lasted from May 1967 until January 1970, when it surrendered to Nigerian forces

Black Rod – formally 'The Gentleman Usher of the Black Rod', also the serjeant-at-arms in attendance upon the lord chancellor; responsible for the security of the House of Lords

Blanco – substance for colouring military accoutrements – it can be either white or khaki colour

Blimp – reactionary and muddle-headed ex-officer type, prone to self-contradictory aphorisms; after the balloon-like cartoon character Colonel Blimp, created by David Low (1891–1963) and appearing in the *Evening Standard*

Bloody Duck (or B.D.) – a private joke between Violet and Churchill, which she sometimes used in signing letters to him; its origin was her emphatic 'yes' to his 1941 offer of a place on the BBC board of governors – 'can a bloody duck swim?'; in saying this she was consciously echoing his own words to Stanley Baldwin in 1924, when he realised that the 'chancellorship' Baldwin (then prime minister) had just offered him was not the duchy of Lancaster, as he half-expected, but the exchequer itself

Blut und Boden – literally 'blood and soil' – a Nazi phrase describing extreme patriotism and a sense of belonging

Bodleian – the Bodleian Library – the main library of the University of Oxford

bon coucheur – an agreeable person – that is, the opposite of the more usual *mauvais coucheur*, meaning 'an awkward customer'

box, on the – next to the driver: from the days of carriages, when the 'box' was the seat where the driver and his companion (usually a footman) sat, at the front of, and usually outside, the main carriage

Brains Trust – BBC radio programme dating from the second world war, in which a panel of five answered listeners' questions; this popular format had a life outside radio, and

Violet participated in many public meetings that were called 'brains trusts'

broadcasting – as used by Violet during an election campaign, this meant the public 'broadcasting' of a message using loudspeakers mounted on cars

Brooks's – a fashionable gentleman's club in St James's Street, SW1, first established in 1764, and of which Bongie was a member

bunched – given a bunch of flowers

Cabinet Particulier – a private office or room

Causerie – restaurant in Claridge's Hotel, popular with Violet and friends, it offered an unlimited smorgasbord at a very reasonable price (5 shillings)

Caxton Hall – in Caxton Street, SW1; late nineteenth-century building designed as the Westminster City Hall and subsequently used for concerts and public meetings; closely associated with the suffrage movement

C.C.O. – Conservative Central Office

C.D.U. – German Christian Democrat Union (Christlich Demokratische Union Deutschlands) – centre right political party

Chamberlainesque – of, or like, appeasement – an allusion to Neville Chamberlain's pursuit of appeasement during the late 1930s; Violet would use it in a derogatory way

Charmeuse [-eaux] – (possibly) black-skinned – from the trade name for cloth with a dull black and semi-glossy surface

Chatham House – in St James's Square, SW1, location of the Royal Institute for International Affairs – of which Violet became the first woman president, 1964; the Institute was formed after the first world war to promote public awareness of international issues and the exchange of ideas between nations

chetif – puny, pitiful

Chiltern Hundreds – parliamentary convention that allows an MP to resign – the stewardship of the Chiltern Hundreds lies within the patronage of the crown and any MP applying for it is therefore effectively disqualified from sitting in the Commons

Cigarren Laden – tobacconist

Cliveden Set – a group of friends who frequented Cliveden, the Buckinghamshire home of Nancy (Lady) Astor during the 1930s and who were popularly associated with appeasement: 'The myth imputing blame to them was started by the gifted Communist journalist Claud Cockburn who, in his small-circulation paper *The Week*, launched the idea of a conspiratorial 'Cliveden Set' engineering a sell-out to the Nazis so that Hitler could become the tool of Western plutocrats against Bolshevism' (Grigg, *Nancy Astor*, 146)

Closed Shop – a trade union practice forbidding anyone from working at a particular site (or 'shop') without belonging to the union controlling it

clumps – a parlour game similar to 'twenty questions'

C.M. – Common Market (see below)

C.N.D. – Campaign for Nuclear Disarmament, which advocated unilateral nuclear disarmament by Britain as a first step towards total world disarmament

Coal and Steel Community – *see* Schuman Plan

Common Market – in common usage this term was virtually synonymous with the 'EEC' (see below); it describes a free trade area, protected by common external tariffs – one of the central aims of the various movements for European unity post-1945

Commons – House of Commons

contrepoids de la gloire – counterweight of glory

Council of Europe – founded by Britain and nine other European states in 1949, and consisting of a committee of foreign ministers and a consultative assembly of parliamentarians; it was a forum in which member states worked towards non-binding agreements on issues of human rights, culture and the environment; based in Strasbourg it was eventually joined by most of the western European states; it is separate from the EEC (EU)

coup de foudre – literally, 'clap of thunder'

C.P. – Communist Party

C.P.O. – Conservative Party Organization

C.R. – Committee Room (in Parliament)

C.V. – Colne Valley – scene of Violet's second (and last) bid to become an MP, at the 1951 general election

D.E.A. – Department of Economic Affairs

déçu(e) – disappointed

dégringolade – fall, tumble

délié – liberated, loosened

dernier cri – the latest; 'state of the art'

désoeuvré – unoccupied, idle

dexedrine tablets – 'energy-giving' glucose tablets, sold in chemists in a variety of flavours

D.P. – 'displaced person'; term in use in Europe immediately after the second world war to describe Holocaust survivors and refugees

draught – sleeping draught – VBC commonly took seconal

Dreyfus case – a *cause célèbre* in 1890s France that centred on a military officer, Alfred Dreyfus, who was wrongly accused of espionage; it exposed anti-semitism in French society and led to Emile Zola's famous letter in Dreyfus's defence, *J'accuse* (1898)

D.T. – the *Daily Telegraph*

Dumbarton – a factory belonging to the Blackburn Company, near Glasgow, and for which Bongie had responsibility as a Blackburn Co. board member

E.C. – European Community, collective name for the ECSC, Euratom and EEC, which merged in 1967; from 1993 it became known as the 'European Union' (EU)

E.C.S.C. – the European Coal and Steel Community, created by the Treaty of Paris, April 1951, between West Germany, France, Italy and Benelux; it established a common market in coal, iron and steel production and manufacture; its institutional structure prefigured that of the EEC, of which it was an early step towards, and by which it was later absorbed (1967) (*see also* Schuman Plan)

E.D.C. – European Defence Community, or 'European Army', created by the May 1952 treaty between West Germany, France, Italy and Benelux – but which failed after the French National Assembly refused to ratify it (August 1954) (*see also* Western European Union)

E.E.C. – European Economic Community, created by the Treaty of Rome, 1957, between Italy, West Germany, France and Benelux; it established internal free trade between the member states with common external tariffs, and anticipated movement towards agreement on political, economic and social questions

effaré – bewildered, scared

E.F.T.A. – European Free Trade Association – an economic organization promoted by Britain as an alternative to the EEC; it came into being on 20 November 1959 with seven full members – Britain, Denmark, Norway, Sweden, Austria, Switzerland and Portugal – establishing a free trade of industrial goods between them; by 1999 all but Norway and Switzerland of the original seven had left to join the European Union

E.L.A.S. – the Greek National People's Liberation Army, established by Communists in 1942

Electoral Reform – in Liberal politics this meant some form of proportional representation in parliamentary elections, as a corrective to the traditional 'first past the post' system, which consistently left the Liberal Party with a much higher proportion of the votes cast than of seats gained

Empire Loyalists – *see* League of Empire Loyalists

en sursaut – 'with a start' (to awake, and so on)

Entente Cordiale – popular name for the 'Anglo-French agreement' of 8 April 1904, which was a resolution of outstanding colonial disputes between Britain and France, principally in North Africa; the 'Entente' paved the way for better relations between the two countries in the following decade

EOKA – 'National Organization of Cypriot Struggle' – underground movement of Greek Cypriots dedicated to driving the British out of Cyprus and to achieving énosis (union) with Greece; established in 1955, it waged a terrorist war until a ceasefire in 1957, though the movement remained active until being disbanded in March 1959

E.P.T. – excess profits tax – a tax on company profits

equal pay – the payment of women and men equally for doing the same work; in reality it means raising women's pay to a level of equality with men's

European Army – *see* E.D.C. and Pleven Plan

European Assembly – the Consultative Assembly of the Council of Europe, established in Strasbourg in 1949, and to which delegations from national parliaments were sent by the member governments (*see also* Council of Europe)

Executive – Liberal Party Executive

F.A. – Foreign Affairs

fardel – a burden, or load of sorrow

Fashoda incident – a diplomatic crisis between Britain and France in 1898, at the root of which was competition over colonial influence in central Africa; on 18 September 1898 Lord

Kitchener, at the head of the British army, discovered a small French garrison at Fashoda on the Nile, under the command of Captain Marchand; the French force had undertaken an epic two-year journey from the west coast of Africa to establish a French presence on the Upper Nile; after a tense stand-off Marchand was ordered to withdraw by his government and in 1899 a settlement was reached between Britain and France over their respective spheres of influence – defined roughly by the Nile-Congo watershed; at the time Fashoda led to deep popular resentment in France towards Britain, but in the longer term it paved the way for better relations between the two countries

F.C.O. – Foreign and Commonwealth Office

F.E. – F. E. Smith, later Lord Birkenhead, Conservative statesman; a barrister by training he was recognized as one of the most brilliant advocates of his day: 'For all the purposes of discussion, argument, exposition, appeal or altercation, F.E. had a complete armoury. The bludgeon for the platform; the rapier for a personal dispute; the entangling net and unexpected trident for the Courts of Law; and a jug of clear spring water for an anxious perplexed conclave' (Churchill, *Great Contemporaries*, 132)

Federalists – a term used in the early days of the movement for European unity to describe those who sought closer ties between the participating states at every level, particularly political; however, the precise definition of what 'federalism' was, and how it was to be attained, was unclear

Federation – *either* the movement for a European 'super state' (as above) *or* the ill-starred union of North Rhodesia, South Rhodesia and Nyasaland, 1953–64

Flüchtlinge – refugees

fons & origo – literally, 'fount and origin' (fons et origo)

Foyle's – W. & G. Foyle, 119–125 Charing Cross Road, W.C.2 – famous London booksellers; established in 1904 by the brothers Gilbert and William Foyle, and continued by successive generations of the family; Violet often attended Foyles 'literary luncheons', held in honour of celebrated authors or to promote special works

frapped flipper – (possibly) a cool greeting – literally a 'cold hand', combining the French 'frappé', meaning iced, with the (archaic) British slang for hand, 'flipper'

Freedom Focus – *see* Peace and Freedom Focus

GATT – General Agreement on Tariffs and Trade; a UN agreement for the liberalization of world trade, first signed in 1948 and periodically renegotiated

Gettysburg Address – delivered by President Lincoln on 19 November 1863 at the dedication of the Gettysburg national cemetery, honouring those who died in the Civil War battle of Gettysburg earlier that year; a concise and classic statement of democratic ideals, with the famous peroration 'government of the people, by the people, and for the people'

Gleichschaltung – literally 'synchronization'; in Nazi Germany it meant forced political conformity – the sense in which Violet uses it

'Go slow' – form of industrial action commonly used in post-war Britain by workers in dispute with their employers – a sort of 'passive disobedience' in the workplace

Götterdämmerung – 'The twilight of the gods'; the last opera in Wagner's *Der Ring des Niebelungen* tetralogy

Green Room – room in a theatre where actors can relax and prepare for a performance

Hauptbahnhof – main railway station (Germany)

H. of C. – House of Commons

H. of C. Star – *see* Star, House of Commons

H. of L. – House of Lords

Herren Volk – upper classes, or social superiors (Herrenvolk)

Hola – location in Kenya of the Hola Detention Camp, at which eleven 'Mau Mau' detainees were beaten to death by guards following a riot there in March 1959; the incident led to severe criticism of the Macmillan government's handling of colonial affairs (*see also* Mau Mau)

Homintern – a nickname invented by Maurice Bowra to describe the homosexual fraternity of public school and university educated men in inter-war Britain; with its obvious play on 'Comintern' it suggests a network devoted to mutual advancement, with its roots in the 'establishment'

hors concours – unrivalled, unequalled

houris – female attendants

House, the – House of Commons

H.P. – Hyde Park – variously, Gardens, Gate, Square, Hôtel, and so on; the park is large and so the distance between, say, the Hôtel to the south and the Bonham Carters' home to the north would represent a fairly long walk

Ken. Gardens – Kensington Gardens, not far from the Bonham Carters' home in Gloucester Square

Königswinter – town on the banks of the Rhine, on the south edge of Bonn – capital of the Federal Republic; it was the location for the annual three-day conference organized by Lilo Milchsack (in later years the conference was held in Cambridge too); 'Although few people realised it, these conferences actually became the corner-stone of Anglo-German relations, helping to turn enemies into allies. Cabinet ministers, politicians, academics and journalists all came together on the banks of the Rhine to grapple, very occasionally with brilliance but always with controversy, with the great questions of the day' (Anthony Glees, obituary in the *Independent*, 8 August 1992).

I.M.F. – International Monetary Fund

Imitas – Winchester College slang for 'imitations' (mimicry)

immonde – impure, unclean

I.T.A. – Independent Television Authority

John Birch Society – right-wing American political society founded in 1958 'to restore and preserve freedom under the U.S. Constitution'; fiercely opposed to Communism it suspects an international conspiracy, with roots in the American government itself, of seeking to subvert freedom in America

lacrimae rerum – tears; 'sunt lacrimae rerum et mentem mortalia tangunt' – literally, 'There are the tears of things and mortal affairs touch the mind' (Virgil)

Lancaster House – large Georgian house in the Stable Yard, St James's Palace, named 'Lancaster House' in 1912 by the future 1st Viscount Leverhulme, who purchased it and later gave it to the nation; used by the government for hospitality, it was the scene of the 1953 coronation banquet

League of Empire Loyalists – extreme right-wing political group founded in Britain in 1954 by the South African-born British fascist Arthur Keith Chesterton; it later fused with the British National Party to form the National Front, opposed to non-white immigration to Britain and British entry to the Common Market

Liberal Nationals – *see* National Liberals

Liberal Party Organization – created in 1936 it was intended as the central policy-making body of the Liberal Party, replacing the National Liberal Federation; Violet served as first woman president, 1945–7

Life Peerages Act 1958 – provided for the creation of life peers and peeresses by the sovereign, acting on the advice of the prime minister, whose nominations were meant to represent the interests of all parties

Limehouse days – an allusion to the radicalism and social reform of the era of Asquith's Liberal government; Limehouse in East London was an area of considerable deprivation and the scene of one of Lloyd George's most famous speeches during the controversy surrounding his 1909 budget

The Listener – respected weekly journal of broadcasting, begun in 1929 and with a peak circulation of over 151,000 in 1949

L.N.U. – the League of Nations Union, founded in Britain in October 1918 from two wartime peace organizations, the League of Nations Society (1915) and the League of Free Nations Association (1917); its aim was to encourage, mobilize and direct public opinion in support of the League of Nations and the cause of world peace; almost 407,000 annual subscriptions were collected in 1931 but the popularity of the movement declined as the League's authority in world affairs diminished; it was led by Lord 'Bob' Cecil, a founder of the League itself, from 1923–45, and Violet was an active member, serving on its executive.

Lords – House of Lords

L.P.O. – *see* Liberal Party Organization

L.P.P. – Liberal Parliamentary Party

Malanism – apartheid – the policy of the South African government under Daniel François Malan (1874–1959), premier, 1948–54

Marshall Aid – popular name for the European Recovery Programme formulated by the US secretary of state George C. Marshall and outlined in a speech at Harvard, 5 June 1947: the speech proposed a programme of American financial aid to Europe designed to rehabilitate the economies of the recipient countries and to create stable conditions in which free political institutions could survive; funds became available in 1948 (*see also* O.E.E.C.)

Marshall Plan (/offer) – *see* Marshall Aid

Mau Mau – a secret organization of militant Kikuyu tribesmen who advocated violent resistance to British rule in Kenya; their campaign of sabotage and assassination was met, from October 1952, with a state of emergency and four years of military operations, during which more than 12,000 lives were lost; 'Mau Mau' became synonymous with atrocities in Britain, although Jomo Kenyatta, jailed in 1953 as a leader of the movement, became first prime minister of independent Kenya a decade later

M.G. – *Manchester Guardian* – daily newspaper established in 1821, it changed its name in 1959 to the *Guardian* and moved its base to London

Millionaires' Row – a colloquialism for Kensington Palace Gardens, W8, on the west side of Hyde Park, where the French embassy residence is situated

Minne/Minis – mini-cab[/s], probably radio controlled and an alternative to the traditional black London taxi; Violet used them increasingly in the 1960s

Miss Joseph – one of Violet's dressmakers

Moss Bros – famous London tailors and a popular place for the hire of men's dress clothes

mot d'ordre – watchword (military usage)

Munich – used by Violet this refers to the September 1938 agreement signed at Munich between Britain, Germany, Italy and France, and which led to the 'Sudetenland' in Czechoslovakia being surrendered to Nazi Germany; Violet shared Churchill's view that it was 'a total and unmitigated defeat' for British diplomacy

N.A.A.F.I. – acronym for the Navy, Army and Air Force Institute, which runs canteens and provisions stores for the armed services

National Liberals – members of the political party that emerged following the 1931 schism in the Liberal Party, over the question of economic policy during the financial crisis of that year; the followers of Sir John (later Lord) Simon ('Simonites') later joined the Conservative dominated 'National government' and thereafter became known as 'National Liberals' (or 'Liberal Nationals'); they enjoyed a reciprocal electoral accommodation with the Conservatives and in Violet's eyes were an appendix of the Conservative Party

N.A.T.O. – North Atlantic Treaty Organization, created by the Treaty of Washington April 1949; a defensive alliance of western European states, the United States and Canada

N.C. – *see News Chronicle*

N.C.B. – National Coal Board

needle – sense of anxiety, tension, or irritability

***News Chronicle* [*News Chron.*]** –

Liberal newspaper created in 1930 by the amalgamation of the *Daily News* and the *Daily Chronicle*; it closed in controversial circumstances in October 1960, thus depriving the Liberal Party of an extremely important source of publicity for its ideas (see also the *Star*)

Nicht Herauslehnen – 'Do not lean out of the window'

1922 Committee – an influential gathering of backbench Conservative MPs, which takes its name from the 1922 revolt of Conservatives against the Lloyd George Coalition, and which led to the government of Bonar Law

N.P.D. – Nationaldemokratische Partei Deutschlands – German National Party; extreme right-wing

N.S. – *New Statesman*

Nunc Dimittis – 'now let (your servant) depart' – from the opening of the Song of Simeon (Luke 2:29–32); used as a canticle

N.U.R. – National Union of Railwaymen

O. & S. – Orkney and Shetland – the constituency represented by Jo Grimond from 1950 to his retirement in 1983

O.E.E.C. – Organisation for European Economic Co-operation – formed in 1948 by western European countries in order to co-ordinate economic policy and the allocation of Marshall Aid (became the OECD in 1961)

Old Vic Trust – trust set up to administer the Old Vic Theatre Company; Violet served as a governor of the trust from 1945

O.R.T.F. – l'Office de Radiodiffusion et Télévision Française – the French government-owned national broadcasting service created in 1964

Osbert Lancasters – people resembling the famous pocket cartoon characters of Osbert Lancaster (1908–86) in the *Daily Express*: 'It was commonly said that he [Lancaster] looked like one of his own cartoon characters and, as he aged, he resembled more and more an effigy of the English gentleman on a French carnival float: bulging eyes, bulbous nose, buffalo-horn moustache, bald head, striped shirt, pinstripe suit from Thresher & Glenny, old-fashioned shoes with rounded toes' (*DNB*)

Other Club – a cross-party parliamentary dining club founded in May 1911 by Winston Churchill and F. E. Smith, partly with the aim of dissipating the party bitterness engendered by the controversies of the day; Churchill frequented it regularly and it remained a favourite assembly even in his old age

Overlap prospectus – political document produced by Rab Butler in the summer of 1950, against the background of Violet's talks with Churchill about the possibility of a Liberal-Conservative alliance; meant to identify the basis for co-operation between the parties

paired – House of Commons practice whereby a pair of members who are going to be absent from the House for a time, and who are of opposing parties, notify their whips of their joint absence; they thus cancel one another out and each party can effectively discount their absence without any disadvantage

Panorama – weekly BBC television

current affairs programme

pass laws – laws introduced by the South African government in 1950 requiring non-whites to carry identification papers; they were the focus of the protest in March 1960 that resulted in the Sharpeville massacre

Pay Pause – phrase used in the 1960s for a statutory prohibition of pay and salary increases, in an attempt to control inflation

P.C. – *see* 'Press Commission'

Peace and Freedom Focus – the Focus in Defence of Freedom and Peace, or more simply Freedom Focus; a loosely organized anti-fascist group that coalesced under Churchill's leadership in the 1930s and in which Violet played a central part

piqûre – injection

pis aller – a last resort

Pleven Plan – October 1950 plan to establish a European army, credited to the French prime minister René Pleven (*see also* E.D.C.)

P.L.P. – Parliamentary Labour Party

Plymouth Brethren – a strict Calvinist religious group, established in Plymouth in Devon around 1830

Potsdam – meeting between Attlee, Truman and Stalin, 17 July-2 August 1945; much was controversial at Potsdam, though there was grudging agreement on German war reparations and the western border of Poland; it marked the end of the wartime alliance and the beginnings of the Cold War tension between East and West

P.P.E. – Philosophy, Politics and Economics – a popular Oxford honour school degree, for which the degree of Bachelor of Arts is awarded

P.P.S. – parliamentary private secretary

P.R. – Proportional Representation – electoral system championed by the Liberal Party after the second world war as a more democratic alternative to the traditional 'first past the post' method of electing MPs (*see also* Electoral Reform)

Press Commission – the Royal Commission on the Press, 1947–9, of which Violet was a member

Quisling – traitor or fifth-columnist; after the leader of the Norwegian Fascist Party, Major Quisling, who proclaimed a puppet government in Norway the day after the German invasion of the country in April 1940

Radio Times – founded in 1923 as a magazine carrying details of radio programmes, including notes about performers, and so on; later extended to cover television

Rathaus – city hall

Rene Clair-ish – after René Clair (1898–1981), French film maker

Reuters – worldwide news service; the name originally referred to a telegraph system

Rhineland occupation – the remilitarization of the Rhineland by the Nazis, in March 1936, in direct contravention of the Treaty of Versailles (1919); the British government took no measures to reverse this step, which was one of the seminal events in the decade leading to the second world war; a key act of 'appeasement' by the British, and a dramatic propaganda coup for the Nazis

Ridderzaal – ('Hall of Knights') public building and historic seat of Dutch parliament, the setting for The Hague Congress of May 1948

Schadenfreude – the sensation of malicious pleasure at the misfortune of another

Schulspeise – free school meal

Schuman Plan – 9 May 1950 blueprint for the European Coal and Steel Community, named after the French foreign minister Robert Schuman – *see* E.C.S.C.

S.C.R. – Senior (or Students') Common Room (of a university or college)

S.D.P. – Social Democratic Party; founded in 1981 by four disillusioned Labour politicians, Roy Jenkins, David Owen, William Rodgers and Shirley Williams; it supported continued British membership of the EEC, electoral reform through proportional representation and a reflationary economic plan; after a period of electoral alliance with the Liberal Party the SDP merged with it, in 1988, to form the Social and Liberal Democratic Party, or 'Liberal Democrats'

Second, a – in British universities a class or 'grade' of honours degree – of which a 'first' is the highest and a 'third' the lowest (nowadays)

S.E.D. – Sozialistische Einheitspartei Deutschlands – German Socialist Unity Party; the Soviet-backed party in Berlin after the second world war

shandigaff – a mixture; from the drink that mixes beer and ginger-beer

Sieges Allee – Avenue of Victory

Sieges Säule – Column of Victory

siren suit – a kind of boiler-suit commonly worn during the 1939–45 war; a one-piece zipped garment, it could be quickly put on when an air raid signal sounded and it was necessary to go down to a cold shelter, often at night; Churchill wore one constantly at 10 Downing Street (though not during cabinet meetings) and *en famille*

Six, the – term describing the original six members of the EEC (and, earlier, the ECSC) – France, West Germany, Italy, Belgium, the Netherlands and Luxembourg

Souls, the – a group of friends in fashionable London society at the end of the nineteenth-century, so-called because their high-minded and intellectual conversation reputedly often turned to spiritual matters; Violet's step-mother Margot Asquith was a prominent member

sound and sight – radio and television – in the era of television Violet often used 'sound' to denote radio

S.P.D. – Socialdemokratische Partei Deutschlands – German Socialist Party; centre left

Star, House of Commons – a diamond star brooch, a wedding gift to VBC from the House of Commons, November 1915

Star – radical newspaper founded in 1888; it later became the sister paper of the *News Chronicle* and closed down with it in October 1960

Sten gun – a type of lightweight sub-machine gun

Strangers' Gallery – in the House of Commons and House of Lords, the gallery in which members of the public can sit to observe proceedings

Suez Group – a group of Conservative MPs, led by Captain Waterhouse, implacably opposed to any compromise on British interests in the Suez Canal; after its nationalization in July 1956 the Suez Group advocated military intervention against Egypt

Syndicalists – political group advocating 'syndicalism' – the revolutionary transformation of society through strike action by workers

tape, the – the 'ticker-tape' strip of paper or ribbon on which the messages are printed in a telegraph system

Telstar – archetypal communications satellite, launched on 10 July 1962, inaugurating a new age of electronic communications; the satellite amplified a signal from the ground and relayed it to another ground station; this technology enabled the Tokyo Olympics to be broadcast across the Pacific two years later

Teutoburger Wald – range of hills forming an arc 25 miles to the north-west of Münster (Germany)

Third Programme – BBC Radio station first on air in September 1946; its output was to be 'of a high cultural level', devoted to the arts and serious discussion

Tischleindeckdich – a German children's fable about a table that sets itself, with food, every time the word 'Tischleindeckdich' is said

Tolpuddle Martyrs – name given to six English labourers sentenced in March 1834 to seven years' banishment to Australia, for organizing trade union activities in the Dorset village of Tolpuddle; the sentences were remitted in March 1836

T.U. – Trade Union

22 Club/Committee – *see* 1922 Committee

Twinnery – a room in Clovelly Court, so called because it was 'given' to Betty Asquith and her twin sister when they were children by the then owner, Christine Hamlyn

***T.W.T.W.*[*T.W.*]** – *That Was The Week That Was*, innovative 1960s satirical television programme presented by David Frost and directed by Ned Sherrin

U.E.M. – *see* United Europe Movement

U.K.C. – the United Kingdom Council of the European Movement – a pro-European political grouping that emerged around 1948 and in which Violet and many MPs participated

U.N.A. – United Nations Association – formed to promote the idea of the UN at a grass-roots level; it was the logical successor in Britain to the League of Nations Union and its membership comprised many old LNU activists – Violet among them; there were 600 branches in Britain, some of which could claim 400 members or more, and the British branch of the movement was the biggest worldwide

United Europe Movement – cross-party political organization founded by Churchill in the winter of 1946–7 to promote the idea of European union

U.N.O. – United Nations Organization

U.N.R.R.A. – United Nations Relief and Rehabilitation Administration, founded during the second world war (1943) to help refugees and provide aid to areas liberated from the Axis powers

Unter den Linden – principal avenue in East Berlin leading to Brandenburg Gate and lined by linden (lime) trees
ur-alt – very old; ancient
Vansittart-ite – anti-German; after Sir Robert (later Lord) Vansittart (1881–1957), who as permanent secretary at the foreign office under Baldwin and Chamberlain warned of the dangers of German rearmament and aggression; his repeated warnings on this count acquired for him a reputation for being anti-German
ventre à terre – at full speed
viva – oral examination used in British universities to give candidates who are borderline after their written exam an opportunity to move up a degree class
W.E.U. – *see* Western European Union
Western European Union – a defensive alliance created in 1954 by the Brussels Treaty powers (Britain, France and Benelux) and Italy and West Germany; it was proposed by the British government following the collapse of the EDC plan, as an alternative means of promoting collective security, and was the means by which Germany was able to rearm and join NATO
White's Club – oldest and grandest of the London gentlemen's clubs, established in 1693 as White's Chocolate House; Edward VII was a member
widerlich – disgusting, repulsive
Yalta – conference between the 'big three' of Churchill, Roosevelt and Stalin at Yalta in the Crimea, 4–11 February 1945; on the agenda was the prosecution of the war to its successful conclusion, and the borders and government of the post-war world, particularly in eastern Europe
Zionist – originally, one who supported the movement for the creation of a Jewish homeland in Palestine

APPENDIX B: *Biographical notes*

The following biographical notes are of family members, prominent historical figures and individuals mentioned frequently in the text. They are mostly confined to the years 1946–69 and have had to be kept concise. It has therefore seldom been possible to include full details. The accumulation of honours, in particular, has been abbreviated so that only the most senior are generally shown – for example, Earl, not Viscount *and* Earl; GCVO, not KCVO *and* GCVO. Marriage details are generally only given where the spouse appears in the text – first marriages are indicated '(1)', second '(2)', and so on. Names in square brackets are commonly used nicknames, those in rounded brackets are unused given names. The colleges identified are all Oxford unless otherwise stated. The principal sources of reference have been *Who's Who, Who Was Who* and the *Dictionary of National Biography.*

Aitken, William Maxwell – see Beaverbrook, Lord.

Asquith, Anthony [Puffin/Puff] (1902–68), Violet's half-brother and godson, the son of H. H. Asquith and his second wife Margot; godfather to Raymond Bonham Carter; educ. Winchester and Balliol College; film director, a founder member of the Film Society in London, and first president of the Association of Cinematographic Technicians (1937–68); he made a major contribution to British film in the years around the second world war and enjoyed particular success with his adaptations of Terence Rattigan plays – for example, *The Winslow Boy* (1948) and *The Browning Version* (1951); he also directed *Pygmalion* (1938) and a highly rated version of *The Importance of Being Earnest* (1951); Violet had strong feelings of maternal protectiveness towards 'Puff', and helped him to overcome his alcoholism, which he once intimated to her was induced by feelings of guilt over his homosexuality; he was involved in a serious car accident in December 1963, from which he never fully recovered; he died of cancer in London, 20 February 1968, and was buried in the churchyard at Sutton Courtenay near his parents.

Asquith, Arthur Melland [Oc] (1883–1939), Violet's brother, godfather to her daughter Cressida; married, 1918, Hon. Betty Constance *née* Manners; educ. Winchester and New College; served with distinction in the Great War (Royal Naval Division; DSO and two bars) and retired as honorary brigadier-general in 1918, after being severely wounded December 1917; afterwards a company director; died of leukaemia, 25 August 1939.

Asquith, Betty Constance *née* Manners (d. 1962) Violet's sister-in-law; married, 1918, Arthur 'Oc' Asquith, with whom she had four daughters – Mary, Jean, Susan and Christine; inherited Clovelly in Devon, one of Violet's favourite places to visit and the scene of many family holidays.

Asquith, Lady Cynthia *née* Charteris (1887–1960), Violet's sister-in-law and exact contemporary, daughter of the 11th Earl of Wemyss; married, 1910, Herbert ('Beb') Asquith; novelist, biographer and diarist.

Asquith, Cyril [Cys] (1890–1954), cr. Baron Asquith of Bishopstone, 1951; Violet's younger brother; educ. Winchester and Balliol College; married, 1918, **Anne Stephanie *née* Pollock** (d. 1964); served in 1914–18 war; barrister and judge; author (with J. A. Spender) of a two-volume life of his father, 1932; lord justice of appeal, 1946; lord of appeal in ordinary and life peer, 1951; declined the lord chancellorship when offered it by Churchill, October 1951, as he felt that he was not physically strong enough and Churchill 'mustn't be saddled with a lame duck on the woolsack' (*DNB*); died in London, 24 August 1954. He was only a year old when his mother died and Violet, three years older, was always extremely protective towards him. On hearing of his death Cynthia Asquith wrote to her: 'How well I remember him, and your love for him – first as the silent, intense, butting-like-a-goat little red-headed boy; and then as the thrilling-looking youth with a flame in his eyes, whose face made one wonder for what he was destined. Alas, that it should have happened so many many years too soon.'

Asquith, Helen Kelsall *née* Melland (1854–91), Violet's mother, the daughter of Frederick Melland and his wife Anne; married, 1877, H. H. Asquith, at the age of twenty-three; died of typhoid fever at the age of thirty-seven, leaving a family of five young children – Raymond (then aged twelve), Herbert ('Beb'), Arthur ('Oc'), Violet and Cyril ('Cys'). Her death had an incalculable effect on her children – Raymond, being the eldest, is said to have taken it the hardest. But Asquith, writing to his future second wife Margot (Tennant) in 1893, wrote of his daughter: 'Violet, who is staying in the country with an Aunt, began to talk to her about Helen & said, after a pause, "You know I sometimes have such a nasty feeling, as if I really couldn't stand it any longer." Asked what she meant she said "About Mother being dead." Isn't that rather pathetic, for she is the least morbid & most high-spirited of children.'

Asquith, Herbert [Beb] (1881–1947), Violet's brother; married, 1910, Lady Cynthia Charteris; educ. Winchester and Balliol College; trained as a barrister; severely shell shocked during the Great War, in which he served with the Royal Field Artillery (captain); wrote poetry, most notably *The Volunteer* (published 1915), a memoir and novels; hearing of his death, 5 August 1947, Violet wrote: 'I feel that his rare shy spirit, which was always a prisoner here, has broken its bonds & is released. No one was ever more valuably sensitive to life & self expression, & release came to him only in poetry & his recognition of beauty wherever it was to be found.'

Asquith, Herbert Henry [H.H.A.] (1852–1928), cr. Earl of Oxford and Asquith,

1925; Violet's father; born in Morley, Yorkshire, the son of a cloth manufacturer; educ. City of London School and Balliol College; married, (1) Helen Kelsall Melland (d. 1891), 1877, four sons, one daughter; (2) Margot Tennant, 1894, one daughter, one son; barrister, 1876; Liberal MP for East Fife, 1886–1918; Paisley, 1920–4; prime minister, 1908–16; Liberal leader 1908–26; died 15 February 1928. In a *Times* obituary of Violet, Michael Foot wrote: 'She was a great upholder of the Asquithian tradition. No father ever had a more faithful daughter.'

Asquith, Katharine *née* Horner (1885–1976), Violet's sister-in-law, godmother to Laura and Raymond Bonham Carter; married, 1907, Raymond Asquith – two daughters and one son. Katharine never remarried after her husband's death in September 1916 and she turned to Catholicism in her widowhood, something that Violet found difficult to accept; the years, though, softened this difference between them, which was in any case tempered by love and mutual respect.

Asquith, (Emma Alice Margaret) Margot *née* Tennant (1864–1945), Countess of Oxford and Asquith; Violet's step-mother, the daughter of the Scots industrialist Sir Charles Tennant, Bt; she married, 1894, H. H. Asquith, with whom she had one daughter (Elizabeth) and one son (Anthony); she died in London, 28 July 1945. A woman of great style and high spirits, Margot did not enjoy an easy relationship with all of her step-children, but was never one to let the threat of disapproval cramp her style: 'She flashed into our lives like some dazzling bird of Paradise – brilliant, incalculable, unexpected – filling us with admiration, amazement, amusement, affection, sometimes even (as children) with a vague uneasiness as to what she might, or might not, do next. We realised of course that she was a law unto herself – but would other people do so too we sometimes wondered with a faint disquiet' (VBC's broadcast 'Margot Oxford', BBC Home Service, 31 May 1953).

Asquith, Raymond (1878–1916), Violet's eldest brother; married, 1907, Katharine *née* Horner; educ. Winchester and Balliol College; barrister and prospective Liberal candidate for Derby before the Great War; volunteered in 1914; lieutenant, Grenadier Guards, 1915. As the Somme approached in 1916 Raymond Asquith steadfastly refused a post on the general staff and he died of wounds sustained in the battle, 15 September 1916.

Asquith of Yarnbury, Lady – see Bonham Carter, (Helen) Violet.

Attlee, Clement Richard (1883–1967), cr. 1st Earl Attlee, 1955; OM, 1951; educ. Haileybury and University College; married, 1922, Violet *née* Millar; Labour MP for Limehouse Stepney, 1922–50; West Walthamstow, 1950–5; leader of the Labour Party, 1935–55; deputy prime minister, 1942–5; prime minister, 1945–51.

Balfour, Arthur James [AJB] (1848–1930), cr. Earl, 1922; educ. Eton and Trinity College, Cambridge; his parliamentary career began as Conservative MP for Hertford in 1874; was Unionist MP for the City of London, 1906–22; prime minister, 1902–5; first lord of the admiralty, 1915–16; foreign secretary, 1916–19; lord president of the council, 1919–22, 1925–9. Balfour became interested in Zionism following a conversation with Chaim Weizmann during the 1906 general election and in November 1917, when foreign secretary, he issued the so-called 'Balfour Declaration' in favour of a Jewish national home in Palestine; this made possible Jewish immigration into Palestine after the Great War, when the territory was a British mandate under the terms of Versailles.

Beaverbrook, Lord – William Maxwell Aitken (1879–1964), cr. Baron Beaverbrook, 1917; born Maple, Ontario; educ. in New Brunswick; newspaper proprietor, owner of the *Daily Express, Sunday Express, Evening Standard*; Unionist MP for Ashton-under-Lyne, Lancashire, 1910–16; a government minister in both world wars, enjoying the patronage of Lloyd George in the first and of Churchill in the second: 'what an evil-looking Ape-Man he is! & how strange that he shld have such knock-down charm for so many people – including Winston' (VBC to Ettie Grenfell, 10 April 1948).

Beddington-Behrens, Sir Edward (1897–1968), Kt, 1957; educ. Charterhouse and Christ Church; married (3) 1958, Mrs Renée Kane; served 1914–18 (MC and bar) and 1939–45; PhD (economics), University of London; vice chairman and one of the founders of the European Movement; chairman and organizer of numerous European conferences; author of *Why Britain Must Join Europe* (1966).

Ben-Gurion, David (1886–1973), Polish-born Israeli statesman, who as leader of the Mapai (Labour) party announced the birth of the state of Israel, May 1948; retired from premiership, 1953, but returned 1955–63.

Benn, Tony (Anthony Wedgwood Benn) (b. 1925), educ. Westminster and Oxford; son of William Wedgwood Benn, 1st Viscount Stansgate; married, 1949, Caroline *née* De Camp; joined Labour Party 1942; MP (Lab.) Bristol South East, 1950–60, August 1963–83; Chesterfield, March 1984–; minister of posts and telecommunications, 1974–5; secretary of state for energy, 1975–9; candidate for Labour leadership, 1976, 1988.

Benson, Leslie *née* Foster (1907–81), mother of Leslie (later Lady) Bonham Carter; born in Winnetka, Illinois, daughter of Albert Volney Foster, investment banker, of Lake Forest, Illinois; she married (1) 1928, Condé Nast, publisher – they had one daughter, Leslie, later Lady Bonham-Carter; (2) 1932, R. L. 'Rex' Benson, merchant banker, two sons; died in Sussex.

Benson, Sir Reginald Lindsay [Rex] (1889–1968), Kt, 1958; educ. Eton and Balliol College; married, 1932, Leslie *née* Foster; joined army (9th Lancers) 1910 and served 1914–18 war (MC, 1914); resigned commission, 1922; rejoined army 1939 – liaison officer to First French Army before Dunkirk; military attaché in Washington, 1941–4; joined his father in Robert Benson & Co. merchant bank, 1924, becoming chairman; later chairman of Robert Benson, Lonsdale & Co.; after a merger with Kleinwort, Son & Co. he served on the board of Kleinwort, Benson, merchant bank.

Bentley, Ada [Nannie] (d. 1956), nanny to the Bonham Carter children; Laura Grimond recalled that she was 'allowed to leave school at 12 .... in order to earn 1 shilling a week pushing a pram to help her mother support 6 or 7 brothers & sisters and her invalid and bad-tempered husband'; she was a highly intelligent woman, a passionate Liberal and Congregationalist; Violet confessed to being somewhat in awe of her.

Berlin, (Sir) Isaiah (1909–97), Kt, 1957; OM, 1971; born in Riga; educ. St Paul's School and Corpus Christi College; married, 1956, Aline *née* de Gunzbourg; fellow of All Souls, 1950–66, 1975–97; Chichele professor of social and political theory, Oxford, 1957–67; founder president, Wolfson College, Oxford, 1966–75; member, board of directors, Royal Opera House, Covent Garden, 1954–65, 1974–87. 'Yes, Isaiah is alpha plus-plus-plus as a talker. I longed to write down every word he said – but his pace wld have defeated short-hand' (VBC to MRBC, 18 April 1948).

Bevan, Aneurin (1897–1960), educ. Serhowy Elementary School and Central Labour College; married, 1934, Jennie Lee, MP; worked as a coal miner and became a trade union activist; Labour MP for Ebbw Vale, Monmouthshire, 1929–60; minister of health, 1945–51; minister of labour and national service, 1951 – resigned over introduction of prescription charges.

Bevin, Ernest (1881–1951), left school aged eleven and worked at delivering mineral water in Bristol, where he became active in the trade union movement; rose to become general secretary of the Transport and General Workers' Union, 1921–40; Labour MP for Central Wandsworth, 1940–50; East Woolwich, 1950–1; minister of labour and national service, 1940–5; foreign secretary, 1945–51; lord privy seal, 1951.

Bibesco, Elizabeth Charlotte Lucy née Asquith (1897–1945), daughter of H. H. Asquith and his second wife, Margot; sister of Anthony Asquith, half-sister of Violet; married, May 1919, Prince Antoine Bibesco (1878–1952), Rumanian diplomat – they had a daughter, Priscilla (Mrs Priscilla Hodgson); a novelist, she lived abroad after her marriage and seldom visited England; she died in Rumania, April 1945.

Birley, (Sir) Robert (1903–82), KCMG 1967; educ. Rugby and Balliol College; headmaster, Charterhouse, 1935–47; educational adviser to military governor, control commission for Germany, 1947–9; a founder of the annual Königswinter conference; headmaster of Eton, 1949–63; his experience of Germany after the war, and in particular the value of education as a medium for social change, inspired him to become a visiting professor at the University of Witwatersrand, 1964–7, where he worked against apartheid; Violet greatly admired Birley, not least for this gesture: 'a delightful man – with great personality, good sense & wonderful looks'; he read the lesson at her memorial service at St Paul's (I Corinthians 15: 20-end).

Bonham Carter, Cressida – see Ridley, (Helen Laura) Cressida

Bonham Carter, Elena Beatrice *née* Propper de Callejon (b. 1934), Violet and Bongie's daughter-in-law; the daughter of HE Señor Eduardo Propper de Callejon and his wife Hélène *née* Fould-Springer; married Raymond Bonham Carter, 26 July 1958 – two sons and one daughter: Edward (b. 1960), Thomas (b. 1961) and Helena (b. 1966).

Bonham Carter, Laura – see Grimond, Laura (Miranda)

Bonham Carter, Leslie *née* Nast (b. 1930), Violet and Bongie's daughter-in-law; the daughter of Condé Nast and Leslie *née* Foster; married (1) 1949 Peter Grenfell, Baron St Just (diss. 1955) – one daughter, Laura (b. 1950); (2) 1955 Mark Bonham Carter – three daughters: Jane (b. 1957), Virginia (b. 1959) and Eliza (b. 1961).

Bonham Carter, Mark Raymond (1922–94), cr. life peer, 1986; third child and elder son of Violet and Maurice Bonham Carter; educ. Winchester and Balliol College; married, 1955, Leslie *née* Nast – one step-daughter and three daughters; served 1941–5 with Grenadier Guards (dispatches); contested Barnstaple (Lib.), 1945; Commonwealth Fund scholar, University of Chicago, 1947–8; director, William Collins & Co., 1955–8; MP (Lib.) Torrington, Devon, March 1958–9; contested Torrington, 1959 and 1964; first chairman of Race Relations Board, 1966–70; chairman, Community Relations Commission, 1971–7; director, Royal Opera House, Covent Garden, 1958–82; governor, Royal Ballet, 1960–94; chairman of governors, 1985–94; vice chairman and a governor of the BBC, 1975–81.

Bonham Carter, Sir Maurice [Bongie] (1880–1960), cr KCB, 1916; KCVO, 1917; Violet's husband, youngest of the eleven sons of Henry Bonham Carter; educ. Winchester and Balliol College; worked in industry before training for the bar (called 1909); private secretary to H. H. Asquith, 1910–16; assistant secretary, ministry of reconstruction, 1917; air ministry, 1918; partner in O. T. Falk & Co., and formerly with Buckmaster and Moore; director, Blackburn & General Aircraft; chairman of Aero Engines, Bristol, and Power Jets, Rugby. He married Violet on 30 November 1915 and together they had two daughters and two sons. Quentin Crewe lodged with the Bonham Carters in London and remembered Bongie as being 'as unalarming' as Violet was 'frightening': '[Bongie] expected nothing of one, except perhaps politeness. When she argued, in her vociferous manner, with some lightly held opinion of mine, foolishly expressed, he would bumble in the background: 'Oh yes, yes. Never mind. I mean, would you like to lunch at Brooks's tomorrow?'' (*Well, I Forget the Rest*, 56).

Bonham Carter, Raymond Henry (b. 1929), youngest of the four children of Violet and Maurice Bonham Carter; educ. Winchester and Magdalen College; Harvard Business School (MBA, 1954); married, 1958, Elena *née* Propper de Callejon – two sons and one daughter; with Irish Guards, 1947–9; read PPE at Magdalen, graduating in 1952; won a Charles and Julia Henry Fellowship in 1952, which he elected to take to Harvard Business School, 1952; graduated from Harvard in 1954 and returned to England, joining J. Henry Schröder & Co., 1954–8; acting adviser, Bank of England, 1958–63; alternate executive director for UK, IMF, and member, UK Treasury and Supply Delegation, Washington, 1961–3; joined S. G. Warburg & Co., 1964; executive director, 1967–77; retired, 1979, following disability.

Bonham Carter, (Helen) Violet *née* Asquith (1887–1969), cr. life peer, 1964 – Baroness Asquith of Yarnbury; DBE, 1953; Hon. LLD Sussex, 1963; born 15 April 1887, in Hampstead, London, fourth child and only daughter of H. H. Asquith and his first wife, Helen Melland; privately educated; 'finished' in Dresden and Paris, 1903–5, and learned to speak German and French; married Maurice Bonham Carter, 30 November 1915 – two daughters (Cressida and Laura) and two sons (Mark and Raymond); president of the Women's Liberal Federation, 1923–5, 1939–45; member of the executive, LNU; member of Churchill's Freedom Focus, 1936–9; governor of the BBC, 1941–5, resigned to contest Wells, 1945, and was reinstated after failing to gain election; became a governor of the Old Vic, 1945; first woman president of the Liberal Party Organization, 1945–7; vice-chair of the United Europe Movement 1947; delegate to the Commonwealth Relations Conference in Canada, 1949; contested Colne Valley, 1951; a trustee of the Glyndebourne Arts Trust 1955–69; president of the Royal Institute of International Affairs, 1964–9; a patron of the United Nations Association; author of *Winston Churchill as I Knew Him* (1965); died in London, 19 February 1969. Quentin Crewe remembered 'an over-developed brand of honesty that prevented her from leaving anything unsaid. At a party she said to me: "There is Tom Driberg, I must go over and tell him how dreadful I thought his article was on Sunday." "But why do you have to tell him? It will merely upset him. Couldn't you just say nothing?" "Certainly not. He might think I had approved of it"' (*Well, I Forget the Rest*, 56).

Boothby, Robert John Graham ('Bob') (1900–86), cr. life peer, 1958; KBE, 1953; educ. Eton and Magdalen College; Unionist MP for East Aberdeenshire, 1924–58; PPS to Winston Churchill (when chancellor of the exchequer), 1926–9; parliamentary secretary, ministry of food, 1940–41; a British delegate to consultative assembly of the Council of Europe, 1949–57; president, Anglo-Israel Association, 1962–75.

Brandt, Willy (1913–92), born in Lübeck 'Herbert Ernst Karl Frahm'; worked as a reporter for the *Lübecker Volksbote*, 1927–33; emigrated to Norway, 1933; involved in anti-Nazi resistance, 1940–5; regained German nationality and became a member of the West German parliament, 1949–57; member of the Berlin Abgeordnetenhaus (House of Delegates), 1950–70; president, 1955–7; internationally known as the mayor of Berlin, 1957–66; foreign minister of Federal Republic, 1966–9; chancellor, 1969–74; awarded 1971 Nobel Peace Prize for his achievement in promoting better understanding between East and West in Germany and in Europe.

Brown, George Alfred (1914–85), cr. life peer, 1970 (George-Brown); educ. West Square Central School, Southwark; MP (Lab.) Belper, Derbyshire, 1945–70; joint parliamentary secretary, ministry of agriculture and fisheries, 1947–51; ministry of works, 1951; secretary of state for economic affairs, 1964–6; for foreign affairs, 1966–8; deputy leader of Labour Party, 1960–70.

Butler, Richard Austen [Rab] (1902–82), cr. life peer, 1965; educ. Marlborough and Pembroke College, Cambridge; MP (Con.) Saffron Walden, 1929–65; chancellor of the exchequer, 1951–5; lord privy seal, 1955–9; leader of the House of Commons, 1955–61; home secretary, 1957–62; deputy prime minister, July 1962–October 1963; foreign secretary, 1963–4; master of Trinity College, Cambridge, 1965–78. 'We discussed Anthony & Rab – & Oliver [Lyttelton] said that tho' he agreed Rab had no personal vanity he had the same kind of massive intellectual arrogance as Cripps' (VBC diary, 6 June 1954). 'Rab was always too clever by half. Every answer he gave, even in cabinet, could be taken either way. No one ever knew where he was or whether they were with him' (Gwilym Lloyd George speaking to William Haley – Haley diary, 16 May 1966).

Byers, Charles Frank (1915–84), cr. life peer, 1964; educ. Westminster and Christ Church; married, 1939, Joan *née* Oliver; Liberal MP for North Dorset, 1945–50; Liberal chief whip, 1946–50; chairman, Liberal Party, 1950–2, 1965–7; vice president, 1954–65; Liberal leader, House of Lords, from 1967: 'Starved of new creations by the Conservatives, the Liberal lords were an ill-organized band before Byers arrived. By common consent he does a good job leading what is still an awkward crew' (*Times* diary, 30 December 1968).

Callaghan, Leonard James [Jim] (b. 1912) cr. life peer, 1987; Labour MP for South Cardiff, 1945–50; South East Cardiff, 1950–83; Cardiff South and Penarth, 1983–7; chancellor of the exchequer, 1964–7; home secretary, 1967–70; prime minister, 1976–9; leader of the Labour Party, 1976–80.

Castle, Barbara Anne *née* Betts (b. 1910), cr. life peer, 1990; educ. Bradford Girls' Grammar School and St Hugh's College; married, 1944, Edward Castle; Labour MP for Blackburn, 1945–50; Blackburn East, 1950–5; Blackburn, 1955–79; minister of overseas development, 1964–5; transport, 1965–8; secretary of state, employment and productivity, 1968–70; later Labour MEP, 1979–89, and leader of British Labour Group in Europe, 1979–85.

Cecil, Robert Arthur James Gascoyne- [Bobbety] (1893–1972), 5th Marquess of Salisbury (succeeded 1947); educ. Eton and Christ Church; married, 1915, **Elizabeth Vere** (d. 1982), daughter of Lord Richard Cavendish; Conservative MP for South Dorset, 1929–41; elevated to Lords as Baron Essendon, 1941; leader of the House of Lords, 1942–5, 1951–7; secretary of state, dominions, 1940–2, 1943–5; colonies, 1942; lord privy seal, 1942–3, 1951–2; secretary of state, commonwealth relations, 1952; lord president of the council, 1952–7.

Churchill, Clementine Ogilvy Spencer *née* Hozier (1885–1977), cr. life peer, 1965 (Spencer- Churchill); GBE, 1946; daughter of Sir Henry and Lady Blanche Hozier;

educ. at Berkhamsted High School for Girls and privately; married Winston Churchill in 1908, with whom she had four daughters and one son (Diana, Sarah, Marigold, Mary, Randolph); president of the YWCA Wartime Fund, 1941–7; chairman of Red Cross Aid to Russia Fund, 1939–46.

Churchill, Randolph (Frederick Edward Spencer) (1911–68), only son of Sir Winston and Lady (Clementine) Churchill; educ. Eton and Christ Church; married (1) 1939 Hon. Pamela Digby, daughter of 11th Baron Digby (diss. 1946); (2) 1948 June *née* Osborne (diss. 1961); served 1939–45 war; Conservative MP for Preston, 1940–5; six times unsuccessful in parliamentary elections, 1935–51; journalist and author; began the monumental biography of his father, continued and completed after his death by Martin Gilbert. 'He is in some ways a pathetic creature – his faults so gross & obvious – & yet possessing qualities of courage & loyalty to friends in which (for instance) Bob Boothby is entirely lacking' (VBC to William Haley, 21 June 1957).

Churchill, Sir Winston Leonard Spencer (1874–1965), KG, 1953; OM, 1946; elder son of Lord Randolph Churchill (1849–95 – third son of 7th duke of Marlborough, and chancellor of the exchequer, 1886–7); educ. Harrow and Sandhurst; married, 1908, Clementine *née* Hozier – four daughters, one son; joined army, 1895, serving in India and Africa (Sudan); correspondent for *Morning Post*, South African war, 1899–1900; first elected to parliament as a Conservative, at Oldham, 1900; thereafter a Liberal, Coalition Liberal and Constitutionalist, before returning to the Conservative Party, and was MP for Woodford, Essex, 1945–64; he became first lord of the admiralty, 1911, was sacked by Asquith, 1915, fought on the Western Front, returned to government as minister of munitions, 1917–19, held numerous cabinet posts, 1919–29, and returned to the admiralty at the outbreak of the second world war, 1939; first taken into government by Asquith, Churchill later served under Lloyd George, Baldwin and Chamberlain; he became prime minister of the war Coalition and minister of defence, 1940–5; briefly premier of a caretaker coalition, 1945; leader of the opposition, 1945–51; premier, 1951–5; he resigned 5 April 1955; author of many histories, including *The World Crisis* (4 vols, 1923–9) and *The Second World War* (6 vols, 1948–54).

Coote, Sir Colin (Reith) (1893–1979), Kt, 1962; educ. Rugby and Balliol College; married (3) 1946, Amalie *née* Lewkowitz; served 1914–18 war; Conservative MP for Isle of Ely, 1917–22; deputy editor of *Daily Telegraph* and *Morning Post*, 1945–50; managing editor, 1950–64.

Cripps, Sir (Richard) Stafford (1889–1952), Kt, 1930; married 1911 Isobel *née* Swithinbank; educ. Winchester and University College, London; Labour MP for East Bristol, 1931–50; South East Bristol, February-October 1950; president of the board of trade, 1945–7; minister for economic affairs, 1947; chancellor of the exchequer, 1947–50.

Crossman, Richard (Howard Stafford) (1907–74), educ. Winchester and New College; assistant editor, *New Statesman*, 1938–55; Labour MP for Coventry East, 1945–74; minister for housing and local government, 1964–6; leader of the Commons and lord president of the council, 1966–8; secretary of state, social security, 1968–70; editor, *New Statesman*, 1970–2; diarist.

Davies, Clement (1884–1962), QC, 1926; Liberal MP for Montgomeryshire, 1929–62; leader of the Parliamentary Liberal Party, 1945–56. Violet was not an admirer of Davies, as Liberal leader, but on hearing of his death she wrote: 'Poor old Clem – one cld not help feeling great affection for him & in one way he inspired respect. He gave up a big income at Levers to serve the Party & refused office in W.'s 1951 Govt. when I thought (perhaps mistakenly?) that it wld have been right for us to go in.... He showed no rancour at his displacement from the leadership by Jo – tho' he must have minded it' (VBC diary, 24 March 1962).

de Gaulle, General Charles André Joseph Marie (1890–1970), educ. Saint-Cyr Academy; wounded and taken prisoner in 1914–18 war; temporary brigadier general and commander 4th French armoured division, 1940; assumed leadership of the Free French in exile; became sole president of the French Committee of National Liberation; returned to Paris as leader of provisional government, 9 September 1944; president of the provisional government and chief of armies, 1944–6; first president of Fifth Republic, 1958–69.

Dietrich, Marlene (1901–92), German actress, born in Berlin; worked in cabaret before being spotted by the film-maker Josef von Sternberg, who cast her in the lead role of a cabaret singer in *The Blue Angel* (1930); under his direction she enjoyed a string of Hollywood successes – *Blonde Venus* (1932), *Scarlet Empress* (1934); opposed Nazis and toured extensively entertaining Allied troops during second world war; appeared in films only intermittently thereafter, but performed regularly in cabaret and in her one-woman show.

Douglas-Home, Alexander Frederick [Alec] (1903–96), cr. life peer, 1974 (Home); Kt, 1962; eldest son of 13th Earl of Home, succeeded in 1951, but disclaimed peerages for life, October 1963; educ. Eton and Christ Church; Unionist MP for South Lanark, 1931–45; Conservative MP for Lanark, 1950–1; Kinross and West Perthshire, November 1963-September 1974; secretary of state, commonwealth relations, 1955–60; deputy leader, House of Lords, 1956–7; leader, and lord president of the council, 1959–60; foreign secretary, 1960–63; prime minister, October 1963–October 1964; leader of the opposition, October 1964–July 1965; foreign secretary, 1970–4.

Eden, Sir (Robert) Anthony (1897–1977), cr. 1st Earl of Avon, 1961; KG, 1954; educ. Eton and Christ Church – read Arabic and Persian; married (2) 1952 Clarissa *née* Churchill (niece of Sir Winston); with KRRC 1915–19 (MC 1917); Conservative MP for Warwick and Leamington, 1923–57; foreign secretary, 1935–8; secretary of state, dominions, 1939–40; for war, 1940; foreign secretary, 1940–5; leader of Commons, 1942–5; deputy leader of opposition, 1945–51; foreign secretary and deputy prime minister, 1951–5; prime minister, April 1955–January 1957.

Edinburgh, duke of – see Philip, Prince

Elizabeth II (b. 1926), Elizabeth Alexandra Mary; born in London, 21 April 1926; married, 20 November 1947, Lieutenant Philip Mountbatten, RN, son of Prince Andrew of Greece; three sons and one daughter – Charles (b. 1948), heir-apparent and Prince of Wales (1958); Anne (b. 1950); Andrew (b. 1960); Edward (b. 1964). Succeeded her father, George VI, and proclaimed queen, 6 February 1952; crowned 2 June 1953.

Elizabeth, Queen *see* George VI

Elliot, Katharine *née* Tennant ['Kay Elliot'] (1903–94), cr. 1958 Baroness Elliot of Harwood; DBE, 1958; daughter of Sir Charles Tennant, Bt, and half-sister of Margot Asquith; educ. Abbot's Hill, Hemel Hempstead, and Paris; married 1934 Walter Elliot (see below); a member of Roxburghshire county council, 1946–75, and of many public committees; a Conservative, she unsuccessfully contested the by-election at Kelvingrove, Glasgow, in March 1958, occasioned by her husband's death; later that year she was included by Harold Macmillan in the first ever creation of life peers.

Elliot, Walter Elliot (1888–1958), educ. Glasgow Academy and University; married (2) 1934 Katharine *née* Tennant; served 1914–18 war (MC and bar); Unionist MP for Lanark, 1918–23; Kelvingrove, Glasgow, 1924–45; Scottish Universities, 1946–50; Kelvingrove, 1950–8; secretary of state, Scotland, 1936–8; minister of health, 1938–40; Elliot's support for appeasement effectively ended his cabinet career; he was in Chamberlain's government up to May 1940 but was excluded from Churchill's Coalition and never held cabinet office again.

Freyberg, Barbara *née* Jeykll (1887–1973), GBE, 1953; daughter of Sir Herbert and Lady (Agnes) Jekyll; married (1) 1911 Hon. Francis McLaren (d. 1917); (2) 1922 Bernard Freyberg – one son, Paul; a childhood friend of Violet, she was a popular governor-general's wife in New Zealand.

Freyberg, Sir Bernard (1889–1963), cr. Baron, 1951; KCB, 1942; born in Richmond, Surrey, his family emigrated to New Zealand, 1891; educ. Wellington College, New Zealand; married, 1922, Barbara, widow of Hon. Francis McLaren; served with great distinction in 1914–18 war (RND and 29th Division – DSO and two bars; VC, 1916; brigadier, 1917); GOC New Zealand Forces, 1939–45 (third bar to DSO, 1945); commander-in-chief Allied forces, Crete, 1941; governor-general of New Zealand, 1946–52; lieutenant-governor and deputy constable, Windsor Castle, 1953–63. Violet first met Freyberg when he served in the RND alongside her brother, Oc Asquith, and she was extremely fond of him.

Gaitskell, Hugh Todd (1906–63); educ. Winchester and New College; married, 1937, **Anna Dora *née* Creditor** (1901–89; Russian-born; cr. life peer, 1963); an economist, he was at ministry of economic warfare and board of trade, 1940–5; Labour MP for South Leeds from 1945; parliamentary secretary, ministry of fuel and power, 1946–7; minister, 1947–50; minister of state for economic affairs, 1950; chancellor of the exchequer, 1950–1; Labour leader from December 1955; tried unsuccessfully to persuade Labour Party to drop the 'socialist' clause iv of its constitution, 1959; died after a short illness, 18 January 1963. 'I got Bellenger to introduce him to me at the F.O. party & thought him quite delightful – echt Wykehamical & 'decent' to the finger-tips. How he manages to shake down with people like Crossman I can't imagine. The answer is he doesn't! He left after lunch on Sunday – Crossman spoke late on Sunday' (VBC diary, 24 April 1954).

George VI (1895–1952), Albert Frederick Arthur George, cr. Duke of York, 1920; second of five sons of George V and Queen Mary; married, 1923, **Lady Elizabeth Angela Marguerite Bowes-Lyon** (b. 1900), youngest daughter of 14th Earl of Strathmore and Kinghorne – two daughters, Princess Elizabeth Alexandra Mary (b. 1926; see above), Princess Margaret Rose (b. 1930; see below); educ. Osborne, Dartmouth and Trinity College, Cambridge; proclaimed King George VI, 12 December 1936, in succession to his brother, Edward VIII (who abdicated December 1936, becoming HRH the Duke of Windsor); died 6 February 1952; buried on 15 February in St George's Chapel, Windsor Castle.

Gollancz, Victor (1893–1967), Kt, 1965; educ. St Paul's and New College; founded Victor Gollancz, publishers, 1928; founded Left Book Club, 1936, in response to the rise of fascism; during the second world war helped found the Committee for Rescue from Nazi Terror, on which Violet also sat; an effective public speaker in post-war years for a variety of causes, he opposed capital punishment and supported nuclear disarmament; a governor of the Hebrew University of Jerusalem, 1944–52; as chairman of the Jewish Society for Human Service he organized relief work for Arabs during the Arab-Israeli war.

Grimond, Joseph [Jo] (1913–93), cr. life peer, 1983; Violet's son-in-law; educ. Eton and Balliol College; married Laura Bonham Carter, 1938 – three sons, one daughter; barrister, 1937; served 1939–45 war, Fife & Forfar Yeomanry (major); Liberal candidate for Orkney and Shetland, 1945; director of personnel, European Office of UNRRA, 1945–7; secretary, National Trust for Scotland, 1947–9; MP for Orkney and Shetland, 1950–83; rector of University of Edinburgh, 1960–3; leader of Parliamentary Liberal Party, 1956–67, May–July 1976.

Grimond, Laura Miranda, *née* Bonham Carter (1918–93), Violet and Maurice Bonham Carter's second child; educated privately; married, 31 May 1938, Joseph Grimond; three sons, one daughter – Andrew (1939–66), Grizelda (b. 1942), John (b. 1946), Magnus (b. 1959); a tireless worker for the Liberal cause, she was the Party's candidate at West Aberdeenshire, 1970.

Hailsham, Lord – see Hogg, Quintin McGarel

Haley, Sir William (John) (1901–87), KCMG, 1946; educ. Victoria College, Jersey; married, 1921, Edith *née* Gibbons; director, Manchester Guardian and Evening News, 1930–43; Reuters, 1939–43; editor-in-chief, BBC, 1943–4; director-general, 1944–52; editor, *The Times*, 1952–66; chairman of Times Newspapers, 1967; editor-in-chief, *Encyclopaedia Britannica*, 1968–9. Violet and Haley became close friends during her time at the BBC and they continued a regular correspondence until her death.

Healey, Denis Winston (b. 1917), cr. life peer, 1992; educ. Bradford Grammar School and Balliol College; secretary, International Department of Labour Party, 1945–52; Labour MP for South East Leeds, 1952–5; Leeds East, 1955–92; secretary of state, defence, 1964–70; later chancellor of the exchequer and deputy Labour leader.

Heath, (Sir) Edward (Richard George) (b. 1916), KG 1992; educ. Chatham House School, Ramsgate, and Balliol College; MP (Con.) for Bexley, 1950–74; Bexley, Sidcup, 1974–83; Old Bexley and Sidcup, 1983–; government chief whip, December 1955–October 1959; minister of Labour, October 1959–July 1960; lord privy seal, 1960–3; secretary of state for industry and president of board of trade, October 1963–October 1964; leader of the opposition, 1965–70, 1974–5; prime minister, 1970–4.

Hogg, Quintin McGarel (b. 1907), cr. life peer, 1970 (Hailsham); QC, 1953; educ. Eton and Christ Church; son of 1st Viscount Hailsham, succeeded 1950, but disclaimed peerages for life, November 1963; Conservative MP for Oxford City, 1938–50; St Marylebone, 1963–70; first lord of the admiralty, 1956–7; minister for education, 1957; deputy leader, House of Lords, 1957–60; leader, 1960–3; minister for science and technology, 1959–64; chairman of Conservative Party Organization, September 1957–October 1959; lord president of the council, 1957–9, 1960–4. 'I wonder what you feel about Hailsham's Presidency, not of the Council but of the Conservative Party organization? Is he "the stuff to give them"? I can't help hoping that he isn't. He bears on his breast the two decorations I should least like to wear – the Munich Medal & the Suez Star' (VBC to WSC, 15 September 1957).

Home, Alec (Douglas-) – see Douglas-Home, Alexander Frederick

Jenkins, Roy Harris (b. 1920), cr. life peer, 1987; OM, 1993; educ. Abersychan Grammar School; University College, Cardiff; Balliol College; married, 1945, (Dame) Jennifer *née* Morris; served 1939–45 war (RA, captain); Labour MP for Central Southwark, 1948–50; Stechford, Birmingham, 1950–76; minister of aviation, 1964–5; home secretary, 1965–7, 1974–6; chancellor of the exchequer, 1967–70; deputy Labour leader, 1970–2; later president of the European Commission and a founder and first leader of the Social Democratic Party; SDP MP for Glasgow, Hillhead, 1982–7; chancellor of the University of Oxford, 1987–; historian and writer, biographer of Asquith (1964) and Gladstone (1995), author of *Mr Balfour's Poodle* (1954).

Johnson, Lyndon Baines (1908–73), 36th president of the United States; first elected 1937 a strong 'New Deal' Democrat representative; senator, 1948; vice president, 1960–3; became president on death of Kennedy, 22 November 1963; returned as president, 1964; saw through the Civil Rights (1964) and Voting Rights (1965) acts, honouring Kennedy's commitment to improve the lot of black Americans; did not seek re-election in 1968 amid growing opposition to the Vietnam war.

Kennedy, John Fitzgerald (1917–63), 35th president of the United States; educ. Harvard and under Laski at the LSE (1938), when his father was ambassador in London, after which he wrote his thesis on Britain's unpreparedness for war *Why England Slept* (1940); married, 1953, Jacqueline Lee Bouvier (later Onassis) (1929–94); served as a torpedo boat commander in the Pacific during war; elected Democrat representative, 1947; senator, 1952; president, 1960 – the youngest ever president and the first Roman Catholic; assassinated in Dallas, Texas, 22 November 1963. Violet discussed Kennedy, *inter alia*, with Dean Acheson in Washington in 1962: 'On Berlin he said the situation had been held in suspense for a year thanks to the Snake-Charmer (Kennedy) who had kept the Cobras writhing in menacing positions but forbearing to strike. He felt the danger lay in what they might do if the snake-charmer grew tired' (VBC diary, 2 May 1962).

Keynes, John Maynard (1883–1946), cr. Baron, 1942; FBA 1929; educ. Eton and King's College, Cambridge; economist and fellow and bursar of King's College; treasury official 1915–19 and principal treasury representative at the Paris Peace Conference, 1919; author of *The Economic Consequences of the Peace* (1919); later treasury adviser, 1940, and leader of the British delegation that negotiated the American loan in Washington, September–December 1945; appointed a governor of the International Bank for Reconstruction and Development, 1946; a leading figure in the promotion of the arts in Britain during and immediately after the war; died of a heart attack on 21 April 1946. Keynes had married, in 1925, **Lydia [Loppy] née Lopokova**, a famous ballerina with the Imperial Ballet at St Petersburg.

Law, Rose (d. 1966), Violet's long-serving and faithful maid, 'given' to her by Pamela Lytton when Victor Lytton went out to be governor of Bengal in the early 1920s; on hearing of her death, Raymond Bonham Carter wrote to his mother: 'It is amazing to think that she must have been already in her late forties when she came to you in 1922 – forty four years ago – the whole of Mark's lifetime – and yet to me during those years, save for deteriorating eyesight and deafness in the last years, she changed remarkably little. She was the prototype neat, trim, nimble cockney sparrow, with rapid movements, darting here and there, eyes and ears cocked' (RBC to VBC, 1 October 1966).

Layton, Sir Walter Thomas (1884–1966), cr. Baron, 1947; Kt, 1930; educ. King's College School; Westminster School; University College, London; Trinity College, Cambridge; married, 1910, Eleanor Dorothea *née* Osmaston (d. 1959); unsuccessful Liberal candidate in 1922, 1923 and 1929 general elections; economist, editor and newspaper proprietor; chairman, News Chronicle, 1930–50; director, Reuters, 1945–63; deputy leader of Liberal Party in the House of Lords, 1952–5; vice-president Consultative Assembly of the Council of Europe, 1949–57.

Leslie, Sir (John Randolph) Shane (1885–1971), 3rd Bt; educ. Eton and King's College, Cambridge; a first cousin of Winston Churchill, Leslie was born into the Anglo-Irish Protestant 'Ascendancy' but became a Roman Catholic and Irish nationalist at King's; unsuccessful parliamentary candidate (Nat.) for Londonderry, 1910; tried to reconcile the religions in Ireland, and the Irish to the English; the author of many works including the wartime *The End of a Chapter* (1916).

Lloyd George, David (1863–1945), cr. 1st Earl Lloyd-George of Dwyfor, 1945; OM, 1919; educ. Llanystumdwy Church School and privately; Liberal MP for Caernarvon Boroughs, 1890–1931; Independent Liberal, 1931–45; chancellor of the exchequer, 1908–15; minister of munitions, 1915–16; secretary for war, 1916; prime minister, 1916–22; leader of the Liberal Party, 1926–31; died 26 March 1945.

Longford, (Lord) 'Frank' see Pakenham, Francis Aungier.

Macmillan, (Maurice) Harold (1894–1986), cr. 1st Earl of Stockton, 1984; OM, 1976; educ. Eton and Balliol College; married, 1920, Lady Dorothy Cavendish (d. 1966), daughter of 9th Duke of Devonshire; served 1914–18 war with Grenadier Guards; Conservative MP for Stockton-on-Tees, 1924–9, 1931–45; Bromley, Kent, November 1945–September 1964; parliamentary secretary, ministry of supply, 1940–2; parliamentary under-secretary for colonies, 1942; minister resident at Allied headquarters, North West Africa, 1942–5; secretary for air, 1945; minister of housing and local government, 1951–4; minister of defence, October 1954–April 1955; foreign secretary, April–December 1955; chancellor of the exchequer, December 1955–January 1957; prime minister, January 1957–October 1963; head of Macmillan, publishers; chancellor of Oxford University, 1960–86.

Margaret, Princess (b. 1930), Margaret Rose; born at Glamis Castle, Scotland, 21 August 1930; Princess Margaret was a beautiful and high-spirited young woman and there was much press speculation as to her possible suitors – Mark Bonham Carter was for a time counted among them; in 1955 she announced her decision not to marry Group-Captain Peter Townsend (1914–95); she married, 1960, Antony Armstrong-Jones (b. 1930), cr. Earl of Snowdon, 1961 (diss. 1978).

Milchsack, Lisalotte *née* Duden [Lilo] (1905–92), hon. DCMG, 1972; born in Frankfurt/Main; educ. at universities of Frankfurt, Geneva, Amsterdam; married, Hans Milchsack (d. 1984, shipowner and mayor of Dusseldorf); she and her husband opposed Hitler and tried to persuade English friends against appeasement; they survived in Germany during Nazi rule only by an 'internal exile', keeping a low profile; after a visit to Britain, 1948, she returned to Germany convinced of the need to foster Anglo-German relations; founded, 1949, the Deutsch-Englische Gesellschaft e.V. (Anglo-German Society), which arranged *inter alia* for British speakers to tour Germany, and was hon. secretary (–1977) and chairman (1977–82); under the auspices of the Society, and with the help of (Sir) Robert Birley, she launched, 1950, the annual Königswinter conference. 'There were those who believed that international relations depended on the great forces of history and economic self-interest. For Milchsack what was important was that people should get to know each other' (Anthony Glees, obituary in the *Independent*, 8 August 1992).

Montagu, (Beatrice) Venetia *née* Stanley (1887–1948), youngest child of the 4th Baron Stanley; educated privately; married, July 1915, Edwin Montagu; one daughter, Judy. A close friend and contemporary of Violet, Venetia became in 1912 the confidante of Violet's father. On Asquith's part at least this developed into intense love and over the course of the next three years he wrote more than 500 letters to her. At the same time Asquith's young colleague Edwin Montagu had also fallen in love with Venetia and she accepted his proposal of marriage in May 1915. News of this shocked and saddened Asquith, and it marked the end of his intimate friendship with Venetia, and of the voluminous correspondence between them. Venetia's many letters to Asquith have disappeared, but his were kept by her and have subsequently been published as *H. H. Asquith: Letters to Venetia Stanley* (1982), edited by Michael and Eleanor Brock.

Montgomery, Field Marshal Sir Bernard Law [Monty] (1887–1976), cr. 1st Viscount Montgomery of Alamein, 1946; KCB, 1942; educ. St Paul's School and Sandhurst; married, 1927, Elizabeth *née* Hobart (d. 1937), one son; commander 8th Army, North Africa, Sicily and Italy, 1942–4; commander-in-chief, British group of armies, Northern France, 1944; commander 21st army group, 1944–5; commander, British Army of the Rhine, 1945–6; chief of the Imperial General Staff, 1946–8; chairman of Western Union commanders-in-chief, 1948–51; deputy supreme commander, NATO forces in Europe, 1951–8.

Morrison, Herbert Stanley (1888–1965), cr. life peer, 1959; educ. at elementary schools; Labour MP for South Hackney, 1923–4, 1929–31, 1935–45; East Lewisham, 1945–51; South Lewisham, 1951–9; minister of supply, 1940; home secretary and minister of home security, 1940–5; member of war cabinet, 1942–5; lord president of the council, leader of the House of Commons and deputy prime minister, 1945–51; foreign secretary, March–October 1951; deputy leader of the opposition, 1951–5.

Murray, (George) Gilbert (Aimé) (1866–1957), OM, 1941; born in Sydney; married, 1889, Lady Mary Howard, eldest daughter of 9th Earl of Carlisle; educ. Merchant Taylor's and St John's College; regius professor of Greek, University of Oxford,

1908–36; chairman, LNU, 1923–38; Murray was a great admirer of H. H. Asquith and of Sir Edward Grey, and of the Liberalism that they represented; he knew Violet from the early 1920s and they corresponded regularly about politics; Violet could not comprehend Murray's support for the Suez venture, 1956, which came between them at the very end of his life.

Nast, Condé (1873–1942), born in St Louis; married 1928 Leslie *née* Foster (marriage diss.); the father of Leslie Bonham Carter; founder and publisher of *Vogue* magazine; died in New York.

Nehru, Jawaharlal (1889–1964), born in Allahabad; educ. Harrow and Trinity College, Cambridge; called to the bar, 1912; returned to India and joined the Indian National Congress, becoming a follower of Gandhi; elected president of the Indian National Congress, 1928; became first premier of independent India, 1947, and minister of external affairs, holding both offices until his death.

Nicolson, Sir Harold (George) [Hatchie] (1886–1968), KCVO, 1953; born in Teheran, Persia; educ. Wellington and Balliol College; married, 1913, Hon. **Victoria Mary Sackville-West** ('Vita'/'Vites') (d. 1962); two sons – Lionel Benedict ('Ben') and Nigel; diplomatic service, 1909–29; National Labour MP for West Leicester, 1935–45; parliamentary secretary, ministry of information, 1940–1; governor, BBC, 1941–6; joined Labour Party, 1947; contested North Croydon, 1948; writer, biographer of George V (1952) and diarist. Violet's nickname for him, 'Hatchie', was her version of 'Hadje', which Vita Sackville-West called her husband, and derived from his time at the legation in Teheran, 1925–7.

Nicolson, Nigel (b. 1917), younger son of Sir Harold Nicolson and Hon. Vita Sackville-West; educ. Eton and Balliol College; married, 1953, Philippa *née* d'Eyncourt (diss. 1970; d. 1987); served 1939–45 with Grenadier Guards; Conservative MP for Bournemouth East and Christchurch, February 1952–September 1959; abstained in a key vote of confidence during the Suez crisis and was subsequently deselected by his constituency association; chairman, Executive Committee of UNA, 1961–6; co-founder of Weidenfeld & Nicolson, publishers, and director from 1948; writer, official historian of the Grenadier Guards 1939–45, and editor of his father's *Diaries and Letters*, 1930–62.

Pakenham, Elizabeth *née* Harman (b. 1906), Countess of Longford; educ. Headington School and Lady Margaret Hall, Oxford; married, 1931, Francis Aungier Pakenham, later Lord Pakenham and Earl of Longford; Labour candidate for Cheltenham, 1935; Oxford, 1950; writer.

Pakenham, Francis Aungier (b. 1905), cr. Baron Pakenham, 1945; 7th Earl of Longford (s. 1961); politician and writer; educ. Eton and New College; married, 1931, Elizabeth *née* Harman (b. 1906); student in politics, Christ Church, 1934–46, 1952–64; personal assistant to Sir William Beveridge, 1941–4; minister of civil aviation, 1948–51; first lord of the admiralty, May–October 1951; later leader of the House of Lords, 1964–8; secretary of state for the colonies, 1965–6; lord privy seal, 1964–5, 1966–8.

Philip, Prince (b. 1921), cr. Duke of Edinburgh (on marriage to Princess Elizabeth, 20 November 1947); OM, 1968; born in Corfu, Philip Mountbatten, son of late Prince Andrew of Greece; educ. Cheam, Gordonstoun and Dartmouth; served with the Royal Navy during the second world war; an active consort to the queen, he inaugurated the Duke of Edinburgh Award Scheme for youth training and development.

Powell, (John) Enoch (1912–98), educ. King Edward's, Birmingham and Trinity College, Cambridge; Conservative MP for Wolverhampton South West, 1950–74; Ulster Unionist, Down South, 1974–83; South Down, 1983–87; minister of health, 1960–3; author and classical scholar.

Rees-Mogg, William (b. 1928), cr. life peer, 1988; Kt, 1981; educ. Charterhouse and Balliol College; married, 1962, Gillian *née* Morris; joined *Financial Times*, 1952; joined *Sunday Times*, 1960; politics and economics editor, 1961–3; deputy editor, 1964–7; editor, *The Times*, 1967–81; contested Chester-le-Street, Co. Durham (Con.), 1956 and 1959.

Ridley, (Sir) Adam Nicholas (b. 1942), Kt, 1985; Violet's grandson, the only son of Jasper and Cressida Ridley; educ. Eton and Balliol College; joined foreign office, 1965, and seconded to DEA, 1965–8; Harkness Fellow, University of California, Berkeley, 1968–9; later executive director of Hambros Bank.

Ridley, (Helen Laura) Cressida *née* Bonham Carter (1917–98), eldest child of Violet and Maurice Bonham Carter, born 22 April 1917; educated privately; married 1939 Jasper Ridley (d. 1943); one son, Adam (b. 1942); worked as an archaeologist, spending time at the British School in Rome.

Russell, Bertrand Arthur William (1872–1970), 3rd Earl Russell (succeeded 1931); OM, 1949; Nobel Prize for Literature, 1950; educ. privately and Trinity College, Cambridge; married (1) 1894 Alys *née* Pearsall Smith (diss. 1921, d. 1951); (2) 1921 Dora *née* Black (diss. 1935); (3) 1936 Patricia *née* Spence (diss. 1952); (4) 1952 Edith *née* Finch; philosopher and social reformer, and fellow of Trinity College; author of *The Principles of Mathematics* (publ. 1930); first president of the Campaign for Nuclear Disarmament (CND), 1958–60; left to form the more militant Committee of 100, dedicated to civil disobedience; he became involved in a strong anti-American campaign in the 1960s, and was briefly imprisoned for his part in a public 'sit-down' protest in 1962.

Salisbury, Lord – see Cecil, Robert Arthur James Gascoyne-.

Samuel, Herbert Louis (1870–1963), cr. Viscount, 1937; educ. University College School and Balliol College; Liberal MP for Cleveland, 1902–18; Darwen, Lancashire, 1929–35; entered cabinet under Asquith; was leader of the Liberal Party, 1931–5;

home secretary under Ramsay MacDonald, 1931–2; Liberal leader in the House of Lords, 1944–55.

Sandys, (Edwin) Duncan (1908–87), cr. life peer (Duncan-Sandys), 1974; educ. Eton and Magdalen College; married (1) 1935, Diana *née* Churchill, daughter of Sir Winston and Lady (Clementine) Churchill (diss. 1960; d. 1963); Conservative MP for Norwood, Lambeth, 1935–45; Streatham, 1950–74; served in war 1939–41 – disabled while on active service; minster of supply, 1951–4; housing and local government, 1954–7; defence, 1957–9; aviation, 1959–60; secretary of state, commonwealth relations, 1960–4; a founder of the European Movement, 1947; chairman of the International Executive of European Movement, 1947–50. In January 1947 Violet considered him a 'scarecrow', who would frighten people away from the UEM. Harold Macmillan, though, thought the success of that movement as being 'primarily due' to his 'tenacity': '[He] proved able to enlist the services and command the respect of a great variety of individuals and organized bodies' (Macmillan, *Tides of Fortune*, 155).

Sassoon, Siegfried Loraine (1886–1967), CBE, 1951; educ. Marlborough and Clare College, Cambridge; married, 1933, Hester *née* Gatty – one son, George (b. 1936) – the marriage ended in separation; served with distinction 1914–18 (lieutenant, Royal Welch Fusiliers; MC, 1916); made famous by his war poetry – *The Old Huntsman* (1917), *Counter-Attack* (1918) – and prose, notably the George Sherston trilogy beginning with *Memoirs of a Fox-Hunting Man* (1928); *Collected Poems* first appeared in 1947, and a critical biography of George Meredith was published the following year. Slim and athletic even in his old age, Sassoon continued to play cricket into his seventies; Violet came to know him well during the 1930s while they were near neighbours in Wiltshire – when she was friendly also with Sassoon's lover, Stephen Tennant, the nephew of her step-mother Margot Asquith.

Selwyn Lloyd, John (1904–78), cr. life peer, 1976 (Selwyn-Lloyd); QC, 1947; educ. Fettes and Magdalene College, Cambridge; MP (Con.) Wirral, Cheshire, 1945–70, 1971–6; foreign secretary, 1955–60; chancellor of the exchequer, 1960–2; lord privy seal and leader of the Commons, 1963–4.

Sinclair, Sir Archibald Henry Macdonald [Archie] (1890–1970), 4th Bt (succeeded 1912); cr. 1st Viscount Thurso, 1952; educ. Eton and Sandhurst; married, 1918, **Marigold *née* Forbes** (godmother to Raymond Bonham Carter); entered army 1910 and was Churchill's second in command when the latter took charge of the 6th Royal Scots Fusiliers, 1916; aide to Churchill at the war office, 1919–21, and colonial office, 1921–2; Liberal MP for Caithness and Sutherland, 1922–45; leader of Liberal Parliamentary Party, 1935–45; secretary of state for air, 1940–5.

Soames, (Arthur) Christopher (1920–87), cr. life peer, 1978; educ. Eton and Royal Military College, Sandhurst; served 1939–45 war (captain); married, 1947, Mary *née* Churchill; Conservative MP for Bedford, Bedfordshire, 1950–66; PPS to the prime minister, Sir Winston Churchill, 1952–5; secretary of state for war, 1958–60; minister of agriculture, fisheries and food, 1960–4; ambassador to France, 1968–72.

Soames, Lady Mary née Churchill (b. 1922), DBE, 1980; youngest daughter of Sir Winston Churchill and Baroness Spencer-Churchill; privately educated; served 1939–45 war, WVS and ATS; married, 1947, Captain Christopher Soames; author of *Clementine Churchill* (1979) and *Speaking for Themselves* (1999).

Spaak, Paul-Henri (1899–1972), Belgian statesman; minister for foreign affairs with government in exile, 1939–45; prime minister, 1946, 1947–9; foreign minister, 1954–7, 1961–6; secretary-general of NATO, 1957–61; as president of the Consultative Assembly of the Council of Europe, 1949–51, Spaak was in the forefront of the movement for European union.

Sparrow, John Hanbury Angus (1906–92), OBE, 1946; educ. Winchester and New College; fellow of All Souls College, Oxford, 1929 (re-elected 1937, 1946); called to bar, 1931; warden of All Souls, 1952–77; fellow of Winchester College, 1951–81.

Stanley, Venetia see Montagu, (Beatrice) Venetia

Steel, (Sir) David (b. 1938) cr. life peer, 1997; KBE, 1990; educ. George Watson's College and Edinburgh University; journalist, broadcaster and politician; Liberal MP for Roxburgh, Selkirk and Peebles, 1965–83; Tweeddale, Ettrick and Lauderdale, 1983–8; Liberal Democrat, 1988–97; youngest member of the 1964–6 parliament; sponsored a private member's bill to reform the law on abortion, 1966–7; leader of Liberal Party, 1976–88; co-founder and leader of the Social and Liberal Democrats, 1988; speaker of the Scottish Parliament, 1999.

Thorpe, (John) Jeremy (b. 1929) educ. Eton and Trinity College; married (1) 1968 Caroline *née* Allpass (d. 1970); (2) 1973 Marion *née* Stein; called to bar, 1954; Liberal candidate for North Devon, 1955; MP for North Devon, 1959–79; leader of the Liberal Party, 1967–76. Violet sat next to him at a dinner at the Oxford Union in the summer of 1951 and gained a mixed impression: 'tho' intelligent & rather nice looking he is pushing & exhibitioniste – terribly anxious to show one that he knows Max Beerbohm etc. (carries on his person snapshots he has taken of him)' (VBC diary, 5 June 1951). She was impressed, though, by his Liberal zeal, writing in 1957, 'I have just had a long & ecstatic account of Southport from Jeremy Thorpe. If faith can move mountains he should be able to flatten out the earth & make the Himalayas skip like young goats – or whatever they do in the Psalms' (VBC to LG, 10 October 1957).

Wilson, (James) Harold (1916–95), cr. life peer, 1983; educ. Wirral Grammar School and Jesus College; married, 1940, Mary *née* Baldwin; Labour MP for Ormskirk, 1945–50; Huyton, Lancashire, 1950–83; president, board of trade, 1947–51; leader of Labour Party, 1963–76; prime minister, 1964–70, 1974–6.

APPENDIX C: *Notes on houses and places mentioned in the text*

The following descriptions are based on information to be found either in the Violet Bonham Carter MSS or in the relevant edition of Nikolaus Pevsner's *The Buildings of England* series (arranged by county). The information here is mostly restricted to the period 1946–69.

I. Houses outside London, and abroad

Balmoral Castle (*Aberdeenshire*) – private residence of the monarch; a nineteenth-century castle in the Scottish baronial style, built on the banks of the River Dee; used as a summer residence, with access to grouse shooting, stalking and highland games.

Beaufort Castle (*Inverness-shire*) – the home of Lord Lovat, near Beauly; a red sandstone Scottish baronial mansion, built in the nineteenth century; Bongie spent summer holidays there.

Birch Grove House (*Sussex*) – near Hayward's Heath, the home of Howard and Dorothy Macmillan; bought by Macmillan's mother, Nellie, after her marriage and rebuilt by her in 1926: 'an imposing mansion, a great neo-Georgian barrack of a house, one of only two or three such major works of residential construction undertaken during the depression' (Horne, *Macmillan, 1894–1956*, 80).

Chartwell (*Kent*) – two miles south of Westerham, the favourite home of Sir Winston Churchill; purchased in 1922 for £5,000, and almost completely rebuilt in 1923.

Chequers Court (*Buckinghamshire*) – set in 1,500 acres about 30 miles north-west of London; a sixteenth-century foundation, extensively rebuilt, the house was given by Viscount Lee of Fareham to the nation, 1917, for use by the prime minister of the day, and it has become the official country residence.

Clovelly Court (*North Devon*) – seat of the Carys and Hamlyns, and then the home of Betty and Oc Asquith; built in the eighteenth century, the house was largely burnt out in 1944, though afterwards it was rebuilt; it was a favourite visiting place of the Bonham Carters, standing on a rugged stretch of the north Devon coast high above the beautiful fishing village of Clovelly, which nestles in a deep cove leading to the sea. 'It was very exciting seeing the new house which is lovely – a real tour de force of Claud Phillimore's. He has put back the clock to 16th century & built it round the old Tower which used to stand unnoticed in the corner where the Twinnery Wing goes off at right angles. It is lovely inside & out – the whole façade stone – the mound near the church flattened out. Lovely colourings inside – washed with Adams green & pink. . . .' (diary, 23 March 1958).

Dalnawillan (*Caithness*) – a shooting lodge belonging to Archie and Marigold

Sinclair; Bongie loved the grouse shooting there, the stalking, and the salmon fishing on the Thurso river.

Drovers (*Sussex*) – the home of Rex and Leslie Benson.

Glebe, the (*Wiltshire*) – in Stockton village, the home for many years after the second world war of Cressida Ridley; it was a farmhouse rented from the Yeatman Biggs, who farmed in Stockton.

Glyndebourne (*East Sussex*) – the home of John Christie, and the location of Glyndebourne Opera; a sixteenth-century house on the South Downs just east of Lewes, extensively rebuilt in Victorian times; in 1933 Christie added a 311-seat opera house, joined to the main building by a music room; the opera house was designed by Edmund Warre.

Heytesbury House (*Wiltshire*) – near Warminster, the home of the poet and writer Siegfried Sassoon: 'We went all over the house which Mark admired enormously. It is I must say most lovely. Every mantelpiece & door & moulding & the proportions of the windows which flood it with light. The "best bedroom" is one of the loveliest I have seen anywhere, with a rounded end over the library. I can't think why the Royal family don't buy houses like that instead of places like "Sunninghill Park"' (diary, 16 August 1947).

Manor Farm, Stockton (*Wiltshire*) – a beautiful farmhouse in the village of Stockton, built in the late sixteenth and early seventeenth centuries, and taken by the Bonham Carters during the war; the farmhouse is close to the east gates of Stockton House.

Mockbeggars (*Suffolk*) – near Claydon, the home of Jasper and Nathalie Ridley.

Mottisfont Abbey (*Hampshire*) – on the River Test, 4½ miles north-west of Romsey, the home of Gilbert and Maud Russell, old friends of Violet and Bongie; a thirteenth-century abbey, rebuilt in eighteenth and twentieth centuries.

Old Manse of Firth (*Orkney*) – purchased by Jo and Laura Grimond in 1951, it became the family home on the island. About 5 miles from Kirkwall, it was the old Church of Scotland manse of the parish of Firth: 'Like many Orkney manses it is unnecessarily tall. Since it is perched on a spur of high ground it catches the full force of all the gales – and there are many. As it is largely one room thick the wind rushes through, no window or door will stop it' (Grimond, *Memoirs*, 158). 'It is a grey house in a most romantic position standing above the sea – a few hundred yds off – square "dignified" rooms with big windows & a rambling tangled garden' (diary, 18 September 1951).

Royaumont (*Asnières-et-Oise, France*) – house belonging jointly to Mrs Mary Wooster and her son le Baron Fould-Springer (Elena Bonham Carter's grandmother and uncle), and from which Raymond and Elena Bonham Carter were married in July 1958; Violet was enchanted by the house, which she described as 'a splendid square "Palais Abbatial" – surrounded by avenues & lakes': 'The beauty of the hall took my breath away – plain stone walls, Doric columns – classical niches holding candelabra – & seen through the pillars a most lovely curve of the spiral staircase against a green background of lime trees – behind a large window. This first glimpse of the stair-case against the leaves is unforgettable' (diary, 24 July 1958).

Sissinghurst Castle (*Kent*) – near Cranbrook, the home of Sir Harold Nicolson and Vita Sackville-West, purchased by the latter in 1930; Sissinghurst consists of farm buildings of various ages, from Tudor to Victorian, dominated by a brick Elizabethan tower; Vita Sackville-West created there one of the most famous, and now most visited, gardens in England.

Stockton House (*Wiltshire*) – owned by Bongie's business partner, O. T. Falk, and used by the Bonham Carters for easter and summer holidays between 1927 and 1934; a large Elizabethan house set in a small park on the edge of Stockton village, in the Wylye valley, some 10 miles north-west of Salisbury.

Thurso Castle (*Caithness*) – a castle built in the Scottish baronial style for Sir John Sinclair, 3rd Bt, 1872–8; home of the Sinclair family.

II. Houses in London

40 Gloucester Square, W.2 – a large house on the fork of two roads just north of Hyde Park; Violet and Bongie lived there, with occasional paying guests, from 1935 until 10 April 1952, when work began on the property to convert it into flats – one of which they subsequently took (*see below*).

21 Hyde Park Square, W.2 – the Bonham Carters moved in to flat 3 on Friday 2 January 1953; the new flat was on the first floor, and was made up of the first floor of the old 40 Gloucester Square address, with rooms from the houses adjoining on either side: 'The noise of hammers is like a Nibelungen Höhle. They are painting outside – which involved not only smell but the presence of 3 men on my balcony who might as well be in my room.... The flat itself is spacious & will be delightful when we get it straight. But oh for Cupboards! No room for blankets – china – glass – filing cabinets!' (diary, 12 January 1953).

15 York House, Kensington Church Street, W.8 – just behind Kensington Palace, Violet and Bongie's temporary home from 10 April 1952 to 2 January 1953, while they waited to move into 21 Hyde Park Square (see above); 'It has 5 bedrooms, 2 bathrooms, 2 sitting-rooms – opens on a quiet courtyard – & has a big empty room in which we cld store furniture' (diary, 10 February 1952).

III. Places

Yarnbury (*Wiltshire*) – an Iron Age hill fort on the South Downs, between Warminster and Amesbury: 'It is a circular camp about a mile round, guarded by a triple rampart of green walls.... Within its solemn orbit aeons dwindle to dust. The green ring holds all time a prisoner in its span. Look down from the high ramparts on the downs, breaking around it, wave upon wave, like a green sea "in fluctuation fixed". The shadows of the moving clouds dapple the plain. All else is still. There is no sound but the cry of the plover, no movement except when a brown hare starts up from among the junipers that grow on the steep banks.... All through the spring and summer there is a carpet of flowers underfoot – milk-wort, blue and white and rose, cushions of golden rock-rose, orchis, wild thyme, purple campanula. But its beauty is as great in winter when the downs have shed their flowery garment and lie cold and pale under grey skies. From Yarnbury you can see the country far and wide....' (from a VBC typescript intended for publication, possibly written during the second world war)

SELECT BIBLIOGRAPHY: *a note on sources and further reading*

I. Manuscript sources

The diaries and letters published here are drawn mostly from the Violet Bonham Carter MSS, with the following exceptions, which are all taken from collections at the Churchill Archives Centre, Churchill College, Cambridge: VBC to Sir Winston Spencer Churchill (Churchill Papers); VBC to Clementine Churchill (Clementine Churchill Papers); Lord Gladwyn to VBC (Gladwyn Papers).

II. Printed sources

The basic research tools have been *The Times* for the detail of daily events, and the relevant volumes of *Who Was Who* and The *Dictionary of National Biography* for biographical information. References to speeches and broadcasts made by Violet Bonham Carter have been taken from the Violet Bonham Carter Papers unless otherwise stated. The 'Harris interview' refers to the transcript of an interview given by VBC to Kenneth Harris, February 1967, the basis of a BBC television programme celebrating her eightieth birthday. Full references of books quoted in footnotes to the text are given below (place of publication is London, unless otherwise stated). Also included are some memoirs of special relevance.

Annan, Noel *Our Age* (1991)

Asquith, Lady Cynthia *Diaries, 1915–1918* (1968)

Asquith, Herbert *Moments of Memory* (1937)

Asquith, H. H. *Memories and Reflections* (2 volumes, 1928)

Asquith, Margot *Places and Persons* (1925)

– *Lay Sermons* (1927)

– *More Memories* (1933)

– *Myself When Young* (1938)

– *Off the Record* (1943)

Barnes, John and Nicholson, David (eds) *The Empire at Bay: The Leo Amery Diaries, 1929–1945* (1988)

Benn, Tony *Years of Hope: Diaries, Letters and Papers, 1940–1962* (edited by Ruth Winstone; 1994) *Out of the Wilderness: Diaries, 1963–1967* (1987)

Berlin, Sir Isaiah *Personal Impressions* (1980)

Blake, Robert *The Unknown Prime Minister* (1955)

Bonham Carter, Mark and Pottle, Mark (eds) *Lantern Slides: The Diaries and Letters of Violet Bonham Carter, 1904–1914* (1996)

Bonham Carter, Violet *Winston Churchill as I Knew Him* (1995)

Brock, M. and Brock E. (eds) *H. H. Asquith: Letters to Venetia Stanley* (1985)

Bullock, Alan *Ernest Bevin: Foreign Secretary, 1945–1951* (1983)

Butler, David *British General Elections since 1945* (1989)
Carlton, David *Anthony Eden* (1981)
Churchill, Sir Winston *Great Contemporaries* (1937)
– *The World Crisis* (4 volumes, 1923–9)
Clark, Ronald W. *The Life of Bertrand Russell* (1975)
Colville, John *The Fringes of Power: Downing Street Diaries, 1939–1955* (1985)
Cook, Chris *A Short History of the Liberal Party, 1900–1988* (1989)
Craig, F. W. S. *Chronology of British Parliamentary By-elections, 1833–1987* (1987)
– *British Parliamentary Election Results, 1950–1970* (1971)
Crewe, Quentin *Well, I Forget the Rest: The Autobiography of an Optimist* (1991)
Freyberg, Paul *Bernard Freyberg, VC: Soldier of Two Nations* (1991)
Gilbert, Martin *Churchill: A Life* (1991)
– *Finest Hour: Winston S. Churchill, 1939–1941* (1983)
– *Never Despair: Winston S. Churchill, 1945–1965* (1988)
Grigg, John *Nancy Astor* (1980)
Grimond, Jo *Memoirs* (1979)
Harris, Kenneth *Attlee* (1982)
Hassall, Christopher *Rupert Brooke: A Biography* (1964)
Horne, Alistair *Macmillan, 1894–1956* (1988)
– *Macmillan 1957–1986* (1989)
Howard, Anthony *RAB: The Life of R. A. Butler* (1987)
Jenkins, Roy *Asquith* (1964)
– *A Life at the Centre* (1991)
Jolliffe, John (ed.) *Raymond Asquith: Life and Letters* (1980)
Koss, Stephen *Asquith* (1976)
Lee, Sir Sidney *King Edward VII: A Biography* (1927)
Longford, Elizabeth *Elizabeth R: A Biography* (1983)
Lycett, Andrew *Ian Fleming* (1995)
Macmillan, Harold *Tides of Fortune, 1945–1955* (1969)
– *Riding the Storm, 1956–1969* (1971)
Minney, R. J. *'Puffin' Asquith* (1973)
Moggridge, D. E. *Maynard Keynes: An Economist's Biography* (1992)
Morgan, Kenneth O. *Labour in Power, 1945–51* (1984)
Nicolson, Nigel (ed.) *Harold Nicolson: Diaries and Letters, 1945–1962* (1968)
Nicolson, Nigel *Long Life* (1997)
Page, Christopher *Command in the Royal Naval Division: A Military Biography of Brigadier General A. M. Asquith, DSO* (1999)
Pottle, Mark (ed.) *Champion Redoubtable: The Diaries and Letters of Violet Bonham Carter, 1914–1945* (1998)
Rhodes James, Robert *Bob Boothby: A Portrait* (1991)
– *Anthony Eden* (1986)
Seymour, Miranda *Ottoline Morrell: Life on the Grand Scale* (1993)
Skidelsky, Robert *Oswald Mosley* (1990)

Soames, Mary *Clementine Churchill* (1979)
– *Speaking for Themselves: The Personal Letters of Winston and Clementine Churchill* (1999)
Young, K. 'Orpington and the "Liberal Revival"', in C. Cook and John Ramsden (eds), *By-elections in British Politics* (1997), 157–79
Wilson, Duncan *Gilbert Murray OM* (Oxford 1987)

INDEX

An asterisk signifies those individuals who are listed in the appendix of 'Biographical notes'. An italicized page number indicates the location of a biographical footnote. A superscript cross identifies houses listed in the appendix of 'Notes on houses'. Entries are sub-divided chronologically rather than alphabetically. The following abbreviations are used: UEM = United Europe Movement; UNA = United Nations. Association; VBC = Violet Bonham Carter; WSC = Winston Spencer Churchill.